11.88

6-21-72

Music for the Voice

MUSIC FOR THE VOICE

A Descriptive List of Concert
and Teaching Material

Sergius Kagen

REVISED EDITION

Indiana University Press Bloomington London

SECOND PRINTING 1971

Library of Congress catalog card number: 68-27348

Published in Canada by Fitzhenry & Whiteside Limited, Scarborough, Ontario

Manufactured in the United States of America

To the memory of
MARCELLA SEMBRICH
*who first introduced me to most of
the music listed in this volume*

CONTENTS

FOREWORD

Sergius Kagen completed the second, revised edition of Music for the Voice shortly before his untimely death in 1964. He defined the scope and purpose of this new edition in his own preface. What I would like to state, since I had the good fortune of working closely with him for several years, is how singularly qualified he was to write this book. Sergius Kagen was not only a superb pianist-accompanist and a devoted teacher who knew vocal literature intimately; he also had expert knowledge of voice production, diction, poetry and prosody. He spoke the most important European languages fluently. He had the insight into music that only a creative person can have, as shown in the seventy-five songs he composed. Above all, he loved the human voice and the music written for it.

Because Sergius Kagen was a practicing musician, he speaks directly to the performer, to the singer, coach, voice student, and accompanist. Because he was a practical man, he succeeds in conveying the result of thirty years' work devoted to the human voice in a few succinct phrases about each of the songs he saw fit to include in his selection.

Robert Starer

New York
March 1968

PREFACE

First Edition

Any descriptive work ought to state with utmost exactitude its aim and scope. It seems only fair that the author and the reader should agree from the outset on what the work in question is or is not.

The aim of this book is to provide the singer, the teacher, the coach, and the amateur in the search of suitable material with a handy guide listing as many composers of vocal solo music as seems practicable and as many examples of each composer's work as seems advisable for the purpose of giving the reader an opportunity to form a fair idea of this composer's vocal music.

Any and every serious student of vocal music will no doubt know most of the compositions listed in this guide. Yet, for many a singer and teacher this guide may prove to be valuable; it may remind one of a composer or a song that had slipped one's memory; it may — and I hope it will — stimulate the reader to acquaint himself with the unlisted compositions of the composers mentioned here and — this being one of the main purposes of this guide — will assist him in selecting material for his type of voice, or for his students.

This guide is not in any way intended as a work of musicology. Vocal literature is so vast that any guide to it, claiming any degree of completeness, would become through sheer volume almost totally useless for any practical purpose. If one considers that a complete list of Bach soli for bass alone would comprise some three hundred entries, and that Handel, Gluck, Piccinni, Grétry, Scarlatti, to name but a very few, would not be far behind in their output, one can easily realize that the perusal of such a list would leave the reader only bewildered.

Again, many a good song or aria has been written by some composer who otherwise has not succeeded in attaining any distinction in his art. The number of such solitary successful efforts must be legion. To try to list them all would, again, seem utterly useless.

The selection of solo excerpts from sacred works has been limited to only those examples which have by now become a part of standard concert repertoire, such as excerpts from the sacred works of Purcell, Handel, Bach, Haydn, Mozart, Mendelssohn, etc. Thus, the entire and very considerable field of sacred music, as such, has not been considered in preparation of this volume, and this volume contains no special section devoted to sacred music. The excerpts included are to be found appended to the lists of the songs of the respective composers.

The selection of nineteenth century operatic excerpts has been deliberately limited to the most celebrated airs only. No attempt was made to include the multitude of effective airs and solo excerpts of minor operatic composers, since such an attempt would obviously lead to an enormously extended list of doubtful practical value. A few widely known airs of minor composers, however, have been included, in instances when such airs are easily available. Twentieth century opera is barely represented in this volume since for the most part it lacks well-defined solo pieces suitable for separate performance with pianoforte accompaniment.

No attempt has been made to list examples of the song literature before the seventeenth century, since that music, in the opinion of this writer, does not lend itself too well to performance with pianoforte accompaniment and is for the most part not easily available in modern reprints.

The bibliographical references found in this volume are simply intended for practical use in the United States only, since practically all of the material that happens to be in the public domain is available in a multitude of editions.

Another consideration presented itself. This guide being primarily intended for use in America, songs and airs from Russian, Eastern European and Scandinavian languages which have no adequate English translations had perforce to be omitted. The same consideration had to govern the selection of folk songs. It seemed best to exclude all but Irish, Scottish, English and American examples.

It seems necessary also to remind the readers of this volume that because of the staggeringly large amount of vocal music, the so-called "standard repertoire" of a singer varies considerably, depending on the country in which the singer lives. A standard repertoire of an instrumentalist is essentially much more stable and more easily defined than that of a vocalist. This volume is primarily devoted to the repertoire at present used in the United States, a repertoire in many respects quite different from that used in Great Britain, not to mention France, Italy or Germany.

To reiterate: this guide does not claim to furnish anything approaching a complete list of all the compositions for solo voice, even by the most celebrated composers. If one is particularly interested in the vocal compositions of some particular composer, one can find the desired information in any of the reliable biographies, music dictionaries, and such works, or obtain it from the catalogues of a good musical library.

This guide is not intended to remind one of the justly or unjustly forgotten works of the celebrated composers, or to remind one of the perhaps very excellent works of composers now totally forgotten.

It is a practical guide, a bare outline, accompanied by a few critical notes and practical performance suggestions, and even as such will no doubt be criticized severely for innumerable omissions, committed wittingly or unwittingly, as well as for the inclusion of numerous entries and their evaluation. But the process of selection and evaluation, in so far as any art is concerned, is unfortunately a largely personal matter.

However, should this guide prove to be of help in stimulating anyone's interest in exploring the realm of music for voice, and should it prove itself useful to a singer attempting to lay the foundation for a repertoire, its purpose will have been accomplished.

I know that many errors will be discovered in this book. I have striven to keep their number as low as possible.

Revised Edition

In preparing the new edition of Music for the Voice I have endeavored to do the following:

(1) To add to each section of the book important new material which has become available since the publication of the first edition of this volume.

(2) To discard material of fleeting importance contained in some sections of the first edition.

(3) To recheck all the bibliographical references and to bring them up to date.

(4) To provide a much needed index of the composers which would greatly facilitate the use of this book.

(5) To provide a uniform code of the publishers' names and thus to standardize the form of bibliographical reference.

(6) To correct all the misprints and inaccuracies which crept into the first edition despite all of my efforts to the contrary.

Thus, in this edition, two large sections "Music before the nineteenth Century" and "American and British Songs" are for all practical purposes newly compiled, for a great wealth of important new material has become available since the publication of the first edition of this volume.

Important additions have been made to practically all other sections, although not to the same extent. As for the correction of misprints, I am by now convinced that a number of newly made mistakes will be found in this edition though I have tried to eliminate them.

Sergius Kagen

New York City
February 1964

xiii

HOW TO USE THIS BOOK

This book is not an encyclopedia of vocal music. Please read the preface.

This book is divided into the following main sections:

(1) Songs and Airs before the Nineteenth Century.
(2) Songs: Nineteenth and Twentieth Centuries.
(3) Folk Songs
(4) Operatic Excerpts (mainly Nineteenth Century)

As noted in the preface, no special section is devoted to excerpts from sacred works. Whenever such excerpts are included they are to be found attached to the song lists of the respective composers.

For the sake of convenience in listing the songs and airs of Bach, Handel, Gluck, Haydn and Mozart, all the material included of each of these five masters is listed in a separate section.

Concert arias are listed in song lists of the respective composers. Arias from dramatic cantatas, such as "L'Enfant Prodigue" by Debussy, are listed with operatic excerpts.

The composers in each section are listed alphabetically. Under the names of the composers all titles are listed alphabetically, in their original languages, with the exception of Russian, Scandinavian and miscellaneous songs and airs which are listed in English translations. In listing the operatic excerpts in the section "Songs and Airs before the Nineteenth Century," the first words of a recitative (when a recitative is listed) are listed first, the first words of the air are listed below and the title of the opera is given in parentheses, after the first words of the air. Thus, an air by Cimarosa, for instance, is listed as follows:

> Recitative:
> Cara, son tutto vostro
> Air:
> Brillar mi sento il core (Il Matrimonio Segreto)

In listing operatic excerpts from the works of the nineteenth and twentieth centuries, however, and in listing excerpts from the operas and oratorios by Handel and Mozart, the title of the opera is given first, the recitative and/or air being listed below it, thus:

> Le Nozze di Figaro
> Recitative:
> Giunse al fin il momento
> Air:
> Deh vieni non tardar
>
> or
>
> Carmen
> Votre toast

As mentioned before, the opera titles are listed by composers.

In listing song titles it seemed advisable sometimes to give the first line of the text in parentheses, when there are two or more songs by the same composer possessing the same title, but different texts (as in the case of many songs by Schubert, for instance). Sometimes an identifying subtitle given by the composer is listed in parentheses.

The following system is used to indicate the pitches:

Thus, for instance, a compass of G-f1 would mean:

a compass of d-b♭1:

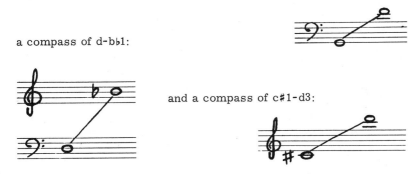

and a compass of c♯1-d3:

In cases where the composer has inserted optional notes, such notes are indicated in parentheses. For instance, the compass (a) c1-g2 (c3) is a-c3, but both a and c3 are optional.

The tessitura is given approximately only, since to establish the tessitura of any vocal piece with precision is obviously an impossibility. When (H) or (L) is added to the pitches of the tessitura it indicates that it was impossible to establish with certainty the original key of the song in question and either a high copy (H) or a low copy (L) was used for the listing. When the word "same" appears in place of the tessitura, the tessitura and the compass seemed identical to this writer. The entries concerning the type of voice for which the song is best suited are primarily suggestions and are to be considered as such by the reader, since it is obvious that any singer who has acquired a more than adequate command of his instrument could, theoretically at least, perform any song, provided it was transposed to suit his voice. In instances when "All voices" is indicated the necessity of such transposition is of course taken for granted. It does not mean, however, that the song is available in transposed editions. The suggestions "Men's voices" and "Women's voices" are as a rule prompted by considerations of the text. It is obvious that such suggestions are largely a matter of personal preference.

In many instances where operatic material is listed, especially in airs intended for soprano, the type of voice for which this writer considers the air most suitable is given first and the type of voice for which the air may be suitable in his opinion is given in parentheses, such as lyric soprano (coloratura soprano) or dramatic soprano (lyric soprano). When only "Soprano" is indicated, it means that in the opinion of this writer the air is suitable for all types of soprano voices. The same procedure is adopted in listing tenor airs.

In some instances, when the composer writes in a manner suitable to all varieties of any type of voice (as Bach and Handel) the Type of Voice remark is omitted. Also in instances when the composer favors some special type of voice (as, for example, Mozart, Wagner and Gluck in their tenor airs), a note prefacing the list discusses the type of voice for which the airs may be most suitable, and the Type of Voice remark is again omitted.

In the remarks column a short description of the characteristics of the song or air is attempted, limited for the most part to its tempo, the character of its vocal line, and its general mood. No critical comment is included, although some obvious performance demands and performance suggestions are from time to time discussed.

"See" followed by the name or names of composers indicates that the same text has been set to music under the same title by the composer or composers mentioned.

In describing operatic airs the terms "Andante, Allegro" and an "Andante, Allegro Air" are often used. They denote a two-movement aria form much in fashion during the second half of the eighteenth and the first half of the nineteenth century. Airs written according to such a pattern consist of a sustained, lyrical slow movement and a brilliant, often very florid final allegro, intended for a display piece. Practically all airs of, for instance, Bellini or Donizetti follow this pattern.

The term "Compound Air" denotes a rather free aria form where several contrasting movements are manipulated according to the demands of the text. An excellent example of a compound air is the "Divinités du Styx" (Alceste) by Gluck. The term "Scena" denotes a very extended recitative, containing independent melodic material. It often seems impossible to establish a clearly defined distinction between a recitative and a scena.

Bibliographical indications are given last in parentheses. As a rule the publisher's name is given; in some instances, however (as in the Songs and Airs before the Nineteenth Century section), a general bibliography is attached, with a list of abbreviations used, and such abbreviations, usually the names of arrangers or editors of collections instead of publishers, are indicated in parentheses. In instances when songs are available in many excellent editions, the editions are discussed in the prefatory note and no bibliographical material is included in the Remarks column.

"Generally available" in parentheses indicates that there are so many separate editions of the song or air that to single out one of them in preference to the others seemed unfair.

"Score" followed by the publisher's name indicates that the most authentic and the most easily obtainable version of the air is to be found in the complete piano score of the opera or oratorio, in the edition indicated.

Whenever possible, biographical data has been included. In some instances, however, it has been omitted since it was not obtainable in standard reference works, and this writer did not have the inclination nor the necessary equipment to embark on such researches, which in most cases seemed fruitless as well as unnecessary. No biographical data is included in the section dealing with contemporary American and British songs.

ACKNOWLEDGMENTS

First Edition

The compilation of this volume, particularly at a time when practically no foreign publications were available in the United States, was a complex task. It was further complicated by the fact that most of our libraries possess rather incomplete collections of songs, especially those of minor composers.

I tender my sincerest thanks to Mr. Ernest Hutcheson, without whose invaluable advice and unfailing interest, this volume would never have been written; to Madame Eva Gauthier, Madame Povla Frijsh, Miss Florence Kimball and Mr. George Fergusson, among many others, for allowing me the use of their collections of vocal music and for giving me much necessary information; to Misses Burnette Bradley, Audrey Goodman, and Mary Williamson Hooker, and Messrs. Norman Farrow and Robert Harmon for their patient and diligent co-operation in the necessary research and clerical work involved in collecting and classifying the material, and to Miss Ruth Neal for her valuable help in preparing the list of folk songs. I also am much indebted to Miss Gwendolyn Mackillop of the Juilliard School of Music Library, to Dr. George S. Dickinson of Vassar College, to G. Schirmer, Inc. (especially to Mr. Lester Hodges, who was kind enough to put the stock of the Schirmer store at my disposal, and to Mr. David Green who located the copies which I needed), and to Mr. M. C. Platte of G. Ricordi and Company.

Revised Edition

I hereby take the opportunity to acknowledge my gratitude to The Martha Baird Rockefeller Fund for Music, Inc. for defraying the clerical expenses incurred while gathering new material and typing the manuscript for the revised edition.

I also wish to thank Mr. Noni Espina for his assistance in collecting, classifying and typing part of the new material for the revised edition of Music for the Voice.

S. K.

New York City
January 1964

CODE OF PUBLISHERS

Publishers Appearing Often

AUG	Augener Music Ltd.	NOV	Novello & Company, Ltd.
AMP	Associated Music Publishers	OX	Oxford University Press
		PI	Peer International
BAER	Baerenreiter Music Publishers	CFP	C. F. Peters Corp.
		TP	Theodore Presser Company
BH	Boosey & Hawkes		
BMC	Boston Music Company	ROW	R. D. Row Music Company
B & H	Breitkopf & Härtel		
BMI	Broadcast Music	RIC	G. Ricordi (c/o Franco Colombo)
CHAP	Chappell Company		
CHES	J. W. Chester	ECS	E. C. Schirmer Music Company
JCC	John Church Company		
CUR	Curwen	GS	G. Schirmer Music, Inc.
OD	Oliver Ditson (c/o Presser)	SCH	Schott & Company
		SMP	Southern Music Publishing Co.
EV	Elkan-Vogel Company		
CF	Carl Fisher, Inc.	S & B	Stainer & Bell, Ltd.
GAL	Galaxy Music Corp.	UE	Universal Edition
HEUG	Heugel	WR	Winthrop Rogers
IMC	International Music Company		

Other Publishers
(identified by the underlined word or words)

Arrow Music Press	Alfred Lengnick & Co., Ltd.
Edwin Ashdown, Ltd.	Edward B. Marks Music Corp.
Choudens	Mercury Music Corp.
Composers Music Corp.	E. H. Morris Co.
Concordia Publishing House	Music Press
Cos Cob Press	Paterson, Ltd.
Cramer	Rouart, Lerolle (c/o Salabert)
Durand	Salabert
Elkin & Co., Ltd.	Schmidt
Enoch & Cie.	N. Simrock
Hargail Music Press	Sonzogno
Harms, Inc.	Valley Music Press
Henmar Press	Weaner-Levant Publishers
Joseph Williams, Ltd.	Weintraub Music Co.
Edwin F. Kalmus	Witmark
Leduc	Suvini Zerboni
Leeds Music Corporation	

1

SONGS AND AIRS BEFORE THE NINETEENTH CENTURY

COMMENTARY ON SONGS AND AIRS BEFORE
THE NINETEENTH CENTURY

The few songs and solo excerpts from the larger vocal works of the seventeenth and eighteenth century composers, listed below, represent but a pitifully small fraction of an extraordinarily extensive literature.

The reasons that limited the listing of this material to so few, standard examples are as follows:

(1) The sheer bulk of the material of this period is so vast that a thoroughly representative list of such music would occupy a larger space than is presently allotted to the entire volume.

(2) Most of the material, at present little known, is as yet available only in editions which are for the most part difficult to obtain.

(3) Each school and mode or manner of composing that arose during those two centuries possesses a certain general uniformity of style, form and texture. This uniformity seems to overshadow the individual characteristics of the minor composers who wrote in the manner of any of such respective schools, at least in so far as the average well-informed performer of today and not an expert musicologist is concerned.

Thus even this scant list can be considered as being to a certain degree representative of the vocal music of the period.

Most of the music for solo voice written before the end of the eighteenth century is published today in the form of various arrangements. This is due to the fact that most such music, in its original form, lacks a written-out piano accompaniment, being either scored for orchestra or confined to the figured or unfigured bass.

Many of these arrangements, admirable as they may be, are nevertheless singularly lacking in much textual information which seems to be desirable. Songs and airs have been frequently transposed in such arrangements, yet the original key is rarely indicated; a translation has often been substituted for the original text, yet no mention of this fact is made. Whole sections of the original are sometimes omitted, yet no indication of the fact that a cut has been made is present; sometimes a recitative of one air is summarily

3

attached to the set musical piece of another; sometimes the editor's own cadenzas are incorporated into the supposedly original melodic line; once in a while one may even encounter a vocal ensemble piece arranged as a solo, though no mention of this fact is made by the arranger. The harmonization of some arrangements is sometimes stylistically indefensible, abounding in chromaticisms, cross relations and chordal progressions unknown or studiously avoided by the composers of the period. In view of all this it seemed best to list only examples found in the most reliable collections available, and to omit most of the multitude of arrangements published singly, and often anonymously, by many publishers.

An overwhelmingly large percentage of the songs and airs listed below is of operatic origin. Yet when an opera ceases to be performed as a stage work and the few airs extracted from it survive only as music, the type of voice for which the air was originally intended by the composer becomes a consideration of little practical import. Since this question is still further complicated by the fact that singing as now practiced differs greatly in one respect from singing as it was practiced during the seventeenth and eighteenth centuries, nothing less than the most extensive and exhaustive research could establish with any amount of certitude the precise type of voice for which some particular air was originally intended. The difference mentioned above lies, of course, in the seventeenth and eigteenth century practice of employing castrati, falsetto singers (not to be confused with the former), as well as boy singers for the singing of alto and soprano parts. This practice, however, was not so prevalent as to exclude the employment of female voices completely. The current practice of considering the old operatic airs as songs, and of singing them in whatever key happens to be most suitable for the individual type of voice, seems therefore fully justified. The procedure adopted by this writer in compiling the following lists is as follows:

In listing airs excerpted from the operas of Mozart, the most frequently performed operas of Gluck, and oratorios and cantatas by Handel, Bach and Haydn, the type of voice is indicated as precisely as his knowledge of the subject permits.

In listing airs excerpted from the now-forgotten operas of the period it seemed best to dispense with precise indications of the type of voice whenever the text and the general character of the vocal line seemed to allow it.

Whenever possible, the title of the opera is listed in parentheses under the title of the air. The arrangement and the edition which this writer considers preferable is indicated in parentheses in the Remarks Column. The material, with few exceptions, is listed by language groups, though the national origin of the composer is thus often disregarded. The airs and songs of Handel, Bach, Gluck, Mozart and Haydn are listed in separate sections. It is hoped that by arranging the material in this way a number of unnecessary duplications and confusing cross references has been avoided.

4

Generally speaking, the Italian vocal music of the seventeenth and eighteenth centuries is now most widely known among singers, due no doubt to the use of much of it for teaching purposes.

The French vocal music of the period is as yet neither widely known nor much appreciated outside of France. This seems a great pity, since in so far as the average present-day English-speaking singer is concerned, his repertoire of music written before the nineteenth century is very limited and, as noticed above, consists largely of Italian airs long since familiar to every singing student. It is sincerely hoped that the perusal of some of the examples of French music of the seventeenth and eighteenth centuries listed below will encourage the readers of this volume to delve further into this extraordinarily rich and rewarding literature.

Much of what applies to the French vocal music of this period applies equally to the English songs and airs, especially those of the seventeenth century. It seems incomprehensible that so little of this music is used in teaching, for instance, in the United States, and that so little of it is performed.

The German composers of this period who wrote in German, with the exception of Mozart and the towering genius of J. S. Bach, whose music transcends all limitations of time and style, have contributed relatively little to vocal literature. It seemed advisable to list but a few examples of minor German masters, since their music is largely of only historical interest, and since most of it is for all practical purposes unavailable now.

SONGS AND AIRS IN ENGLISH BEFORE THE NINETEENTH CENTURY

Bibliography

The name found in parentheses after the Remarks indicates one of the following collections:

Bantock: <u>One Hundred Songs of England</u>, edited by Bantock, published by O. Ditson.

Dolmetsch: <u>Selected English Songs and Dialogues</u>, edited by Dolmetsch, published by Boosey.

Duncan: <u>The Minstrelsy of England</u>, Vol. II, edited by Duncan, published by Augener.

Fellowes 40: <u>Forty Elizabethan Songs</u>, edited by Fellowes, published by Stainer and Bell.

Hatton and Fanning: <u>Songs of England</u>, edited by Hatton and Fanning, published by Boosey.

Keel: <u>Elizabethan Love Songs</u>, edited by Keel, published by Boosey.

Moffat: <u>The Minstrelsy of England</u>, edited by Moffat, published by Bayley and Ferguson.

Potter: <u>Reliquary of English Song</u>, edited by Potter, published by G. Schirmer.

Wilson: <u>Old English Melodies</u>, edited by Wilson, published by Boosey.

TITLE	COMP.	TESS.	TYPE	REMARKS
Ah! Willow	bb-c2	d1-bb1	All voices	Slow, sustained. (Wilson)
Come, let's be merry	bb-eb2 (f2)	f1-c2	Not too suitable for very light, high voices	Spirited, gay. (Wilson)
Drink to me only with thine eyes	f1-f2	f1-c2	All voices	Sustained. (gen. av.)
False Phillis	a-d2 (e2)	d1-b1	Men's voices	Animated, graceful, humorous. (Wilson)
Have you seen but a whyte lillie grow	e1-f2	f1-d2	All voices	Sustained, delicate. (Dolmetsch)
Ralph's ramble to London	c1-e2	e1-c2	Most suitable for men's voices	Animated. Demands facile articulation. Humorous. (Wilson)
The happy lover	bb-eb2	eb1-c2	Most suitable for men's voices	Sustained, graceful. Demands some flexibility. (Wilson)
The slighted swain	c1-d2	e1-c2	All voices	A graceful, humorous minuet. (Wilson)
Willow song	d1-d2	d1-c2	All voices	Slow, sustained. (Fellowes 40)

MICHAEL ARNE
(1740-1786)

Lass with the delicate air	b-g2	g1-e2	Not too suitable for very low voices	Light and graceful. Demands some flexibility and lightness of tone. (gen. av.)
The topsails shiver in the wind	Ab-f1	eb-eb1	Baritone	Vigorous. Demands some flexibility. (Moffat)
This cold flinty heart	d#1-g#2	g#1-e2	Soprano	Graceful. Demands some flexibility. (Duncan)

DR. THOMAS AUGUSTINE ARNE
(1710-1778)

Many, if not most of the astonishingly large number of songs and airs by Dr. Arne are now almost totally forgotten, since only a few are obtainable in modern reprints.

Although one could hardly consider Dr. Arne a composer of great importance, practically all of his vocal music possesses a certain distinctive charm and grace and seems to have lost little, if any of its effectiveness. Like all the minor eighteenth century composers Arne was an expert craftsman who fashioned his music in accordance with the conventional pattern of his day, a pattern largely dominated by the dance forms of his time, such as the minuet, the gavotte, etc.

Musically his songs present no problem, being unabashedly simple in their harmonic and rhythmic scheme. His treatment of the vocal line, however, though invariably effective and considerate of the singer, demands often a more than elementary technical proficiency.

In the opinion of this writer his songs and airs could be most successfully used as teaching material designed to acquaint the present-day English-speaking singer with the stylistic problems of the vocal music of the eighteenth century.

Barrett in parentheses indicates <u>Twenty Songs of Arne</u>, edited by Barrett, published by Novello.

TITLE	COMP.	TESS.	TYPE	REMARKS
Bacchus god of mirth and wine	A-e1	d-d1	Bass or baritone	A vigorous, animated, drinking song. (Barrett)
Blow, blow, thou winter wind	c1-f2	f1-d2	All voices	Sustained. Demands some flexibility. (Potter)
By dimpled brook (Comus)	d1-g2	g1-e2	All voices	Graceful, sustained. (Potter)
By the gaily circling glass	B♭-e♭1	f-c1	Bass or baritone	Animated, vigorous. (Barrett)
Cast, my love, thine eyes around	d1-g2	g1-e2	Most suitable for high voices	Graceful, sustained. Demands some flexibility. (Duncan)
Decrepit winter limps away	d1-e♭2	e♭1-c2	All voices	Animated, graceful, spirited. Demands facile articulation. (Moffat)
Despairing beside a clear stream	c1-f2	f1-e2	High or medium voices	Sustained, graceful. Demands some flexibility. (Barrett)

7

TITLE	COMP.	TESS.	TYPE	REMARKS
Fresh and strong the breeze is blowing	a1-e2	same	All voices	Sustained. (Barrett)
Honest lover	d1-f#2	g1-d2	All voices	A saraband. (Duncan)
In infancy	c1-f2	f1-d2	Women's voices	Sustained. Has some florid pas-sages. (Barrett)
My dog and my gun	c1-f2	e1-c2	Men's voices	A gay, spirited song in praise of hunting. Demands some flexibility. (Duncan)
Now Phoebus sinketh in the west (Comus)	A-e1 (f1)	c-c1	Bass or baritone	Recitative and spirited air. De-mands some flexi-bility. A trans-posed edition for tenor can be found in Hatton and Fan-ning. (Potter)
Peggy	eb1-g2	g1-f2	Most suit-able for men's voices, ex-cepting bass.	Graceful. Demands some flexibility. (Potter)
Phillis, we don't grieve	d1-g2	g1-e2	Not too suitable for very low voices	Graceful. Demands some flexibility. (Potter)
Preach me not your musty rules (Comus)	d1-g2	d1-d2 (H)	Men's voices	Spirited, vigorous. Demands some flexibility. (Arr., Samuel Endicott, (ROW)
Sally	d1-g2	f1-eb2	Not too suitable for very low voices	Graceful. Demands some flexibility. (Moffat)
Strephon on the hill	e1-f2	f1-d2	Women's voices	Graceful, light. Demands some flexibility. (Mof-fat)
Sweet Nan of the vale	d1-f2	f1-eb2	Not too suitable for very low voices	Graceful. (Moffat)

8

TITLE	COMP.	TESS.	TYPE	REMARKS
Tell me where is fancy bred	b-g2	g1-eb2 (H)	All voices	Animated, graceful. Demands some flexibility. (Bantock)
The arch denial	c1-f2	f1-c2	All voices	Animated, light humorous. (Moffat)
The echoing horn	f1-g2	f1-eb2	Men's voices	A spirited, vigorous hunting song. Demands facile articulation and some flexibility. (Duncan)
The faithful lover	d#1-g2	g1-e2	Not too suitable for very low voices	Sustained. Demands some flexibility. (Potter)
The maiden's complaint	e1-gb2	g1-eb2	Women's voices	Recitative and a sustained air. Demands some flexibility. (Moffat)
The plague of love	d1-g2	g1-eb2	All voices	Sustained, graceful. Demands some flexibility. (Wilson)
The shepherd	d#1-e2	f#1-d2	Most suitable for men's voices	Slow. Demands some flexibility. (Barrett)
The soldier tired of war's alarms	c#1-b2	f#1-a2	Soprano	Most suitable for high voices. A spirited, in parts florid, display piece. Could be sung by a mezzo-soprano, tenor, or high baritone if transposed. (Hatton and Fanning)
The sycamore shade	bb-f2	f1-eb2	Alto or mezzo-soprano	Sustained, graceful. Demands some flexibility. A trifle long. (Barrett)
Under the greenwood tree	c1-f#2	f#1-d2	All voices	Spirited, light. (Potter)

TITLE	COMP.	TESS.	TYPE	REMARKS
Water parted from the sea	e♭1-g2	f1-e♭2	All voices	Sustained. Demands some flexibility. (Potter)
We all love a pretty girl under the rose	c1-f2	e♭1-c2	All voices	Light, animated, humorous. Demands facile articulation. (Hatton and Fanning)
When daisies pied	d1-e♭2	f1-e♭2	Not too suitable for very low voices	Graceful, delicate. Demands some flexibility. (Moffat)
When forced from dear Hebe to go	d1-f2	f1-d2	Men's voices	Sustained. (Hatton and Fanning)
Where the bee sucks	c1-f2	f1-d2	Not too suitable for very low voices	Graceful, animated. Demands some flexibility. (Bantock)
Why so pale and wan?	a-e2	d1-d2	Not too suitable for light, high voices	Rather vigorous, gently humorous. (Duncan)

For other songs to poems by Shakespeare, see Songs to the Plays of Shakespeare, edited by Philip Miller, Music Press.

DR. SAMUEL ARNOLD
(1740-1802)

Amo, amas, I love a lass	g1-g2	g1-e2	Men's voices	Spirited, humorous. (Duncan)

JOHN ATTEY
(d. 1640?)

On a time the amorous Silvy	d1-g2	g1-d2	Not too suitable for light, high voices	Sustained, graceful. (Fellowes 40)
Sweet was the song	e1-a2	a1-f2	Most suitable for light soprano	Delicate, sustained. Demands some flexibility. A Christmas lullaby. (Keel)

10

THOMAS ATTWOOD
(1765–1838)

TITLE	COMP.	TESS.	TYPE	REMARKS
At early dawn	e1-f#2	a1-e2	Not too suitable for very low voices	Animated, graceful. Demands some flexibility. (Potter)

JOHN BARTLET
(Early 17th Century)

TITLE	COMP.	TESS.	TYPE	REMARKS
A pretty, pretty ducke	f1-g2	a1-f2	Most suitable for light soprano	Animated, graceful. Gently humorous. (Keel)
If there be anyone	f1-f2	a1-f2	Not too suitable for very low voices	Graceful. (Keel)
I heard of late	d1-g2	g1-e2	Not too suitable for very low voices	Graceful, sustained. (Keel)
Of all the birds that I do know	g1-g2	g1-e2	All voices	Animated, humorous. Demands facile articulation. (Fellowes 40)
What thing is love	e1-f#2	a1-e2	Most suitable for men's voices	Animated, graceful. Gently humorous. (Keel)
When from my love I lookte	e1-g2	g1-e2	Most suitable for men's voices	Graceful. (Keel)
Whither runneth my sweetheart?	d1-g2	g1-e2	Most suitable for high voices	Animated, light. Demands facile articulation. (Keel)
Who doth behold my mistress' face?	a1-f#2	same	Most suitable for men's voices	Light, graceful. (Keel)

THOMAS H. BAYLY
(1797–1839)

TITLE	COMP.	TESS.	TYPE	REMARKS
I'd be a butterfly	g1-c3	b1-g2	Light so-prano	Graceful. Has florid cadenzas by La Forge. (Arr., La Forge, CF)
Long, long ago	eb1-f2	ab1-eb2 (H)	All voices	Sustained. (gen. av.)
We met	d1-f2	d1-b1	Women's voices	Sustained. (Hatton and Fanning)

JOHN BENET
(1570–1615)

TITLE	COMP.	TESS.	TYPE	REMARKS
My mistress is as fair as fine	c1-c2	same	Men's voices	Sustained. (Duncan)
Weep, O mine eyes	d1-e2	g1-d2	All voices	Slow, sustained. A transcription of a four-part madrigal. (Bantock)

SIR HENRY R. BISHOP
(1786–1855)

The inclusion of songs by Bishop in this section was primarily prompted by stylistic considerations. Bishop's pleasing and effective songs could hardly be classed as belonging to the nineteenth century, since harmonically and melodically they are written in a manner which most probably must have seemed "old-fashioned" to the listeners of his day. Of no great consequence, most of his songs which have survived did so mainly as florid display pieces for coloratura soprano.

TITLE	COMP.	TESS.	TYPE	REMARKS
Bid me discourse	b-a2	g1-g2	Soprano	A brilliant, somewhat florid display song. (Hatton and Fanning)
Echo song	d1-c3 (eb3)	g1-g2	Coloratura soprano	A florid display piece. (Arr., La Forge, GS)
Home, sweet home	e1-e2	same	All voices	Sustained. (gen. av.)

TITLE	COMP.	TESS.	TYPE	REMARKS
Lo, here the gentle lark	e1-c3	f1-g2	Coloratura soprano or light soprano	Animated, brilliant display song. Has florid cadenza. Flute obbligato. (gen. av.)
Love has eyes	f1-g2	bb1-f2	Most suitable for women's voices	Light, animated. Demands facile articulation. (gen. av.)
Pretty mocking bird	d1-ab2	g1-f2	Coloratura or light soprano	Animated, has florid cadenzas. Demands facile articulation. (Hatton and Fanning)
Rest, my child	f1-f2	same	Women's voices	Sustained, subdued. (Duncan)
Should he upbraid	d1-d3	g1-e2	Light soprano	Light and spirited. Demands some flexibility. (For a shortened version see the Liebling edition, GS)
Tell me, my heart	d1-ab2	g1-f2	Light soprano	A sustained introduction and an animated and rather florid andantino. (Hatton and Fanning)

JOHN BLOW
(1648–1708)

It is not that I love you less	d1-g2	g1-e2	Men's voices	Sustained. (Bantock)
Since the spring comes on	d1-g#2	d1-d2	Most suitable for men's voices	Graceful. (Duncan)
Tell me no more	d1-g2	e1-e2 (H)	All voices	Animated, graceful. Demands some flexibility. (Bantock)

DR. WILLIAM BOYCE
(1710–1779)

Declare my pretty maid	a-d2	d1-c#2	Men's voices	Animated, lively. (Mulinar, AUG)

TITLE	COMP.	TESS.	TYPE	REMARKS
Heart of oak	bb-f2	f1-d2	Most suitable for men's voices	Animated. Strophic. A setting to nationalistic words by David Garrick. (Potter)
Of all the torments	c#1-d2	d1-b1	All voices	Graceful. (Mullinar, AUG)
Tell me no more I am deceived	d1-ab2	g1-e2	Men's voices	Animated, graceful.
The happy pair	b-e2	e1-c2	Men's voices	In the style of a minuet. Graceful. (Mullinar, AUG)
The sword within the scabbard keep (from Dryden's "Secular Masque")	bb-eb2	eb1-c2	Medium or low voices	Animated, vigorous. (Arr., G. E. P. Arkwright, OX)
Tho' Chloe out of fashion	b-e2	e1-c#2	Men's voices	Animated, florid. (Mullinar, AUG)
Venus to soothe my heart	b-c2	d1-b1	Men's voices	Sustained, graceful. (Mullinar, AUG)

THOMAS BROWN
(18th Century?)

TITLE	COMP.	TESS.	TYPE	REMARKS
Shepherd! thy demeanor vary	e1-c3	a1-f2	Light soprano	Animated, light. Has florid passages. (Wilson)

WILLIAM BYRD
(1542–1623)

TITLE	COMP.	TESS.	TYPE	REMARKS
I thought that love had been a boy	e1-g2	g1-e2 (H)	All voices	Delicate, sustained. A transcription of a madrigal. (Bantock)
My mind to me a kingdom is	bb-eb2	eb1-bb1	All voices	Sustained. (Moffat)
O mistress mine	g1-g2	g1-e2 (H)	Most suitable for men's voices	Sustained. (Bantock)

THOMAS CAMPIAN (CAMPION)
(1567–1620)
(See prefatory note to John Dowland)

TITLE	COMP.	TESS.	TYPE	REMARKS
Beauty is but painted hell	e1-f♯2	g♯1-e2	All voices	Sustained. (Keel)
Breake now my heart and die	e1-g2	f♯1-e2	Men's voices	Graceful, sustained. (Keel)
Come, you pretty false eyed wanton	g♯1-f♯2	a1-e2	Men's voices	Spirited, light. (Keel)
Every dame affects good fame	e1-g2	a1-f2	Most suitable for men's voices	Graceful, humorous. (Keel)
Fair, if you expect admiring	e1-f♯2	a1-e2	Men's voices	Animated, graceful. (Fellowes 40)
Follow thy fair sun	f♯1-f♯2	b1-f♯2	Men's voices	Sustained, somber. (Fellowes 40)
Follow your saint	d1-d2	f1-b1	Most suitable for men's voices	Sustained. (Fellowes 40)
Here she her sacred bower adornes	d1-d2	same	Men's voices	Animated, graceful. Demands some flexibility. (Keel)
Her rosie cheeks	e1-f♯2	g♯1-e2	Men's voices	Sustained. Demands some flexibility. Graceful. (Keel)
Jack and Joan	g1-f♯2	a1-e2	All voices	Spirited. (Fellowes 40)
Move now with measured sound	e1-e2	g1-e2	All voices	Sustained. (Duncan)
My sweetest Lesbia	f1-g2	a1-f2 (H)	Most suitable for men's voices	Sustained, not slow. (Fellowes 40)
Never weather beaten sail	d1-e2	g1-d2	All voices	Sustained. A religious song taken from Divine and Moral Songs. Originally written for four parts. (Bantock)
Now hath Flora robb'd her bow'rs	d1-e2	g1-d2	All voices	Sustained. (Duncan)

15

TITLE	COMP.	TESS.	TYPE	REMARKS
O deare, that I with thee might live	f#1-f#2	b1-f#2	Most suitable for men's voices	Sustained. (Keel)
Oft have I sighed for him	f1-f2	g1-db2	Women's voices	Sustained, somber. (Keel)
Shall I come, sweet love, to thee	f1-f2 (H)	same	Most suitable for men's voices	Sustained. Originally for two voices with lute accompaniment. (Bantock)
The cypress curtain of the night	g1-f2	same	All voices except a very light soprano	Slow, sustained, somber. (Fellowes 40)
There is a garden in her face	e1-f#2	a1-e2 (H)	Most suitable for men's voices	Graceful, not slow. (Fellowes 40)
Thrice tosse these oaken ashes in the air	e1-g2	g1-e2	All voices	Sustained. A magic incantation to break love's spell. (Keel)
The peaceful western winde	f1-g2	bb1-f2	Most suitable for men's voices	Sustained. (Keel)
When to her lute Corinna sings	b-d2	e1-b1 (L)	Most suitable for men's voices	Sustained, somewhat declamatory. (Fellowes 40)

HENRY CAREY
(1690–1743)

TITLE	COMP.	TESS.	TYPE	REMARKS
A pastoral	c1-g2 (a2)	g1-e2	Soprano	Animated, florid, graceful. (Wilson)
Divinest fair	d1-g2	g1-e2	Most suitable for men's voices	Sustained, graceful. (Duncan)
Here's to thee, my boy	bb-eb2	eb1-eb2	Men's voices, except a very light tenor	A spirited, vigorous, somewhat rowdy drinking song. Demands some flexibility. (Moffat)

TITLE	COMP.	TESS.	TYPE	REMARKS
The plausible lover	d1-g2	g1-e2	Most suitable for light, high voices	Graceful, delicate. Demands considerable flexibility and a good command of high pp. (Potter)

MICHAEL CAVENDISH
(c. 1565-1628)

TITLE	COMP.	TESS.	TYPE	REMARKS
Finetta fair and feat	f#1-f#2	a#1-e2	Men's voices	Sustained, graceful. (Fellowes 40)

JEREMIAH CLARK
(1659-1707)

TITLE	COMP.	TESS.	TYPE	REMARKS
The bonny grey-eyed morn	c1-g2	g1-e2	All voices	Graceful. Demands some flexibility. (Duncan)

WILLIAM CORKINE
(Early 17th Century)

TITLE	COMP.	TESS.	TYPE	REMARKS
Deare, though your mind	b-d2	e1-c2	Most suitable for men's voices	Animated, graceful. (Keel)
Down, down, proud mind	e1-g2	a1-g2 (H)	Not too suitable for very light voices	Very sustained, grave. (Fellowes 40)
Shall a smile or a guileful glance	g1-g2	g1-e2	Most suitable for men's voices	Graceful. (Keel)
Sweete cupid, ripen her desire	d1-d2	same	Men's voices	Animated, graceful. (Keel)

WILLIAM CROFT
(1678-1727)

TITLE	COMP.	TESS.	TYPE	REMARKS
Musidora	d1-g2 (a2)	g1-e2	Most suitable for high voices	Sustained. (Duncan)

17

JOHN DAVY
(1763–1824)

TITLE	COMP.	TESS.	TYPE	REMARKS
Just like love is yonder rose	f1–g2	g1–e2	Not too suitable for very low voices	Graceful. Requires some flexibility. (Duncan)

WILLIAM de FESCH
(1700–1758)

TITLE	COMP.	TESS.	TYPE	REMARKS
Daphne	d1–e2	f♯1–d2	All voices	Graceful, humorous. (Potter)

For other songs and airs see under "Italian" in this section (page 44).

CHARLES DIBDIN
(1745–1814)

TITLE	COMP.	TESS.	TYPE	REMARKS
Blow high, blow low	G–c1	B♭–b♭	Bass	A vigorous sailor's song. (Potter)
Jolly young waterman	d1–e2	g1–d2	Men's voices	Animated. Demands facile articulation. (Bantock)
The tinker's song	d♭1–f2	d♭1–d♭2	Men's voices	Spirited, vigorous, humorous. (Wilson)
The wily fox	a–g2	e1–e2	Men's voices	A spirited hunting song. Demands facile articulation. (Duncan)

JOHN DOWLAND
(1563–1626)

The songs of John Dowland, Thomas Campian, and a number of lesser known Elizabethan composers for one or more voices with lute accompaniment, have been made popularly available only comparatively recently, mainly in the admirable transcriptions of Dr. Edmund H. Fellowes.

Every singer, especially in the English-speaking countries, ought to be thoroughly familiar with these remarkable songs. None of them are vocally taxing, their compass rarely exceeds a tenth and for the most part being confined to an octave or a ninth. Stylistically, however, they may present a number of difficulties to those who are used to the more flamboyant manner of delivery considered desirable in certain types of nineteenth century vocal music.

A competent performance of these songs would seem to demand above all a considerable degree of rhythmic precision, as well as a certain amount of understatement in the delivery of the text. Under no circumstances, however, should the search for such precision and simplicity terminate in superficial pedantry, for these songs are by no means "quaint" examples of the music of the past. Unless the present-day singer can accept these songs as an artistically valid combination of poetry and music it would be best for him not to attempt to perform them.

One should note that in the edition of Dr. Fellowes no time signatures whatsoever are used. The very frequent meter changes occur without any written warning. Likewise the bar line and the accent often do not coincide, the bar line being used as a purely visual convenience and not as an indication of a strong beat.

Most of the other transcriptions of these songs (including Keel) distort the original assymetrical structure by adding and subtracting beats to make the measures of uniform length.

Dowland 50 in parentheses indicates <u>Fifty Dowland Songs</u> (High and Low), edited by Fellowes, published by Stainer and Bell.

TITLE	COMP.	TESS.	TYPE	REMARKS
A shepherd in a shade	f♯1-f♯2	a♯1-e2	All voices	Animated, graceful. (Dowland 50)
Awake, sweet love, thou art returned	e1-f2	g1-e2	Most suitable for men's voices	Animated, graceful. (Dowland 50)
Away with these self-loving lads	e1-f♯2	g♯1-e2	Most suitable for men's voices	Animated, graceful. (Keel)
By a fountain where I lay	f♯1-f2	g1-f2	All voices	Sustained, graceful. (Dowland 50)
Clear and cloudy	f1-g2	b1-f2	All voices	Slightly animated. (Dowland 50)
Come again! sweet love doth now invite	e♭1-f2	a♭1-e♭2	All voices	Graceful, animated. (Dowland 50)
Come away, come, sweet love	f♯1-f2	a1-d2	Not too suitable for very low voices	Graceful, light. (Dowland 50)

TITLE	COMP.	TESS.	TYPE	REMARKS
Come, heavy sleep	e1-f♯2	g1-e2	All voices	Slow, sustained. Somewhat subdued. (Dowland 50)
Dear, if you change	e1-f♯2	f♯1-f♯2	All voices	Slow, sustained. (Dowland 50)
Disdain me still	f1-g2	a1-f2	All voices	Sustained. (Dowland 50)
Farewell, unkind, farewell	g♯1-f♯2	a1-e2	All voices	Sustained. (Keel)
Fine knacks for ladies	e1-f2	f1-d2	Most suitable for men's voices	An animated, somewhat vigorous "peddler's song." (Fellowes 40)
Flow, my tears	f1-g2	g1-eb2	All voices, excepting a very light soprano	Slow, sustained, somber. (Fellowes 40)
Flow not so fast, ye fountains	g1-g2	c2-f2	All voices	Very sustained, somber. (Dowland 50)
Go, crystal tears	a1-f2	a1-eb2	Most suitable for men's voices	Slow, sustained. (Dowland 50)
I saw my lady weep	g1-g2	bb1-f2	Men's voices	Slow, sustained, somber. (Fellowes 40)
If my complaints could passions move	f♯1-f2	g1-e2	All voices	Sustained. (Fellowes 40)
If that a sinner's sighs	f♯1-g2	a1-d2	All voices	Slow, sustained. (Dowland 50)
In darkness let me dwell	eb1-g2	g1-f2	Not suitable for light, high voices	Slow, sustained, somber. (Dowland 50)
It was a time when silly bees	e1-f2	a1-e2	All voices	Sustained. (Dowland 50)
Lady, if you so spite me	g1-f2	a1-eb2	Men's voices	Sustained. (Dowland 50)
Mourn! Day is with darkness fled	f1-f2	same	All voices	Slow, sustained. (Dowland 50)
My heart and tongue were twins	d1-f♯2	f♯1-e2	All voices	Sustained. (Dowland 50)

TITLE	COMP.	TESS.	TYPE	REMARKS
Now, O now, I needs must part	f♯1-f♯2	f♯1-e2	All voices	Sustained, graceful. An arrangement of a four-part madrigal. (Dowland 50)
O what hath overwrought?	f♯1-f2	g1-d2	All voices	Animated. (Dowland 50)
Say, love, if ever thou didst find	a1-f2	b♭1-e♭2	Most suitable for men's voices	Animated, graceful. (Fellowes 40)
Shall I strive with words to move?	a1-g2	a1-e2	Men's voices	Graceful. Demands facile articulation. (Dowland 50)
Shall I sue?	g1-g2	g1-d2	Most suitable for men's voices	Light, graceful. Demands facile articulation. (Dowland 50)
Sleep, wayward thoughts	e♭1-c2	same	Most suitable for men's voices	Sustained. (Fellowes 40)
Sorrow, sorrow, stay	c1-c2	e1-b1	All voices	Slow, somber, somewhat declamatory. (Fellowes 40)
Stay, time, awhile thy flying	g1-f2	same	All voices	Sustained, graceful. (Keel)
Tell me, true love	f♯1-f♯2	a1-f♯2	All voices	Slow, sustained. (Dowland 50)
The lowest trees have tops	f♯1-f♯2	a1-e2	All voices	Sustained. (Dowland 50)
Unquiet thoughts	g1-f2	a1-e2	All voices	Sustained. (Dowland 50)
Weep you no more, sad fountains	d1-g2	g1-d2	All voices	Slow, sustained. (Fellowes 40)
Were every thought an eye	g1-g2	b1-f2	Men's voices	Animated, graceful. (Dowland 50)
What if I never speed?	e1-f2	a1-e2	Most suitable for men's voices	Animated, graceful. (Dowland 50)
Where sin sore wounding	g1-g2	a♭1-f2	All voices	Slow, sustained. (Dowland 50)

TITLE	COMP.	TESS.	TYPE	REMARKS
Woeful heart with griefe oppressed	c1-e♭2	e♭1-c2	Not too suitable for very high voices	Slow, sustained, somber. (Keel)

JOHN ECCLES
(1650–1735)

TITLE	COMP.	TESS.	TYPE	REMARKS
The avowal	e1-g2	g1-e2	Men's voices	Sustained, graceful. (Duncan)

THOMAS FORD
(1580–1648)

TITLE	COMP.	TESS.	TYPE	REMARKS
Come, Phillis, come into these bowers	g♯1-g2	a1-e2	Most suitable for men's voices	Sustained, graceful. (Fellowes 40)
Fair, sweet, cruel	b-d2	d1-b1	All voices	Somewhat declamatory. Not fast. (Fellowes 40)
Not full twelve years	c♯1-g♯2	g♯1-e2	Not too suitable for very light, high voices	Slow, sustained, somber. Demands some flexibility. (Fellowes 40)
Now I see thy looks were feigned	e1-g2	a1-e2	Men's voices	Sustained, not slow. (Fellowes 40)
Passing by	d1-e2	g1-d2	Men's voices	Sustained. (Duncan)
Since first I saw your face	f1-f2	f1-c2	Most suitable for men's voices	Sustained. (Bantock)
What then is love, sings Corydon	c1-d2	same	All voices	Sustained, not slow. (Fellowes 40)

JOHN ERNEST GALLIARD
(1687–1749)

TITLE	COMP.	TESS.	TYPE	REMARKS
The early horn	c1-g2	f1-f2	Men's voices	Recitative and a spirited rather florid hunting song. (Potter)

TITLE	COMP.	TESS.	TYPE	REMARKS
The lover's message	d1-e2	f#1-d2	All voices	Sustained, graceful. (Potter)

ORLANDO GIBBONS
(1583-1615)

TITLE	COMP.	TESS.	TYPE	REMARKS
The silver swan	f1-g2	bb1-f2	All voices	Slow, sustained. A transcription of a five-part madrigal. One of Gibbons' few secular songs. (Bantock)
Like as a huntsman	f1-f2	same	Most suitable for men's voices	Animated, demands some flexibility. (Duncan)
Orpheus with his lute	f1-g2	f1-e2	Most suitable for high voices	Animated. Demands flexibility. (Duncan)
The nymph that undoes me	f1-f2	same	Men's voices	Graceful. (Duncan)

JAMES HOOK
(1746-1827)

TITLE	COMP.	TESS.	TYPE	REMARKS
Bright Phoebus	eb1-f2	ab1-eb2	Men's voices	A spirited hunting song. Demands considerable flexibility. (Neitzel, Gems of Antiquity, JCC)
Lass of Richmond Hill	c1-f2	f1-d2	Most suitable for men's voices	Graceful. (Bantock)
Love's call	db1-eb2	f1-db2	Men's voices	Sustained, graceful. (Duncan)
Mary of Allendale	eb1-ab2	g1-eb2	Most suitable for high voices	Sustained. Demands good command of high pp. (Wilson)
Softly waft, ye southern breezes	e1-g2	a1-f#2	Soprano	Animated, graceful. Demands some flexibility. (Potter)

TITLE	COMP.	TESS.	TYPE	REMARKS
The sweet little girl that I love	f1-a2	a1-f2	Most suitable for tenor.	Sustained, graceful. Demands good command of high pp. (Wilson)

FRANCIS HOPKINSON
(1737–1791)

The songs of Francis Hopkinson, one of the first American composers, have lately attained a considerable popularity. Pleasant and tuneful, these songs are as typical of the period as any of Dr. Arne, though perhaps not as skillfully executed.

TITLE	COMP.	TESS.	TYPE	REMARKS
Beneath a weeping willow's shade	d1-g2	g1-d2	All voices	Graceful. Demands some flexibility.
Come, fair Rosina	e1-f♯2	a1-d2	All voices	Sustained, graceful.
My days have been so wondrous free	e♭1-g2 (a♭2)	a♭1-e♭2 (H)	All voices	Graceful.
My generous heart disdains	d1-g2	g1-d2	Most suitable for men's voices	Graceful, gently humorous. A trifle long.
O'er the hills	c♯1-g2	f♯1-d2	All voices	Spirited, vigorous hunting song. Demands some flexibility.
The traveler benighted	d1-g2	f1-d2	All voices	Sustained, graceful.

All songs arranged by H. V. Milligan, Arthur Schmidt edition.

TITLE	COMP.	TESS.	TYPE	REMARKS
Ode from Ossian's poems	d1-a2	e1-e2	High voices	A short solo cantata in several contrasting movements. Demands some flexibility. (Arr., Carl Deis, GS)

CHARLES EDWARD HORN
(1786–1849)

TITLE	COMP.	TESS.	TYPE	REMARKS
Cherry ripe	d1-g2	g1-e♭2	Not too suitable for very low voices	Animated, graceful. Demands some flexibility. (gen. av.)

TITLE	COMP.	TESS.	TYPE	REMARKS
I've been roaming	c#1-f#2	f#1-d2	Women's voices	Animated, graceful. Demands facile articulation. (Bantock)
The deep, deep sea	a-g2	f#1-d2	Most suitable for men's voices	Sustained, graceful. (Hatton and Fanning)

SAMUEL HOWARD
(1710–1782)

TITLE	COMP.	TESS.	TYPE	REMARKS
The diffident lover	f#1-g2	g1-e2	Not too suitable for very low voices	Sustained, delicate. Demands some flexibility. (Potter)

TOBIAS HUME
(d. 1648)

TITLE	COMP.	TESS.	TYPE	REMARKS
Fain would I change that note	d1-g2	g1-e2	All voices, except a very light soprano	Sustained. (Fellowes 40)

PELHAM HUMFREY (HUMPHREY)
(1647–1674)

TITLE	COMP.	TESS.	TYPE	REMARKS
A hymne to God the Father	c#1-f2	eb1-eb2 (H)	Not suitable for light, high voices	Slow, sustained. Declamatory throughout, in parts somewhat dramatic. An impressive setting of powerful texts by John Donne. (Tippett and Bergmann, SCH)
I pass all my hours	e1-f2	g#1-e2	Most suitable for men's voices	Sustained. (Bantock)
O the sad day	c1-g2	f1-eb2	All voices	Sustained, somewhat declamatory. (Bantock)

TITLE	COMP.	TESS.	TYPE	REMARKS
Wherever I am	c#1-f2	f#1-eb2	Men's voices	Graceful. (Moffat)

WILLIAM JACKSON
(1730–1803)

TITLE	COMP.	TESS.	TYPE	REMARKS
To fairest Delia's grassy tomb	g1-g2	g1-eb2 (H)	Most suitable for men's voices	Sustained. (Bantock)
What shepherd or nymph of the grove?	c1-g2	g1-eb2 (H)	Most suitable for men's voices	Sustained. Demands some flexibility. (Bantock)
Ye shepherds, give ear to my lay	d1-g2	a1-f2	Not too suitable for very low voices	Sustained, graceful. (Moffat)

ROBERT JOHNSON
(c. 1583–1633)

TITLE	COMP.	TESS.	TYPE	REMARKS
As I walked forth one summer day	c1-f2	f1-c2	Not too suitable for very light, high voices	Slow, sustained. (Bantock)
Dear, do not your fair beauty wrong	c1-g2	f1-e2 (H)	All voices	Sustained. (Bantock)

ROBERT JONES
(d. 1617)

TITLE	COMP.	TESS.	TYPE	REMARKS
Go to bed, sweet muse	c1-eb2	f1-c2	All voices	Animated, humorous. (Keel)
In Sherwood lived stout Robin Hood	d1-g2	g1-e2 (H)	All voices	Spirited, animated. (Fellowes 40)
Love is a bable	a-d2	d1-d2 (L)	Most suitable for men's voices	Animated, humorous. (Fellowes 40)

TITLE	COMP.	TESS.	TYPE	REMARKS
Love's god is a boy	g1-g2	same	All voices	Animated, humorous. Demands in parts facile articulation. (Fellowes 40)
My love bound me with a kisse	e1-e2	e1-b1	Men's voices	Sustained. (Moffat)
Now what is love	c1-c2	f1-c2	All voices	Animated, gently humorous. (Fellowes 40)
Sweet Kate	d1-d2	e1-c2	All voices	A humorous dialogue between Kate and her lover. Demands some flexibility. (Keel)
What if I seek for love	c#1-e2	f#1-c#2	All voices	Not fast. Demands rather facile articulation. (Keel)
What if I speede	e1-g2	a1-e2	Not too suitable for very low voices	Animated, gay. (Keel)

HENRY LAWES
(1595–1662)

Amarantha sweet and fair	f1-f2	same	Men's voices	Sustained. (Duncan)
About the sweet bag of a bee	g1-f2	same	All voices	Sustained. (Potter)
Ask me why I send you here	f1-f2	same	All voices	Sustained. (Duncan)
Beauty and love	c#1-e2	f#1-c#2	All voices	Graceful. (Potter)
Bid me but live	g1-f2	same	All voices	Sustained, graceful. (Bantock)
Chloris, yourself you so excel	c1-e2	e1-c2	Men's voices	Sustained, graceful. (Duncan)
Come, lovely Phillis	d1-d2	same	Men's voices	Graceful. (Potter)
How happy art thou	c1-e2	g1-c2	Men's voices	Spirited. (Potter)
I am confirmed a woman can	c1-e2	g1-c2	Most suitable for men's voices	Animated, humorous. (Dolmetsch)

TITLE	COMP.	TESS.	TYPE	REMARKS
I do confess thou'rt smooth and fair	d1-d2	g1-d2	All voices	Sustained. (Potter)
I prithee, send me back my heart	eb1-eb2	g1-c2	All voices	Sustained. (Moffat)
If the quick spirit of your eye	f#1-f#2	g1-d2	Men's voices	Animated, graceful. (Potter)
Tavola	c#1-e2	d1-d2	All voices	Lawes wrote this song as a satire upon the Italian songs of his day. The text is the Index of a volume of Italian songs and madrigals. (Bridge, Seventeenth Century Songs, NOV)
The angler's song	f1-f2	same	Most suitable for men's voices	Spirited. Words by Izaak Walton. (Dolmetsch)
The nightingale	c#1-c#2	e1-b1 (L)	All voices	Sustained, delicate. (J. Woodside, Seven Centuries of Solo Song, Vol. II, BMC)
To a lady weeping	e1-d2	same	All voices	Sustained. (Moffat)
Unfading beauty	g1-f2	same	All voices	Sustained. (Duncan)
While I listen to thy voice	d1-eb2	g1-d2	Men's voices	Sustained. (Neitzel, Gems of Antiquity, JCC)

WILLIAM LAWES
(1602–1645)

TITLE	COMP.	TESS.	TYPE	REMARKS
Gather ye rosebuds while you may	g1-e2	same	All voices	Sustained, graceful. (Potter)

RICHARD LEVERIDGE
(1670–1758)

TITLE	COMP.	TESS.	TYPE	REMARKS
Black eyed Susan	d1-f#2	f#1-d2	Women's voices	A narrative song. The tune has become as popular as a folk song. (Bantock)

TITLE	COMP.	TESS.	TYPE	REMARKS
Jilted	f1-g2	a1-f2	Not too suitable for very low voices	Graceful. Demands some flexibility. (Duncan)
Send back my longstrayed eyes to me	d1-f2	e1-e2	All voices	Sustained. One of Leveridge's appealing songs. (Duncan)
Sweet are the charms of her I love	d1-f2	g1-eb2	Men's voices	Sustained, graceful. Demands some flexibility. (Moffat)
The beggar's song	(g)a-d2	d1-b1	Men's voices, except a very light tenor	Spirited, vigorous. (Wilson)
The fairies (Now the hungry lions roar)	e1-g2	g1-e2	All voices	Animated. (Duncan)
The maid's resolution	d1-f♯2	f♯1-e2	Women's voices	Sustained, graceful. The words are of an amusingly moral character. (Potter)
The sweet rosy morning	eb1-eb2	same	Men's voices	A spirited hunting song. Demands facile articulation. (Moffat)
When dull care	b-e2 (g2)	d1-c2	Men's voices	A spirited, vigorous drinking song. (Wilson)

THOMAS LINLEY
(1732–1795)

TITLE	COMP.	TESS.	TYPE	REMARKS
Here's to the maiden of bashful fifteen	d1-d2	d1-b1	Men's voices	A spirited toast to women of all ages. Demands facile articulation. (Bantock)
Lawn, as white as driven snow	b-e2	e1-c2	Medium or low voices	A spirited setting of Autolycus' song from The Winter's Tale. (Neitzel, Gems of Antiquity, JCC)

TITLE	COMP.	TESS.	TYPE	REMARKS
No flower that blows	e1-f♯2	a1-e2	All voices	Sustained, delicate. (Potter)
O, bid your faithful Ariel fly	b-g♯2	d1-d2	High voices	Animated. Quite florid in parts. (Hatton and Fanning)
Primroses deck the bank's green side	b-e2	e1-c♯2	Most suitable for men's voices	Sustained, graceful. Demands some flexibility. (Hatton and Fanning)
Still the lark finds repose	e1-f♯2	g1-f♯2	Not too suitable for very low voices	Sustained, graceful. (Duncan)
While the foaming billows roll	b♭(a♭)-e♭2	e♭1-c2	Men's voices	A vigorous, patriotic sea song. (Wilson)

MATTHEW LOCKE
(1630–1677)

TITLE	COMP.	TESS.	TYPE	REMARKS
My lodging, it is on the cold ground	c1-e♭2	f1-c2	Women's voices	Sustained. (Bantock)

THOMAS MORLEY
(1557–1603)

TITLE	COMP.	TESS.	TYPE	REMARKS
Flora, wilt thou torment me?	d1-g2	g1-e2	Most suitable for men's voices	Animated, graceful. A transcription of a two-part canzonet. (Keel)
It was a lover and his lass	f1-f2 (H)	same	All voices	Animated, light. Demands facile articulation. (Bantock)
Now is the month of maying	d1-d2 (H)	same	All voices	Animated. (Bantock)
Sweet nymph, come to thy lover	b-e2	e1-b1	Most suitable for men's voices	Animated, graceful. Demands some flexibility. A transcription of a two-part canzonet. (Keel)

TITLE	COMP.	TESS.	TYPE	REMARKS
When lo! by breake of morning	a-e2	d1-d2	Most suitable for men's voices	Animated, graceful. A transcription of a two-part canzonet. (Keel)

GEORGE MUNRO
(18th Century)

My lovely Celia	d1-g2	g1-d2	All voices	Sustained, graceful. Demands good command of high pp. and some flexibility. (Wilson)

JAMES OSWALD
(1712-1769)

Peace, the fairest child of heaven	d1-g2	f1-eb2	All voices	Sustained. Demands some flexibility. (Potter)

FRANCIS PILKINGTON
(1562-1638)

Diaphenia	f1-f2	b1-f2	Men's voices	Sustained, graceful. (Fellowes 40)
Down a down thus Phyllis sung	f1-f2	bb1-f2	Not too suitable for very low voices	Graceful. (Fellowes 40)
Now peep, Bo-peep	e1-g2	a1-e2	Men's voices	Sustained. (Fellowes 40)
Rest, sweet nymphs	g1-f2	g1-eb2 (H)	All voices	Sustained, subdued. (Fellowes 40)
Underneath a cypress tree	eb1-eb2	f1-c2	All voices	Sustained. (Keel)

DANIEL PURCELL
(1663-1717)

Phillis, talk no more of passion	d1-f2	a1-d2	All voices	Graceful. Demands some flexibility. (Potter)

HENRY PURCELL
(1658–1695)

Purcell's name, generally speaking, seems to be much more familiar than his music to the majority of performers and music lovers of today. In this respect the somewhat paradoxical nature of his fame is rather similar to that of Rameau and Lully.

One of the greatest seventeenth century composers, Purcell wrote in a remarkably individual manner. His songs and airs are perhaps among the most striking examples of his style of writing. Never unnecessarily florid, powerfully descriptive in the delineation of the mood and character of the text, impeccable in prosody, his songs and airs are nevertheless often marred, at least for the present-day performer and listener, by their undistinguished and antiquated texts. Musically, however, Purcell's songs and airs are so extraordinarily powerful that the limitations of his poetic material seem to vanish during the actual performance.

Purcell's songs and airs demand from the vocalist a peculiarly delicate balance between dramatic delivery and the impeccably clear delineation of the musical line. In singing Purcell the vocalist should always remember that the florid passages are never intended for mere display, but serve as an intensification of the dramatic context, and are for the most part strikingly descriptive of the word upon which they occur. One must also remember that Purcell's bass line is melodically as important as his vocal line. This writer believes that many a scholarly and well-intentioned editor of Purcell's songs and airs, which were originally written for bass (figured or unfigured) and voice, has obscured the magnificently eloquent bass line by overloading the accompaniment with too many independent inner parts. Purcell was very fond of the basso ostinato, and in certain editions the recurrence of the bass figure in some of his songs is almost inaudible in the maze of unnecessarily elaborate added counterpoint in the inner voices.

Purcell, when not writing for alto or bass often favors very high tessituras. In most of the available present-day editions his soprano or tenor songs are transposed, sometimes as much as a fourth lower than the original. The original keys can be easily ascertained by consulting the Purcell Society edition.

The name found in parentheses in the remarks column indicates one of the following collections:

Edmunds: Henry Purcell (high and low), available singly and in collection, realized and edited by J. Edmunds, published by Row Music Co.

Kagen: 40 Songs (4 volumes, high and low) and 6 Songs for Bass, realized and edited by S. Kagen, published by International Music Co.

Moffat: 6 Songs by Purcell (original keys), edited by A. Moffat, published by Bayley and Ferguson.

32

Purcell Society: <u>Popular Edition</u> (2 volumes, high and low), compiled by the Purcell Society, published by Novello.
Somervell 15; 17: <u>15 Songs by Purcell and 17 Songs by Purcell</u> (original keys), edited by A. Somervell, published by Novello.

TITLE	COMP.	TESS.	TYPE	REMARKS
Adam's sleep	c1-g2	g1-f2	All voices	Very sustained, broad. (Edmunds)
Ah, Belinda, I am prest! (Dido and Aeneas)	c1-f2	g1-eb2	Soprano or mezzo-soprano	Sustained. (Kagen)
Ah! how pleasant 'tis to love	g1-g2	a1-g2	All voices	Sustained, graceful. (Kagen)
Ah, how sweet it is to love (Tyrannick love)	f#1-g2	a1-eb2	All voices	Not fast, graceful. Demands some flexibility. Originally written for soprano. (Kagen)
Ah what pains	d1-g2	g1-f2	High voices	Sustained. Demands some flexibility. (Somervell 17)
An evening hymn	d1-g2	f#1-e2	All voices, except a very light soprano	Slow, very sustained, broad. Ostinato bass. Has majestic Hallelujah section in the second half. Demands flexibility. (Kagen)
Anacreon's defeat	F-e1	c-c1	Baritone or bass	A short solo cantata in three contrasting movements. Has florid passages. Demands in parts considerable flexibility. (Kagen)
April who till now has mourn'd	e1-f2	a1-e2	Not too suitable for very low voices	Animated, graceful. Has florid passages. (Moffat)
Arise, ye subterranean winds (The Tempest)	E-d1	c-c1	Bass	Animated, vigorous, florid. (Kagen)
Ask me to love no more	d1-g2	g1-eb2	Soprano	Graceful. Demands some flexibility. (Moffat)

TITLE	COMP.	TESS.	TYPE	REMARKS
Bess of Bedlam	c1-g2	e1-e2	Women's voices	A dramatic, cantata-like song with many recitatives. Interpretatively and stylistically not easy. Compare with Purcell's "From rosy bowers." (Kagen)
Cease, o my sad soul	g1-g2	g1-eb2	All voices	Slow, sustained. (Kagen)
Come all ye songsters	f1-g2	a1-f2	All voices	Short recitative and sustained song with some florid passages. Joyous. One tone higher in original. (Kagen)
Fairest isle (King Arthur)	eb1-gb2	g1-eb2	All voices	Sustained, graceful. An "Address to Britain." One tone higher in original. (Kagen)
Fly swift, ye hours	B-e1	e-d1	Baritone	Vigorous, animated, quite florid. The final section is slow and sustained. Rather long. (Somervell 15)
From rosy bowers	d1-g2	eb1-g2	Soprano or mezzo-soprano	A rather long cantata-like song describing the phases of madness of a "lady distracted by love." The phases are as follows: "sullenly mad, mirthfully mad, melancholy madness, fantastically mad, stark mad." Has some florid passages. Interpretatively and stylistically not easy. (Kagen)
Hail to the myrtle shade (Theodosius)	e1-d2	f1-c2(L)	Most suitable for men's voices	Sustained, graceful. (Purcell Society)

TITLE	COMP.	TESS.	TYPE	REMARKS
Halcyon days (The Tempest)	d1-g2	g1-f2	All voices	Mostly sustained. Has florid passages. (Edmunds)
Hark! how all things	d1-f2	e1-e2	All voices	Spirited, quite florid. Demands flexibility. (Kagen)
Hark! the ech'ing air sings (Fairy Queen)	e1-a2	a1-g2	All voices	Spirited, florid. Demands some flexibility. (Kagen)
Hence with your trifling deity! (Timon of Athens)	F-eb1	c-c1	Bass	Spirited, vigorous. Has florid passages. (Kagen)
Here let my life	c1-eb2	eb1-db2 (L)	All voices	Sustained, somewhat slow. Ostinato bass used throughout. (Purcell Society)
How delightful's the life	d1-f#2	g1-e2	All voices	Graceful. Demands some flexibility. (Somervell 17)
Hush, be silent (The Fairy Queen)	c1-f2	c1-c2	All voices	Slow, sustained, subdued. (Edmunds)
I am come to lock all fast (The Fairy Queen)	d1-g2	eb1-eb2	All voices	Animated. Demands some flexibility. (Purcell Society)
I attempt from love's sickness to fly (The Indian Queen)	d#1-f#2	a1-e2	All voices	Graceful, light. Demands some flexibility. (Kagen)
I envy not a monarch's fate	c#1-e2	e1-c#2	Men's voices	Graceful. Demands some flexibility. (Somervell 15)
I fain would be free	e1-g2	g1-e2	All voices	Graceful, humorous. (Somervell 17)
I saw that you were grown so high	d1-f2	f1-f2	All voices	Sustained, short. (Kagen)
I see she flies me ev'rywhere (Aureng-Zebe)	b-e2	e1-d2 (L)	Men's voices	Fast, animated, light first section; slower, sustained ending section. (Purcell Society)
I take no pleasure	d1-f2	e1-e2	Men's voices	Slow, sustained. Somber text. Emotionally intense. (Edmunds)

TITLE	COMP.	TESS.	TYPE	REMARKS
If music be the food of love (First version)	d1-g2	f1-f2	All voices	Sustained. Demands some flexibility. (Kagen)
If music be the food of love (Third version)	d1-a2	g1-g2	Not suitable for low, heavy voices	Sustained, very florid. Demands flexibility. (Kagen)
I'll sail upon the Dog-star (A fool's preferment)	c1-g2	f1-d2	Men's voices	Spirited, vigorous; in parts quite florid. Sometimes called "The mad Tom." (Kagen)
In Cloris all soft charms agree	bb-eb2	eb1-c2	All voices	Sustained, graceful. (Somervell 15)
Let each gallant heart	c1-g2	g1-e2	All voices	Sustained, graceful. Demands some flexibility. Somervell 17)
Let us dance, let us sing (Dioclesian)	d1-f#2	g1-d2	All voices	Animated. Demands considerable flexibility. (Potter)
Lord, what is man	d1-a2	f#1-g2	All voices, except a very light soprano	A cantata-like sacred song which is neither interpretatively nor vocally easy. Has florid, dramatic recitative, a minuet-like allegretto and a florid, spirited, vigorous allegro. (Kagen)
Love quickly is pall'd (Timon of Athens)	c1-e2	e1-d2 (L)	All voices	Animated. (Purcell Society)
Man is for the woman made	e1-g2	e1-e2	All voices	Spirited, vigorous, humorous. (Kagen)
More love or more disdain	d1-g2	f1-f2	All voices	Sustained. Has alternating sections in 4/4 and 3/4 rhythms. (Kagen)
Music for awhile (Oedipus)	e1-f2	a1-e2	All voices	Sustained. Has a few florid passages. (Kagen)

TITLE	COMP.	TESS.	TYPE	REMARKS
My heart, whenever you appear	d1-f2	f1-d2	Men's voices	Sustained. Demands some flexibility. (Somervell 15)
Next winter comes slowly (The Fairy Queen)	G-d1	d-b♭	Bass	Slow, sustained. Demands some flexibility. (Potter)
No watch, dear Celia	d1-e2	e1-d2	Most suitable for men's voices	Delicate, graceful. Has florid passages. (Somervell 15)
Not all my torments	d1-a♭2	f1-f2	All voices	A free, recitative-like, florid, rather slow song. Perhaps one of Purcell's most remarkable songs. (Kagen)
Nymphs and shepherds (The Libertine)	d1-g2	f1-e2	All voices	Animated, light, graceful. Has florid passages. Demands flexibility. (Kagen)
O! fair Cedaria	b♭-f2	e♭1-e♭2	Most suitable for men's voices	A very sustained ground bass song, preceded and followed by a recitative which demands some flexibility. (Somervell 15)
O, lead me to some peaceful gloom	d1-a♭2	e♭1-g2	All voices	Recitative-like section followed by a sustained air. Has florid passages. (Kagen)
O! let me forever weep (The Fairy Queen)	d1-g2	g1-g2	Women's voices	Sustained, rather slow. Somber text. (Purcell Society)
O Lord, rebuke me not	c1-g2	f1-f2	All voices	Sustained and minuet-like sections followed by one that is more florid and ended with an animated, quite florid Alleluia.

TITLE	COMP.	TESS.	TYPE	REMARKS
				Demands consider-able flexibility (Edmunds)
One charming night	c#1-d2	f#1-d2	All voices	Sustained. De-mands some flexi-bility. (Purcell Society)
Phillis, I can ne'er forgive it	c#1-e2	e1-e2	Men's voices	Sustained. (Mof-fat)
Retir'd from any mortal's sight (King Richard the Second)	d1-f2	f#1-f2	All voices	Sustained. (Pur-cell Society)
Since from my dear (The Prophetess)	d1-f2	e1-e2	Most suit-able for men's voices	Sustained. De-mands some flexi-bility. (Kagen)
Solitude	a-e2	e1-d2	Low voices	A slow, sustained, ground bass song. Quite long. (Som-ervell 15)
Sound the trumpet	d1-ab2	f1-f2	All voices	Spirited, vigorous, very florid. Orig-inally written for male alto or counter tenor. Trumpet obbligato. One tone higher in orig-inal. (Kagen)
Strike the viol	d1-eb2	f1-d2	All voices	Sustained. Osti-nato bass. Has some florid pas-sages. Demands considerable flexi-bility. (Kagen)
Sweet, be no longer sad	g#1-g2	a1-e2	All voices	Sustained. (Kagen)
Sweet tyranness	e1-f2	g1-e2	Men's voices	Sustained. (Som-ervell 15)
Sweeter than roses	d1-a2	eb1-g2	Most suit-able for women's voices	Recitative-like first section, fol-lowed by marked, animated second section. Florid. (Kagen)
Sylvia, now your scorn	g1-g2	a1-f2	Men's voices	Graceful, gently humorous. (Pur-cell Society)

38

TITLE	COMP.	TESS.	TYPE	REMARKS
Take not a woman's anger ill (The Rival Sisters)	c1-eb2	eb1-d2	Men's voices	Spirited, humorous. (Purcell Society)
The airy violin (Ode on St. Cecilia's Day)	g-bb1	b-g1	Alto	Graceful. Demands some flexibility. Has a very low tessitura. (Score, NOV)
The arrival of the royal barge	f1-ab2	a1-g2	All voices	Sustained, joyous. Has some florid passages. A welcome song in 1681 for the king. (Edmunds)
The blessed virgin's expostulation	db1-gb2	f1-f2	Women's voices	A cantata-like piece on religion-inspired text. Has florid passages. Interpretatively not easy. (Kagen)
The fatal hour	d#1-g2	e1-f#2	All voices	A dramatic, florid recitative and an andantino air. (Kagen)
The fife and all the harmony of war (Ode on St. Cecilia's Day)	a-d1	d1-a1	Alto	Spirited, vigorous. Demands some flexibility. Has a very low tessitura. (Score, NOV)
The knotting song	f1-g2	g1-f2	All voices	Graceful. Demands some flexibility. (Kagen)
The message	c#1-e2	f#1-c#2	Most suitable for men's voices	Sustained. Demands some flexibility. (Moffat)
The queen's epicedium	d1-g2	f1-g2	All voices	Free recitative and sustained air. Cantata-like in structure. Has florid passages. Latin text. An elegy on the death of Queen Mary, 1695. (Kagen)
There's not a swain	b-g2	e1-e2	All voices	Graceful, light, humorous. (Kagen)

TITLE	COMP.	TESS.	TYPE	REMARKS
Thou tunest this world (Ode on St. Cecilia's Day)	f1-g2	bb1-g2	Soprano	Graceful, not fast. Demands flexibility. Although a solo with chorus, this song could be sung as a solo piece. (Score, NOV)
Thrice happy lovers (The Fairy Queen)	d1-g2	g1-f2	All voices	Sustained. Demands some flexibility. Has florid passages. (Kagen)
Thus to a ripe consenting maid (The Old Bachelor)	d1-g2	e1-f2	Most suitable for women's voices	Animated. Demands facile articulation. (Purcell Society)
Recitative: Thy hand, Belinda! Air: When I am laid in earth (Dido and Aeneas)	c#1-g2	f#1-eb2	Women's voices, except a light soprano	Slow and very sustained. (Kagen)
'Tis nature's voice (Ode on St. Cecilia's Day)	eb1-a2	g1-g2	All voices	Slow, very florid. Originally written for male alto or counter tenor. (Kagen)
Turn then thine eyes	e1-a2	a1-f2	Not suitable for very heavy voices	Animated, florid, graceful. Demands flexibility and facile articulation. (Edmunds)
We sing to him	c#1-g2	f1-f2	Not too suitable for very light, high voices	Broad, sustained first section; graceful and lighter second section. Has some rhythmic complexity. (Kagen)
Welcome, more welcome does he come	c1-eb2	eb1-d2	All voices	Sustained. Taken from the welcome song "From those serene and rapturous joys." (Purcell Society)
What can we poor females do	e1-g2	g1-f2	Women's voices	Animated, accented. Slightly humorous. Has one florid passage. (Kagen)

TITLE	COMP.	TESS.	TYPE	REMARKS
What shall I do	eb1-g2	g1-eb2	Men's voices	Sustained. (Kagen)
When I a lover pale do see	c1-g2	f1-d2	All voices	Graceful, gently humorous. (Bridge, Seventeenth Century Songs, NOV)
When I have often heard (The Fairy Queen)	c1-g2	f1-f2	Women's voices	Animated. (Potter)
Whilst I with grief did on you look	b-e2	e1-c2	Most suitable for baritone or bass	A recitative-like slow, florid introduction, and a spirited rather florid air. (Moffat)
Wondrous machine (Ode on St. Cecilia's Day)	B-e1	e-c1	Bass or baritone	Slow, sustained. Demands flexibility; has some florid passages. (Kagen)
Ye twice ten hundred deities (The Indian Queen)	G-eb1	d-d1	Bass or baritone	Recitative and a spirited air, followed by a slow, sustained final section. Has some florid passages. (Kagen)
Your awful voice	d1-g2	f1-g2	All voices	Short recitative and an animated, energetic and florid air. Demands flexibility. (Kagen)

PHILIP ROSSETER
(1575–1623)

TITLE	COMP.	TESS.	TYPE	REMARKS
If I urge my kind desires	f#1-e2	same	Men's voices	Animated, graceful. (Fellowes 40)
If she forsake me	e1-f#2	a1-f#2	Men's voices	Animated, graceful. (Fellowes 40)
What then is love but mourning?	g1-f2	g1-d2	Men's voices	Sustained. (Fellowes 40)
When Laura smiles	e1-f#2	a1-e2	All voices	Animated, graceful. (Fellowes 40)

TITLE	COMP. TESS.	TYPE	REMARKS

WILLIAM SHIELD
(1748–1829)

Eve around the huge oak	bb-g2	eb1-bb1	Men's voices	Animated. (Neitzel, <u>Gems of Antiquity</u>, JCC)

RICHARD J. S. STEVENS
(1757–1837)

Sigh no more, ladies	d1-e2 (g2)	g1-d2	All voices	Animated. Demands some flexibility. (gen. av.)

STEPHEN STORACE
(1763–1796)

A sailor loved a lass	c1-eb2 (f2)	c1-bb1	All voices, except a very light soprano	Animated, humorous. (Wilson)
Peaceful slumbering	bb-f2	f1-d2	Most suitable for women's voices	Sustained, subdued. (Potter)
The pretty creature	c1-d2 (f2)	e1-c2	Most suitable for men's voices	Animated, light. Demands facile articulation. (Wilson)
The summer heat's bestowing	e1-b2	a1-f#2	Soprano	Sustained. (Neitzel, <u>Gems of Antiquity</u>, JCC)

THOMAS WEELKES
(1575–1623)

Cease sorrows now	d#1-g2	f#1-e2 (H)	All voices	Sustained and grave. (Bantock)

JOHN WELDON
(1676–1736)

Celia, let not pride undo you	b-e2	d1-d2	All voices	Animated, graceful. Demands

TITLE	COMP.	TESS.	TYPE	REMARKS
				some flexibility. (Potter)
Prithee, Celia	d1-f♯2	d1-d2	All voices	Graceful. Demands some flexibility. (Potter)

JOHN WILBYE
(1574–1638)

TITLE	COMP.	TESS.	TYPE	REMARKS
Flora gave me fairest flowers	f1-g2	a1-f2 (H)	Most suitable for men's voices	Animated, graceful. A transcription of a five-part madrigal. (Bantock)

JOHN WILSON
(1595–1674)

TITLE	COMP.	TESS.	TYPE	REMARKS
In the merry month of May	d1-e2	f♯1-d2	All voices	Animated, graceful. Demands some flexibility. (Moffat)

ANTHONY YOUNG
(c.1685–c.1720)

TITLE	COMP.	TESS.	TYPE	REMARKS
Phillis has such charming graces	e1-g♭2	b♭1-f2	Most suitable for high voices	Sustained, graceful. Demands some flexibility. (Wilson)

SONGS AND AIRS IN ITALIAN BEFORE THE NINETEENTH CENTURY

Bibliography

The name found in parentheses after the Remarks indicates one of the following collections:

Dallapiccola: Italian Songs of the 17th and 18th Centuries, edited by Luigi Dallapiccola, published by International Music Co. (2 volumes, high, medium, low). One of the most accurate and reliable editions available.

Echos de l'Italie: Echos de l'Italie, Vol. VI edited by Viardot-Garcia, published by Durand, Paris.

Ewerhart: Cantio Sacra, edited by Rudolf Ewerhart, published by Ed. Bieler, Köln.

Floridia: Early Italian Songs and Airs, 2 volumes, edited by Floridia, published by O. Ditson (high and low). A very popular collection but stylistically very poor.

Fuchs: Italian Songs of the 18th Century, edited by Albert Fuchs, published by International Music Co.

Gevaert: Les Gloires de l'Italie, edited by Gevaert, published by Heugel, Paris.

Jeppesen: La Flora, 3 volumes, edited by Knud Jeppesen, published by Wilhelm Hansen. One of the most accurate and reliable editions available.

Krehbiel: Voices from the Golden Age, edited by Krehbiel, published by G. Schirmer.

Landshoff: Alte Meister des Bel Canto, 2 volumes, edited by Landshoff, published by C. F. Peters.

Parisotti, Ricordi: Arie Antiche, 3 volumes, edited by Parisotti, published by Ricordi. (All songs and airs of this and the following collection published by G. Schirmer are also available separately in Ricordi edition.)

Parisotti, Schirmer: Italian Anthology, 2 volumes, edited by Parisotti, published by G. Schirmer. (Almost all songs and airs in this collection as well as in the one published by Ricordi are transposed to suit medium voices.)

Zanon: Arias by Old Italian Masters, 2 volumes, edited by Zanon, published by Boston Music Co.

See also the catalogues of Ricordi, Ashdown, and Oxford University Press for many other excellent transcriptions and arrangements, as well as Maîtres du Chant, edited by Prunieres, published by Heugel, Paris.

TITLE	COMP.	TESS.	TYPE	REMARKS

ANTONIO MARIA ABBATINI
(1595–1677)

TITLE	COMP.	TESS.	TYPE	REMARKS
Quanto è bello il mio diletto	g1-g2	b1-e2	Soprano	Not fast, rather florid. Has a sustained middle section. (Landshoff)

TOMASSO ALBINONI
(1671–1750)

TITLE	COMP.	TESS.	TYPE	REMARKS
Rusceletto limpidetto	c1-d2	e1-c2	Most suitable for medium and low voices	Rather sustained. Demands some flexibility. (Jeppesen)

GIOVANNI FRANCESCO ANERIO
(c.1567–c.1630)

TITLE	COMP.	TESS.	TYPE	REMARKS
Hodie apparuerunt	F-c1	A-a	Bass	Sustained. (Ewerhart)
Sicut lilium inter spinas	E-f1	G-d1	Bass	Sustained. Has some florid passages. Wide range. (Ewerhart)
Tu es pastor ovium	F-e1	B-c1	Bass	Sustained. Has some florid passages. (Ewerhart)

PANCRAZIO ANIELLO
(Late 18th Century)

TITLE	COMP.	TESS.	TYPE	REMARKS
Lo so che pria mi moro	a-c#2	d1-b1	Medium or low voices	A rather slow, sustained Siciliana. (Zanon)

ANONYMOUS

TITLE	COMP.	TESS.	TYPE	REMARKS
Amar il caro bene (17th Century)	c#1-g#2	f#1-f#2	High voices	An extended cantata in several contrasting movements interspersed with

TITLE	COMP.	TESS.	TYPE	REMARKS
				recitatives. Has a few florid passages. (Jeppesen)
Care mie selve (c.1600)	c1-e2	e1-e2	All voices except a very light soprano	Sustained, grave, rather declamatory. (Jeppesen)
"Lamento" Chi sa le mie pene (Neapolitan school, 18th Century)	b-f2	eb1-eb2	Medium or low voices	A slow, sustained air on a ground bass. (Gevaert, Répertoire Classique du chant Français. (Lemoine, Paris)
Occhi, fonti del core	d1-e2	e1-d2	Most suitable for medium or low voices	Sustained, declamatory. This song is attributed to Monteverdi. (Jeppesen)

MARIA ANTONIA (E. T. P. A.)
(1724–1782)

TITLE	COMP.	TESS.	TYPE	REMARKS
Prendi l'ultimo addio	bb-eb2	eb1-c2	All voices	Slow, for the most part sustained. Demands some flexibility. (Fuchs)

ATTILIO ARIOSTI
(1666–c.1740)

TITLE	COMP.	TESS.	TYPE	REMARKS
Vuci, che parta! (Lucio Vero)	e1-g#2	a1-f#2	Soprano	Slow, in parts quite florid. (Landshoff)

EMANUELE D'ASTORGA
(1680–c.1757)

TITLE	COMP.	TESS.	TYPE	REMARKS
Auretta vezzosa	b-e2	e1-c2	Medium or low voices	Graceful. Demands some flexibility. (Echos de l'Italie)
Fiore ingrato	bb-d2	d1-c2	Medium or low voices	Sustained. Demands in parts some flexibility. (Jeppesen)

TITLE	COMP.	TESS.	TYPE	REMARKS
L'immago tua	f1-g2	bb1-f2	Most suitable for light, high voices	Animated, graceful. Somewhat florid. (Echos de l'Italie)
Morir vogl'io	d1-e2	f#1-d2	Most suitable for medium or low voices	Slow, sustained. (Floridia; also Neitzel, Gems of Antiquity, JCC)
Ti parlo	d1-g2	g1-eb2	Soprano	Recitative and a graceful air. Demands some flexibility. (Echos de l'Italie)
Vo cercando in queste valli	d1-g2	g1-e2 (H)	All voices	Light and delicate. (Floridia)

JOHANN CHRISTIAN BACH
(1735–1782)

TITLE	COMP.	TESS.	TYPE	REMARKS
Non è ver (Caratacco)	f1-bb2	bb1-g2	Soprano	Not fast, quite florid. (Landshoff)

(See also J. C. Bach, 12 Konzert und Opern Arien, edited by Landshoff, published by C. F. Peters.)

GIOVANNI BATTISTA BASSANI
(1657–1716)

TITLE	COMP.	TESS.	TYPE	REMARKS
Dormi, bella, dormi tu?	eb1-f2	eb1-eb2	Most suitable for men's voices	A graceful, sustained air. Has rapid sections. (Parisotti, GS)
Posate, dormite	eb1-f2	bb1-eb2	All voices	Recitative and a sustained cavatina. Demands good command of pp. The tessitura is somewhat high. (Parisotti, GS)
Seguita a piangere	d1-f2	f1-db2	Most suitable for medium voices	Recitative and a graceful arietta, interrupted by several recitative

47

passages. De-
mands some flexi-
bility. (Parisotti,
GS)

DOMENICO BELLI
(Early 17th Century)

Title	Comp.	Tess.	Type	Remarks
Di vostri occhi le facelle	bb-f2	f1-d2	Most suitable for medium voices	Animated, light. Demands very facile articulation. (Gevaert)

ANDREA BERNASCONI
(1712–1784)

Title	Comp.	Tess.	Type	Remarks
Se non ti mora allato (Adriano)	c#1-e2	g1-d2	Mezzo-soprano or alto	Sustained. Demands some flexibility. A little long. (Krehbiel)

GIOVANNI PIETRO BERTI
(c.1600)

Title	Comp.	Tess.	Type	Remarks
Dove sei gita	d1-f2	f1-e2	All voices	Sustained, grave. The middle section is lighter and somewhat florid. (Jeppesen)

FRANCESCO BIANCHI
(1752–1811)

Title	Comp.	Tess.	Type	Remarks
La mia virtù non ceve (L'Orfano della China)	c1-f2	f1-c2	Mezzo-soprano or alto	Recitative and a dramatic air. Has some florid passages. (Krehbiel)
Tu seconda i voti miei (L'Orfano della China)	d1-e2	f#1-c#2	Medium or low voices	Recitative and a slow, sustained air. (Krehbiel)

GERARDO BIANCOSI
(c. 1600)

TITLE	COMP.	TESS.	TYPE	REMARKS
Ben ch'in me giri	f1-f2	g1-d2	Most suitable for men's voices	Animated. (Jeppesen)

GIOVANNI BONONCINI
(Sometimes listed as Giovanni Battista)
(1670–1747)

TITLE	COMP.	TESS.	TYPE	REMARKS
Ben che speranza	b1-e2	g1-d2	Medium or low voices	Vigorous, rhythmical. (Echos de l'Italie)
Deh lascia o core (Astianatte)	b-g2	e1-e2	Mezzo-soprano or dramatic soprano	Slow. Has florid passages. (Gevaert)
Deh più a me non v'ascondete	eb1-f2	ab1-eb2	All voices	Delicate. Demands some flexibility. (Parisotti, GS; also Floridia)
La speranza i cori affida	c1-f2	f1-db2	All voices	Sustained. In parts florid. (Fuchs)
L'esperto nocchiero (Astarte)	d1-g2	g1-e2 (H)	All voices	Spirited. Has some florid passages. (Floridia)
Lungi da te	c1-f2	f1-d2	All voices	A sustained, graceful da capo air. Has some florid passages, especially in the middle section, which is in a different meter. (Fuchs)
Per la gloria d'adorarvi	d1-f2	g1-d2	All voices	Sustained. (Parisotti, GS; also Floridia)
Pieta, mio caro bene	d1-g2	a1-e2 (H)	All voices	Slow and very sustained. (Floridia)
Più non ti voglio credere	d1-ab2	bb1-ab2	Soprano	Demands facile articulation. The tessitura is quite high, the ab2 being

TITLE	COMP.	TESS.	TYPE	REMARKS
				used very fre-quently. The violin obbligato part can be easily played by the pi-anist. (Lands-hoff)
Più vaga e vezzosetta	a-e2	d1-d2	All voices	Graceful, light. Demands some flexibility. (Fuchs)
Se mai vien tocca	d1-f2	g1-d2 (H)	Not too suitable for very light voices	Sustained. De-mands some flexi-bility. (Floridia)
Se ti piace	b-f2	eb1-c2	All voices	Recitative and a graceful, sustained air. Demands some flexibility. (Fuchs)
Si che fedele	eb1-g2	g1-f2	Light soprano	Graceful. De-mands facile artic-ulation and some flexibility. (Echos de l'Italie)

COSIMO BOTTEGARI
(1554–1620)

TITLE	COMP.	TESS.	TYPE	REMARKS
Mi parto	e1-e2	f1-c2	All voices	Slow, sustained. (Ricci, Antiche Gemme Italiane, RIC)

GIOVANNI BATTISTA BREVI
(17th Century?)

TITLE	COMP.	TESS.	TYPE	REMARKS
Catenae terrenae	F-d1	c-d1	Bass	A solo cantata in three movements. Has recitatives and ends with a vigorous, florid alleluja section. Has florid pas-sages throughout. (Ewerhart)

DOMENICO BRUNI
(Late 18th Century)

TITLE	COMP.	TESS.	TYPE	REMARKS
La vezzosa pastorella	c1-g2	f1-d2	Not too suitable for very low voices	Animated, graceful, light. Demands flexibility. (Zanon)
Se meritar potessi	eb1-g2	g1-eb2	Most suitable for high voices	Graceful. Demands flexibility. (Zanon)

CHERUBINO BUSATTI
(c.1644)

TITLE	COMP.	TESS.	TYPE	REMARKS
Dite ch'io canti	d1-f2	e1-c2	Men's voices	Animated. (Jeppesen)
È tornato il mio ben	c1-e2	e1-d2	All voices	Animated, graceful. Has a few florid passages. (Jeppesen)
Morto son io	c1-f2	e1-d2	Not suitable for light, high voices	Grave, declamatory. In parts dramatic. (Jeppesen)
Pupillette	d1-g2	g1-e2	Not suitable for low, heavy voices	Light, delicate. Demands facile articulation. High tessitura. (Jeppesen)

GIOVANNI BUZZOLENI
(c.1680)

TITLE	COMP.	TESS.	TYPE	REMARKS
Non fuggirai	c1-g2	f1-eb2	All voices	Recitative and a minuet-like sustained air. (Jeppesen)
Sì che morte	d1-a2	e1-f2	Most suitable for soprano	Graceful, quite florid. Has many large skips. High tessitura. (Jeppesen)
Volgimi, o cara filli	e1-g2	a1-f2	Most suitable for	Recitative and a slow, sustained

TITLE	COMP.	TESS.	TYPE	REMARKS
			men's voices	air, followed by a minuet-like movement. (Jeppesen)

GUILIO CACCINI
(c.1546–1618)

TITLE	COMP.	TESS.	TYPE	REMARKS
Al fonte, al prato	f#1-f2	g1-d2	All voices	Animated. (Jeppesen)
Amarilli	d1-e2	f#1-d2	All voices	Slow, very sustained. (Jeppesen, also Dallapiccola)
Amor, ch'attendi	f#1-e2	g1-d2	All voices	Animated, graceful. (Jeppesen)
Aur' amorosa	d1-e2	g1-e2	All voices	Sustained. Has some florid passages. (Jeppesen)
Belle rose purpurine	g1-e2	same	Not too suitable for low, heavy voices	Graceful, light. (Dallapiccola)
Deh, dove son fuggiti	e1-e2	g1-e2	All voices	Sustained. (Jeppesen)
Fere selvaggie	e1-e2	f#1-e2	All voices	Slow and very sustained. (Jeppesen)
Non piango e non sospiro (Euridice)	d1-d2	e1-bb1	Medium or low voices	Sustained, grave. (Krehbiel)
O, che felice giorno	f#1-f2	g1-eb2	All voices	Sustained. Has some florid passages. Rhythmically interesting. (Jeppesen)
Occhi immortali	f#1-e2	g1-d2	All voices	Sustained. (Jeppesen; also Dallapiccola)
Sfogava con le stelle	e1-f2	g1-d2	Most suitable for men's voices	Sustained. Has florid passages. (Dallapiccola)
Tu, ch'hai le penne, amore	f#1-d2	g1-c2	Not too suitable for very high, light voices	Slow, sustained. (Parisotti, RIC)

TITLE	COMP.	TESS.	TYPE	REMARKS
Udite amanti	g1-f2	a1-e2	All voices	Sustained, vigorous. (Jeppesen)

ANTONIO CALDARA
(1670–1736)

TITLE	COMP.	TESS.	TYPE	REMARKS
Alma nel core	a1-f#2 (H)	b1-e2	All voices	A graceful minuet. Demands lightness of tone. (Floridia)
Come raggio di sol	c#1-e2	e1-c2	Most suitable for medium or low voices	Slow and very sustained. (Parisotti, GS; also Floridia)
Mirti, faggi	b-c2	e1-b1	Low or medium voices	Slow. Demands some flexibility. (Landshoff)
Sebben crudele	d1-e2	g1-d2	All voices	Sustained. (Parisotti, GS)
Selve amiche	e1-e2	a1-d2	All voices	Sustained. Has florid passages. Demands some flexibility. (Dallapiccola)
Si t'intendo	eb1-f2	db1-eb2	All voices	Sustained. Has some florid passages. (Fuchs)
Vaghe luci	bb-c2	c1-ab1	Low or medium voices	Slow. The violin obbligato part can be easily played by the pianist. (Landshoff)

VINCENZIO CALESTANI
(c.1600)

TITLE	COMP.	TESS.	TYPE	REMARKS
Accorta lusinghiera	d1-d2	f1-bb1	All voices	Graceful. Strophic. (Jeppesen)
Ferma, Dorinda mia	d1-eb2	e1-c2	Men's voices	Slow, declamatory. (Jeppesen)

RINALDO DA CAPUA
(1715–1780)

TITLE	COMP.	TESS.	TYPE	REMARKS
Dal sen del caro sposo (Vologeso)	d1-a2	a1-f#2	Soprano	A very sustained air. Has short,

TITLE	COMP.	TESS.	TYPE	REMARKS
				spirited sections. The tessitura is somewhat high. (Krehbiel)
Nell orro di notte oscura (Vologeso)	bb-bb2	g1-g2	Soprano	Recitative and a florid, brilliant air. (Krehbiel)

GIACOMO CARISSIMI
(1604–1674)

TITLE	COMP.	TESS.	TYPE	REMARKS
Ah, morire!	d1-f2	a1-e2 (H)	All voices	Slow, sustained. Demands some flexibility. (Floridia)
Come sete importuni	c#1-g2	f1-eb2	All voices	A short cantata with many contrasting short sections. A few florid passages. (Jeppesen)
Così volete, così sarà	d1-a2	g1-eb2	Soprano	Sustained. The middle section is animated and florid. (Landshoff)
Deh, contentatevi	e1-g2	ab1-eb2 (H)	All voices	Very sustained. (Floridia)
Filli, non t'amo più	d#1-f#2	a1-e2 (H)	Men's voices	Spirited. Demands some flexibility. (Floridia)
Fuggite, fuggite	d1-g2	f1-e2	All voices	Graceful. Has a few florid passages. (Jeppesen)
La mia fede altrai giurata	f#1-ab2	g1-d2	High voices	Not fast, rather sustained. (Landshoff)
Ma no, non fuggir	d1-a2	f1-g2	Not too suitable for very light voices	Sustained, grave. Demands considerable dramatic intensity. (Jeppesen)
No, no, mio core	d1-g2	g1-e2 (H)	All voices	Sustained. (Floridia)
No, no, non si speri	f-g1	g-eb1	Alto or bass	Slow, sustained. Has some florid passages. (Landshoff; also Floridia)

TITLE	COMP.	TESS.	TYPE	REMARKS
Non posso vivere	f1-g2	g1-f2	All voices	Animated, vigorous. (Jeppesen)
O vulnera doloris	G-d1	A-c1	Bass	A short solo cantata. Sustained. (Ewerhart)
Piangete aure	d1-f2	f1-e2	Not suitable for very light, high voices	A short cantata; somewhat declamatory in parts. Dramatic. (Echos de l'Italie)
Piangete ohimè, anime innamorate	b-e2	e1-c#2	Not suitable for very light, high voices	Slow, sustained. (Parisotti, RIC)
Soccorretemi	c1-g2	eb1-eb2	High voices, except a very light soprano	Sustained. Somewhat declamatory. Has some florid passages and some recitatives. Somewhat long. (Landshoff)
Sventura, cuor mio	d1-g2	g1-f2	Not suitable for light voices	Sustained, grave. Demands considerable dramatic intensity. (Jeppesen)
Vittoria, mio core	d1-g2	f#1-f#2	All voices	Spirited. Has florid passages. (Jeppesen; Parisotti, GS)

EMILIO DEL CAVALIERI
(c. 1550–1602)

TITLE	COMP.	TESS.	TYPE	REMARKS
Il tempo fugge (La Rappresentatione di Anima e di Corpo)	f1-f2	g1-eb2	Not suitable for light, high voices	Declamatory, in parts dramatic. (Dallapiccola)

PIETRO FRANCESCO CAVALLI
(1602–1676)

TITLE	COMP.	TESS.	TYPE	REMARKS
Affè mi fate ridere	d1-f2	g1-d2	High or medium voices	Spirited, gay. Demands facile articu-

TITLE	COMP.	TESS.	TYPE	REMARKS
				lation and some flexibility. (Parisotti, RIC)
Beato chi può (Serse)	A-d1	d-b	Bass or baritone	Also suitable for alto. Sustained. Has some florid passages. (Gevaert)
Chi si pasce (Eritrea)	f1-f2	g1-d2	High or medium voices	Spirited. Demands some flexibility. (Echos de l'Italie)
Delizie contente, che l'alma beate (Giasone)	f1-eb2	g1-c2	All voices	Graceful. (Parisotti, GS)
Dell'antro magico (Giasone)	c1-g2	e1-e2	Dramatic soprano or mezzo-soprano	Vigorous, dramatic, majestic. (Gevaert; also Neitzel, Gems of Antiquity, JCC)
Dolce amor, bendato dio	d1-g2	a1-e2 (H)	Not too suitable for very heavy, low voices	Delicate and graceful. (Floridia)
Donzelle fuggite	e1-g2	g1-e2 (H)	All voices	Rapid and light. Demands facile articulation. (Floridia)
Gran pazzia (Eritrea)	e1-f#2	g#1-e2	High voices, except a very light soprano	Vigorous. Demands some flexibility. (Echos de l'Italie)
In amor (Eritrea)	c1-g2	f1-f2	Most suitable for light soprano	Graceful. Demands some flexibility. Two very florid variations by Lorenzo Pagans are attached. (Echos de l'Italie)
Son ancor pargoletta	d1-g2	g1-e2	Most suitable for soprano or high mezzo-soprano	Animated, graceful. The refrain demands facile articulation. (Jeppesen)
Sospiri di foco	f1-f2	g1-eb2	All voices	Animated, graceful. Has some florid passages. (Jeppesen)

TITLE	COMP.	TESS.	TYPE	REMARKS
Speranze	e1-g2	g1-f2	All voices	Slow, sustained, has a more animated refrain. Demands some flexibility. (Jeppesen)
Troppo soavi i gusti	g1-g2	ab1-eb2	All voices	Very sustained, but has rapid parlato passages. (Floridia)
Vaghe stelle	d1-g2	e1-e2	All voices	Very sustained. Not slow. (Jeppesen)

CARLO F. CESARINI
(1660–1720)

Recitative:
  Filli, Filli nol niego
Air:

	COMP.	TESS.	TYPE	REMARKS
Compatite me, sono infermo	f#1-ab2	ab1-f2	Soprano or tenor	Recitative and a sustained air. Has a florid passage. (Landshoff)

MARCANTONIO CESTI
(1618–1669)

Recitative:
  Addio Corindo
Air:
  Vieni Alidoro

	COMP.	TESS.	TYPE	REMARKS
Addio Corindo	f1-g2	g1-f2	Soprano	Slow, sustained. Has florid passages. (Landshoff)
Ah, quanto è vero (Il pomo d'Oro)	a1-a2	c1-f2 (H)	All voices	Very sustained. (Floridia)
Che angoscia, che affanno (Il pomo d'Oro)	e1-f2	a1-e2 (H)	All voices	Very sustained. (Floridia)
E dove t'aggiri (Il pomo d'Oro)	d#1-f2	a1-e2 (H)	Most suitable for medium or low voices	Very slow and sustained. Sarabande. (Floridia)
Intorno all'idol mio	d1-f2	g1-d2	All voices	Sustained, graceful. (Parisotti, GS)

TITLE	COMP.	TESS.	TYPE	REMARKS
O del ben che acquistero (Il pomo d'Oro)	e1-g2	a1-f2 (H)	Most suitable for men's voices	Very sustained. (Floridia)
Tu mancavi a tormentarti	c1-g2	g1-d2	All voices	Sustained. Has an animated middle section which demands some flexibility. (Gevaert; also Parisotti, GS)

LUIGI CHERUBINI
(1760-1842)

Recitative: Ahi! che forse ai miei di Air: Ahi, sola quand'io vivea (Demofonte)	db1-gb2	f1-db2	Soprano or high mezzo soprano	Recitative and a sustained air. (Parisotti, RIC)
Ave Maria	e1-a2	f1-f2	Soprano or tenor	Very sustained. Demands in parts some flexibility. (GS)

For other songs and airs see under "French" in this section (page 105).

ANTONIO CIFRA
(1584-1629)

La violetta	g1-f2	g1-d2	All voices	Animated, graceful. (Jeppesen)

DOMENICO CIMAROSA
(1749-1801)

Ah, tornar la bella aurora (La Vergine del Sole)	c#1-c3	g#1-g2	Soprano	An andante, allegro air. In parts quite florid. (Landshoff)
Bel nume che adoro	d1-eb2	g1-eb2	High voices	Sustained. (Parisotti, RIC)
Bramar di perdere (Artaserse)	f#1-b2	a1-g2	Soprano, most	Graceful, in parts florid. Demands

TITLE	COMP.	TESS.	TYPE	REMARKS
			suited for light, high voices	flexibility and good command of high p. High tessitura. (G. Campese, Dieci Arie Inedite, Zerboni)
Recitative: Cara, son tutto vostro Air:				
Brillar mi sento il core (Il Matrimonio Segreto)	f-a1	a-f1	Lyric tenor	Spirited, in parts quite florid. (Parisotti, RIC)
Che terrore, che paura (I Finti Nobili)	d1-b2	g1-f2	Dramatic soprano or mezzo-soprano	An andante aria. Demands flexibility and in parts facile articulation. (G. Campese, Dieci Arie Inedite, Zerboni)
Di ve' pozza scanzare (La Finta Parigina)	e1-g2	g1-e2	Soprano	Sustained, graceful. (G. Campese, Dieci Arie Inedite, Zerboni)
È ver che le villane (Chi Dell'altrui si Veste Presto si Spoglia)	e1-b2	b1-g2	Most suitable for light, high soprano	Graceful, in parts demands some flexibility. (G. Campese, Dieci Arie Inedite, Zerboni)
È vero che in casa io sono padrone (Il Matrimonio Segreto)	e1-a2	a1-f2	Soprano or mezzo-soprano	Animated. Demands facile articulation and some flexibility. In the opera assigned to contralto. The tessitura, however, seems somewhat high for this type of voice. (Parisotti, RIC)
Fanciulla sventurata (I Nemici Generosi)	d1-c3	a1-g2	Soprano	Sustained aria. Demands good command of high p and some flexibility. (G. Campese, Dieci Arie Inedite, Zerboni)

TITLE	COMP.	TESS.	TYPE	REMARKS
Recitative: Misero Bernardone				
Aria:				
Maritati poverelli (Gianina e Bernardone)	A♭-f1	f-d1	Baritone	A buffo scena, andante, allegro. Demands in parts facile articulation. (Gevaert)
Mio signor (Il Falegname)	c#-e1	e-d1	Baritone	A buffo scena, allegro. Demands facile articulation. (G. Campese, Dieci Arie Inedite, Zerboni)
Nel lasciarti (Olimpiade)	b♭-b♭2	f1-e♭2	Mezzo- soprano or dra- matic so- prano	An andante, alle- gro aria. Demands some flexibility. (Parisotti, RIC)
Perdonate signor mio (Il Matrimonio Segreto)	d#1-a2	a1-f#2	Colora- tura so- prano (lyric so- prano)	Spirited. Demands facile articulation and considerable flexibility. (Score, RIC)
Pria che spunti in cielo (Il Matri- monio Segreto)	e♭-b♭1	b♭-g1	Lyric tenor	An andante, allegro aria. Demands some flexibility and facile articu- lation. (Score, RIC)
Quel soave e bel diletto	b-g2	e1-d2	High voices	Slow. Has florid passages. (Pari- sotti, RIC)
Resta in pace, idolo mio	b♭-f2	f1-e♭2	Soprano or mezzo- soprano	Sustained. De- mands some flexi- bility. (Parisotti, RIC)
Se lo specchio (Il Falegname)	c-e1	e-d1	Baritone	Animated aria. Demands facile articulation and some flexibility. (G. Campese, Dieci Arie Inedite, Zerboni)
Se son vendicata (Il Matrimonio Segreto)	d#1-a2	a1-e2	Soprano	A spirited andante, allegro aria. In parts very florid;

TITLE	COMP.	TESS.	TYPE	REMARKS
				demands facile articulation. (Score, RIC)
Tengo la palettella (Il Fanatico per gli Antichi Romani)	g1-a2	b1-e2	Soprano	Graceful, light. Demands good command of pp. (G. Campese, Dieci Arie Inedite, Zerboni)
Udite tutti, udite (Il Matrimonio Segreto)	A-e1	d-d1	Bass or baritone	A spirited buffo aria. Demands facile articulation. (Score, RIC)
Vedrai la forte (Don Calandrino)	B-f#1	f#-d1	Baritone	A very spirited compound buffo aria. Demands in parts very facile articulation. (Gevaert)
Vi dirò, sentite bene (L'amante Disperato)	f#1-a2	a1-f#2	Soprano	Sustained, in parts demands flexibility. (G. Campese, Dieci Arie Inedite, Zerboni)
Voi avete, o mia signora (Il Mercato Malmantile)	eb1-bb2	a1-f2	Soprano	An andante aria. Demands flexibility and facile articulation. (G. Campese, Dieci Arie Inedite, Zerboni)

GIOACCHINO COCCHI
(1720–1804)

Gli sbirri già l'aspettano (La Scaltra Governatrice)	B-d1	c-c1	Bass or baritone	A spirited, buffo air. Demands facile articulation. (Gevaert)

WILLIAM DEFESCH
(1700–1758)

Tu fai la superbetta	d#1-c#3	f#1-f#2	Coloratura soprano	A theme and two florid, brilliant

variations. (Arr. by Estelle Liebling, GS)

For other songs and airs see the section Songs and Airs in English before the Nineteenth Century. See also Alfred Moffat's collection, Old Mastersongs, 17th and 18th Centuries, published by Augener.

FRANCESCO DURANTE
(1684–1755)

TITLE	COMP.	TESS.	TYPE	REMARKS
Danza, danza fanciulla gentile	bb-f2	f1-db2	Most suitable for men's voices	Spirited and light. Demands facile articulation and some flexibility. (Dallapiccola)
Vergin, tutto amor	d1-f2	a1-e2	Not too suitable for very light, high voices	Very sustained. (Dallapiccola)

ANDREA FALCONIERI
(1586–1656)

TITLE	COMP.	TESS.	TYPE	REMARKS
Bella fanciulla	d1-f2	f1-eb2	Most suitable for men's voices	Animated. Rhythmically interesting. (Jeppesen)
Bella porta di rubini	f#1-f2	g1-d2	All voices	Animated, graceful. (Jeppesen)
Donn' ingrata	d1-eb2	f1-d2	Most suitable for men's voices	Sustained. (Jeppesen)
Non più d'amore	eb1-f2	ab1-eb2 (H)	All voices	Spirited. Demands facile articulation. The accompaniment is quite elaborate. (Floridia)
Nudo arciero	db1-ab2	ab1-f2 (H)	All voices	Spirited. Demands facile articulation. The accompaniment is quite elaborate. (Floridia)

TITLE	COMP.	TESS.	TYPE	REMARKS
O bellissimi capelli	d1-f2	g1-d2 (H)	Most suitable for men's voices	Graceful. (Parisotti, RIC; also Floridia)
Occhietti amati	d1-f2	f1-d2	All voices	Animated. Has one florid passage. (Jeppesen)
Segui, segui dolente core	d1-f#2	f#1-d2	All voices	Graceful, not fast. (Parisotti, RIC)
Vezzosette e care	c#1-e2	e1-c#2	All voices	Light and graceful. Demands facile articulation. A gavotte. (Parisotti, GS)

GIOVANNI BATTISTA FASOLO
(16..–16..)

TITLE	COMP.	TESS.	TYPE	REMARKS
Cangia, cangia tue voglie	c1-g2	e1-d2	All voices	Graceful. Demands some flexibility. (Parisotti, GS)
Lungi, lungi è amor da me	d1-f2	f1-d2	All voices	Sustained. (Parisotti, RIC)

RUGGIERO FEDELLI (FEDELI)
(16..–1722)

TITLE	COMP.	TESS.	TYPE	REMARKS
Il mio core	d1-f2	f1-d2	All voices	Animated, graceful. (Fuchs; also Floridia)

GIROLAMO FRESCOBALDI
(1583–1643)

TITLE	COMP.	TESS.	TYPE	REMARKS
A piè della gran croce	eb1-f2	ab1-eb2	Women's voices, except a light, high soprano	A recitative-like piece with text based on the story of Magdalene at the foot of the cross. (Dallapiccola)
Dove, dove, signor	e1-f#2	a1-e2	All voices	In recitative style throughout. Sacred text. (Dallapiccola)

TITLE	COMP.	TESS.	TYPE	REMARKS
Se l'aura spira	d1-f2	g1-d2	All voices	Animated. (Jeppesen)

BERNARDO GAFFI
(Early 17th Century)

TITLE	COMP.	TESS.	TYPE	REMARKS
Luci vezzose	f1-g2	bb1-f2 (H)	All voices	A graceful minuet. (Floridia)

GIOVANBATISTA DA GAGLIANO
(c.1580)

TITLE	COMP.	TESS.	TYPE	REMARKS
Pupille arciere	d1-d2	e1-c2	All voices	Graceful. (Jeppesen)

MARCO ZANOBI DA GAGLIANO
(c.1575-1642)

TITLE	COMP.	TESS.	TYPE	REMARKS
Chi da'lacci d'amor (Dafne)	d1-d2	f1-c2	Soprano or mezzo-soprano	Graceful and delicate. Has some florid passages. (Krehbiel)
Dormi amore (La Flora)	e1-g2	a1-d2 (H)	All voices	Sustained and delicate. Demands good command of pp. (Floridia)
Mie speranze	c1-e2	e1-d2	All voices	Animated. Interesting alternating 3/2 and 6/4 rhythms. (Jeppesen)
Valli profonde (Il Dannato)	c1-f2	d1-e2	Not suitable for light, high voices	Sustained. Has a number of florid passages. (Jeppesen; also Gevaert)

BALDASSARE GALUPPI
(1706-1785)

TITLE	COMP.	TESS.	TYPE	REMARKS
È ingrato, lo veggio (Adriano in Siria)	b-d2	g1-d2	Mezzo-soprano or alto	Spirited. Has florid passages. (Krehbiel)

TITLE	COMP.	TESS.	TYPE	REMARKS
La pastorella al prato (Il Filosofo di Campagna)	e1-g2	g1-e2	High voices	A graceful pastoral. (Echos de l'Italie)
Prigioniera, abbandonata (Adriano in Siria)	d1-a2	b1-g2	Soprano	Florid. Most suitable for lyric or coloratura soprano. (Krehbiel)
Son io semplice fanciulla (L'Inimico delle Donne)	d1-ab2	g1-eb2	Light soprano	Graceful, quite florid. (Gevaert)
Son troppo vezzose (Enrico)	c-g1	f-d1	Tenor	Graceful. Demands some flexibility. (Krehbiel, Songs from the Operas, Tenor, OD)

FRANCESCO GASPARINI
(1665–1737)

TITLE	COMP.	TESS.	TYPE	REMARKS
Augellin vago e canoro	d1-f2	f#1-d2	High voices	Andante and a spirited allegro; the spirited allegro has a florid passage. (Parisotti, RIC)
Caro laccio, dolce nodo	eb1-eb2	f1-c2	All voices	Graceful. Demands lightness of tone. (Parisotti, GS)
Lasciar d'amarti	eb1-f2	ab1-eb2	All voices	Sustained, graceful. (Parisotti, GS; also Floridia)

GIUSEPPE GIORDANI
(c.1753–1798)

TITLE	COMP.	TESS.	TYPE	REMARKS
Caro mio ben	d1-f2	g1-eb2	All voices	Sustained. (Dallapiccola)

BONIFATIO GRATIANI
(1605–1664)

TITLE	COMP.	TESS.	TYPE	REMARKS
Gaudia, pastores, optate	d1-a2	f1-g2	Soprano or tenor	A short solo cantata. Has some

| | | | | floril passages. Sacred text. Ends with extended jovial "Noe" section. (Ewerhart) |

KARL HEINRICH GRAUN
(1704–1759)

TITLE	COMP.	TESS.	TYPE	REMARKS
Recitative: Disperata Porcia Air: Quanto dolce	f1-c3	bb1-g2	Soprano	Recitative and a slow, rather sustained air. Has florid passages. (Landshoff)

For other songs and airs, see under "German" in this section (page 138).

JOHANN ADOLPH HASSE
(1699–1783)

TITLE	COMP.	TESS.	TYPE	REMARKS
Agnus Dei (Mass in d minor)	c#1-d2	e1-b1	Alto	Sustained. Has florid passages. Latin text. (Alt Arien. B & H)
La tua virtù mi dice	d1-f2	g1-d2	Soprano	Graceful. Demands some flexibility. (Landshoff)
Padre, perdona (Demofoonte)	b-f#2	e1-e2	Dramatic soprano or mezzo-soprano	Sustained. Demands some flexibility. The middle section is a spirited allegro. (Gevaert)
Ritornerai fra poco	d1-a2	g1-g2	Most suitable for light soprano	Animated, graceful. Rather florid. (GS)
Salve Regina	a-e2	b-b1	Alto	Slow, sustained. Demands some flexibility. Latin text. (Alt Arien. B & H)

TITLE	COMP.	TESS.	TYPE	REMARKS
Voi che credete	d1-f#2	f#1-d2	Not too suitable for very light, high voices	Rather vigorous and animated. Demands some flexibility. (Fuchs)

See also J. A. Hasse, Ausgewählte Geistliche Gesänge, edited by O. Schmidt, published by Breitkopf und Härtel.

NICCOLO JOMMELLI
(1714—1774)

Recitative:
  Bella mia fiamma, addio
Air:

TITLE	COMP.	TESS.	TYPE	REMARKS
Resta o cara (Cerere placata)	d1-g2 (bb2)	eb1-eb2	Lyric soprano (dramatic soprano)	Scena, andante, allegro. Demands in parts considerable flexibility. (Gevaert)
Chi vuol comprar la bella calandrina	b-g2	g1-e2	Most suitable for high voices	Light. Demands some flexibility. (Parisotti, GS)

GAETANO LATILLA
(1713—1789)

TITLE	COMP.	TESS.	TYPE	REMARKS
Fra degno ed amore (Siroë)	e1-a2	a1-e2	Soprano	Majestic. Has florid passages. (Krehbiel)
Sgombra dall'anima (Siroë)	d1-a2	a1-eb2	Soprano	Graceful and light. Demands some flexibility. (Krehbiel)

GIOVANNI LEGRENZI
(1626—1690)

TITLE	COMP.	TESS.	TYPE	REMARKS
Che fiero costume	d1-e2	g1-d2	All voices	Rapid. Demands facile articulation. (Dallapiccola)
Farci pazzo	c1-g2	g1-f2	High voices	Animated, light. Demands some

TITLE	COMP.	TESS.	TYPE	REMARKS
				flexibility and facile articulation. (Gevaert)
Non mi dir di palesar	c#1-f2	e1-e2	High or medium voices	Sustained. Rhythmically quite interesting. (Landshoff)

LEONARDO LEO
(1694–1744)

TITLE	COMP.	TESS.	TYPE	REMARKS
Ahi, che la pena mia	d1-g2	a1-f2	High voices	A graceful Siciliana. Demands some flexibility. Has a vigorous middle section. (Gevaert)
Ah si! che di Betleme	d1-a2	e1-g2	High voices	Recitative and a sustained arioso. Demands good command of high pp. (Phyllis James, AUG)
Di contento	d1-a2	e1-g2	Most suitable for light, high soprano	Graceful, lively. Has some florid passages. Demands some flexibility. (Phyllis James, AUG)
Dirti, ben mio, vorrei (Allessandro in Persia)	eb1-f2	eb1-eb2	Soprano	Sustained, graceful. (GS)
Dunque si sforza (La morte d'Abel)	bb(f)-f2	d1-d2	Low voices	Vigorous, grave. Demands some flexibility. (Echos de l'Italie)
Praebe, virgo, benignas aures	e1-c3	g1-a2	Lyric soprano or coloratura soprano	A solo cantata with sacred Latin text. Florid. Demands considerable flexibility. Ends with a secco recitative. (Ewerhart)

Recitative:
  Io vado
Air:

| Se cerca, se dice (Olimpiade) | bb-eb2 | c1-c2 | Medium or low voices | Recitative and a spirited, vigorous air. (Landshoff) |
| Se mai senti (La Clemenza di Tito) | d1-g2 | g1-d2 (H) | All voices | Sustained. Demands some flexibility. Originally written for alto, b-e2. (Gevaert; also Floridia) |

ARCANGELO DEL LEUTO
(15..–16..)

| Dimmi, amor | c1-f2 | e1-c2 | All voices | Sustained. (Parisotti, GS) |

CARLO AMBROGIO LONATI
(1650–1710)

| Tu paristi idolo amato | d1-ab2 | g1-f2 | High voices | Sustained. (Landshoff) |

ANTONIO LOTTI
(1667–1740)

| Pur dicesti, o bocca bella | d1-f#2 | a1-d2 | All voices | Light and delicate. Demands some flexibility. (Parisotti, GS) |

S. DE LUCA
(Early 16th Century)

| Non posso disperar | d1-f#2 | g1-d2 | All voices | Graceful. Demands facile articulation. (Parisotti, GS) |

FRANCESCO DE MAJO
(1740–1770)

	COMP.	TESS.	TYPE	REMARKS
Recitative: Accresca pietoso Air: Se il labbro si lagra (Ifigenia in Tauride)	e1-a2	a1-f2	Soprano	Recitative, andante, allegro. (Landshoff)

FRANCESCO MANCINI
(1679–1739)

	COMP.	TESS.	TYPE	REMARKS
Dir ch'io t'ami	b#-e2	e1-c#2	Not too suitable for very light voices	Sustained, vigorous. (Fuchs; also Floridia)
Son prigioniero	f#1-ab2	a1-g2	High voices	Animated, graceful, florid. Demands good flexibility. (Jeppesen)

LUIGI MANZIA
(c.1680)

	COMP.	TESS.	TYPE	REMARKS
Hai core, o crudele	eb1-fb2	eb1-c2	Not too suitable for very light voices	Recitative and a slow, sustained air. (Fuchs)
Son povera donzella	g1-e2	a1-e2	Women's voices	Graceful, not fast. (Jeppesen)
Toglietemi, pietosi	f1-g2	bb1-f2	Women's voices	Recitative and a sustained air. High tessitura. (Jeppesen)
Voglio farti dire il vero	g1-g2	a1-e2	Most suitable for high voices	Rapid. Rhythmical. Demands facile articulation. High tessitura. (Jeppesen)

TITLE	COMP.	TESS.	TYPE	REMARKS

BENEDETTO MARCELLO
(1686–1739)

TITLE	COMP.	TESS.	TYPE	REMARKS
Che inviolabile	d#1-f#2	f#1-e2	Not suitable for light, high voices	Sustained, vigorous, rather grave. Has a two-measure basso ostinato with curious chromatic changes in the second half of the piece. (Jeppesen)
Didone	bb-c3	d1-g2	Dramatic soprano (lyric soprano)	A long cantata (22 pages) arranged by Respighi. Has several contrasting movements interrupted by recitative passages. Demands in parts considerable flexibility as well as considerable dramatic intensity. (RIC)
Il mio bel foco	c1(a)-g2	f1-d2	Not too suitable for very light, high voices	Recitative and an animated air. (Parisotti, GS; also, Floridia)
Le Pecorelle	bb-d2	bb-bb1	Medium or low voices	A sustained Siciliana. (Jeppesen)
Lontananza e gelosia	a#-e2	e1-c#2	All voices	Slow, sustained. Has a few florid passages. (Fuchs)
Non m'è grave morir per amore	c1-e2	g1-d2	All voices	Recitative and a graceful aria. (Parisotti, GS)
O, signor, chi sara	e1-a2	f#1-e2	Most suitable for high voices	Animated, spirited. (Jeppesen)
Vedi quel rusceletto	d1-g2	f1-d2	All voices	Graceful, light. Demands some flexibility. (Fuchs)

NICOLA MATTEIS
(1650–1700)

TITLE	COMP.	TESS.	TYPE	REMARKS
Caro volto	e1-g2	g1-eb2	High	Rapid, light. De-

TITLE	COMP.	TESS.	TYPE	REMARKS
pallidetto			voices	mands facile articulation. (Landshoff)

GIOVANNI BATTISTA MAZZAFERRATA
(16..-1691)

TITLE	COMP.	TESS.	TYPE	REMARKS
Presto, presto io m'innamore	e1-g2	g1-eb2	All voices	Rapid and light. (Floridia)

DOMENICO MAZZOCCHI
(c.1590-c.1650)

TITLE	COMP.	TESS.	TYPE	REMARKS
Piu non sia, che m'innamori	e1-f2	g1-e2	High or medium voices	Graceful. Demands some flexibility. (Landshoff)

ANTONIO MAZZONI
(1718-17..)

TITLE	COMP.	TESS.	TYPE	REMARKS
Io veggio in lontananza (Demetrio)	c1-g2	f1-f2	Dramatic soprano (lyric soprano)	Spirited and florid. (Krehbiel)

ALESSANDRO MELANI
(c.1630-1703)

TITLE	COMP.	TESS.	TYPE	REMARKS
Vezzosa aurora	e1-g2	f#1-eb2	All voices	A minuet-like song. Has some florid passages. (Jeppesen)

TOMAS MILANS
(18th Century?)

TITLE	COMP.	TESS.	TYPE	REMARKS
Dominus regnavit	F#-e1	d-e1	Bass or Bass-baritone	A vigorous, spirited song with a recitative in the middle of the two sections. Second section is florid

TITLE	COMP.	TESS.	TYPE	REMARKS
				and demands flexibility. Sacred Latin text. (Ewerhart)
Quem vidistic, pastores	d1-g2	e1-f2	Soprano or tenor	Sustained, but ends with a slightly animated florid Alleluja. Sacred Latin text. (Ewerhart)
Sanctum, et terrible nomen ejus	c1-f2	e1-e2	Soprano or tenor	Spirited. Demands some flexibility. Sacred Latin text. (Ewerhart)

CLAUDIO MONTEVERDI
(1567-1643)

Monteverdi, one of the first composers to write in the monodic style, could be considered one of the inventors of vocal solo music as we know it today.

His airs and songs are strangely "modern," not in their harmonic idiom but in their treatment of the vocal line, which is fashioned not as a self-contained melodic pattern but primarily as a musical intensification of speech. Insofar as musical form is concerned, Monteverdi wrote as freely as any late romantic composer, and much more freely than most twentieth century composers, though naturally within the frame of the stylistic conventions of his time.

The singer wishing to do justice to a Monteverdi air would do well to train himself to recite the text as such, by memory, for Monteverdi's music is shaped and dominated by the text to a greater degree, perhaps, than any other vocal music written before the latter part of the nineteenth century.

As a rule Monteverdi's airs and songs are sustained and do not contain any florid passages of the type encountered in the operatic soli of his successors, and are best suited to rather heavy voices.

Editions: Complete edition of Monteverdi's works, under the editorship of Malipiero, was being prepared by the Universal Edition (fourteen volumes had appeared by 1933).
Combattimento di Clorinda e Tancredo, published by Ricordi.
Incorazione di Poppea (French text only), edited by d'Indy, published by Rouart, Lerolle.

TITLE	COMP.	TESS.	TYPE	REMARKS
Ahi, troppo e duro (Il Balletto delle Ingrate)	d1-f2	a1-d2 (H)	Not too suitable for light, high voices	Very sustained, grave and declamatory. (Floridia)

TITLE	COMP.	TESS.	TYPE	REMARKS
Con che soavità	d1-e2	f1-d2	Medium or low voices	Sustained. Has some florid passages. (Landshoff)
Dal mio permesso amato (Pròlogo: La Musica L'Orfeo)	f1-e2	a1-d2	Not suitable for light, high voices	Sustained, solemn, declamatory. Has an allegro interlude. (Jeppesen)
Di misera regina (Il Ritorno d'Ulisse in Patria)	d#1-f#2	g#1-e2	Women's voices, except a light, high soprano	A lengthy, dramatic recitative. Interpretatively and stylistically not easy. Listed under the title "Monologo del Tempo." (Dallapiccola)
Ecco pur ch'a voi ritorno (Orfeo)	f1-d2	g1-c2	Medium or low voices	Very sustained. (Krehbiel)
Eri già tutta mia	c1-g2	g1-e2	High voices	Sustained. Strophic. (Hunter and Palisca, Five Songs, TP)
Et è pur dunque vero	c1-g2	g1-f2	Most suitable for men's voices	Sustained, somber, somewhat intense. (Hunter and Palisca, Five Songs, TP)
Exulta filia	c1-g2	d1-e2	High voices	A solo motet in five movements plus a ritornello. Ends with an extended, florid Alleluja. (SCH)
Illustratevi, o cieli (Il Ritorno d'Ulisse in Patria)	eb1-eb2	g1-d2	Women's voices	Animated, florid, joyous. Demands some flexibility. (Dallapiccola)
In un fiorito prato (Orfeo)	c1-e2	d1-c2	Not suitable for light, high voices	Slow, declamatory. (Parisotti, RIC)
Lasciatemi morire (Lamento d'Arianna)	d1-d2	e1-bb1	Medium or low voices	Very sustained, grave, declamatory. (Jeppesen; also Parisotti)
Quel sguardo sdegnosetto	c1-a2	g1-g2	High voices	Sustained, in parts florid. (Hunter and

TITLE	COMP.	TESS.	TYPE	REMARKS
Se i languidi miei sguardi	c1-f2	e1-d2	Most suitable for men's voices	Palisca, <u>Five Songs</u>, TP) Sustained, free rhythm. Composer's note: "A love letter for solo voice, composed in expressive, dramatic stile rappresentativo and therefore to be sung without regular measure." (Hunter and Palisca, <u>Five Songs</u>, TP)
Tu se'morta (Orfeo)	c1-e2	f1-d2	Medium or low voices	Very sustained, grave, declamatory. (Krehbiel)

FERNANDO ORLANDI
(1777–1848)

TITLE	COMP.	TESS.	TYPE	REMARKS
Degli angelletti al canto (Il Podesta di Chioggia)	c1-d2	g1-c2	Mezzo-soprano or alto	Graceful. Demands some flexibility. (Krehbiel)

GIOVANNI MARIA ORLANDINI
(1690–1745)

TITLE	COMP.	TESS.	TYPE	REMARKS
Caro, son tua così (Temistocle)	c#1-e2	e1-c#2	Mezzo-soprano or alto	Graceful. (Krehbiel)

FERDINANDO PAER
(1771–1839)

TITLE	COMP.	TESS.	TYPE	REMARKS
Ecco de'miei trascorsi (Agnese)	d1-f2	f1-e2	Soprano or light mezzo-soprano	Animated, graceful. (GS)

For other songs and airs, see under "French" in this section (page 105).

GIOVANNI PAESIELLO
(1741–1816)

TITLE	COMP.	TESS.	TYPE	REMARKS
Chi vuol la Zinga-rella	c1-f2	d1-c2	Women's voices	Light and some-what humorous. Demands facile articulation. (Parisotti, GS)

Recitative:
Dove, ahi dove son io?
Air:

Mentre ti lascio o figlia (La Disfatta di Dario)	c-bb1	bb-f1	Lyric tenor	A scena, andante, allegro. In parts very florid. (Ge-vaert)
Il mio ben quando verrà	c1-a2	a1-f2	Soprano	Delicate. Demands good flexibility. (Parisotti, GS)
Nel cor più non mi sento (La Molinara)	d1-f2	f1-d2	Light so-prano	Graceful and light. (Parisotti, GS; also Floridia)

For other songs and airs, see under "French" in this section (page 105).

PIETRO DOMENICO PARADIES
(1710–1792)

TITLE	COMP.	TESS.	TYPE	REMARKS
M'ha preso alla sua ragna	eb1-f2	ab1-eb2	High or medium voices	Animated, light. Demands facile articulation and flexibility. (Pari-sotti, GS)
Quel ruscelletto	d1-a2	g1-g2	Soprano	Graceful, florid. (Arr., La Forge, CF)

BERNARDO PASQUINI
(1637–1710)

TITLE	COMP.	TESS.	TYPE	REMARKS
Bella bocca	e1-e2	same	All voices	Animated, grace-ful. Demands good flexibility and facile articu-lation. (Jeppesen)

TITLE	COMP.	TESS.	TYPE	REMARKS
Quanto è folle quell' amante	c1-f2	f1-d2	Soprano	Animated, light. Demands facile articulation. Has florid passages. (Landshoff)
So ben s'io peno	f#1-g2	g1-f2	Women's voices	Sustained, rather somber. (Jeppesen)

GIOVANNI BATTISTA PERGOLESI
(1710–1736)

TITLE	COMP.	TESS.	TYPE	REMARKS
A Serpina penserete (La Serva Padrona)	d1-g2	a1-f2	Light soprano	Light and gently humorous. Has rapid sections demanding facile articulation. (Score, RIC)
Confusa, smarrita, spiegarti vorrei (Catone)	c1-f2	f1-d2	Mezzo-soprano or alto	Spirited and dramatic. (Krehbiel)
Dite ch'ogni momento	f1-g2	a1-f2	Not too suitable for very low voices	Sustained, graceful. Demands some flexibility. (Zanon)
Gemo in un punto e fremo (L'Olimpiade)	a-b2	a1-f#2	Dramatic soprano	Spirited. Demands some flexibility. (Krehbiel)
Recitative: Io vado Air: Se cerca e dice: L'amico dov'è? (L'Olimpiade)	db1-gb2 (bb2)	ab1-f2	Soprano	Recitative and a compound aria (andante, allegro repeated). Demands some flexibility. (Gevaert; also Parisotti, RIC)
Mentre dormi, amor fomenti	f1-a2	f1-f2	Soprano	Not fast, quite florid. (Landshoff)
Ogni pena più spietata	b-e2	e1-c2	Most suitable for high or medium voices	Graceful. Demands some flexibility. (Parisotti, GS)

77

TITLE	COMP.	TESS.	TYPE	REMARKS
Se al labbro mio non credi (L'Olimpiade)	a-eb2	f1-c2	Alto or mezzo-so-prano	Slow, sustained. Has some florid passages. (Krehbiel)
Se tu m'ami	bb-f2	g1-eb2	Women's voices	Graceful, delicate. (Parisotti, GS)
Sempre in contrasti con te si sta (La Serva Padrona)	F-f1	c-d1	Bass or bass-baritone	Very animated buffo air. Has a florid passage. Demands facile articulation. (RIC)
Son imbrogliato io già (La Serva Padrona)	Eb-eb1	Bb-c1	Bass or bass-baritone	A very animated buffo air. Demands facile articulation. (RIC)
Stizzoso, mio stizzoso (La Serva Padrona)	e1-a2	a1-f#2	Soprano	Light and humorous. (Parisotti, GS; transposed one-half tone lower)
Tre giorni	e1-f2	ab1-eb2 (H)	Men's voices	The authorship of this famous air is not definitely established. It exists in many arrangements, sometimes named "Nina." Very sustained. (Floridia)

AIRS FROM THE "STABAT MATER"
(The score is generally available)

Cujus animam gementem	f1-ab2	bb1-g2	Soprano	Animated, graceful.
Fac ut portem	c1-eb2	eb1-c2	Alto or mezzo-soprano	Slow, has florid passages.
Pia mater, fons amoris	b-eb2	c1-bb1	Alto or mezzo-soprano	Sustained. Demands some flexibility.
Quae moerebat	d1-f2	eb1-c2	Alto or mezzo-soprano	Animated. Demands some flexibility.
Vidit suum dulcem natum	f1-ab2	g1-f2	Soprano	Sustained. Demands some flexibility.

78

See also "Salve Regina," a solo cantata for soprano, published by Music Press.

JACOPO PERI
(1561–1633)

TITLE	COMP.	TESS.	TYPE	REMARKS
Al fonte, al prato	g1-e2	g1-d2	All voices	Animated, vigorous. (Jeppesen)
Funeste piaggie (Euridice)	d1-d2	g1-d2	Baritone (mezzo-soprano or alto)	Sustained, majestic. (Krehbiel)
Gioite al canto mio (Euridice)	g#1-f#2	a1-e2	Not suitable for light, high voices	Sustained, majestic. (Dallapiccola)
Nel puro ardor (Euridice)	g1-e2	g1-d2	All voices	Very sustained. (Dallapiccola)
O miei giorni fugaci	f1-d2	g1-d2	Not too suitable for light, high voices	Sustained, grave. Sacred text. (Jeppesen)
Un di soletto	f#1-e2	g1-d2	Most suitable for men's voices	Animated. Has interesting rhythms. (Jeppesen)

JACOPO ANTONIO PERTI
(1661–1756)

TITLE	COMP.	TESS.	TYPE	REMARKS
Begli occhi, io non mi pento	d1-f2 (g2)	g1-e2	All voices	A recitative and a graceful minuet-like air. Has a few florid passages. (Fuchs; also Floridia)
Dolce, scherza	c1-eb2	g1-eb2	All voices	A graceful, minuet-like canzonetta. (Fuchs)
Io son zittella	e1-g2	g1-e2	Soprano	Very animated, light. (Landshoff)
Mai non intesi	d#1-e2	a1-d2	All voices	Animated, graceful. (Jeppesen)
Mi fa vezzi	g1-f2	a1-e2	All voices	Animated, spirited. (Jeppesen)
Scioglie omai le nevi	c1-f2	f1-f2	All voices	Animated. Rather vigorous. Has

TITLE	COMP.	TESS.	TYPE	REMARKS
				some florid pas-sages. (Jeppesen)
Sperar io non dovrei	f1-f2	a1-d2	All voices	A sustained Sicili-ana. (Jeppesen)

MARTINO PESENTI
(c.1600–c.1648)

TITLE	COMP.	TESS.	TYPE	REMARKS
Cosi Nilio canto	c1-g2	f1-d2	Not too suitable for very light voices	Sustained. Rather majestic. (Jeppe-sen)
O biondetta lascivetta	c1-f2	e1-e2	Most suit-able for men's voices	Animated, grace-ful, light. De-mands facile artic-ulation. Strophic. (Jeppesen)

NICOLA PICCINNI (PICCINI)
(1728–1800)

Piccinni, primarily remembered now as Gluck's Parisian rival, seems to have suffered the fate of most of his contemporaries, name-ly, polite neglect. Hardly any of the songs and airs from his eighty or more operas are now available in reprints and of those available only a few are still encountered occasionally on concert programs. Of these the "Se il ciel mi divide" from "Alessandro nelle Indie" is perhaps most widely known, having been included in the Parisotti collection as well as in the Gevaert "Les Gloires de l'Italie."

TITLE	COMP.	TESS.	TYPE	REMARKS
Giammai provai (La Donna Vana)	f#1-g2	g1-e2	Not too suitable for very low voices	Graceful, delicate tempo di minuetto. (Zanon)
Non sarei si sventurata	g1-b2	a1-f#2	Soprano	Animated. De-mands consider-able flexibility. (Landshoff)
Se il ciel mi divide (Alessandro nelle Indie)	c#1-g2	f1-d2	Mezzo-soprano or drama-tic soprano	Scena and a spirited air. Transposed a third lower than the original. A cut from bar 3, page 139, to bar

8, page 143, is
recommended.
(Parisotti, GS).
This air in the
original key can
be found in Ge-
vaert's "Les Gloires
de l'Italie" (Heugel).
See Vinci.

For other songs and airs see under "French" in this section (page 105).

CARLO PIETRAGRUA
(c.1700)

Title	Comp.	Tess.	Type	Remarks
Tortorella	b-c#2	d#1-b1	All voices	Slow, plaintive, in parts quite florid. (Jeppesen)

GIUSEPPE PIGNATTA
(c.1700)

Title	Comp.	Tess.	Type	Remarks
Cieco si finse amor	c#1-f#2	e1-e2	All voices	Animated. Demands considerable flexibility. (Fuchs)

NICOLO (NICOLA) ANTONIO PORPORA
(1686-1768)

Title	Comp.	Tess.	Type	Remarks
Come la luce è tremola	c1-f2	eb1-db2	All voices	Sustained, graceful. In parts demands considerable flexibility. (Fuchs)
Contemplar almen	b-d2	d1-c2	Medium or low voices	Graceful, quite florid, demands good flexibility. (Jeppesen)
Già la Notte	d1-g2	g1-e2	Soprano or light tenor	Slow, has florid passages. See also "Già la Notte" by Viardot (an arrangement of a

TITLE	COMP.	TESS.	TYPE	REMARKS
				movement from a Haydn string quartet). (Echos de l'Italie)
Ne' campi e nelle selve	b-eb2	e1-d2	Medium or low voices	Not fast, graceful, in parts florid. A trifle long. (Jeppesen)
Non più fra sassi	e1-a2	g1-f2	Most suitable for light soprano	Animated, graceful, very florid. Rather high tessitura. (Jeppesen)
Poscia quando il pastor	b-d2	d1-c2	Medium or low voices	Recitative and a rather florid da capo air. (Jeppesen)
Sei mio ben	f1-a2	a1-g2	High voices	A rather florid da capo air. (Jeppesen)
Senza il muero piacer	d1-eb2	f#1-d2	Medium or low voices	Slow, sustained, in parts quite florid. (Jeppesen)
So ben che la speranza	d1-a2	g1-f2	High voices	Animated, graceful da capo air. Demands flexibility. (Jeppesen)
Vigilate, oculi mei	e1-a2	a1-f#2	Soprano or tenor	A solo cantata in three movements with short recitatives in between. Arias are florid. Ends with an extended, florid alleluja section. Sacred Latin text. (Ewerhart)

FRANCESCO PROVENZALE
(1640–1700)

TITLE	COMP.	TESS.	TYPE	REMARKS
Deh, rendetemi	f1-f2	a1-eb2 (H)	Most suitable for medium or low voices	Delicate. Demands good command of pp. (Floridia) This air in the original key (a sixth lower) can

TITLE	COMP.	TESS.	TYPE	REMARKS
				be found in the Landshoff collection "Alte Meister des Bel Canto," CFP.

PAOLO QUAGLIATI
(15..–16..)

TITLE	COMP.	TESS.	TYPE	REMARKS
Apra il suo verde seno	g1-e2 (H)	same	All voices	Delicate and graceful. The accompaniment is somewhat elaborate. (Floridia) A simpler version can be found in Landshoff.

VINCENZO RIGHINI
(1756–1812)

TITLE	COMP.	TESS.	TYPE	REMARKS
Amor, che cieco sei (La Gerusalema liberata)	c1-f2	f1-c2	Soprano or mezzo-soprano	Graceful. Demands some flexibility. (Krehbiel)

RAFAELLO RONTANI
(? –1622)

TITLE	COMP.	TESS.	TYPE	REMARKS
Caldi sospiri	e1-eb2	f1-d2	All voices	Animated, light. Demands facile articulation. (Jeppesen)
O primavera	d1-f2	e1-e2	All voices	Sustained, rather declamatory. (Jeppesen)
Or ch'io non segno più	eb1-gb2	eb1-eb2 (H)	All voices	Animated, light. Somewhat humorous. Demands facile articulation. (Floridia)
Pescatrice ligurina	d1-f2	d1-eb2	All voices	Spirited, demands facile articulation and some flexibility. (Ricci, Antiche Gemme Italiane, RIC)

83

TITLE	COMP.	TESS.	TYPE	REMARKS
Se bel rio	f1-f2	a1-d2	All voices	Graceful. Demands lightness of tone. (Parisotti, GS; also Floridia)

SALVATORE ROSA
(1615-1673)

TITLE	COMP.	TESS.	TYPE	REMARKS
Selve, voi che le speranza	d1-g2	g1-d2	All voices	Very sustained. (Floridia)
Star vicino	f1-g2	bb1-f2 (H)	Most suitable for men's voices	Demands good command of pp and some flexibility. (Floridia)
Vado ben spesso	c1-g2	g1-e2	Most suitable for men's voices	Graceful, rhythmic. (Dallapiccola). Liszt made a piano transcription of this tune, "Canzonetta di Salvator Rosa." (Floridia) This song is attributed to either Salvatore Rosa or Giovanni Bononcini.

LUIGI ROSSI
(1598-1653)

TITLE	COMP.	TESS.	TYPE	REMARKS
Ah, rendimi (Mitrane)	g-f#2	b-b1	Mezzo-soprano or alto	An andante, allegro air. Rather vigorous. (GS)
Che sventura	e1-g2	g1-e2	High voices	Not fast. Demands some flexibility. (Landshoff)
Fanciulla son io	f1-g2	bb1-f2	Light soprano	Animated, graceful. Demands facile articulation. Has florid passages. The verse beginning "Tuo strale dorato" could be omitted. (Neitzel, Gems of Antiquity, JCC)

84

TITLE	COMP.	TESS.	TYPE	REMARKS
Gelosia, che a poco a poco (Cantata)	c1-g2	eb1-eb2	Mezzo-soprano (dramatic soprano) or tenor	A solo cantata in several contrasting movements. In parts very florid. (Gevaert)
Non la volete intendere	f1-g2	g1-f2	High voices	Sustained; has a slower middle section. (Landshoff)
Se mi toglie ria sventura	f1-g2	g1-eb2	Soprano	Sustained. Demands good command of high pp. Has some florid passages. (Landshoff)

ANTONIO SACCHINI
(1734–1786)

TITLE	COMP.	TESS.	TYPE	REMARKS
Recitative: Deh calma, o cara Air: Cara, ascondi a me quel pianto (Motezuma)	b-g#2 (a2)	f#1-e2	Dramatic soprano (lyric soprano) or tenor	Recitative and a sustained air. In parts florid. (Gevaert)
Se mai più sarò (Alessandro nell' Indie)	d#1-a2	g#1-e2	High voices	Sustained. Has some florid passages. (Gevaert, reprinted by GS)

For other songs and airs see under "French" in this section (page 105).

GIOVANNI FELICE SANCES
(c.1600–1679)

TITLE	COMP.	TESS.	TYPE	REMARKS
Pietosi, allontanatevi	c#1-f2	f1-e2	Not too suitable for light, high voices	Very sustained, grave, declamatory (Jeppesen)

DOMENICO SARRI
(1678–1745)

TITLE	COMP.	TESS.	TYPE	REMARKS
Non ha ragione	e1-f2	f1-e2	Soprano	Not fast, grace-

TITLE	COMP.	TESS.	TYPE	REMARKS
ingrato				ful. Demands some flexibility. (Landshoff)
Sen corre l'agne-letta	c1-f2	f1-c2	All voices	Graceful. Demands lightness of tone and some flexibility. (Parisotti, GS)

GIUSEPPE SARTI
(1729–1802)

TITLE	COMP.	TESS.	TYPE	REMARKS
Mia speranza io pur vorrei	b(a)–b2	e1-e2	Dramatic soprano (lyric soprano)	An andante, allegro aria. Demands some flexibility. (Gevaert)
S'inganna chi crede (Medoro)	f#1-a2	g#1-e2	Soprano or tenor	Graceful. Demands some flexibility. (Zanon)

ANTONIO SARTORIO
(1620–1681)

TITLE	COMP.	TESS.	TYPE	REMARKS
Oh, che umore stravagante	c1-e2	e1-c2	Most suitable for men's voices	Very spirited. Demands some flexibility and facile articulation. (Parisotti, RIC)

ALESSANDRO SCARLATTI
(1660–1725)

The few airs and songs of Alessandro Scarlatti available in modern reprints are too well known to every singer to need any sort of comment. Beautifully written for the voice, extraordinarily perfect in the elegance of their form, powerfully characteristic in the musical delineation of their poetic content, they have long been used as teaching material, no doubt because of their comparative harmonic simplicity. Yet if one considers that Scarlatti wrote 115 operas, 200 masses, and a great number of miscellaneous vocal works, one wonders why, in view of the obvious popularity of the few of his airs available in modern reprints, no publisher has found it advisable to issue a comprehensive anthology of Scarlatti's songs and airs.

Scarlatti's vocal music, like that of Rameau and Purcell, seems, with few exceptions, to have suffered the same polite neglect accorded to the work of their lesser contemporaries. It seems a pity that these three great composers are not as yet fully appreciated, and that their music is largely looked upon as a sort of relic of olden times, instead of being treated as music which is as magnificently alive today as it was when first conceived.

"Moriarty Soprano" and "Moriarty Medium," both in parentheses, indicate "Scarlatti—Songs for Soprano" and "Scarlatti—Songs for Medium Voice," respectively. Both collections are edited by J. Moriarty, published by R. D. Row.

TITLE	COMP.	TESS.	TYPE	REMARKS
All' acquisto di gloria (Tigrane)	c1-g2	f1-d2	Medium or low voices	Spirited. Has florid passages. (Parisotti, GS)
Bellezza, che s'ama	g#1-f#2	a1-e2	All voices	Animated, graceful. Rather high tessitura. (Jeppesen)
Caldo sangue (Il Sedecia, Re di Gerusalemene)	f#1-a2	a1-f#2	Soprano	Slow, sustained. Demands some flexibility. An air from an oratorio. (Landshoff)
Cara e dolce	d1-eb2	f1-d2	All voices	Graceful. (Jeppesen)
Chi vuole innamorarsi	f#1-g2	a1-e2 (H)	Most suitable for high voices	Rapid and light. Demands facile articulation. (Floridia)
Da te lungi	c1-f2	eb1-eb2	Not suitable for light, high voices	Recitative and a very sustained air. (Moriarty Medium)
Diffesa non ha	d1-eb2	f1-d2	All voices	Graceful, not fast. (Jeppesen)
Elitropio d'amor	d#1-e2	same	All voices	A solo cantata consisting of two rapid and brilliant arias, each introduced by a recitative. Florid passages. Demands flexibility. (G. Tintori, 4 Cantate, RIC)

TITLE	COMP.	TESS.	TYPE	REMARKS
Fermate omai fermate	a-b1	d1-b2	Alto	A solo cantata in two movements, the first very sustained and the other lively and detached. Each is introduced by a recitative. Has a few florid passages. (G. Tintori, 4 Cantate, RIC)
Già il sole dal Gange	e1-f♯2	a1-e2	Not too suitable for very light, high voices	Vigorous and spirited. (Dallapiccola)
Già mai	d1-g2	g1-eb2	High voices	A sustained, graceful Siciliana. (Echos de l'Italie)
Io dissi	c1-d2	d1-c2	Medium or low voices	Moderate, rather grave. Somewhat long and rhythmically repetitious. (Jeppesen)
Io morirei contento	b-a2	e1-g2	All voices	A solo cantata with several recitatives and ariosos. Has long florid passages and sustained phrases. Demands considerable flexibility. (G. Tintori, 4 Cantate, RIC)
La fortuna è un pronto ardir	d1-d2	e1-c♯2 (L)	All voices	Graceful. Demands some flexibility. (J. Woodside, Seven Centuries of Solo Song, BMC)
La speranza	d1-f♯2	g1-e2	All voices	Animated, rhythmical, rather vigorous. (Jeppesen)
La tua gradita fé	d1-f2	f1-e2	All voices	Sustained. (Jeppesen)
Marmi adorati e cari	d1-d2	f♯1-c2	Not suitable for low, heavy voices	Animated, lively. Demands some flexibility. (Moriarty Medium)
Nevi intatte	d♯1-e2 (a2)	g1-e2	Most suitable for	Sustained, graceful. Demands

TITLE	COMP.	TESS.	TYPE	REMARKS
			men's voices	some flexibility. (Fuchs)
Non dar più pene, o caro (La Rosaura)	e1-f♯2	a1-e2	Soprano	Animated, light. The violin obbligato can be easily incorporated into the piano part. (Krehbiel)
Non vogl'io se non vederti	f♯1-e2	g1-d2 (H)	All voices	A minuet. Demands lightness of tone. (Floridia)
O cessate di piagarmi	d♯1-d2	f♯1-c2	All voices	Very sustained. (Parisotti, GS). In the Jeppesen edition a fourth higher.
O di Betlemme altera	c1-a2	f1-f♯2	Soprano	A solo cantata in three movements with recitatives and arioso sections. Has florid passages. Published with string quartet and harpsichord accompaniment; piano reduction available. English translation is awkward. (E. J. Dent, OX)
O, dolcissima speranza	d1-f♯2	f1-d2	All voices	Sustained, graceful. (Jeppesen)
Pensieri	d1-g2	f1-e♭2	Most suitable for high voices	A rather extended cantata. Has several recitatives and contrasting movements. In parts quite florid. (Jeppesen)
Per formare la Betta	d1-e2 (g2)	g1-d2	Most suitable for men's voices	Animated, rather vigorous. Demands considerable flexibility. (Fuchs)
Piu m'impiaga quel ciglio nero	d1-d2	f1-c2	All voices	Animated, graceful. (Moriarty Medium)
Povera pellegrina	f1-f2	a♭1-e♭2	Soprano	A sustained, graceful siciliana. (Gevaert)

TITLE	COMP.	TESS.	TYPE	REMARKS
Quanto peni, anima mia	c1-eb2	f1-db2	All voices	Sustained. (Moriarty Medium)
Rugiadose, odorose	f1-g2	bb1-eb2 (H)	All voices	Animated, light. Demands facile articulation and lightness of tone. Exists in many arrangements. Sometimes named "Le Violette" or "Violette." (Floridia)
Recitative: Qual mia colpa Air:				
Se delitto è l'adorarti	c1-f2	g1-eb2	All voices	Sustained. (Parisotti, RIC)
Se delitto è l'essere amante	g#1-a2	a1-g2	All voices	Sustained. Has two short, florid passages. (Moriarty Soprano)
Se Florindo è fedele	eb1-eb2	ab1-db2	Women's voices	Light and delicate. (Parisotti, GS)
Se tu della mia morte	c1-eb2	f1-db2	All voices	Sustained. (Parisotti, GS)
Sento nel core	d#1-e2	f#1-d2	All voices	Slow, sustained. (Dallapiccola)
Siete estinte, o mia speranza	b-d2	e1-c2	All voices	Sustained. (Moriarty Medium)
Solitudine avvenne	d1-b2	f1-g2	Soprano	A solo cantata with several recitatives and movements. Florid. Has a long cadenza. The flute obbligato can be incorporated into the piano part. (Zimmermann, Frankfurt Am Main)
Son tutta duolo	d1-eb2	g1-d2	Most suitable for medium or low voices	Grave and declamatory. (Parisotti, GS)
Sono unite a tormentarmi	e1-ab2	g1-f2	High voices	Slow, sustained first part; animated, light, florid second section. (Moriarty Soprano)

TITLE	COMP.	TESS.	TYPE	REMARKS
Speranze mie	a-f2	d1-e2	All voices	A short solo cantata with a recitative and three movements. Has florid passages; demands flexibility. (G. Tintori, <u>4 Cantate</u>, RIC)
Su, venite a consiglio	d1-f#2	g1-d2	Not too suitable for very light, high voices	An amusing, spirited dialogue between the composer and his thoughts. Demands facile articulation. (Parisotti, GS)
Toglietemi la vita ancor	d#1-f2	g#1-e2	All voices	Animated, demands facile articulation. (Jeppesen)
Tu lo sai	f#1-f#2	f#1-d2	All voices	Sustained, graceful. (Ricci, <u>Antiche Gemme Italiane</u>, RIC)
Un cor da voi ferito (La Rosaura)	b-b1	e1-b1	Alto or mezzo-soprano	Very sustained. (Krehbiel)
Va per lo mare	b-e2	e1-d2	All voices	Animated, rather vigorous. Very florid. (Fuchs)
Voglio Amar	eb1-g2	g1-eb2	All voices	Spirited, graceful. (Moriarty Soprano)

DOMENICO SCARLATTI
(1685-1757)

Consolati e spera	bb-e2	f1-d2	Not too suitable for very light, high voices	Sustained. (Parisotti, GS)
Dire non voglio	d1-a2	f#1-e2	High voices	Spirited, vigorous. Demands some flexibility. A trifle long. (OX)
Qual farfaletta amante	f#1-ab2	g1-g2 (H)	Not too suitable	Animated, graceful. Demands

91

TITLE	COMP.	TESS.	TYPE	REMARKS
			for very low voices	some flexibility. (Ascherberg, Hopwood and Crew, London)
Sono amante e	d1-g2	g1-f2	High voices	Sustained. Demands some flexibility. (OX)
Tuo mi chiami	e1-g2	g1-e2	High voices	Sustained. Has some florid passages. (OX)
Vorresti, si vorresti	e1-a2	g#1-f#2	High voices	Sustained. Has a vigorous, animated middle section. (OX)

GAETANO MARIA SCHIASSI
(16..-1754)

TITLE	COMP.	TESS.	TYPE	REMARKS
Digli, ch'io son fedele (Alessandro nell' Indie)	c1-d2	e1-b1	Alto or mezzo-soprano	Majestic. Demands some flexibility. (Krehbiel)

ANTONIO SECCHI
(1761-1833)

TITLE	COMP.	TESS.	TYPE	REMARKS
Lungi dal caro bene	c1-a2	a1-f2 (H)	All voices	Very sustained. The authorship of this famous air has not been definitely established. Another very effective arrangement by Bruno Huehn. (GS; Floridia)

AGOSTINO STEFFANI
(1654-1748)

TITLE	COMP.	TESS.	TYPE	REMARKS
Sei si caro (Marco Aurelio)	d#1-f2	a1-e2 (H)	Women's voices	Slow, sustained. Demands flexibility. (Floridia)

ALESSANDRO STRADELLA
(1642-1682)

TITLE	COMP.	TESS.	TYPE	REMARKS
A Porfiria vec-	f#1-g2	g1-e2	All voices	A short, animated

TITLE	COMP.	TESS.	TYPE	REMARKS
chiarella				satirical song. Demands facile articulation. (Jeppesen)
Col mio sangue comprenderei	e♭1-a♭2	g1-e♭2 (H)	All voices	Slow and very sustained. (Floridia)
Cosi, amor, mi fai languir	e♭1-f2	g1-e♭2	All voices	Graceful. (Jeppesen)
Ombre, voi che celate	c#1-g2	f1-f2	Not too suitable for very light, high voices	A cantata with several contrasting movements interspersed with recitatives. Has some florid passages. (Jeppesen)
Per pietà (Il Floridoro)	f1-a♭2	a♭1-e♭2 (H)	All voices	Very sustained. (Floridia)
Pietà signore	c1-f2	g1-e♭2 (H)	Not suitable for very light voices	Very sustained. (Floridia)
Ragion sempre addita	d1-g2	e1-e2	All voices	Spirited. Demands facile articulation. Has florid passages. (Parisotti, GS)
Se amor m'annoda il piede	b♭-f2	f1-d2	Most suitable for medium voices	A short cantata. (Parisotti, GS)
Se nel ben	e1-f#2	f#1-e2	All voices	Animated, rhythmical. (Jeppesen)
So ben che mi saettano	c1-a2	g1-f2	Soprano	Animated, graceful. Demands facile articulation. (Landshoff)

BARBARA STROZZI
(1583-1660)

TITLE	COMP.	TESS.	TYPE	REMARKS
Amor dormiglione	f1-g2	a♭1-f2 (H)	Not too suitable for very light, high voices	Spirited. (Floridia)

TITLE	COMP.	TESS.	TYPE	REMARKS
Chiamata a nuovi amori	c1-g2	e1-e2	All voices	Animated. Some rather florid sections interspersed with graceful, more sustained passages. (Ricci, Antiche Gemme Italiane, RIC)
Soccorete, luci avare	d1-g2	g1-eb2	All voices	First part very sustained and slow, second part animated, demanding facile articulation and flexibility. (Jeppesen)
Spesso per entro al petto	c1-f2	f1-c2	All voices	Not fast. Has some florid passages and a staccato refrain. (Jeppesen)

FRANCESCO SUPRIANI
(attributed to)
(16..-17..)

Potrà lasciare il rio	e1-g#2	b1-f#2 (H)	All voices	Delicate. (Floridia)

ANTON FRANCESCO TENAGLIA
(1600-16..)

Begil occhi, mercè	c#1-e2	e1-c2	Not too suitable for very light, high voices	Sustained. Demands some flexibility. (Parisotti, RIC)
Quando sarà quel di	d1-d2	g1-c2	Most suitable for medium voices	Animated, light. (Parisotti, GS)

GIUSEPPE TORELLI
(1658-1709)

Tu lo sai	bb-eb2	f1-db2	All voices	Sustained. In this

| | | | | edition transposed for low voice. See also the arrangements by Floridia and one in the G. Schirmer edition of twenty-five songs. (Fuchs) |

TOMMASO TRAETTA
(1727–1779)

TITLE	COMP.	TESS.	TYPE	REMARKS
Dovrei . . . ma no	b-f2	e1-d2	Soprano or mezzo-soprano	Sustained, somewhat declamatory. (Parisotti, RIC)
Ombra cara, amorosa	b-g2	g1-e2	Not too suitable for very light, high voices	Scena and aria. Dramatic. (Parisotti, GS; also Floridia)

FRANCESCO MARIA VERACINI
(1685–1750)

TITLE	COMP.	TESS.	TYPE	REMARKS
Pastorale	c1-g2 (a2)	a1-f2	Soprano	Light and delicate. Demands some flexibility and a good command of high pp. (Arr. by A. L., BH)

LEONARDO VINCI
(1690–1730)

TITLE	COMP.	TESS.	TYPE	REMARKS
Deh respirar lasciatemi (Artasere)	d1-g2	g1-eb2	Soprano	Sustained. Demands some flexibility. (Gevaert)
Se il ciel mi divide (Alessandro nelle Indie)	eb1-ab2	ab1-f2	Soprano	Animated. Demands some flexibility. (Gevaert) See Piccinni.
Sentirsi dire	c1-e2	e1-d2	Medium or low voices	Very spirited. Demands some flexibility. (Parisotti, RIC)

TITLE	COMP.	TESS.	TYPE	REMARKS
Si bella mercede	c1-f2	f1-d2	High voices	Animated. Demands some flexibility. (Parisotti, RIC)
Teco, si, vengo anch'io	d1-f2	f1-eb2	High voices	Graceful. Has some florid passages. (Parisotti, RIC)
Vedovella afflitta e sola	c1-d2	e1-c2	Mezzo-soprano or alto	Animated. Demands facile articulation. (Parisotti, RIC)
Vo solcando un mar crudele (Artaserse)	d1-a2	f#1-e2	Soprano	Spirited, florid. (GS)

FILIPPO VITALI
(c.1600–1653)

TITLE	COMP.	TESS.	TYPE	REMARKS
O bei lumi	d1-e2	g1-d2	All voices	Animated, graceful. Has a few florid passages. (Jeppesen)
Pastorella	d1-d2	g1-c2	Most suitable for men's voices	Animated, light. Demands facile articulation. (Jeppesen)

ANTONIO VIVALDI
(c.1669–1741)

Until very recently hardly any editions of Vivaldi's vocal music were available. The "rediscovery" of Vivaldi which took place during the last decade has completely changed his stature so far as the general public is concerned. Now the music of one of the most important Baroque composers is beginning to be a little better known and appreciated. A great number of collections of Vivaldi's songs and airs are in preparation and it seems that in another few years much of his magnificent work will finally become available to the performer.

Bibliography

The name found in parentheses after the remarks indicates one of the following collections:

Edmunds: Five Arias from Solo Cantatas (high and low), edited by J. Edmunds, published by Row Music Co.

Turchi: <u>4 Arias</u>, edited by G. Turchi, published by International Music Co.

Gentili: <u>Sei Arie</u>, edited by A. Gentili, published by G. Ricordi.

Füssl 2; 5: <u>2 Songs for Contralto and 5 Arias for Soprano</u>, edited by K. H. Füssl, published by International Music Co.

See also the vocal score of "Gloria," published by both International Music Co. and G. Ricordi.

TITLE	COMP.	TESS.	TYPE	REMARKS
Amato ben	d#1-f2	f#1-d2	High voices	Graceful. Demands considerable flexibility. (Füssl 5)
Armatae face et anguibus (Juditha Triumphans)	c1-g2	f1-eb2	Not too suitable for very heavy, low voices	Animated, fast, florid. Demands flexibility and facile articulation. (Gentili)
Di due rai	e1-a2	f1-e2	High voices	Animated, graceful, demands flexibility. (Turchi)
Dille ch'il viver mio	e1-g2	f1-f2	Most suitable for high voices	Sustained, graceful, delicate. Has some florid passages. (Turchi)
Domine Deus (Gloria)	f1-f2	same	Soprano	Very slow, sustained. Has some florid passages. Sacred Latin text. (Score, RIC; IMC)
Far min dirti	d1-d2	f#1-d2	Medium or low voices	Not fast, has some florid passages. (Füssl 2)
Filli di gioia vuoi farmi morir	f#1-e2	g1-e2	All voices	Spirited. (Edmunds)
Ingrata si mi svena	e1-e2	f#1-d2	All voices	Animated, graceful. (Edmunds)
La farfaletta	g1-a2	c1-g2	Most suitable for coloratura soprano	Animated, light, very florid. High tessitura. (Füssl 5)
La pastorella sul primo albore	e1-a2	g1-f2	Most suitable for light soprano	Animated, light. Demands facile articulation and flexibility. (Turchi)
Lascera l'amato salma	d1-ab2	g1-eb2	Most suitable for light soprano	Animated, graceful, florid. (Füssl 5)

TITLE	COMP.	TESS.	TYPE	REMARKS
O di tua man	c1-c2	same	Most suitable for medium and low voices	Sustained. Has a few florid passages. (Jeppesen; also Edmunds)
O servi, volate (Juditha Triumphans)	e1-g2	f#1-f#2	Not suitable for heavy, low voices	Animated, graceful. Has florid passages. (Gentili)
Piango, gemo	a-b1	same	Medium or low voices	A sustained, vigorous passacaglia. The basso ostinato is a descending chromatic scale between tonic and dominant. (Jeppesen; also Edmunds)
Pur ch'à te grata	c1-f2	e1-db2	All voices	Animated. Demands some flexibility. (Edmunds)
Qui sedes ad dexteram (Gloria)	c#1-d2	same	Alto	Spirited, florid. Demands flexibility. Sacred Latin text. (Score, RIC; IMC)
Quo cum patriae (Juditha Triumphans)	c1-d2	d1-c2	Women's voices except heavy alto	Animated, graceful. Has some florid passages. (Gentili)
Se cerca, se dice (L'Olimpiade)	d1-g2	f1-f2	Soprano or mezzosoprano	A song of contrasting moods and tempi. Has parts with some dramatic intensity. (Gentili)
Sebben sente	f1-bb2	bb1-g2	Most suitable for light soprano	Animated, graceful. Quite florid. (Füssl 5)
Sento con quel diletto	d1-f#2	same	Most suitable for light, high voices	Florid, graceful. (Füssl 5)
Si fulgida per te (Juditha Triumphans)	d1-e2	e1-d2	All voices	Sustained, graceful. (Gentili)
Stabat mater	ab-d2	c1-c2	Alto	A cantata in five movements. Has one recitative. In

TITLE	COMP.	TESS.	TYPE	REMARKS
				parts florid; demands some flexibility. Sacred Latin text. (Alfredo Casella, Carisch)
Ti sento	b-b1	d1-b1	Medium or low voices	Animated, light. Has some florid passages. (Füssl 2)
Un certo non so che	c1-f2	e1-c2	Most suitable for medium voices	Sustained. Demands some flexibility. (Parisotti, GS; also Floridia)
Vieni, vieni o mio diletto	d1-f♯2	f♯1-e2	All voices	Animated, graceful. (Turchi)

DIONIGI ZAMPERELLI
(18th Century)

TITLE	COMP.	TESS.	TYPE	REMARKS
So che godendo vai (Catone)	a-f2	e♭1-c2	Mezzo-soprano or alto	Sustained and majestic. (Krehbiel)

FRANCESCO MARIA ZANETI
(c.1680)

TITLE	COMP.	TESS.	TYPE	REMARKS
Avvezzati, mio core	f1-a2	g1-f2	All voices	Slow, very sustained; the middle section is animated and rather florid. (Jeppesen)

99

SONGS AND AIRS IN SPANISH BEFORE THE NINETEENTH CENTURY

Bibliography

The name found in parentheses after the remarks indicates one of the following collections:

Ewerhart: <u>Cantio Sacra</u>, edited by Ewerhart, published by Bieler, Köln.

Nin: <u>14 Airs Anciens</u>, 2 volumes, edited by Nin, published by Eschig.

Subirá: <u>Spanish Songs of the 18th Century</u>, edited by Subirá, published by International Music Co.

TITLE	COMP.	TESS.	TYPE	REMARKS
		ANONYMOUS		
		(18th Century)		
Ave Maria	f1-g2	a1-f2	Tenor or soprano	A sustained and florid solo motet. Sacred Latin text. (Ewerhart)
Beata mater	F-f1	c-c1	Bass	Sustained, in parts florid. Has wide skips. Demands some flexibility. Sacred Latin text. (Ewerhart)
Canción de cuna (El Gurrumino)	g♯1-e2	a1-e2	Most suitable for women's voices	Sustained, somewhat slow, gentle. (Subirá)
Ecce homo sine querela	g-a1	b-g1	Alto	A sustained and florid solo motet. Sacred Latin text. (Ewerhart)

100

JOSÉ BASSA
(1670–1730?)

Minué cantado	g1-e2	same	All voices	A delicate minuet. (Nin)

MARIANO BUSTOS
(c.1790)

Canción contra los violetistas (La Necedad)	f#1-g2	g1-e2	High voices	Spirited. Demands facile articulation. (Subirá)

JOSÉ CASTEL
(c.1776)

Canción de la gitana habilidosa (La Gitanilla en el Coliseo)	e1-f2	f1-e2	Women's voices	Rhythmic, dance-like, graceful. (Subirá)

SEBASTIAN DURON
(1645–1716?)

Cloris hermosa	d#1-f#2	e1-c2	Most suitable for men's voices	Sustained, not slow, rather delicate. (Nin)

PABLO ESTEVE
(c.1730–1794)

Alma sinatmos	a1-gb2	bb1-eb2	High voices, except a very light soprano	Very sustained, somber. (Nin)
Canción satírica de pronósticos (El Juicio del Año)	d1-e2	g1-d2	All voices, except bass	Animated, graceful. Humorous, satirical. (Subirá)

TITLE	COMP.	TESS.	TYPE	REMARKS

FERNANDO FERNANDIERE
(c. 1778)

Minueto en alabanza de la música seria (La Consulta)	c1-f2	f1-e2	All voices except bass	A graceful minuet. The vocal line is florid. (Subirá)

VENTURA GALVAN
(c. 1770)

Seguidillas del oficial cortejante (Vagamundos y ciegos fingidos)	c1-eb2	f1-c2	Women's voices	Sustained, somewhat humorous. Spoken ending. Accompaniment is in imitation of the guitar. (Subirá)

BLAS DE LASERNA
(1751-1816)

El jilguerito con pico de oro (Los Amantes Chasquesados)	f#1-a2	g1-e2	High voices	An animated, graceful, brilliant minuet air. Demands considerable flexibility and an accomplished pianist. (Nin)
Seguidillas majas (El Majo y la Italiana fingida)	e#1-e2	g#1-d2	Women's voices	Animated. (Subirá)

ANTONIO LITERES
(1680-1755?)

Aria: Si de rama en rama (Acis y Galatea)	c1-g2	g1-d2	Soprano	Recitative and an animated, somewhat florid air. See also "Confiado Jilquerillo," an arrangement by Obradors of the same air for coloratura soprano. (Nin)

TITLE	COMP.	TESS.	TYPE	REMARKS

JOSÉ MARIN
(1619–1699)

TITLE	COMP.	TESS.	TYPE	REMARKS
Corazón que en prisión	c1-f2	eb1-eb2	Not suitable for very light, high voices	Slow, very sustained, somber. (Nin)
Desengañemonos ya	d1-gb2	gb1-eb2	High voices, except a very light soprano	Very sustained. (Nin)

TOMAS MILANS
(18th Century?)

TITLE	COMP.	TESS.	TYPE	REMARKS
Dominus regnavit	F#-e1	d-e1	Bass or bass-baritone	A vigorous, spirited song with a recitativ in the middle of the two sections. Secon section is florid, demands flexibility. Sacred Latin text. (Ewerhart)
Quem vidistic, pastores	d1-g2	e1-f2	Soprano or tenor	Sustained, but ends with a slightly animated, florid Alleluia. Sacred Latin text. (Ewerhart)
Sanctum, et terrible nomen ejus	c1-f2	e1-e2	Soprano or tenor	Spirited. Demands some flexibility. Sacred Latin text. (Ewerhart)

LUIS MISÓN
(? –1766)

TITLE	COMP.	TESS.	TYPE	REMARKS
Sequidilla dolorosa de una enamorada (Una Mesonera y en Arriero)	d1-e2	f#1-b1	Women's voices	Sustained, somewhat slow. Somber text. (Subirá)

JOSÉ PALOMINO
(c.1769)

TITLE	COMP.	TESS.	TYPE	REMARKS
Canción Picaresca	c#1-e2	f#1-d2	All voices	Animated, humor-

TITLE	COMP.	TESS.	TYPE	REMARKS
(El Canape)				ous. Demands facile articulation. (Subirá)

MANUEL PLA
(c.1857)

TITLE	COMP.	TESS.	TYPE	REMARKS
Seguidillas religiosas (La Lepra de Constantino)	d1-e2	f#1-d2	All voices	Sustained. Religious text. (Subirá)

ANTONIO ROSALES
(c.1775)

TITLE	COMP.	TESS.	TYPE	REMARKS
Canción contra las madamitas gorgoriteadoras (El Recitado)	d1-g2	g1-e2	All voices	Animated, humorous. Has florid passages. (Subirá)

JACINTO VALLEDOR
(c.1768)

TITLE	COMP.	TESS.	TYPE	REMARKS
Canción de timida (El Apasionado)	e1-e2	g1-e2	All voices	Graceful, sustained. (Subirá)

See also:
 Nin, "Dix Noëls Espagnols"—medium or high voices. (Transcriptions of ten old Spanish Christmas carols, published by Eschig.)
 Nin, "Vingt Chants Populaires Espagnol"—not too suitable for very light, high voices. Demand an accomplished pianist. (Transcriptions of Spanish folksongs, 2 volumes, published by Eschig.)

SONGS AND AIRS IN FRENCH BEFORE THE
NINETEENTH CENTURY

Bibliography

The name found in parentheses after the remarks indicates one of the following collections:

Echos de France: Echos de France, 3 volumes, edited anonymously, published by Durand. (Not overly accurate.)

Ewerhart: Cantio Sacra, edited by Ewerhart, published by Ed. Bieler, Köln.

Gevaert: Répertoire classique du chant Français, 25 volumes, edited by Gevaert, published by Lemoine, Paris. One of the most comprehensive and reasonably accurate collections available. Each song or air is also available separately in the Lemoine edition.

Grovlez: Les plus beaux airs de l'Opéra François, 8 volumes (2 for each type of voice), edited by Grovlez, published by Chester, London.

See also Maîtres du Chant, edited by Prunières, published by Heugel, Paris; Echos du temps passé, 3 volumes, edited by Weckerlin, published by Durand.

TITLE	COMP.	TESS.	TYPE	REMARKS

PIERRE BERTON
(1727–1780)

TITLE	COMP.	TESS.	TYPE	REMARKS
Oui, c'est demain que l'hyménée (Montano et Stéphanie)	g1-ab2	ab1-eb2	Soprano	An andante, allegro air. Demands flexibility. (Gevaert)

FELICE BLANGINI
(1781–1841)

TITLE	COMP.	TESS.	TYPE	REMARKS
Il est parti	b-f2	eb1-eb2	Women's voices	Sustained. (Parisotti, Arie Antiche. RIC)

TITLE	COMP.	TESS.	TYPE	REMARKS
C'est une misère que nos jeunes gens	b-e2	e1-c2	Women's voices	A graceful, humorous arietta. (Parisotti, Arie Antiche. RIC)

FRANÇOIS BOÏELDIEU
(1775-1834)

TITLE	COMP.	TESS.	TYPE	REMARKS
Ah! quel plaisir d'être soldat (La Dame Blanche)	f-c2	a-f#1	Tenor	Spirited, martial air. Rather long. (Gevaert)
Recitative: Qu'à mes ordres ici Air: C'est la Princesse de Navarre (Jean de Paris)	Bb-f1	eb-c1	Baritone	A spirited, buffo air. (Krehbiel, Songs from the Operas. OD)
Essayons, s'il se peut, de parler son langage (Les Voitures Versées)	a-bb2	eb1-f2	Coloratura soprano or lyric soprano	A very florid, comic bravura aria. Requires good command of medium and low voice, as the singer is required to mockingly imitate a man. (Gevaert)
Il me semble (Beniowsky)	e1-b2	g1-e2	Soprano	Scena and an andante, allegro air. (Gevaert)
Oui, je saurai combattre et plaire (Bayard à Mézières)	c#-a1	f#-f#1	Dramatic tenor	Robust, vigorous character air. Demands considerable flexibility. (Gevaert)
Recitative: Maintenant observons Air: Viens, gentille dame (La Dame Blanche)	d-c2	bb-g1	Lyric tenor	A graceful compound aria, in parts quite florid. (Krehbiel, Songs from the Operas. OD)

LOUIS T. BOURGEOIS
(1676–1750)

TITLE	COMP.	TESS.	TYPE	REMARKS
Paisible nuit (Les Amours Déguisés)	f1-a2	a1-g2	Lyric tenor or soprano	Slow and very sustained. The final section is more animated. Very high tessitura. (Grovlez)

FRANÇOIS BOUVARD
(1683–1760)

TITLE	COMP.	TESS.	TYPE	REMARKS
Ruisseau dont le bruit charmant (Cassandre)	g#-a1	a-f#1	Lyric tenor (or soprano)	Slow, sustained. (Grovlez)

SÉBASTIEN DE BROSSARD
(1655–1730)

TITLE	COMP.	TESS.	TYPE	REMARKS
O plenus irarum dies	G-eb1	bb-d1	Bass or bass baritone	A solo cantata in five movements with a recitative. Has long, florid passages. Sacred Latin text. (Ewerhart)
Quemadmodum desiderat cervus	d#1-a2	g1-g2	Soprano or tenor	A short cantata in three movements. Has a few florid passages. Sacred Latin text. (Ewerhart)

ANDRÉ CAMPRA
(1660–1744)

TITLE	COMP.	TESS.	TYPE	REMARKS
Air Italien (Ad un cuore)(L'Europe Galante)	d1-f2	a1-f2	Soprano or mezzo-soprano	Delicate. Demands some flexibility. The tessitura is somewhat high for mezzo-soprano. Italian text. (Grovlez)

TITLE	COMP.	TESS.	TYPE	REMARKS
Charmant papillon (Les Fêtes Vénitien- nes)	d1-g2	g1-eb2	Soprano	Light and florid. (gen. av.)
Naissez brillantes fleurs (Les Fêtes Vénitiennes)	f-a1	c1-g2	Lyric tenor or soprano	Animated, grace- ful. Has florid passages. Very high tessitura. (Grovlez)
O dulcis amor	d1-g2	f1-f2	Soprano or tenor	A short cantata; has a graceful middle section. Sacred Latin text. (Ewerhart)
Recitative: Irène, paraissez Air: Rassurez votre coeur timide (Les Fêtes Vénitiennes)	c-d1	e-c1	Baritone or bass	Graceful. (Grov- lez)
Seuls confidents de mes peines (Iphigénie)	d#1-f#2	g#1-e2	Soprano or mezzo- soprano	Very sustained. The tessitura is somewhat high. (Grovlez)
Venez, venez, fières beautés (Les Fêtes Vénitiennes)	eb1-ab2	c1-g2	Light so- prano	Recitative and a florid air. (Grov- lez)

CHARLES CATEL
(1773–1830)

TITLE	COMP.	TESS.	TYPE	REMARKS
J'avais cru que ces dieux (Semiramis)	d1-bb2	g1-eb2	Soprano	Recitative and a dramatic, vigor- ous air. (Grovlez)
Recitative: Du doute où je vous vois Air: Pleurez, mais chantez ma victoire (Les Bayadères)	e1-a2	a1-f#2	Dramatic soprano or lyric soprano	Recitative and an andante, allegro air. (Gevaert)

MARC-ANTOINE CHARPENTIER
(1634–1704)

TITLE	COMP.	TESS.	TYPE	REMARKS
Que d'horreurs, que de maux (Médée)	d1-g2	f#1-e2	Mezzo-soprano or soprano	Declamatory and dramatic. (Grovlez)
Quel prix de mon amour (Médée)	e1-f2	a1-e2	Mezzo-soprano or soprano	Slow and very sustained. (Grovlez)

LUIGI CHERUBINI
(1760–1842)

TITLE	COMP.	TESS.	TYPE	REMARKS
Guide mes pas (Les Deux Journées)	eb-eb1	g-d1	Baritone	Animated, rather vigorous. (Krehbiel, Songs from the Operas. OD)
Recitative: Suspendez à ces murs Air: J'ai vu disparaître (Les Abencérages)	f#-a1	a-f1	Dramatic tenor	Recitative and an andante, allegro air. Has dramatic climaxes. (Gevaert)
Jeunes filles aux regards doux (Anacréon)	eb1-bb2	g1-f2	Soprano	Rather animated, the vocal line sustained. (Gevaert)
Loin de celui (Rondo intercalé dans l'Italiana in Londra de Cimarosa)	eb1-ab2	ab1-gb2	Soprano	Sustained. Demands some flexibility. (Gevaert)
Vous voyez de vos fils (Médée)	db1-ab2	f1-f2	Dramatic soprano	Slow, sustained. Demands some flexibility. The final section, declamatory and dramatic. (Gevaert)

For other songs and airs see under "Italian" in this section (page 44).

PASCAL COLASSE
(1649–1709)

TITLE	COMP.	TESS.	TYPE	REMARKS
Tristes honneurs,	d1-f2	f1-d2	Mezzo-	Slow and sustained.

TITLE	COMP.	TESS.	TYPE	REMARKS
gloire cruelle (Thétis et Pélée)			soprano or soprano	(Grovlez)

FRANÇOIS COUPERIN
(1668-1733)

Leçons de Tenebres: Sacred solo cantatas on text from the Book of Jeremiah. Realized from the figured bass. (Ewerhart)

TITLE	COMP.	TESS.	TYPE	REMARKS
Première leçon	c1-a2	e1-g2	Soprano or tenor	Has some extended florid passages. Demands considerable flexibility.
Seconde leçon	d1-g2	e1-g2	Soprano or tenor	Generally sustained throughout. Has some florid passages. A shorter work than the first.

NICOLAS DALAYRAC
(1753-1809)

Recitative:
Cent esclaves ornaient
Air:

TITLE	COMP.	TESS.	TYPE	REMARKS
Ah! que mon âme était ravie (Gulistan)	d-c2	g-f♯1	Lyric tenor (or soprano)	Recitative. Andante, allegro. Has some florid passages. (Grovlez)
D'un époux chéri	d1-g2	g1-d2	Soprano	Graceful arietta in contrasting tempi. Demands lightness of tone and some flexibility. (Echos de France)
Hélas! c'est prés de vous (Sargines)	f-b♭1	g-g1	Tenor	Sustained. (Gevaert)
O ma Georgette	c1-f2	e1-c2	Men's voices	Sustained. (Echos de France)
Quand le bien aimé reviendra	d1-e2	e1-b1	Women's voices	Graceful, light. (Echos de France; also Parisotti, RIC)

ANTOINE DAUVERGNE
(1713–1797)

TITLE	COMP.	TESS.	TYPE	REMARKS
D'un amant incon-stant (Les Troqueurs)	f1-b♭2	a1-f2	Light so-prano	Spirited, light. Demands consid-erable flexibility. (Gevaert)
J'ai cru faire un bon coup (Les Troqueurs)	A-e1	f#-d1	Bass-baritone or baritone	Recitative and a spirited air. (Grov-lez)

HENRI DESMARETS
(1662–1741)

TITLE	COMP.	TESS.	TYPE	REMARKS
Qu'un triste éloignement (Vénus et Adonis)	d#1-a2	g1-e2	Soprano	Delicate, sustained. Demands in parts considerable flexi-bility and a good command of p. (Grovlez)

ANDRÉ-CARDINAL DESTOUCHES
(1672–1749)

TITLE	COMP.	TESS.	TYPE	REMARKS
Brillez dans ces beaux lieux (Les Eléments)	e♭1-g2	g1-e♭2	Soprano	Majestic, sustained. Has florid passages. (Grovlez)
Le feu qu'en ce temple (Les Eléments)	A-e1	d-d1	Bass or baritone	An andante, allegro air. Vigorous. Has florid pas-sages. (Grovlez)

FRANÇOIS DEVIENNE
(1759–1803)

TITLE	COMP.	TESS.	TYPE	REMARKS
Dans l'asile de l'innocence	d1-f2	f1-d2	High or medium voices	Sustained, grace-ful. (Echos de France)

EGIDIO R. DUNI
(1709–1775)

TITLE	COMP.	TESS.	TYPE	REMARKS
Ah! que l'amour	c1-a2	e1-e2	Soprano	Sustained, grace-

TITLE	COMP.	TESS.	TYPE	REMARKS
est chose jolie			(or tenor)	ful. (Echos de France; Durand)
Les temps passé (Les Moissonneurs)	d1-g2	g1-e2	Soprano	Animated, graceful. (Gevaert)

FRANÇOIS GOSSEC
(1734–1829)

TITLE	COMP.	TESS.	TYPE	REMARKS
Ah! faut-il me venger (Thésée)	f#1-a2	g1-g2	Dramatic soprano	A compound, rather sustained air interrupted by recitative passages. (Gevaert)
Dors, mon enfant (Rosine)	c#1-f#2	a1-d2	Mezzo-soprano or soprano	Slow, sustained. Demands good command of pp. (Grovlez)
Doux repos, innocente paix (Thésée)	eb1-bb2	g1-g2	Soprano	A compound dramatic air. Demands flexibility. (Gevaert)
Ne verrais-je paraître (Thésée)	f1-bb2	g1-g2	Dramatic soprano	Sustained. (Gevaert)
Songe: Aux douceurs du sommeil (Sabinus)	A-f#1 (g1)	e-d1	Bass-baritone or baritone	A scena and a compound air with a spirited final allegro. (Gevaert)
Un tendre engagement va plus loin (Thésée)	f1-bb2	f1-f2	Dramatic soprano	Recitative and a rather vigorous, dramatic compound air. (Gevaert)

ANDRÉ GRÉTRY
(1741–1813)

Grétry, in his time one of the most popular and elegant of the French opera composers, was extremely prolific, even when judged by the severe standards of his time. Much of his music is now forgotten and unavailable, yet judging by the few songs and airs available in modern reprints, one wonders why the publishers of today have not found it advisable to make a comprehensive anthology of his songs and airs.

112

Grétry's humor, his beautifully conceived vocal line, always considerate of the singer, his melodic gift, and his unfailingly felicitous, though perhaps not invariably powerful or individual manner of expression ought to make him a most popular representative of the late eighteenth century French vocal music.

He seems to have favored the high voices, seldom writing anything for bass or alto, and being especially fond of high baritone, tenor and light soprano voices.

Soprano

TITLE	COMP.	TESS.	TYPE	REMARKS
Ah, quel tourment! (Le Huron)	c1-a2	g1-f2	Soprano or mezzo-soprano	A scena and an andante, allegro air. (Gevaert)
Ah! si parfois (L'Ami de la Maison)	e1-b2	f#1-f#2	Lyric soprano (coloratura soprano)	Delicate, sustained. In parts quite florid. (Gevaert)
Cher objet (Aucassin et Nicolette)	cb1-ab2	ab1-f2	Soprano	Sustained; has a rapid middle section. (Gevaert)
En conscience (La Fausse Magie)	c1-a2	f1-e2	Lyric soprano (coloratura soprano)	A spirited buffo arietta. Demands facile articulation and some flexibility. (Gevaert)
Eprise d'un feu (Anacréon chez Polycrate)	g1-c3	bb1-g2	Lyric soprano	A sustained larghetto and a spirited allegro. Demands some flexibility. (Grovlez)
Il est certains barbons (Le Tableau Parlant)	c1-g2	g1-e2	Lyric soprano (coloratura soprano)	A spirited subrette air. Demands facile articulation and some flexibility. (Gevaert)
Il va venir (Sylvain)	b-bb2	g1-f2	Soprano	A sustained, subdued andante and a spirited allegro. (Gevaert)
Je crains de lui (Richard Coeur de Lion)	e1-ab2	f1-db2	Lyric soprano (coloratura soprano)	Animated, graceful. (Gevaert)

TITLE	COMP. TESS.	TYPE	REMARKS
Je ne fais semblant de rien (L'Ami de la Maison)	c♯1-a2 g1-e2	Lyric so-prano (coloratura soprano)	Delicate and light. (Gevaert)
Je ne le dis qu'à vous (La Fausse Magie)	eb1-ab2 eb1-eb2	Lyric so-prano (coloratura soprano)	Not fast. Very florid. (Gevaert)
Je ne sais pas si ma soeur (Sylvain)	eb1-bb2 f1-f2	Lyric so-prano (coloratura soprano)	Animated, deli-cate air. De-mands flexibility. (Gevaert)
La fauvette avec ses petits (Zémire et Azor)	d1-b2 g1-g2	Coloratura soprano	A spirited, bril-liant air. The middle section is sustained and del-icate. (Gevaert)
Recitative: C'est ici que le beau Céphale Air: Naissantes fleurs (Céphale et Procris)	d1-a2 g1-e2	Lyric so-prano (coloratura soprano)	Graceful, sus-tained, delicate. Demands some flexibility. (Gevaert)
O douce nuit (L'Amant Jaloux)	eb1-bb2 f1-f2	Soprano	Sustained com-pound air. (Gevaert)
Oui, mes amis, la bienfaisance (Pierre-le-Grand)	eb1-ab2 ab1-eb2	Soprano or mezzo-soprano	An andante, allegro air. (Gevaert)
Plus de dépit (Les Deuz Avares)	c1-bb2 ab1-f2	Lyric so-prano (coloratura soprano)	Graceful, delicate, sustained. Has some florid pas-sages. (Gevaert)
Rose chérie (Zémire et Azor)	c1-a2 g1-e2	Lyric so-prano (coloratura soprano)	Sustained, delicate. Demands good com-mand of high pp. (Gevaert)

Alto

| A quels maux tu me livres (L'Amitié à l'Epreuve) | b-e2 e1-c♯2 | Alto or mezzo-soprano | Very sustained. This charming cantilena, origi-nally written for |

TITLE	COMP.	TESS.	TYPE	REMARKS
				soprano, is transposed a fourth lower in the Gevaert edition to make it suitable for alto. "The classic French repertoire has but a very few arias suitable for this type of voice." (Gevaert)
A, quel tourment! (Le Huron)	c1-a2	g1-f2	Soprano or mezzo-soprano	A scena and an andante, allegro air. (Gevaert)
Du destin qui m'opprime (Le Jugement de Midas)	a-f2	d1-d2	Alto or mezzo-soprano	Sustained. Demands some flexibility. Originally written for tenor; transposed a minor third lower in the Gevaert edition. (Gevaert)
Oui, mes amis, la bienfaisance (Pierre-le-Grand)	e♭1-a♭2	a♭1-e♭2	Soprano or mezzo-soprano	An andante, allegro air. (Gevaert)

Tenor

TITLE	COMP.	TESS.	TYPE	REMARKS
Ah! Quel tourment (Zémir et Azor)	d-g♭1	f-f1	Tenor	Sustained. Demands some flexibility. (Gevaert)
Assuré de ton innocence (Le Comte d'Albert)	e-a1	a-f1	Tenor	Sustained. (Gevaert)
Certain coucou, certain hibou (Le Jugement de Midas)	c-a1	g-f1	Lyric tenor (or soprano)	Light, graceful, humorous, in parts quite florid. (Grovlez)
Doux charme de la vie (Le Jugement de Midas)	e-a♭1	a♭-f1	Tenor	Graceful, sustained air. (Gevaert)
Du moment qu'on aime (Zémire et Azor)	d♯-g1	g♯-e1	Lyric tenor	Sustained, graceful. Demands some flexibility. (Gevaert)

TITLE	COMP.	TESS.	TYPE	REMARKS
Par une grâce touchante (Le Jugement de Midas)	f-g1	a-f1	Lyric tenor	Andante, allegro air. Demands considerable flexibility and good command of high pp. (Gevaert)
Qu'il est cruel d'aimer (Les Evénements Imprévus)	(d)f-a♭1	a♭-f1	Tenor	Grave, sustained. (Gevaert)
Si l'univers entier m'oublie (Richard Coeur de Lion)	(A♭)f-b♭1	b♭-f1	Dramatic tenor	Rather animated. Has florid pas-pages and dramatic climaxes. Demands an extensive range. (Gevaert)
Tandis que tout sommeille (L'Amant Jaloux)	f♯-g1	b♭-g1	Lyric tenor	Delicate, light serenade. Demands good command of pp and rather facile articulation. (Gevaert)

Baritone

TITLE	COMP.	TESS.	TYPE	REMARKS
Adieu, Marton, adieu, Lisette (L'Epreuve Villageoise)	e-f♯1	g-e1	Baritone	Animated, light, humorous. Demands some flexibility. (Gevaert)
Ah, ma femme! Qu'avez vous fait? (Lucille)	A♭-g♭1	e♭-e♭1	Baritone	Slow, sustained, somewhat declamatory. In parts demands considerable dramatic intensity. (Gevaert)
Déesse des beaux jours (Céphale et Procris)	B-g1	d-d1	Baritone	Graceful, sustained. Demands some flexibility. (Gevaert)
De ma barque légère (Anacréon)	c♯-d♯1 (f♯1)	e♯-c♯1	Baritone (bass-baritone)	Light, graceful. (Gevaert)
Laisse en paix le dieu des combats (Chanson Bachique) (Anacréon)	B-e1	e-d1	Baritone (bass-baritone)	Spirited, vigorous. Demands some flexibility. (Gevaert)

TITLE	COMP.	TESS.	TYPE	REMARKS
Le pauvre enfant ne savait pas (Zémire et Azor)	c-f1	d-c1	Baritone	Sustained. In parts demands considerable dramatic intensity. Originally written for tenor. In this edition transposed a minor third lower than the original. (Gevaert)
Nièces, neveux (Les Deux Avares)	A-g1	e-d1	Baritone	A comic, spirited air. (Gevaert)
O fortune ennemie (Anacréon chez Polycrate)	Bb-eb1	f#-d1	Baritone (bass-baritone)	Vigorous and spirited. (Grovlez)
O Richard, ô mon roi (Richard Coeur de Lion)	Bb-g1	f-d1	Baritone	An andante, allegro air. Demands some flexibility. Originally written for tenor. (Gevaert)
Quand l'âge vient l'Amour nous laisse (La Fausse Magie)	A-f#1 (g1)	d-d1	Baritone	Sustained, graceful. Demands some flexibility. (Gevaert)
Songe enchanteur (Anacréon)	A-f#1	d-d1	Baritone	Slow, sustained. (Gevaert)

NICOLO ISOUARD
(1775–1818)

TITLE	COMP.	TESS.	TYPE	REMARKS
Ah! Pour moi quelle peine extrême (Jeannot et Colin)	c1-c3	f1-f2	Dramatic soprano or lyric soprano	Andante, allegro air. Very spirited and dramatic. (Gevaert)
Dieu puissant! (Michel-Ange)	f1-c3	g1-f2	Soprano	Rather animated, sustained. Interrupted by a recitative passage. (Gevaert)
Scena and rondo: Non, je ne veux pas chanter (Le Billet de Loterie)	d1-c3 (eb3)	f1-f2	Coloratura soprano	Brilliant, spirited. Very florid. A little long. Was once a celebrated bravura piece. (Gevaert)

JEAN MARIE LECLAIR
(1697–1764)

TITLE	COMP.	TESS.	TYPE	REMARKS
Chantez, chantez l'amour (Scylla et Glaucus)	f-b♭1	a-f1	Lyric tenor (or soprano)	Animated, in parts very florid. Very high tessitura. (Grovlez)
Serments trompeurs (Scylla et Glaucus)	e♭1-f2	f1-d♭2	Mezzo-soprano or alto	Slow, grave. Demands some flexibility. (Grovlez)

JEAN F. LESUEUR
(1760–1837)

TITLE	COMP.	TESS.	TYPE	REMARKS
Hélas! Sans m'entendre (Ossian ou les Bardes)	c1-e2	e1-c2	Mezzo-soprano or alto	Dramatic. Somewhat declamatory, vigorous. (Grovlez)

JEAN BAPTISTE LULLY
(1632–1687)

Most of the songs and airs of Lully are but rarely performed at present. It may be that the severe simplicity of his style seems too bare and forbidding to the majority of present-day singers. It may, however, be that the difficulty of procuring most of Lully's music in modern reprints is primarily responsible for this neglect, since the few readily available airs like "Bois Epais" are frequently performed. In the opinion of this writer, Lully's music is as remarkably alive today as it was some three hundred years ago. Nobly declamatory in style and devoid of any unnecessary embellishments, Lully's songs and airs seem to be most suitable for rather heavy voices and are, superficially at least, rather similar to Monteverdi's in the character of their vocal line.

Lully and the French composers of his time developed a curious form of rhythmic notation with which many musicians of today seem to be poorly acquainted. (Rameau continued using this notation nearly fifty years later.)

Lully's and Rameau's time signatures denoted only the number of beats (pulses) within a measure, since the length of all beats within any given composition was supposed to be of the same duration, no matter how expressed on paper. Thus only the numerator was used of the fraction which we today associate with any time signature. Many find it difficult to read music in which ♩ and ♪ are often of the same duration.

The time signatures used were ¢ (meaning $\frac{2}{2}$), C (meaning $\frac{4}{4}$), and **3** (meaning either $\frac{3}{4}$ or $\frac{3}{2}$). Thus Lully's ¢ ♩♩♩♩ | ¢ ♩♩ | **3** ♩♩♩ would equal in modern notation either $\frac{4}{2}$ 𝅗𝅥𝅗𝅥𝅗𝅥𝅗𝅥 | $\frac{2}{2}$ 𝅗𝅥𝅗𝅥 | $\frac{3}{2}$ 𝅗𝅥𝅗𝅥𝅗𝅥 or $\frac{4}{4}$ ♩♩♩♩ | $\frac{2}{4}$ ♩♩ | $\frac{3}{4}$ ♩♩♩. Only in the Gevaert edition such a transcription into modern notation is consistently and accurately effected.

TITLE	COMP.	TESS.	TYPE	REMARKS
Admirons le jus de la treille	d-f1	f-eb1	Baritone	A vigorous, rhythmical drinking song. (Rouart)
Ah! faut-il me venger (Thésée)	d1-f2	g1-d2	Soprano	Sustained, grave. Short. (Gevaert)
Ah! Mortelle douleurs (Fêtes de Versailles)	e1-f2	same	Women's voices, except a light soprano	Slow, sustained. In parts demands considerable dramatic intensity. Somewhat long. (HEUG)
Ah! Quel tourment (Roland)	f-ab1	ab-f1	Tenor	Sustained, rather grave air. (Gevaert)
Ah! Quelle cruauté (Ballet de Flore)	d1-f2	e1-d2	Mezzo-soprano or alto	Sustained introduction and a rather vigorous second movement. Demands in parts considerable dramatic intensity. (HEUG)
Ah! Si la liberté (Armide)	e1-g2	a1-f2	Soprano	Majestic. (Grovlez)
Allez, éloignezvous (Armide)	f-ab1	f-f1	Tenor	Short, sustained arioso. (Gevaert)
Allez remplir ma place (Armide)	f-ab1	ab-eb1	Tenor	A recitative with a spirited main section. (Gevaert)
Amants, aimez vos chaines (Cadmus et Hermione)	e1-f2	a1-e2	All voices except a heavy bass	A graceful minuet. (Rouart)
Amour que veux tu de moi? (Amadis)	d1-f2	g1-eb2	Not suitable for light voices	Grave, declamatory, in parts demands considerable dramatic intensity. (Rouart; Gevaert)

119

TITLE	COMP.	TESS.	TYPE	REMARKS
Amour, vois quels maux (Cadmus et Hermione) Recitative: J'aime Atys Air: Atys est trop heureux (Atys)	f1-f2	g1-eb2	Soprano or mezzo-soprano	Sustained, grave. (Gevaert)
Atys est trop heureux (Atys)	e1-f2	f1-d2	Women's voices	Recitative and a sustained, graceful air. (Rouart)
Bacchus veut qu'on boive (Psyché)	d1-eb2	f1-d2	Most suitable for men's voices	A vigorous, animated, drinking song followed by a minuet-like movement. See also the Tagliaferre collection. (Rouart)
Barbacola (Son dottor) (Les Noces de Village) Recitative: Quel coeur n'est pas fait Air:	G-e1	B-c1	Bass	A comic, animated air. The Italian text is by Lully. (HEUG)
Belle Hermione (Cadmus et Hermione)	d-e1	e-d1	Baritone or bass	Slow, sustained. One of Lully's most remarkable airs. (Rouart). In the Gevaert edition the recitative is omitted and a postlude for the piano added.
Bois épais (Amadis)	d1-f2	f1-c2	Most suitable for medium or low voices	Originally written for tenor. Very sustained. Perhaps Lully's most famous air. (Krehbiel, Songs from the Operas, Alto. OD; also arranged by A. L., BH)
Dans un piège fatal (Amadis)	Bb-eb1	eb-d1	Bass or baritone	Sustained, majestic. (Grovlez)
Dépit mortel (Thésée)	e1-f2	e1-e2	Women's voices, except a light soprano	Declamatory, majestic. (Rouart)

120

TITLE	COMP.	TESS.	TYPE	REMARKS
Dieu, qui vous déclarez mon père (Phaéton)	c#-f1	f-e1	Baritone	Grave, declamatory, in parts demands considerable dramatic intensity. (Rouart)
Dormons tous! (Atys)	g1-a2	a1-g2	Lyric tenor (or soprano)	Very sustained. Very high tessitura. (Grovlez)
Espoir si cher (Atys)	e1-e2	same	Women's voices, except a very light soprano	Declamatory, majestic. (Rouart)
Fermez-vous pour jamais (Amadis)	d1-g2	f1-d2	Soprano or mezzo-soprano	Very sustained and grave. (Gevaert)
Grand Dieu des Enfers (La Naissance de Vénus)	d1-f2	d1-d2	Not suitable for light, high voices	A stately, grave sarabande. (HEUG)
Hymen! o doux Hymen! (Persée)	e1-e2	same	Not too suitable for very light voices	A sustained, somewhat solemn invocation. (Rouart)
Il faut passer tôt ou tard (Alceste)	G-d1	c-c1	Bass or bass-baritone	Rather animated compound air. (Gevaert)
Le héros que j'attends (Alceste)	e1-f2	same	Soprano or mezzo-soprano	Sustained. (Gevaert)
Ne troublez pas nos jeux (Le Triomphe de L'Amour)	g1-g2	bb1-g2	Soprano or tenor	Animated, graceful, light. (HEUG)
Recitative: Je ne puis plus braver				
Air: Nuit charmante	e1-g2	a1-f2	Soprano	Recitative and a compound air. Rather declamatory. (HEUG)
Pauvres amants (Le Sicilien)	g-a1	b-f#1	Lyric tenor (or soprano)	Sustained, graceful. Demands some flexibility. (Grovlez)

TITLE	COMP.	TESS.	TYPE	REMARKS
Plus j'observe ces lieux (Armide)	f#-a1	a-g#1	Lyric tenor or soprano	Slow, sustained. Very high tessitura. (Grovlez)
Que notre vie (Proserpine)	e1-f2	a1-e2	Soprano or tenor	A graceful minuet. (HEUG)
Que rien ne trouble ici (Thésée)	G-d1	c-c1	Bass or bass-baritone	An andante, allegro air. Has some florid passages. (Grovlez)
Que soupirer d'amour (Le Carnaval)	d1-f#2	f#1-d2	All voices except a heavy bass	A graceful minuet. (Rouart; see also Tagliaferre and Gevaert collections)
Que vois-je, ô spectacle effroyable (Amadis)	e1-g2	g1-eb2	Soprano or mezzo-soprano	A rather dramatic recitative and a sustained air. (Gevaert)
Que vos âmes (Psyché)	d1-f2	f1-eb2	Women's voices, except a light soprano	Sustained, grave. (Rouart)
Réponds, charmante nuit (Le Carnaval)	d1-e2	f#1-d2	All voices	Sustained, rather subdued. (Rouart; see also the Tagliaferre collection)
Revenez, revenez amours (Thésée)	d1-f2	g1-d2	Soprano	Sustained, graceful. Has a few declamatory passages. (Grovlez)
Rochers, vous êtes sourds (La Naissance de Vénus)	d1-eb2	f1-d2	Women's voices, except a light soprano	Sustained, majestic, rather declamatory. (Rouart)
Sommes-nous pas trop heureux (Ballet de l'Impatience)	d1-g2	f1-e2	All voices, except a heavy bass	Graceful, delicate. (HEUG)
Soyez fidèle (Le Carnaval)	d1-e2	f#-d2	All voices	A graceful minuet. (HEUG)
Trop heureux qui moissonne (Thésée)	f1-f2	g1-eb2	All voices, except a heavy bass	Sustained, graceful. (Rouart)

TITLE	COMP.	TESS.	TYPE	REMARKS
Vous êtes le charme (Air de Rafrina)	d1-f♯2	e1-d2	All voices, except a heavy bass	A graceful minuet. Has a few florid passages. (Rouart)

LULLY ET COLASSE

TITLE	COMP.	TESS.	TYPE	REMARKS
Amour, tu m'as soumise encor (Les Saisons)	f♯1-g2	a1-e2	Soprano	Sustained, delicate. Has florid passages. (Gevaert)
Charmants ruisseaux (Les Saisons)	f-g1	b♭-g1	Tenor	Sustained, graceful. (Gevaert)
L'affreuse discorde (Les Saisons)	f♯-a1	b-g1	Tenor	Animated. (Gevaert)
Le doux printemps (Les Saisons)	c-e♭1	f-c1	Baritone or bass	Short, recitative and a sustained air. (Gevaert)
Me plaindrai-je toujours, Amour (Les Saisons)	d1-g2	f1-f2	Soprano	Sustained, graceful air. Demands flexibility. (Gevaert)
Mon retour des mortels (Les Saisons)	G-d1	c-c1	Baritone or bass	Animated, vigorous air. (Gevaert)
Que mon destin est déplorable (Les Saisons)	B-e1	e-d1	Baritone or bass	Sustained. Demands some flexibility. (Gevaert)
Tout cède à vos doux appas (Les Saisons)	f1-a♭2	a♭1-f2	Soprano	Sustained, graceful. (Gevaert)

JEAN PAUL MARTINI
(1741–1816)

TITLE	COMP.	TESS.	TYPE	REMARKS
Plaisir d'amour	b♭-e♭2	e♭1-c2	All voices	Very sustained. (Parisotti, Italian Anthology, GS)

ETIENNE MÉHUL
(1763–1817)

TITLE	COMP.	TESS.	TYPE	REMARKS
Ah, lorsque la mort trop cruelle (Joseph)	f♯1-e2	same	Soprano (mezzo-soprano)	Graceful, animated. Vocally not taxing. (Score, CFP)

TITLE	COMP.	TESS.	TYPE	REMARKS
A peine au sortir de l'enfance (Joseph)	g-f1	f-e1	Tenor	Sustained, vocally not taxing. (Score, CFP)
Recitative: Vainement Pharaon Air: Champs paternels (Joseph)	d#-a1	a-e1	Tenor	Recitative, andante, allegro. (Gevaert)
Femme sensible, entends-tu? (Ariodant)	eb-eb1	ab-db1	Baritone	Very sustained. (Gevaert)
Recitative: Mais que dis-je? Air: O des amants le plus fidèle (Ariodant)	g#-a2	d1-e2	Mezzo-soprano (dramatic soprano)	Recitative, andante, allegro. In parts very dramatic. (Gevaert; also Krehbiel, Songs from the Operas, OD)
Sur le sort de son fils (Stratonice)	B-f1	f-d1	Baritone	Recitative, andante, allegro. (Grovlez)
Versez tous vos chagrins (Stratonice)	e-ab1	g-f1	Tenor	Short recitative and an andante, allegro air. (Gevaert)

JEAN-JOSEPH MONDONVILLE
(1711–1772)

TITLE	COMP.	TESS.	TYPE	REMARKS
Sur les pâles humains (Titon et l'Aurore)	G-f1	d-bb	Bass-baritone or baritone	Rapid and vigorous. Demands considerable flexibility. (Grovlez)
Venez, venez sous ce riant feuillage (Titon et l'Aurore)	e1-b2	a1-f#2	Coloratura soprano or lyric soprano	Animated, delicate, florid. (Grovlez)

PIERRE A. MONSIGNY
(1729–1817)

TITLE	COMP.	TESS.	TYPE	REMARKS
Adieu, chère Louise (Le Déserteur)	d-f1	g-eb1	Baritone	Slow and very sustained. (Gevaert)

TITLE	COMP.	TESS.	TYPE	REMARKS
C'est ici que Rose respire (Rose et Colas)	f-g1	g-e1	Tenor	Very sustained, delicate. (Gevaert)
Il m'eut été si doux de t'embrasser (Le Déserteur)	B-e1	e-d1	Baritone	Sustained, somewhat declamatory. In parts demands considerable dramatic intensity. (Gevaert)
Il regardait mon bouquet (Le Roi et le Fermier)	d#1-g#2	f#1-f#2	Light soprano	A delicate buffo arietta. Demands facile articulation. (Adler, Operatic Anthology, GS)
Je ne déserterai jamais (Le Déserteur)	c-f1	f-d1	Baritone	Spirited, vigorous. Demands some flexibility. (Gevaert)
L'art surpasse ici la nature (La Belle Arsene)	eb1-c3	ab1-f2	Light soprano or coloratura soprano	Sustained. Has some florid cadenzas. (Gevaert)
Un jeune coeur (Les Aveuz Indiscrets)	d1-a2	a1-f#2	Light soprano	Graceful. Demands considerable flexibility and a good command of staccato. (Grovlez)

MICHEL MONTÉCLAIR
(1667-1737)

TITLE	COMP.	TESS.	TYPE	REMARKS
Qu'ai je entendu! (Jephté)	e1-f2	f1-d2	Mezzo-soprano	Sustained, stately. Somewhat declamatory. (Grovlez)
Quel funeste appareil (Jephté)	B-eb1	d-c1	Bass or baritone	Sustained, majestic. Somewhat declamatory. (Grovlez)

JEAN J. MOURET
(1682–1738)

Doux plaisirs (Pirithoüs)	c1-f2	eb1-c2	Mezzo-soprano or alto	Graceful, delicate. Demands good command of p. (Grovlez)

FERDINANDO PAER
(1771–1839)

Hélas! C'est près de vous	d1-f2	g1-e2	Most suitable for men's voices	Sustained, graceful. (Echos de France)
Si l'hymen a quelque douceur	d1-g2	g1-d2	High voices	Graceful. (Echos de France)

For other songs and airs see under "Italian" in this section (page 44).

GIOVANNI PAESIELLO
(1740–1816)

Recitative: De l'aurore au couchant Air: Déserts écartés (Proserpine)	bb-bb2	eb1-eb2	Dramatic soprano or high mezzo-soprano	Very sustained. Demands some flexibility. (Gevaert)

For other songs and airs see under "Italian" in this section (page 44).

ANDRÉ D. PHILIDOR
(1647–1730)

Belle Ernelinde (Ernelinde)	(G)c-e1 d-d1		Bass or bass-baritone	Majestic, not slow. Demands some flexibility. (Gevaert)

TITLE	COMP.	TESS.	TYPE	REMARKS
Dans la magie (Le Sorcier)	c-g1	f-f1	Tenor	A compound air. Has alternate sections of mock majesty and graceful gaiety. (Gevaert)
Né dans un champ (Ernelinde)	c-g1	f-d1	Baritone	Sustained, rhythmical. Has some florid passages. (Grovlez)
Non, cher objet que j'adore (Melide or Le Navigateur)	d-ab1	ab-g1	Tenor	A dramatic scena and air. (Gevaert)
O toi qui ne peux m'entendre (Tom Jones)	eb1-bb2	g1-e2	Soprano	Scena and an andante, allegro air. Demands flexibility. (Gevaert)
Quand pour le grand voyage (Le Maréchal-ferrant)	d-a1	a-f#1	Tenor	Animated, delicate air. Demands facile articulation. (Gevaert)

NICOLA PICCINNI (PICCINI)
(1728–1800)

	COMP.	TESS.	TYPE	REMARKS
Recitative: Qu'ai-je donc fait, cruel Air: Ah! Prends pitié de ma faiblesse (Didon)	c1-ab2	f1-f2	Dramatic soprano or lyric soprano	Sustained. Has dramatic climaxes. (Gevaert)
Recitative: Amants qui vous plaignez Air: Brûle d'une flamme (Atys)	c-ab1	g-f1	Tenor	Subdued recitative and a graceful air. Demands flexibility. (Gevaert)
J'ai mérité qu'on me punisse (Atys)	g-ab1	ab-f1	Dramatic tenor	Spirited. Has dramatic climaxes. Demands flexibility. (Gevaert)

TITLE	COMP.	TESS.	TYPE	REMARKS
Je mourrai (Roland)	d#1-f#2	f#1-e2	Not too suitable for very light, high voices	Sustained. (Echos de France)
L'amour fait verser trop de pleurs (Atys)	g-a1	a-f#1	Tenor	Delicate. Has animated sections. Demands some flexibility. (Gevaert)
O nuit, déesse du mystère (Le Faux Lord)	b-e2	g1-d2	Mezzo-soprano or alto	Sustained. Has dramatic climaxes. (Parisotti, Italian Anthology, GS)
Recitative: Je t'aime plus que moi Air: Oreste, au nom de la patrie (Iphigénie en Tauride)	c-d1 (f1)	e-c1	Bass-baritone or bass	Sustained. (Gevaert)
Recitative: O funeste amitié Air: Quel trouble agite non coeur? (Atys)	e-bb1	c1-a1	Dramatic tenor	Dramatic and spirited. Demands flexibility. Very high tessitura. (Gevaert)

For other songs and airs see under "Italian" in this section (page 44).

JEAN PHILIPPE RAMEAU
(1683-1764)
(See prefatory note to Lully)

Rameau's name is unfortunately much more widely known among the present-day singers than his music. In the opinion of this writer the neglect of Rameau's music coupled with the veneration accorded to his name is as inexplicable as it is unjustified; for not much of the early eighteenth century vocal music can equal Rameau's in vitality, elegance and simplicity.

Rameau's airs, although in no way difficult musically, present a number of rather complex stylistic problems for the present-day singer; one of such problems, that of proper declamation of the text, seems to demand not only a considerable knowledge of French prosody, but also of the French dramatic conventions of the period. Another is the problem of a rhythmically satisfactory performance of short embellishments in which Rameau's music abounds.

In the opinion of this writer it would often seem more practical and satisfactory to dispense with such embellishments unless one can learn to perform them gracefully, casually and in a rhythmically impeccable fashion.

As in the case of most of the eighteenth century vocal music a knowledge of classical mythology would add greatly to the understanding of Rameau's texts.

Editions:
> Complete works, piano score, published by Durand.
> Collection of Airs, edited by Saint-Saëns, published by Durand.
> The most authentic reprints of excerpts from operas and cantatas are to be found in the following collections:
> Gevaert: Répertoire classique du chant Français. Lemoine, Paris.
> Grovlez: Les plus beaux airs de l'Opéra François. Chester, London.
> Prunières: Maîtres du chant. Heugel, Paris.

TITLE	COMP.	TESS.	TYPE	REMARKS
A l'amour rendez les armes (Hippolyte et Aricie)	d1-f2	f1-d2	All voices	A graceful gavotte. (Durand Collection; also Echos de France)
Accourez riante jeunesse (Les Fêtes d'Hébé)	d1-f2	g1-e2	Soprano	Animated, graceful. Has florid passages. (Gevaert)
Amour quand du destin (Les Indes Galantes)	e1-g2	a1-f2	Soprano	Delicate, sustained, demands some flexibility. (Durand Collection)
Arrachez de mon coeur (Dardanus)	c1-d2	f♯1-d2	Medium or low voices	Sustained. (Echos de France)
Aux langueurs d'Apollon (Platée)	d1-a2	e1-e2	Soprano	Animated, rather florid. (Gevaert)
Chassons de nos plaisirs (Acanthe et Céphise)	e1-f2	g1-d2	Soprano (or tenor)	Sustained, graceful. (Gevaert)
Dans ces doux asiles (Castor et Pollux)	c1-f2	d1-d2	High or medium voices	A graceful, delicate minuet. (Gevaert) The original is a third higher, a solo with chorus. Known as "Menuet Chanté."

TITLE	COMP.	TESS.	TYPE	REMARKS
Recitative: Vous excitez la plus sincère ardeur Air: Et vous, jeune beauté (La Prin- cesse de Navarre)	e1-g2	a1-f♯2	Soprano	Graceful, demands some flexibility. Rather high tessi- tura. (Durand Collection)
Recitative: Ah! que me faites-vous entendre? Air: Il faut que l'amour (Les Indes Galantes)	a-e2	d1-d2	Medium or low voices	A graceful minuet. Demands some flexibility. (Durant Collection)
Les plaisirs et les jeux (Zoroastre)	c♯1-e2	g1-e2	Soprano	Rather slow, sus- tained. Demands some flexibility. (Gevaert)
Recitative: Voici les tristes lieux Air: Monstre affreux	F-f1	c-d1	Bass or baritone	Very sustained, vigorous and maj- estic. (Gevaert)
Nature, amour, qui partagez mon coeur (Castor et Pollux)	d-e1	e-d1	Bass or baritone	Sustained. (Grovlez)
O jour affreux (Dardanus)	e1-g2	f1-f2	Soprano	Grave, sustained air. (Gevaert) In the Durand Collec- tion transposed a tone lower, suit- able for lower voices.
O mort, n'exerce pas ta rigueur (Les Fêtes d'Hébé)	e1-g2	a1-f2	Soprano	Slow, sustained, grave. (Durand Collection)
Papillon inconstant (Les Indes Galantes)	f♯1-b2	b1-f♯2	Light so- prano	Animated, grace- ful, quite florid. (Durand Collection)

130

TITLE	COMP.	TESS.	TYPE	REMARKS
Permettez, astre du jour (Les Indes Galantes) Recitative: Les oiseaux d'alentour Air:	c#1-e2	f#1-d2	Medium or low voices	Graceful, light. (Durand Collection)
Pourquoi leur envier (L'Impatience)	e1-f2	f1-d2	All voices	Graceful. (Durand Collection)
Puisque Pluton est inflexible (Hippolyte et Aricie)	bb-eb2	eb1-c2	Medium or low voices	Rather vigorous, stately. (Durand Collection)
Puissant Maître des flots (Hippolyte et Aricie) Recitative: Ciel! Tandis qu'au sommeil Air:	B-e1	f#-d1	Bass or baritone	Slow, very sustained. (Grovlez)
Quand le silence (Diane et Actéon)	d1-f2	f1-d2	All voices	A rather extended recitative and a graceful, sustained air. (Durand Collection)
Ranimez vos flambeaux (Les Indes Galantes)	d1-g2	a1-g2	Soprano	Animated, graceful, in parts quite florid. (Durand Collection)
Rossignols amoureux (Hippolyte et Aricie)	e1-a2	a1-f#2	Light soprano	Slow, delicate. Has many florid passages. (Grovlez) In the Gevaert edition transposed a half tone lower and provided with some cadenzas. This edition also reprinted by Ditson. In the Durand Collection transposed a tone lower.
Séjour de l'éternelle le paix (Castor et Pollux)	c1-f2	f1-d2	All voices	Slow, sustained, graceful air. Has a recitative in the middle section. (Durand

TITLE	COMP.	TESS.	TYPE	REMARKS
				Collection) The original is a fourth higher, for light soprano or tenor.
Soleil! On a détruit tes superbes asiles (Les Indes Galantes)	A♭-e♭1	e♭-d♭1	Bass or baritone	A declamatory, majestic, compound air. Demands some flexibility. A trifle long. Known as "Invocation et Hymne au Soleil." (Gevaert)
Sur les ombres fugitives (Castor et Pollux)	e1-a2	b1-f♯2	Light soprano	A somewhat florid gavotte. (Durand Collection)
Tristes apprêts (Castor et Pollux)	e♭1-g2	g1-e♭2	Soprano or tenor	Very sustained. (Grovlez) In the Durand Collection transposed to suit medium voices.
Troubles cruels (Dardanus)	c1-b♭2	f1-f2	Most suitable for light soprano	An andante, allegro air. Most of this air is quite spirited and florid. (Gevaert)
Tu veux avoir la préférence (Les Fêtes d'Hébé)	g♯-a1	a-f1	Lyric tenor (or soprano)	Graceful, sustained. (Grovlez)
Vents furieux (La Princesse de Navarre)	d1-b♭2	g1-g2	Soprano	Animated, quite florid, rather vigorous. Has a short, sustained, slow middle section. (Durand Collection)
Recitative: Les nymphes de Diane Air: Vole, lance tes traits! (Zéphyre)	e1-b♭2	a1-f2	Most suitable for light soprano	Animated, graceful, quite florid. (Durand Collection)

JEAN FERRY REBEL
(1669–1747)

TITLE	COMP.	TESS.	TYPE	REMARKS
Souffrirai-je toujours (Ulysse)	c1-f2	f1-d♭2	Mezzo-so-prano or alto	Slow, sustained, somewhat declamatory. (Grovlez)
Volez, zéphirs amoureux	c♯1-e2	same	All voices	An animated "Tambourin." Demands rather facile articulation. (Echos du Temps Passé, Durand)

JEAN JACQUES ROUSSEAU
(1712–1778)

TITLE	COMP.	TESS.	TYPE	REMARKS
Je vais revoir ma charmante maîtresse (Le Devin du Village)	d-b♭1	g-g1	Lyric tenor	Graceful. Has a very high tessitura. (Grovlez)
Le Rosier	g1-e2	Same	All voices	Sustained, graceful. (Echos du Temps Passé, Durand)
Que le jour me dure	g1-b1	Same	All voices	Sustained. A song on three notes. (Echos de France)

ANTONIO SACCHINI
(1730–1786)

TITLE	COMP.	TESS.	TYPE	REMARKS
Recitative: D'un penchant si fatal Air: Arrachez de mon coeur (Dardanus)	d1-a♭2	g1-e♭2	Dramatic soprano (lyric soprano)	Slow and sustained. Majestic. Demands in parts some flexibility. (Gevaert)
Recitative: Je tombe à vos genoux Air: C'est votre bonté que j'implore (Chimène)	f1-a♭2	a♭1-f2	Dramatic soprano (lyric soprano)	Sustained. Demands some flexibility. (Gevaert)

TITLE	COMP.	TESS.	TYPE	REMARKS
Recitative: Appesanti par l'âge Air: Dieux! ce n'est pas pour moi (Oedipe à Colone)	eb1-ab2	f1-f2	Dramatic soprano (lyric soprano)	An andante, allegro air. (Gevaert)
Recitative: Mon fils, tu ne l'es plus Air: Elle m'a prodigué sa tendresse (Oedipe à Colone)	Bb-eb1	d-c1	Bass or bass-baritone	Very sustained, majestic. (Gevaert)
Jour heureux (Dardanus)	f-g2 (bb2)	bb-f1	Tenor	Sustained. Demands in parts some flexibility. (Gevaert)
Juge mieux un frère qui t'aime (Evelina)	eb-g1	ab-eb1	Tenor	Graceful air. Demands some flexibility. (Gevaert)
Recitative: Douce et modeste Evelina Air: Justes dieux que j'implore (Evelina)	A-eb1	d-d1	Bass or bass-baritone	Animated, majestic. (Gevaert)
Recitative: J'aime la sombre horreur Air: O ma patrie! (Evelina)	Bb-f1	e-d1	Bass or bass-baritone	Very sustained, majestic. (Gevaert)
Tout mon bonheur (Oedipe à Colone)	eb1-ab2	ab1-f2	Soprano	Slow and sustained. (Gevaert)

For other songs and airs see under "Italina" in this section (page 44).

GASPARO SPONTINI
(1774-1851)

TITLE	COMP.	TESS.	TYPE	REMARKS
Dans le sein d'un ami (La Vestale)	d-f1	g-eb1	Baritone	Sustained. Demands some flexibility. Has high tessitura. (Anthology, CFP)

TITLE	COMP.	TESS.	TYPE	REMARKS

Recitative:
  Cruels! Délivrez-
  moi de ces apprêts
Air:				

Hélas! Si de ma
  faible vie (Fer-
  nando Cortez)
	d1-g2	g1-eb2	Dramatic
			soprano
			(lyric so-
			prano)
				Sustained.
				(Gevaert)

Il faut hélas!
  Bien peu de
  chose
	c1-f2	f1-d2	Women's
			voices
				Graceful. De-
				mands some flex-
				ibility. (Parisotti,
				RIC)

O des infortunés (La Vestale)	c#1-f#2	f#1-d2	Dramatic soprano or mezzo- soprano	Very slow, sus- tained. Vocally not taxing. (Ge- vaert)

O patrie, o lieux
  pleins de charmes
  (Fernando Cortez)
	e-f#1	f#-e1	Baritone	An andante, al-
				legro air. In
				parts very vig-
				orous and dra-
				matic. High tes-
				situra. (Anthol-
				ogy, CFP)

Recitative:
  Dieux secourez
  Cassandre
Air:				

O saintes lois (Olympie)	f1-a2 (c3)	a1-f2	Dramatic soprano (lyric so- prano)	A majestic an- dante, allegro air. (Gevaert)

O toi, dont
  l'univers (Hym-
  ne au soleil)
  (Milton)
	db-f1	db-ab1	Baritone	Very sustained.
				Demands some
				flexibility. (Ge-
				vaert)

Toi, que je laisse
  sur la terre (La
  Vestale)
	db1-f2	f1-eb2	Dramatic
			soprano
			or lyric
			soprano
				Slow, very sus-
				tained. Demands
				some flexibility.
				(Gevaert)

Toi que j'implore
  avec ferveur
  (often sung in the
  Italian version:
  Tu che invoco con
  orrore) (La
  Vestale)
	eb1-bb2	g1-g2	Dramatic
			soprano
				A sustained an-
				dante, a dramat-
				ic scena, and a
				vigorous allegro.
				Demands some
				flexibility. (Ge-
				vaert)

Appendix: Bergerettes

The so-called "bergerettes," or French popular songs, of the seventeenth and eighteenth centuries occupy a rather unique position, since they are neither folk songs nor traditional airs in the proper sense of the word. Composed and sung for the most part for and by the upper strata of French prerevolutionary society, they could be perhaps best defined as old popular songs, which have survived because of the extraordinary charm and grace of their tunes and words.

Musically and vocally these songs present no problems even to an untrained singer. Stylistically, however, they demand great elegance and an extraordinarily fluent command of the language. Their great popularity now is largely due to the efforts of J. B. Weckerlin, who has collected and admirably arranged a great number of such songs (Echos du Temps Passé, 3 vols., Durand). A rather representative collection of his arrangements is available in the O. Ditson and G. Schirmer editions. The short list below is limited to the bergerettes available in American reprints.

See also, among many other excellent collections, those by Yvette Guilbert (Augener) and Perilhou (Heugel).

TITLE	COMP.	TESS.	TYPE	REMARKS
Aminte	c1–d2	e1–c2	Most suitable for men's voices	Delicate. Demands light, facile articulation.
Bergère légère	d1–e2	f♯1–d2	All voices	Delicate. Demands lightness of tone.
Chantons les amours de Jean	d1–e2 (g2)	g1–d2	All voices	Spirited. Demands facile articulation.
Chaque chose à son temps	c1–c2	f1–b♭1	All voices	Light.
Je connais un berger discret	e♭1–f2	g1–e♭2	All voices	Light.
Jeunes fillettes	g1–e2	a1–e2	All voices	Light and spirited. Demands some flexibility.
L'amour s'envole	e1–g2	g1–d2	Not too suitable for very heavy, low voices	Demands some flexibility.

TITLE	COMP.	TESS.	TYPE	REMARKS
La Mère Bontemps	d1-d2	g1-d2	Women's voices	Light. Demands facile articulation.
Lisette	e1-g2	g1-d2	All voices	Delicate.
Maman, dites-moi	e1-f♯2	g1-d2	Women's voices	Light. Demands facile articulation.
Menuet d'Exaudet (Cet étang)	d1-g2	f♯1-c2	All voices	Delicate. Demands good sense of rhythm.
Nanette	e1-g2	g1-d2	All voices	Light.
Non, je ne crois pas	e1-e2	f1-c2	Women's voices	Light.
Non, je n'irai plus au bois	e1-f2 (a2)	a1-e2	Women's voices	Light.
O ma tendre musette	g♯1-e2	d1-d2	All voices	Delicate. Has a delightful accompaniment.
Par un matin	f1-d2	g1-c2	All voices	Light.
Philis plus avare que tendre	d1-d2	g1-c2	All voices	Sustained, delicate.
Que ne suis-je la fougère	f♯1-e♭2	g1-d2	All voices	Sustained, delicate.
Trop aimable Sylvie	d1-e2	g1-c2	Most suitable for men's voices	Delicate. Demands facile articulation.
Venez, agréable printemps	c1-f2	f1-c2	All voices	Demands facile articulation.

MARIE ANTOINETTE

TITLE	COMP.	TESS.	TYPE	REMARKS
Chanson de Marie Antoinette	d♯1-g♯2	e1-e2	Soprano	Graceful, light. This melody is supposedly by Marie Antoinette, the queen of France; arranged by Myron Jacobson. (CF)

SONGS AND AIRS IN GERMAN BEFORE
THE NINETEENTH CENTURY

Bibliography

The name found in parentheses in the remarks column indicates one of the following collections:

Reimann 4: Das deutsche Lied, 4 volumes, edited by Reimann, published by Simrock.

Reimann 6: Das deutsche geistliche Lied, 6 volumes, edited by Reimann, published by Simrock.

Moser: Alte Meister des deutschen Liedes, edited by Moser, published by C. F. Peters.

JOHANN GEORG AHLE
(1651–1706)

TITLE	COMP.	TESS.	TYPE	REMARKS
Brünstiges Ver- langen einer Seele	e1-e2	e1-c2	Not suit- able for high, light voices	Slow and very sus- tained. Religious text. (Reimann 4)

JOHANN RUDOLF AHLE
(1625–1673)

Auf die Zukunft unseres Heilandes	c1-f2	e1-c2	Not too suitable for very light, high voices	A sacred dialogue between the Herald and the Soul in con- trasting moods and tempi. (Reimann 4)

CARL PHILIPP EMANUEL BACH
(1714–1788)

TITLE	COMP.	TESS.	TYPE	REMARKS
Das Gebet	c1–ab2	f1–f2	High voices	Sustained, in parts florid. (Reimann 4)
Der Frühling	e1–f#2	g#1–e2	High or medium voices	Graceful, rather florid. (Reimann 6)
Der gestirnte Himmel	e1–f#2	g#1–e2	High or medium voices	Graceful. Demands some flexibility. (Reimann 6)
Der Phönix	d1–eb2	f1–d2	All voices	Sustained. In a manner of a minuet. (Reimann 4)
Der Tag des Weltgerichts	d1–eb2	g1–d2	Heavy voices	Majestic, vigorous, dramatic. (Reimann 6)
Die Himmel rühmen des Ewigen Ehre	c#1–g#2	e1–e2	Most suitable for heavy voices	Very sustained, majestic, vigorous. Religious text. (Reimann 6)
Gottes Grösse in der Natur	d1–f2	a1–f2	High or medium voices	Graceful. Demands some flexibility. Religious text. (Reimann 6)
Jesus in Gethsemane	e1–eb2	f#1–d2	Medium or low voices	Slow, somewhat declamatory, grave. Religious text. (Reimann 6)
Passionslied	d1–g2	g1–eb2	Most suitable for high or medium voices	Sustained, somber. Religious text. (Reimann 6)

See also C. P. E. Bach, <u>Geistliche Lieder</u>, edited by Roth, published by C. F. Peters.

W. FRIEDEMANN BACH
(1710–1784)

TITLE	COMP.	TESS.	TYPE	REMARKS
Kein Hälmlein wächst auf Erden	bb–eb2	eb1–c2	Most suitable for medium or low voices	Very sustained. (Neitzel, <u>Gems of Antiquity</u>. JCC)

GEORG BÖHM
(1661–1733)

Title	Comp.	Tess.	Type	Remarks
Mein Freund ist mein (from Cantata, Mein Freund ist mein)	a-c2	c1-b1	Alto	Sustained. Demands some flexibility. (Collection of Arias for Alto. B&H)

DAVID CORNER
(16..–16..)

Title	Comp.	Tess.	Type	Remarks
Ein neues andächtiges Kindelwiegen	f1-eb2	same	All voices	Sustained, delicate, graceful. Religious text. (Reimann 6)

JOHANN GEORG EBELING
(1637–1676)

Title	Comp.	Tess.	Type	Remarks
Ich steh an deiner Krippe hier	eb1-f2	g1-d2	All voices	Sustained. Religious text. (Reimann 6)

JOHANN WOLFGANG FRANCK
(1644–c. 1710)

Title	Comp.	Tess.	Type	Remarks
Auf, auf! zu Gottes Lob	g1-g2	g1-e2	High voices	Animated, vigorous. Has a sustained, majestic ending. Religious text. (Reimann 6)
Die bitt're Leidenszeit	c1-g2	g1-eb2	High voices	Sustained. Religious text. (Reimann 6)
Jesus neight sein Haupt und stirbt	e1-e2	same	All voices	Slow and sustained. For the most part very subdued. Religious text. (Reimann 6)
Mein Gott, ich bin bereit	c1-g2	g1-eb2	High voices	Very slow and sustained. Religious text. (Reimann 6)

TITLE	COMP.	TESS.	TYPE	REMARKS
Wie seh' ich dich, mein Jesu, bluten	e1-f♯2	same	All voices	Slow. Rather florid. Religious text. (Reimann 6)

MELCHIOR FRANCK
(c. 1579–1639)

TITLE	COMP.	TESS.	TYPE	REMARKS
Ach, treuer Gott, Herr Jesu Christ	a1-f2	same	All voices	Sustained. Religious text. (Reimann 6)
Kommt ihr Gespielen	eb1-eb2	same	All voices	Animated, gay. (Reimann 4)

KARL HEINRICH GRAUN
(1704-1759)

Der Tod Jesu (An Oratorio)
(Score, C. F. Peters)

	COMP.	TESS.	TYPE	REMARKS
Recitative: Gethsemane! Wen hören deine Mauern				
Air: Du Held!	eb1-bb2	bb1-f2	Lyric soprano (coloratura soprano)	A rather extended recitative and an animated, quite florid air. Has a sustained middle section.
Recitative: Ach mein Immannel				
Air: Ein Gebet um neue Stärke	e1-a2	g1-e2	Lyric soprano (coloratura soprano)	A rather extended recitative and a graceful, in parts quite florid air.
Recitative: Nun klingen Waffen				
Air: Ihr Weichgeschaff'nen Seelen	e-ab1	a-gb1	Tenor	A rather extended recitative and a slow, sustained, in parts quite florid air, which has a rapid middle section.

TITLE	COMP.	TESS.	TYPE	REMARKS

Recitative:
  Wer ist der
  Heilige
Air:
  Singt dem gött-
  lichen Propheten
	e♭1-c3	a1-g2	Lyric so-
			prano (col-
			oratura
			soprano)
				Animated, bril-
				liant, in parts
				very florid air.
				This air, with
				English words
				"Lo! the heaven
				descended Proph-
				et" is published
				by Novello.

Recitative:
  Jerusalem,
  voll Mordlust
Air:
  So stehet ein
  Berg Gottes
	B♭-f♯1	e-e1	Baritone	A dramatic scena
				and a vigorous,
				animated aria.
				Has florid pas-
				sages.

Schäfer und Schäferin	d♯1-e2	e1-c♯2	All voices	A delicate, grace- ful dialogue with a sprightly final section. (Rei- mann 4)

For other songs and airs see under "Italian" in this section (page 44).

CHRISTOPHER GRAUPNER
(1683–1760)

TITLE	COMP.	TESS.	TYPE	REMARKS
Jesü, führe meine Seele (A cantata for voice, unison violins and continuo or piano)	c-e1	d-d1	Baritone or bass	Vivace, allegro. Has a recitative separating the two movements. Has florid passages. (F. Noack, Merse- burger, Berlin)

HANS LEO HASSLER
(1564–1612)

TITLE	COMP.	TESS.	TYPE	REMARKS
Gagliarda	f♯1-f2	a1-e2	All voices	Vigorous, spirited. (Reimann 4)

TITLE	COMP.	TESS.	TYPE	REMARKS
Mein G'müth ist mir ver- wirret	e1-e2	f♯1-d2	All voices	Slow, sustained. Originally writ- ten for five voices. (Reimann 4)
Tanzlied	d♯1-e2	f♯1-d2	All voices	Light and delicate. The final section is sustained. (Rei- mann 4)

JOHANN A. HILLER
(1728-1804)

TITLE	COMP.	TESS.	TYPE	REMARKS
Aeol	c1-f2	g1-e2	Not too suitable for very light, high voices	Spirited, humor- ous, vigorous. De- mands facile ar- ticulation. (Rei- mann 4)

FRIEDRICH H. HIMMEL
(1765-1814)

TITLE	COMP.	TESS.	TYPE	REMARKS
Der Lockvogel	f1-f2	g1-d2	All voices	Light, gently hu- morous. Demands some flexibility. (Reimann 4)
Der Rosenstock	c1-g2	a1-e2	All voices	Delicate, sustained. Demands some flexibility. (Rei- mann 4)
Die Gewalt des Blickes	e♭1-g♭2	g1-e♭2	Most suit- able for men's voices	Animated. (Rei- mann 4)
Die Sendung	e♭1-e♭2	f1-c2	Women's voices	Sustained. (Rei- mann 4)

GEORG JOSEPH
(16..-17..)

TITLE	COMP.	TESS.	TYPE	REMARKS
Die Psyche jubiliert über die Aufer- stehung Jesu Christi	d1-e2	g1-d2	Not too suitable for very light voices	Animated, rather vigorous. Reli- gious text. (Rei- mann 6)

REINHARD KEISER
(1674–1739)

TEXT	COMP.	TESS.	TYPE	REMARKS
Von dem Land-leben	c1-g2	f♯1-d2	Soprano	A short cantata, "arietta," recitative, and a spirited aria. Has florid passages. (Reimann 4)

JOHANN PH. KIRNBERGER
(1721–1783)

Schön sind Rosen	c1-f2	f1-d2	All voices	Delicate. Demands some flexibility. (Reimann 4)

BERNHARD KLEIN
(1793–1832)

Ein Seufzer	g1-e2	same	All voices, except a very light soprano	Animated. (Reimann 4)
Heil'ge Nacht	d♯1-e2	f♯1-c♯2	Medium or low voices	Slow, very sustained. (Reimann 4)

ADAM KRIEGER
(1634–1666)

Der hat gesiegt, den Got vergnügt	c1-b♭1	same	Medium or low voices	Sustained. Religious text. (Reimann 6)

JOHANN LÖHNER
(16..–17..)

O Ewigkeit	d♯1-f♯2	f♯1-d2	Not too suitable for very light, high voices	Sustained. Somewhat declamatory. Religious text. (Reimann 6)

144

TITLE	COMP.	TESS.	TYPE	REMARKS

CHRISTIAN GOTTLOB NEEFE
(1748–1798)

TITLE	COMP.	TESS.	TYPE	REMARKS
Die frühen Gräber	c1-g2	d1-bb1	Not too suitable for very light voices	Slow and very sustained. (Reimann 4)
Die Wassernymphe	c♯1-e2	e1-e2	All voices	Animated, delicate. Demands some flexibility. (Moser)
Serenade	c1-f2	ab1-db2	Most suitable for men's voices	A song in contrasting moods and tempi. Demands some flexibility. (Moser)

VALENTIN RATHGEBER
(1682–1750)

TITLE	COMP.	TESS.	TYPE	REMARKS
Von der edlen Musik	c1-e2	d1-d2	All voices	A minuet in praise of music. (Moser)

JOHANN FR. REICHARDT
(1752–1814)

TITLE	COMP.	TESS.	TYPE	REMARKS
Das Lösegeld	e1-f2	a1-e2	All voices	Gently humorous. Somewhat declamatory. (Reimann 4)
Lied an die Nacht	bb-f2	eb1-bb1	Most suitable for medium or low voices	Slow and sustained. (Reimann 4)
Mailied	c♯1-e2	d1-d2	All voices	Animated, gay. (Moser)
Rhapsodie	bb-f2	eb1-eb2	Medium or low voices	Sustained, majestic. See Alto Rhapsody by Brahms (for alto, male chorus and orchestra). (Moser)

TITLE	COMP.	TESS.	TYPE	REMARKS

LUISE REICHARDT
(1779–1826)

TITLE	COMP.	TESS.	TYPE	REMARKS
Wenn die Rosen blühen (In the time of Roses)	f#-g2	a1-e2	All voices	Sustained, subdued, delicate. (OD)

FRIEDRICH W. RUST
(1739–1796)

TITLE	COMP.	TESS.	TYPE	REMARKS
An die Nachtigall	c1-d2	d1-c2	Not too suitable for very light, high voices	Very sustained. (Reimann 4)

J. A. P. SCHULZE
(1747–1800)

TITLE	COMP.	TESS.	TYPE	REMARKS
Der Schmetterling	e1(a)-f#2	a1-e2	All voices	Light. Demands facile articulation. (Reimann 4)
Die Mutter bei der Wiege	f1-d2	same	Women's voices	Delicate, sustained, gently humorous. (Reimann 4)
Frühlingsliebe	c1-f2	f1-d2	All voices	Delicate, sustained. (Reimann 4)
Liebeszauber	e1-f#2	a1-e2	All voices	Light, animated. Demands facile articulation and some flexibility. (Reimann 4)
Sagt, wo sind die Veilchen hin?	bb-eb2	eb1-eb2	All voices, except a very light soprano	Delicate, sustained. (Reimann 4)
Ständchen	d1-g2	g1-d2	Not too suitable for very low voices	A light, graceful waltz song. (Reimann 4)

HEINRICH SCHÜTZ
(1585–1672)

Gore in parentheses indicates <u>Five Sacred Songs</u>, edited by R. Gore, published by Concordia Publishing House.

TITLE	COMP.	TESS.	TYPE	REMARKS
Aus dem 119ten Psalm	c1-d2	f1-c2	All voices	Sustained. Religious text. (Reimann 4)
Bringt her dem Herren	d1-f2	eb1-eb2	All voices	Animated, bright. Has some florid passages and impressive Alleluia sections. Religious text. (Gore)
Eile, mich, Gott, zu erretten	c1-g2	d1-e2	All voices, except light, high soprano	Declamatory. In parts demands considerable dramatic intensity. Religious text. (Gore)
Ich danke dem Herrn	c1-f2	d1-e2	All voices	Sustained. Demands rhythmic clarity. Imposing and stately climax. Religious text. (Gore)
Ich will den Herren loben allezeit	c1-g2	d1-e2	All voices	Animated, bright. Has some florid passages and impressive Alleluia sections. Religious text. (Gore)
Paratum cor meum	d1-f2	e1-e2	All voices	An aria for voice, two violins, and continuo or piano. Graceful, rhythmic. Has florid passages. Impressive ending. Sacred Latin text. (Hinrichsen)
Was hast du verwirket	db1-f2	eb1-eb2	All voices	Declamatory for the most part. In parts demands considerable dramatic intensity.

TITLE	COMP.	TESS.	TYPE	REMARKS
				Admirable and impressive setting of text from St. Augustine's "Meditations." (Gore)

GEORG PHILIPP TELEMANN
(1681-1767)

TITLE	COMP.	TESS.	TYPE	REMARKS
Die rechte Stimmung	f1-f2	same	All voices	Humorous. Demands some flexibility. (Reimann 4)
Gott will Mensch und sterblich werden (A cantata for soprano, violin and continuo [or piano])	d1-g2	same	Soprano	Rapid and sustained air, recitative and a vigorous, florid, brilliant air. (BAER)

See also a collection of Telemann's songs and airs published by C. F. Peters.

FRANZ TUNDER
(1614-1667)

TITLE	COMP.	TESS.	TYPE	REMARKS
Ein kleines Kindelein	c1-f2	eb1-eb2	All voices	Graceful, jubilant. Has a recitative and an arioso section. (Concordia)

CARL F. ZELTER
(1758-1832)

TITLE	COMP.	TESS.	TYPE	REMARKS
Der Arme Thoms	c1-f2	f1-db2	All voices	Sustained. (Reimann 4)
Félicité passée	c1-g2	a1-f2	All voices	Sustained. The poem is by J. J. Rousseau. French text. (Reimann 4)
Geistergrass	bb(f)-c2	c1-g1	Low voices	Slow and very sustained. (Reimann 4)

TITLE	COMP.	TESS.	TYPE	REMARKS
Ständchen	e1-f♯2	a1-e2	Most suitable for high voices	Light and delicate. Demands some flexibility and a good sense of rhythm. (Reimann 4)

JOHANN R. ZUMSTEEG
(1760–1802)

TITLE	COMP.	TESS.	TYPE	REMARKS
Una	e♭1-d2	f1-b♭1	Most suitable for medium or low voices	Slow, sustained, somewhat dramatic. (Reimann 4)

JOHANN SEBASTIAN BACH
(1685–1750)

It seems unnecessary, as well as impossible, to try to evaluate the vocal music of Bach in a short prefatory note. A few practical suggestions pertaining to matters of performance may, however, be of some value.

1. Although not popularly considered so, Bach's airs are for the most part not vocal solo pieces, but chamber music with a vocal part, since he very frequently employs an obbligato part or parts of equal importance with the vocal line. The transference of such an obbligato line, possessing its own distinctive sonority (such as oboe, flute, or a string instrument), into the pianoforte "accompaniment" is for the most part a musically unsatisfactory and even reprehensible practice. Some Bach airs lose so much by this procedure as to become almost unintelligible.

In Bach's airs the vocal line as such is seldom paramount in importance, as it is for instance in his songs, or in the airs of Gluck and Handel. The singer must learn to accompany the instrumental passages, when this is necessary. Often this is forgotten, and the resulting emphasis on a contrapuntal detail contained in the vocal part is responsible for the harsh and unintelligible effects which would never arise were the vocal part considered in the proper perspective—as one of the active melodic parts and not as the only melodic part.

2. Many of the available pianoforte reductions of the instrumental part of Bach's airs seem to be overloaded with contrapuntal detail, added by the arrangers and not found in the original obbligato and figured bass parts. These obscure the melodic expressiveness of the vocal line, the obbligato line, and the bass line.

For concert performance of Bach's airs, when pianoforte is employed as the only instrument and some of the available pianoforte reductions are used, the pianist would do well to allow the original obbligato part and the bass line to stand out at the expense of many a contrapuntal passage in the middle voices, often of doubtful authenticity. The best way to attain the desired balance would be to compare

the pianoforte arrangement with the original score, and to reduce
the pianoforte part to the absolute minimum, so that the bass and
the obbligato part stand out as melodically important parts.

3. One must bear in mind the fact that Bach's soprano and alto
airs were originally intended for boy singers or male falsetto singers (not to be confused with castrati).

4. Most singers, especially tenors and soprani, would do well
to sing Bach airs a half tone lower than the original, since much of
the available evidence seems to prove almost conclusively that the
pitch in Bach's time was considerably lower than the present-day
440 or 442 a. Unless the vocal line can be negotiated without strain
in its original key, there seems to be no reason, aesthetic or otherwise, to disregard this now almost conclusively established difference in pitch.

5. The often enormously long florid passages vocalized on one
vowel do not have to be sung in one breath. A tied note, such as
♩ ♫♫ or ♪♩ ♫♫ offers an excellent opportunity for the intake
of breath without disturbance to the melodic line or to the rhythmic
pattern. The now often-encountered practice of rushing through
such passages at top speed and minimum volume for the sake of pre-
serving them on one breath seems to me to be pedantic and harmful
to the music, even if it may afford some slight gratification to the
performer by offering him an opportunity to display the excellence
of his breath control. Only in instances where taking a phrase on
one breath does not in any way affect the tempo, the volume, and the
melodic expressiveness of the phrase in question is such a practice
artistically valid. As soon as singing a phrase in one breath becomes a problem and the singer has to exert himself in every possible way to keep up this self-imposed race against time, it seems
better to break the phrase vocally (which can be easily done without
breaking it musically), instead of keeping it intact at the cost of im-
pairing the tone quality and the steady rhythm.

6. Although a metronomically rigid, totally inflexible rhythm
is undesirable in performing Bach's music, as in performing any
music, a nineteenth century romantic rubato is even less desirable.

Bach's counterpoint is essentially polyrhythmic and the bar
line in his music does not necessarily signify a "strong" beat. One
of the most troublesome ensemble problems in performing Bach is
to find the proper accentuation in each melodic line. These accents
often do not coincide either with the bar lines nor with each other.
Thus a "strong" beat in the bass or an obbligato instrument may not
be a "strong" beat in the voice part, and both "strong" beats may occur on some of the "weak" beats within the measure. However, one
must not forget that Bach frequently employed strict dance forms
such as the minuet, gavotte and sarabande in his airs, and that such
dance forms demand a precise accentuation and a steady tempo.

7. The present-day singer is apt to forget that the manner of
dramatic delivery of the text of Bach's airs is very different from

151

the one employed by the nineteenth century composers, or even Gluck or Mozart.

Bach, in his own way, is perhaps as conscious of the dramatic possibilities of his texts as Wagner, but he uses entirely different means to achieve the desired effect. The text never dominates his music, though it most definitely influences its pattern and is as important, in so far as the entire mood of an air is concerned, as the text is in a song by Hugo Wolf. The means of expression, however, remain at all times purely musical, and never enter the province of acting as opposed to singing. The stylistically untenable violence and "expressive declamation" so often employed by present-day singers in performing Bach's airs is as repulsive as the suppression of any normal emotional reaction toward the text accorded to Bach's vocal music by those who seem to believe it to be nothing more than a contrapuntal vocalise.

8. One of the most frequently encountered malpractices in singing Bach is the practice of over-phrasing, as well as of overloading each phrase with too many dynamic shadings. One must remember that in doing so the singer may easily disturb and sacrifice the line and the mood of a large phrase, which in some instances is of considerable duration (often as long as sixteen bars). This of course by no means implies that Bach should be sung with no dynamic shadings whatsoever.

9. Bach's airs make very severe demands upon the musicianship of the vocalist, since Bach hardly ever uses any doubling of the vocal line for the purpose of helping the singer (as Gluck, for instance, almost invariably does). Since Bach's music is chromatic to a degree not encountered in vocal music until the latter half of the nineteenth century, and since more than one melodic line is almost constantly employed, the singer would do well to acquaint himself thoroughly with the obbligato parts before attempting to sing his own part.

10. In closing I want to remind the reader that the da capo aria form which Bach used often can sometimes be cut down to fit the present-day requirements of length, by substituting the instrumental ritornel for the entire recapitulation, or by singing the da capo section and omitting the ritornel. The desirability of such cuts is questionable, however, since by shortening one of the three sections the architecture of the piece as a whole is undoubtedly endangered.

The selection of Bach airs for this list was extraordinarily difficult, since hardly one Bach air seems to be superior to another. In selecting the following list the airs available in collections have been favored.

The name (or names) in parentheses in the remarks column indicate one of the following collections:

Prout: Bach Songs and Airs, 2 volumes for each voice, edited by Dr. E. Prout, published by Augener.

Straube: <u>Bach Arien</u>, 1 volume for each type of voice, edited by K. Straube, published by C. F. Peters. (This edition, though accurate, abounds in a variety of expression marks by Straube which are of questionable value.)

Whittaker: <u>The Oxford Series of Bach Arias</u>, edited by W. G. Whittaker, published by Oxford University Press (English texts only, available separately).

When no biographical reference is given, the Breitkopf & Härtel or the C. F. Peters edition of the complete piano score is meant.

All of Bach's 214 cantatas are published in piano score edition by Breitkopf & Härtel. The last revision of this edition is by far the best because in it all the additions (realizations of the figured bass by the editor) appear in small print.

Larger works:

<u>Matthäus Passion</u> (St. Matthew Passion): C. F. Peters (German text only); G. Schirmer (English text only, not the most accurate edition).

<u>Johannes Passion</u> (St. John Passion): G. Schirmer, edited by A. Mendel, German and English text, a model edition of Bach.

<u>Weihnachts Oratorium</u> (Christmas Oratorio): C. F. Peters, Breitkopf & Härtel (German text only); G. Schirmer, Novello (English text only).

<u>Mass in B minor</u>: Bärenreiter (most accurate of all editions), G. Schirmer, C. F. Peters, Breitkopf & Härtel.

<u>Magnificat in D major</u>: G. Schirmer, C. F. Peters, Novello.

Songs: Breitkopf & Härtel.

Airs from the cantatas, with pianoforte and obbligato instruments, are published by the "Neue Bach Gesellschaft," Breitkopf & Härtel. This is no doubt the most practical of all modern editions of Bach airs. One volume of this edition (soprano) has been reprinted by Kalmus.

A collection of Bach airs (English text only) is published by Novello in 4 volumes, one for each type of voice. The identifying numbers of cantatas are unfortunately omitted in this collection.

A number of Bach airs are to be found in the Breitkopf & Härtel Arien Album as well as in the Arien Album published by C. F. Peters and the Arien Album published by Universal Edition.

Since Bach wrote within a rather uniform compass and tessitura for each of the four main types of voice, and since the character of each air, as described in the remarks column, seems sufficient to indicate the type of voice for which the air is possibly best suited, it seemed best to dispense with the mention of the type of voice column in each of the following entries.

Soprano

TITLE:AIR	TITLE:WORK	COMP.	TESS.	REMARKS
Auch mit ge- dämpften, schwachen Stimmen Recitative: Er hat uns allen wohl- getan (To all men Jesus good hath done) Air:	Cantata 36: Schwingt freudig euch empor	d1-g2	f#1-e2	Not fast. Has a florid middle sec- tion. (Straube)
Aus Liebe will mein Heiland sterben (In love my Sav- iour now is dying)	Matthäus Passion (St. Matthew Passion)	e1-a2	a1-f2	Very slow. Has florid passages.
Blute nur (Bleed and break)	Matthäus Passion (St. Matthew Passion)	e1-g2	g1-e2	Sustained. Demands some flexibility.
Die Armen will der Herr um- armen	Cantata 186: Ärge dich, o Seele, nicht	d1-g2	g1-eb2	Sustained. (Straube)
Die Seele ruht in Jesu Händen	Cantata 127: Herr Jesu Christ, wahr'r Mensch und Gott	c1-ab2	g1-eb2	Slow, sustained. Demands some flexibility. (Straube, also Prout)
Ei! Wie schmeckt der Kaffee süsse	Cantata 211: (Kaffee Can- tata): Schwei- get stille plaudert nicht	d1-a2	a1-f2	Graceful, gently hu- morous. Demands flexibility.
Es ist und bleibt der Christen Trost	Cantata 44: Sie werden euch in den Bann thun	d1-a2	g1-eb2	Animated and florid. (Straube)

TITLE:AIR	TITLE:WORK	COMP.	TESS.	REMARKS
Flösst, mein Heiland, flösst dein Namen (Ah! my Saviour)	Weihnachts Oratorium (Christmas Oratorio)	d1-g2	g1-e2	Graceful. Demands some flexibility. This air is not too suitable for concert performance because of the occasional chorus entrances.
Gedenk'an uns mit deiner Liebe	Cantata 29: Wir danken dir, Gott, wir danken dir	f#1-a2	a1-f#2	Graceful, sustained. Demands some flexibility. (Prout)
Gottes Engel weichen nie	Cantata 149: Man singet mit Freuden vom Sieg	c#1-a2	g1-e2	Delicate, graceful. (Straube, also Prout)
Gottlob! Gottlob!	Cantata 28: Gottlob, nun geht das Jahr zu Ende	d1-a2	g1-f2	Spirited, has florid passages.
Gott versorget alles Leben	Cantata 187: Es wartet alles auf dich	d1-ab2	f1-f2	Slow, somewhat florid. Has a graceful middle section.
Heil und Segen	Cantata 120: Gott, man Lobet dich in der Stille	d1-g2	g1-e2	Slow, very sustained. Demands some flexibility. (Straube)
Herr, deine Güte reicht (Lord, wide as heaven above)	Cantata 17: Wer Dank opfert, der preiset mich	e1-g#2	f#1-e2	Animated, spirited. Demands flexibility. (Whittaker)
Herr, der du stark und mächtig bist	Cantata 10: Meine Seel' erhebt den Herren	c1-a2	g1-g2	Vigorous, very spirited, florid.
Höchster, Höchster	Cantata 51: Jauchzet Gott in allen Landen	e1-a2	g1-e2	Not fast, sustained. Has florid passages.
Höchster, Tröster	Cantata 183: Sie Werden euch in den Bann thun	d1-a2	g1-f2	Graceful and florid.

TITLE:AIR	TITLE:WORK	COMP.	TESS.	REMARKS
Hört, ihr Augen, auf zu weinen	Cantata 98: Was Gott thut das ist wohlgetan	c1-ab2	g1-eb2	Not fast. Demands considerable flexibility. (Straube)
Hört, ihr Völker	Cantata 76: Die Himmel erzählen die Ehre Gottes	d1-g2	g1-e2	Graceful. Demands flexibility.
Ich esse mit Freuden	Cantata 84: Ich bin vergnügt mit meinem Glücke	d1-a2	g1-e2	Animated and graceful.
Ich folge dir gleichfalls	Johannes Passion (St. John's Passion)	d1-ab2	a1-f2	Animated, florid. (Score, GS)
Ich nehme mein Leiden	Cantata 75: Die Elenden sollen essen	c1-a2	f1-e2	Graceful and delicate. Has rapid florid passages. (Prout)
Ich säe meine Zähren	Cantata 146: Wir müssen durch viel Trübsal	c1-g2	a1-e2	Not fast. Has florid passages. (Straube)
Recitative: . Wiewohl mein Herz (Although my heart) Air: Ich will dir mein Herze schenken (Lord, to thee my heart I proffer)	Matthäus Passion (St. Matthew Passion)	c1-g2	e1-e2	Animated. Demands considerable flexibility.
Ich wünschte mir den Tod	Cantata 57: Selig ist der Mann	c1-ab2	g1-eb2	Slow and sustained, grave. (Prout)
Ihm hab' ich mich ergeben	Cantata 97: In allen meinen Thaten	c1-g2	e1-c2	Animated and graceful. Has florid passages.
Jauchzet Gott in allen Landen	Cantata 51: Jauchzet Gott in allen Landen	e1-c3	a1-f2	Animated, brilliant, florid.

TITLE:AIR	TITLE:WORK	COMP.	TESS.	REMARKS
Komm in mein Herzenshaus	Cantata 80: Ein feste Burg ist unser Gott	e1-a2	a1-f#2	Not fast, florid. (Prout)
Lass der Spötter Zungen schmähen	Cantata 70: Wachet, betet	d1-a2	g1-e2	Not fast. Demands some flexibility.
Lass uns, o höchster Gott	Cantata 41: Jesu nun sei gepreiset	d1-a2	a1-f#2	Graceful. Has some florid passages. (Straube, also Prout)
Meinem Hirten bleib' ich treu	Cantata 92: Ich hab in Gottes Herz und Sinn	d1-a2	g1-e2	Graceful. (Straube)
Mein gläubiges Herze (My heart ever faithful)	Cantata 68: Also hat Gott die Welt geliebt	f1-a2	a1-f2	Animated. Demands some flexibility. This famous air exists also in many transposed editions, and is sometimes sung by alti. (gen. av.)
Mein Jesus will es thun	Cantata 72: Alles nur nach Gottes willen	d1-a2	f1-e2	Animated, graceful. Has some florid passages. (Straube)
Mein Seelenschatz ist Gottes Wort!	Cantata 18: Gleich wie der Regen und Schnee vom Himmel fällt	eb1-ab2	g1-eb2	Animated. Demands flexibility. (Prout)
Nur ein Wink von seinen Händen (Naught against the pow'r He wieldeth)	Weihnachts Oratorium (Christmas Oratorio)	c#1-a2	a1-f#2	Not fast. Demands considerable flexibility.
Öffne dich, mein ganzes Herze	Cantata 61: Nun komm, du Heiden Heiland	d1-g2	g1-d2	Rather slow, sustained.

TITLE:AIR	TITLE:WORK	COMP.	TESS.	REMARKS
Patron das macht der Wind	Phoebus und Pan	d1-a2	g1-e2	Spirited, humorous. Demands facile articulation and some flexibility. G. Schirmer has published a transposed edition of this air, one tone lower than the original. (Prout)
Quia respexit (Latin text)	Magnificat in D Major	d1-f♯2	g1-e2	Slow, Has florid passages.
Ruhet hie, matte Sinne	Cantata 210: O holder Tag	d♯1-a2	g♯1-e2	Sustained. Demands some flexibility. (Prout)
Schafe können sicher weiden	Geburtstagscantate: Was mir behagt ist nur die muntre Jagd	f1-a♭2	b♭1-f2	Sustained, delicate. Published by Galaxy a whole tone lower than the original, edited by W. Kramer; by C. Fischer (in the original key), edited by LaForge.
Sei Lob und Preis mit Ehren	Cantata 51: Jauchzet Gott in allen Landen	c1-c3	g1-e2	First part, a sustained solo choral; second part animated and very florid.
Seufzer, Tränen, Kummer, Not	Cantata 21: Ich hatte viel Bekümmernis	d1-a♭2	g1-f2	Slow, sustained, subdued. Demands good command of high pp. (Prout)
Stein, der über alle Schätze	Cantata 152: Tritt auf die Glaubensbahn	d1-g2	g1-e2	Slow and sustained. (Straube)
Süsser Trost, mein Jesus kömmt	Cantata 151: Süsser Trost, mein Jesus kömmt	f♯1-a2	a1-f♯2	Very sustained, delicate. Has a more animated, florid middle section. (Straube, also Prout)
Was die Welt in sich hält (Little worth is found on earth)	Cantata 64: Sehet! welch eine Liebe hat uns der Vater erzeiget	d1-g2	f♯1-f♯2	Slow and sustained. (Whittaker)
Wie lieblich klingt es in den Ohren	Cantata 133: Ich freue mich in dir	e1-a2	a♯1-g2	Not fast. Demands some flexibility. (Straube)

TITLE:AIR	TITLE:WORK	COMP.	TESS.	REMARKS
Wie Zittern und wanken	Cantata 105: Herr, gehe nicht ins Gericht	c1-ab2	g1-f2	Rather animated. Has florid passages.
Wir beten zu dem Tempel an	Cantata 51: Jauchzet Gott in allen Landen	e1-a2	g1-e2	Slow. Has florid passages.
Recitative: Mein Gott, wie lang', ach lange? Air: Wirf, mein Herze, wirf dich noch	Cantata 155: Mein Gott, wie lang'	c1-a2	f1-f2	A sustained recitative (has a florid final passage) and a vigorous, majestic air, which demands some flexibility. (Prout)
Zerfliesse, mein Herze	Johannes Passion (St. John Passion)	c1-ab2	ab1-g2	Slow, quite florid. (Score, GS)

Mezzo-Soprano or Alto

Ach, schläfrige Seele- wie?	Cantata 115: Mache dich, mein Geist, bereit	a-d2	c1-c2	Sustained. Has a rapid middle section. Florid. (Prout)
Ach Herr! Was ist ein Menschenkind?	Cantata 110: Unser Mund, sei voll Lachens	c#1-d#2	e1-c#2	Sustained. Demands some flexibility. (Prout)
Ach, lege das Sodom der sündlichen Glieder	Cantata 48: Ich elender Mensch, wer wird mich erlösen	bb-eb2	eb1-c2	Not fast, graceful Demands flexibility.
Agnus Dei (Latin text)	Mass in B Minor	a-eb2	d1-bb1	Very slow and sustained.

TITLE:AIR	TITLE:WORK	COMP.	TESS.	REMARKS
Bereite dich Zion (Prepare thyself, Zion) Recitative: Du lieber Heiland du (O blessed Saviour) Air:	Weihnachts Oratorium (Christmas Oratorio)	b-e2	e1-c2	Animated. Has florid passages.
Buss und Reu (Grief and pain)	Matthäus Passion (St. Matthew Passion)	b-e2	f#-d2	Sustained. Demands some flexibility.
Doch Jesus will	Cantata 46: Schauet doch und sehet, ob irgend ein Schmerz sei	g-eb2	d1-c2	Not fast. Demands flexibility.
Du Herr, du krönst allein	Cantata 187: Es wartet Alles auf dich	bb-eb2	e1-c2	Graceful. Has florid passages. (Prout) A simplified version of "Domine Fili unigenite" from Mass in G Minor.
Du machst, o Tod	Cantata 114: Ach, lieben Christen, seid getrost	bb-eb2	eb1-c2	Animated, rather vigorous. Demands flexibility. (Prout; also Straube)
Ein unbarmherziges Gerichte	Cantata 89: Was soll ich aus dir machen, Ephraim?	bb-e2	e1-c2	Animated and vigorous.
Erbarme dich mein Gott (Have mercy, Lord, on me)	Matthäus Passion (St. Matthew Passion)	c#1-e2	f#1-d2	Slow, very sustained. Demands some flexibility.
Es ist vollbracht (It is finished)	Johannes Passion (St. John Passion)	b-d2	d1-b1	Very slow, sustained, grave. Has a spirited, somewhat florid middle section. (Score, GS)
Esurientes implevit bonis (Latin text)	Magnificat in D Major	g#-d2	d#1-b1	Not fast, graceful, florid.

TITLE:AIR	TITLE:WORK	COMP.	TESS.	REMARKS
Et exultavit spiritus meus (Latin text)	Magnificat in D Major	c#1-f#2	e1-d2	Animated. Has florid passages.
Geist und Seele wird verwirret	Cantata 35: Geist und Seele wird verwirret	b-e2	e1-d2	Slow. Has florid passages.
Gelobet sei der Herr	Cantata 129: Gelobet sei der Herr, mein Gott	c#1-e2	e1-c2	Not slow, graceful. Has florid passages. (Prout)
Getrost, getrost! (Be glad)	Cantata 133: Ich freue mich in dir	a-e2	e1-c#2	Spirited. In parts quite florid. (Whittaker)
Gott hat Alles wohlgemacht	Cantata 35: Geist und Seele wird verwirret	c1-e2	e1-c2	Rather vigorous. In parts quite florid.
Gott ist unser Sonn' und Schild	Cantata 79: Gott der Herr ist Sonn' und Schild	c#1-e2	e1-d2	Spirited. Has florid passages. (Prout)
Gott man lobet dich, in der Stille	Cantata 120: Gott man Lobet dich	a-e2	e1-d2	Slow, sustained. In parts very florid. (Straube)
Halleluja, Stärk und Macht	Cantata 29: Wir danken dir Gott, wir danken dir	a-e2	d1-b1	Vigorous, spirited, quite florid.
Herr, was du willst soll mir gefallen	Cantata 156: Ich steh' mit einem Fuss im Grabe	f-e2	d1-d2	Vigorous, animated. Has florid passages. (Prout)
Leget euch dem Heiland unter (Lowly bend before the Saviour)	Cantata 182: Himmelskönig sei willkommen	a-d2	d1-b1	Slow, sustained. Demands some flexibility. (Whittaker)
Hochgelobter Gottesohn	Cantata 6: Bleib bei uns, denn es will Abend werden	bb-eb2	eb1-c2	Not fast. Rather florid.

TITLE:AIR	TITLE:WORK	COMP.	TESS.	REMARKS
Ich sehe schon im Geist	Cantata 43: Gott fähret auf mit Jauchzen	b-e2	e1-c2	Graceful. Has florid passages.
Ich will dich all mein Leben lang	Cantata 117: Sei Lob und Ehr	a-e2	e1-c#2	Animated. Demands some flexibility.
Ich wünsche mir bei Gott zu leben	Cantata 35: Geist und Seele wird verwirret	c1-e2	d1-c2	Rather animated. In parts quite florid.
In deine Hände	Cantata 106: Gottes Zeit ist die aller- beste Zeit	bb-eb2	f1-db2	Slow, sustained.
In Jesu De- muth kann ich Trost	Cantata 151: Süsser Trost mein Jesus kömmt	a-e2	e1-c2	Not slow. Demands flexibility. (Prout)
Jesu, lass dich finden	Cantata 154: Mein liebster Jesus is ver- loren	b-d#2	e1-b1	Subdued, graceful. Demands some flexibility. (Prout)
Jesus schläft	Cantata 81: Jesus schläft was soll ich hoffen?	a-d2	b-b1	Sustained, subdued. (Prout)
Komm, leite mich	Cantata 175: Er rufet seinen Scha- fen mit Na- men	b-e2	e1-b1	Not fast, sustained. (Straube)
Kommt, ihr angefocht'- nen Sünder	Cantata 30: Freue dich erlöste Schaar	a-e2	e1-c2	Not fast. Demands flexibility. Has in- teresting syncopated rhythm. (Straube)
Recitative: Erbarm' es Gott (O gracious God) Air: Können Trä- nen meiner Wangen (If my tears be un- availing)	Matthäus Passion (St. Matthew Passion)	c1-eb2	g1-d2	Not slow. Demands considerable flexi- bility.

TITLE:AIR	TITLE:WORK	COMP.	TESS.	REMARKS
Laudamus te (Latin text)	Mass in B Minor	c#1-e2	e1-c#2	Not fast, florid.
Leg ich mich späte nieder	Cantata 97: In allen meinen Thaten	b-eb2	eb1-c2	Grave. Demands some flexibility. (Straube)
Liebt, ihr Christen in der That	Cantata 76: Die Himmel erzählen die Ehre Gottes	b-d2	e1-c2	Grave and sustained.
Mein Jesu, ziehe mich nach dir	Cantata 22: Jesus nahm zu sich die Zwölfe	bb-eb2	g1-c2	Flowing and subdued, graceful. (Straube)
Menschen, glaubt doch dieser Gnade	Cantata 7: Christ unser Herr zum Jordan kam	b-e2	d#1-c2	Very vigorous, dramatic. Has some florid passages. (Prout)
Recitative: O sel'ger Christ Arioso: Herr, so du willt Air: Mit Allem was ich hab und bin	Cantata 72: Alles nur nach Gottes willen	bb-e2	e1-c2	Recitative, and a sustained arioso, followed by a spirited air requiring great flexibility. (Straube)
Mund und Herze steht dir offen	Cantata 148: Bringet dem Herrn Ehre seines Namens!	b-e2	f#1-d2	Graceful. Demands flexibility. (Prout)
Murre nicht, lieber Christ	Cantata 144: Nimm, was dein ist, und gehe hin	a-d2	b-b1	Not slow, sustained, graceful. (Prout)
Nichts kann mich erretten	Cantata 74: Wer mich liebet, der wird mein Wort halten	g-e2	d1-c2	Animated and vigorous. Has florid passages. (Prout)

TITLE:AIR	TITLE:WORK	COMP.	TESS.	REMARKS
O Mensch, errette deine Seele	Cantata 20: O Ewigkeit, du Donnerwort	c#1-e2	f1-c2	Slow, grave. Demands some flexibility.
Qui sedes (Latin text)	Mass in B Minor	c#1-e2	e1-c#2	Gently animated. Has florid passages.
Schlafe, mein Liebster (Slumber beloved)	Weihnachts Oratorium (Christmas Oratorio)	a-e2	e1-c2	Slow, very sustained. Has florid passages.
Schläfert aller Sorgen Kummer	Cantata 197: Gott ist unsere Zuversicht	a-e2	e1-c#2	Very sustained. Has a spirited, florid middle section.
Schlage doch gewünschte Stunde	Cantata 53 (for alto solo): Schlage doch, gewünschte Stunde	b-e2	e-c#2	Very sustained, grave. (Prout)
Schliesse, mein Herze, dies selige Wunder (Keep, o my spirit)	Weihnachts Oratorium (Christmas Oratorio)	b-e2	e1-d2	Sustained, rather vigorous.
Recitative: Ach Golgotha (Ah Golgotha) Air: Sehet, Jesus hat die Hand (Look ye Jesus waiting stands)	Matthäus Passion (St. Matthew Passion)	g-eb2	eb1-db2	Slow. Demands considerable flexibility.
Recitative: O Wort, das Geist und Seel erschreckt Air: Vergib, o Vater	Cantata 87: Bisher habt ihr nichts gebeten	bb-e2	d1-c2	Slow, sustained. Demands flexibility.

TITLE:AIR	TITLE:WORK	COMP.	TESS.	REMARKS
Vergnügte Ruh, beliebte Seelenlust	Cantata 170: Vergnügte Ruh, beliebte Seelenlust	b-e2	e1-d2	Sustained. Demands some flexibility.
Von den Stricken meiner Sünden	Johannes Passion (St. John Passion)	bb-eb2	d1-c2	Not fast. Demands flexibility. (Score, GS)
Von der Welt verlang' ich nichts (Of this world I ask for nought)	Cantata 64: Sehet! welch eine Liebe hat uns der Vater erzeiget	b-e2	e1-c2	Not fast; graceful. Demands flexibility. (Whittaker)
Wann kommt der Tag	Cantata 70: Wachet, betet, seid bereit	a-d2	d1-b1	Sustained. Has some florid passages.
Was Gott thut	Cantata 100: Was Gott thut, das ist wohlgethan	a-e2	d1-a1	Animated and graceful. Demands some flexibility. (Prout)
Weh! der Seele	Cantata 102: Herr, deine Augen sehen nach dem Glauben	b-eb2	f1-c2	Sustained, grave. Demands some flexibility. (Straube)
Wer Gott bekennt	Cantata 45: Es ist dir gesagt, Mensch, was gut ist	b#-d#2	e1-c#2	Not fast, grave. Has florid passages.
Wer Sünde tut	Cantata 54 (for alto solo): Widerstehe doch der Sünde	f-c2	c1-g1	Not fast, grave. Has florid passages.
Widerstehe doch der Sünde	Cantata 54 (for alto solo): Widerstehe doch der Sünde	f-bb1	c1-f1	Rather slow and sustained, grave. (Prout)
Wie furchtsam wankten meine Schritte	Cantata 33: Allein zu dir Herr Jesu Christ	a-d2	d-b1	Not fast. Demands flexibility. (Straube)

TITLE:AIR	TITLE:WORK	COMP.	TESS.	REMARKS
Wo Zwei und Drei versammelt sind in Jesu theurem Namen	Cantata 42: Am Abend aber desselbigen Sabbaths	b-e2	e1-c2	Not fast. Has florid passages. (Straube)
Wohl euch, ihr auserwählten Seelen	Cantata 34: O Ewiges Feuer	b-e2	e1-c♯2	Sustained. Demands some flexibility. (Straube)

Tenor

TITLE:AIR	TITLE:WORK	COMP.	TESS.	REMARKS
Ach, mein Sinn	Johannes Passion (St. John Passion)	e-a1	a-f♯1	Sustained. (Score, GS)
Ach, schlage doch bald	Cantata 95: Christus, der ist mein Leben	d-b1	a-f♯1 (g1)	Not fast. Demands flexibility. (Straube; in the Prout edition this air is transposed one tone lower)
Adam muss in uns verwesen (He who would in Christ be living)	Cantata 31: Der Himmel lacht, die Erde jubilieret	c-g1	g-e1	Animated, very short. (Whittaker)
Auf, auf, Gläubige	Cantata 134: Ein Herz, das seinen Jesum	d-b♭1	f-f1	Vigorous. Has florid passages. (Straube)
Bäche von gesalznen Zähren	Cantata 21: Ich hatte viel Bekümmernis	c-g1	a♭-e♭1	Slow, rather florid. (Prout)
Benedictus	Mass in B Minor	e-a1	a-f♯1	Sustained. Demands flexibility.
Bewundert, o Menschen	Cantata 62: Nun komm, der Heiden Heiland	c-a1	a-f1	Animated and florid.
Deposuit potentes (Latin text)	Magnificat in D	c♯-a1	f♯-d1	Animated, quite florid, robust.

TITLE:AIR	TITLE:WORK	COMP.	TESS.	REMARKS
Die schäu- menden Wellen	Cantata 81: Jesus schläft, was soll ich hoffen?	d-a1	a-f1	Spirited. Has rapid florid pas- sages. Has sev- eral recitative pas- sages interrupting the set musical piece. (Prout)
Die Welt kann ihre Lust und Freud'	Cantata 94: Was frag' ich nach der Welt	c♯-b1	f-f1	Animated, rather florid. (Prout)
Erbarme dich	Cantata 55: Ich armer Mensch, ich Sünden Knecht	f-b♭1	a-f1	Not fast. For the most part sustained. Demands flexibility.
Erfreue dich Seele	Cantata 21: Ich hatte viel Bekümmernis	c-a1	a-f1	Very spirited. De- mands considerable flexibility.
Erwäge, wie sein blutgefärb- ter Rücken	Johannes Passion (St. John Passion)	e-a1	g-f1	Slow. Has florid passages. (Score, GS)
Ewigkeit, du machst mir bange	Cantata 20: O Ewigkeit, du Donner- wort	c-a♭1	g-e♭1	Slow, grave. Has florid middle sec- tion. (Straube)
Frohe Hirten, eilt (Haste, ye shepherds) Recitative: Mein Jesus schweigt (He holds his peace) Air:	Weihnachts Oratorium (Christmas Oratorio)	d-a1	g-e1	Graceful, very florid
Geduld, ge- duld, wenn mich falsche Zungen stechen (Be still, be still)	Matthäus Passion (St. Matthew Passion)	e-a1	a-f1	Slow, quite florid.
Gott, dem der Erdenkreis zu Klein	Cantata 91: Gelobet seist du, Jesus Christ	e-a1	g-e1	Spirited, somewhat declamatory. De- mands flexibility.

TITLE:AIR	TITLE:WORK	COMP.	TESS.	REMARKS
Handle nicht nach deinen Rechten	Cantata 101: Nimm von uns, du treuer Gott	d-ab1	g-e1	Not fast; rather sustained. Demands flexibility.
Hasse nur, hasse mich recht	Cantata 76: Die Himmel erzählen die Ehre Gottes	c-g1	g-e1	Dramatic and vigorous. Has florid passages.
Hebt euer Haupt empor	Cantata 70: Wachet, betet, seid bereit allezeit	c-g1	g-e1	Animated. Demands some flexibility. (Prout)
Ich traue seiner Gnaden	Cantata 97: In allen meinen Thaten	d-ab1	g-eb1	Sustained and grave. Has florid passages.
Ich weiss dass mein Erlöser lebet	Cantata 160: Ich weiss dass mein Erlöser lebet	d-g1	g-e1	Not fast, rather sustained. Demands in parts some flexibility. (Prout)
Ich will leiden	Cantata 87: Bisher habt ihr nichts gebeten in meinem Namen	f-bb1	g-g1	Rather slow. Demands some flexibility. (Straube, also Prout)
Ich will nur dir zu Ehren leben ('Tis thee I would be praising)	Weihnachts Oratorium (Christmas Oratorio)	c-g1	f-d1	Animated, florid.
Ihr Menschen rühmet Gottes Liebe	Cantata 167: Ihr Menschen rühmet Gottes Liebe	d-a1	g-f1	Animated. Has florid passages. (Straube)
Ja tausendmal	Cantata 43: Gott fähret auf mit Jauchzen	d-a1	f#-f#1	Very animated, spirited, and florid.
Jesu lass durch Wohl und Weh (Jesu, paths of weal and woe)	Cantata 182: Himmelskönig sei willkommen	d-g1	f#-e1	For the most part sustained. Has two florid passages. (Whittaker)
Jesus Christus, Gottessohn	Cantata 4: Christ lag in Todesbanden	d#-f#1	e-e1	Very spirited. The vocal line consists of a sustained chorale

TITLE:AIR	TITLE:WORK	COMP.	TESS.	REMARKS
				melody, except the final phrase which is florid. (Prout)
Kann ich nur Jesum mir zum Freunde machen (If my Lord Jesus)	Cantata 105: Herr, gehe nicht ins Gericht	d-a♭1	f-e♭1	Not fast. Demands flexibility. (Whittaker)
Komm, Jesu	Cantata 61: Nun komm, der Heiden Heiland	c-f1	f-d1	Subdued and graceful.
Kommt, eilet!	Cantata 74: Wer mich liebet, der wird mein Wort halten	d-a1	a-f♯1	Rapid and very florid.
Man halte nur ein wenig stille	Cantata 93: Wer nur den lieben Gott lässt walten	d-b♭1	a-f1	Sustained. Has a florid closing passage. (Straube)
Mein alles in Allem, mein ewiges Gut (O treasure of treasures)	Cantata 22: Jesus nahm zu sich die Zwölfe	d-g1	f-d1	Graceful. In parts demands considerable flexibility. (Whittaker)
Meine Seufzer, meine Thränen	Cantata 13: Meine Seufzer, meine Thränen	d-a♭1	g-e1	Sustained, grave. Has one florid passage. (Straube)
Mein Jesus ist erstanden	Cantata 67: Halt' im Gedächtnis Jesum Christ	e-a1	b-g♯1 (b-f♯1)	Spirited. Demands flexibility. The tessitura is very high. (Prout)
Mein Jesus soll mein Alles sein	Cantata 75: Die Elenden sollen essen	d-g1	g-e1	Animated and graceful. (Straube)
Mein liebster Jesus ist verloren	Cantata 154: Mein liebster Jesus ist verloren	f♯-a1	a-f♯1	Sustained. (Prout)
Recitative: Welt, deine Lust Air: Mein Verlangen	Cantata 161: Komm, du süsse Todesstunde	c-g1	f-e1	Very sustained. (Straube)

TITLE:AIR	TITLE:WORK	COMP.	TESS.	REMARKS
Nimm mich dir zu eigen hin	Cantata 65: Sie werden aus Saba alle kommen	d-a1	g-e1	Animated. Has florid passages. (Prout)
Nun mögt ihr stolzen Feinde schrecken (Ye foes of man)	Weihnachts Oratorium (Christmas Oratorio)	d-a1	a-f♯1	Rather vigorous. Demands some flexibility.
O Seelen-paradies	Cantata 172: Erschallet, ihr Lieder	c-g1	g-e1	Sustained. Has some florid passages. (Prout)
Sanfte soll mein Todes-kummer	Oster Orato-rium	c♯-a1	f-f1	Slow, sustained, subdued. Demands some flexibility. (Straube, also Prout)
Seht, was die Liebe thut	Cantata 85: Ich bin ein guter Hird	d-b♭1	a-g1	Not fast; sustained and graceful. (Straube, also Prout)
Recitative: Was Gott den Vätern alter Zeit				
Arioso: Sein Same musste sich so sehr	Cantata 10: Meine Seel' erhebt den Herren	d-g1	a-g1	Recitative and a short sustained arioso.
Stürmt, nur stürmt	Cantata 153: Schau lieber Gott wie meine Feind'	e-a1	g-f1	Vigorous, florid. (Straube)
Tröste mir Jesu mein Gemüte	Cantata 135: Ach Herr, mich armen Sünder	c-a1	g-f1	For the most part sustained. Has a few florid passages. (Prout)
Was des Höchsten Glanz er-füllt	Cantata 194: Höchster-wünschtes Freudenfest	d-g1	f-f1	Not fast; rather florid. Originally written in bass clef, for high baritone. (Prout)
Welch' Über-mass der Gü-te schenkst du mir	Cantata 17: Wer Dank opfert, der preiset mich	d-a1	g-e1	Animated. Has flor-id passages. (Straube, also Prout)

TITLE:AIR	TITLE:WORK	COMP.	TESS.	REMARKS
Ach, soll nicht dieser grosse Tag	Cantata 70: Wachet, betet, seid bereit allezeit	G-f1	c-c1	Majestic, closes with a florid passage.
Ächzen und erbärmlich Weinen	Cantata 13: Meine Seufzer, meine Thränen	G-eb1	eb-c1	Sustained. In parts demands some flexibility.
Am Abend, da es kühle war	Matthäus Passion (St. Matthew Passion)	G-eb1	c-c1	A sustained arioso.
An irdische Schätze	Cantata 26: Ach wie flüchtig, ach wie nichtig	G-e1	d-b	Rather animated. Has florid passages. (Straube)
Auf, auf mit hellem Schall	Cantata 128: Auf Christi Himmelfahrt allein	F#-e1	d-d1	Animated, vigorous. Has florid passages. The final section is a short recitative followed by the instrumental ritornel. (Prout)
Beglückte Herde	Cantata 104: Du Hirte, Israel, höre	F#-d1	B-b	Rather subdued, graceful. Requires flexibility. (Prout, also Straube)
Betrachte meine Seel'	Johannes Passion (St. John Passion)	Bb-eb1	eb-db1	Slow, sustained. (Score, GS)
Darum sollt ihr nicht sorgen	Cantata 187: Es wartet alles auf dich	(G)c-eb1	f-d1	Vigorous, animated. (Prout)
Das Brausen von den rauhen Winden	Cantata 92: Ich hab' in Gottes Herz und Sinn	A-e1	c-c1	Rapid and very florid.
Dein Geburtstag ist erschienen	Cantata 142: Uns ist ein Kind geboren	E-d1	e-c1	Sustained. Demands some flexibility. (Galaxy)
Dein Wetter zog sich auf von Weitem	Cantata 46: Schauet doch und sehet, ob irgend ein Schmerz sei	Bb-e1	eb-c1	Majestic. Has very florid passages. (Straube)

TITLE:AIR	TITLE:WORK	COMP.	TESS.	REMARKS
Doch weichet ihr tollen vergeblichen Sorgen	Cantata 8: Liebster Gott, wann werd' ich sterben	A-e1	e-d1	Animated, grace-ful, quite florid. (Prout)
Eilt, ihr an-gefocht'nen Seelen	Johannes Passion (St. John Passion)	G-e1	c-c1	Animated, florid. With chorus, but could be sung as a solo piece. (Score, GS)
Endlich, endlich	Cantata 56: Ich will den Kreuzstab gerne tragen	G-e1	c-c1	Spirited and florid.
Erleucht auch meine finstre Sin-nen (O Lord, my darkened heart en-lighten)	Weihnachts Oratorium (Christmas Oratorio)	b-e1	e-d1	Not fast. Has many florid passages.
Es ist voll-bracht	Cantata 159: Sehet, wir geh'n hinauf	G-e♭1	d-d1	Sustained. Has some florid passages. (Prout)
Et in Spiritum Sanctum	Mass in B Minor	A-e1	e-c♯1	Not fast. Demands some flexibility. The tessitura is somewhat high.
Fürst des Lebens, starker Streiter (Prince eternal)	Cantata 31: Der Himmel lacht, die Er-de jubilieret	G-d1	c-a	Not fast; florid. (Whit-taker)
Gebt mir meinen Je-sum wieder (Bring him back is all my prayer)	Matthäus Passion (St. Matthew Passion)	G-e1	d-c1	Not slow. Has florid passages.
Recitative: Der Heiland fällt vor sei-nem Vater nieder (The Saviour low before his Fath-er bending)				

TITLE:AIR	TITLE:WORK	COMP.	TESS.	REMARKS
Air:				
Gerne will ich mich be- quemen (Glad- ly would I be enduring)	Matthäus Passion (St. Matthew Passion)	G-eb1	d-c1	Sustained. Demands some flexibility.
Gewaltige stösst Gott vom Stuhl hinunter	Cantata 10: Meine Seel' erhebt den Herren	F-eb1	c-c1	Animated, vigorous, dramatic. Has flor- id passages.
Grosser Herr, und starker König (Mighty Lord and King all Glorious)	Weihnachts Oratorium (Christmas Oratorio)	A-e1	e-d1	Vigorous. Demands some flexibility.
Gute Nacht du Weltge- tümmel	Cantata 27: Wer weiss wie nahe mir mein Ende	G-eb1	d-c1	Grave, sustained. Has florid passages. (Straube, also Prout)
Hat man nicht mit seinen Kin- dern	Cantata 211: Kaffee Canta- ta (Schweiget stille, plaudert nicht)	B-e1	d-d1	Animated, humorous. Demands facile articu- lation and some flexi- bility. (Prout)
Heiligste Dreieinig- keit Recitative: Ach unser Wille bleibt verkehrt	Cantata 172: Erschallet ihr Lieder	G-d1	c-c1	Majestic. Demands some flexibility. (Prout)
Air:				
Herr, so du willst	Cantata 73: Herr, wie du willst, so schick's mit mir	G-eb1	eb-d1	Recitative and a sus- tained, grave air. (Prout)
Hier, in meines Va- ters Stätte	Cantata 32: Liebster Jesu, mein Verlan- gen	G-e1	e-c1	Slow and sustained. Demands some flexi- bility. (Prout)
Hier ist das rechte Osterlamm	Cantata 4: Christ lag in Todes- banden	E-e1	e-b	Slow, grave, and sus- tained. Has a very majestic, vigorous ending.

TITLE:AIR	TITLE:WORK	COMP.	TESS.	REMARKS
Höllische Schlange, wird dir nicht bange	Cantata 40: Dazu ist er- schienen der Sohn Gottes	G-e1	d-c1	Vigorous. (Straube)
Ich freue mich auf meinen Tod	Cantata 82: Ich habe ge- nug	G-e♭1	B-b	Very animated. Has florid passages.
Ich habe ge- nug	Cantata 82: Ich habe ge- nug	G-e♭1	f-c1	Sustained, grave. Demands some flexi- bility. (Straube)
Ich will den Kreuzstab	Cantata 56: Ich will den Kreuzstab gerne tragen	G-e1	e-c1	Fairly sustained. Demands some flexi- bility. (Prout)
Arioso: Ihr Klein- gläubigen Air: Schweig, schweig	Cantata 81: Jesus schläft, was soll ich hoffen?	G-e1	c-c1	Grave arioso followed by a fast, vigorous air. (Prout, also Straube)
Ja, ja, ich kann die Feinde schlagen	Cantata 57: Selig ist der Mann	G-e♭1	e-c1	Animated, vigorous. Demands flexibility. (Prout)
Johannis freudenvol- les Springen (John filled with joy) Recitative: Ja! freilich will in mir (In truth, to bear the cross) Air: Komm süs- ses Kreuz (Come, heal- ing cross)	Cantata 121: Christum wir sollen loben schon

Matthäus Passion (St. Matthew Passion) | G-e1

A-e1 | c-c1

d-d1 | Spirited, quite florid. (Whittaker)

Slow, quite florid. |
| Lasset dem Höchsten | Cantata 66: Erfreut euch, ihr Herzen! | A-e1 | d-c1 | Vigorous, animated. Has florid passages. (Straube) |

TITLE:AIR	TITLE:WORK	COMP.	TESS.	REMARKS
Mache dich mein Herze rein (Make thee clean my heart from sin)	Matthäus Passion (St. Matthew Passion)	A-eb1	c-c1	Sustained. Demands some flexibility.
Meinen Jesum lass' ich nicht (Never Jesus will I leave)	Cantata 98: Was Gott thut, das ist wohlgetan	A-eb1	eb-c1	Animated, rather vigorous. Demands considerable flexibility. (Whittaker)
Mein Erlöser und Erhalter	Cantata 69: Lobe den Herrn, meine Seele	A-e1	e-b	Rather grave and sustained. Has some florid passages.
Merke mein Herze beständig nur dies	Cantata 145: So du mit deinem Munde	A-e1	d-d1	Animated. In parts quite florid. (Prout)
Mit Verlangen	Phoebus und Pan	B-f#1	e-e1	Sustained. Has florid passages. (Prout)
O Menschen, die ihr täglich sündigt (We mortals)	Cantata 122: Das Neugebor'ne Kindelein	(G)c-eb1	c-c1	Vigorous. Has florid passages. (Whittaker)
Quia fecit mihi magna (Latin text)	Magnificat in D Major	G#-d#1	c#-c#1	Not fast, rather florid.
Quoniam tu solus sanctus (Latin text)	Mass in B Minor	G#-e1	B-b	Slow. Has florid passages.
Schlummert ein	Cantata 82: Ich habe genug	Bb-eb1	c-c1	Rather slow, sustained and subdued. (Prout)
Selig ist der Mann	Cantata 57: Selig ist der Mann	G-eb1	e-c1	Slow and very sustained. Has one florid passage.
Seligster Erquickungstag	Cantata 70: Wachet, betet, seid bereit allezeit	G-d1	c-c1	Slow and rather sustained at the beginning and end. Rapid and florid middle section. (Prout, also Straube)

175

TITLE:AIR	TITLE:WORK	COMP.	TESS.	REMARKS
So löschet im Eifer	Cantata 90: Es reifet euch ein schreck-lich Ende	B♭-e♭1	d-b	Vigorous and majes-tic. Demands flexi-bility.
Recitative: Siehe, siehe, ich komme				
Air: Starkes Lieben (Great thy love, Lord)	Cantata 182: Himmels-könig, sei Wilkommen	E-c1	c-b	Not fast. Demands flexibility. (Whit-taker)
Tag und Nacht	Cantata 71: Gott ist mein König	F-e1	c-c1	Slow, sustained. Has florid middle section.
Verachtest du den Reichtum seiner Gnade	Cantata 102: Herr, deine Augen sehen nach dem Glauben	G-e♭1	e♭-c1	Spirited. (Prout)
Verstumme, Höllenheer	Cantata 5: Wo soll ich fliehen hin	A-e1	d-d1	Animated, vigorous. Demands some flexi-bility. (Prout)
Wacht auf ihr Adern und ihr Glieder	Cantata 110: Unser Mund sei voll La-chen	F♯-e1	d-d1	Vigorous. In parts quite florid. (Prout)
Wacht auf	Cantata 20: O Ewigkeit, du Donner-wort	G-e1	c-d1	Majestic, vigorous. Has florid passages. (Prout)
Wahrlich, ich sage euch	Cantata 86: Wahrlich, ich sage euch	G-d1	d-b	Majestic, rather vigorous.
Was Gott thut	Cantata 100: Was Gott thut, das ist wohl-gethan	A-e1	e-c1	Animated. Has florid passages.
Weicht all', ihr Übel-täter	Cantata 135: Ach Herr, mich armen Sünder	A-e1	d-d1	Animated, vigorous. Has rather unusual florid passages. (Prout)
Wie will ich lustig lachen (How jovial is my laughter)	Cantata 205: Der Zufrie-dengestellte Aeolus	F♯-f♯1	e-e1	Spirited, vigorous, florid. In the Oxford edition, transposed one tone lower. (Whittaker)

SONGS

Edition: Breitkopf & Härtel

TITLE	COMP.	TESS.	TYPE	REMARKS
Bist du bei mir	d1-ab2	ab1-f2	All voices	Sustained. (gen. av.)
Dir, dir Jehova	f1-g2	a1-eb2	Not too suitable for very light voices	Majestic, vigorous.
Es ist vollbracht	d1-f#2	f#1-d2	All voices	Sustained, grave.
Komm, süsser Tod	c1-g2	g1-eb2	Not too suitable for very light voices	Slow and sustained; grave. (gen. av.)
Liebster Herr Jesu	g1-f2	a1-d2	All voices	Sustained.
Meine Seele, lass es gehen	f1-ab2	ab1-g2	All voices	Slow and sustained.
So oft ich meine Tabakspfeife	d1-f2	g1-d2	Most suitable for men's voices	Humorous, sustained.
Vergiss mein nicht	d#1-g2	a1-f2	All voices	Very slow and sustained; grave.
Willst du dein Herz mir schenken	d1-g2	g1-eb2	All voices	Sustained. Demands in parts considerable flexibility.

GEORGE FREDERICK HANDEL
(1685-1759)

Handel's songs and airs are perhaps more frequently performed now than the vocal music of any of his contemporaries, including Bach. One of the main reasons for this popularity, aside from the magnificent nature of Handel's music, is the fact that Handel's manner of writing for the voice is so extraordinarily considerate of the singer. Even his most difficult display pieces, written for the famed vocal virtuosi of his time and demanding optimum vocal endowment as well as a maximum of control, are never vocally awkward. His idiom is largely diatonic in character, and is thus extremely well suited to the human voice, as well as easily comprehended by the listener. Employing the flatteringly vocal manner of writing of his Italian contemporaries, and as aware of the limitations and possibilities of each type of voice as any servile hack composer of his period, Handel, with a truly miraculous sense of balance, perhaps not possessed by any composer save Mozart, nonetheless never permitted this manner or this awareness to influence the content of his vocal music.

Thus it is not surprising that Handel's songs and airs are seemingly as satisfying to the singer and the listener of today as they were to the singer and the listener of some two hundred years ago.

Since Handel wrote magnificently for all types of voice, from bass to coloratura soprano, and since he wrote in every conceivable manner, from extremely florid display pieces to sustained airs of inconceivable majesty and nobility, it would seem superfluous to attempt to formulate any general suggestions pertaining to the performance of his vocal music. Every singer at any stage of development, will be able to find at least a few of Handel's songs and airs suitable to his type of voice and singing.

As most of Handel's Italian operas are now forgotten, being dramatically too static for present-day audiences, the airs extracted from them can now be easily performed by voices other than those for which they were originally intended. The peculiarly apt and adroit manner of writing for the voice in which Handel excelled makes many of his Italian tenor airs suitable for performance by soprano voices, and many of his bass and baritone airs suitable for performance by alto and mezzo-soprano voices, as well as vice versa. Natually the characteristics of each individual air and voice will have to be taken into account when considering such a procedure. It would also seem advisable to mention the fact that many of his airs are suitable for all types of voices, if transposed.

The number of editions in which Handel's Italian airs are available is so great that anything approaching a bibliographical survey even in a most limited sense of the word would comprise several hundred entries.

The editions mentioned below are by no means the only ones in which the airs listed can be obtained. In the opinion of this writer, however, the editions referred to in the list below are either the most accurate or the most easily available.

The famous English oratorios are of course generally available in piano scores in a variety of editions. The mention of publishers in the lists devoted to airs with English text is intended only as a matter of convenience, since, for all practical purposes nearly all of these airs could be classed generally available.

Bibliography

The name in parentheses indicates one of the following collections:

Best: Fifty Arias by Handel, edited by Best, published by Boosey and Hawkes.
B & H: Handel Arias, published by Breitkopf & Härtel.
Jeppesen: La Flora, 3 volumes, edited by K. Jeppesen, published by W. Hansen.
Kagen: Forty-five Arias by Handel, edited by S. Kagen, published by International Music Co. (high and low).
Prout: Handel Songs and Airs, 2 volumes, edited by Dr. E. Prout, published by O. Ditson (high and low).
Whittaker: Arias from Handel's Italian Operas, edited by Whittaker, published by Oxford University Press.
Wolff: Eight Handel Arias for Bass, edited by E. V. Wolff, published by Music Press.

There are numerous other collections. Most of the famous airs are now available in a variety of editions in transposed keys, to suit almost all types of voice (see the catalogues of Ashdown, Ltd., and Augener, London). An excellent collection of Handel's airs with English text only, edited by Ford, is now published by Boosey in seven volumes, each containing airs for one type of voice only, such as dramatic soprano, light soprano, bass, baritone, and so on.

Since Handel wrote within a rather uniform compass and tessitura for each of the four main types of voice, and since the character

of each air, as described in the remarks seems sufficient to indicate
the type of voice for which the air is possibly best suited, it seemed
best to dispense with the type of voice statement in the following lists.
Note: the title of the opera or oratorio is placed above the title of the
air.

ITALIAN TEXT

Soprano

TITLE	COMP.	TESS.	REMARKS
Admeto Luci care	e♭1-g2	g1-e♭2	Slow, sustained. (Prout)
Admeto Quanto godrà	e1-g2	a1-f2	Spirited. Has florid passages. (Best)
Admeto Spera, si	c1-g2	f1-d♭2	Not fast. Demands some flexibility. (Best)
Agrippina Bel piacere	d♭1-g♭2	g♭1-e♭2	Graceful. Demands lightness of tone and some flexibility. Has a very interesting rhythmic pattern. (Kagen)
Agrippina Ogni vento	d1-g2	f♯1-d2	Spirited. Demands some flexibility. (Best)
Alcina Ah! Mio cor	f1-a♭2	b♭1-g2	Sustained, somewhat declamatory. Has a spirited middle section. This air is published in the Parisotti collection, transposed a fourth lower, with the middle section omitted. (Best)
Alcina Ama, sospira	e1-a2	a1-g2	Not fast, graceful. Very high tessitura. (Jeppesen)
Alcina Mi restano le lagrime	e♯1-a2	a1-f♯2	Sustained, graceful. Most suitable for a light voice. (Best)

180

TITLE	COMP.	TESS.	REMARKS
Alcina			
Un momento di contento	e1-g♯2	g♯1-e2	Animated, florid, graceful. (Jeppesen)
Alessandro			
Recitative:			
Ne trionfa d'Alessandro			
Air:			
Lusinghe più care	d1-g2	g1-d2	Florid, spirited. (gen. av.)
Amadigi			
Gioje, venite in sen	e♭1-a♭2	g1-e♭2	A graceful, rather slow Siciliana. Has florid passages. (Whittaker)
Atalanta			
Care selve	f♯1-a2	a1-f♯2	Slow, very sustained. (Kagen)
Atalanta			
Riportai, gloriosa palma	e1-a2	a1-e2	Spirited, vigorous. Has florid passages. (Best)
Deidamia			
Se pensi amor tu solo	f♯1-a2	b1-g2	Animated. Has florid passages. Best for light voice. (Best)
Floridante			
Amor comanda	f1-b♭2	b♭1-f2	Animated. In parts florid. (Kagen)
Giulio Cesare			
Da tempeste	d♯1-a2	e1-e2	Spirited. Quite florid. (Best)
Giulio Cesare			
Recitative:			
E pur così in un giorno			
Air:			
Piangerò la sorte mia	e1-a2	g♯-e1	A very sustained air with a spirited, florid middle section. (Kagen)
Giulio Cesare			
Se pietà di me non senti	e1-a2	a1-f♯2	Slow, sustained. Demands some flexibility. Optional for tenor. (Arr. by S. Endicott. ROW)

181

TITLE	COMP. TESS.		REMARKS

Giulio Cesare
V'adoro, pupille saette d'amore — f1-g2 — a1-f2 — Slow, sustained. Demands in parts some flexibility. (Best)

TITLE	COMP.	TESS.	REMARKS
Giulio Cesare			
V'adoro, pupille saette d'amore	f1-g2	a1-f2	Slow, sustained. Demands in parts some flexibility. (Best)
Ottone			
Affanni del pensier	eb1-ab2	ab1-eb2	Slow, graceful, sustained. Demands some flexibility. (Parisotti; Best)
Ottone			
O grati orrori	f1-a2	g1-f2	Scena and graceful air. Demands some flexibility. (Arr. by Wintter Watts. RIC)
Ottone Recitative: Ben a ragion Air: Vieni o figlio	d#1-f#2 (g#2)	same	Sustained. Optional for alto. (Arr. by F. Bibb. GS)
Partenope			
Qual farfaletta	e1-a2	a1-f#2	Animated, graceful. Quite florid. Best for light voices. (gen. av.)
Radamisto			
Quel nave smarrita	c#1-g2	f#1-d2	Slow, rather vigorous. Demands some flexibility. (Best; Prout)
Radamisto			
Sommi Dei	g1-a2	g1-e2	Majestic, declamatory, grave. Best for dramatic soprano. (Kagen)
Rinaldo Recitative: Armida, dispietata Air: Lascia ch'io pianga	f1-g2	a1-f2	Very sustained. Best for dramatic soprano. Optional for alto. (Kagen)
Rinaldo			
Parolette, vezzi e sguardi	e1-a2	g1-g2	Animated, quite florid. (Jeppesen)
Rinaldo			
Vò far guerra	d1-g2	f#1-d2	Spirited, vigorous. Has florid passages. Optional for tenor. (Kagen)

182

TITLE	COMP.	TESS.	REMARKS
Rodelinda Ho perduta il caro sposo	e♭1-a♭2	g1-e♭2	Slow and sustained. Demands some flexibility. (Whittaker)
Rodelinda L'empio rigor del fato	d1-b♭2	b♭1-g2	Animated, spirited. Has florid passages. Best for light voice. (Whittaker)
Rodelinda Mio caro bene	f♯1-a2	a1-e2	Animated, spirited. Has florid passages. Best for light voice. (Whittaker)
Rodelinda Morrai si	d♯1-g♯2	g♯1-e2	Vigorous, spirited. Has florid passages. (Best)
Rodelinda Ombre, piante	f♯1-a2	b1-f♯2	Slow, sustained. Demands some flexibility. (Whittaker)
Rodelinda Ritorna, oh caro	g1-a2	a1-e2	Sustained. (Whittaker)
Rodelinda Spietati io vi giurai	f1-a♭2	a1-f2	Spirited. Demands some flexibility. (Best)
Serse Caro voi siete	e1-a2	a1-e2	Sustained, graceful, high tessitura. Rather short. (Jeppesen).
Serse Di tacere e di schernirmi	d1-g2	g1-e2	Sustained. Has florid passages. (Jeppesen)
Serse Dirà che amor per me	f1-a2	a1-e2	Animated, graceful. Demands facile articulation and some flexibility. (Whittaker)
Serse Ne men con l'ombre	e1-a2	g♯1-e2	Delicate, quite florid. Demands some flexibility. Rather short. (Jeppesen)
Serse Và godendo vez- zoso e bello	e1-a2	a1-e2	Animated, graceful, florid. Best for light voice. (Kagen)
Serse Voi mi dite	f1-g2	g1-f2	Sustained, rather short. Optional for tenor. (Jeppesen)

TITLE	COMP.	TESS.	REMARKS
Siroe Ch'io mai vi possa	d#1-g2	g1-e2	Animated. Has florid passages. (Kagen)
Siroe Mi lagnero tacendo	f-a2	a1-f2	Graceful, sustained. (Best)
Siroe Recitative: Si diversi sembianti Air: Non vi piacque	e1-g#2	g#1-e2	Slow, somewhat florid. (Best)
Sosarme Recitative: Rasserena, o madre Air: Rend'il sereno al ciglio	f#1-g#2	g#1-e2	Slow, sustained. (Kagen)
Tamerlano Cor di padre	d1-a2	g1-e2	Slow, grave, somewhat declamatory. Demands some flexibility. (Whittaker)
Tamerlano Deh! Lasciatemi	e#1-g#2	a1-f#2	Slow, quite florid. Demands some flexibility. (Jeppesen)
Tamerlano Par che mi nasca in seno	e1-g2	g1-e2	Sustained, graceful. Demands some flexibility. (Whittaker)
Teseo Vieni, torna idol mio	d1-f2	a1-d2	Not fast; graceful. (Whittaker)
Tolomeo Voi dolce surette al cor	d1-g2	g1-e2	Graceful. Demands some flexibility. <u>Best for light voice.</u> (Arr. by Frank Bibb. GS)

Mezzo-soprano or Alto

TITLE	COMP.	TESS.	REMARKS
Admeto Cangiò d'aspetto	a-d2	d1-b1	Animated, graceful. Has florid passages. (Kagen)

TITLE	COMP.	TESS.	REMARKS
Alcina La bocca vaga	b-e2	e1-c#2	Graceful. (B & H)
Alcina Verdi prati	c#1-e2	e1-c#2	Slow and very sustained. (Kagen)
Amadigi Ah! Spietato!	b-d2	e1-c2	Very sustained. <u>Optional for baritone</u>. (Kagen)
Amadigi O rendetemi il mio bene	c#1-eb2	f1-d2	Slow, grave. <u>Optional for baritone</u>. (Whittaker)
Amadigi Recitative: D'un sventurato amante Air: Pena tiranna	c1-eb2	e1-c2	Vigorous, majestic. (Kagen)
Amadigi Tu mia speranza	b-d2	d1-b1	Animated. Demands some flexibility. (Prout)
Arminio Vado a morir	d1-eb2	eb1-bb1	Slow, sustained, grave. <u>Option- al for baritone</u>. (Whittaker)
Atalanta Ben'io sento l'ingrata	b-db2	d1-c2	Not fast; vigorous. Has florid passages. (Whittaker)
Atalanta Come alla tortorella	b-e2	e1-c#2	Sustained, somewhat subdued. Demands some flexibility. (Whittaker)
Atalanta Soffri in pace	bb-eb2	eb1-c2	Sustained, graceful. Has florid passages. (Whittaker)
Berenice No! Soffrir non può il mio amore	c1-e2	same	Sustained. Demands some flexibility. <u>Optional for bass</u>. (Wolff)
Berenice Si tra i ceppi	b-d2	c1-c2	Spirited. Has florid passages. <u>Optional for bass</u>. (Kagen)

TITLE	COMP.	TESS.	REMARKS
Ezio Quanto mai felici siete	c#1-d2	e1-b1	Animated. Has florid passages. (Best)
Faramondo Sento che un giusto sdegno	bb-f2	eb1-c2	Animated. Has florid passages. (Whittaker)
Flavio Chi può mirare	g-eb2	c1-c2	Animated. Demands some flexibility. (B & H)
Flavio L'armellin' vita non cura	b-e2	e1-c#2	Animated. Demands considerable flexibility. (Best)
Flavio O Amor! Nel mio penar	bb-db2	db1-bb1	Very sustained. (B & H)
Floridante Alma mia	c#1-e2	d1-d2	Sustained, graceful. Optional for baritone. (Kagen)
Floridante Se dolce m'era già	b-eb2	eb1-c2	Graceful. Demands some flexibility. (B & H)
Lotario Già mi sembra	a-e2	e1-c2	Vigorous, spirited. Demands some flexibility. (Prout)
Lotario Per salvarti idol mio	b-d2	d#1-b1	Not fast; sustained. Has florid passages. (Best)
Muzio Scevola Volate più dei venti	a-f2	f1-d2	Animated, vigorous. Demands some flexibility. Has slow, sustained middle section. Optional for bass. (Wolff)
Orlando Vaghe pupille, no non piangete	a-d2	d1-bb1	In three sections; allegretto, larghetto on a basso ostinato, and a somewhat florid allegro. (Best)
Ottone Ah! Tu non sai	c1-d2	e1-c2	Slow, graceful, delicate. (Kagen)
Ottone Recitative: Ben a ragion			

TITLE	COMP.	TESS.	REMARKS
Air: Vieni o figlio	d#1-f#2 (g#2)	same	Sustained. Optional for so- prano. (Arr. by F. Bibb. GS)
Partenope Furibondo spira il vento	b-e2	e1-d2	Rapid, florid, vigorous. Optional for baritone. (Kagen)
Poro Che vive amante	c1-d2	e1-c2	Animated, graceful. (Ashdown)
Poro E prezzo leggiero	a-d2 (eb2)	d1-c2	Spirited. Has florid passages. (Prout)
Radamisto Ombra cara	c1-e2	d1-b1	Very sustained. Optional for tenor. A minor third higher, though Prout collection lists it as for alto. (Kagen)
Radamisto Perfido, di a quell'empio	bb-eb2	eb-c2	Animated, vigorous. Has flor- id passages. Optional for bass. (Wolff)
Radamisto Quando mai spietata	db1-eb2	eb1-c2	Slow, sustained. Demands some flexibility. (Best)
Rinaldo Cara sposa	b-e2	e1-c2	A very sustained andante; mid- dle section is an allegro which demands facile articulation. (Prout)
Rinaldo Recitative: Armida, dispi- etata Air: Lascia ch'io pianga	f1-g2	a1-f2	Very sustained. Optional for dramatic soprano. (Kagen)
Rodelinda Con rauco mor- morio	bb-d1	eb1-c2	Graceful, sustained. Optional for baritone. (Kagen)
Rodelinda Recitative: Pompe vane di morte Air: Dove sei?	b-e2	e1-b1	An extended recitative and a slow, sustained air. (Best, also Prout, Kagen without the recitative)

TITLE	COMP.	TESS.	REMARKS
Rodelinda Scacciata dal suo nido	bb-eb2	eb1-c2	Animated. In parts quite florid. <u>Optional for bass.</u> (Wolff)
Scipione Recitative: Nulla temer Air: Generoso, chi sol brama	b-d♯2	e1-b1	Recitative and a sustained air. Demands some flexibility. (Kagen)
Scipione Ombra cara	c1-e2	d1-c2	Very sustained. (Kagen)
Scipione Pensa, oh bella	a-d2	c1-c2	Graceful, rather florid. <u>Optional for baritone.</u> (Whittaker)
Scipione Recitative: Quando timor costate Air: Son pellegrino	b-d2	e1-c♯2	Not fast. Has florid passages. (B & H)
Scipione Tutta raccolta ancor	a-f2	e1-c2	Grave, sustained. <u>Optional for bass.</u> (Kagen) Also now widely known as "Hear Me, Ye Winds and Waves" with an added recitative from Julius Caesar. (BH)
Serse Non so se sia la speme	d1-e2	e1-c2	Slow. Demands some flexibility. (Best)
Siroe Recitative: Son stanco ingiusti numi Air: Deggio morire, o stelle	bb-eb2	f1-db2	Slow, grave. (B & H)

Tamerlano
Recitative:
  Il Tartaro ama
  Asteria
Air:
  Bella Asteria | a-d2 | c1-c2 | Sustained. In parts quite florid. Demands some flexibility. (Jeppesen)

Teseo
Più non cerca
  libertà | c1-d2 | f1-c2 | Animated, graceful. Demands some flexibility. (B & H)

Teseo
Ricordati, oh
  bella | b-d2 | d1-b1 | Not slow. Demands some flexibility. Optional for baritone. (Whittaker)

Tolomeo
Recitative:
  Inumano fratel
Air:
  Stille amare | bb-db2 | f1-c2 | A dramatic recitative and a very sustained, grave air. (Kagen)

Tenor

Alcina
Semplicetto! A
  donna credi? | e-g1 | g-f1 | Spirited, graceful. Has florid passages. (Prout)

Alcina
Un momento di
  contento | e1-g#2 | g#1-e2 | Animated, florid, graceful. (Jeppesen)

Atalanta
Dì ad Irene | d-ab | g-eb1 | Spirited. Has florid passages. (Prout)

Atalanta
Lascia ch'io
  parta solo | e-bb1 | g-f1 | Sustained. Has florid passages. (Whittaker)

Atalanta
M'allontano | d-g1 | f-eb1 | Not fast. Has florid passages. (Whittaker)

Atalanta
S'è tuo piacer
  ch'io mora | e-a1 | f#-d1 | Sustained. (Whittaker)

TITLE	COMP.	TESS.	REMARKS
Deidamia Due bell'alme	f-bb1	a-f1	Sustained. (Best)
Giulio Cesare Se pietà di me non senti	e1-a2	a1-f#2	Slow, sustained. Demands some flexibility. <u>Optional for soprano</u>. (Arr. by S. Endicott. ROW)
Radamisto Cara sposa, amato bene	e-f#1	f#-e1	Slow, sustained. (Kagen)
Radamisto Ombra cara	eb-g1	f-d1	Very sustained. (Kagen)
Rinaldo Vò far guerra	d-g1	f#-d1	Spirited, vigorous. Has florid passages. <u>Optional for soprano</u>. (Kagen)
Rodelinda Recitative: Fatto inferno Air: Pastorello d'un povero Armento	d-g1	g-d1	Sustained, graceful. (Whittaker)
Rodelinda Prigioniera, ho l'alma in pena	e-a1	g#-e1	Animated. Has florid passages. (Best)
Rodrigo Allor che sorge astro lucente	d-g1	f#-d1	Sustained. Demands some flexibility. (Best)
Serse Recitative: Frondi tenere e belle Air: Ombra mai fu	c1-f2	f1-d2	Very slow and sustained. <u>Optional for all voices except a very light soprano</u>. (Kagen)
Serse Quella che tutta fe	c1-f2	e1-db2	A sustained Siciliana. Rather short. (Jeppesen)
Serse Voi mi dite	f1-g2	g1-f2	Sustained, rather short. (Jeppesen)

TITLE	COMP.	TESS.	REMARKS

Tamerlano
A sui piedi padre

(a♯)d-g1 (a1) e-e1 — Vigorous, sustained. (Whittaker)

Tamerlano
Recitative:
  E il soffrirete
Air:
  Empio, per farti guerra

c-a1 f-eb1 — Animated, vigorous, dramatic. Has some florid passages. (Whittaker)

Tamerlano
Recitative:
  Si figlia, io moro
Air:
  Figlia mia, non pianger, no

eb-ab1 g-eb1 — Declamatory, dramatic. (Whittaker)

Tamerlano
Forte e lieto a morte andrei

d-a1 g-f♯1 — Not fast; vigorous. Has florid passages. (Whittaker)

Tamerlano
No, il tuo sdegno mi placo

c♯-g1 a-e1 — Vigorous. Has florid passages. (Whittaker)

Baritone or Bass

Admeto
Signor lo credi a me

A-e1 d-c1 — Animated, vigorous. Has florid passages. (Best)

Agrippina
Io di Roma il Giove sono

G-e1 d-c1 — Vigorous. Has florid passages. (Best)

Agrippina
Se ben nemica sorte Col raggio placido

G-eb1 c-c1 — Vigorous, spirited. Has florid passages. (GS)

Amadigi
Ah! Spietato!

B-d1 e-c1 — Very sustained. Optional for alto. (Kagen)

Amadigi
O rendetemi il mio bene

c♯-eb1 f-d1 — Slow, grave. Optional for alto. (Whittaker)

TITLE	COMP.	TESS.	REMARKS

Amadigi
Recitative:
 D'un sventurato
 amante
Air:

Pena tiranna	c-eb1	e-c1	Sustained. Optional for alto. (Kagen)

Ariodante

Al sen ti stringo e parto	G#-e1	c#-c#1	Sustained, graceful. (Prout)

Arminio

Vado a morir	d-eb1	eb-bb	Slow, sustained, grave. Optional for alto. (Whittaker)

Berenice
Recitative:
 No, soffrir non può
Air:

Il mio amore	c-e1	same	Sustained. Demands some flexibility. Optional for alto. (Wolff)

Berenice

Si tra i ceppi	B-d1	c-c1	Spirited. Has florid passages. Optional for alto. (Kagen)

Deidamia

Nel riposo e nel contento	G-d1	Bb-c1	Slow, sustained, subdued. Demands some flexibility. (Prout)

Ezio

Nasce al bosco	(F)A-f1	c-c1	Vigorous, stately. Has florid passages. (Kagen)

Ezio

Se un bell'ardire	G-e1	c-c1	Vigorous, spirited. Has florid passages. (Prout)

Ezio

Tutta raccolta ancor	d-f1	g-c1	Vigorous, short. (Kagen)

Floridante

Alma mia	C#-e1	d-d1	Sustained, graceful. Optional for alto. (Kagen)

Floridante

Finchè lo strale	Bb-f1	eb-eb1	Vigorous, spirited. Has florid passages. (Kagen)

TITLE	COMP.	TESS.	REMARKS
Floridante Non lasciar	B♭-f1	e♭-e♭1	Spirited, vigorous. Has florid passages. (Prout)
Giulio Cesare Dal fulgor di questa spada	B♭-f1	d-d1	Spirited, vigorous, quite florid. (Prout)
Muzio Scevola Volate piu dei venti	A-f1	f-d1	Animated, vigorous, with a slow, sustained middle section. Demands some flexibility. Optional for alto. (Wolff)
Orlando Lascia amor	A-e♭1	d-d1	Vigorous. Has florid passages. (Ashdown)
Orlando Sorge infausta	G-e♭1	e♭-c1	Vigorous, spirited. Has florid passages. (Prout)
Ottone Del minacciar del vento	A-f1	d-d1	Vigorous, spirited. Has florid passages. (Kagen)
Partenope Furibondo spira il vento	B-e1	e-d1	Rapid, florid, vigorous. Optional for alto. (Kagen)
Radamisto Perfido, di a quell'empio	B♭-e♭1	e♭-c1	Animated, vigorous. Has florid passages. Optional for alto. (Wolff)
Riccardo Nel mondo e nell'abisso	G-f1	d♭-e♭1	Vigorous, animated. Has florid passages. (Best)
Rinaldo Il tricerbero umiliato	A-f1	c-c1	Vigorous, spirited. Has florid passages. (Best)
Rodelinda Con rauco mormorio	B♭-d1	d-b♭	A sustained Siciliana. Optional for alto. (Kagen)
Rodelinda Confusa si miri	B-d1	c♯-c♯1	Animated, vigorous. Has florid passages. (Whittaker)

TITLE	COMP.	TESS.	REMARKS
Rodelinda Di cupido impiego	Bb-f1	eb-eb1	Spirited, vigorous. Has florid passages. (Whittaker)
Rodelinda Scacciata dal suo nido	Bb-eb1	eb-c1	Animated. In parts quite florid. Optional for alto. (Wolff)
Scipione Pensa, oh bella	A-d1	c-c1	Graceful, rather florid. Optional for alto. (Whittaker)
Scipione Tutta raccolta ancor	A-f1	e-c1	Grave, sustained. Optional for alto. (Kagen) Also now widely known as "Hear Me, Ye Winds and Waves" with an added recitative from Julius Caesar. (BH)
Serse Del mio caro Bacco amabile	G-e1	e-c1	A spirited drinking song. Demands some flexibility. (Best)
Siroe Gelido, in ogni vena	E-f#1	f#-c#1	Slow, sustained. (Best)

Tamerlano
Recitative:
  Il Tartaro ama
  Asteria
Air:
  Bella Asteria
	A-d1	c-c1	Sustained. In parts quite florid. (Jeppesen)

Teseo Ricordati, oh bella	B-d1	d-b	Not slow. Demands some flexibility. Optional for alto. (Whittaker)

Tolomeo
Recitative:
  Inumano fratel
Air:
  Stille amare
	Bb-db1	eb-c1	A dramatic recitative and a very sustained, grave air. Optional for alto. (Wolff)

Soprano

TITLE	COMP.	TESS.	REMARKS
Acis and Galatea As when the dove laments her love	d1-g2	a1-f2	Graceful, delicate. Demands some flexibility and good command of pianissimo. (Kagen)
Acis and Galatea Would you gain the tender creature	e1-g2	a1-f2	Animated, graceful. Optional for tenor. (Prout)
Alexander Balus Recitative: Calm thou my soul Air: Convey me to some peaceful shore	d#1-f#2	f#1-d#2	Sustained. (Prout)
Alexander Balus Here amid the shady woods	d1-f2	f1-e2	Sustained, graceful. (Prout)
Alexander Balus Subtle love, with fancy viewing	e1-f#2	f#1-e2	Not fast; quite florid. (GS)
Athalia Will God, whose mercies ever flow	f1-ab2	g1-f2	Sustained. Demands some flexibility. (Prout)
Esther Hallelujah	e1-a2	g1-f2	Rapid and very florid. (Kagen)
Hercules My father! Ah, methinks I see	c1-f2	f1-eb2	Slow, sustained, somewhat declamatory. Suitable for either dramatic or lyric soprano. (Prout)
Hercules Recitative: O Hercules! Why art thou absent Air: The world when day's career is run	c1-g2	f#1-d2	Slow, sustained. Demands some flexibility. (Score, gen. av.)

TITLE	COMP.	TESS.	REMARKS
Jephtha Farewell ye limpid spring and floods	d♯1-g2	f♯1-e2	Sustained. (Prout)
Jephtha The smiling dawn of happier days	c1-a♭2	g1-e♭2	Animated, graceful. Demands some flexibility. (Score, NOV)

Jephtha
Recitative:
  Deeper and
  deeper still
Air:
  Waft her, angels, to the skies
	d1-a2	g1-g2	A scena and a rather slow, somewhat florid air. <u>Optional for tenor.</u> (Kagen)

Joshua Hark! 'Tis the linnet	d1-g2	f♯1-e2	Animated, graceful, rather florid. (Score, NOV)
Joshua O had I Jubal's lyre	d♯1-f♯2	g♯1-e2	Spirited; quite florid. (gen. av.)
Judas Maccabaeus Come, ever smiling liberty	e1-a2	a1-e2	Graceful. Demands some flexibility. (gen. av.)

Judas Maccabaeus
Recitative:
  O let eternal honours crown his name
Air:
  From mighty kings he took the spoil
	d1-a2	g♯1-e2	Florid; not fast. The middle section is spirited. (gen. av.)

Judas Maccabaeus
Recitative:
  To heaven's almighty King we kneel
Air:
  O liberty! Thou choicest treasure
	d♯1-f♯2	f♯1-e2	Slow, sustained. Demands some flexibility. <u>Optional for mezzo-soprano.</u> <u>Usually sung by tenor.</u> (gen. av.)

Judas Maccabaeus Pious orgies	d1-g2	g1-e2	Slow, sustained. Originally written for bass (B♭-e♭1; e♭-c1), (gen. av.)

TITLE	COMP.	TESS.	REMARKS
Judas Maccabaeus So shall the lute and harp awake	d1-g2	g1-eb2	Spirited, light, florid. (Kagen)
Judas Maccabaeus Wise men, flatt'ring, may deceive you	d1-a2	f1-f2	Graceful, sustained. (gen. av.)
L'Allegro But o, sad virgin	d#1-a2	f#1-f#2	Slow, in parts very florid. Demands good command of short trills. Best for light voices. (Score, NOV)
L'Allegro Come, come, thou goddess fair and free	f1-bb2	a1-f2	Animated. Demands some flexibility. (Score, NOV)
L'Allegro Hide me from day's garish eye	f1-ab2	ab1-f2	Slow, sustained, subdued. (Prout)
L'Allegro Let me wander not unseen	d1-g2	a1-f2	A graceful, sustained, subdued Siciliana. <u>Optional for tenor.</u> Often sung together with "Or Let the Merry Bells Ring Round" from L'Allegro, which air is in the same key and follows nicely as a sort of contrasting movement. (Kagen)
L'Allegro Oft on a plat of rising ground	f1-g2	a1-f2	Slow, sustained. Demands some flexibility. (Prout)
L'Allegro Or let the merry bells ring round	d1-a2	a1-e2	Animated, spirited. Demands some flexibility. <u>Optional for tenor.</u> See L'Allegro, "Let Me Wander Not Unseen." (Kagen)
L'Allegro Sweet bird that shun'st the noise of folly	d1-a2	a1-f#2	Slow, delicate. In parts very florid. <u>Best for light voice.</u> (Kagen)
Messiah Come unto Him	f1-g2	a1-f2	Slow, sustained, rather subdued. (gen. av.)

TITLE	COMP.	TESS.	REMARKS
Messiah How beautiful are the feet of them	f1-g2	g1-eb2	Slow, sustained, delicate. (gen. av.)
Messiah I know that my Redeemer liveth	e1-g#2	g#-e2	Slow, very sustained. (gen. av.)
Messiah If God be with us who can be against us	eb1-ab2	g1-f2	Slow, sustained. Has florid passages. (gen. av.)
Messiah Rejoice greatly	eb1-ab2	g1-eb2	Animated, florid. The mid- dle section is sustained. (gen. av.)
Ode for St. Cecilia's Day The soft com- plaining flute	d1-g2	a#1-f#2	Sustained. Has florid passages. Best for light voice. (Score, gen. av.)
Samson Let the bright Seraphim	d1-a2	a1-f#2	Rather vigorous, quite florid. (Kagen)
Saul Fell rage and black despair	e1-a2	f#1-e2	Sustained. (Prout)
Saul Oh God-like youth	f1-ab2	a1-f2	Sustained. Demands some flexibility. (Score, NOV)
Semele O sleep, why dost thou leave me	d#1-g#2	e1-e2	Slow and sustained. Demands some flexibility. Optional for tenor. (Kagen)
Solomon With thee th'un- sheltered moor I'd tread	d1-g2	f#1-d2	Very sustained. (Prout)
Susanna Ask if yon damask rose	d1-g2	g1-eb2	Animated, graceful. Optional for tenor. (Score, NOV)
Susanna Recitative: I know the pangs			

TITLE	COMP.	TESS.	REMARKS
Air:			
Beneath the cypress' gloomy shade	d1-f2	f1-d2	Recitative and a sustained, graceful Siciliana. (Score, NOV)
Susanna			
Recitative:			
Lead me to some cool retreat			
Air:			
Crystal streams in murmurs flowing	d1-g2	f#1-d2	Not fast. Demands considerable flexibility. (Score, NOV)
Susanna			
If guiltless blood be your intent	c#1-g2	f1-e2	Spirited. Has florid passages. Middle section is very sustained. Suitable for either dramatic or lyric voice. (Prout)
Theodora			
Recitative:			
O worse than death indeed			
Air:			
Angels ever bright and fair	d1-f2	f1-d2	Very sustained. Suitable for either dramatic or lyric soprano. (Kagen)

Mezzo-soprano or Alto

	COMP.	TESS.	REMARKS
Athalia			
Recitative:			
O Judah, chosen seed			
Air:			
O Lord, whom we adore	bb-c2	d1-bb1	Slow, sustained. (GS)
Belshazzar			
Great God! who yet but darkly known	c1-d2	e1-c2	Very sustained. (Prout)
Belshazzar			
O sacred oracles of truth	bb-eb2	c1-c2	Slow, rather sustained. (Prout)

Belshazzar
Recitative:
  Rejoice, my
  countrymen
Air:

Thus saith the Lord to Cyrrus	a-d2	d1-b1	Recitative and a majestic arioso. Demands some flexi- bility. (Prout)

Deborah

All dangers dis- daining	a-d2	d1-d2	Spirited, vigorous. Has florid passages. (B & H)

Deborah

In the battle fame pursuing	(a)b-d2	d1-b1	Not fast; rather florid. (Prout)

Hercules

The smiling hours, a joyful train	b♭-e2	d1-c2	Animated, graceful, florid. (GS)

Israel in Egypt

Thou shalt bring them in	b-e2	e1-b1	Sustained. Demands some flexibility. (Score, gen. av.)

Jephtha
Recitative:
  'Twill be a pain-
  ful separation
Air:

In gentle mur- murs will I mourn	b-e2	e1-c2	Slow, sustained. Demands some flexibility. (Score, NOV)

Joseph

The peasant tastes the sweets of life	a-d2	e1-c2	A graceful, sustained pasto- rale. The middle section is florid and more robust. (Score, NOV)

Joshua
Recitative:
  But who is he?
Air:

Awful, pleasing being, say	b-e2	d♯-b1	Sustained. Demands some flexibility. (Score, NOV)

Joshua
Recitative:
  Now give the
  army breath

TITLE	COMP.	TESS.	REMARKS
Air:			
Heroes when with glory burning	c1-f2	e1-c2	A spirited gavotte. Demands some flexibility. (Prout)
Judas Maccabaeus			
Father of heaven	c1-eb2	e1-c2	Slow, sustained. Demands some flexibility. (Kagen)
Judas Maccabaeus Recitative: To heaven's almighty King we kneel Air:			
O liberty, thou choicest treasure	d#1-f#2	f#1-e2	Slow, sustained. Demands some flexibility. Optional for soprano or tenor. (gen. av.)
Messiah			
He was despised	bb-bb1	d1-ab1	Slow, grave, sustained. Somewhat declamatory. (gen. av.)
Messiah Recitative: Then shall the eyes of the blind be opened Air:			
He shall feed his flock	c1-d2	e1-c2	Slow, sustained, rather subdued. (gen. av.)
Messiah Recitative: Behold! A virgin shall conceive Air:			
O thou that tellest good tidings to Zion	a-b1	d1-a1	Spirited, vigorous. Has florid passages. (gen. av.)
Samson			
Return, o God of hosts	bb-eb2	eb1-c2	Slow and sustained. (Score, gen. av.)
Samson			
Ye sons of Israel, now lament	bb-db2	eb1-c2	Slow, sustained. (Score, gen. av.)

TITLE	COMP.	TESS.	REMARKS
Saul Brave Jonathan his bow ne'er drew	b-e2	d1-d2	Very sustained. (B & H)
Saul O Lord, whose mercies number- less	bb-d2	c1-bb1	Slow, very sustained. (Prout)
Semele Hence, Iris, hence away	bb-eb2	eb1-c2	Spirited, vigorous. Has florid passages. (B & H)
Semele Hymen, haste! Thy torch pre- pare	a-c2	bb-bb1	Spirited. Has florid pas- sages. (Prout)
Solomon What though I trace	c#1-e2	e1-c#2	Slow and sustained. <u>Optional for heavy soprano voice.</u> (Prout)
Susanna Recitative: A love like mine Air: When first I saw my lovely maid	c1-e2	e1-d2	Recitative and sustained, graceful air. (GS)
Theodora As with rosy steps the morn	c1-e2	e1-c2	Slow, rather sustained. De- mands some flexibility. (Prout)
Theodora Defend her, heaven	d#1-f#2	e1-e2	Very sustained. Demands some flexibility. <u>Optional for baritone.</u> (Arr. by L. Lebell. S & B)
Theodora Lord, to thee each night and day	c#1-e2	e1-d2	Slow, sustained. The middle section is animated and has florid passages. (Prout)

Tenor

TITLE	COMP.	TESS.	REMARKS
Acis and Galatea Love in her eyes sits playing	f-ab1	bb-g1	Graceful, sustained. Demands some flexibility. (Prout)

TITLE	COMP.	TESS.	REMARKS
Acis and Galatea			
Would you gain the tender creature	e-g1	a-f1	Animated, graceful. <u>Optional for soprano</u>. (Prout)
Athalia			
Gentle airs, melodious strains	e-f#1	g#-e1	Slow, quite florid. (Prout)
Chandos Anthem			
Recitative:			
O come let us sing			
Air:			
O come let us worship	e-a1	g-f1	Slow, sustained. Demands flexibility. (Prout)
Esther			
O beauteous queen	e-g1	a-f1	Sustained. (Prout)
Esther			
Recitative:			
O God, who from the suckling's mouth			
Air:			
Sing songs of praise	f-a1	a-f1	Sustained. (Randegger, NOV)
Hercules			
From celestial seats descending	c-g1	f-f1	A sustained Siciliana. (GS)
Israel in Egypt			
The enemy said	d-a1	g-e1	Spirited; quite florid. (Score, NOV)
Jephtha			
Recitative:			
Deeper and deeper still			
Air:			
Waft her, angels, to the skies	d-a1	g-g1	A scena and a rather slow, somewhat florid air. <u>Optional for soprano</u>. (Prout)
Judas Maccabaeus			
Recitative:			
'Tis well, my friends			
Air:			
Call forth thy powers	d-a1	a-f#1	Spirited, vigorous. Has florid passages. (Score, gen. av.)

TITLE	COMP.	TESS.	REMARKS

Judas Maccabaeus
Recitative:
  Thanks to my
  brethren
Air:

How vain is man who boasts	d-g1	g-f1	Vigorous. Demands considerable flexibility. (gen. av.)

Judas Maccabaeus
Recitative:
  Ambition! If e'er
  honour was thine
  aim
Air:

No, unhallowed desire	f-g1	g-e1	Spirited. In parts quite florid. (Score, gen. av.)

Judas Maccabaeus
Recitative:
  To heaven's almighty King we
  kneel
Air:

O liberty thou choicest treasure	d#-f#1	f#-e1	Slow, sustained. Demands some flexibility. <u>Optional for soprano or mezzo-soprano.</u> (gen. av.)

Judas Maccabaeus

So rapid thy course is	B-g1	d-d1	Spirited. Demands considerable flexibility. (Score, gen. av.)

Judas Maccabaeus

Sound an alarm	d-a1	a-e1	Spirited, vigorous. Has florid passages. (gen. av.)

Judas Maccabaeus
Recitative:
  O Judas! May
  those noble views
Air:

'Tis liberty	e-g#1	e-e1	Not fast. Has florid passages. (Score, gen. av.)

Judas Maccabaeus

With honor let desert be crowned	d-a1	a-e1	Not fast. In parts quite florid. (Score, gen. av.)

TITLE	COMP.	TESS.	REMARKS

L'Allegro
Come and trip it   eb-ab1   g-eb1   Graceful, animated. Has florid passages. An air with chorus, but can be sung as a solo. (Kagen)

L'Allegro
Let me wander not unseen   d-g1   a-f1   A graceful, sustained, subdued Siciliana. Often sung together with "Or Let the Merry Bells Ring Round" from L'Allegro, which air is in the same key and follows nicely as a sort of contrasting movement. <u>Optional for soprano</u>. (Kagen)

L'Allegro
Recitative:
  Hence, loathed melancholy
Air:
  Mirth, admit me of thy crew   f♯-g1   a-e1   Very animated, spirited. Demands some flexibility. (Score, NOV)

L'Allegro
Or let the merry bells ring round   d-a1   a-e1   Animated, spirited. Demands some flexibility. <u>Optional for soprano</u>. See L'Allegro, "Let Me Wander Not Unseen." (Kagen)

Messiah
Recitative:
  Thy rebuke hath broken his heart
Air:
  Behold and see   d♯-g1   g-e1   Slow, sustained. (Score, gen. av.)

Messiah
Recitative:
  He was cut off
Air:
  But thou didst not leave his soul in hell   e-g1   f♯-e1   Slow, sustained. (Score, gen. av.)

Messiah
Recitative:
  Comfort ye my people

TITLE	COMP.	TESS.	REMARKS
Air: Every valley shall be exalted	d#-g#1	e-e1	A sustained, accompanied recitative (arioso) and a rather spirited, florid air. (gen. av.)
Messiah Recitative: He that dwelleth Air: Thou shalt break them	e-a1	a-e1	Vigorous. Has florid passages. (Score, gen. av.)
Occasional Oratorio Jehovah! To my words give ear	d#-f#1	f#-e1	Sustained. (Score, NOV)
Occasional Oratorio Then will I Jehovah's praise	e-f#1	e-e1	Spirited. Demands some flexibility. (Prout)
Samson Thus when the sun	d-g1	f-d1	Sustained. Demands some flexibility. (Prout)
Samson Total eclipse	e-g1	g-e1	Slow, somewhat declamatory. (Kagen)
Samson Recitative: My grief for this Air: Why does the God of Israel sleep	d-ab1	f-f1	Spirited. Has many florid passages. (Score, NOV)
Saul Sin not, o King	d-f1	f-eb1	Slow and sustained. (Prout)
Semele O sleep, why dost thou leave me	d#-g#1	e-e1	Slow and sustained. Demands some flexibility. Optional for soprano. (gen. av.)
Semele Where'er you walk	f-g1	g-d1	Slow, sustained. Demands some flexibility. (gen. av.)
Susanna Ask if yon damask rose	d-g1	g-eb1	Animated and graceful. Optional for soprano. (Score, NOV)

Susanna
Recitative:
  Tyrannic love
Air:

Ye verdant hills	d-f#1	f#-d1	A scena and a sustained air. (Score, NOV)

Baritone or Bass

Acis and Galatea
Recitative:
  I rage, I melt,
  I burn
Air:

O ruddier than the cherry	F-f1	Bb-d1	Spirited, vigorous. Has florid passages. (Kagen)

Alexander's Feast

Bacchus, ever fair and young	c-f1	f-d1	Very sustained. (Bass Arias, CFP)

Alexander's Feast

Revenge, Timo- theus cries	G-e1	d-d1	Animated, vigorous. Has florid passages. The slow middle section of this rather long da capo air, "Behold a Ghastly Band," as well as the allegro are sometimes sung separately. (Kagen; Prout)

Deborah

Tears such as ten- der fathers shed	Bb-eb1	eb-bb	Slow, sustained. (Prout)

Dettinger Te Deum

Vouchsafe, o Lord	d-d#1	e-c#1	Slow, majestic, very sustained. (Kagen)

Dettinger Te Deum

When Thou tookest upon Thee	d#-e1	e-c#1	Slow, sustained. Demands some flexibility. (Score, CFP)

Esther

Turn not, o queen, thy face away	c-d1	d-c1	Slow and sustained. (Prout)

Jephtha
Recitative:
  It must be so

TITLE	COMP.	TESS.	REMARKS
Air: Pour forth no more unheeded prayers	A-eb1	c-c1	Spirited, vigorous. Demands some flexibility. (Score, NOV)
Joshua See the raging flames arise	A-e1	d-d1	Spirited, vigorous. Has florid passages. (Kagen)
Joshua Shall I in Mamre's fertile plain	G-eb1	eb-c1	Slow, sustained. (Prout)
Judas Maccabaeus Recitative: I feel the Deity within Air: Arm, arm, ye brave	B-e1	c-c1	Spirited, vigorous. Demands some flexibility. (gen. av.)
Judas Maccabaeus Recitative: Be comforted Air: The Lord worketh wonders	A-e1	c-c1	Spirited, vigorous, florid. (Score, gen. av.)
Judas Maccabaeus Recitative: Enough! To heaven we leave the rest Air: With pious hearts	G-e1	d-c1	Sustained. (Score, gen. av.)
L'Allegro Come with na- tive lustre shine	c-eb1	e-c1	Stately, sustained. Has some florid passages. (Score, NOV)
L'Allegro Recitative: If I give thee honour due Air: Mirth, admit me of thy crew	Ab-eb1	eb-eb1	A spirited hunting song. Has florid passages in which the voice imitates the call of a horn. (Score, NOV)
Messiah Recitative: Thus saith the Lord			

TITLE	COMP.	TESS.	REMARKS
Air:			
But who may abide the day of His coming	G-e1	d-d1	The recitative is florid. The air consists of two repeated contrasting sections—a sustained larghetto and a vigorous presto which has florid passages. (gen. av.)
Messiah			
Recitative: For behold, darkness shall cover the earth			
Air: The people that walked in darkness	(F#)G-e1	B-b	Slow, somber. Demands some flexibility. (gen. av.)
Messiah			
Thou art gone up on high	B-e1	e-d1	Vigorous, animated. Has florid passages. (Score, gen. av.)
Messiah			
Recitative: Behold, I tell you a mystery			
Air: The trumpet shall sound	A-e1	f#-d1	Very vigorous. Has florid passages. (gen. av.)
Messiah			
Why do the nations so furiously rage together	B-e1	c-c1	Vigorous, very animated. Has florid passages. (gen. av.)
Occasional Oratorio			
Recitative: Humbled with fear			
Air: His sceptre is the rod of righteousness	G#-e1	c#-d1	Vigorous, spirited. Has many florid passages. (Spicker, Anthology of Sacred Song, GS)
The Passion			
My Father, look upon my anguish	Bb-eb1	d-c1	Slow and sustained. Has a recitative for the middle section. (Spicker, Anthology of Sacred Song, GS)

TITLE	COMP.	TESS.	REMARKS
Samson Honour and arms	G-eb1	Bb-d1	Vigorous, spirited. Has florid passages. (gen. av.)
Samson How willing my paternal love	B-e1	B-b	Slow and sustained. Demands some flexibility. (Kagen)
Samson Thy glorious deeds inspired my tongue	Bb-f1	d-d1	Spirited. Has many florid passages. The middle section is slow and sustained. (Prout; Kagen)
Semele Leave me, loathsome light	A-d1	d-b	Very sustained. (Prout)
The Triumph of Time and Truth False, destructive ways of pleasure	Ab-f1	eb-d1	Spirited, quite florid. (Prout)
The Triumph of Time and Truth Loathsome urns, disclose your treasure	Bb-db1	c-c1	Sustained. (Prout)
Theodora Defend her, heaven	d-f♯1	e-e1	Very sustained. Demands some flexibility. Optional for alto or mezzo-soprano. (Arr. by L. Lebell. S & B)

MISCELLANEOUS AIRS

TITLE	COMP.	TESS.	TYPE	REMARKS
Alcina Ah! Mio cor (Italian text)	c1-eb2	f1-d2	Not suitable for very light, high voices	Grave, somewhat declamatory. (Parisotti, Italian Anthology, GS)
Almira (Handel's first opera) Zweier Augen Majestät (German text)	Bb-eb1	eb-c1	Bass or alto	Sustained. Demands some flexibility. (Wolff)

TITLE	COMP.	TESS.	TYPE	REMARKS
Dank sei Dir, Herr (German text)	e1-g2	g1-e2 (H)	Not suitable for light, high voices	Very sustained, majestic. Of questionable authenticity. (Kagen)
Ottone				
Affanni del pensier (Italian text)	c1-eb2	f1-c2	Most suitable for medium or low voices	A sustained, graceful Siciliana. (Parisotti, Italian Anthology, GS)
Pack clouds away	b-e2	e1-c#2 (L)	All voices	Animated, graceful. Demands some flexibility. (Arr. by Henry Coleman. Paterson, Glasgow)
La Passione (The Passion)				
Chi sprezzando il sommo bene (Italian text)	eb1-f2	eb1-eb2	Not suitable for light, high voices	Slow and very sustained. Has also the original German text. (Kagen)
Rinaldo Recitative: Armida dispietata Air: Lascia ch'io pianga (Italian text)	f1-g2	a1-f2	All voices, except a very light soprano	Very sustained. (Kagen)
Rinaldo Scorta rea	bb-c2	d1-c2	Low voices	Vigorous, florid, animated. (Jeppesen)
Rinaldo Sorge nel petto	b-d2	d1-c2	Low voices	Slow and sustained. (Jeppesen)
Serse Recitative: Frondi tenere e belle Air: Ombra mai fu (Italian text)	c1-f2	f1-d2	All voices, except a very light soprano	Very slow and sustained. Originally written for tenor. (Kagen)

TITLE	COMP.	TESS.	TYPE	REMARKS
Silent worship	e1-f♯2	a1-e2 (H)	Most suitable for men's voices	Spirited, graceful. An arrangement by A. Somervell of "Non lo diro col labbro" from Ptolemy and provided with an excellent English text. (CUR)
Tamerlano				
Dammi pace	c1-d2	d1-c2	Low voices	Animated, vigorous, in parts florid. (Jeppesen)

CHRISTOPH WILLIBALD GLUCK
(1714–1787)

Gluck's revolt against the stultifying conventions of the eighteenth century Italian opera led him to abandon one of the salient features of the 18th century operatic form, the florid da capo aria, designed almost solely to provide the singer with a suitable vehicle for the exhibition of his virtuosity. This allowed Gluck to experiment widely with the form of his vocal soli. His airs are for the most part of compound form; that is, they consist of two or more movements manipulated freely in accordance with the demands of the text. However, his airs often conform to a strict dance form such as the minuet, gavotte or sarabande, which apparently did not seem dramatically restrictive to him.

In studying Gluck's airs one would do well to acquaint oneself thoroughly with the respective libretti of his operas and their classical archetypes. The easiest and most enjoyable way of doing the latter would be to consult a standard work on mythology, such as Bulfinch's Mythology (available in many inexpensive reprints) and to have a classical dictionary handy (such as the one published in the Everyman's Library series).

As a musical dramatist, Gluck is perhaps nearer to Wagner than to any eighteenth century composer. One of the essential attainments he demands of the singer is the ability to recite texts with the proper dramatic inflection. As a sort of standard procedure that may be most helpful in studying his airs, the singer should endeavor to learn to recite their texts by memory before attempting to sing them. Through such a comparison of the spoken sentence with the musical phrase the singer may be able to realize more fully the extraordinary dramatic impact that underlies and directs the flow of Gluck's melodic line.

Stylistically Gluck's airs are quite complex. The eighteenth century conception of the classical drama differed greatly from ours, abounding in peculiar anachronisms which seem strangely out of place to the present-day actor and singer whose conception of the classical drama has been greatly influenced by the intervening one

213

hundred fifty years of exhaustive historical and archaeological research. Yet notwithstanding his inadequate historical knowledge,
Gluck, in his music, seems to have approximated the spirit of the
classical drama better than anyone before or after him.

Gluck's important soprano airs are for the most part best suited to rather heavy dramatic voices, and if transposed a tone lower
than the original are excellently suited to the high dramatic mezzo-
soprano type of voice. His smaller dance-form airs are, however,
very suitable for light soprano voices. In his mature period Gluck
seems to have written no airs designed specifically for coloratura
soprano.

His alto and mezzo-soprano airs are few, the most famous of
these being of course the Orfeo airs. Gevaert in his "Répertoire
Classique du Chant Français" has transposed several dramatic soprano airs to suit the lower voices, a perfectly justified and sensible
procedure in the opinion of this writer.

Gluck's tenor and baritone airs often seem to lie too high for
present-day singers. Since there are indications that the pitch in
Gluck's time was considerably lower than the present 440-442 a, it
seems only sensible to recommend the transposition of these airs
in preference to the comparative oblivion to which they are now subject, due no doubt largely to their forbiddingly high tessitura.

Editions: Orfeo, Alceste, Iphigénie en Tauride, Iphigénie en Aulide,
and Armide are generally available in piano scores.

Excerpted airs from these and other operas can be found in Gevaert, Répertoire Classique du Chant Français, published by Lemoine,
Paris; and the Breitkopf & Härtel collections of airs for soprano, alto,
tenor and bass.

A few celebrated airs are generally available in a variety of editions.

Note: In the following list, the name Gevaert indicates Répertoire
Classique du Chant Français, edited by Gevaert, published by Lemoine.

FRENCH TEXT

Soprano

TITLE	COMP.	TESS.	TYPE	REMARKS
Adieu! Conservez dans votre âme (Iphigénie en Aulide) Recitative: Grands dieux soutenez mon courage	d1-ab2	f1-eb2	Soprano	Slow, sustained, short. Vocally not too taxing. (Score, NOV)

TITLE	COMP.	TESS.	TYPE	REMARKS
Air:				
Ah, divinités im- placables (Alceste)	d1-a2	f1-f2	Dramatic soprano	A very dramatic scena and a sus- tained air. (Ge- vaert)
Recitative: Dérobez-moi Air:				
Ah! Malgré moi (Alceste)	eb1-a2	g1-f2	Dramatic soprano	Recitative, an- dante, allegro. Vigorous, ma- jestic, dramatic. (Gevaert)
Ah! Si la liberté (Armide)	e1-g2	g1-e2	Dramatic soprano (lyric soprano)	Sustained. In the Gevaert edition, this aria is trans- posed a whole tone lower. (Score, CFP)
Amour, sors pour jamais (Armide)	f1-f2	g#1-eb2	Dramatic soprano (mezzo- soprano)	Animated, vigorous. (Score, CFP)
Armez vous d'un noble courage (Iphigénie en Aulide)	d1-a2	f1-d2	Dramatic soprano (mezzo- soprano)	Animated, vigorous, dramatic. (Score, NOV)
Recitative: Hélas, c'est mon coeur que je crains! Air:				
De mes plus doux regards (Armide)	f1-g2	a1-f2	Soprano	Short, sustained. (Score, CFP)
Divinités du Styx (Alceste)	c1-bb2	f1-f2	Dramatic soprano	A majestic, vig- orous, compound air. Sometimes sung by mezzo- soprani transposed a third lower. (gen. av.)
Recitative: Je cède à vos désirs Air:				
D'une image hélas! trop chérie (Iphigénie en Tauride)	f1-g2	g1-eb2	Soprano	Recitative and a sustained, grace- ful air. (Score, NOV)

TITLE	COMP.	TESS.	TYPE	REMARKS
Recitative: Hélas! dans ce malheur extrême Air: Grands dieux! Du destin qui m'ac- cable (Alceste)	e1-bb2	f1-f2	Dramatic soprano (lyric soprano)	An andante, al- legro air. Ma- jestic, dramatic. (Reprinted by G. Schirmer from the Gevaert edi- tion.)
Recitative: L'ai-je bien entendu? Air: Hélas! mon coeur sensible et tendre (Iphigénie en Aulide)	f1-g2	g1-f2	Dramatic soprano	Recitative and a dramatic, com- pound air. (Ge- vaert)
Heureux guerriers, volez à la victoire (Iphigénie en Aulide)	g1-a2	a1-e2	Lyric soprano (dramatic soprano)	Graceful, minuet- like air. (Score, NOV)
Il faut de mon destin subir la loi (Iphigénie en Aulide)	bb-g2	f1-eb2	Soprano or mezzo- soprano	Short, sustained. (Score, NOV)
Iphigénie, hélas! vous a trop fait connaître (Iphigénie en Aulide)	f#1-f#2	g#1-d2	Soprano	Short, sustained. Vocally not tax- ing. (Score, NOV)
Jamais dans ces beaux lieux (Armide)	f1-f2	a1-f2	Soprano	Short, graceful, sustained. (Score, CFP)
Recitative: Les dieux ont entendu Air: Je n'ai jamais chéri la vie (Alceste)	c#1-a2	a1-e2	Dramatic soprano (lyric soprano)	Sustained. (Ge- vaert)
Recitative: Non, cet affreux devoir				

TITLE	COMP.	TESS.	TYPE	REMARKS
Air:				
Je t'implore et je tremble (Iphigénie en Tauride)	d#1-a2	a1-e2	Dramatic soprano (lyric soprano)	Animated, dramatic, majestic. (Score, NOV)
Jeunes coeurs! tout vous est favorable (Armide)	d1-e2	g1-d2	Soprano (mezzo-soprano)	Short, graceful. Vocally not taxing. (Score, CFP)
Recitative: Dieux puissants, que j'atteste!				
Air:				
Jupiter, lance ta foudre (Iphigénie en Aulide)	d1-g2	g1-e2	Dramatic soprano or mezzo-soprano	A very dramatic scena and an animated, vigorous, dramatic air. (Score, NOV)
La chaîne de l'Hymen m'étonne (Armide)	e1-f#2	g#1-e2	Soprano	Sustained, graceful. Vocally not taxing. (Score, CFP)
Le perfide Renaud me fuit (Armide)	g1-a2	a1-f2	Dramatic soprano	A very dramatic scena. (Score, CFP)
Les voeux dont ce peuple (Iphigénie en Aulide)	d1-a♭2	g1-e2	Soprano	Short, sustained, vocally not taxing. (Gevaert)
Recitative: Où suis-je?				
Air:				
Non! ce n'est pas un sacrifice (Alceste)	f#1-a2	a1-f#2	Dramatic soprano (lyric soprano)	A scena and a sustained, majestic air. (Gevaert)
O malheureuse Iphigénie (Iphigénie en Tauride)	b-a2	g1-g2	Dramatic soprano	Very sustained, majestic. Not slow. (Gevaert)
Recitative: Cette nuit, j'ai revu le palais de mon père				
Air:				
O toi, qui prolongeas mes jours (Iphigénie en Tauride)	f1-a2	a1-f#2	Dramatic soprano (lyric soprano)	A very extended, interpretatively taxing scena and a sustained air. (Gevaert)

TITLE	COMP.	TESS.	TYPE	REMARKS
On s'étonnerait moins (Armide)	f♯1-a2	a1-f♯2	Light soprano	Graceful, delicate. (Score, CFP)
Recitative: Vous essayez en vain de bannir mes alarmes				
Air: Par la crainte et par l'espérance (Iphigénie en Aulide)	d1-a2	f1-f2	Dramatic soprano (lyric soprano)	Recitative and a vigorous, sustained, dramatic air. (Score, NOV)
Recitative: Seigneur! j'embrasse vos genoux				
Air: Par son père cruel à la mort condamnée (Iphigénie en Aulide)	e1-g2	f♯1-d2	Dramatic soprano (mezzo-soprano)	Recitative and a sustained air. (Score, NOV)
Que j'aime à voir (Iphigénie en Aulide)	g1-e2	same	Soprano or mezzo-soprano	Very short, sustained. Vocally not taxing. (Gevaert)
Si je dois m'engager (Armide)	f♯1-g2	a1-e2	Soprano	Short, sustained, majestic. (Score, CFP)
Son front est couronne (Iphigénie en Aulide)	d1-f♯2	g♯1-d2	Soprano	Very short, sustained, vocally not taxing. (Score, NOV)
Recitative: Enfin il est en ma puissance				
Air: Venez, secondez mes désirs (Armide)	d1-a2 (b2)	g1-f♯2	Dramatic soprano	A dramatic scena, a graceful andantino, and a sustained, rather vigorous andante. (Gevaert)
Recitative: Il m'aime? quel amour!				
Air: Venez, venez, haine implacable (Armide)	f1-a2	a1-f2	Dramatic soprano	Scena and a vigorous, dramatic air. (Score, CFP)

TITLE	COMP.	TESS.	TYPE	REMARKS
Vivez, vivez pour Oreste (Iphigénie en Aulide)	e1-e2	g1-d2	Soprano	Short, sustained. Vocally not taxing. (Gevaert)
Voici la charmante retraite (Armide)	f1-f2	g1-d2	Soprano	Short, graceful. Vocally not taxing. (Score, CFP)
Vous troublez-vous (Armide)	g1-ab2	bb1-f2	Soprano	Short, sustained, graceful. (Score, CFP)

Mezzo-soprano or alto

TITLE	COMP.	TESS.	TYPE	REMARKS
Amour, sors pour jamais (Armide)	f1-g2	g#1-eb2	Mezzo-soprano or alto	Animated, vigorous. (Score, CFP)
Armez-vous d'un noble courage (Iphigénie en Aulide)	bb-g2	eb1-eb2	Mezzo-soprano or alto	Animated, vigorous, dramatic. Transposed into this key in the Gevaert edition.
Il faut de mon destin subir la loi (Iphigénie en Aulide)	bb-g2	f1-eb2	Mezzo-soprano or soprano	Short, sustained. (Score, NOV)
Je n'ai jamais chéri la vie (Alceste)	a-f2	d1-d2	Alto	Sustained, grave. Originally written for soprano. This aria is transposed into this key in the Gevaert edition.
Jeunes coeurs! tout vous est favorable (Armide) Recitative: Dieux puissants que j'atteste! Air:	d1-e2	g1-d2	Mezzo-soprano or soprano	Short, graceful. Vocally not taxing. (Score, CFP)
Jupiter, lance ta foundre (Iphigénie en Aulide) Recitative: Seigneur! J'embrasse vos genoux	d1-g2	g1-e2	Mezzo-soprano or dramatic soprano	A very dramatic scena and an animated, vigorous, dramatic air. (Gevaert)

TITLE	COMP.	TESS.	TYPE	REMARKS
Air: Par son père cruel, à la mort condamnée (Iphigénie en Aulide)	c1-eb2	d1-d2	Mezzo-soprano or alto	Recitative and a sustained air. Originally written for soprano; transposed into this key in the Gevaert edition.
Que j'aime à voir (Iphigénie en Aulide)	g1-e2	same	Mezzo-soprano or soprano	Very short, sustained. Vocally not taxing. (Score NOV)

Tenor

Since practically all of the Gluck tenor airs listed below are most suitable for a rather heavy type of voice, it seems best to dispense with the "type of voice" remark.

TITLE	COMP.	TESS.	REMARKS
Ah, mon ami (Iphigénie en Tauride)	a-ab1	bb-eb1	Animated. The vocal line is sustained. (Score, NOV)
Recitative: Vivre sans toi, moi, vivre sans Alceste?			
Air: Alceste, au nom des Dieux, sois sensible (Alceste)	f-a1	ab-f1	Recitative and a sustained, dramatic air. (Score, CFP)
Allez éloignez-vous de moi (Armide)	g-a1	b-g1	Sustained, short. (Score, CFP)
Recitative: O moment délicieux			
Air: Bannis la crainte et les alarmes (Alceste)	e-a1	a-e1	Animated. (Score, CFP)
Recitative: Tu veux mourir			
Air: Barbare, non, sans toi je ne puis vivre (Alceste)	e-a1	a-f1	A scena and a sustained, dramatic air with a vigorous, rapid middle section. (Score, CFP)

TITLE	COMP.	TESS.	REMARKS
Recitative: Éh bien! obéissez, barbares! Air: Calchas, d'un trait mortel blessé (Iphigénie en Aulide)	g♯-b1	b-g1	Animated, vigorous, dramatic. (Score, NOV)
Recitative: S'il était vrai Air: Cruelle, non, jamais votre insensible coeur (Iphigénie en Aulide)	g♯-b1	a-f1	Recitative and a sustained, majestic air. (Score, NOV)
De l'amitié touchante (Echo et Narcisse)	f-a♭1	a♭-f1	Scena, sustained air, and closing scena. (Gevaert)
Divinité des grandes âmes (Iphigénie en Tauride)	g-a1	b-e1	Animated, majestic. (Score, NOV)
Recitative: Divinité des eaux Air: Je ne puis m'ou- vrir ta froide de- meure (Echo et Narcisse)	f♯-g1	g♯-f1	An extended scena and a sustained air. (Gevaert)
Par ma voix (Echo et Narcisse)	f-g1	g-e♭1	Recitative and a sustained dramatic air with a florid closing passage. (Gevaert)
Plus j'observe ces lieux (Armide)	g-a1	b-f♯1	Sustained. The tessitura is very high. (Score, CFP)
Recitative: Quel Langage accablant Air: Unis dès la plus tendre enfance (Iphigénie en Tauride)	f♯-a1	a-e1	Sustained, graceful. (Score, NOV)
Viens! Du froid de la mort (Echo et Narcisse)	f-a♭1	g-e♭1	Recitative and a sustained arioso. Demands some flexibility. (Gevaert)

TITLE	COMP.	TESS.	TYPE	REMARKS
Recitative: Diane impitoyable Air: Brillant auteur de la lumière (Iphigénie en Aulide)	c-e1	f♯-d1	Baritone	A sustained, ma- jestic scena and a compound air, ending in a recita- tive. (Gevaert)
Caron t'appelle, entends sa voix! (Alceste) Recitative: Au pouvoir de la mort je saurai la ravir	c♯-e1 (f♯1)	e-d1	Bass (bass- baritone)	Animated, very vigorous. (Score, CFP)
Air: C'est en vain que l'enfer compte sur sa victime (Alceste)	d♯-e1	e-d1	Baritone (bass- baritone)	Animated, vigor- ous. (Score, CFP)
C'est un torrent (Les pélerins de la Mecque) Recitative: Le ciel par d'éclatants miracle	c♯-f1	f-d1	Baritone	A spirited allegro and a graceful an- dante. (Gevaert)
Air: De noirs pres- sentiments (Iphigénie en Tauride)	e♯-g1	a-e1	High baritone	Recitative and a sustained, dramat- ic air. Transposed a third lower in the Gevaert edition.
Recitative: Tes destins sont remplis! Air: Déjà la mort s'apprête (Alceste) Recitative: Je t'ai donné la mort	c-f1	e♭-e♭1	Baritone (bass- baritone)	Majestic, sus- tained, vigorous. (Score, CFP)

TITLE	COMP.	TESS.	TYPE	REMARKS
Air: Dieux! qui me poursuivez (Iphigénie en Tauride) Recitative: Armide, que le sang qui m'unit avec vous Air:	f♯-f♯1	a-e1	Baritone	Animated, vigorous, dramatic. (Score, NOV)
Je vois de près la mort (Armide) Recitative: Dans ta fureur enfin j'ai lu mon triomphe! Air:	c-e♭1	f-d1	Baritone	Recitative, andante, allegro. (Gevaert)
En cet instant suprême (Ezio)	B-e1	e-c♯1	Bass-baritone or bass	Recitative and a sustained air. The Gevaert edition does not have the original Italian text. (Gevaert)
Hector et les Troyens (Iphigénie en Aulide) Recitative: Dieux! protecteurs de ces affreux rivages Air:	B-e1	e-e1	Baritone	Short, vigorous. (Score, NOV)
Le calme rentre dans mon coeur (Iphigénie en Tauride) Recitative: Tu décides son sort Air:	d-f♯1	a-d1	Baritone	A short scena and a sustained, majestic air. (Score, NOV)
O toi, l'objet le plus aimable (Iphigénie en Aulide)	c-f♯1	e-d1	Baritone	A very long scena (which could be omitted if so desired) and a majestic, dramatic compound air. (Gevaert)

TITLE	COMP.	TESS.	TYPE	REMARKS
Peuvent-ils ordonner qu'un père (Iphigénie en Aulide)	d-f1	g-d1	Baritone	Sustained, vigorous, dramatic. (Gevaert)
Pour vous, quand il vous plaît (Armide)	e-f1	g#-e1	Baritone	Animated, rather vigorous. (Score, CFP)

ITALIAN TEXT

TITLE	COMP.	TESS.	TYPE	REMARKS
Ah, ritorna (Il trionfo di Clelia)	d1-b2	g1-f2	Soprano	A graceful minuet. Demands some flexibility. (Landshoff, Alte Meister, CFP)
Ah, non chiamarmi ingrato (Telemacco)	eb-ab1	ab-eb1	Tenor (or soprano)	Sustained, graceful. (Krehbiel, Songs from the Operas, OD)
Recitative: Ahimè! Dove trascorsi Air: Che farò senza Euridice (Orfeo)	b-f2	e1-c2	Alto	A dramatic recitative and a very sustained air. (gen. av.)
Recitative: Qual vita è questa mai Air: Che fiero momento, che barbara sorte (Orfeo)	d#1-ab2	g1-eb2	Dramatic soprano (lyric soprano)	Recitative and a vigorous, animated, dramatic air. (gen. av.)
Che puro ciel! (Orfeo)	c1-e2	d1-c2	Alto	A sustained "quasi recitative"; somewhat declamatory. (Score, gen.av.)
Chiamo il mio ben così (Orfeo)	a-eb2	c1-c2	Alto	A short, sustained air which is repeated three times with two interpolated recitatives. (Score, gen. av.)

TITLE	COMP.	TESS.	TYPE	REMARKS
Deh placatevi con me (Orfeo)	bb-eb2	eb1-c2	Alto	Air with chorus. Sustained, rather vigorous. (Score, gen. av.)
Di questa cetra (Parnasso Confuso)	d1-g2	g1-d2	Soprano	Graceful. Demands lightness of tone. (Gevaert)
È quest' asilo ameno e grato (Orfeo)	e1-a2	g1-f2	Soprano	A graceful, delicate, sustained air with chorus. (Score, gen. av.)
Gli sguardi trattieni (Orfeo)	d1-g2	g1-e2	Soprano	Graceful. (Score, gen. av.)
Numi offesi (Aristeo)	(a)e1-d2	e1-c2	Alto	Very sustained, slow. (B & H, Alt Arien, Vol. II)
O del mio dolce ardor (Elena e Paride)	b-f#2	f#1-d2	All voices	Very sustained. (Parisotti, Italian Anthology. GS) Originally written for soprano.
Oscura il sol le stelle (Semiramide)	g-c2	c1-c2	Alto	Majestic, sustained. (B & H, Alt Arien, Vol. II)
Recitative: Ferma crudele, ferma Air: Prenditi, il figlio (Le Donne Chinese)	a#-d2 (f#2)	d1-c#2	Alto	Vigorous, dramatic, spirited. (B & H, Alt Arien, Vol. II)
Spiagge amate (Elena e Paride)	d1-g2	f1-eb2	All voices	Very sustained. (RIC) Originally for soprano.
Tradita, sprezzata, che piango? (Semiramide)	bb-eb2	d1-d2	Alto	Vigorous, dramatic. (B & H, Alt Arien, Vol. II)
Vieni, che poi sereno (Semiramide)	b-e2	g1-d2	All voices	A graceful minuet. Originally written for alto. (Krehbiel, Songs from the Operas. OD) A transposed edition, a minor third higher for soprano or tenor. (GS)

225

FRANZ JOSEPH HAYDN
(1732–1809)

Most of Haydn's best vocal music is to be found in his oratorios. His songs, as those of Mozart, charming and pleasant as they are, can hardly be called in any way representative of his style of writing for the voice. The canzonettas to English texts, among them the delightful "Mermaid's song," as well as the more widely known "My mother bids me bind my hair," "The spirit's song," and "She never told her love" are perhaps the most representative and rewarding among his few songs.

Editions: C. F. Peters
Augener
Novello
Numerous reprints of single songs by many American publishers

Note: "Füssl" in parentheses refers to "Arien für Sopran," 2 volumes, edited by Füssl, published by Haydn-Mozart Presse, Salzburg.

TITLE	COMP.	TESS.	TYPE	REMARKS
Ah, crudel!	c1-f2	e1-d2	Soprano	Has slow, sustained, and fast sections. The latter somewhat spirited. Demands some flexibility. Italian text. Used in Gazzaniga's "La Vendemmia." (Füssl)
Ausgesandt vom Strahlenthrone	eb1-bb2	eb1-g2	Soprano	Sustained. In "Alfred." (Füssl)

TITLE	COMP.	TESS.	TYPE	REMARKS
Chi vive amante	d1-ab2	f1-f2	Soprano	Sustained. Demands some flexibility. Has some florid passages. Italian text. Used in Bianchi's "Alessandro nell' Indie." (Füssl)
Costretta a piangere	c1-c3	g1-g2	Most suitable for light, high soprano	Graceful, light, demands flexibility. Has some florid passages. Italian text. Probably from the lost "Commedia." (Füssl)
Der erste Kuss	d1-g2	g1-eb2	Not too suitable for very low voices	Sustained, graceful. Demands some flexibility.
D'una spossa meschinella	a-a2	g1-g2	Soprano	Generally sustained. Has both adagio and presto sections, florid passages. Demands considerable flexibility. Ending phrase has an interval skip of full two octaves. Italian text. Used in Paisiello's "La Frascatana." (Füssl)
Eine sehr gewöhnliche Geschichte	d1-e2	g1-d2	All voices	Light and humorous. Demands facile articulation.
Il meglio mio carattere	bb-g2	eb1-f2	Soprano	Short recitative and a graceful aria. Light. Italian text. Used in Cimarosa's "L'impresario in Augustie." (Füssl)
In felice sventurata	d1-bb2	f1-g2	Soprano	Sustained section followed by one which is faster, spirited. Demands some flexibility.

TITLE	COMP.	TESS.	TYPE	REMARKS
				Italian text. Used in Cimarosa's "I due supposti conti." (Füssl)
Jeder meint, der Gegenstand	e1-f2	f1-d2	All voices	Light, delicate.
La moglie quando è buona	g-f2	eb1-eb2	Mezzo-soprano	Short, sustained andante and a faster, somewhat spirited song. Demands flexibility. Italian text. Used in Cimarosa's "Giannina e Bernadone." (Füssl)
Liebes Mädchen, hör mir zu	e1-e2	f#1-c#2	Most suitable for men's voices	Delicate.
Lob der Faulheit	c1-f#2	g1-e2	All voices	A mock-serious hymn in praise of laziness.
My mother bids me bind my hair	e1-e2	a1-e2	Women's voices	Light, delicate.
O tuneful voice	b-g2	f1-eb2	All voices	A beautiful cantilena, unfortunately marred by poor English prosody. The German translation may be preferable.
Pensi a me	c#1-g2	g1-e2	All voices	A slow arietta. Italian text.
Quando la rosa	f#1-b2	g1-g2	Soprano	Sustained, gentle, graceful. Italian text. Used in Anfossi's "La Metilde ritrovata." (Füssl)
Sailor's song	e-f#1	a-e1	Men's voices	A spirited, rollicking song extolling the British Navy.
She never told her love	d1-f2	ab1-eb2	All voices except a very light soprano	Slow and grave.

TITLE	COMP.	TESS.	TYPE	REMARKS
Signor, voi sapete senz' altre parole	e1-g2	f1-f2	Soprano	Has sustained and spirited sections. Demands some flexibility. Italian text. Used in Anfossi's "Il Matrimonio per Inganno." (Füssl)
Solo è pensoso i più deserti campi	c1-b♭2	f1-f2	Soprano	Sustained. In two sections, the second slightly faster and more graceful than the first. Italian text. Used in Francesco Petrarca's "Il Canzoniere." (Füssl)
Son pietosa, son bonina	d♯1-f♯2	d♯1-e2	Soprano, except light, high voices	Sustained section followed by one that is faster, rhythmical and dancelike. Italian text. Used in Cimarosa's "La Circe" or "L'isola Incantata." (Füssl)
Sono Alcina	e1-f2	same	Soprano	Sustained, somewhat slow. Italian text. Used in Gazzaniga's "L'isola di Alcina." (Füssl)
The Mermaid's Song	c1-g2	e1-d2	Soprano or mezzo-soprano	Light, spirited, demands some flexibility and an accomplished pianist.
The Spirit's Song	b-g♭2	f1-d♭2	Medium or low voices	Slow and somber.
The Wanderer	d1-e♭2	f1-d2	Medium or low voices	Slow and sustained.
Un tetto umil	d♯1-g♯2	e1-e2	All voices	A delicate and sustained arietta. Italian text.
Vada adagio, signorina	f1-b♭2	g1-g2	Soprano, except light, high voices	Spirited, has some florid passages. Demands flexibility and facile articulation.

| | | | | Italian text. Used in Pietro Gugliel-mi's "La Quakera Spiritosa." (Füssl) |

AIRS FROM THE ORATORIOS

(Scores of "The Creation" and "The Seasons" are generally available.)

TITLE	COMP.	TESS.	TYPE	REMARKS
The Seasons Recitative: Lo! where the plenteous harvest wav'd Air: Behold, along the dewy grass	G-f1	c-d1	Bass	Vigorous, spirited. Has some florid passages and some very wide leaps.
The Seasons Recitative: 'Tis noon and now intense the sun Air: Distressful nature fainting sinks	b♯-f♯1	e-e1	Tenor	Slow and sustained. Not suitable for light, high voices.
The Seasons From out the fold the shepherd drives	B♭-f1	f-c1	Bass	Sustained and grace-ful. Has florid pas-sages.
The Creation Recitative: And God created man Air: In native worth	f♯-a1	g-e1	Tenor	Sustained, graceful. Demands some flexi-bility.
The Seasons Light and life de-jected languish	c1-f2	e1-c2	Soprano	A short, slow and sustained air. Also suitable for mezzo-soprano or alto.
The Creation Recitative: And God said: Let the earth bring forth the living creature	F-d1	d-c♯1	Bass	An extended recita-tive, and a vigorous, majestic air. De-mands some flexibility

TITLE	COMP.	TESS.	TYPE	REMARKS
Air: Now Heav'n in fullest glory shone The Seasons Recitative: O welcome now Air: O, how pleasing to the senses	bb-bb2	a1-f2	Soprano	An extended reci- tative and an andan- te, allegro air. De- mands considerable flexibility.
The Creation Recitative: And God said: Let the waters Air: On mighty pens	e1-bb2	g1-f2	Soprano	Graceful. Has florid passages.
The Creation Recitative: And God said: Let the waters Air: Rolling and foaming billows	G-f1	d-d1	Bass or baritone	Rapid, vigorous, de- mands some flexibility. The vocal line is sus- tained, the final sec- tion subdued.
The Creation The marvelous work behold amazed	c1-c3	g1-f2	Soprano	A spirited solo with choral accompani- ment. May be used as a solo excerpt. Demands some flexi- bility.
The Seasons Recitative: A crystal pave- ment lies the lake Air: The trav'ler stands perplexed	d-b1	e-e1	Tenor	Fast. Has some florid passages.
The Seasons Recitative: At last the bounteous sun Air: With joy the im- patient husbandman	Bb-e1	c-c1	Bass	Graceful. Demands some flexibility.

TITLE	COMP.	TESS.	TYPE	REMARKS

The Creation
Recitative:

And God said:	e1-bb2	a1-f2	Soprano	Graceful. Has
Let the earth				florid passages.
bring forth grass				

Air:
With verdure clad

OPERATIC AIRS

"Vállalat" in parentheses after the remarks column refers to "Arie Dalle Opere," published by Z. Vállalat, Budapest.

Der Apotheker
(German text. Score published by Gutmann)

Diese Püppchen	G#-d1	e-b	Bass	A rapid buffo air. Demands extremely facile articulation.
Es Kam ein Pascha aus Türkenland	d1-g#2	e1-e2	Mezzo-soprano or soprano	Graceful, comic narrative. Demands considerable flexibility.
Sitzt Einem hier im Kopf das Weh'	d#-a1	e-e1	Tenor	Spirited comic air. Has florid passages.
Wie Schleier seh' ich's nieder-schweben	c-bb2	f1-e2	Soprano	Sustained.
Wo Liebesgötter lachten	b-g2	f1-e2	Mezzo-soprano or soprano	Rapid comic air. Demands considerable flexibility and facile articulation.

Il Mondo della
Luna

O luna lucente	d1-eb2	same	All voices, except a light, high soprano	Sustained. Italian text. (Vállalat)

Il Mondo della
Luna

Un poco di denaro	bb-g2	eb1-eb2	Tenor	Very slow, sustained. Italian text. (Vállalat)

TITLE	COMP.	TESS.	TYPE	REMARKS
La Canterina (an intermezzo) Non v'è chi miajuta	d1-g2	g1-e♭2	Soprano	Animated. Italian text. (Vállalat)
Le Pescatrici Questa mano	c♯1-d2	same	Mezzo-soprano	Animated, graceful. Italian text. (Vállalat)
Le Pescatrici Voglio amar e vuo scherzare	d1-d3	g1-a♭2	Lyric soprano or coloratura soprano	Sustained, florid. Demands considerable flexibility. Italian text. (Vállalat)
L'Infedeltà Delusa Chi s'impaccia di moglie cittadina (Nencio's serenade)	b♭-c3	e♭1-g2	Tenor	Sustained, somewhat slow. Demands flexibility and facile articulation. Italian text. (Vállalat)
L'Infedeltà Delusa È la pompa un grand imbroglio	b♭-b♭2	f1-g2	Soprano	Sustained vocal line. Has some long, florid passages. Italian text. (Vállalat)

WOLFGANG AMADEUS MOZART
(1756–1791)

OPERATIC AIRS AND CONCERT ARIAS

The operatic airs of Mozart often follow a pattern of a recitative (sometimes so extended as to reach the proportions of a dramatic "scena"), a sustained cantabile movement and a more or less florid, spirited allegro. For the most part Mozart avoids the older da capo aria form. Yet perhaps fully as often he abandons the andante, allegro form in favor of a more unified single-movement song form, as for instance in the "Porgi Amor" (Nozze di Figaro) or "Finche han dal vino" (Don Giovanni).

Vocally, Mozart arias, although magnificently written for the voice, are for the most part quite difficult, demanding considerable flexibility, excellent breath control and a good command of dynamics. Sometimes they demand a voice possessing a very extensive range, but only in a few instances does Mozart demand a voice of unusual power.

His concert arias are extraordinarily difficult display pieces. Seldom performed now because of their difficulty, they would seem to be of considerable value to any virtuoso vocalist's repertoire, especially to the repertoire of a coloratura soprano. In the opinion of this writer, the tenor concert arias, as well as the tenor airs from Idomeneo and La Clemenza di Tito, can now be performed effectively by soprani, or in some instances by high mezzo-soprani, since these two works have not been performed as stage works for nearly a hundred years, and the association between the air and the character of the drama is now, for all practical purposes, forgotten.

In studying Mozart's airs one should bear in mind the fact that, as a musical dramatist, Mozart is unique and perhaps unequaled. One can safely say that Mozart never wrote a piece of vocal music in which the text and the music were not in complete and miraculous accord; even his use of florid passages, which to many a present-day singer may imply a non-dramatic approach to the problem of setting words to music, is emotionally significant, naturally within the stylistic frame of his time.

To appreciate the dramatic expressiveness of a florid air of

Mozart, one should compare it with a florid air of a composer like Galuppi, for instance, who, like most composers of the period, wrote delightful florid passages without being able to endow them with much, if any, emotional significance.

A singer who is trying to learn a Mozart air would do well to study the libretto of the entire opera—a procedure which of course is always helpful, but which would add little to his appreciation of an air by composers like Cesti, Bononcini, or even Handel in some instances.

The soprano airs of Mozart are, generally speaking, written for the following types of voices: the rather heavy lyric soprano (Spinto), the light soubrette soprano and the coloratura soprano. In some instances (the Queen of the Night airs in Zauberflöte, some Constanza airs in the Entführung, and the Fiordiligi airs in Così fan Tutte, as well as in his concert arias) Mozart writes for a voice of an unusually wide range and power; these airs are not recommended for the student, as the problems of both range and volume could hardly be mastered if the instrument itself is not adequate to the demands made upon it.

Mozart wrote hardly any airs for alto and only a few for mezzo-soprano. Most of his mezzo-soprano airs can easily be sung by heavy dramatic soprano voices, for which his soprano airs may be too high in tessitura.

His tenor airs are, practically without exception, written for a rather light lyric voice, and demand considerable facility in florid work. The tessitura is for the most part rather high and would seem to be too taxing for a heavy voice.

There are not many airs of Mozart suitable for high baritone; most of his baritone airs are best suited for heavier bass-baritone voices. His bass airs, with the exception of the two Sarastro airs in Zauberflöte and the Concert Aria, are almost always of the buffo character.

Bibliography

The name found in parentheses after the remarks indicates one of the following collections:

Becker: Arie Scelte, edited by G. Becker, published by G. Ricordi.
Füssl: 7 Arias for Contralto, edited by K. H. Füssl, published by International Music Co.
Kagen: Arias from Operas, 4 volumes for soprano, 1 volume for mezzo-soprano, 1 volume for tenor, 2 volumes for baritone, 1 volume for bass. Edited by S. Kagen, published by International Music Co.
21 Arias: 21 Concert Arias, published by G. Schirmer.

Note: Publisher's name in parentheses signifies that the aria is available singly.

TITLE	COMP.	TESS.	TYPE	REMARKS

TITLE	COMP.	TESS.	TYPE	REMARKS
Ascanio in Alba L'ombra de' rami tuoi	d1-g2	g1-g2	Soprano	Animated, spirited aria. In parts florid. Demands some flexibility. (Kagen)
Ascanio in Alba Si, ma d'un altro amore	eb1-ab2	g1-f2	Soprano	Recitative and an andante aria. Demands some flexibility. (Kagen)
Così fan Tutte Recitative: Temerari, sortite fuori Air: Come scoglio	a-c3	f1-f2	Dramatic soprano (lyric soprano)	Recitative and a vigorous, animated air. Has many florid passages. Demands a voice of unusually extensive range. (Kagen; Becker)
Così fan Tutte E amore un ladroncello	f1-g2	bb1-f2	Soprano	Light and rapid. Gently humorous. Demands some flexibility and facile articulation. (Kagen)
Così fan Tutte In uomini, in soldati	c1-a2	f1-f2	Soprano	Animated, light. Gently humorous. Demands facile articulation. (Kagen)
Così fan Tutte Recitative: Ei parte, senti, ah no . . . . . . Air: Per pietà ben mio perdona	a-b2	e1-e2	Dramatic soprano (lyric soprano)	Recitative, andante, allegro. Has florid passages. Demands a voice of very extensive range, possessing a well-developed lower register. (Kagen; Becker)
Così fan Tutte Una donna a quindici anni	d1-b2	g1-e2	Soprano	Animated, light, humorous. Demands facile articulation. (Kagen)

TITLE	COMP.	TESS.	TYPE	REMARKS
Der Schauspiel- direktor Bester Jüngling	e♭1-b♭2	g1-g2	Soprano	An andante, al- legro air. Has florid passages. German text. (IMC)
Der Schauspiel- direktor Da Schlägt die Abschiedsstunde	f♯1-d3	b♭1-g2	Coloratura soprano	An andante, al- legro air. In parts very florid. German text. (IMC)
Die Entführung aus dem Serail Ach ich liebte	f1-d3	b♭1-f2	Coloratura soprano	An andante, al- legro air. In parts very florid. German text. (gen. av.)
Die Entführung aus dem Serail Durch Zärtlichkeit	e1-e3	a1-f♯2	Lyric soprano (coloratura soprano)	Graceful, gently humorous. Has florid passages. German text. (gen. av.)
Die Entführung aus dem Serail Martern aller Arten	b-d3	a1-a2	Coloratura soprano	Dramatic, spirited, brilliant and florid. Demands a rather unusual coloratura voice, having a good command of forte and of medium register. German text. (Kagen)
Die Entführung aus dem Serail Welche Wonne, welch Lust	g1-a2	b1-g2	Lyric soprano (coloratura soprano)	Rapid, light. Demands facile articulation. German text. (Kagen)
Die Entführung aus dem Serail Welcher Kummer herrscht in mei- ner Seele	f♯1-b♭2	g1-g2	Lyric soprano (coloratura soprano)	Slow, very sustained. Demands some flexi- bility. German text. (Kagen)

TITLE	COMP.	TESS.	TYPE	REMARKS
Don Giovanni				
Ah, fuggi il traditor	f#1-a2	a1-f#2	Dramatic soprano (lyric soprano)	Dramatic, spirited. Has florid passages. (Kagen)
Don Giovanni				
Batti, batti o bel Masetto	c1-bb2	f1-f2	Soprano	A graceful andante, allegro aria. Has florid passages. Gently humorous. (gen. av.)
Don Giovanni				
Recitative: Un quali eccessi o Numi Air: Mi tradi quel alma ingrata	d1-bb2	bb1-g2	Dramatic soprano (lyric soprano)	Recitative and an animated, florid air. (gen. av.)
Don Giovanni				
Recitative: Crudele? Ah no, mio bene Air: Non mi dir	e1-bb2	g1-g2	Dramatic soprano (lyric soprano)	Recitative, andante, allegro. Has florid passages. (gen. av.)
Don Giovanni				
Or sai chi l'onore	f1-a2	a1-g2	Dramatic soprano (lyric soprano)	Dramatic, vigorous. (Kagen)
Don Giovanni				
Vedrai carino	g1-g2	g1-e2	Soprano	Graceful. Vocally not taxing. (gen. av.)
Idomeneo				
Recitative: O smania! O furie! Air: D'Oreste, d'Ajace!	eb1-c3	g1-g2	Dramatic soprano (lyric soprano)	Recitative and a dramatic, spirited, vigorous air. (Kagen)
Idomeneo				
Idol mio, se ritroso altro	f#1-a2	a1-g2	Soprano	Sustained, florid. Demands some flexibility. (Kagen)
Idomeneo				
Recitative: Qundo avran' fine o mai				

TITLE	COMP. TESS.	TYPE	REMARKS
Air:			
Padre! Germani!	e1-ab2 g1-g2	Soprano	Sustained. Demands some flexibility. (Score, IMC)
Idomeneo			
Se il padre perdei	eb1-bb2 g1-eb2	Soprano	Slow. Demands considerable flexibility. (Score, IMC)
Idomeneo			
Recitative:			
Estinto è Idomeneo	c1-a2 a1-f2	Dramatic soprano (high mezzosoprano)	An extended recitative and a spirited, vigorous, dramatic air. (Kagen)
Air:			
Tutte nel cor vi sento			
Idomeneo			
Recitative:			
Solitudini amiche	e#1-a2 g#1-e2	Soprano	Recitative and a sustained, graceful air. In parts quite florid. (IMC)
Air:			
Zeffiretti lusinghieri			
Il re pastore			
Recitative:			
Ditelo, voi pastori	e1-bb2 a1-g2	Soprano (lyric or coloratura)	An andante recitative and an allegro air. Has some long, very florid passages. Demands flexibility and facile articulation. (Becker)
Air:			
Aer tranquillo			
Il re pastore			
Alla selva, al prato	f#1-c3 a1-g2	Soprano (lyric or coloratura)	An animated aria. Has some long, florid passages. Demands flexibility. (Becker)
Il re pastore			
Barbaro! O Dio!	f1-c3 a1-g2	Soprano (lyric or coloratura)	Andante, allegro. Has florid passages. (Becker)
Il re pastore			
Recitative:			
No: voi non siete	eb1-bb2 g1-g2	Soprano	Recitative and a florid allegro aria. (Becker)
Air:			
Di tante sue procelle			

TITLE	COMP.	TESS.	TYPE	REMARKS
Il re pastore L'amerò, sarò costante	e♭1-b2	g1-g2	Soprano	Sustained, graceful, with violin obbligato. An elaborate cadenza by J. Lauterbach is added near the end. (Kagen)
Il re pastore Se tu di me fai dono	g♯1-a2	a1-f♯2	Most suitable for light, high soprano	A sustained, graceful air. Very high tessitura. (IMC)
La Clemenza di Tito Deh per questo istante solo	c♯1-f♯2	a1-e2	Soprano or mezzo-soprano	An andante, allegro air. Demands some flexibility. (Kagen)
La Clemenza di Tito Deh, se piacer mi vuoi	b-b2	g1-d2	Dramatic soprano or high mezzo-soprano	An andante, allegro air. Quite florid. (Kagen)

La Clemenza di Tito
Recitative:
  Ecco il punto
Air:
  Non più di fiori
	c1(g)-a2	f1-f2	Dramatic soprano or mezzo-soprano	Scena, andante, allegro. Demands some flexibility. (Kagen)

La Clemenza di Tito Parto, parto, ma tu, ben mio	c1-b♭2	g1-e♭2	Soprano or mezzo-soprano	Clarinet obbligato. An andante, allegro air. Has florid passages. (IMC)
La Clemenza di Tito Saltro che lacrime	f♯1-a2	a1-f♯2	Lyric soprano (coloratura soprano)	A graceful minuet. (Kagen)
La Clemenza di Tito Torna di Tito a lato	d1-g2	g1-d2	Soprano or mezzo-soprano	Graceful. Demands some flexibility. (Score, IMC)

TITLE	COMP.	TESS.	TYPE	REMARKS
La Clemenza <u>di Tito</u> Tu fosti tradito	e1-a2	g1-f2	Soprano	Sustained. Demands some flexibility. (Score, IMC)
La finta <u>giardiniera</u> Crudeli, fermate	eb1-ab2	ab1-g2	Soprano	Animated. In some parts demands some flexibility. (Kagen)
La finta <u>giardiniera</u> Geme la tortorella	f#1-c3	a1-g2	Most suitable for light, high soprano	Sustained, florid. High tessitura. (Kagen)
La finta semplice Senti l'eco ove t'aggiri	eb1-a2	g1-g2	Soprano	Sustained andante sections followed by graceful allegro passages. In parts florid. (Kagen)
Le nozze di Figaro Al desio	b-a2	f1-f2	Dramatic soprano (high mezzo-soprano)	Andante, allegro. Has florid passages. An alternate air for the role of the Countess; no longer used in stage performances of the opera. (Kagen)
Le nozze di Figaro Recitative: Giunse al fin il momento Air: Deh vieni non tardar	c1(a)-a2	f1-f2	Soprano	Recitative and a sustained, delicate air. In bar fifteen of the andante, the "bb" and "a" are often sung as "bb1, a1." (gen. av.)
Le nozze di Figaro Recitative: E Susanna non vien Air: Dove sono	d1-a2	g1-f2	Dramatic soprano (lyric soprano)	Recitative, a very sustained andante, and a spirited allegro. (gen. av.)

TITLE	COMP.	TESS.	TYPE	REMARKS
Le nozze di Figaro				
L'ho perduta, me meschina	f1-f2	ab1-e#2	Soprano	Sustained, short. Vocally not taxing. (Score, gen.av.)
Le nozze di Figaro				
Non so più	eb1-g2	g1-eb2	Soprano (mezzo-soprano)	Rapid, light. Demands very facile articulation. (gen. av.)
Le nozze di Figaro				
Porgi amor	d1-ab2	bb1-f2	Dramatic soprano (lyric soprano)	Slow, very sustained. (gen. av.)
Le nozze di Figaro				
Un moto di gioia	b-g2	g1-d2	Soprano	Animated, light. Vocally not taxing. An alternate arietta for the role of Susanna, no longer used in stage performances of the opera. (Kagen)
Le nozze di Figaro				
Venite, inginocchiatevi	d1-g2	g1-e2	Soprano	Gently humorous. Vocally not too taxing. (Score, gen. av.)
Le nozze di Figaro				
Voi che sapete	c1-f2	f1-eb2	Soprano (mezzo-soprano)	Sustained, graceful. Vocally not taxing. (gen. av.)
Lucio Silla				
Frà i pensier	d1-ab2	g1-g2	Soprano	A very sustained andante and an allegro. (Kagen)
Lucio Silla				
Pupille amate	e1-a2	g#1-f#2	Soprano	A graceful minuet. Demands some flexibility. (Kagen)
Mitridate, rè di Ponto				
Parto: nel gran cimento	e1-b2	a1-g#2	Soprano (dramatic)	Andante and florid allegro sections. Demands considerable flexibility. (Kagen)

TITLE	COMP.	TESS.	TYPE	REMARKS
Mitridate, rè di Ponto				
Tu sai per chi m'accese	e1-b2	a1-g2	Soprano	Sustained. Has some florid passages. (Kagen)
Zaide				
Ruhe sanft, mein holdes Leben	g1-b2	a1-g2	Most suitable for light, high soprano	A graceful minuet with an andante middle section. Has florid passages. Demands flexibility. German text. (Kagen)
Zaide				
Tiger! Wetze nur die Klauen	d1-a2	g1-g2	Dramatic soprano	A dramatic, vigorous aria with a sustained larghetto in the middle. Demands some flexibility. German text. (Kagen)
Zaide				
Trostlos schluchzet Philomele	e1-a2	a1-a2	Most suitable for light, high soprano	Sustained aria. Demands flexibility. German text. (Kagen)
Zauberflöte				
Ach ich fühl's	c#1-bb2	g1-g2	Most suitable for lyric soprano	Slow, very sustained. Demands in parts some flexibility. German text. (gen. av.)
Zauberflöte				
Der Hölle Rache	f1-f3	a1-a2	Coloratura soprano	Dramatic, brilliant, florid allegro. Demands a rather unusual coloratura voice, possessing a good command of forte and of medium register. German text. (gen. av.)
Zauberflöte Recitative: O zittre nicht mein lieber Sohn				

TITLE	COMP.	TESS.	TYPE	REMARKS
Air: Zum Leiden bin ich auserkoren	d1-f3	bb1-g2	Coloratura soprano	Recitative, andante, allegro. Florid. Demands a rather unusual coloratura voice, possessing a good command of forte and of medium register. German text. (gen. av.)

CONCERT AIRS — Soprano

TITLE	COMP.	TESS.	TYPE	REMARKS
A questo seno, deh! vieni!	eb1-bb2	g1-g2	Soprano	Recitative and a light, animated rondo. Demands considerable flexibility. (IMC)
Ah, lo previdi!	eb1-bb2	g1-g2	Soprano	Recitative and an allegro, andante, allegro air. (21 Arias)
Ah se in ciel, benigne stelle	d1-d3	a1-a2	Soprano	Animated, quite florid in parts. (21 Arias)
Alma grande e nobil core	c1-g2	f1-f2	Not suitable for light, high soprano	Allegro, allegro assai. Inserted by Mlle Villeneuve in Cimarosa's "I due Baroni." (21 Arias)
Basta, vincesti. . . Ah non lasciarmi, no	eb1-bb2	g1-g2	Soprano	Two recitatives, each followed by a sustained air. (21 Arias)
Bella mia fiamma. . . Resta, oh cara	d1-a2	g1-g2	Not suitable for light, high soprano	Recitative and a sustained andante, allegro air. (21 Arias)
Chi sa, chi sa, qual sia	d1-a2 (g2)	g1-g2	Soprano	Sustained air with some florid passages. Inserted by Mlle Villeneuve in V. Martin's opera "Il burbero di buon cuore." (21 Arias)

TITLE	COMP.	TESS.	TYPE	REMARKS
Ch'io mi scordi di te? . . . . Non temer, amato bene	ab-bb2 (ab2)	eb1-g2	Not suitable for light, high soprano	Recitative and an andante, allegretto rondo air. Has some florid passages. Text, in part, identical to K. 490, Idamante's aria. (21 Arias)
Kommet her, ihr frechen Sünder	e1-g2	g1-f2	Soprano	Sustained, strophic. A Lenten hymn "probably composed to be included in an oratorio." (21 Arias)
Ma che vi fece, o stelle. . . . Sperai vicino il lido	f1-f3	a1-a2	Soprano	Two sections of recitative and a sustained allegretto, allegro air. The allegro is in parts quite florid. (21 Arias)
Mia speranza adorata	c1-f3	a1-a2	Coloratura soprano	Recitative, andante, allegro. Florid. Demands a rather unusual coloratura voice, commanding a good forte and having a well-developed medium register. (21 Arias)
Misera, dove son!	f1-bb2	g1-g2	Soprano	Recitative, andante, allegro. Demands considerable flexibility. (IMC)
Nehmt meinen Dank	f#1-a2	a1-f2	Soprano	Sustained. German text. (21 Arias)
No, no, no, che non sei capace	d1-e3	a1-a2	Soprano	Sustained air. Allegro section. Florid, demands flexibility. Inserted by Lange into Anfossi's "Il curioso indiscreto." (21 Arias)
Non piu. Tutto ascoltavi	e1-bb2	bb-g2	Soprano	Recitative, andante, allegro. Has florid passages. Written to replace original beginning of Act II

TITLE	COMP.	TESS.	TYPE	REMARKS
				in private performance of "Idomeneo." (21 Arias)
Popoli di Tessaglia!	f1-g3	ab1-a2	Soprano (dramatic coloratura)	Extended recitative and sustained air. In parts extremely florid. Demands considerable flexibility. Text is from Gluck's opera, "Alceste." (21 Arias)
Vado, ma dove?	d1-g2	f1-f2	Not suitable for light, high soprano	Sustained aria. Inserted by Mlle Villeneuve in V. Martin's opera "Il burbero di buon cuore." (21 Arias)
Voi avete un cor fedele	d1-b2	g1-g2	Soprano	Graceful andantino sections followed by allegro sections with some long, florid passages. (21 Arias)
Vorrei spiegarvi, oh Dio!	e1-e3	a1-a2	Soprano	Sustained. In parts florid. Inserted by Lange into Anfossi's opera "Il curioso indiscreto." (21 Arias)

OPERATIC AIRS — Mezzo-Soprano and Contralto

Così fan Tutte				
Recitative:				
Ah, scostati!	d1-ab2	eb1-eb2	Mezzo-soprano (dramatic soprano)	Recitative and a spirited, vigorous, dramatic air. (Kagen)
Air:				
Smanie implacabili				
Idomeneo				
Recitative:				
Estinto è Idomeneo				

TITLE	COMP.	TESS.	TYPE	REMARKS
Air: Tutte nel cor vi sento	c1-a2	a1-f2	High mezzo- soprano or dra- matic soprano	An extended reci- tative and a spirit- ed, vigorous, dra- matic air. (Kagen)
La Clemenza di Tito Deh per questo istante solo	c#1-f#2	a1-e2	Mezzo- soprano or so- prano	An andante, allegro air. Demands some flexibility. (Kagen)
La Clemenza di Tito Deh, se piacer mi vuoi	b-b2	g1-d2	High mezzo- soprano or dra- matic soprano	An andante, allegro air. Quite florid. (Score, IMC)
La Clemenza di Tito Recitative: Ecco il punto Air: Non più di fiori	c1(g)-a2	f1-f2	Mezzo- soprano or dra- matic soprano	Scena, andante, al- legro. Demands some flexibility. (Kagen)
La Clemenza di Tito Parto, parto, ma tu, ben mio	c1-bb2	g1-eb2	Mezzo- soprano or soprano	Clarinet obbligato. An andante, allegro air. Has florid passages. (IMC)
La Clemenza di Tito Torna di Tito a lato	d1-g2	g1-d2	Mezzo- soprano or soprano	Demands some flexibility. (Score, IMC)
Le Nozze di Figaro Al desio	b-a2	f1-f2	High mezzo- soprano or dra- matic soprano	Andante, allegro. Has florid passages. An alternate air for the role of the Countess; no longer used in stage performances of the opera. (Kagen)

TITLE	COMP.	TESS.	TYPE	REMARKS
Le Nozze di Figaro Il capro e la capretta	f#1-b2	b1-g2	High mezzo- soprano or soprano	Originally in- tended for a high mezzo-soprano. A graceful minuet and a spirited al- legro. In parts quite florid. (Ka- gen)
Le Nozze di Figaro Non so più	eb1-g2	g1-eb2	Mezzo- soprano or soprano	Rapid, light. De- mands very facile articulation. (gen. av.)
Le Nozze di Figaro Voi che sapete	c1-f2	f1-eb2	Mezzo- soprano or soprano	Sustained, graceful. Vocally not taxing. (gen. av.)
Mitridate, rè di Ponto Già daglia occhi	a-d2	d1-c2	Contralto	Andante, allegro. Has some florid passages. In parts demands some flexi- bility. (Füssl)
Mitridate, rè di Ponto Son reo; l'error confesso	a-e2	d1-d2	Contralto	A majestic adagio and an allegro. In parts demands some flexibility. (Füssl)
Mitridate, rè di Ponto Va, l'error mio palesa	a-e1	d1-c2	Contralto	Animated. Has some fairly florid passages (Füssl)
Mitridate, rè di Ponto Venga pur, minacci e frema	a-d2	d1-c2	Contralto	Allegro, andante, al- legro. Has some florid passages. In parts demands some flexibility. (Füssl)

CONCERT AIRS — Bass and Contralto

TITLE	COMP.	TESS.	TYPE	REMARKS
Io ti lascio	bb-d1	d1-c2	Alto (or bass)	Slow and sustained. (IMC)

TITLE	COMP.	TESS.	TYPE	REMARKS
Ombra felice	g-d2	c1-c2	Low, heavy contralto	An accompanied recitative and an extended rondo, alternating between an andante and an allegro assai. (IMC)

OPERATIC AIRS — Tenor

TITLE	COMP.	TESS.	REMARKS
Così fan Tutte Recitative: Non sperarlo Air: Ah, lo veggio quella anima bella	f-bb1	bb-g1	Recitative and an animated air. Demands considerable flexibility and lightness of tone. The tessitura is uncommonly high, the bb1 occurring frequently. (Score, gen. av.)
Così fan Tutte Recitative: In qual fiero contrasto Air: Tradito, schernito, dal perfido cor	f-a1	a-g1	Recitative and a vigorous allegro. Demands some flexibility. (Score, gen. av.)
Così fan Tutte Un'aura amorosa	d-a1	a-f#1	Sustained. Demands considerable flexibility. (gen. av.)
Die Entführung aus dem Serail Constanze! Dich wieder zu sehen	e-a1	a-e1	Slow, quite florid. German text. (Score, gen. av.)
Die Entführung aus dem Serail Frisch zum Kampfe	d-b1	a-f#1	A spirited, vigorous, mock-heroic air. German text. (Score, gen. av.)
Die Entführung aus dem Serail Hier soll ich dich denn sehen	g-a1	c-g1	Sustained. Demands some flexibility. German text. (Score, gen. av.)
Die Entführung aus dem Serail Ich baue ganz auf deine Stärke	eb-bb1	bb-g1	Sustained. Quite florid. German text. (Kagen)

TITLE	COMP.	TESS.	REMARKS
Die Entführung aus dem Serail Im Mohrenland	e#-d1	a-d1	A delicate, subdued serenade. Vocally not taxing. Demands good command of pianissimo. German text. (Score, gen. av.)
Die Entführung aus dem Serail Wenn der Freude Thränen spriessen	C-ab1	bb-f1	Andante, allegro. Has some florid passages. German text. (Score, gen. av.)
Don Giovanni Dalla sua pace	d-g1	b-g1	Very sustained. Demands some flexibility. (gen. av.)
Don Giovanni Il mio tesoro	d-a1	bb-f1	Sustained. Has florid passages. (gen. av.)
Idomeneo Recitative: Qual mi contrubai sensi Air: Fuor del mar hò un mar in seno	d-g1	g-d1	A spirited, florid air. Somewhat long. Can be cut easily, beginning with the recapitulation "Fuor del mar" second time. (Score, IMC)
Idomeneo Recitative: Ah, qual gelido orror m'ingombrai i sensi Air: Il padre adorato	e-g1	g-f1	A vigorous, dramatic air. (Score, IMC)
Idomeneo No la morte, la morte io non pavento	e-g1	g-e1	Spirited. Vigorous. Has a sustained middle section. Demands some flexibility. (Score, IMC)
Idomeneo Non ho colpa	e-a1	a-f1	Spirited. Demands some flexibility. (Score, IMC)
Idomeneo Recitative: Sventurata Sidon Air: Se colà nè fato è scritto	e-a1	g#-e1	Recitative and a sustained air. Has florid passages. (Score, IMC)

TITLE	COMP.	TESS.	REMARKS
Idomeneo			
Se il tuo duol, se il mio desio	d-a1	g-e1	Spirited. In parts quite florid. (Kagen)
Idomeneo			
Recitative:			
Popoli! a voi l'ultima legge impone Idomeneo	f-g1	a-f1	A very extended recitative. The air is sustained, has a graceful allegretto for the middle section. Demands some flexibility. (Score, IMC)
Air:			
Torna la pace al core			
Idomeneo			
Vedrommi intorno	e-g1	g-e1	Andante, allegro. Demands some flexibility. (Score, IMC)
Il re Pastore			
Se vincendo vi rendo felici	c1-a2	g1-g2	An allegro aria. Florid. (Becker)
Il re Pastore			
Si spandi al sole	e1-g2	a1-g2	An allegro aria. Florid. (Becker)
Il re Pastore			
Voi che fausti	b-g2	g1-g2	Sustained, florid. Demands considerable flexibility. (Becker)
La Clemenza di Tito			
Ah, se fosse intorno al trono	f♯-a1	a-f♯1	Animated. Demands some flexibility. (Score, IMC)
La Clemenza di Tito			
Del piu sublime soglio	e-a1	g-e1	Sustained. Demands some flexibility. (Kagen)
La Clemenza di Tito			
Se all'impero, amici Dei	f-b♭1	a-f1	Allegro, andantino, allegro. In parts quite florid. (Score, IMC)
La Clemenza di.Tito			
Tu fosti tradito	e1-a2	g1-g2	Sustained. (Becker)
La Finta Giardiniera			
Che beltà, che leggiadria	d1-g2	a1-f2	Sustained. Has some florid passages. Demands flexibility. (Kagen)
Le Nozze di Figaro			
In quegli'anni	e♭-g1	a-f1	Andante, minuet, allegro. A comic air. Demands facile articulation. (Score, gen. av.)

251

TITLE	COMP.	TESS.	REMARKS
Lucio Silla			
Guerrier, che d'un acciaro	d1-a2	g1-g2	Spirited, vigorous, florid. (Kagen)
Zaide			
Herr und Freund!	f♯1-g2	b1-g2	Sustained. German text. (Kagen)
Zauberflöte			
Alles fühlt der Liebe Freuden	d-e1	g-d1	A rapid buffo verse song. Demands good command of p. and very facile articulation. German text. (Score, gen. av.)
Zauberflöte			
Dies Bildnis ist bezaubernd schön	f1-ab1	bb-g1	Slow, sustained. Demands some flexibility. German text. (gen. av.)

CONCERT AIRS — Tenor

TITLE	COMP.	TESS.	REMARKS
Recìtative: Misero! Air: O sogno, o son desto?	eb-ab1	bb-g1	Recitative, andante, and a brilliant allegro. (CFP: B & H)
Per pieta, non ricercare	c-ab1	g-g1	Andante, allegro. (CFP: B & H)

OPERATIC AIRS — Baritone and Bass

TITLE	COMP.	TESS.	TYPE	REMARKS
Così fan Tutte				
Donne mie, la fatte a tanti	B-e1	g-d1	Bass or bass-baritone	A spirited buffo air. Demands facile articulation. (gen. av.)
Così fan Tutte				
Non siate ritrosi	d-e1	same	Baritone or bass-baritone	A short andantino air. (Score, gen. av.)
Così fan Tutte				
Vorrei dir e cor non ho	eb-eb1	g-c1	Baritone or bass-baritone	Animated, short. (Score, gen. av.)

TITLE	COMP.	TESS.	TYPE	REMARKS
Die Entführung aus dem Serail O! wie will ich triumphieren	D-e1	d-d1	Bass	Rapid, vigorous buffo air. Demands very facile articulation, some flexibility, and a good command of low D. German text. (gen. av.)
Die Entführung aus dem Serail Solche herge-laufene Laffen	F-f1	c-c1	Bass	A spirited, vigorous buffo air. Demands some flexibility, and facile articulation. German text. (gen. av.)
Die Entführung aus dem Serail Wer ein Liebchen hat gefunden	G-d1	d-bb	Bass	A sustained verse song with variated accompaniment. German text. (Score, gen. av.)
Don Giovanni Ah pietà, Signori miei	A-e1	d-c1	Bass or bass-baritone	Rapid. Demands facile articulation. (Score, gen. av.)
Don Giovanni Deh vieni alla finestra	d-e1	a-d1	Bass-baritone or baritone	A graceful, light, animated serenade. (gen. av.)
Don Giovanni Finchè han dal vino	d-eb1	f-d1	Bass-baritone or baritone	Extremely rapid. Demands very facile articulation. (gen. av.)
Don Giovanni Ho capito, Signor, si	c-c1	same	Bass-baritone or baritone	A rapid buffo air. Demands facile articulation. (gen. av.)
Don Giovanni Madamina! Il catalogo è questo	A-e1	d-d1	Bass or bass-baritone	A rapid buffo air. Demands very facile articulation. (gen. av.)
Don Giovanni Metà di voi quà vadano	c-e1	f-c1	Baritone or bass-baritone	Animated. Demands facile articulation. (Score, gen. av.)

TITLE	COMP.	TESS.	TYPE	REMARKS
La Clemenza di Tito Tardi s'avvede	B-e1	f#-d1	Bass or baritone	Animated. Demands some flexibility. (Score, IMC)
La Finta Giardiniera A forza del martelli	d-e1	g-d1	Baritone	Animated, vigorous, demands some flexibility. High tessitura. (Kagen)
La Finta Giardiniera Con un vezzo all'Italiana	e-e1	same	Baritone	Andantino, andante, allegretto. Gently animated, light. Demands some flexibility. A "flirtation" aria. (Kagen)
La Finta Giardiniera Un marito, o Dio, vorresti	e-d1	f-d1	Baritone	Graceful, light. Demands some flexibility. (Kagen)
La Finta Semplice Con certe persone	A-e1	d-d1	Bass-baritone or baritone	Spirited, light air. Demands facile articulation. (Kagen)
La Finta Semplice Ella vuole ed io torrei	Bb-d1	c-c1	Baritone or bass-baritone	Majestic, generally sustained. Humorous. (Kagen)
La Finta Semplice Non c'è al mondo	A-e1	d-d1	Baritone or bass-baritone	Animated. (Kagen)
La Finta Semplice Troppa briga a prender moglie	G-e1	c-e1	Baritone or bass-baritone	Recitative-like section followed by a spirited air. Demands flexibility and facile articulation. (Kagen)
La Finta Semplice Ubriaco non son io	c-d1	same	Baritone or bass	A spirited air. (Kagen)

TITLE	COMP.	TESS.	TYPE	REMARKS
La Finta Semplice Vieni, vieni, o mia Ninetta	G-f1	c-c1	Baritone or bass- baritone	Not fast, humor- ous. Demands facile articulation. (Kagen)
Le Nozze di Figaro Recitative: Tutto e disposto Air: Aprite un po'quegli occhi	Bb-eb1	eb-c1	Bass- baritone or baritone	An extended recita- tive and a spirited, comic air. De- mands facile articu- lation. (Kagen)
Le Nozze di Figaro La vendetta, oh la vendetta	A-e1	d-d1	Bass	A vigorous, spirited buffo aria. Demands facile articulation. (Kagen)
Le Nozze di Figaro Non più andrai	c-e1	e-c1	Baritone	Spirited, vigorous, rhythmical. De- mands facile ar- ticulation. (gen. av.)
Le Nozze di Figaro Se vuol ballare	c-f1	f-c1	Baritone	A spirited allegretto and a presto which demands facile ar- ticulation. (gen. av.)
Le Nozze di Figaro Recitative: Hai già vinta la causa Air: Vedrò mentr'io sospiro	A-f♯1	d-d1	Baritone	An extended recita- tive and a vigorous, spirited air. (Kagen)
Zaide Ihr Mächtigen, seht ungerührt	A-f1	Bb-c1	Bass or bass- baritone	A rather dramatic, compound air. De- mands some flexi- bility. German text. (Kagen)
Zaide Nur mutig, mein Herz	B-f1	e-f1	Baritone	Sustained, majestic. Demands flexibility. Has long phrases and some florid pas- sages. German text. (Kagen)

TITLE	COMP.	TESS.	TYPE	REMARKS
Zaide Wer hungrig bei der Tafel sitzt	c-f1	f-d1	Baritone or bass- baritone	An animated buffo air. Demands facile articulation. German text. (Kagen)
Zauberflöte Der Vogelfänger bin ich ja	d-e1	g-c1	Baritone	A spirited, gay verse song. De- mands some flexi- bility and facile articulation. Ger- man text. (gen. av.)
Zauberflöte Ein Mädchen oder Weibchen	B-d1	f-c1	Baritone	A spirited light verse song. De- mands some flexi- bility. German text. (Score, gen. av.)
Zauberflöte In diesen heilgen Hallen	F♯-c♯1	B-b	Bass	Sustained, very slow, stately. German text. (gen. av.)
Zauberflöte O Isis und Osiris	F-c1	c-a	Bass	Slow, very sustained, grave. German text. (gen. av.)

CONCERT AIRS — Bass

TITLE	COMP.	TESS.	TYPE	REMARKS
Recitative: Alcandro, lo confesso Air: Non so donde viene	E-e1	b♭-d1	Bass	A vigorous recitative and an animated rondo. Demands flexibility; has an unusually wide range. (IMC) See so- prano version, "21 Concert Arias," GS.
Recitative: Così dunque tradisci Air: Aspri rimorsi atroci	F(D)-f1	c-c1	Bass or bass- baritone	Recitative and a vigorous allegro air. Has an unusually wide range. (IMC)

TITLE	COMP.	TESS.	TYPE	REMARKS
Io ti lascio	bb-d1	d1-c2	Bass (or alto)	Slow, sustained. (IMC)
Mentre ti lascio	A-eb1	d-c1	Bass or bass-baritone	An andante, allegro air. Demands some flexibility. (IMC)
Per questa bella mano	F#-d1	B-b	Bass	An andante, allegro air. Originally for bass, orchestra and string bass obbligato. In this transcription the obbligato string bass part is arranged for cello. (IMC)
Rivolgete a luí lo sguardo	G-f#1	d-d1	Baritone	Vigorous, spirited, humorous. Demands facile articulation. Originally intended to be included in the opera "Così fan Tutte" in the place of the aria No. 15, "Non siate ritrosi." (IMC)
Un bacio di mano	B-e1	e-c1	Baritone	A graceful, light, humorous arietta. (IMC)

SOLO EXCERPTS FROM SACRED WORKS

Betulia Liberata
(Oratorio)

Del pari infeconda	g-d2	d1-c2	Contralto (mezzo-soprano)	Sustained. Has florid passages. Demands some flexibility. (Füssl)

Bétulia Liberata
(Oratorio)

Parto inerme, e non pavento	a-d2	d1-c2	Contralto	Allegro, adagio. Mainly sustained vocal lines. (Füssl)

Betulia Liberata
(Oratorio)

Prigionier, che fa ritorno	a-c#2	c#1-b1	Contralto	Sustained. Has a short, graceful, light section toward the end. (Füssl)

257

TITLE	COMP.	TESS.	TYPE	REMARKS
Exsultate, Jubilate (Motet in three movements):			Soprano	The very brilliant, florid Alleluja is widely known and
(1) Exsultate, Jubilate Recitative	d1-a2	g1-f2		often performed separately. The two other move-
(2) Tu Virginum Corona	e1-a2	a1-e2		ments, however, the somewhat flor-
(3) Alleluja	f1-a2 (c3)	a1-f2		id, spirited "Exsulta-te, Jubilate" and the sustained "Tu Virginum Corona" deserve to be as widely known. The entire motet can form a most effective recital group. Latin text. (IMC; "Alleluja" gen. av.)
Mass in C Minor Et Incarnatus est	b-c3	g1-g2	Lyric soprano (dramatic soprano)	Not fast. In parts very florid, elaborate air. Latin text. (IMC)
Mass in C Minor Laudamus Te	a-a2	f1-f2	Mezzo-soprano or alto	Spirited. In parts quite florid. Latin text. (IMC)

SONGS

The songs of Mozart are for the most part simple, almost sketch-like occasional pieces, written perhaps primarily for home entertainment. Their very small number, if compared with Mozart's fantastically prodigious output in all other musical forms, is in itself significant as a possible indication of their relative unimportance among Mozart's vocal compositions, which are almost exclusively for either the operatic stage or the church.

Delightful as his songs are, their study could hardly assist one in forming an adequate idea of Mozart's unparalleled and miraculous genius as a composer of vocal music. His operatic airs are much more representative of his style of writing; curiously enough, a great number of them seem to be but little known or performed.

Editions: C. F. Peters
         Breitkopf & Härtel
         Universal Edition

TITLE	COMP.	TESS.	TYPE	REMARKS
Abendempfindung	e1-f2	g1-eb2	All voices	Slow and sustained.
Ah, spiegarti, oh Dio (Italian text)	d1-a2	f1-d2	Soprano	A concert arietta, sustained.
Als Louise die Briefe ihres un-getreuen Lieb-habers verbrannte	a1-f2	g1-eb2	Women's voices, except a very light soprano	Dramatic, some-what declamatory.
An Chloe	eb1-ab2	g1-eb2	Not too suitable for very heavy voices	Light and delicate. Note the time signa-ture ¢. Often taken too slowly.
Dans un bois solitaire (French text)	eb1-ab2	g1-eb2	All voices	An animated ariet-ta. Has a recita-tive passage in the middle section. De-mands some flexi-bility.
Das Kinderspiel	e1-e2	g♯1-d2	All voices	Light and gay. De-mands some flexi-bility. Verses 2 and 3 could be omit-ted.
Das Veilchen	f1-g2	bb1-e2	Most suit-able for high voices	A miniature canta-ta. Delicate, inter-pretatively not easy.
Die Alte	b-e2	e1-b1	Mezzo-soprano or alto	An amusing charac-ter song. Note Mozart's direction "to be sung a bit through the nose."
Die ihr des uner-messlichen Welt-alls	d1-a2	g1-g2	High voices, except a very light soprano	A solo cantata. Recitative and sev-eral short contrast-ing movements. Rather grave and declamatory.
Die kleine Spinnerin	e1-f2	g1-d2	Women's voices	Light and animated. Verse 2 or 3 could be omitted.
Gesellenreise	f1-g2	bb1-eb2	All voices	Sustained. A Masonic song.
Ich würd auf meinem Pfad	c♯1-g2	a1-e2	All voices	Sustained. Verse 2, 3, or 4 could be omitted.

259

TITLE	COMP.	TESS.	TYPE	REMARKS
Oiseaux, si tous les ans (French text)	g1-g2	b1-g2	Most suitable for high voices	A delicate arietta.
Ridente la calma	c1-a2	a1-f2	Most suitable for high voices	A slow, sustained arietta. Demands some flexibility. Italian text.
Sehnsucht nach dem Frühling	f1-f2	f1-c2	Not too suitable for very low, heavy voices	Delicate and gay. Verses 3 and 4 could be omitted.
Verdankt sei es dem Glanz	c1-f2	g1-e2	Not too suitable for very light, high voices	Very sustained. Verse 2 or 3 could be omitted.
Warnung	c1-d2	f1-c2	All voices	A delightful, humorous song. Demands facile articulation.
Wiegenlied	f1-f2	f1-c2	Women's voices	This delicate little song has been attributed to Mozart for so long that it seemed best to list it here. The composer is B. Flies, Mozart's contemporary.

2

SONGS OF THE NINETEENTH AND TWENTIETH CENTURIES

GERMAN

Many excellent songs by German and Austrian composers could not be included in the following list. Were one to try to list all the noteworthy German songs one could easily extend this list to the size at present allotted to the entire volume, since practically every German and Austrian composer of note has written a considerable number of songs. Moreover, practically every German and Austrian musician, including those who have been primarily performing artists, can boast at least a few songs of undeniable merit.

Confronted with this extraordinary wealth of material it seemed best to limit this list to the most famed songs of the outstanding German and Austrian composers.

The very great number of songs by mid- and late-nineteenth century composers of comparatively small stature, such as Marschner, Lassen, Raff, had to be omitted to provide space for the somewhat extended lists of songs by such towering figures as Schubert, Schumann, Brahms, and Hugo Wolf. The inclusion of a few songs of some minor composers, like Bohm, for instance, seemed justified in view of their great popularity.

As in the case of the French list, the contemporary German and Austrian composers, particularly those whose writing tends toward extremes in experimentation, are not represented here, with the exception of some songs of Hindemith, Schönberg and Berg. Historically, therefore, this list is admittedly in no way complete. For all practical purposes, however, it can be considered as representative of the German Lied, for the extraordinary songs of Schubert, Schumann, Brahms and Wolf are as fully represented here as the scope of this volume can allow.

For songs with original German texts listed elsewhere, see the lists of the following composers: Grieg, Griffes, Kilpinen, Sibelius, Sinding, Medtner, Rubinstein and Tschaikovsky.

263

LUDWIG VAN BEETHOVEN
(1770–1827)

As a composer of songs, Beethoven does not occupy the same towering position he holds in the realm of instrumental music. Nevertheless, songs like "Adelaide" and "An die ferne Geliebte" can at the very least be considered equal to the best examples of the German Lied, or any other type of song.

Beethoven wrote but sixty-eight songs: sixty-one to German texts (including two comic arias for Bass and Orchestra) and seven to texts in Italian, including the concert aria, "Ah, Perfido."

The songs intended for tenor or heavy voices present no extraordinary vocal difficulties. It is only in the treatment of the vocal line in the songs for a light soprano that Beethoven deviates somewhat from the usual procedure, whereby the entire or almost the entire range of the voice is as a rule utilized. Ordinarily, if a composer intends a song for a soprano possessing a range of approximately $c1$-$e3$, for example, he is almost certain to make use of the $g2$-$e3$ section of the voice. Thus the character of the voice intended is established beyond doubt and the singer is given a chance to display the high voice. Beethoven, not concerned in his songs with furnishing a singer with an opportunity of displaying the voice, abandons the usage. His soprano songs seem, at first glance, to demand a voice of limited range $c1$-$a2$. Yet for such a voice, the tessitura and the prosody seem cruelly high and demanding; the reason for this, of course, is simply that these songs are intended for a voice with a much wider range—approximately up to $e3$.

This curious discrepancy between the seemingly short total compass and the handling of the tessitura and prosody is perhaps responsible for the oft-repeated charge that Beethoven wrote badly for the voice.

Most of the soprano songs by Beethoven will gain if transposed down, should they be sung by a soprano of $c1$-$c3$ range. But many of his songs, in their original keys, would provide a most welcome addition to the concert repertoire of coloraturas. The following list ought to prove itself useful in the study of Beethoven songs.

Editions: Novello
C. F. Peters
Breitkopf & Härtel
Universal Edition

TITLE	COMP.	TESS.	TYPE	REMARKS
Adelaide	e♭1-a2	a1-g2	Most suitable for men's voices	Sustained. Has an animated final section. Interpretatively not easy. Demands an accomplished pianist.

TITLE	COMP.	TESS.	TYPE	REMARKS
Ah, Perfido (concert air)	bb-bb2	eb1-f2	Dramatic soprano	A dramatic scena and a compound brilliant air. Has a very sustained slow movement. The final allegro demands in parts considerable flexibility.
An die ferne Geliebte (A cycle of six connected songs)	eb1-g2	eb1-eb2	Most suitable for men's voices	Interpretatively not easy. Demands an accomplished pianist. Really a piece of chamber music.
An die Geliebte	e1-e2	f#1-d2	All voices except a very light soprano	Animated, not fast.
Andenken	d1-g2	f#1-e2	High or medium voices	Graceful, sustained.
Aus Goethe's Faust	c1-d2	eb1-c2	Men's voices	Animated, rather vigorous. See Mussorgsky, "The Song of the Flea."
Busslied (From Sechs Geistliche Lieder, op. 48)	e1-g2	f#1-e2	Not suitable for light, high voices	Sustained. Has a more animated final section.
Das Geheimnis	g1-e2	same	All voices	Sustained.
Der Kuss	e1-g#2	f#1-e2	Men's voices	An animated, humorous character song of no particular distinction.
Der Liebende	f#1-f#2	g1-e2	All voices	Animated.
Die Ehre Gottes aus der Natur (From Sechs Geistliche Lieder, op. 48)	c1-g2	e1-e2	Heavy voices	Majestic, vigorous, sustained.
Die Prüfung des Küssens	G-e1	c-c1	Bass or bass-baritone	A humorous andante allegro aria. Demands in parts facile articulation. Originally for Bass and Orchestra. (IMC)

265

TITLE	COMP.	TESS.	TYPE	REMARKS
Die Trommel gerühret	f1-f2	g1-e2	Women's voices, except a light soprano	Vigorous, very animated, rhythmic.
Freudvoll und leidvoll	g#1-a2	a1-f#2	Women's voices except a very heavy alto	A song of contrasting moods and tempi. Interpretatively not easy. See Liszt; Schubert, "Die Liebe"; Rubinstein, "Clärchens Lied."
Ich liebe dich	d1-f2	g1-d2	All voices	Sustained, delicate.
In questa tomba	c1-e2	eb1-c2	Low or medium voices	Slow, somber. Beethoven has six songs and a concert air to Italian texts of which this song and "La Partenza" are best known. Somewhat of a curiosity is the "L'amanto impaziente" which Beethoven set to music twice, once in a buffo style and once in an exaggeratedly serious vein.
Lied aus der Ferne	e1-g2	f1-f2	Most suitable for rather light, high voices	Animated, graceful. Demands lightness of tone, some flexibility, and an accomplished pianist.
Mailied	eb1-eb2	same	Not too suitable for very low voices	Animated, graceful. Demands facile articulation and some flexibility.
Marmotte	e1-e2	a1-d2	All voices	A very short, graceful, simple song undeservedly neglected.
Mignon (Kennst du das Land)	e1-f#2	g#1-e2	Women's voices	Sustained. Has contrasting animated sections. Interpretatively not easy. See Schubert, Schumann, Liszt, Wolf.

TITLE	COMP.	TESS.	TYPE	REMARKS
Mit einem gemal- ten Band	e1-a2	a1-f2	Most suit- able for rather light, high voices	Animated, grace- ful. Demands light- ness of tone and some flexibility. The tessitura is higher than it may appear at first glance.
Mit Mädeln sich vertragen	A-e1	d-d1	Baritone or bass- baritone	Very animated buffo aria. De- mands facile ar- ticulation. Origi- nally for Bass and Orchestra. (IMC)
Neue Liebe, neues Leben	e1-a2	g1-f2	Not too suitable for very heavy low voices	Very animated, rhythmic. De- mands facile ar- ticulation.
Resignation	e1-f♯2	a1-e2	All voices	Not fast, somewhat declamatory.
Sehnsucht	e♯1-f♯2	f♯1-d2	All voices	Animated, graceful. Demands facile ar- ticulation and an accomplished pianist.
Vom Tode (From Sechs Geistliche Lieder, op. 48)	c♯1-g2	f♯1-e2	Not suit- able for light, high voices	Sustained, somber.
Wonne der Weh- mut	d♯1-g2	f♯1-d♯2	All voices except a very light soprano	Slow. Interpreta- tively not easy. See Franz.

ALBAN BERG
(1885–1936)

Alban Berg, the composer of Wozzeck, one of the most stirring of contemporary operas, has written only a few songs; most of them belong to his earliest efforts. For the most part they are musically quite complex and are not recommended to inexperienced singers.

Edition: Universal Edition

TITLE	COMP.	TESS.	TYPE	REMARKS
Im Zimmer (from Sieben frühe Lieder)	d1-g2	f1-d2	High voices	Delicate, sustained.
Liebesode (from Sieben frühe Lieder)	c1-f♯2	e1-e2	Medium or high voices, except a very light soprano or tenor	Slow, sustained. Has very imposing climaxes. See Joseph Marx, "Selige Nacht."
Schilflied (from Sieben frühe Lieder)	e♭1-f2	f1-e2	High voices	Sustained, rather subdued. Demands an accomplished pianist. See Charles Griffes, "By a Lonely Forest Pathway."

Vier Lieder: opus 2
"Der Glühende": three songs

(1) Schlafend trägt man mich	b-f♭2	f-d♭2	Medium or low voices	Slow, short, rather sustained. Musically not easy.
(2) Nun ich der Riesen stärksten überwand	c♭1-e2	e♭1-c2	Medium or low voices	Somewhat declamatory. Musically not easy.
(3) Warm die Lüfte	a-g♯2	e1-e2	Medium or low voices	Slow, somewhat declamatory. Has a very dramatic climax. Musically complex. Demands an accomplished pianist.

Schlafen, schlafen	a-f2	e1-b1	Medium or low voices	Slow, subdued, sustained. Musically not easy.

LEO BLECH
(b. 1871)

Edition: Universal Edition

Der Sandmann	d♯1-g♯2	b1-f♯2	High voices	Light. Demands good command of pp and an excellent

TITLE	COMP.	TESS.	TYPE	REMARKS
				pianist. See Schumann. One of the series of thirty-two songs "to be sung for children."
Heimkehr vom Feste	bb-g2	a1-f2	Most suitable for high or medium voices	Light and gently humorous. One of the series of thirty-two songs "to be sung for children."
Herr Hahn und Fräulein Huhn	bb-ab2	same	Most suitable for high or medium voices	A droll burlesque. One of the series of thirty-two songs "to be sung for children."

CARL BOHM
(1844–1920)

TITLE	COMP.	TESS.	TYPE	REMARKS
Still wie die Nacht	d1-ab2	g1-eb2 (H)	All voices	Very sustained. Effective. (gen. av.)

JOHANNES BRAHMS
(1833–1897)

The manner in which Brahms sets a poem to music could be perhaps best understood if one would give serious consideration to the fact that he was earnestly and actively engaged in collecting, harmonizing and imitating folk songs of German, as well as of western Slavic, origin.

The attempt to combine the purely melodic expressiveness of a folk song with the more elaborate musicodramatic conception of a nineteenth century song seems to be one of the predominant characteristics of Brahm's vocal works.

Brahms never seems to sacrifice his melodic line for any consideration; often complex pianistically, harmonically and rhythmically in his accompaniments, he keeps the melodic line as simple and as expressive in itself as that of any folk song. This is not to be understood as meaning that Brahms lacked the dramatic sensitivity of a Hugo Wolf, for instance; even a cursory examination of his songs would make such a statement untenable; but he differs widely in his choice of methods of expression from the then fashionable manner of insisting upon the dramatic and poetic content of a song in preference to its purely musical content.

Thus a song of Brahms demands above all a melodically satisfactory manner of vocalization; there are hardly any instances of a demand for a parlato style, for even in his rapid songs, requiring a syllable on almost every note, as it sometimes happens, the melodic line is superbly in evidence.

Brahms has been popularly identified with writing songs suitable mostly for heavy, low voices. It is true that among his best songs one finds a great number intended for this type of voice; it is equally true, however, that among his best songs one finds an equal, if not a greater number of songs intended for light, high voices. A coloratura soprano, for instance, could easily sing several groups of Brahms songs without finding it necessary to transpose any of them to suit her voice. For some unknown reason this fact has never been sufficiently emphasized in popular discussions of Brahms songs.

For the most part Brahms demands an accomplished pianist for his songs, well versed in the art of adjusting the sonority of his instrument to that of the voice of the singer for whom he is playing. Often Brahms writes thickly for the piano, and although the resulting balance of sonorities must by all means be preserved, it can, if overstressed, overpower and distort the vocal line of the song.

Editions: C. F. Peters, 4 vols. (H & L).
70 songs selected by Sergius Kagen, International Music Co. (H & L).
German Folk Songs, Breitkopf & Härtel and International Music Co. (H & L).
Numerous albums by many publishers.

TITLE	COMP.	TESS.	TYPE	REMARKS
Ach wende diesen Blick	eb1-g2	ab1-f2	Not suitable for very light, high voices	Dramatic. Demands an accomplished pianist.
Agnes	g1-g2	bb1-f2	Women's voices, except a very light soprano	Animated, rhythmical, somber. See Wolf.
Alte Liebe	d1-f2	eb1-eb2	Not too suitable for very light, high voices	Animated, somber.

270

TITLE	COMP.	TESS.	TYPE	REMARKS
Am Sonntag Morgen	e1-a2	a1-f#2	Not too suitable for very light, high voices	Dramatic. Demands an accomplished pianist.
An den Mond	e#1-g2	a#1-f#2	Not too suitable for very heavy voices	Very sustained.
An die Nachtigall	d#1-g2	a1-f#2	All voices	Sustained.
An ein Veilchen	d#1-g#2	a1-f#2	All voices	Slow and sustained. Demands good command of high pp.
An eine Aeolsharfe	eb1-a2	ab1-f#2	Women's voices	Very sustained. Demands an accomplished pianist. Note the time signature ₵. Often sung too slowly. See Wolf.
Anklänge	e1-g2	a1-f2	All voices	Very sustained. Demands good command of pp.
Auf dem Kirch- hofe	b-eb2	eb1-c2	Not too suitable for very light, high voices	Grave and somber. Interpretatively not easy. Demands an accomplished pianist.
Auf dem Schiffe	g1-a2	b1-f#2	High voices	Rapid and light. Demands an excellent pianist.
Auf dem See (An dies Schifflein)	d#1-a2	g#1-f#2	Not too suitable for very heavy, low voices	Graceful. Demands an accomplished pianist.
Auf dem See (Blauer Himmel)	d#1-f#2	g#1-e2	All voices	The vocal line is very sustained.
Bei dir sind meine Gedanken	e1-f#2	a1-f2	All voices	Animated, delicate. Demands an accomplished pianist.
Bittres zu sagen denkst du	e1-g2	a1-e2	All voices	Delicate.

271

TITLE	COMP.	TESS.	TYPE	REMARKS
Blinde Kuh	g1-g2	bb1-f2	Not too suitable for very low voices	Rapid. Demands facile articulation and an excellent pianist.
Botschaft	f1-ab2	ab1-gb2	Not too suitable for very low voices	Light and spirited. Demands some flexibility and an excellent pianist. The tempo mark "grazioso" is often disregarded and the song taken at too fast a tempo. Sounds best in the original high key.
Dämmrung senkte sich von oben	g-e2	d1-d2	Low or medium voices	Slow and sustained. Demands an accomplished pianist. Sounds best in the original low key.
Das Mädchen	f#1-g#2	a1-f#2	Women's voices	Spirited. Interpretatively not easy.
Das Mädchen spricht	e1-f#2	a1-e2	Soprano or mezzo-soprano	Light, animated. Demands some flexibility, facile articulation, and an accomplished pianist.
Dein blaues Auge	bb-g2	g1-eb2	Not too suitable for very light, high voices	Slow and sustained.
Der Gang zum Liebchen	b-e2	e1-c#2	All voices	A delicate waltz song in folk vein. Demands an accomplished pianist.
Der Jäger	f1-f2	a1-f2	Women's voices	Light and rapid. In folk vein. Demands facile articulation.
Der Schmied	f1-f2	bb-eb2	Heavy soprano, mezzo or contralto	Spirited and very vigorous. Demands an accomplished pianist.
Der Tod das ist die kühle Nacht	c1-a2	f#1-f#2	All voices	Slow and sustained. Interpretatively and vocally not easy.

TITLE	COMP.	TESS.	TYPE	REMARKS
Der Überläufer	b-d2	e1-b1	Men's voices	Very sustained. In folk vein.
Des Liebsten Schwur	c1-f2	f1-d2	Soprano or mezzo-soprano	Rapid and light. In folk vein. Demands facile articulation, some flexibility, and an accomplished pianist.
Die Mainacht	bb-fb2	g1-eb2	Not too suitable for very light, high voices	Very sustained. Interpretatively and vocally not easy.
Dort in den Weiden	a1-a2	b1-f#2	Soprano or mezzo-soprano	Spirited. In folk vein. Demands facile articulation.
Eine gute, gute Nacht	g1-a2	a1-f#2	Most suitable for high voices	Delicate.
Erinnerung	e1-g2	g1-g2	All voices	Very sustained.
Es hing der Reif	d1-a2	a1-f2	Not too suitable for very heavy, low voices	Very sustained.
Es liebt sich so lieblich im Lenze	d1-g2	a1-f#2	Not too suitable for very heavy, low voices	Animated. Interpretatively not easy. Demands an accomplished pianist. See R. Franz.
Es schauen die Blumen	f#1-g#2	b1-f#2	Most suitable for high voices	Animated. Demands an accomplished pianist.
Es träumte mir	g1-f#2	b1-f#2	All voices	Slow and very sustained. Interpretatively not easy. Demands good command of high pp.
Feldeinsamkeit	c1-eb2	e1-db2	All voices	Slow and very sustained.
Geheimnis	f#1-a2	c#2-g2	Not too suitable for very heavy, low voices	Light and delicate. Demands good command of high pp.

TITLE	COMP.	TESS.	TYPE	REMARKS
Heimkehr	e1-g♯2	b1-f♯2	Most suitable for men's voices	Rapid and very vigorous.
Ich schleich umher betrübt	d1-d2	e1-b♭1	Low or medium voices	Very sustained.
Immer leiser wird mein Schlummer	a-f2	c♯1-d2	Women's voices	Slow and very sustained. Interpretatively not easy. Note the time signature ₵. Often sung too slowly.
In der Fremde	g♯1-g2	b1-f♯2	All voices	Sustained. See Schumann, "In der Fremde" ("Aus der Heimat").
In der Gasse	c♯1-g♭2	f1-e♭2	Not too suitable for very light, high voices	Dramatic.
In Waldeseinsam-keit	f♯1-g2	b1-f♯2	All voices	Slow and very sustained. Interpretatively not easy. Demands good command of high pp.
Juchhe!	d1-a♭2	f1-c2	All voices	Spirited and gay. Demands facile articulation and an excellent pianist. The tessitura is curiously low, considering the frequent use of f2, g2, and a♭2. Very suitable for medium or low voices if transposed down.
Klage (Aus dem Böhmischen)	d1-f♯2	f♯1-d2	All voices, except a very light soprano	Animated. In folk vein.

TITLE	COMP.	TESS.	TYPE	REMARKS
Komm bald	d#1-g2	g1-f2	All voices	Delicate, sustained.
Lerchengesang	f#1-g#2	b1-f#2	Not suitable for very heavy, low voices	Very delicate and sustained. Demands good command of pp.
Liebe kam aus fernen Landen	db1-f2	eb1-db2	Men's voices	No. 4 of the "Romanzen aus Magelone" cycle of songs, opus 33. Sustained. Has an animated middle section. Interpretatively not easy.
Liebestreu	eb1-ab2	ab1-gb2	Women's voices, except a light soprano	Very slow and sustained. Dramatic.
Mädchenfluch	e1-a2	a1-e2	Women's voices	Dramatic. In folk vein. In parts very rapid. Demands an accomplished pianist.
Mädchenlied (Ach und du mein kühles Wasser)	a1-g2	c2-g2	Women's voices	Slow and sustained. In folk vein.
Mädchenlied (Am jüngsten Tag)	f1-f2	a1-f2	Women's voices	Delicate and gently humorous.
Mädchenlied (Auf die Nacht in der Spinnstub'n)	f#1-f#2	b1-e2	Women's voices	Sustained. Demands in parts considerable dramatic intensity. See Schumann, "Die Spinnerin."
Maienkätzchen	f1-g2	g1-eb2	All voices	Delicate, graceful.
Meerfahrt	e1-ab2	a1-f#2	All voices, except a very light soprano	Somber. Interpretatively and vocally not easy. Demands an accomplished pianist. See R. Franz; H. Wolf, "Mein Liebchen, wir sassen zusammen."
Meine Lieder	e#1-f#2	g#1-e2	All voices	Delicate. Animated.

TITLE	COMP.	TESS.	TYPE	REMARKS
Mein wundes Herz	e1-g2	g1-e2	Not too suitable for very light, high voices	Animated.
Meine Liebe ist grün	e♯1-a2	a♯1-f♯2	All voices, except a very light soprano	Spirited and vigorous. Demands an accomplished pianist.
Minnelied	d1-g2	g1-f2	Men's voices	Very sustained. See Mendelssohn.
Mit vierzig Jahren	f♯-d2	b-b1	Low voices	Grave and sustained.
Mondenschein	d1-g2	f1-d2	All voices	Slow and sustained.
Muss es eine Trennung geben	f♯1-f♯2	g1-d2	All voices, except a very light soprano	Very sustained. No. 12 of the Romanzen aus Magelone, opus 33.
Nachklang	f♯1-a2	b1-f♯2	All voices	Delicate. Demands some flexibility. The melodic material of this song and of the "Regenlied" is employed in the first movement of the G major violin sonata.
Nachtigall	d1-a2	a1-g2	All voices	Slow and sustained. Interpretatively and vocally not easy.
Nachtigallen schwingen	f1-g2	b♭1-f2	Not too suitable for very low voices	Animated. Demands lightness of tone and an excellent pianist. Interpretatively not easy. Sounds best in the original high key.
Nicht mehr zu dir zu gehen	c♯1-e♭2	d1-c2	Low or medium voices	Dramatic; somewhat declamatory. Interpretatively not easy. Sounds best in the original low key.
O komme, holde Sommernacht	c♯1-f♯2	f♯1-e2	Most suitable for light, high voices	Very rapid and light. Demands an excellent pianist. Sounds best in the original high key.

TITLE	COMP.	TESS.	TYPE	REMARKS
O kühler Wald	d1-eb2 (f2)	ab1-eb2	Not too suitable for very light, high voices	Slow and very sustained.
O liebliche Wangen	f♯1-a2	a1-f♯2	All voices	Spirited. Demands facile articulation and good rhythmic sense.
O wüsst ich doch den Weg zurück	e1-f♯2	g♯1-e2	All voices	Slow and sustained. Demands an accomplished pianist.
Ruhe, Süssliebchen	eb1-f♯2	g1-eb2	Men's voices	Slow and sustained. No. 9 of the Romanzen aus Magelone, opus 33. See R. Franz, "Schlummerlied."
Salome	g1-g2	b1-f♯2	Women's voices	Spirited and vigorous. Demands good sense of rhythm. See Wolf, "Singt mein Schatz."
Sandmännchen	d1-e2	g1-d2	All voices	Delicate. In folk vein.
Sapphische Ode	a-d2	a-a1	Low voices	Very slow and sustained. Note the time signature ₵. Often sung too slowly and too loudly.
Schön war, das ich dir weihte	e1-g2	ab1-f2	All voices	Slow and sustained. A remarkably beautiful song, neglected for some unknown reason.
Schwermut	d1-f2	ab1-eb2	Not too suitable for very light, high voices	Slow and very sustained.
Sehnsucht (Hinter jenen dichten Wäldern)	eb1-ab2	c2-gb2	Not suitable for light voices	Spirited and vigorous. The vocal line is very sustained.

277

TITLE	COMP.	TESS.	TYPE	REMARKS
Serenate	f♯1-g♯2	b1-f♯2	All voices	Delicate, sustained.
Sind es Schmerzen sind es Freuden	c1-g2	a♭1-f2	Men's voices	No. 3 of the "Romanzen aus Magelone," opus 33. A complex song of many moods. Interpretatively not easy. Demands an accomplished pianist. See Weber.
So willst du den Armen	e♭1-g2	a1-f2	Men's voices	No. 5 of the "Romanzen aus Magelone," opus 33. Spirited.
Sommerabend	d1-d2	f1-c2	Not too suitable for very light, high voices	Slow and sustained.
Sonntag	c1-f2	f1-d2	All voices	Graceful. In folk vein.
Spanisches Lied	e1-f♯2	a1-e2	Women's voices	Light and delicate. See Wolf, "In dem Schatten meiner Locken." Also Jensen.
Ständchen	d1-g♯2	g1-f♯2	All voices	Light. Demands facile articulation, good command of high pp and an excellent pianist.
Steig auf, geliebter Schatten	b♭-e♭2	e♭1-b♭1	Medium or low voices	Very sustained.
Tambourliedchen	e1-a2	a1-f♯2	All voices	Very spirited. Demands facile articulation and an accomplished pianist.
Therese	b-d2	f♯1-b1	Women's voices	Delicate, sustained. Interpretatively not easy. See Wolf, "Du milchjunger Knabe."

TITLE	COMP.	TESS.	TYPE	REMARKS
Todessehnen	a#-d#2	c#1-a1	Not too suitable for light high voices	Slow and sustained.
Treue Liebe	d#1-e2	f#1-d2	Medium or low voices	Slow and sustained. In parts demands considerable dramatic intensity.
Über die Heide	d#1-f2	a1-e2	All voices	Somber. Interpretatively not easy.
Über die See	f#1-g2	g1-e2	Women's voices	Very sustained.
Vergebliches Ständchen	e1-f#2	a1-e2	All voices	Light, humorous. In folk vein. Demands facile articulation.
Verrat	F#-d#1	d-b	Bass or baritone	A dramatic narrative song (ballade). Could be sung by a dramatic tenor if transposed.
Verzagen	c#1-f#2	f#1-e2	Not suitable for light, high voices	Somber. Has a sustained vocal line over an elaborate accompaniment. Demands an excellent pianist.

Vier Ernste Gesänge: opus 121, for bass or baritone

(1) Denn es gehet dem Menschen	A-f1	d-d1		Sustained, somber. Has animated sections. Demands an excellent pianist.
(2) Ich wandte mich	G-eb1	d-d1		Very sustained, grave.
(3) O Tod, wie bitter bist du	B-f#1	c#-c#1		Very sustained, grave.
(4) Wenn ich mit Menschen und mit Engelszungen	A(Ab)-f1(g1)	c-c#1		Rather animated, vigorous. Has very sustained slow sections.
Von ewiger Liebe	a-f#2	e1-e2	Not suitable for light, high voices	Dramatic. Vocally and interpretatively not easy. Demands an excellent pianist.

TITLE	COMP.	TESS.	TYPE	REMARKS
Vorschneller Schwur	d1-a2	a1-f#2	All voices	Animated. Gently humorous. In folk vein.
Wenn du nur zu- weilen lächelst	g1-g2	bb1-f2	All voices	Slow and sus- tained. Interpreta- tively not easy.
Wie bist du meine Königin	d1-f#2	ab1-f2	Men's voices	Slow and sus- tained.
Wie froh und frisch	d1-g2	g1-e2	Not suit- able for very light voices	No. 14 of the "Ro- manzen aus Mage- lone," opus 33.
			"	Spirited and vig- orous. Demands an accomplished pianist.
Wie Melodien zieht es	a-e2	e1-d2	All voices	Very delicate. In- terpretatively not easy. Note the time signature ₵. Often sung too slowly.
Wie schnell ver- schwindet so Licht als Glanz	c1-eb2	f1-c2	Not too suitable for very light, high voices	No. 11 of the "Ro- manzen aus Mage- lone," opus 33. Slow and sustained.
Wiegenlied	eb1-eb2	g1-eb2	All voices	Delicate, sus- tained.
Willst du dass ich geh?	d1-f#2 (a2)	a1-f#2	All but very light, high voices	Rapid, dramatic. Demands facile ar- ticulation and an excellent pianist.
Wir müssten uns trennen	db1-g2	ab1-f2	Men's voices	No. 8 of the "Ro- manzen aus Mage- lone," opus 33. A complex song, of many moods. In- terpretatively not easy. Demands an accomplished pianist.
Wir wandelten	eb1-gb2	ab1-f2	All voices	Slow and very sus- tained. Demands an accomplished pianist.

"Zigeunerlieder": eight songs, opus 103 (originally written for vocal quartet and pianoforte, arranged for solo voice by Brahms).

TITLE	COMP.	TESS.	TYPE	REMARKS
(1) He! Zigeuner	d#1-g2	a1-e2 (H)	Not suitable for very light voices	Rapid and vigorous. Demands an accomplished pianist.
(2) Hochgetürmte Rimaflut	d1-g2	a1-e2 (H)	Not suitable for light voices	Very rapid. Vigorous.
(3) Wüsst ihr wann mein Kindchen	f#1-g2	a1-d2 (H)	All voices	Light, spirited.
(4) Lieber Gott, du weisst	f1-f2	a1-e2 (H)	All voices	Light, spirited.
(5) Brauner Bursche	d1-g2	f#1-d2 (H)	Not too suitable for very light voices	Spirited, rhythmical. Demands an accomplished pianist.
(6) Röslein dreie	eb1-g2	a1-e2 (H)	All voices	Rapid, light. Demands facile articulation and an accomplished pianist.
(7) Kommt dir manchmal in den Sinn	d#1-g#2	g#1-e2 (H)	All voices	Very sustained.
(8) Rote Abendwolken	eb1-ab2	ab1-eb2 (H)	Not suitable for very light voices	Spirited, vigorous.

See also the arrangements of German folk songs, "Deutsche Volkslieder" among them, the famous "Schwesterlein" and "Mein Mädel hat einen Rosenmund," the "Volkskinderlieder," the two songs for alto with viola obbligato, opus 91.

PETER CORNELIUS
(1824–1874)

With the exception of a few, one rarely encounters songs by Cornelius on the present-day concert program. This neglect does not seem justified; Cornelius' songs deserve a permanent and esteemed place in every serious singer's repertoire. They are, apart from their poetic and musical qualities, well written for the voice. This consideration alone has too often brought a long life to much music immeasurably inferior to his.

Cornelius, like Wagner and in some instances Debussy and Mussorgsky, wrote for the most part his own texts. He had a remarkable poetic gift and would undoubtedly be still considered one of the important minor poets of his time had he not written anything but the texts to his songs.

Editions: Breitkopf & Härtel (complete ed. 2 vols.)
Brautlieder, International Music Co.
Weihnachtslieder, Boston Music Co.
A few reprints of single songs by G. Schirmer and others.

TITLE	COMP.	TESS.	TYPE	REMARKS
Angedenken	c1-d2	d1-a1	Not too suitable for very light, high voices	Very slow and somber. From "Trauer und Trost," a cycle of 6 songs.

"Brautlieder": a cycle of six songs; text by the composer

(1) Ein Myrtenreis	e1-f#2	g#1-e2	Women's voices	Sustained, delicate.
(2) Der Liebe Lohn	b-f#2	e1-c#2	Women's voices, except a very light soprano	Animated. Demands an accomplished pianist.
(3) Vorabend	c#1-g2	g1-d2	Women's voices	Sustained.
(4) Am Morgen	d1-g2	f#1-d2	Women's voices	Slow, somewhat declamatory.
(5) Aus dem hohen Liede	d1-a2	g1-e2	Women's voices, except a very light soprano	Spirited, vigorous.
(6) Märchenwunder	d#1-g#2	g#1-e2	Women's voices	Animated. Demands an accomplished pianist.
Ein Ton			All voices	This celebrated song, in which the voice part consists of one incessantly repeated note is

282

TITLE	COMP.	TESS.	TYPE	REMARKS
Komm, wir wandeln	f1-g♯2	ab1-f2	All voices	originally written in e minor, the voice note being b1. From "Trauer und Trost," a cycle of 6 songs. Sustained. One of Cornelius' best known and very representative songs.

"Weihnachtslieder": a cycle of six songs; text by the composer

(1) Christbaum	d1-e2	g1-d2	All voices	Spirited.
(2) Die Hirten	c♯1-eb2	e1-c♯2	All voices	Sustained.
(3) Die Könige	b-e2	d1-b1	All voices	Slow. The accompaniment is an independent choral.
(4) Simeon	b-d2	e1-b1	All voices	A narrative song.
(5) Christus der Kinderfreund	c1-c2	eb1-bb1	All voices	Slow, rather delicate.
(6) Christkind	c1-eb2	eb1-c2	All voices	Spirited.

See also the following cycles: "Vater unser," "Rheinische Lieder," "An Bertha."

WERNER EGK
(b. 1901)

Chanson	f1-bb2	a1-g2	Soprano, most suitable for light, high voices	Sustained. Demands good command of high pp. French text. (SCH)
La romance du Comte Olinos et de Blanche	eb1-e3	a1-a2	Coloratura soprano (lyric soprano)	Generally sustained. In parts florid. Musically difficult. Demands good command of high pp. French text. (SCH)

283

TITLE	COMP.	TESS.	TYPE	REMARKS

Natur-Liebe-Tod   A cantata for bass, originally scored for voice and chamber orchestra. Demands an accomplished pianist. (SCH)

TITLE	COMP.	TESS.	REMARKS
(1) In Silberhüllen	F#-e1	B-d1	Sustained, tranquil.
(2) Die Nachtigall	Ab-eb1	d-c1	Very sustained. Demands some flexibility.
(3) Grabe Spaten	G-e1	c-c1	Forceful, majestic. Has dramatic intensity.

See also "La tentation de Saint Antoine" (French text) for contralto and string quartet, and "Quattro canzoni" (Italian text) both published by Schott.

GOTTFRIED VON EINEM
(b. 1918)

Acht Hafis-Lieder (Op. 5)   Eight songs for high voices. All demand an accomplished pianist.

TITLE	COMP.	TESS.	REMARKS
(1) Wahrlich	f#1-a2	a1-ab2	Animated. The vocal line is in parts rhythmically complex. (UE)
(2) Wenn mein heisses Herz	ab1-ab2	c2-ab2	Sustained. Strong climax. (UE)
(3) Ich Unglückseliger!	eb1-g2	eb1-e2	Declamatory in parts. Rhythmically complex. Demands good command of high pp. (UE)
(4) Fort ist die Sonne	e1-ab2	e1-c2	Animated, in parts declamatory. Forceful ending. Accompaniment is mainly percussive. (UE)
(5) Nichtswürdig bist du	g#1-a2	a1-g2	Very fast. Demands flexibility and a good command of high pp. Short. (UE)
(6) Jawohl	d1-g2	a1-d2	Sustained, subdued, short. (UE)

TITLE	COMP.	TESS.	TYPE	REMARKS
(7) Das sind die Kostbarkeiten dieser Erde	e1-a2	b1-g2		Sustained for the most part. Subdued ending. The accompaniment is mainly percussive. (UE)
(8) Die Tulpen haben ihre Kelche	f1-g2 (c3)	g1-g2		Fast, animated. Demands flexibility. Effective ending. (UE)

Fünf Lieder aus dem Chinesischen (Op. 8)   Five songs for
medium voice.   Texts by various Chinese poets, translated into
German.   (SCH)

(1) Die geheimnisvolle Flöte	f♯1-g♯2	b1-f♯2		Sustained.
(2) In der Fremde	f♯1-d♯2	same		Slow, very sustained. Subdued throughout. Demands good command of high ppp.
(3) Die Einsame	e1-f2	e1-e2		Sustained, with gentle declamation.
(4) Ein junger Dichter denkt an die Geliebte	g-g♭2	b-e♭2		Sustained for the most part. A song of contrasting moods.
(5) Abend	b♯-g♯2	e1-f♯2		Sustained. Demands good command of high p.

Japanische Blätter (Op. 15)   Sixteen songs for high voice, some of
which are brief, one unaccompanied.   c♯1-a2   g1-e2   These songs
have generally little melodic variety, in some cases, narrow range,
in simulation to Oriental style.   Some are highly chromatic both in
the vocal line as well as in the accompaniment which, in many cases,
is percussive in imitation of plucked strings.   Texts by various Japanese authors and from traditional sources, translated into German.
(SCH)

Sieben Lieder nach verschiedenen Dichtern (Op. 19)   Seven
songs for high voices.   All songs demand an accomplished pianist.
(Bote & Bock)

(1) Auf dem Nachhausenweg 1945	e1-g2	g1-g2		Animated sections alternate with sustained and quiet ones.

285

TITLE	COMP.	TESS.	TYPE	REMARKS
(2) Erste Blume	e1-ab2	f1-g2		Slow, sustained.
(3) Finsternisse fallen Dichter	f1-gb2	f1-eb2		Animated, fast.
(4) Liebeslied	g1-f2	ab1-eb2		Slow, sustained. Demands rhythmical flexibility. Generally subdued.
(5) Und wie manche Nacht	db1-gb2	db1-eb2		Slow, sustained. Generally subdued; contemplative.
(6) Verzweiflung	d1-a2	g#1-g2		Animated, vigorous. Demands facile articulation and flexibility.
(7) Weit aus den Wäldern	eb1-f2	g1-eb2		Sustained, subdued.

ROBERT FRANZ
(1815–1892)

Practically none of the songs of Robert Franz make any unusual technical demands upon the singer or the pianist.

One of the outstanding characteristics of his manner of writing is its unassuming, almost self-effacing simplicity, and although he is uncommonly inventive and extremely fastidious in regard to part leading (especially in the treatment of the inner parts of his accompaniments), his reluctance to employ any violent harmonic or rhythmic effects makes his songs appear utterly devoid of complexity. Even though his technical demands upon the vocalist are moderate, his treatment of the vocal line is such that his songs at first glance invariably appear even less exacting than they are. Thus, it seems only natural that many of his songs have been used extensively for teaching purposes; this has undoubtedly contributed to the undeserved neglect of most of his songs by many a concert singer, branding Franz, in his eyes as a composer of "teaching songs."

Although it is true that a more or less adequate performance of many of his songs may be within the powers of almost any competent vocalist, a more satisfactory performance of a song by Franz requires a rare poetic insight and a considerable musical sensitivity. The very outward simplicity of his songs tends to emphasize any inadequacy of this kind on the part of the singer, an inadequacy which may be much less apparent in a more elaborate musical setting of a poem.

Out of nearly three hundred songs that Franz wrote, the following list of fifty-six seemed adequate for the purpose of this volume, as his writing is rather uniform in style and his choice of poetic material, though nearly impeccable in taste, seems to be on the whole somewhat limited in scope.

It is claimed on good authority that Franz always had a mezzo-soprano voice in his mind when composing his songs and resented any attempts to transpose them to fit other voices, although, as one writer puts it, "he did not object to having his songs sung by men."

Editions: C. F. Peters
Breitkopf & Härtel
G. Schirmer
Musicians Library, Oliver Ditson
Numerous reprints of single songs

TITLE	COMP.	TESS.	TYPE	REMARKS
Abends	d♯1-g2	g1-e2	All voices	Delicate, sustained.
Ach, wenn ich doch ein Immchen wär	e♯1-f♯2	a♯1-d♯2	Most suitable for light, high voices	Light and delicate. Demands an accomplished pianist.
Altes Lied	b-f♯2	g1-e2	Most suitable for medium or low voices	A rather curious poem. Interpretatively not easy.
Auf dem Teich, dem regungslosen	e♭1-g2	b♭1-f2	All voices	Delicate, sustained. Demands good command of p. See Mendelssohn, "Schilflied," and the setting of this Lenau poem by C. Griffes.
Auf dem Meere (Das Meer hat seine Perlen)	c♯1-g♯2	e1-d♯2	Not too suitable for very light, high voices	Slow and sustained.
Auf geheimem Waldespfade	g♭1-g♭2	b♭1-e♭2	All voices	Sustained. Demands good command of p. See C. Griffes, "By a Lonely Forest Pathway."

TITLE	COMP.	TESS.	TYPE	REMARKS
Aus meinen grossen Schmerzen	c#1-e2	f1-c2	All voices	Slow and sustained. See H. Wolf.
Bitte	db1-db2	f1-c2	Medium or low voices	Slow and very sustained.
Da die Stunde kam	d1-f2	g1-d2	All voices	Delicate.
Das Meer erstrahlt im Sonnenschein	c1-g2	g1-c2	Not too suitable for very light, high voices	Slow and very sustained.
Denk ich dein	d1-g2	g1-e2	All voices	Delicate. Very sustained.
Der Fichtenbaum	db1-gb2	f1-db2	All voices	Slow and very sustained. See Liszt.
Der Schalk	e#1-f#2	a#1-e2	Not too suitable for very low voices	Light and delicate.
Die blauen Frühlingsaugen	c#1-g#2	f#1-d#2	All voices	Graceful, delicate. Demands lightness of tone and an accomplished pianist.
Die Lotosblume (Geibel)	f1-g2	bb1-f2	All voices	Sustained. Demands good command of pp.
Du liebes Auge	f#1-f#2	g#1-d#2	All voices	Very sustained.
Durch den Wald im Mondenschein	c#1-f#2	g#1-e2	All voices	Rapid. Demands an accomplished pianist. See Mendelssohn, "Neue Liebe."
Ein Friedhof	c1-eb2	eb1-c2	Medium or low voices	Grave and very sustained. Demands good command of p.
Ein Stündlein wohl vor Tag	c1-g2	e1-c2	Women's voices	Delicate, graceful. Demands some flexibility. See Wolf.
Er ist gekommen	eb1-f2	ab1-eb2	Women's voices, except a very light soprano	Rapid, vigorous.

TITLE	COMP.	TESS.	TYPE	REMARKS
Es hat die Rose sich beklagt	d♭1-f2	e♭1-b♭1	All voices	Delicate, graceful. See Rubinstein.
Es ragt in's Meer der Runenstein	g-f2	c1-c2	Most suitable for medium or low voices	Grave, somewhat declamatory.
Frühling und Liebe	e1-f#2	a1-e2	Not suitable for very heavy low voices	Graceful, delicate.
Frühlings-gedränge	f1-a♭2	a♭1-f2	High voices	Light and animated. See R. Strauss.
Für Musik	g♭1-a♭2	b♭1-e♭2	All voices	Slow and sustained. See Rubinstein, "Nun die Schatten dunkeln." Also see Jensen.
Gute Nacht	e1-e2	a1-d2	All voices	Delicate, subdued.
Hör' ich das Liedchen klingen	e1-g2	b1-e2	Not too suitable for very heavy voices	Delicate. Demands some flexibility. See Schumann.
Ich hab' in deinem Auge	e♭1-f2	a♭1-e♭2	All voices	Very sustained.
Im Herbst	c1-a♭2	g1-e♭2	Not suitable for light voices	Dramatic, somber.
Im Rhein, im heiligen Strome	c#1-e2	e1-c#2	All voices	Delicate, sustained. Demands good command of p. See Schumann and Liszt.
In meinen Armen wieg' ich dich	c1-e♭2	a♭1-e♭2	All voices	Slow and very sustained. Interpretatively not easy.
Kommt feins Liebchen heut'	b#-f#2	f#1-c#2	Most suitable for men's voices	Very sustained, subdued. See Schumann, "Morgens steh' ich auf und frage."

TITLE	COMP.	TESS.	TYPE	REMARKS
Lieb Liebchen	a-e2	a1-d2	Most suitable for men's voices	Animated. Interpretatively not easy. See Schumann.
Lieber Schatz sei wieder gut mir	d1-f2	g1-d2	Women's voices	Delicate, graceful. In folk vein.
Mädchen mit dem roten Mündchen	e♭1-g♭2	a♭1-e♭2	All voices	Graceful, delicate.
Marie	d1-f2	f1-c2	All voices	Sustained, delicate. See Jensen.
Meerfahrt	c♯1-d♯2	f♯1-c♯2	All voices	Delicate. See Brahms, and H. Wolf, "Mein Liebchen, wir sassen beisammen."
Mein Schatz ist auf der Wanderschaft	e♭1-g2	g1-e♭2	Women's voices	Light and animated. Demands facile articulation.
Mit schwarzen Segeln	c1-f2	g1-e♭2	Not suitable for light voices	Somber, animated and vigorous.
Mutter, o sing' mich zur Ruh'	e1-g2	a1-e2	Women's voices	Slow and sustained. Demands an accomplished pianist.
O Lüge nicht	e1-e2	g1-d2	Not too suitable for very light, high voices	Very sustained.
O säh ich auf der Heide dort	f1-f2	g1-d2	Not suitable for very light voices	Rapid and vigorous. See also Mendelssohn's version of this Burns poem (Duet for two soprani).
Sag mir	c1-a2	a1-e2	Most suitable for light voices	Gently humorous. Interpretatively not easy.
Schlummerlied	e1-f♯2	g♯1-d♯2	All voices	Delicate, sustained. See Brahms, "Ruhe Süssliebchen."
Sie liebten sich beide	d♯1-e♯2	g♯1-d♯2	All voices	Delicate. Interpretatively not easy.

TITLE	COMP.	TESS.	TYPE	REMARKS
Sonnenuntergang: schwarze Wolken ziehn	c#1-f#2	f#1-d#2	Not suitable for light, high voices	Somber, animated and vigorous.
Sterne mit den goldnen Füsschen	d#1-e2	g#2-e2	All voices	Graceful, delicate. Demands lightness of tone.
Stille Sicherheit	e1-f2	ab1-eb2	All voices	Delicate, sustained.
Umsonst	f1-e2	a1-d2	All voices	Slow, sustained and subdued.
Und die Rosen die prangen	c1-g2	g1-eb2	All voices	Delicate, sustained.
Waldfahrt	d1-g2	b1-e2	All voices	Spirited.
Wandl' ich in dem Wald	d#1-f#2	f#1-d#2	All voices	Delicate, sustained.
Widmung	eb1-f2	ab1-eb2	All voices	Slow and very sustained.
Wie des Mondes Abbild	gb1-f2	bb1-f2	Most suitable for light voices	Slow and very sustained. Demands good command of pp.
Willkommen, mein Wald	c1-g2	g1-eb2	All voices, except a very light soprano	Spirited.
Wonne der Wehmut	f1-g2	ab1-db2	All voices	Slow and sustained. See Beethoven.

PAUL HINDEMITH
(1895–1965)

Paul Hindemith, perhaps one of the outstanding composers of our time, has written only a comparatively small number of songs. The most remarkable among them are perhaps those contained in the "Marienleben" cycle, of which a few are listed below. Hindemith's songs may seem very complex and dissonant at first reading, but upon closer acquaintance one becomes aware of their extraordinary logic and simplicity. They are expertly written for the voice and can under no circumstances be considered vocally taxing. The short list here is primarily intended for those who are not at all familiar with his songs. It is sincerely hoped that it will stimulate the reader to acquaint himself more fully with songs by Hindemith.

Editions: Schott
Associated Music Publishers, New York

TITLE	COMP.	TESS.	TYPE	REMARKS
Argwohn Josephs (from "Marienleben" a cycle of 15 songs, opus 27)	c1-g2	f1-f2	Mezzo-soprano or soprano	Rapid. Musically not easy. Demands an accomplished pianist.
Auf der Treppe sitzen meine Öhrchen (8 songs, opus 18)	eb1-f2	ab1-d2	High or medium voices	Not fast. Subdued. Demands facile articulation. Musically and interpretatively not easy.
Cum natus esset	c#1-c3	f1-gb2	Soprano	A motet on sacred Latin text. Generally sustained; has some animated sections and recitative-like passages.
Geburt Marias (from "Marienleben" a cycle of 15 songs, opus 27)	e1-a2	a1-f#2	Soprano	Very delicate. Sustained.
Nuptiae factae sunt	c1-f#2	f#1-eb2	All voices	A motet on sacred Latin text. Generally sustained. Demands flexibility.
Pastores loquebantur	d1-g2	eb1-e2	High or medium voices	Motet on sacred Latin text. Sustained. Demands some flexibility and an accomplished pianist.
Pietà (from "Marienleben," a cycle of 15 songs, opus 27)	c1-e2	same	Mezzo-soprano or soprano	Slow and declamatory; grave. Musically and interpretatively not easy.
Trompeten (8 songs, opus 18)	b(ab)-ab2	g1-eb2	Most suitable for high voices	Slow, somewhat declamatory. Demands good command of high pp. Musically and interpretatively not easy.

English Songs

Echo	d1-f#2	same	High or medium voices	Animated.

292

TITLE	COMP.	TESS.	TYPE	REMARKS
Envoy	eb1-f#2	f#1-e2	High or medium voices, except a very light soprano	Slow, sustained. In parts demands considerable dramatic intensity. Musically not easy.
La belle dame sans merci	d#1-g2	f#1-eb2	High or medium voices	A song of contrasting moods and tempi. Interpretatively not easy. A setting of Keat's famous poem.
On a fly drinking out of his cup	e1-f2	f#1-e2	All voices	Slow, sustained, subdued.
On hearing "The last rose of summer"	d1-f2	f1-f2	High or medium voices	Very slow, sustained. For the most part subdued.
Sing on there in the swamp	c#1-g#2	f#1-f#2	High or medium voices	Very slow, subdued. Interpretatively not easy.
The moon	d#1-eb2	f#1-c#2	Not suitable for very light, high voices	Very animated. Has a slow, rather declamatory and subdued ending. Interpretatively not easy. Demands an accomplished pianist.
The wild flower's song	e1-g2	f1-e2 (H)	Not too suitable for very low voices	Sustained.
The whistling thief	e1-f2	same	High or medium voices	An animated comic song.
To music to becalm his fever	c#1-f#2	f#1-e2	High or medium voices	Sustained. Demands flexibility and an accomplished pianist. Text by Robert Herrick.

See also "Die Junge Magd," 6 songs for mezzo-soprano and chamber orchestra.

ENGELBERT HUMPERDINCK
(1854–1921)

TITLE	COMP.	TESS.	TYPE	REMARKS
Am Rhein	c1–g2	f1–f2	Not too suitable for very light, high voices	Sustained, effective. (AMP)
Wiegenlied	c1–f2	f1–d2	Women's voices	Sustained, subdued. (AMP)

ADOLF JENSEN
(1837–1879)

Jensen's songs, though very popular at the turn of the century, seem of but little importance or interest now, and have, perhaps justly, almost disappeared from the present-day repertoire. They are, however, expertly written, possess a certain not inconsiderable elegance and are, if well performed, quite effective.

Editions: C. F. Peters
A very comprehensive collection by O. Ditson (Musician's Library).
Numerous reprints of single songs.

TITLE	COMP.	TESS.	TYPE	REMARKS
Am Ufer des Flusses, des Manzanares	d1–f♯2	f♯1–d2	Not too suitable for very heavy, low voices	Spirited and light. Demands an accomplished pianist.
Barcarole	f1–f2	a1–e2	Not too suitable for very heavy, low voices	Light and delicate.
Lehn' deine Wang'	c1–eb2	g1–d2	All voices	Very sustained. See Schumann.
Leis' rudern hier	f♯1–g2	a1–e2	Men's voices	Light and delicate. See Schumann, "Venetianisches Lied."
Marie	f1–d2	a1–c2	All voices	Very sustained, delicate. See Franz.
Margreta	f1–f2	ab1–eb2	Men's voices	Light and spirited. Demands facile articulation. One of Jensen's best songs.

TITLE	COMP.	TESS.	TYPE	REMARKS
Mein Herz ist im Hochland	c♯1-e2	e1-c♯2	Not suitable for very light voices. Best for baritone	Vigorous and spirited. The original words by Burns ("My heart's in the Highlands") can be substituted. One of Jensen's best songs.
Murmelndes Lüftchen	e1-a♭2	d♭2-g♭2	Most suitable for high, light voices	Very light and delicate. Demands good command of high pp.
Nun die Schatten dunkeln	f1-a♭2	a♭1-e♭2	All voices	Very sustained. See Rubinstein and Franz, "Für Musik."
Süss und sacht	d♭1-g♭2	g1-e♭2	Women's voices	Delicate, sustained. The original words by Tennyson ("Sweet and low") can be substituted.
Wenn durch die Piazzetta	e1-g2 (a2)	a1-f2	Most suitable for men's voices	Light and delicate. Demands an accomplished pianist. See Schumann, "Venetianisches Lied," and Mendelssohn, "Venetianisches Gondellied."
Wie so bleich	d♯1-e2	f♯1-b1	Mezzo-soprano or alto	Grave and very sustained. (From Dolorosa cycle.) One of Jensen's best songs.

ERICH WOLFGANG KORNGOLD
(1897–1957)

Edition: Associated Music Publishers

TITLE	COMP.	TESS.	TYPE	REMARKS
Das Ständchen	c1-f♯2	e1-e2	Not too suitable for very light, high voices	Animated. Demands an accomplished pianist. See H. Wolf, "Ständchen."

TITLE	COMP.	TESS.	TYPE	REMARKS
Liebesbriefchen	d#1-f#2	g#1-d#2	All voices	Sustained.
Nachtwanderer	c#1-f2	d1-d2	Most suitable for medium or low voices	Dramatic. Interpretatively not easy.
Schneeglöckchen	c1-g2	f1-d2	All voices	Delicate, sustained.

ERNST KŘENEK
(b. 1900)

Ernst Křenek, best known as the composer of the so-called "jazz opera" Johnny Spielt Auf, has written a considerable number of songs. Two cycles: "Fiedellieder," opus 64, 7 songs, most suitable for baritone or mezzo-soprano (ab-f#1) and "Reisebuch aus den Oesterreichischen Alpen," opus 62, 20 songs for medium or high voices, are among the most representative of his manner of writing.

Edition: Universal Edition

See also: Vier Gesänge (Op. 53) for mezzo-soprano.
Drei Gesänge (Op. 56) for baritone.
Die Nachtigall (Op. 68) for soprano.

ROLF LIEBERMANN
(b. 1910)

Chinesische Liebeslieder   A cycle of four short Chinese lovesongs for all voices. (UE)

(1) Mir tat die	d#1-g2	g#1-d2		Slow, sustained.
(2) Der Strom floss	e1-a2	g#1-f#2		Sustained. Demands good command of high pp.
(3) Wenn ich an deinem Munde	e1-a2	a1-g2		Sustained.
(4) Die Libelle schwebt	db1-a2	g1-f2		Waltz-like, gentle.

FRANZ LISZT
(1811–1886)

Some of Liszt's songs, not unlike some of his instrumental music, seem to have lost much of their former appeal, even though the histor-

296

ical significance of his music appears to be more generally recognized and appreciated now than ever before.

Yet songs like "Die drei Zigeuner," "Comment, disaient-ils," and "Oh, quand je dors" are masterpieces of such remarkable individuality and power that it seems strange to have to recommend them to the present-day singer.

Liszt's songs demand for the most part considerably developed vocal technique, as well as a highly developed dramatic instinct, and his accompaniments, like the piano part in "Die drei Zigeuner," often demand a pianist of soloist stature.

Editions: Breitkopf & Härtel
Universal Edition
Excellent selection Musician's Library, O. Ditson
12 songs (2 vols.), G. Schirmer
Numerous reprints of single songs

TITLE	COMP.	TESS.	TYPE	REMARKS
Angiolin dal biondo crin (Italian text)	c1-e♭2	f1-d2	Women's voices	Sustained, graceful.
Comment, disaient-ils (French text)	c♯1-a♭2 (b2)	same	Most suitable for light soprano	Rapid, delicate. Demands good command of high pp and an accomplished pianist. See Lalo.
Das Veilchen	d1-e♭2	g1-d2	All voices	Graceful, delicate.
Der Fischer-knabe	d♯1-a♭2	a♭1-f2	Soprano or mezzo-soprano	Delicate, sustained. Demands good command of high pp and an accomplished pianist.
Der König von Thule	b(g♯)-f2	e♭1-c2	Not suitable for light voices	A dramatic narrative song. See a simple setting by Schubert.
Der du von dem Himmel bist	e1-g♯2	b1-f♯2	All voices	Very slow, sustained. Somewhat declamatory. See Schubert and Löwe.
Die drei Zigeuner	b-g2	d1-d2	Not suitable for very light voices	Dramatic, descriptive. Interpretatively not easy. Demands an excellent pianist. One of Liszt's most remarkable songs.

TITLE	COMP.	TESS.	TYPE	REMARKS
Die Lorelei	b-g1 (bb2)	g1-e2	Heavy voices	A dramatic, narrative song. Demands an accomplished pianist.
Du bist wie eine Blume	e1-g2	a1-e2	All voices	Slow, very sustained. See Schumann, Rubinstein.
Ein Fichtenbaum steht einsam	d1-f2	ab1-eb2	All voices	Slow, very sustained. Demands good command of high pp. See R. Franz's version among many others.
Es muss ein Wunderbares sein	c1-eb2	f1-db2	All voices	Very sustained.
Freudvoll und leidvoll	eb1-g2 (ab2)	ab1-f2	Women's voices	Sustained. In parts demands considerable dramatic intensity. See Schubert, "Die Liebe"; and Rubinstein, "Clärchens Lied."
Kling leise mein Lied	e1-g♯2	f♯1-f♯2	Not too suitable for very low, heavy voices	Animated, delicate. Demands good command of sustained pp.
Lasst mich ruhen	d♯1-eb2	f♯1-c♯2	All voices	Slow and sustained. Demands good command of pp.
Mignon's Lied (Kennst du das Land)	b♯-f♯2	f♯1-d♯2	Women's voices, except a very light soprano	Dramatic. Demands an excellent pianist. See Schubert, Beethoven, Schumann, H. Wolf.
Oh, quand je dors (French text)	d♯1-a2	g♯1-e2	Most suitable for high voices	Very sustained. In parts demands considerable dramatic intensity, also good command of high pp.
Schlüsselblümchen	eb1-f2	f1-eb2	All voices	Animated, graceful. Demands lightness of tone.

TITLE	COMP.	TESS.	TYPE	REMARKS
S'il est un charmant gazon (French text)	e♭1-f2	a♭1-e♭2	All voices	Delicate, graceful. See G. Fauré, "Rêve d'amour."
Wanderers Nachtlied (Über allen Gipfeln)	b-e2	f1-d2	Not too suitable for very light, high voices	Slow and very sustained. See Schubert, C. Löwe, and Schumann, "Nachtlied."
Jeanne D'Arc au bucher (French text)	c1-g♯2 (a2)	e1-e2	Dramatic soprano (mezzo-soprano)	A "dramatic scene" originally written for voice and orchestra. A declamatory adagio and a somewhat martial animato. (Album of Concert Arias, GS)

CARL LÖWE
(1796–1869)

Most of the ballades (narrative songs) and songs of Löwe, with but few exceptions, are written for heavy dramatic voices.

Löwe's unerring dramatic instinct enabled him to create extraordinarily forceful effects with elementary harmonic and melodic devices. In performing his songs and ballades one should perhaps try to emulate this simplicity by avoiding as much as possible an overdramatization in the manner of delivery.

Editions: Schlesinger (complete)
Albums: C. F. Peters
Breitkopf & Härtel
G. Schirmer

TITLE	COMP.	TESS.	TYPE	REMARKS
Archibald Douglas	g-e♭2	d1-d2	Not suitable for light voices; most suitable for baritone	A dramatic, narrative song of considerable length. Demands an accomplished pianist.
Canzonetta	b-a2	g♯1-f♯2	Most suitable for high voices	Slow and sustained. Demands considerable flexibility.

TITLE	COMP.	TESS.	TYPE	REMARKS
Der Heilige Franziskus	a-e2	e1-b1	Low or medium voices	Slow, sustained.
Die nächtliche Heerschau	b♭(g)-f2	d1-d2	Low or medium voices	An animated, march-like dramatic narrative song (ballade).
Der Mohrenfürst auf der Messe	b-g2	e1-e2	Not suitable for light, high voices	A dramatic narrative song (ballade). Demands an excellent pianist. One of the best examples of Löwe's musico-dramatic style. No. 3 of the trilogy, opus 97; "Der Mohrenfürst," "Die Mohrenfürstin," and "Der Mohrenfürst auf der Messe."
Der Mummelsee	a-g2	d1-d2	Mezzo-soprano or soprano; not suitable for very light, high soprano	A narrative song (ballade). Very florid. Demands an accomplished pianist.
Der selt'ne Beter	a-e2	b-b1	Medium or low voices	A dramatic narrative song (ballade).
Der Zahn	c1-f2	e1-e2	All voices	A jolly song in praise of a baby's first tooth.
Des Glocken-thürmers Töchterlein	c♯1-a2	a1-f♯2	Most suitable for high, light voices	Light, gently humorous. Quite florid.
Die Uhr	b♭-f2	d1-d2	Not too suitable for light, high voices	A simple narrative song.
Edward	b♭(a♭)-g♭2	e♭1-e♭2	Not suitable for	A dramatic narrative song (bal-

TITLE	COMP.	TESS.	TYPE	REMARKS
			very light, high voices	lade). One of the best examples of Löwe's musico-dramatic style. Demands an accomplished pianist.
Erlkönig	a1-g2	d1-d2	Not suitable for light voices	A dramatic, narrative song (ballade). One of the best examples of Löwe's musico-dramatic style. See Schubert and an admirable essay on Löwe's "Erlkönig" by D. Tovey.
Mädchen sind wie der Wind	b(g)-e2	d1-d2	Medium or low voices	Light and rapid. Demands an accomplished pianist.
Niemand hat's geseh'n	d♯1-f♯2 (a2)	e1-e2	Most suitable for light soprano	Very animated, light. Demands considerable flexibility.
Odins Meeres-Ritt	b-f♯2	e1-e2	Not suitable for light, high voices	A dramatic narrative song.
O Süsse Mutter	d1-g2	g1-e2	Women's voices	Animated. Demands facile articulation. See H. Wolf, "Die Spinnerin."
Süsses Begräbnis	d♯1-e2	g♯1-d♯2	All voices	Sustained.
Walpurgisnacht	g-g2	c1-c2	Women's voices, except a very light soprano	Very animated, dramatic. Demands facile articulation.

See also: "Die Verfallene Mühle"
"Tom der Reimer"   all dramatic narrative songs.
"Der Nöck"

GUSTAV MAHLER
(1860-1911)

The songs of Gustav Mahler, as characteristic of his manner of writing as are his symphonies, seem to possess a much wider popular appeal. Of great melodic simplicity, they are nevertheless not too easy vocally or interpretatively, being written for the most part for rather heavy voices possessing a somewhat extensive range and capable of commanding a great variety of dynamics. Practically all of them are written for voice and orchestra; the pianoforte arrangements of the orchestral score are, however, Mahler's own, in most cases.

The "Lieder eines fahrenden Gesellen," "Wer hat dies Liedlein erdacht," "Ich atmet' einen linden Duft," "Liebst du um Schönheit," "Ich bin der Welt abhanden gekommen" are recommended to those not at all acquainted with his manner of writing.

Editions: International Music Co.
Universal Edition.
Some reprints by Boosey & Hawkes.

TITLE	COMP.	TESS.	TYPE	REMARKS
Blicke mir nicht in die Lieder	c1-f2	c1-c2	All voices	Very animated. Demands an excellent pianist.
Das irdische Leben	bb-gb2 (H)	same	Dramatic soprano or mezzo-soprano	Dramatic, animated. Demands an excellent pianist.
Der Tambours-g'sell	A-g1	c-c1	Most suitable for baritone	A marchlike, dramatic song. Interpretatively not easy.
Des Antonius von Padua Fischpredigt	d1(a)-g2(H)	same	Not too suitable for very light, high voices	Humorous. Demands some flexibility and an excellent pianist. A trifle long.
Erinnerung	d1-f2 (a2)	g1-eb2	All voices	Slow, sustained and subdued.
Frühlingsmorgen	d1-g2	g1-e2	Most suitable for high voices	Light, delicate. Demands some flexibility and an accomplished pianist.

TITLE	COMP.	TESS.	TYPE	REMARKS
Hans und Grethe	c1-f2 (c3)	same	Not too suitable for very low voices	A waltz. In folk vein.
Ich atmet einen Linden Duft	bb-f#2	f#1-d2	Not suitable for very low, heavy voices	Slow, sustained, very delicate. Demands good command of high pp.
Ich bin der Welt abhanden gekommen	bb-f2	eb1-eb2	All voices	Slow, subdued. Interpretatively not easy. Demands some flexibility and good command of high pp.

Kindertotenlieder

A cycle of five songs for low or medium voice and orchestra. Piano reduction of orchestral score available. (Intended to be sung without interruption as a unit.)

(1) Nun will die Sonn' so hell aufgeh'n!	d1-eb2	e1-bb1		Slow, sustained, somber. Interpretatively not easy.
(2) Nun seh' ich wohl, warum so dunkel Flammen	a-f2	d1-d2		Sustained, somber. Demands good command of high pp. Interpretatively not easy.
(3) Wenn dein Mütterlein	g-f2	c1-c2		Sustained, somber. Demands in parts considerable dramatic intensity. Interpretatively not easy.
(4) Oft denk' ich, sie sind nur ausgegangen	bb-gb2	eb1-eb2		Not fast. Sustained, somber. In parts very dramatic. Demands good command of high pp. Interpretatively not easy.

TITLE	COMP.	TESS.	TYPE	REMARKS
(5) In diesem Wetter!	b♭-f2	d1-d2		Animated, somewhat declamatory, dramatic. The final section sustained and delicate. Interpretatively not easy. Demands an accomplished pianist.
Liebst du um Schönheit	e♭1-f2	same	Most suitable for women's voices	Sustained. Demands good command of high pp.

Lieder eines fahrenden Gesellen

TITLE	COMP.	TESS.	TYPE	REMARKS
(1) Wenn mein Schatz Hochzeit macht	b-g2	a1-e2	High baritone or mezzo-soprano	Sustained. This magnificent cycle of four songs is originally written for voice and orchestra. The piano arrangement is by Mahler. The songs can be sung separately, but are best performed as a unit. They are interpretatively complex and demand an accomplished pianist.
(2) Ging heut Morgen über's Feld	a-f♯2 (g2)	f♯1-e2		Animated, delicate. Demands good command of high pp.
(3) Ich hab ein glühend Messer	b♭-g♭2 (g2)	f1-e♭2		Very dramatic and rapid.
(4) Die zwei blauen Augen	a-g2	e1-c2		Very subdued, in march tempo. Demands good command of high pp.
Lob des hohen Verstandes	a-b♭2	d1-d2	Not suitable for	Humorous. Demands an excellent

TITLE	COMP.	TESS.	TYPE	REMARKS
			very light, high voices	pianist. The bb2 is not sung, but is used in an imitation of a donkey's bray.
Phantasie	b-f♯2	f♯1-d2	All voices, except a very light soprano	Sustained, very subdued.
O Röschen rot (alto solo from Symphony No. 2)	db1-eb2	db1-db2	Alto	Sustained. In the manner of a choral.
Revelge	d-a1	f-eb1	Most suitable for dramatic tenor or high baritone	Marchlike, dramatic. Interpretatively not easy. Demands an accomplished pianist.
Rheinlegendchen	b-f♯2	e1-e2	Soprano or mezzo-soprano	Light, gently humorous. Demands some flexibility and an accomplished pianist.
Serenade	e1-g2	f♯1-d2	Most suitable for men's voices	Sustained, delicate.
Um Mitternacht	b-g2	e1-e2	Not too suitable for light voices	Very sustained. Demands in parts considerable dramatic intensity. Interpretatively not easy.
Wer hat dies Liedlein erdacht	c-f1 (a2)	f1-d2 (H)	All voices	Light, gently humorous. Demands considerable flexibility and an excellent pianist.
Wo die schönen Trompeten blasen	a-g2	f♯1-f♯2	Not too suitable for very light, high voices	Very subdued. Interpretatively not easy. Demands good command of sustained pp.

See also nine early songs to texts from "Des Knaben Wunderhorn"; solo excerpts from symphonies Nos. 3, 4, 8, and "Das Klagende Lied," for soprano, alto, tenor, chorus and orchestra. See also "Das Lied von der Erde," 6 songs for tenor and alto (or baritone) and orchestra. (Not overly suitable for performance with piano.)

TITLE	COMP.	TESS.	TYPE	REMARKS

FRANK MARTIN
(b. 1890)

| Sechs Monologe aus Jedermann | a-f2 | d1-d2 | Alto or baritone | Originally for voice and orchestra. The piano reduction is by the composer. The six songs, somewhat in the nature of recitative, are highly dramatic and are both musically and interpretatively rather complex. They are obviously intended to be performed as a cycle. (UE) |

See also "Quatre sonnets" (French texts) for mezzo-soprano, flute, viola and violoncello, published by Hug Frères.

JOSEPH MARX
(b. 1882)

Marx's many songs, effective and well written as they are, seem sometimes to suffer from a certain overornateness and overelaboration of the accompaniment. The extremely effective and well-known "Hat dich die Liebe berührt" and "Der Ton" are perhaps not so direct and moving as "Marienlied," "Selige Nacht," and "Nocturne," which can perhaps be classed among the outstanding examples of Marx's style at its best.

    Editions: Universal Edition
                  Associated Music Publishers

| An einen Herbstwald | c#1-f#2 | f#1-c#2 | Not suitable for light, high voices | Grave, vigorous. Demands an accomplished pianist. |

TITLE	COMP.	TESS.	TYPE	REMARKS
Der bescheidene Schäfer	e1-a2	g1-e2	Soprano or mezzo-soprano	Humorous, light.
Der Rauch	c#1-f#2	f#1-c#2	All voices	Slow, sustained and subdued.
Der Ton	c1-f2	f1-db2	Medium or low voices	Very effective. Has a sustained vocal line over an elaborate accompaniment. Demands an excellent pianist.
Hat dich die Liebe berührt	eb1-g2 (bb2)	g1-eb2	Not suitable for light voices	Slow and sustained. Has very effective, dramatic climaxes. Demands an accomplished pianist.
Lied eines Mädchens	c#1-f#2	f#1-d#2	Women's voices	Slow, sustained, rather delicate.
Marienlied	d1-ab2	g1-eb2	Not too suitable for very low voices	Delicate, sustained.
Nocturne	eb1-ab2	ab1-f2	High voices	Has a sustained vocal line over an elaborate accompaniment. Demands an excellent pianist. The extremely important piano part would lose too much of its sonority if transposed.
Selige Nacht	db1-gb2	gb1-eb2	All voices	Sustained, delicate.
Tuch der Tränen	c1-ab2	g1-eb2	All voices	Sustained, rather subdued, somber.
Und gestern hat er mir Rosen gebracht	e1-a2	a1-f#2	Soprano	Light, animated. Very effective. Demands an accomplished pianist.
Valse de Chopin	c#1-g#2	c#1-c#2	Not too suitable for very light, high voices	Animated. Interpretatively not easy. Demands an excellent pianist.
Waldseligkeit	d#1-a2	a1-e2	All voices	Sustained, effective.

TITLE	COMP.	TESS.	TYPE	REMARKS
Wie einst	d1-g2	e♭1-e♭2	All voices	Slow, sustained, delicate.

FELIX MENDELSSOHN
(1809–1847)

Mendelssohn's songs are seldom encountered on concert programs today. The general reaction so prevalent during the past twenty or thirty years against their so-called "sentimentality" seems to have prejudiced many a singer against Mendelssohn; although it may be questioned how many of such singers have taken the pains to acquaint themselves with his songs. The curious fact is that Mendelssohn in his songs is perhaps less sentimental than, for instance, Schumann or Franz, and that most of his songs demand an almost Mozartean clarity, restraint and precision of execution, especially in regard to rhythm and phrasing. Songs like "Neue Liebe," "Jagdlied," "Lieblingsplätzchen," "Pagenlied," "Frühlingslied" (In Schwäbischer Mundart), "Erndtelied," to name but a few, are magnificent examples of the German Lied at its best and it seems rather peculiar that any serious singer should have to be reminded of their existence.

Editions: C. F. Peters
G. Schirmer
Novello, and many others.

TITLE	COMP.	TESS.	TYPE	REMARKS
Altdeutsches Lied	e1-e2	a1-e2	All voices	Very sustained.
An die Entfernte	f1-f2	g1-d2	All voices	Delicate, light. Demands facile articulation.
Auf Flügeln des Gesanges	e♭1-f2	b♭1-e♭2	All voices	Very sustained.
Bei der Wiege	f1-f2	f1-d2	Women's voices	Delicate. Demands lightness of tone.
Das erste Veilchen	f1-f2	a1-e♭2	All voices	Graceful, sustained.
Das Waldschloss	e1-e2	g1-d2	Not too suitable for very light, high voices	Vigorous, dramatic.
Der Blumenstrauss	e1-f♯2	a1-e2	All voices	Graceful.
Der Mond	e1-g♯2	g♯1-e2	All voices	Very sustained.

308

TITLE	COMP.	TESS.	TYPE	REMARKS
Erndtelied (Es ist ein Schnitter, der heisst Tod)	d1-d2	e1-b1	Not too suitable for very light, high voices	A chorale-like setting of a beautiful old religious poem. Verses 2, 4 and 5 could be omitted. A little known, remarkable song.
Frühlingslied (In dem Walde)	e1-f♯2	a1-e2	All voices	Very sustained.
Frühlingslied (In Schwäbischer Mundart)	d♯1-g♯2	g♯1-e2	Most suitable for light soprano	Light and graceful. In dialect, but German words can be easily substituted. Demands some flexibility and an accomplished pianist.
Gruss	d♯1-f♯2	a1-d2	All voices	Sustained, delicate.
Hirtenlied	d1-g2	g1-e2	Most suitable for high voices	Sustained, graceful.
Im Grünen	c♯1-g♯2 (b2)	b1-f♯2	Most suitable for high voices	Rapid and gay. Demands facile articulation.
Jagdlied	b-e2	e1-b1	All voices	Spirited.
Lieblingsplätzchen	f♯1-e2	g1-d2	All voices	Delicate.
Maienlied	d1-f♯2	a1-e2	All voices	Animated, delicate.
Minnelied (Wie der Quell)	e1-f♯2	a1-e2	All voices	Very sustained.
Minnelied im Mai	f1-g2	a1-d2	Most suitable for men's voices	Graceful, sustained. See Brahms, "Minnelied."
Nachtlied	d1-a♭2	g1-e♭2	All voices	Slow. Interpretatively not easy.
Neue Liebe	c♯1-a2	a1-f♯2	Most suitable for high, light voices	Very rapid and light. Demands facile articulation and an excellent pianist. One of the most remarkable of Mendelssohn's songs. See

TITLE	COMP.	TESS.	TYPE	REMARKS
				R. Franz, "In dem Mondenschein im Walde."
O Jugend, o schöne Rosen- zeit	e1-a2	a1-f#2	All voices	Animated, the vocal line is sustained. In folk vein.
Pagenlied	e1-e2	g1-d2	All voices	Light and delicate.
Reiselied (Der Herbstwind rüttelt)	e1-g2	g1-e2	Not too suitable for very light, high voices	Rapid, vigorous, dramatic. De- mands an accom- plished pianist.
Schilflied	c#1-f#2	g#1-d2	All voices	Somber. In parts demands consider- able dramatic in- tensity. See R. Franz, "Auf dem Teich dem regungs- losem," and C. Griffes.
Sonntagslied	e1-f#2	a1-e2	Women's voices	Animated. In folk vein.
Suleika (Was bedeutet die Bewegung)	e1-g#2	g#1-e2	Women's voices	Spirited. See Schubert.
Tröstung	d1-f#2	f#1-d2	All voices	Very sustained.
Venetianisches Gondellied	e1-f#2	b1-f#2	Most suit- able for men's voices	Delicate. See Schumann and A. Jensen, "Wenn durch Piazzetta."
Wenn sich zwei Herzen scheiden	e1-f#2	g1-d2	All voices	Sustained.
Infelice! Già dal mio sguardo (concert air) (Italian text)	d1-bb2	f1-f2	Dramatic soprano (lyric soprano)	Recitative, an- dante, allegro. (GS, Album of Concert Arias)

Solo Excerpts from English Oratorios
Note: All these excerpts are generally available.

Soprano

Elijah

Hear ye, Israel	d#1-a#2	a1-f#2	Dramatic soprano (lyric soprano)	A very sustained adagio and a spirited, vigorous, dramatic allegro maestoso.

TITLE	COMP.	TESS.	TYPE	REMARKS
Hear my prayer (Motet) O for the wings of a dove	d1-g2	g1-d2	Soprano	Sustained, rather delicate.
Lauda Sion Caro cibus (Lord at all times)	d1-g2	f1-f2	Lyric soprano (dramatic soprano)	Sustained.
St. Paul Recitative: So they being filled Air: I will sing of thy great mercies	e1-f2	g1-e2	Lyric soprano (dramatic soprano)	Sustained, graceful.
St. Paul Jerusalem, thou that killest the prophets	f1-f2	bb1-f2	Lyric soprano (dramatic soprano)	Slow, very sustained.

Alto or Mezzo-soprano

TITLE	COMP.	TESS.	TYPE	REMARKS
Elijah O rest in the Lord	b-d2	e1-c2		Slow, very sustained.
Elijah Woe unto them	b-e2	d#1-b1		Slow, sustained.
St. Paul Recitative: And he journeyed with companions Air: But the Lord is mindful of His own	a-d2	d1-a1		Slow, very sustained.

Tenor

TITLE	COMP.	TESS.	TYPE	REMARKS
Elijah Then shall the righteous shine forth	eb-ab1	ab-f1		Slow, sustained.

TITLE	COMP.	TESS.	TYPE	REMARKS

Elijah
Recitative:
  Ye people,
  rend your hearts
Air:
  If with all your
  hearts
— COMP. f#-ab1, TESS. bb-eb1, REMARKS: Sustained.

TITLE	COMP.	TESS.	TYPE	REMARKS
Elijah Recitative: Ye people, rend your hearts Air: If with all your hearts	f#-ab1	bb-eb1		Sustained.
Hymn of Praise Recitative: Sing ye praise Air: He counteth all your sorrows	d-g1	g-d1		Animated. The vocal line is very sustained.
Hymn of Praise The sorrows of death	c-ab1	g-e1		Sustained. In parts demands considerable dramatic intensity. Not too suitable for separate performance.
St. Paul Be thou faithful unto death	d-g1	g-e1		Very sustained.

Bass or Baritone

TITLE	COMP.	TESS.	TYPE	REMARKS
Elijah Recitative: I go on my way Air: For the mountains shall depart	B-e1	e-d1		Slow, sustained.
Elijah Is not his word like a fire	B-f1	e-d1		Very animated, vigorous, dramatic. Demands some flexibility.
Elijah It is enough	A-e1	f#-d1		Slow, very sustained. Has a very animated, dramatic, vigorous middle section.
Elijah Lord, God of Abraham	Bb-eb1	d-bb1		Sustained, majestic.

TITLE	COMP.	TESS.	TYPE	REMARKS
St. Paul Consume them all	B-d1	f#-c#1		Rapid, vigorous. The vocal line sustained.
St. Paul For know ye not	A-d1	d-d1		Very sustained, vigorous.
St. Paul O God, have mercy	B-d1	f#-d1		A very sustained adagio; the middle section is somewhat declamatory; vigorous allegro maestoso.

GIACOMO MEYERBEER
(1791–1864)

TITLE	COMP.	TESS.	TYPE	REMARKS
Der Mönch	F-e1	c-c1	Bass	Sustained, dramatic, effective. Has a vigorous, animated middle section. At one time one of the most popular bass songs. Demands good command of low f. (gen. av.)
Du schönes Fischersmädchen	c1-f2	f1-c2	Most suitable for men's voices	Light, graceful. (gen. av.)

HANS (ERICH) PFITZNER
(1869–1949)

Pfitzner's music has never become widely known outside of Germany. A prolific composer, he has written a large number of songs, rather uniform in quality, basically post-romantic in idiom. This short list is primarily designed for those who are not at all familiar with Pfitzner's vocal music.

TITLE	COMP.	TESS.	TYPE	REMARKS
Der Bote	f#1-a2	a1-e2	High voices	Animated. Demands an accomplished pianist. Effective climax. (Adolphe Fürstner)

TITLE	COMP.	TESS.	TYPE	REMARKS
Die Einsame	e1-e2	f#1-b1	All voices	Sustained, gentle. Animated accompaniment. Demands an accomplished pianist. (Max Brockhaus)
Gretel	a-a2	d1-e2	All voices, except bass	Graceful, jovial. (Max Brockhaus)
Herbstgefühl	d#1-f#2	e1-e2	High or medium voices	Sustained. Demands good command of high pp and an accomplished pianist. (CFP)
Ich und du	d1-eb2	eb1-d2	All voices	Slow, very sustained, very subdued. (Max Brockhaus)
Ist der Himmel darum im Lenz so blau?	c#1-d#2	d#1-c#2	All voices	Sustained, folklike. (Max Brockhaus)
Leuchtende Tage	e1-f#2	g1-e2	High or medium voices	Sustained vocal line. Fast. Climactic ending. (CFP)
Lied	b#-f#2	f#1-e2	All voices	Slow, sustained. (Max Brockhaus)
Sehnsucht	d1-gb2	e1-d2	All voices	Slow, sustained. Short. (CFP)
Sonst	d1-g2	f#1-f#2	All voices	A song of contrasting moods and tempi. Has a short recitative-like section near the end. (Max Brockhaus)
Stimme der Sehnsucht	c#1-g2 (ab2)	e1-e2	All voices, except bass	Sustained vocal part. Very fast. Has some parts with dramatic intensity. Demands an accomplished pianist. (Max Brockhaus)

TITLE	COMP.	TESS.	TYPE	REMARKS
Wiegenlied	d1-f♯2	f♯1-e2	Soprano	Graceful, gentle, subdued. (Adolph Fürstner)

MAX REGER
(1873–1916)

Reger's music has never become widely known outside of Germany. An extraordinarily prolific composer, he has written a startlingly large number of songs. The few examples listed here could be considered quite representative, since Reger's style is rather uniform.

Editions: Universal Edition
Bote & Bock

TITLE	COMP.	TESS.	TYPE	REMARKS
Aeolsharfe	c1(c♭1)-f2	f1-d♭2	All voices	Slow, sustained. Musically not easy.
Beim Schnee-wetter	b-e2	e1-c2 (L)	All voices	Delicate, sustained.
Darum	d1-f♯2	f♯1-d2	Women's voices	Animated, gently humorous. Demands some flexibility and an accomplished pianist.
Des Kindes Gebet	f1-g2	a1-f2 (H)	All voices	Delicate. Demands good command of pp.
Es blüht ein Blümlein rosenrot	e♭-a♭♭2	a♭1-f2 (H)	All voices	Slow and sustained. Demands good command of high pp.
Es schläft ein stiller Garten	a-e2	e♭1-c2	Most suitable for low voices	Slow, very sustained. In parts demands considerable dramatic intensity.
Friede	e♭1-g2	a♭1-f2 (H)	All voices	Very sustained.
Frühlingsmorgen	e♭1-f♯2	g1-e2	High or medium voices	Very sustained. Demands in parts considerable dramatic intensity.
Mariä Wiegenlied	f1-f2	a1-d2	Women's voices	Sustained, delicate. Demands good command of high pp. (gen. av.)

TITLE	COMP.	TESS.	TYPE	REMARKS
Mit Rosen bestreut	c♯1-d2	f♯1-d2 (L)	Women's voices	Delicate, sustained.
Sommernacht	a♯-e1	e1-b1	Most suitable for medium or low voices	Sustained. In parts demands considerable dramatic intensity.
Waldeinsamkeit	a-d2	d1-b1 (L)	Women's voices	Graceful, gently humorous.

OTHMAR SCHOECK
(1886–1957)

This highly respected Swiss composer has written a large number of songs in traditional late romantic idiom. All of his songs are expertly made, beautifully written for the voice, and in excellent taste. The short list below is merely intended to serve as an introduction to his vocal music.

Editions: Universal Edition
Breitkopf & Härtel

Distichen	d1-g2	f1-e2	All voices	Lively, has some humor. Strophic, folk-like. Demands facile articulation.
Einst	f1-f2	same	All voices	Sustained, folk-like. Strophic.
Leidenschaft	f♭1-a2	f1-f♯2	High or medium voices	Sustained, demands a somewhat free delivery. Demands an accomplished pianist.
Liederfrühling	f♯1-a2	a1-g2	High or medium voices	Animated. Demands an accomplished pianist.
Muttersprache	f1-g2	a1-f2	All voices	Recitative-like, free delivery.
Nacht, Muse und Tod	f1-f♯2	g1-d2	High or medium voices	Sustained, generally subdued. In parts contemplative. A conversation between three characters.

TITLE	COMP.	TESS.	TYPE	REMARKS
Rückkehr	e1-a2	g1-f♯2	High or medium voices	Sustained, in flowing style.
Spruch	d1-g2	g1-d2	All voices	Recitative-like, short.
Unmut. Trost.	e♭1-a2	g1-f2	High or medium voices	Two songs to be performed together. The first is sustained and introspective; the second and the shorter one is more free, brighter, and ending broadly.
Vorwurf	f♯1-a2	a1-f♯2	All voices	Sustained, in flowing style.
Waldeinsamkeit	d1-g2	g1-d2	All voices	Sustained, quiet.

ARNOLD SCHÖNBERG
(1874–1951)

The songs of Arnold Schönberg, a figure of immense importance in contemporary music, can be roughly classified as falling in two categories—the early songs, which are highly chromatic, somewhat complex, but nevertheless adhere to the principles of tonality, and the songs of the later period, in which a definite break with the conventional system of tonality is attempted. The still controversial nature of Schönberg's later music makes the inclusion of examples of this latter style into this volume somewhat questionable. Anyone interested in acquainting himself with this facet of Schönberg's style of writing is referred to the catalogue of the Universal Edition which lists all his songs. The somewhat fragmentary list here is primarily designed for those who are not at all familiar with Schönberg's vocal music.

Edition: Universal Edition

Das schöne Beet betracht' ich	c♯1-e♯2	e1-c2	All voices	Slow and sustained. Musically complex.
Der verlorene Haufen (opus 12)	A♭-g1	d-e1	Baritone	A vigorous, animated, dramatic ballade. Demands an accomplished pianist. Musically and interpretatively not easy.

TITLE	COMP.	TESS.	TYPE	REMARKS
Erhebung	e#1-a2	e#1-e2	High voices, except a very light soprano	Sustained. Demands in parts considerable dramatic intensity.
Geübtes Herz (opus 3, no. 5)	a#-f2	f#1-d#2	Most suitable for medium voices (preferably baritone)	Sustained.
Ghasel (opus 6)	c1-g#2	f1-e2	High voices, except a light soprano	Sustained. Demands in parts considerable dramatic intensity.

Excerpts from "Gurrelieder" for soli, chorus and orchestra

TITLE	COMP.	TESS.	TYPE	REMARKS
Lied der Waldtaube: "Tauben von Gurre"	a-bb2	db1-eb2	Mezzo-soprano or alto	Dramatic. Interpretatively and musically not easy.
Tove: "Nun sag ich dir zum ersten mal"	b-f#2	d#1-d2	Dramatic soprano	Sustained.
Waldemar: "Du wunderliche Tove"	c#-a1	f-f1	Tenor	Sustained. In parts demands considerable dramatic intensity.
Waldemar: "So tanzen die Engel"	c#-g1	f#-eb1	Tenor	Sustained.
Hochzeitslied (opus 3, no. 4)	d1-f#2	f#1-d2	Not too suitable for very light, high voices	Sustained, not slow.
Ich darf nicht dankend	a-f2	d1-eb2	Medium or low voices	Slow, rather sustained.
In diesen Wintertagen	b-g2	d-e2	Not suitable for very light, high voices	Not fast. Demands in parts considerable dramatic intensity.
Mädchenlied (opus 6)	d#1-a2	f1-f2	Soprano	Rapid, dramatic. Musically not easy. Demands an accomplished pianist.

318

TITLE	COMP.	TESS.	TYPE	REMARKS
Verlassen (opus 6)	b-g♭2	e1-d2	Not suitable for very light, high voices	Sustained, somber, dramatic. Musically not easy.
Warnung (opus 3, no. 3)	b♭-e♭2	d♭1-d♭2	Medium or low voices (preferably baritone)	Very animated, dramatic. Interpretatively and musically not easy. Demands an accomplished pianist.

FRANZ SCHREKER
(1878–1934)

TITLE	COMP.	TESS.	TYPE	REMARKS
Dass er ganz ein Engel werde	c♯1-e2	f♯1-c♯2	Women's voices, except a very light soprano	Slow and somber. Demands good command of pp. (UE)
Einst gibt ein Tag mir alles Glücken eigen	b♭-e♭2	b♭-b♭1	Low voices	Slow, declamatory. Musically and interpretatively not easy. (UE)
O Glocken, böse Glocken	b♭-g♭2	d1-d2	Women's voices, except a very light soprano	Sustained. Demands in parts considerable dramatic intensity. (UE)

FRANZ SCHUBERT
(1797–1828)

So much has been written about Schubert that it seems best to dispense with anything in the nature of general remarks concerning his unequaled importance as a composer of songs, especially in a brief prefatory note.

Specifically, however, one observation in regard to the performance of his songs may be of some value. The considerable and probably only difficulty facing a present-day singer who is attempting to sing Schubert lies in the domain of style. By this is meant that in order to sing Schubert properly one must try to adjust one's attitude toward art in general, and toward music, poetry and singing in particular, to the attitude that was prevalent in the Vienna of Schubert's time and that influenced him to no small degree.

The problem of such an adjustment is of course ever present in the attempt to perform any music. Yet, in the case of Schubert songs it seems to be of special importance, due perhaps to the fact that the stylistic conventions of his time are not so obviously and unmistakably different from ours, as those, for instance, which governed Bach and Mozart's mode of musical expression.

The present-day singer is liable to forget that vocalization in Schubert's time had reached an almost unprecedented and probably never afterward equaled degree of elegance, that the musicodramatic conception, existing as it did since the time of Peri and Monteverdi, was still subject to purely musicotheoretic considerations, that the poetic climate tended toward refined sentimentality, not yet fully released from the eighteenth century gallant and mythological patterns, and that Schubert, notwithstanding the fact that he was the possessor of a great and miraculous genius, was none the less a man living in the Vienna of that time.

I know of no easy and simple way of attaining stylistic sensitivity. One must first of all become familiar with the attitudes and standards of the period; this necessitates some familiarity with the poetry, literature, painting, and other arts of the period, with its aesthetic writings, social usages, and living conditions.

Then, if one possesses sufficient imagination, one may instinctively arrive at the attitude one is trying to establish.

Practically, the following advice may be of some slight help:

(1) Do not try to dramatize Schubert, in the Wagnerian sense of the word, that is, never sacrifice the phrase (sentence) to the single word.

(2) The melodic line should at all times be kept flowing smoothly and elegantly.

(3) The rhythm must at no time be allowed to become slack or vague.

(4) Do not try to use Schubert songs as vehicles for exhibition of vocal powers; remember that the size of a voice was not considered as important, even in opera, at Schubert's time, as a singer's elegance and the perfection of his vocalization. (Mozart and Rossini were the most admired composers of vocal music at that time.)

(5) Have a classical dictionary handy, for the number of mythological allusions in the poetry used by Schubert is very great.

Schubert's accompaniments, simple as they seem harmonically, are often pianistically complex demanding an instrumentalist of polish. In many of his songs the balance between the voice part and the piano is of the type more often encountered in the chamber music than in the songs of that period, though, of course, the piano part is hardly ever treated independently, even in songs like "Erlkönig," where it demands a virtuoso technique.

Editions: Complete: Breitkopf & Härtel (Mandyszewski).
Complete: C. F. Peters, 7 vols. (Friedländer), (Vols. I) & II, H, M & L).

200 songs selected by Sergius Kagen (3 vols.), International Music Co. (H & L).
Numerous albums by many publishers.

TITLE	COMP.	TESS.	TYPE	REMARKS
Abendbilder	e1-a2	b1-g2	Most suitable for high, light voices	Delicate, animated. Demands lightness of tone and an accomplished pianist.
Abendstern	e1-g2	a1-e2	All voices	Sustained.
Abschied	d1-ab2	ab1-eb2	Men's voices	Animated, graceful. Demands lightness of tone and facile articulation. Verses 4 and 5 may be omitted.
Am Bach im Frühling	ab-db2	db1-bb1	Medium or low voices	Sustained. In parts declamatory.
Am Flusse	d1-f♯2	a1-d2	All voices	Sustained.
Am Grabe Anselmo's	d1-g2	g1-fb2	Women's voices	Slow and sustained, somber.
Am Meer	d1-f2	g1-e2	All voices, except a very light soprano	Slow and sustained. In parts demands considerable dramatic intensity. Interpretatively not easy.
Am See	d1-f2	g1-eb2	All voices	Sustained, delicate. Demands some flexibility.
Am Strome	d♯1-f♯2	b1-e2	All voices	Sustained.
An den Mond (Gruss lieber Mond)	f1-gb2	ab1-eb2	All voices	Slow, sustained, delicate.
An den Tod	bb-c♯2	d1-b1	Medium or low voices	Very sustained, majestic.
An die Entfernte	f♯1-g2	c2-f2	All voices	The tessitura is somewhat high. Slow and sustained. In parts demands considerable dramatic intensity.

TITLE	COMP.	TESS.	TYPE	REMARKS
An die Laute	d1-f♯2	a1-d2	All voices	Light and delicate.
An die Leyer	b♭-f2	e♭1-c2	Not suitable for very light, high voices	Very sustained. In parts declamatory. Interpretatively not easy.
An die Musik	c♯1-f♯2	f♯1-d2	All voices	Note the tempo mark mässig, ℂ. Sustained. Often sung too slowly.
An die Nachtigall	g1-g2	c2-f2	Most suitable for light voices	Delicate, sustained.
An die Türen will ich schleichen	g♯1-g2	b1-f2	Men's voices	Sustained. Demands good command of pp. See Schumann and H. Wolf.
An Schwager Kronos	a-f♯2	f1-e2	Heavy voices	Dramatic, very vigorous. Demands an excellent pianist. Interpretatively not easy.
An Sylvia	e1-f♯2	a1-e2	All voices	Delicate, sustained.
Auf dem Wasser zu singen	e♭1-g♭2	a♭1-e♭2	Not too suitable for very low voices	Animated, delicate. Demands lightness of tone, some flexibility and an excellent pianist.
Aufenthalt	b-g2	e1-e2	Heavy voices	Vigorous, sustained, somber.
Aus Heliopolis (Fels an Felsen)	g-d2	d1-c2	Heavy medium or low voices	Dramatic, vigorous.
Aus Heliopolis (Im kalten, rauhen Norden)	a(g♯)-e2	e1-c♯2	Medium or low voices	Sustained.
Ave Maria	f1-f2	g1-e♭2	Most suitable for women's voices	Slow and very sustained. Care should be taken to sing the sixteenths evenly. The substitution of the Latin prayer text for the original poem is not recommended in view of the fact

TITLE	COMP.	TESS.	TYPE	REMARKS
				that the accents of the Latin text do not coincide with the accents of the melodic line.
Blumenlied	e1-g♯2	g♯1-e2	Not too suitable for very low voices	Delicate. Demands some flexibility.
Das Fischermädchen	c1-g♭2	a♭1-e♭2	Men's voices	Animated. Demands lightness of tone.
Das Lied im Grünen	e1-a2	a1-e2	All voices	Delicate. Demands lightness of tone and facile articulation. The song is somewhat long, but cuts are permissible and in some respects desirable.
Das Rosenband	f1-f2	a♭1-e♭2	All voices	Delicate and graceful.
Dass sie hier gewesen	g1-g2	c2-f2	All voices	Slow and very sustained. Demands good command of pp. The tessitura is somewhat high.
Dem Unendlichen (Third version)	c1-a♭2	f1-e♭2	Heavy voices	Majestic and declamatory. Interpretatively complex.
Der Alpenjäger	c1-f♯2	f1-d2	Not suitable for light voices	Spirited and vigorous.
Der Atlas	d1-a♭2	g1-e2	Heavy voices	Dramatic, very vigorous. Demands an accomplished pianist.
Der Doppelgänger	b1-g2	d1-d2	Not suitable for light voices	Dramatic, slow. Often sung and played slovenly in regard to time values, thus losing much of its dramatic impact.

TITLE	COMP.	TESS.	TYPE	REMARKS
Der Einsame	d1-g2	g1-e2	All voices	Delicate. Demands lightness of tone, facile articulation, and an accomplished pianist.
Der Erlkönig	c1-g2	a1-f2	Not suitable for very light voices	Dramatic narrative song. Demands a virtuoso pianist. Observe Schubert's MM ♩ = 152. See C. Löwe, "Erlkönig," and an admirable essay upon it by Donald Tovey.
Der Jüngling am Bache	eb1-f2	g1-eb2	All voices	Sustained. Demands some flexibility.
Der Jüngling an der Quelle	e1-a2	a1-g2	All voices	Slow and sustained. Delicate.
Der Jüngling auf dem Hügel	c1(g)-f2	g1-e2	Medium or low voices	Slow, sustained. Interpretatively not easy.
Der Knabe	a1-a2	c♯2-g2	Light, high voices	Delicate, graceful.
Der Liebliche Stern	d1-f2	g1-d2	Most suitable for light voices	Delicate. Demands lightness of tone and some flexibility.
Der Musensohn	f♯1-g2	b1-e2	All voices	Light, graceful, very animated. Demands facile articulation and an excellent rhythmic sense.
Der Schiffer	bb-eb2	eb1-c2	Medium or low voices	Rapid and vigorous. Demands facile articulation and an accomplished pianist.
Der Schmetterling	e1-f2	f1-c2	Not too suitable for very heavy or very low voices	Delicate, graceful, animated.
Der Tod und das Mädchen	a(d)-eb2	d1-a1	Mezzo-soprano	This celebrated song has seemingly

TITLE	COMP.	TESS.	TYPE	REMARKS
		or alto		become an almost exclusive property of alti no doubt because of the optional final d, mostly used for exhibitionistic purposes, often without much success. However, should this one note be omitted and d1 taken instead, this song can be most effectively sung by a lighter voice, even a soprano, as the entire low passage is expressly marked pp, which is, incidentally, very rarely obeyed. The tempo, according to Schubert's own markings, is $\d$= 54 about twice as fast as this song is often taken.
Der Wachtelschlag	d♯1-f♯2	a1-e2	Most suitable for light, high voices	Light and animated. Demands some flexibility and an accomplished pianist.
Der Wanderer	g♯(e)-e2	e1-c♯2	Medium or low voices	Slow, somber. Interpretatively not easy.
Der Wanderer an den Mond	d1-f2	g1-d2	All voices	Demands lightness of tone and good sense of rhythm. Delicate, animated.
Der Winterabend	e1-f2	a1-e2	All voices	Delicate. Demands lightness of tone and an accomplished pianist. A trifle long.

325

TITLE	COMP.	TESS.	TYPE	REMARKS
Der Zürnende Barde	a-e2	f1-c2	Bass, baritone or heroic tenor	Vigorous, animated. Demands facile articulation.
Der Zwerg	a-g♭2	f♯1-e2	Not suitable for light voices	A dramatic narrative song.
Des Mädchens Klage	c1-e♭2	g1-c2	Women's voices	Slow and sustained.
Die Allmacht	c1-a2 (b♭2)	b♭1-g2	Heavy voices	Very sustained, majestic, vigorous. Vocally not easy.
Die Forelle	e♭1-g♭2	a♭1-e♭2	All voices	Demands facile articulation and an accomplished pianist. Light and animated.
Die junge Nonne	c1-g♭2	a♭1-e2	Women's voices, except a very light soprano	Not slow. Dramatic. Demands an accomplished pianist.
Die Liebe	g1-b♭2	d2-g2	Soprano or mezzo-soprano	Slow and very sustained. Has a high tessitura. See "Freudvoll und Leidvoll" by Beethoven and by Liszt; and Rubinstein, "Clärchens Lied."
Die Liebe hat gelogen	g1-f2	b♭1-e♭2	All voices, except a very light soprano	In parts demands considerable dramatic intensity. Sustained.
Die Männer sind Mechant!	e1-f2	e1-c♯2	Women's voices	Sustained. Somewhat humorous.
Die Rose	g1-g2	b♭1-e♭2	Most suitable for light, high voices	Graceful and delicate.

Die Schöne Müllerin

A cycle of twenty songs, opus 25, text by W. Müller

As in the case of some other song cycles, it seemed advisable to list these songs under one heading, and in their original order, instead

of alphabetically. This cycle follows a definite plot; ideally, therefore, it is desirable to perform the whole as a unit, which of course
is, to say the least, a rather ambitious undertaking.

The practice of performing these songs separately is widespread,
however, and is by no means to be condemned, although one must admit that many a song loses thus some of its meaning. The cycle was
originally intended for tenor, but, it can and has been performed by
practically every type of voice, by men as well as women. Generally
speaking, it seems to suit high voices best.

TITLE	COMP.	TESS.	TYPE	REMARKS
(1) Das Wandern	f1-f2	b♭1-e♭2	All voices	Spirited. Demands lightness of tone and excellent sense of rhythm.
(2) Wohin	d1-g2	f♯1-e2	All voices	Light and animated. One of the best known songs in this cycle. Demands facile articulation, lightness of tone, and an accomplished pianist. Often taken at too fast a tempo.
(3) Halt	f1-g2	g1-e2	All voices	Animated.
(4) Danksagung an den Bach	f♯1-g2	b1-f♯2	All voices	Slow, very sustained. The tessitura is somewhat high. Demands good command of high p.
(5) Am Feier-abend	c1-g2	a1-f2	Not too suitable for very light, high voices	Rapid, dramatic. Demands facile articulation and an accomplished pianist.
(6) Der Neugierige	e♯1-g2	b1-e2	All voices	Slow, sustained. One of the best known songs in this cycle. Observe the 3/8 rest before the "Sehr langsam" section.
(7) Ungeduld	e1-a2	a1-f♯2	All voices	Rapid. One of the best known songs in this cycle. Demands very facile

TITLE	COMP.	TESS.	TYPE	REMARKS
				articulation, good command of high voice, and an excellent pianist. Often taken at too fast a tempo. Verse 3 may be omitted.
(8) Morgengruss	g1-f2	c1-e2	All voices	Sustained.
(9) Des Müllers Blumen	e1-f♯2	a1-e2	All voices	Delicate and sustained. Demands lightness of tone.
(10) Thränenregen	d♯1-e2	f♯1-d2	All voices	Sustained. Interpretatively not easy.
(11) Mein	d1-f♯2	f♯1-d2	All voices	Spirited. Demands facile articulation and some flexibility. In some editions marked 𝄵.
(12) Pause	e1-f2	g1-e♭2	All voices	Sustained. Interpretatively not easy.
(13) Mit dem grünen Lautenbande	e1-f2	b♭1-e♭2	All voices	Graceful. In folk vein.
(14) Der Jäger	c1-g2	g1-e♭2	All voices	Very rapid. Demands exceptionally facile articulation. Seldom performed separately.
(15) Eifersucht und Stolz	d1-g2	g1-e♭2	All voices	Very rapid. Demands facile articulation and an excellent pianist.
(16) Die liebe Farbe	f♯1-f♯2	b1-e2	All voices	Slow and very sustained.
(17) Die böse Farbe	d♯1-g2	b1-f♯2	Not too suitable for very light soprano	Dramatic, vigorous. Demands very facile articulation in parts and an excellent pianist.
(18) Trockne Blumen	f♯1-g2	g1-e2	All voices	Slow and sustained. One of the best known songs in this cycle. Demands

TITLE	COMP.	TESS.	TYPE	REMARKS
				good command of pp, excellent rhythmic sense, and an accomplished pianist.
(19) Der Müller und der Bach	f#1-g2	g1-e2	All voices	Slow and very sustained.
(20) Des Baches Wiegenlied	g#1-g#2	b1-e2	All voices	Sustained. Seldom sung separately. Note the tempo mark, mässig₵. Often sung too slowly.
Die Spinnerin	f#1-a2	b1-f#2	Light soprano	Delicate. Demands some flexibility. Verses 4, 5, 6 could be omitted.
Die Stadt	c1-g2	g1-eb2	All voices, except a very light soprano	Sustained, somber. Demands in parts considerable dramatic intensity. Interpretatively not easy. Demands an accomplished pianist. Often sung rather slovenly in regard to time values, thus losing much of its dramatic impact.
Die Taubenpost	f1-g2	a1-e2	All voices	Delicate, sustained. Demands lightness of tone.
Du bist die Ruh'	f1-ab2	bb1-f2	All voices	Slow and very sustained. Note the full bar rests.
Du liebst mich nicht	e1-f#2	a1-e2	All voices, except a very light soprano	Sustained. Demands in parts considerable dramatic intensity.
Ellens zweiter Gesang	eb1-eb2	bb1-eb2	Mezzo-soprano or alto	Animated. Demands good sense of rhythm.

329

TITLE	COMP.	TESS.	TYPE	REMARKS
Erlafsee	e1-g2	a1-f2	Most suitable for high, light voices	Sustained, delicate. Demands lightness of tone and some flexibility.
Erster Verlust	c2-f2	e2-f2	All voices	Very slow and sustained. The tessitura is somewhat high. See Mendelssohn.
Fahrt zum Hades	a(f)-d2	d1-bb1	Medium or low voices	Dramatic, somber, somewhat declamatory.
Fischerweise	d1-e2	f#1-d2	Medium or low voices	Spirited. Demands facile articulation.
Fragment aus dem Aeschylus	c1-gb2	f1-eb2	Heavy voices	Dramatic, declamatory. Interpretatively complex.
Frühlingsglaube	eb1-f2	g1-eb2	All voices	Slow and sustained.
Frühlingslied	e1-g2	g1-d2	All voices	Animated, light.
Frühlingssehnsucht	e1-g2	bb1-f2	All voices	Rapid and light. Demands facile articulation. The second verse may be omitted.
Ganymed	d#1-f2	ab1-e2	All voices	Sustained. Interpretatively not easy. Demands an accomplished pianist. See H. Wolf.
Gebet während der Schlacht	c#1-e2	f1-d2	Bass, baritone, or heroic tenor	Dramatic; in parts declamatory.
Geheimes	eb1-ab2	ab1-f2	All voices	Graceful, delicate, light.
Gott im Frühling	e1-g#2	g#1-e2	Not too suitable for very low voices	Graceful, delicate.
Gretchen am Spinnrade	e1-a2	a1-f2	Women's voices,	Sustained. Demands considerable

TITLE	COMP.	TESS.	TYPE	REMARKS
			except a very light soprano	dramatic intensity in parts, and an excellent pianist. Observe Schubert's MM mark ♩= 72.
Gretchens Bitte	b-g2	ab1-f2	Women's voices, except a very light soprano	Slow, sustained. In parts demands considerable dramatic intensity.
Grenzen der Menschheit	bb(a)-ab2	f♯1-e2	Heavy voices	Majestic, declamatory. Interpretatively complex. See H. Wolf.
Gruppe aus dem Tartarus	c1-eb2	e1-c2	Heavy voices	Dramatic. Interpretatively not easy. Demands an excellent pianist.
Heiden Röslein	g1-g2	d1-g2	All voices	Graceful, delicate.
Ihr Bild	f1-eb2	g1-d2	All voices	Slow and sustained. Interpretatively not easy.
Ihr Grab	d1-gb2	bb1-f2	Men's voices	Very slow and sustained.
Im Abendroth	eb1-f2	ab1-eb2	All voices	Slow and very sustained. Demands good command of pp.
Im Frühling	d1-f♯2	g1-e2	Not too suitable for very heavy voices	Delicate. Interpretatively not easy. Demands an accomplished pianist.
Im Haine	c♯1-g2	a1-f♯2	Most suitable for light, high voices	Very delicate, sustained. Demands some flexibility.
In der Ferne	b-g2	f♯1-e2	Heavy voices	Sustained, dramatic. Interpretatively not easy.
Jägers Abend-lied	g1-gb2	bb1-eb2	All voices	Very slow and sustained. Demands good command of pp.

TITLE	COMP.	TESS.	TYPE	REMARKS
Kriegers Ahnung	a-f2	g1-e2	Baritone or bass	Dramatic. Interpretatively not easy.
Lachen und Weinen	e♭1-f2	a♭1-e♭2	All voices	Delicate, graceful. Demands lightness of tone. Interpretatively not easy.
Liebesbotschaft	e1-g2	a1-e2	All voices	Delicate, graceful. Demands lightness of tone, facile articulation, and an accomplished pianist. Often taken at too fast a tempo.
Liebe schwärmt auf allen Wegen	g1-g2	g1-e2	Soprano	Delicate, animated, graceful.
Lied der Mignon (Heiss mich nicht reden)	c1-g2	g1-e2	Women's voices, except a very light soprano	Sustained. Demands in parts considerable dramatic intensity.
Lied der Mignon (Nur wer die Sehnsucht kennt)	g1-f2	c2-f2	Women's voices	Slow and sustained. See Beethoven, Schumann, H. Wolf, Tchaikovsky, among many others.
Lied der Mignon (So lasst mich scheinen)	d♯1-f♯2	b1-e2	Women's voices, except a very light soprano	Sustained. Demands in parts considerable dramatic intensity. See Schumann and H. Wolf.
Lied eines Schiffers an die Dioskuren	c1-e♭2	f1-d♭2	Not too suitable for very high voices	Slow and very sustained.
Litaney	c1-e♭2	g1-d2	Not too suitable for very high light voices	Slow and very sustained. The poem has 9 verses, of which 7 are as a rule omitted.
Lob der Thränen	f♯1-f♯2	a1-e2	All voices	Slow and sustained.

TITLE	COMP.	TESS.	TYPE	REMARKS
Meeresstille	b-d2	d♯1-a1	Medium or low voices	Very slow and sustained. Demands good command of pp.
Memnon	ab-f2	f1-db2	All voices, except a very light soprano	Slow and sustained. Interpretatively not easy. Demands an accomplished pianist.
Minnelied	d♯1-f♯2	g♯1-e2	Most suitable for men's voices	Delicate, sustained. See Brahms and Mendelssohn.
Nachtgesang	bb-eb2	c1-g1	Low or medium voices	Very slow and sustained.
Nacht und Träume	d♯1-e2	f♯1-d♯2	Not too suitable for very high voices	Very slow and sustained. Demands good command of pp. Vocally not easy.
Nachtviolen	a1-a2	c1-f2	Most suitable for light voices	Slow and sustained. Demands good command of pp.
Nähe des Geliebten	f1-gb2	db1-gb2	All voices	Very slow and sustained. The tessitura is quite high.
Prometheus	cb1-f2	f1-eb2	Heavy voices, preferably heroic tenor or baritone	Majestic, declamatory, dramatic. Interpretatively complex. Demands an accomplished pianist. See H. Wolf.
Rastlose Liebe	d♯1-a2	b1-g2	Not too suitable for very light voices	Rapid, vigorous. Demands an excellent pianist. See R. Franz.
Romanze (from Rosamunde)	c1-eb2	g1-db2	Most suitable for medium voices	Sustained.
Schäfers Klagelied	c1-fb2	g1-eb2	All voices	Sustained. Demands in parts considerable dramatic intensity.

TITLE	COMP.	TESS.	TYPE	REMARKS
Schlaflied (some-times called Schlummerlied)	c1-f2	f1-d2	All voices	Delicate, sustained. Demands good command of pp.
Schwanengesang	eb1-g2	g1-eb2	All voices	Slow and very sustained.
Sei mir gegrüsst	g1-g2	bb1-f2	All voices	Slow and sustained.
Sprache der Liebe	d1-g#2	g#1-e2	Most suitable for high voices	Delicate.
Ständchen (Horch, horch die Lerch)	f1-g2	c2-f2	All voices	Delicate, animated, graceful.
Ständchen (Leise flehen)	d1-g2	a1-f2	All voices	Sustained. Demands lightness of tone. Note the tempo mark, "mässig." Often sung too slowly.
Suleika I (Was bedeutet die Bewegung)	d#1-g2	a1-f#2	Soprano or mezzo-soprano	Animated. Interpretatively not easy. Demands an accomplished pianist.
Suleika II (Ach um diese feuchten Schwingen)	f1-bb2	bb1-f2	Soprano or mezzo-soprano	Animated. Interpretatively and vocally not easy. Demands an accomplished pianist. See Mendelssohn.
Thekla	bb1-e2	same	Mezzo-soprano or alto	Very slow and sustained.
Todesmusik	d1-g2	g1-e2	All voices	Slow, sustained. Interpretatively not easy.
Totengräbers Heimweh	a-f2	f1-f2	Baritone	Dramatic, animated. Demands good command of pp. Interpretatively not easy.
Über Wildemann	c#1-g2	f1-e2	Men's voices	Rapid and vigorous. Demands facile articulation and an accomplished pianist.

TITLE	COMP.	TESS.	TYPE	REMARKS
Wanderers Nachtlied (Der du von dem Himmel bist)	eb1-g2	g1-eb2	All voices	Slow, sustained. See H. Wolf, Liszt, C. Löwe.
Wanderers Nachtlied (Über allen Gipfeln)	f1-f2	bb1-d2	All voices	Slow and sustained. Demands good command of pp. See Schumann, "Nachtlied," and "Wanderers Nachtlied" by Liszt and by C. Löwe.
Wehmut	d1-f2	a1-d2	All voices	Slow and very sustained.
Wer nie sein Brot	e1-g2	a1-e2	Men's voices, except a light tenor	Slow and sustained; in parts dramatic. See Schumann, Liszt and H. Wolf.
Wer sich der Einsamkeit ergibt	c1-fb2	a1-e2	Men's voices, except a light tenor	Slow and sustained; in parts dramatic. See Schumann and H. Wolf.
Wiegenlied	eb1-f2	bb1-eb2	Women's voices	Delicate, sustained. Demands lightness of tone.

Winterreise

A cycle of twenty-four songs, opus 89, text by W. Müller

As in the case of some other song cycles, it seemed advisable to list these songs under one heading, and in their original order instead of alphabetically.

Although the 24 songs comprising this cycle are somewhat more loosely connected than those in the "Schöne Müllerin" they should ideally be performed as a unit. Needless to say this is a formidable task. The practice of performing these songs separately is widespread, however, and is by no means to be condemned, although one must admit that many a song loses thus some of its poignancy and impact.

The cycle was originally intended for tenor, of a heavier, darker timbre than the one demanded by the "Schöne Müllerin." It can and has been performed by practically every type of voice, by men as well as women. Generally speaking it does not seem to suit high, light voices too well.

335

TITLE	COMP.	TESS.	TYPE	REMARKS
(1) Gute Nacht	c1-f♯2	e1-d2	All voices	Sustained. Note the tempo mark, "mässig in gehender Bewegung." The second verse is sometimes omitted. Often sung too slowly.
(2) Die Wetterfahne	e1-g2	g♯1-e2	All voices	Animated. Interpretatively not easy. Demands some flexibility and an excellent pianist.
(3) Gefrorene Tränen	c1-f2	f1-e♭2	Not too suitable for very high, light voices	Sustained, somber. Note the tempo mark, "Nicht zu langsam"₵. Often sung too slowly.
(4) Erstarrung	f1-a♭2	g1-f2	All voices	Rapid and dramatic. Demands facile articulation and an excellent pianist.
(5) Der Lindenbaum	c1-e2	e1-b1	All voices	Very sustained. One of the best known songs in this cycle. Demands an excellent pianist.
(6) Wasserflut	b-g2	e1-e2	All voices	Very slow and sustained, somber.
(7) Auf dem Flusse	b(a♯)-g2(a2)	e1-e2	All voices	Slow. Interpretatively not easy. Demands in parts considerable dramatic intensity.
(8) Rückblick	d1-g2	g1-e2	All voices	Animated. Rhythmically not easy. Demands facile articulation and an excellent pianist.
(9) Irrlicht	b-g2	f♯1-f♯2	Not too suitable for very light voices	Slow and somber. Demands some flexibility.

TITLE	COMP.	TESS.	TYPE	REMARKS
(10) Rast	b-g2	g1-e♭2	All voices	Sustained. Demands in parts considerable dramatic intensity. Demands some flexibility.
(11) Frühlingstraum	e1-f♯2	a1-e2	All voices	Delicate, graceful. One of the best known songs in this cycle. In parts dramatic. Interpretatively not easy.
(12) Einsamkeit	c♯1-f♯2	f♯1-e♭2	Not too suitable for very light, high voices	Very sustained. Demands in parts considerable dramatic intensity.
(13) Die Post	e♭1-a♭2	a♭1-f2	All voices	Animated. One of the best known songs in this cycle. Demands facile articulation and an accomplished pianist.
(14) Der greise Kopf	c1-f2	e♭1-e♭2	All voices	Sustained; in parts dramatic.
(15) Die Krähe	c1-g2	f1-d2	Not too suitable for very light, high voices	Very sustained. Demands in parts considerable dramatic intensity. Note the tempo mark, "Etwas langsam" 2/4. Often sung too slowly in 4/8.
(16) Letzte Hoffnung	b♭-g2	g1-e♭2	All voices	Sustained. In parts demands considerable dramatic intensity. Interpretatively not easy.
(17) Im Dorfe	d1-e2	f♯1-d2	All voices	Sustained. Seldom sung separately. The accompaniment is not so easy as it may seem.

TITLE	COMP.	TESS.	TYPE	REMARKS
(18) Der stür- mische Morgen	c#1-eb2	d1-bb1	Most suit- able for heavy voices	Spirited, vigorous.
(19) Täuschung	d#1-e2	e1-c#2	All voices	Animated, delicate. Seldom sung sepa- rately.
(20) Der Weg- weiser	f#1-g2	g1-e2	All voices, except a very light soprano	Sustained, somber. One of the best known songs in this cycle. Inter- pretatively not easy.
(21) Das Wirtshaus	e1-f2	f1-d2	All voices	Very slow and sustained, somber.
(22) Mut	bb-g2	d1-bb1	Most suit- able for heavy voices	Spirited and vig- orous.
(23) Die Neben- sonnen	a1-f2	a1-d2	All voices	Very slow and sustained. One of the best known songs in this cycle.
(24) Der Leier- mann	e1-f2	a1-e2	All voices	Slow. One of the best known songs in this cycle. Vocal- ly and musically of utmost simplicity, this song is inter- pretatively very difficult.

ROBERT SCHUMANN
(1810–1856)

Schumann was perhaps more conscious and articulate in regard
to his objectives as a composer than any composer before him, with
the possible exception of Gluck, who stated his objectives so nobly
and clearly in his short preface to Alceste.

The best way to acquaint oneself with Schumann's aesthetic
theories is to read his writings on music, which are available in English translations. These writings are of course recommended not
so much for their intrinsic value, which, considerable as it may be,
has but little bearing on musical matters of today, as for the light
they shed on his style and the objectives he tried to attain as a composer.

338

For any prospective performer of Schumann's music, even a casual acquaintance with Schumann the music critic and the aesthetic theorist ought to prove of great value.

The songs of Schumann, presenting as they do with few exceptions hardly any musical or vocal problems, demand a singer and a pianist of considerable poetic sensitivity. For the most part, they are best suited to voices possessing a well-controlled medium register. The greatest danger facing a present-day singer attempting to perform Schumann is the tendency to overlook the fact that sentiment is by no means synonymous with sentimentality, and that feelings can be expressed without violence.

In his songs Schumann demands considerable elegance in phrasing, a rubato that must stay within the frame of the rhythmic pulse, and a simplicity and sincerity of recitation almost naive in its lack of artifice. Thus, it may be superfluous to add that, unless the singer can unreservedly and enthusiastically accept the poem of any particular song by Schumann, he would be wise not to sing it, even though it may seem musically and vocally to his liking, for under such circumstances he will not be able to achieve the synthesis between the poetry and the music so overwhelmingly important in Schumann's approach to the problem of setting a poem to music.

Schumann's accompaniments are almost always of great importance. He often uses the device of dividing the melodic line between the voice and the piano ("Der Nussbaum," for instance) thus achieving an effect more often associated with instrumental chamber music than with songs. Often his accompaniments are independently pianistic, and sometimes, as in "Aufträge," they demand an almost virtuoso technique.

Editions: 3 vols., C. F. Peters. (Vol. I, H & L)
Breitkopf & Härtel
Selection: International Music Co.
85 songs selected by Sergius Kagen, International
Music Co. (H & L)
Numerous albums by many publishers.

TITLE	COMP.	TESS.	TYPE	REMARKS
An den Mond	e1-f2	g1-eb2	Most suitable for medium or low voices	Slow and sustained. See Mendelssohn, "Schlafloser Augen Leuchte," and H. Wolf, "Sonne der Schlummerlosen."
An die Türen will ich schleichen	c-eb1	g-c1	Baritone	Slow and sustained. Demands good command of pp. See Schubert and H. Wolf.

TITLE	COMP.	TESS.	TYPE	REMARKS
An den Sonnen-schein	d1-g2	f1-d2	All voices	Sustained. In folk vein.
Auf einer Burg (Liederkreis, no. 7)	c1-c2	e1-b1	Medium or low voices	Very slow and sustained.
Aufträge	e1-f#2 (a2)	a1-e2	Not too suitable for very low voices	Light and rapid. Demands facile articulation and an excellent pianist. Sounds best in the original key, sung by a light, high voice.
Aus den hebrä-ischen Ge-sängen	a-f#2	e1-c#2	Heavy voices	Slow. Interpretatively not easy. Demands an accomplished pianist.
Aus den öst-lichen Rosen	d1-eb2	g1-c2	All voices	Delicate, sustained.
Belsatzar	c1-g2	g1-eb2	Not too suitable for light voices	A dramatic, narrative song (ballade). Demands an accomplished pianist.
Da liegt der Feinde ge-streckte Schaar	F-c1	c-ab	Bass or bass-bari-tone	Grave, dramatic.
Das verlassene Mägdlein	d1-d2	f1-c2	Women's voices	Somber, slow and very sustained. See Wolf.
Dein Angesicht	d1-gb2	bb1-eb2	All voices	Slow and very sustained.
Der arme Peter	b-g2	g1-e2	Not too suitable for light, high voices	Three poems by Heine, set as one continuous piece (in the manner of Beethoven's "An die ferne Geliebte"). Dramatic.
Der Contra-bandiste	A-g1	f-d1	Baritone	A rapid character song. Demands facile articulation, some flexibility, and an excellent pianist.

TITLE	COMP.	TESS.	TYPE	REMARKS
Der Himmel hat eine Träne ge- weint	d1-f2	ab1-db2	All voices	Slow and very sustained.
Der Husar, trara!	d-d1 (eb1)	f-c1	Baritone	Vigorous and spirited.
Der Nussbaum	d1-f♯2	g1-e2	All voices	Delicate. De- mands an accom- plished pianist.
Der Sandmann	c1-f2	a1-e2	Not too suitable for very low voices	Light and deli- cate. Demands facile articulation and an accom- plished pianist. See L. Blech.
Der schwere Abend	eb1-gb2	ab1-eb2	All voices	Slow and very sustained.
Der Soldat	c1-f2	a1-d2	Men's voices	Dramatic. Inter- pretatively not easy. Demands an accomplished pianist.
Der Zeisig	e1-g2	f1-d2	All voices	Light.

Dichterliebe
A cycle of sixteen songs, opus 48, text by H. Heine

As in the case of some other song cycles, it seemed advisable to list these songs under one heading, and in their original order in- stead of alphabetically.

Generally speaking, it is best to perform these songs as a unit. However, Nos. 1 to 7 inclusively are sometimes sung together, as a sort of abbreviated version of the cycle, and Nos. 10, 13 and 14 are sung separately occasionally, as well as Nos. 3, 4, 6 and 7.

Although the texts of these songs sound most convincing when sung by a man, this cycle has been much sung by women.

Like most of Schumann's songs, these songs present no obvious vocal difficulties. Yet a satisfactory performance of this cycle, con- sidered by many to be one of the most notable examples of chamber music for voice and piano demands two accomplished artists in abso- lute command of their instruments.

These Heine poems, as well as most of his poetry, have been admirably translated into English by Louis Untermeyer.

TITLE	COMP.	TESS.	TYPE	REMARKS
(1) Im wunder-schönen Monat Mai	f#1-g2	b1-e2	All voices	Delicate, sustained. This song and the following one are harmonically connected. Thus a separate performance of this song seems unadvisable; the second song, however, could be sung by itself if so desired. See R. Franz.
(2) Aus meinen Tränen spriessen	f#1-d2	a1-c#2	All voices	Very delicate.
(3) Die Rose, die Lilie	d1-e2	a1-d2	All voices	Spirited and light. Demands facile articulation. Often sung at too fast a tempo. Bar 10: Heine's original text, "Aller Liebe Bronne" instead of "Wonne," a mistake by Schumann, dutifully reprinted in most editions. See R. Franz.
(4) Wenn ich in deine Augen seh'	f#1-f2 (g2)	g1-d2	All voices	Slow. Interpretatively not easy.
(5) Ich will meine Seele tauchen	a#1-f#2	b1-e2	All voices	Animated, very delicate. Demands an accomplished pianist. Often sung too slowly.
(6) Im Rhein, im heiligen Strome	d1-f2	e1-c2	Not too suitable for very light, high voices	Heavy, sustained. See R. Franz and Liszt.
(7) Ich grolle nicht	c1-e2 (a2)	e1-c2	Not too suitable for light voices	Very sustained, dramatic. The optional a2, g2, f2 in the final climax

TITLE	COMP.	TESS.	TYPE	REMARKS
				ought not be at-tempted if the recitation of the poem would be in any way im-peded by the high tessitura of this passage.
(8) Und wüssten's die Blumen, die kleinen	g#1-f2	a1-e2	All voices	Animated. De-mands an ac-complished pia-nist. No tempo mark in the original. Ap-proximately MM ♩ = 66.
(9) Das ist ein Flöten und Geigen	c1-f2	a1-e2	Not too suitable for very light, high voices	Animated. De-mands an excel-lent pianist.
(10) Hör' ich das Liedchen klingen	d1-db2	eb1-bb1	All voices	Slow and sustained. The postlude for piano solo demands an accomplished pianist. See R. Franz.
(11) Ein Jüngling liebt ein Mädchen	bb1-f2	f1-d2	Not too suitable for very high, light voices	A spirited almost crudely satirical song. Demands fac-ile articulation. In Ms. marked allegro.
(12) Am leuchten-den Sommer-morgen	f1-d2	g1-c2	All voices	Delicate and sus-tained. The post-lude for piano solo, utilized in the ex-tended postlude to the cycle, demands an accomplished pianist.
(13) Ich hab' im Traum gewei-net	db1-fb2	eb1-bb1	Not too suitable for very light, high voices	Slow. Interpreta-tively difficult. Often sung slovenly in re-gard to time values, thus losing much of its dramatic impact. See R. Franz, C. Löwe, and "J'ai pleuré en rêve" by G. Huë.

TITLE	COMP.	TESS.	TYPE	REMARKS
(14) Allnächtlich im Traume	a#-d#2	f#1-c#2	All voices	Delicate. See Mendelssohn.
(15) Aus alten Märchen	b-g#2	g#1-e2	All voices	Animated. Demands facile articulation and an accomplished pianist.
(16) Die alten, bösen Lieder	c#1-g#2	f#1-c#2	Not suitable for very light voices	Dramatic, vigorous. Demands an accomplished pianist. The extended postlude for piano solo makes a separate performance of this song seem unadvisable.
Dichters Genesung	c#1-e2	e1-b1	Most suitable for medium or low voices	Animated. Interpretatively not easy. Demands an accomplished pianist.
Die beiden Grenadiere	bb(a)-d2	d1-bb1	Men's voices, except a light tenor	A dramatic narrative song (ballade). See Wagner's setting of the French version of this Heine poem.
Die Kartenlegerin	bb-eb1	eb1-bb1	Mezzo-soprano or alto	An amusing, light character song. Demands facile articulation and an accomplished pianist.
Die Lotosblume	c1-g2	a1-e2	All voices	Delicate and sustained. See R. Franz.
Die Meerfee	c#1-f#2	a1-e2	Most suitable for high voices	Light and delicate.
Die Sennin	e#1-f#2	g#1-e2	All voices	Delicate and sustained. Demands some flexibility.
Die Soldatenbraut	c1(bb)-f2	f1-d2	Women's voices	Rhythmic and delicate.

TITLE	COMP.	TESS.	TYPE	REMARKS
Die Spinnnerin	c#1-e2	f#1-c#2	Women's voices	Sustained. Demands an accomplished pianist. See Brahms, "Mädchenlied" (Auf die Nacht).
Die Stille (Liederkreis, no. 4)	d1-e2	g1-d2	Women's voices (if sung separately)	Delicate. Demands lightness of tone. See Mendelssohn, "Es weiss und rät es doch keiner."
Die Tochter Jephtha's	c1-gb2	eb1-eb2	Women's voices, except a light soprano	Dramatic.
Du bist wie eine Blume	g1-f2	bb1-eb2	All voices	Slow and sustained. This Heine poem has been set to music innumerable times. See Liszt, Rubinstein, and many British and American composers (Chadwick, F. Bridge).
Einsamkeit	d1-e2	f1-b1	Most suitable for medium or low voices	Slow and sustained, somber.
Er ist's	e1-a2	b1-f#2	Not too suitable for very low voices	Spirited. Sounds best in the original key. See H. Wolf.
Erstes Grün	d1-d2	g1-c1	All voices	Very delicate, sustained.
Es fiel ein Reif	e1-c2	same	All voices	Slow and somber, very subdued. Exceedingly simple musically. Interpretatively not easy. No. 2 of the cycle of two songs

TITLE	COMP.	TESS.	TYPE	REMARKS
				and a duet to the poems of Heine, entitled "Tragödie."
Es leuchtet meine Liebe	c1-g2	g1-eb2	Not too suitable for very light voices	Animated. Interpretatively not easy. Demands an excellent pianist. Should not be transposed too low.
Es treibt mich hin	d1(a#)-f#2(g2)	f#1-d2	Men's voices, except a very light tenor	Rapid and dramatic.
Flügel, Flügel um zu fliegen	c#1-a2	f#1-f#2	Not too suitable for very light voices	Dramatic, very animated. Demands an excellent pianist.
Frage	eb1-ab2	ab1-eb2	All voices	Slow and very sustained.

Frauenliebe und Leben

A cycle of eight songs, opus 42, text by A. Chamisso

As in the case of some other song cycles it seemed best to list these songs under one heading and in their original order instead of alphabetically. All the songs in this cycle save No. 8 lend themselves well to the individual performance; however, it is best to sing these songs as a unit. These songs lend themselves best to a rather high mezzo-soprano voice; they have been, however, performed by practically every type of women's voices, save perhaps a coloratura soprano.

(1) Seit ich ihn gesehen	eb1-eb2	f1-bb1	Women's voices	Slow and sustained.
(2) Er, der Herrlichste von Allen	c1-gb2	g1-eb2	Women's voices	Rhythmic and spirited. Demands good command of medium voice.
(3) Ich kann's nicht fassen, nicht glauben	c1-f2	g1-d2	Women's voices	Animated, dramatic. Demands facile articulation.
(4) Du Ring an meinem Finger	c1-f2	eb1-c2	Women's voices	Slow and very sustained.
(5) Helft mir, ihr Schwestern	bb-g2	f1-d2	Women's voices	Animated. Often sung at too fast a tempo.

TITLE	COMP.	TESS.	TYPE	REMARKS
(6) Süsser Freund du blickest	e1-e2	g1-d2	Women's voices	Slow. Interpretatively not easy.
(7) An meinem Herzen an meiner Brust	d1-f♯2	a1-d2	Women's voices	Spirited. Demands facile articulation.
(8) Nun hast du mir den ersten Schmerz getan	c♯1-d2	d1-a1	Women's voices	Grave and declamatory. The extended postlude for piano solo, utilizing the material employed in the first song of this cycle, makes a separate performance of this song seem unadvisable.
Frühlingsfahrt	c♯1-f♯2	a1-e2	Not too suitable for very light, high voices	Narrative, vigorous. Interpretatively not easy.
Frühlingslust	d1-g2	f♯1-d2	Not too suitable for very low voices	Light and delicate.
Frühlingsnacht (Liederkreis, No. 12)	d♯1-f♯2	e1-b1	All voices	Rapid. Demands facile articulation and an excellent pianist. See A. Jensen.
Geisternähe	e1-f♯2 (a2)	a1-f♯2	Most suitable for high voices	Animated. Interpretatively not too easy.
Geständnis	e1-g2	g1-e2	All voices	Animated, exuberant. Interpretatively not easy. Demands an accomplished pianist.
Heiss mich nicht reden	b-g2	f1-d2	Women's voices, except a light soprano	Dramatic, declamatory. See Schubert, H. Wolf.
Hoch, hoch sind die Berge	a-f2	e♭1-c2	Mezzo-soprano or alto	Slow and very sustained.

TITLE	COMP.	TESS.	TYPE	REMARKS
Ich wandelte unter den Bäumen	d♯1-g♯2	f♯1-d♯2	All voices	Slow and very sustained.
Ihre Stimme	d1-g2	f1-eb2	All voices, except a very light soprano	Very sustained. Demands good command of medium voice.
Im Walde (Liederkreis, No. 11)	c♯1(a)-d2	e1-b1	Most suitable for medium or low voices	Animated. Interpretatively not easy.
Im Westen	f1-f2	g1-e2	Women's voices	Very sustained.
In der Fremde (Liederkreis, No. 1)	f♯1-e2	a1-d2	Not too suitable for very light, high voices	Very sustained. See Brahms.
In der Fremde (Liederkreis, No. 8)	e1-f2	a1-e2	All voices	Delicate. Interpretatively not easy.
Intermezzo (Liederkreis, No. 2)	e1-f♯2	a1-d2	All voices	Delicate and sustained.
Jasminenstrauch	f♯1-f♯2	b1-e2	Most suitable for light, high voices	Very delicate. Being extremely short it is sometimes sung twice without interruption.
Jemand	e1-g2	g1-e2	Women's voices	A short song of contrasting moods and tempi.
Jung Volkers Lied	c♯1-e2	f♯1-c♯2	Men's voices	Spirited and vigorous.
Lieb Liebchen	b-e2	e1-b1	Men's voices	Interpretatively not easy. See R. Franz.
Liebster, deine Worte stehlen	d1-g2	e1-d2	Women's voices, except a very light soprano	Animated. Interpretatively not easy
Lied der Suleika	e1-f♯2	a1-e2	Women's voices	Sustained.

TITLE	COMP.	TESS.	TYPE	REMARKS
Lieder der Braut				
No. 1	d1-a2	a1-e2	Women's	These two songs
No. 2	e1-e2	a1-d2	voices	ought to be per-
				formed together.
				Very delicate and
				sustained.
Lorelei	e1-e2	g#1-d#2	All voices	Delicate, sustained.
Kommen und	eb1-f#2	bb1-d2	All voices	Slow and subdued.
Scheiden				Interpretatively
				not easy.
Marienwürmchen	f1-f2	g1-d2	Most suit-	Light and delicate.
			able for	A setting of an old
			women's	rhyme (Lady bug,
			voices	lady bug, fly away
				home). Must be
				sung very simply.
Märzveilchen	e1-e2	g1-d2	All voices	Very delicate.
				See Gade.
Meine Rose	db1-gb2	gb1-d2	All voices	Delicate and sus-
				tained. Interpreta-
				tively not easy.
				Demands an ac-
				complished pianist.
Mein schöner	eb1-g2	a1-f2	All voices	Written for tenor.
Stern				Very sustained.
Meine Töne still	f#1-a2	a1-e2	Men's	Written for tenor.
und heiter			voices	Light and delicate.
				Demands good
				sense of rhythm.
Melancholie	d1-g2	f1-d2	Not too	Declamatory.
			suitable	
			for very	
			light, high	
			voices	
Mignon (Kennst	f#1-g2	bb1-f2	Women's	Dramatic, sus-
du das Land)	(a2)		voices,	tained. See Bee-
			except	thoven, Schubert,
			a very	Liszt, and H. Wolf.
			light	
			soprano	
Mit Myrten und	d1-g2	a1-f#2	Not too	Sustained. De-
Rosen			suitable	mands in parts con-
			for very	siderable dramat-
			light, high	ic intensity. Inter-
			voices	pretatively not easy.

TITLE	COMP.	TESS.	TYPE	REMARKS
Mondnacht (Liederkreis, No. 5)	e1-f♯2	b1-e2	All voices	Slow. Very sustained. Demands good command of pp and an accomplished pianist.
Morgens steh' ich auf und frage	d1-e2	e1-b1	Men's voices	Delicate, sustained. See R. Franz, "Kommt feins Liebchen heut," and Liszt.
Muttertraum	a-e♭2	e1-c2	Mezzo-soprano or alto	Somber and subdued. Interpretatively not easy.
Nachtlied	d1-f2	g1-e2	All voices	Slow and very sustained. See Schubert, "Wanderers Nachtlied" (Über allen Gipfeln); Löwe, and Liszt.
Nur wer die Sehnsucht kennt	d1-a♭2	g1-e♭2	Women's voices, except a very light soprano	Slow and sustained. In parts demands considerable dramatic intensity. See Beethoven, Schubert, H. Wolf, Tchaikovsky among many others.
O Freund, mein Schirm, mein Schutz	d1-e♭2	g1-d2	Women's voices, except a very light soprano	Slow and sustained. Interpretatively not easy.
O wie lieblich ist das Mädchen	f1-b♭2	b♭1-g2	Most suitable for high voices	Light and delicate. Demands facile articulation. See Schumann, "Weh, wie zornig ist das Mädchen."
Provenzalisches Lied	e1-g2	a1-f2	Men's voices	Written for tenor. Spirited, graceful.
Requiem	e♭1-g2	g1-e♭2	All voices, except a light soprano	Slow and very sustained.

TITLE	COMP.	TESS.	TYPE	REMARKS
Romanze	d1-f♯2	a1-d2	Men's voices	Sustained, graceful. Demands an accomplished pianist.
Röselein, Röselein	f♯1-f♯2	a1-e2	Not too suitable for very low voices	Delicate. Interpretatively not easy. Demands an accomplished pianist.
Schneeglöckchen (Der Schnee, der gestern)	d1-g2	g1-e♭2	All voices	Very delicate.
Schöne Fremde (Liederkreis, No. 6)	f♯1-g♯2	g♯1-e2	Not too suitable for very light, high voices	Animated. Interpretatively not easy. Demands considerable dramatic intensity in parts and an accomplished pianist.
Schöne Wiege meiner Leiden	d♯1-f2	e1-e2	Not too suitable for very light, high voices	Animated. In parts dramatic. Demands an accomplished pianist.
Sehnsucht	c1-g2	f1-c2	Not too suitable for very light voices	Dramatic, animated.
Ständchen	d1-g2	d1-b1	Men's voices	Light and delicate.
So lasst mich scheinen	e1-a2	a1-f♯2	Women's voices	Slow and sustained. Interpretatively not easy. In parts demands considerable dramatic intensity. See Schubert, H. Wolf.
Stille Liebe	e♭1-a♭2	g1-e♭2	All voices	Very sustained.
Stille Tränen	g1-a2 (b♭2)	c2-g2	All voices	Slow and very sustained. Vocally perhaps the most exacting song that Schumann wrote. Demands exceptionally good command of breath and

TITLE	COMP.	TESS.	TYPE	REMARKS
				of high voice. In the original key most suitable for a lyric soprano capable of singing a db3 or d3 with ease.
Stiller Vorwurf	d1-g2	a1-e2	All voices	Slow. Interpretatively not easy.
Talismane	b-d2(g2)	e1-c2	Heavy voices	Vigorous and declamatory.
Tief im Herzen trag' ich Pein	f1-f2	g1-d2	All voices	Written for soprano. Slow and sustained.
Viel Glück zur Reise, Schwalbe	d1-f2	f1-d2	Not suitable for very low voices	Delicate and light. Demands facile articulation and an accomplished pianist. Being extremely short, it can be sung twice without interruption.
Venetianisches Lied No. 1 (Leis rudern hier)	d1-d2	g1-c2	Most suitable for men's voices	Light and gently humorous. Demands facile articulation. See A. Jensen.
Venetianisches Lied No. 2 (Wenn durch Piazzetta)	f#1-e2	g1-d2	Most suitable for men's voices	Light and delicate. See Mendelssohn, "Venetianisches Gondellied," and A. Jensen, "Wenn durch Piazzetta."
Volksliedchen	d1-g2	a1-e2	Women's voices	Light and delicate. Demands facile articulation.
Waldesgespräch (Liederkreis, No. 3)	e1(b)-e2(g#2)	g#1-e2	Not too suitable for very light voices	Dramatic, animated.
Wanderlied	d1-a2	bb1-f2	Men's voices	Spirited and vigorous.
Wanderung	eb1-g2	f1-d2	Most suitable for men's voices	Spirited and light.

TITLE	COMP.	TESS.	TYPE	REMARKS
Was will die einsame Träne	e1-f#2	g1-e2	All voices	Slow and sustained. See R. Franz, P. Cornelius.
Weh, wie zornig ist das Mädchen	f1-g2	a1-eb2	All voices	Light and gently humorous. Demands facile articulation. Often used as a companion piece to "O wie lieblich ist das Mädchen."
Wehmut (Liederkreis, No. 9)	e1-e2	f#1-c#2	All voices	Slow and very sustained.
Wer nie sein Brot	G-f1	g-d1	Bass or bass-baritone	Sustained. In parts demands considerable dramatic intensity. See Schubert, Liszt, H. Wolf.
Wer machte dich so krank	eb1-eb2	eb1-bb1	All voices	Written for baritone. Sustained. Same melody with another set of words, also by J. Kerner, "Alte Laute."
Wer sich der Einsamkeit ergibt	eb-f1	g-eb1	Baritone	Slow and sustained. In parts demands considerable dramatic intensity. See Schubert and H. Wolf.
Widmung	b-gb2	ab1-eb2	All voices	Spirited. Demands good command of medium voice. Note the tempo mark "Innig, Lebhaft 3/2." Often sung too slowly.
Zum Schluss	f1-f2	ab1-db2	All voices	Very slow and sustained.
Zwielicht (Liederkreis, No. 10)	a#-e2	g1-d2	Not too suitable for very high voices	Slow and sustained. Interpretatively not easy.

RICHARD STRAUSS
(1864–1949)

In his songs, in contrast to his operas and orchestral works, Richard Strauss seems deliberately to avoid any attempts at experimentation. Many of the songs of Liszt, for instance, are fully as "modern" as some of Strauss' songs, written some fifty years later.

Strauss writes expertly for the voice. The vocal line in his songs is always magnificently effective, and contrary to the popular belief most considerate of the singer. But he often demands a voice of operatic dimensions, in both range and volume. Sometimes this is not realized, and many a singer with a voice of less imposing proportions, concludes, after vainly trying to master a Strauss song, not intended for his type of voice, that the fault lies with the composer.

Most of the well-known songs of Strauss are neither musically nor interpretatively complex, though they may present some vocal, dramatic and pianistic problems not likely to be encountered in Schubert or Brahms, for instance.

Strauss is very direct in his treatment of the poetic text, so direct sometimes that some critics have found him obvious. In his choice of text, he seems to prefer poetry that possesses an easily definable mood and thus lends itself well to either a naturalistically dramatic setting or to a purely lyrical, melodic interpretation.

Strauss' treatment of the piano part varies considerably. Often his accompaniments demand a purely orchestral approach, but fully as often they are superbly pianistic. Sometimes, again, he uses the piano only for the purpose of providing a harmonic background for the melodic line.

Editions: Fürstner - Boosey & Hawkes (H, L).
Universal Edition (H, M, L).
27 songs selected by Sergius Kagen, International Music Co. (H, M. L).
40 songs (Musician's Library), Oliver Ditson (H, L).
3 songs, C. F. Peters (H).

TITLE	COMP.	TESS.	TYPE	REMARKS
Ach, Lieb, ich muss nun scheiden	d1-g2	a♭1-f2	All voices	Slow and sustained.
All' mein Gedanken, mein Herz und mein Sinn	e1-g♯2	b1-f♯2	Not too suitable for very low voices	Light and delicate. See Max Reger.
Allerseelen	d1-a♭2	a♭1-f2	All voices	Slow and sustained.

TITLE	COMP.	TESS.	TYPE	REMARKS
Am Ufer	a♯-f♯2	c♯1-d2	Not too suitable for very light, high voices	Very slow and sustained. Demands good command of pp.
Amor	c♯1-d3	a1-a2	Coloratura soprano	Sustained, animated, light. Has florid passages. Demands great flexibility and an accomplished pianist.
Barkarolle	d♭1-b♭2	b♭1-g♭2	Most suitable for high, light voices	Animated, delicate. Demands good command of high pp and an accomplished pianist.
Befreit	b-e♯2	f♯1-e♭2	Not suitable for light voices	Slow, very sustained. Interpretatively not easy.
Begegnung	d1-f2	e1-e2	Soprano	Rapid, brilliant, effective. Demands an excellent pianist.
Beim schlafengehn	d♭1-b♭2	g1-f2	Soprano or tenor	Sustained. Demands flexibility, good command of high pp, and an excellent pianist. Has long, sustained phrases.
Blauer Sommer	c♯1-g♯2	f♯1-f♯2	All voices	Slow and very sustained. Demands an accomplished pianist.
Breit über mein Haupt	g♭1-a♭2	d♭1-a♭2	All voices	Slow and very sustained, very effective. The tessitura is quite high.
Cäcilie	e1-b2	b1-g2	Heavy voices	Rapid, vigorous; very effective. Demands an excellent pianist.
Der Einsame	F-c1	A♭-f	Bass	Very slow, sustained. No. 2 of the two songs for bass and orchestra, opus 51.

TITLE	COMP.	TESS.	TYPE	REMARKS
Die erwachte Rose	e1-f#2	e1-e2	High voices	Animated, light, graceful. Demands an accomplished pianist.
Die Nacht	f1-g2	a1-f#2	All voices	Slow and sustained. Demands good command of p.
Die Zeitlose	c#1-g2	g1-e2	All voices	Slow and sustained. Interpretatively not easy.
Du meines Herzens Krönelein	db1-gb2	gb1-eb2	All voices	Slow and sustained. Demands good command of high pp. See Max Reger.
Freundliche Vision	d1-g2	f#1-f#2	All voices	Slow and sustained. Demands good command of pp and an accomplished pianist.
Frühling	c1-b2	eb1-g#2	Soprano or tenor	Sustained. Vocally not easy. Has long, sustained phrases. Demands good command of high pp and an excellent pianist.
Frühlingsgedränge	f#1-a2	b1-g#2	Not suitable for very low voices	Light, very rapid. Demands an excellent pianist. See R. Franz.
Für fünfzehn Pfennige	b-b2	g1-g2	Not too suitable for very low voices	Rapid. A comic character song. Demands facile articulation, some flexibility and an accomplished pianist. See Max Reger.
Glückes genug	c#1-g#2	f#1-f#2	All voices	Slow and sustained. Demands good command of p. See Max Reger.
Hat gesagt, bleibts nicht dabei	b-b2	f#1-f#2	Women's voices	A humorous character song. Demands some flexibility and an accomplished pianist.

TITLE	COMP.	TESS.	TYPE	REMARKS
Heimkehr	b-e2	e1-c♯2	All voices	Slow and sustained. Demands good command of high pp.
Heimliche Aufforderung	d♯1-ab2	f1-f2	All voices	Rapid, brilliant and effective. Demands an excellent pianist.
Ich schwebe	e1-a♯2	a1-f♯2	Not suitable for very low voices	Animated, the vocal line sustained.
Ich trage meine Minne	c♯1-ab2	gb1-gb2	All voices	Very sustained, subdued.
Im Abendroth	db1-g2	g1-eb2	Soprano or tenor	Slow, sustained. Demands good vocal control and an excellent pianist.
Im Spätboot	gb-db2	c1-bb1	Not suitable for light, high voices	Slow and very sustained. Interpretatively not easy. Demands an accomplished pianist.
Kling!	g1-c3	c2-g2	Most suitable for high heavy voices	Very animated, has imposing climaxes.
Leise Lieder	c1-e♯2	g1-e2	All voices	Very sustained, subdued. Demands an accomplished pianist.
Liebeshymnus	f1-bb2	bb1-gb2	All voices	Very sustained.
Madrigal	eb1-gb2	g1-e2	Men's voices	Slow and very sustained. Demands in parts considerable dramatic intensity.
Mein Auge	bb-g2	d1-d2	Not too suitable for very low voices	Slow and very sustained. Interpretatively and musically not easy. Demands an accomplished pianist.
Mein Herz ist stumm	eb1-ab2	ab1-gb2	Most suitable for high voices	Slow and somber. Demands good command of pp and an accomplished pianist.

TITLE	COMP.	TESS.	TYPE	REMARKS
Meinem Kinde	d1-g2	g1-f2	All voices	Very sustained. Demands good command of pp and an accomplished pianist.
Mit deinen blauen Augen	c1-g♯2	a1-f♯2	All voices	Slow and sustained. Demands an accomplished pianist.
Morgen	f♯1-g2	g1-e2	All voices	Slow. Interpretatively not easy. Demands an accomplished pianist.
Muttertändelei	b-f♯2	e1-e2	Women's voices	Light and spirited. Demands considerable flexibility and an accomplished pianist.
Nachtgang	db1-gb2	eb1-eb2	All voices	Slow and sustained. Demands good command of pp. Interpretatively not easy.
Rote Rosen	db1-f2	d1-db2	High voices	Slow, sustained. Mostly subdued. Demands good command of high pp.
Ruhe, ruhe, meine Seele	c1-f♯2	f1-f2 (H)	Not suitable for very light voices	Slow, declamatory and dramatic.
Schlagende Herzen	d1-a2 (b2)	g1-g2	Most suitable for high voices	Animated, light, graceful. Demands an accomplished pianist.
Schlechtes Wetter	bb-bb2	f1-f2	Not too suitable for very low voices	Animated. A characteristic satirical song. Interpretatively not easy. Demands an excellent pianist.
Seitdem dein Aug' in meines schaute	c1-ab2	f1-f2	All voices	Slow, very sustained.
September	d1-g2	f♯1-e2	Soprano or tenor	Very sustained. Has long, slightly florid sustained phrases. Demands some flexibility and an excellent pianist.

TITLE	COMP.	TESS.	TYPE	REMARKS
Ständchen	c#1-a#2	f#1-f#2	All voices	Rapid and light. Demands an excellent pianist. The last "hochglühen" on a#2 is traditionally held two bars.
Traum durch die Dämmerung	c#1-g♭2	d#1-d#2	All voices	Slow and sustained, subdued. Demands good command of pp. See Christian Sinding.
Von dunklem Schleier umsponnen	e♭1-g#2	g♭1-e♭2	Not too suitable for very low voices	Very slow and sustained. Demands good command of pp.
Weisser Jasmin	c#1-g#2	g#1-e2	Not too suitable for very low voices	Delicate. Demands an accomplished pianist.
Wer lieben will, muss leiden	b-f#2	d1-d2	Women's voices, except a very light soprano	Sustained. In folk vein.
Wie sollten wir geheim sie halten	d1-a2	a1-g#2	All voices	Rapid, brilliant and effective. Demands an excellent pianist.
Wiegenlied	d1-g#2	f#1-e2	Women's voices	Very sustained vocal line over a rapid arpeggio accompaniment. Demands good command of pp.
Wiegenliedchen	a-f#2	d#1-d#2	Women's voices, except a very light soprano	Very delicate.
Winternacht	c1-f#2	g1-e♭2	Not suitable for light voices	Rapid and vigorous. Demands an accomplished pianist.

TITLE	COMP.	TESS.	TYPE	REMARKS
Wozu noch, Mädchen	f♯1-a2	c1-f♯2	Men's voices	Light, animated. Demands facile articulation, good command of high p, and an accomplished pianist.
Zueignung	e1-a2	g1-f2	All voices, except a very light soprano	Animated, effective.

RICHARD TRUNK
(b. 1879)

Trunk is chiefly known in the United States for his charming and simple "In meiner Heimat." His many songs, which include such fine examples of lyric writing as "Die Stadt," "Wunsch," "Sommerfäden," are worthy of any serious singer's attention.

Editions: Breitkopf & Härtel
Otto Halbreiter (Munich)

TITLE	COMP.	TESS.	TYPE	REMARKS
Das Hemd	f♯1-a2	g♯1-e2	Women's voices	Very rapid and humorous. Demands facile articulation.
Der Feind	c1-e♭2 (e♯2)	e1-d2	Heavy voices	Dramatic. Demands an excellent pianist.
Die Stadt	c♯1-f2	f1-d2	Not too suitable for very light, high voices	Slow. Interpretatively not easy. Demands an accomplished pianist.
In der Nacht	d♯1-g♯2	g♯1-e♯2	All voices	Slow and sustained.
In meiner Heimat	e♭1-a♭2	a♭1-f♭2 (H)	All voices	Delicate and sustained.
Meine Mutter hat's gewollt	d1-f2 (a2)	a1-f2	Women's voices, except a very light soprano	Dramatic.

TITLE	COMP.	TESS.	TYPE	REMARKS
Nachtgesang	db1-g2	f1-db2	All voices	Very sustained.
Schlafen, schlafen	b-d2	d1-b1	Most suitable for medium or low voices	Very slow and sustained.
Schmerz	c#1-g2	g#1-e2	Heavy voices	Dramatic.
Sommerfäden	d1-d2	f#1-c#2	All voices	Delicate.
Tanzlied	d1-f2	g1-eb2	All voices	Delicate and light.
Wunsch	d#1-g2	f#1-d#2	All voices	Very delicate. Extremely short (13 bars).

RICHARD WAGNER
(1813–1883)

The "Fünf Gedichte für eine Frauenstimme," containing the two celebrated studies for Tristan and Isolde (Träume and Im Treibhaus), are the only songs that Wagner has written as a mature composer. The five other songs—four of them to French text—were written between 1838 and 1840 and can hardly be considered representative, although one can by no means dismiss them as mere "youthful efforts."

Editions: Schott
Fünf Gedichte—G. Schirmer and many other publishers.

TITLE	COMP.	TESS.	TYPE	REMARKS
Der Engel	c#1-g2	g1-e2	All voices	Originally written for soprano. Very sustained and subdued.
Dors, mon enfant (French text)	d1-f2	g1-e2	Women's voices	Sustained. Demands good command of pp.
Im Treibhaus	c#1-f#2	e1-d2	Most suitable for soprano	Very slow and sustained. Demands good command of high pp. Interpretatively not easy. A study for Tristan.
Les deux grenadiers (French text)	A-e1	e-c#1	Bass-baritone or baritone	A dramatic narrative song. See Schumann, "Die beiden Grenadiere," written in 1839 and dedicated to H. Heine.

TITLE	COMP.	TESS.	TYPE	REMARKS
				It is curious to note that Schumann in his setting of this Heine poem also makes use of the "Marseillaise" in the final section.
Schmerzen	c1-a♭2	f1-e♭2	Not suitable for light voices	Originally written for soprano. Sustained. Demands in parts considerable dramatic intensity. Interpretatively not easy.
Stehe still	c1-g2	f1-e2	Not suitable for very light voices	Originally written for soprano. Animated. Interpretatively not easy. Demands an accomplished pianist.
Träume	c1-g♭2	e♭1-c2	Not suitable for very light voices	Originally written for soprano. Very sustained. Demands an accomplished pianist. Interpretatively not easy. A study for Tristan.

See also "Mignonne," "Attente," "Der Tannenbaum."

CARL MARIA von WEBER
(1786–1826)

Weber's operas and concert arias are by far more representative of his style of writing for the voice than most of his songs. His numerous settings of folk songs and his songs in folk vein are, however, most interesting and like "Die Zeit," "Elfenlied," "Das Mädchen und das erste Schneeglöckchen," to name but a few, deserve to be heard more often than they are.

Editions: C. F. Peters
Universal Edition

TITLE	COMP.	TESS.	TYPE	REMARKS
Das Mädchen und das erste Schneeglöckchen	d1-g2	f♯1-e♭2	Women's voices	Slow and sustained.

TITLE	COMP.	TESS.	TYPE	REMARKS
Die gefangenen Sänger	d1-g2	f1-d2	All voices	Sustained.
Die Zeit	c1(a)-e2	e1-c2	Not suitable for light, high voices	Very sustained, somber.
Elfenlied	e1-f♯2	a1-e2	Light soprano	Rapid and light. Demands some flexibility.
Heimlicher Liebe Pein (Mein Schatz, der ist)	b-b1	e1-b1	Mezzo-soprano or alto	Slow, sustained and somber. In folk vein.
Herzchen, mein Schätzchen	e1-f♯2	f♯1-d2	Most suitable for men's voices	Animated. In folk vein.
Ich denke dein	e1-g2	f1-d2	All voices	Slow and sustained. In parts demands considerable dramatic intensity. See Beethoven.
Reigen	a-g2	d1-d2	High baritone	A lively, rollicking dance tune. In folk vein.
Sind es Schmerzen sind es Freuden	a-g2	c1-c2	Men's voices, except a very light tenor	Animated, dramatic. See Brahms.
Wiegenlied	c1-e2	e1-c2	Women's voices	Delicate, sustained. Verses 2 and 3 could be omitted.

See also the four solo songs from the "Leyer und Schwert" 10 songs, 6 for unaccompanied male chorus.

ANTON von WEBERN
(1883–1945)

An extremely daring experimentor, Anton von Webern has exercised an enormous influence upon contemporary music. His songs are difficult vocally, rhythmically and intervallically and are not recommended to singers possessing an average ear.

TITLE	COMP.	TESS.	TYPE	REMARKS
Edition: Universal Edition				
Der Tag ist vergangen	b♭-a♭2	e1-e2	High voices	Sustained, quiet. Demands good command of high pp and considerable flexibility.
Das Geheimnisvolle Flöten	c1-e♭2	d1-c2	High or medium voices	Slow, sustained, quiet. Demands flexibility.
Fünf Lieder (Op. 3)	b♭-a2	e♭1-f2		Five short songs for mezzo-soprano. Musically difficult. Demands good command of high pp, considerable flexibility and an accomplished pianist. Highly chromatic. Keys are not written in.
Fünf Lieder (Op. 4)	b-a2	e1-e2	High or medium voices	Five short songs. Musically difficult. Demands good command of high pp, considerable flexibility and an accomplished pianist. Keys are not written in.
Gleich und Gleich	c1-g2	f1-c2	High or medium voices	Sustained, generally quiet. Demands flexibility and good command of high pp. Text by Goethe.
Schien mir's, als ich sah die Sonne	a-a2	e1-e2	High or medium voices	Sustained. Demands considerable flexibility and an accomplished pianist. Demands good command of high p.

See also "Vier Lieder" (Op. 13) for voice and orchestra (piano score available) and "Drei Lieder" (Op. 25).

HUGO WOLF
(1860–1903)

Most of the songs of Hugo Wolf are so dominated by their texts that unless one approaches them from a musicodramatic standpoint their melodic line may often seem disjointed and their harmonic and rhythmic structure may even seem unmotivated. The singer who attempts to sing Hugo Wolf must above all and at all times be conscious of the relationship between the text and the music, in the same sense in which Wolf himself seems to regard this relationship; namely, that the music of a song must not merely be inspired by the poetic idea embodied in the text, but that it must follow, interpret and illustrate the poem, sentence by sentence, or even word by word. This approach to the relationship between the text and the music, although popularly considered "Wagnerian," is almost as old as the composed song itself. The "nuovi musici" of the Italian Renaissance have often tried to approach their texts in a like manner. To a greater or lesser degree, practically every composer writing for solo voice has at least in isolated instances followed the same procedure. In the songs of Wolf, however, this attitude is so prevalent and sometimes so extreme that, when one tries to describe the demands his songs make upon the singer, the demand for a definite and a sympathetic approach to his manner of setting the text to music seems to be of primary importance.

Most of his songs are musically not overcomplex; in some instances, however, his chromaticism and his use of certain rhythmic devices, designed to ensure the proper recitation of the poem, may make a song seem complex at first reading.

An adequate performance of a song by Wolf always demands a pianist uncommonly sensitive to the poem and Wolf's musical reaction to it. Often the piano part demands a technique of great brilliancy; sometimes almost the entire burden of musical illustration and interpretation of the text is left to the pianist; the instances where Wolf uses the piano for the purpose of merely providing a harmonic background for the melody are extremely rare.

Wolf wrote little outside of songs (one opera, Corregidor, a symphonic poem and a string quartet). Most of his 245 songs are written for the c1-a2 high voice and are vocally not taxing. However, a very light soprano (c1-e3) as well as a bass or bass-baritone can both find among his songs a great number that would prove most welcome additions to their concert repertoire.

Editions: International Music Co. (complete), original keys.
           C. F. Peters (complete), original keys.
           65 songs selected by Sergius Kagen, International Music Co. (H, L).
           Numerous albums by many publishers.

TITLE	COMP.	TESS.	TYPE	REMARKS
Ach des Knaben Augen	eb1-f2	bb1-f2	All voices	Sustained and subdued. Interpretatively not easy.
Ach im Maien	e1-g♯2	a1-e2	All voices	Animated, delicate. The vocal line is very sustained.
Agnes	f1-gb2	g1-db2	Women's voices	Slow and sustained. Interpretatively not easy. See Brahms.
Alle gingen, Herz, zur Ruh'	d1-f2	f1-d2	Not too suitable for very high, light voices	Slow and sustained. Demands in parts considerable dramatic intensity.
Alles endet was entstehet	F♯-c♯1	B♯-a	Bass	Slow and somber. Interpretatively not easy.
Anakreon's Grab	d1-d2	f♯1-d2	All voices	Slow and sustained.
An den Schlaf	f♯1-f♯2	ab1-f2	All voices	Slow and sustained. Demands good command of pp.
An die Geliebte	eb1-ab2	ab1-f2	All voices	Very slow, declamatory. Musically and interpretatively not easy. Demands good command of high pp.
An eine Aeolsharfe	c♯1-g♯2	g♯1-e2	Women's voices	Very sustained. Interpretatively and musically complex. Demands an accomplished pianist. Sounds best in the original high key. See Brahms.
Auch kleine Dinge	e1-f♯2	a1-e2	All voices	Very delicate and sustained.
Auf dem grünen Balkon	e1-f♯2	a1-e2	All voices	Animated, light. Demands an accomplished pianist.
Auf ein altes Bild	f♯1-e♯2	b1-d2	All voices	Slow and sustained. Demands good command of pp.

TITLE	COMP.	TESS.	TYPE	REMARKS
Auf eine Christblume I	c-f2	f#1-d2	All voices	Slow and interpretatively complex. Demands an accomplished pianist.
Auf eine Christblume II	c#1-g2	e1-d#2	All voices	Slow and sustained. Demands good command of pp.
Auf einer Wanderung	b-g2	g1-eb2	Not too suitable for very light, high voices	Animated. Musically and interpretatively complex. Demands an excellent pianist. The extremely important piano part loses much of its sonority if transposed.
Bedeckt mich mit Blumen	d1-f2	g1-eb2	All voices	Slow and sustained. Musically not easy. Demands an accomplished pianist.
Begegnung	d1-gb2	g1-eb2	All voices	Animated. Interpretatively not easy.
Biterolf	d1-f1	f-d1	Bass or bass-baritone	Very slow and sustained.
Blumengruss	eb1-f2	g1-eb2	All voices	Delicate, sustained.
Citronenfalter im April	e1-a2	c2-f#2	Most suitable for light, high voices	Very delicate. Demands an accomplished pianist.
Dank des Paria	c1-gb2	ab1-eb2	Heavy voices	Grave, declamatory.
Das Köhlerweib ist trunken	c1-g2	a1-f2	Not too suitable for very light voices	Very rapid, dramatic. Musically and interpretatively complex. Demands an excellent pianist.
Das Ständchen	c#1-gb2	f#1-eb1	All voices	Has a very sustained vocal line over an independent, somewhat complex accompaniment. See Korngold.

TITLE	COMP.	TESS.	TYPE	REMARKS
Das verlassene Mägdlein	e1-f2	a1-e2	Women's voices	Slow and sustained. See Schumann.
Das Vöglein	c#1-f#2	f#1-e2	High voices	Light and animated. Demands facile articulation and an excellent pianist.
Denk' es, o Seele	b#-d2	g1-c#2	All voices, except a very light soprano	Somber and sustained. Interpretatively not easy. Has a very dramatic climax. See Pfitzner.
Der Feuerreiter	c1-g2	same	Heavy voices	Rapid, dramatic. An uncommonly long, difficult song. Demands an excellent pianist.
Der Freund	c#1-f#2	e1-e2	Most suitable for heavy voices	Vigorous, dramatic. Demands an accomplished pianist.
Der Gärtner	a1-g2	b1-f#2	Most suitable for light, high voices	Light and delicate. See Schumann.
Der Genesene an die Hoffnung	bb-ab2	f#1-e2	Not too suitable for very light voices	Grave and sustained. Musically and interpretatively not easy. Demands an accomplished pianist.
Der Knabe und das Immlein	c#1-a2	bb1-g2	Most suitable for light, high voices	Delicate and gently humorous. Interpretatively not easy. Demands an excellent pianist.
Der Mond hat eine schwere Klag' erhoben	bb-db1	eb-bb1	Medium or low voices	Slow and very sustained.
Der Musikant	d#1-e2	e1-c#2	Most suitable for men's voices	Gently humorous. Interpretatively not easy.

TITLE	COMP.	TESS.	TYPE	REMARKS
Der Rattenfänger	c1-f2	e1-e2	Heavy voices, preferably baritone or dramatic tenor	Rapid and vigorous. Demands an excellent pianist.
Der Soldat I	e1-f♯2	g1-e2	Men's voices	Humorous, lively.
Der Soldat II	e♭1-a♭2	g♭1-f2	Men's voices	Very rapid and dramatic. Demands facile articulation and an excellent pianist.
Der Tambour	b♯-g♯2	g♯1-f♯2	Most suitable for men's voices	Humorous. Demands an accomplished pianist.
Die ihr schwebet	g1-g2	c♯2-f♯2	Women's voices, except a very light soprano	Animated. Demands considerable dramatic intensity in parts and an accomplished pianist. See "Geistliches Wiegenlied" by Brahms, opus 91 no. 2.
Die Geister am Mummelsee	a♯-g2	same	Heavy voices	Dramatic. A very difficult song. Demands an excellent pianist.
Die Spinnerin	d♯1-f♯2	same	Women's voices, except a light soprano	Very animated, dramatic. Interpretatively complex. Demands an excellent pianist. See C. Löwe.
Die Zigeunerin	c1-a2	f1-f2	Soprano or mezzo-soprano	Musically and interpretatively quite complex. Demands considerable flexibility and an excellent pianist.
Du denkst mit einem Fädchen mich zu fangen	e♭1-f2	g1-e♭2	Women's voices	Light and delicate. Interpretatively not easy.

369

TITLE	COMP.	TESS.	TYPE	REMARKS
Ein Ständchen euch zu bringen	c♯1-g2	g1-d2	Men's voices	Light and animated. Demands facile articulation and an excellent pianist.
Ein Stündlein wohl vor Tag	a♭1-g2	c2-f2	Women's voices	Slow and sustained. Interpretatively not easy. See R. Franz.
Elfenlied	d1-f2	f1-d2	Not too suitable for very heavy, low voices	Light and gently humorous. Demands very facile articulation and an accomplished pianist.
Er ist's	d1-g2	b1-g2	All voices	Spirited and brilliant. Demands an excellent pianist. See Schumann.
Erstes Liebeslied eines Mädchens	e♭1-a♭2	a1-f2	Women's voices, except a very light soprano	Very rapid. Interpretatively complex. Demands an excellent pianist.
Epiphanias	d1-b♭2	g1-e♭2	Not too suitable for very light voices	Humorous, characteristic. Demands an excellent pianist.
Frage und Antwort	d1-a♭2	b♭1-f2	Most suitable for high voices	Sustained. Musically and interpretatively not easy. Demands good command of high pp.
Frühling übers Jahr	d♯1-a2	a1-e2	High, light voices	Very delicate and light. Demands an accomplished pianist.
Fühlt meine Seele	A-d1	e-c1	Bass or bass-baritone	Slow, declamatory. Musically and interpretatively not easy. Demands an accomplished pianist.

TITLE	COMP.	TESS.	TYPE	REMARKS
Fussreise	c♯1-e2	f♯1-c♯2	All voices, except a very light soprano	Spirited. Demands good sense of rhythm.
Ganymed	f♯1-g2	a1-f♯2	All voices	Interpretatively and musically complex. Demands an accomplished pianist. Sounds best in the original high key. See Schubert.
Gebet	d1-f♯2	f♯1-d2	All voices, except a very light soprano	Slow and sustained.
Geh, Geliebter, geh jetzt	c♯1-g♭2	f♯1-e2	Women's voices, except a very light soprano	Animated, dramatic. Musically and interpretatively complex. Demands an excellent pianist.
Gesang Weyla's	d♭1-f2	a♭1-d♭2	Not too suitable for very high, light voices	Slow and very sustained.
Gesegnet sei durch den die Welt entstund	d1-g2	f1-f2	All voices	Slow and declamatory.
Geselle, woll'n wir uns in Kutten hüllen	d1-f2	e1-d2	Men's voices	A humorous character song. Demands an accomplished pianist.
Gleich und Gleich	f♯1-a♭2	b1-f♯2	Most suitable for high, light voices	Delicate, light.
Grenzen der Menschheit	F-e♭1	e-c1	Bass	Slow and sustained, declamatory. Interpretatively complex. See Schubert.
Harfenspieler I (Wer sich der Einsamkeit ergibt)	B-f1	f-d1	Baritone	Slow. Interpretatively not easy. See Schubert and Schumann.

TITLE	COMP.	TESS.	TYPE	REMARKS
Harfenspieler II (An die Türen will ich schleichen)	c-d1	g-c1	Bass or baritone	Very sustained. Demands good command of pp. See Schubert and Schumann.
Harfenspieler III (Wer nie sein Brot)	c-e1	f-d♭1	Bass or baritone	Slow. In parts demands considerable dramatic intensity. See Schubert, Schumann, Liszt.
Heb' auf dein blondes Haupt	f1-f2	a♭1-e♭2	Men's voices	Very sustained.
Heimweh (Anders wird die Welt)	c♭1-f2	g1-e♭2	All voices	Slow and sustained. Demands good command of pp.
Herr, was trägt der Boden hier	b-e2	a1-d2	All voices	Slow. Interpretatively not easy.
Heut Nacht erhob' ich mich	c♯1-f2	f1-d2	All voices	Delicate. Interpretatively not easy.
Ich hab' in Penna	c1-a2	g1-d2	Women's voices	Very rapid, humorous. Demands facile articulation and an excellent pianist.
Im Frühling	b-g2	e1-e2	All voices	Sustained. Musically and interpretatively complex. Demands an accomplished pianist.
In dem Schatten meiner Locken	d1-f2	g1-e♭2	Women's voices	Light and delicate. Interpretatively not easy. Demands an accomplished pianist. See Brahms, "Spanisches Lied," and A. Jensen.
In der Frühe	b-g2	e1-e2	Medium or low voices	Slow and grave.
Jägerlied	e1-a2	a1-e2	Men's voices	Light. Demands facile articulation and a good sense of rhythm.

TITLE	COMP.	TESS.	TYPE	REMARKS
Karwoche	b-ab2	ab1-f2	All voices	Slow. Musically and interpretatively not easy. Demands an accomplished pianist.
Klinge, klinge mein Pandero	db1-f2	g1-d2	All voices, except a very light soprano	Animated. Demands an excellent pianist. See A. Jensen.
Köpfchen, Köpfchen nicht gewimmert	f1-g2	c2-f2	Light soprano	Delicate and light. See Cornelius.
Lebe wohl	db1-ab2	ab1-f2	All voices	Slow. Demands in parts considerable dramatic intensity.
Liebe mir im Busen	e1-f♯2	a1-f2	Women's voices	Very rapid dramatic. Demands an excellent pianist.
Lied vom Winde	c1-g2	a1-e2	High voices	Very animated. Musically and interpretatively not easy. Demands an excellent pianist. The extremely important piano part loses much in sonority if transposed.
Mansfallensprüchlein	db1-g2	a1-f2	Most suitable for women's voices	Light and delicate. Interpretatively not easy. Demands an accomplished pianist.
Mein Liebster hat zu Tische mich geladen	c1-g2	f1-e2	Women's voices	Light, gently humorous.
Mein Liebster singt am Haus	d1-f2	g1-eb2	Women's voices	Sustained. Demands an accomplished pianist.
Mignon (Kennst du das Land?)	bb-ab2	gb1-f2	Women's voices, except a very light soprano	Sustained, in parts very dramatic. Musically and interpretatively not easy. Demands an excellent pianist. See Beethoven, Schubert, Schumann, Liszt.

TITLE	COMP.	TESS.	TYPE	REMARKS
Mignon I (Heiss mich nicht reden)	c1-f2	f1-d2	Women's voices, except a very light soprano	Slow, declamatory. Demands in parts considerable dramatic intensity. See Schubert and Schumann.
Mignon II (Nur wer die Sehnsucht kennt)	d1-g2	g1-f2	Women's voices, except a very light soprano	Animated. Interpretatively not easy. See Beethoven, Schubert, Schumann, Tchaikovsky.
Mignon III (So lasst mich scheinen)	c♯1-g2	g1-e2	Women's voices	Slow and sustained. Musically not easy. Demands good command of pp. See Schubert and Schumann.
Mögen alle bösen Zungen	f♯1-f♯2	a1-e2	Women's voices	Animated. Interpretatively not easy. Demands an accomplished pianist.
Morgenstimmung	b♮-g♯2	f♯1-e2	Not suitable for very light voices	Slow and sustained. Demands an accomplished pianist and considerable dramatic intensity in the final climax. See "Morning Hymn" by Henschel.
Morgentau	e1-e2	a1-e2	All voices	Delicate, sustained.
Mühvoll komm' ich und beladen	d1-g2	a♭1-e2	Not too suitable for very light voices	Slow and grave. Musically and interpretatively not easy.
Nachtzauber	c♯1-f♯2	f♯1-d♯2	All voices	Very sustained. Demands good command of pp and an accomplished pianist. Musically not easy.
Nein, junger Herr	d1-f2	f♯1-d2	Women's voices	Animated, graceful. Interpretatively not easy. Demands an accomplished pianist.

TITLE	COMP.	TESS.	TYPE	REMARKS
Neue Liebe	c1-ab2	g1-f2	Not suit-able for very light voices	Slow, declama-tory. Demands in parts consider-able dramatic in-tensity.
Nicht Gelegenheit macht Diebe	c#1-g2	f1-d2	All voices	Animated. De-mands an accom-plished pianist.
Nimmersatte Liebe	eb1-ab2	ab1-eb2	All voices	Humorous. In-terpretatively complex.
Nixe Binsefuss	e1-g2	b1-f#2	Light soprano	Rapid and light. Demands facile articulation and an excellent pia-nist.
Nun lass uns Frieden schliessen	eb1-eb2	bb1-eb2	All voices	Very sustained, delicate.
Nun wandre, Maria	g1-f#2	b1-e2	All voices	Slow and sus-tained. Inter-pretatively not easy. Demands an accomplished pianist.
Prometheus	B-e1	f-eb2	Bass or bass-baritone	Dramatic and declamatory. De-mands an excel-lent pianist. A very difficult song. See Schubert.
Schlafendes Jesuskind	c#1-ab2	a1-e2	All voices	Slow and very sustained. De-mands good com-mand of pp.
Schweig einmal still	e1-f2	a1-e2	Women's voices	An amusing, char-acter song. De-mands an accom-plished pianist.
Seemann's Abschied	c#1-a2	c1-f2	Men's voices, except a very light tenor	Rapid, dramatic. Demands an ex-cellent pianist.
Sonne der Schlummerlosen	c#1-e2	d1-b1	Medium or low voices	Slow. Interpreta-tively not easy. See Schumann, "An den Mond," and

TITLE	COMP.	TESS.	TYPE	REMARKS
				Mendelssohn, "Schlafloser Augen Leuchte."
St. Nepomuks Vorabend	d1-ab2	a1-f2	Most suitable for light, high voices	Slow, very sustained and delicate. Demands good command of pp.
Storchenbotschaft	c1-bb2	g1-f2	Most suitable for high voices	A humorous, narrative song. Interpretatively not easy. Demands an excellent pianist.
Tief im Herzen trag' ich Pein	c1-eb2	eb1-c2	Not suitable for very light, high voices	Slow, declamatory. Interpretatively not easy. See Schumann.
Treibe nur mit Lieben Spott	d1-f2	g1-eb2	Most suitable for men's voices	Light and delicate. Demands facile articulation. Interpretatively not easy.
Tretet ein hoher Krieger	c#1-g2	a1-e2	Women's voices	Gently humorous. Demands good sense of rhythm.
Trunken müssen wir alle sein	e#1-f#2	b1-f#2	Men's voices, except a very light tenor	Very vigorous and spirited. Demands an accomplished pianist.
Über Nacht	d1-g2	g1-eb2	Not suitable for very light, high voices	A dramatic song in contrasting moods and tempi.
Um Mitternacht	g#-e2	c#1-c#2	Low voices	Very slow and sustained. See R. Franz.
Und willst du deinen Liebsten sterben sehen	eb1-fb2	same	Most suitable for men's voices	Very slow, sustained, delicate. Musically not easy.
Verborgenheit	d1-g2	bb1-eb2	All voices	Sustained. See R. Franz.

TITLE	COMP.	TESS.	TYPE	REMARKS
Verschwiegene Liebe	c♯1-f♯2	f♯1-e♭2	All voices	Delicate and very sustained. Demands good command of high pp.
Waldmädchen	e1-g♯2	c1-g2	Soprano	Very rapid. Demands facile articulation and an excellent pianist.
Wanderers Nachtlied (Der du von dem Himmel bist)	d♯1-g2	g♭1-e♭2	All voices	Very slow and sustained. See Schubert, C. Löwe, and Liszt.
Was für ein Lied soll dir gesungen werden	e♭1-e♭2	same	All voices	Slow and sustained.
Was soll der Zorn	d♭1-f2	f1-e♭2	Not suitable for light voices	Dramatic.
Wenn du zu den Blumen gehst	d♯1-g2	a1-f♯2	All voices	Delicate and sustained. Musically not easy. Demands an accomplished pianist.
Wer rief dich denn?	d♭1-g♭2	f1-f2	Women's voices	Dramatic. Interpretatively not easy.
Wie glänzt der helle Mond	b-e2	g1-e♭2	Women's voices	Slow and very sustained. Demands good command of pp.
Wieviel Zeit verlor' ich	d1-e♭2	same	All voices	Delicate and sustained.
Wir haben beide lange Zeit geschwiegen	b♭-f2	f1-d♭2	All voices	Slow and sustained. Interpretatively not easy.
Wo find' ich Trost	d1-a♭2	g1-f2	Not suitable for very light voices	Slow, declamatory. Musically and interpretatively not easy. Demands an accomplished pianist.
Wohl denk' ich oft	c-e1	e-c1	Bass or bass-baritone	Grave and declamatory.

TITLE	COMP.	TESS.	TYPE	REMARKS
Zum neuen Jahr	d1-b2	c#1-g#2	Very high, light voices	Animated. The tessitura is uncommonly high.
Zur Ruh', zur Ruh'	b-ab2	eb1-eb2	Not suitable for very light voices	Grave and very sustained. Demands considerable dramatic intensity in the climax.

ERICH WOLFF
(1874–1913)

Erich Wolff, whose excellent "Alle Dinge haben Sprache" has become one of the very popular concert songs, has written a great number of most effective and distinguished songs. He is perhaps at his best in his least elaborate moments, for songs like, for instance, "Fäden," "Spaziergang," "Märchen" are in many ways sufficiently remarkable to be classed among the best examples of the post-Wagnerian German school.

Editions: Harmonie, Berlin
Bote & Bock, Berlin
Reprints by Harmonie Edition (with English titles), New York
and some songs by G. Schirmer

TITLE	COMP.	TESS.	TYPE	REMARKS
Alle Dinge haben Sprache	bb-gb2	f1-f2	Not suitable for very light, high voices	Sustained. Has an imposing climax. Demands an accomplished pianist.
Aus der Ferne in die Nacht	c#1-f#2	f#1-d2	All voices	Delicate. Demands good command of high pp.
Das Gärtlein dicht verschlossen	c1-f2	g1-eb2	All voices	Slow and very sustained. Demands good command of pp.
Der Kuckuk ist ein braver Mann	b-g#2	e1-e2	All voices	Light and humorous.
Du bist so jung	a#-f#2	e1-e2	Most suitable for baritone	Slow, somewhat declamatory. Demands an accomplished pianist.

TITLE	COMP.	TESS.	TYPE	REMARKS
Einsamkeit	bb-f2	e1-b1	Medium or low voices	Slow and somber.
Ein Sonntag	e1-g2	b1-g2	Most suitable for light, high voices	Very delicate. Demands good command of pp.
Ewig	bb-fb2	eb1-c2	Heavy voices	Sustained, majestic.
Fäden	c#1-f#2	a#1-e2	All voices	Very delicate, sustained.
Friedhof	c1-f#2	e1-e2	All voices	Somber. Interpretatively not easy. Demands an accomplished pianist.
Ich bin eine Harfe	b-f#2	f#1-d#2	Not suitable for high, light voices	Slow. Interpretatively not easy. Demands good command of p and an accomplished pianist.
Immer wieder	d1-f#2	f1-d2	All voices	Slow and sustained. Demands good command of p.
Knabe und Veilchen	d1-d2	a1-d2	All voices	Light and delicate.
Märchen	d1-e2	same	All voices	Very delicate, sustained. Demands good command of pp.
Mich tadelt der Fanatiker	d1-g2	same	Men's voices	Spirited and humorous. Demands an accomplished pianist.
Schlafe ruhig ein	c#1-f#2	f#1-e#2	Soprano or mezzo-soprano	Delicate, sustained.
Spaziergang	c#1-g2	a#1-f#2	Most suitable for light, high voices	Very delicate. Demands good command of high pp.

FRENCH

The list of French songs in this volume is primarily designed
to be of some practical value to a present-day singer outside of
France. Thus it is admittedly not as representative as it would be
were it intended as a historical survey of French song.

Most of the examples of the nineteenth century "drawing room"
music, for instance, have little if any practical value for the present-
day performer. Thus it seemed best to limit to a minimum the listing of songs of Chaminade, Godard, Thomas, and to include just a
few of the many songs of Gounod, although historically they have no
inconsiderable importance.

Extraordinarily popular some fifty years ago, these songs are
almost forgotten today, particularly outside of France. It has seemed
rather unnecessary to try to revive interest in them by listing them
in this volume. Naturally, masters like Gounod and Thomas are represented in the section devoted to operatic excerpts; their operas do
not seem to have lost any of their validity on the stage of today, even
if their songs seem to have lost much, if not all, of their former appeal.

Again, with the exception of some of the most representative
examples of the most significant contemporary French composers,
it seemed best not to try to list too many songs of avowedly experimental nature or of extraordinary complexity and difficulty. To list
a great number of such songs in a volume, the purpose of which is
primarily to provide the singer with a foundation upon which an individual repertoire could be built, seemed unwarranted.

The inclusion of some songs by such minor composers as
Fourdrain, Bemberg, Poldowski, Szulc, etc., seemed warranted by
the still rather powerful appeal they seem to possess for the performer as well as the public outside of France. The exclusion, however,
of many fine examples of a number of French composers of equal
stature seemed equally proper in view of the fact that their songs
seem for one reason or another never to have attained sufficient
popularity outside of France.

Songs by Chausson, Duparc, Fauré, Debussy, Honegger, Milhaud, Poulenc and Ravel form the backbone of this list. It does not seem unreasonable to assume that any list of French songs which includes a sufficient number of examples of these eight masters could fail to represent, for all practical purposes, the most important and significant examples of French song literature.

Naturally, a multitude of fine and effective French songs, old and new, could easily be added. Yet such an amplification would hardly effect any change in the general complexion of this list; in so far as the present-day singer and public are concerned it would still be dominated by the work of these eight composers, which rightfully seem to represent the French song to the world in general.

Note: For songs with original French texts listed elsewhere see the lists of the following composers: Albéniz, Barber, Borodin, Britten, Carpenter, Castelnuovo-Tedesco, De Falla, Delius, Egk, Liszt, Loeffler, Martin, Mozart, Santoliguido, Stravinsky, Thomson, Tchaikovsky, Villa Lobos and Wagner.

"40 IMC" in parentheses after the remarks column refers to "40 French Songs" selected and edited by S. Kagen, 2 volumes, high, medium and low, published by International Music Co.

Publisher's name in parentheses indicates that the song is available singly or in a collection.

EVA DELL'ACQUA
(b. 1860)

TITLE	COMP.	TESS.	TYPE	REMARKS
Chanson provençale	(bb)d1-bb2(c3)	g1-g2	Light soprano	Light, somewhat florid. Demands good command of high pp. (GS)
Villanelle	eb1-d3	bb1-g2	Coloratura soprano	A very florid display piece. (GS)

ADOLPHE ADAM
(1803-1856)

Cantique pour Noël	eb1-g2	g1-eb2 (H)	All voices	Sustained. Religious text. (OD)
Variations on: Ah, vous dirai-je, maman	b-e3	g1-b2	Coloratura soprano	A brilliant, florid display piece. Flute obbligato ad lib. (Edited by E. Liebling. GS)

LOUIS AUBERT
(b. 1877)

Edition: Durand

TITLE	COMP.	TESS.	TYPE	REMARKS
La lettre	e1-a2	g1-f2 (H)	All voices	Slow and subdued. Somewhat declamatory. Interpretatively not easy. Demands good command of pp.
Sérénade	e1-g2	f#1-e2	All voices	Animated, rhythmical.
Si de mon premier rêve	eb1-g2	g1-eb2	All voices	Sustained. (From "Rimes Tendres," three songs)
Vieille chanson espagnole	e1-a2	a1-e2 (H)	All voices	A sustained habanera.

GEORGES AURIC
(b. 1899)

TITLE	COMP.	TESS.	TYPE	REMARKS
Alphabet	c1-f2	f1-e2	High or medium voices	Seven short, amusing songs. Demand an accomplished pianist. Interpretatively not easy. (Eschig)
Attendez le prochain bateau	c#1-g2	e1-e2	High or medium voices	Slightly animated. (Eschig)
Enfance	f1-f#2	e1-f2	High or medium voices	Animated, light. (Eschig)
La jeune sanguine	c#1-d#2	same	All voices, except bass	Sustained, demands an accomplished pianist. (Eschig)
La chale	c#1-f#2	d1-d2	High or medium voices	Sustained, light, graceful. (Eschig)
Nuit blanche	db1-f#2	g1-f2	High voices	Sustained. (Eschig)
Printemps	e1-f#2	a1-e2	Light soprano	An animated, delicate waltz song. Demands some flexibility. (Durand)

382

TITLE	COMP.	TESS.	TYPE	REMARKS
Regrets	c1-e2	e1-c#2	All voices	Sustained, calm, subdued. (Eschig)

ALFRED BACHELET
(1864-1944)

TITLE	COMP.	TESS.	TYPE	REMARKS
Chère nuit	d1-bb2	bb1-gb2	Most suitable for light, high voices	Slow and very sustained. Demands an accomplished pianist. (40 IMC)
Vocalise	c1-bb2	f1-f2	High voices	Sustained. (Hettich, Répertoire Moderne de Vocalises. Leduc, Paris)

HERMAN (HENRI) BEMBERG
(1859-1931)

TITLE	COMP.	TESS.	TYPE	REMARKS
Chant hindou	c#1-f#2	f#1-d2	Women's voices	Slow, sustained, effective. (GS)
Du Christ avec ardeur (La Mort de Jeanne d'Arc)	db1-ab2	f1-eb2	Dramatic soprano or mezzo-soprano or alto	Sustained, effective. In parts demands considerable dramatic intensity. (GS; OD)
Il neige	f#1-g2	b1-f#2 (H)	Not too suitable for very low voices	Light, animated. Demands facile articulation. (40 IMC)

HECTOR BERLIOZ
(1803-1869)

The very few songs of Berlioz are perhaps among his least representative compositions. The three songs and the cycle below seem to be the most representative of his manner of writing for the voice.

Editions: Augener Music Ltd.
Costellat
International Music Co.

TITLE	COMP.	TESS.	TYPE	REMARKS
La captive	a-f#2	d1-d2	Mezzo-soprano or alto	Sustained. Demands some flexibility. (Originally for voice and orchestra.)

TITLE	COMP.	TESS.	TYPE	REMARKS
Le repos de la Sainte Famille (L'Enfance du Christ. Part II, No. 3)	e-a1	a-e1	Tenor	Sustained, graceful. (Score, Costellat)
Recitative: Toujours ce rêve Air: O misère des rois (L'Enfance du Christ. Part I, No. 3)	F-e♭1	c-c1	Bass	Grave, sustained. In parts dramatic. (Score, Costellat)
Les nuits d'été (A cycle of six songs)				
(1) Villanelle	e1-f♯2	a1-e2	Not too suitable for very heavy, low voices	Light and delicate.
(2) Le spectre de la rose	a-f2	d♯1-d2	Women's voices, except a light soprano	Slow, sustained. In parts demands considerable dramatic intensity.
(3) Sur les lagunes (Lamento)	d♭1(g♭)-g2	g1-f2	Most suitable for men's voices	Sustained, in parts demands considerable dramatic intensity. Demands good command of pp.
(4) L'absence	c♯1-f♯2	f♯1-d♯2	All voices	Slow, somewhat declamatory. Demands in parts considerable dramatic intensity, as well as a good command of high pp.
(5) Au cimetière (Clair de lune)	e1-g2	g1-f2	All voices	Very sustained. Demands good command of pp and ppp. See "Lamento" by Duparc.

TITLE	COMP.	TESS.	TYPE	REMARKS
(6) L'Ile inconnue	db1-g2	g1-f2	All voices	Spirited. Demands some flexibility and facile articulation.

PAUL BERNARD
(1827–1879)

Ca fait peur aux oiseaux	g#1-f2	a1-e2	Soprano	Graceful, delicate. Demands facile articulation. (GS)

GEORGES BIZET
(1838–1875)

Perhaps because of the extraordinary popularity of Carmen, the rest of Bizet's music seems to have suffered comparative neglect. His songs, for instance, among them such charming and individual things as "Chanson d'avril," "Douce mer," "Après l'hiver," to name but a few, deserve an esteemed place in any singer's French repertoire. Though by no means of extraordinary importance, they undoubtedly belong among the few artistically still valid examples of the mid-nineteenth century French "Romance."

> Editions: G. Schirmer, 2 volumes
> Choudens, Paris.
> Various reprints of single songs by many publishers

TITLE	COMP.	TESS.	TYPE	REMARKS
Adieux de l'hôtesse arabe	(bb)c1-g2(ab2)	g1-f2	Women's voices	Sustained. Demands some flexibility, especially in the final florid passage.
Après l'hiver	e1-g2	f1-eb2	All voices	Animated, delicate.
Chanson d'avril	e1-g2	f1-f2	All voices	Light, delicate. Demands facile articulation. (40 IMC)
Douce mer	eb1-ab2	ab1-f2	Most suitable for high voices	Demands good command of high pp and some flexibility.

TITLE	COMP.	TESS.	TYPE	REMARKS
Ma vie a son secret	b♭-g2	f1-e♭2	All voices, except a very light soprano	Sustained.
Ouvre ton coeur	d♯1-g♯2 (b2)	b1-f♯2	Most suitable for women's voices	An effective, spirited serenade in Spanish style. Demands some flexibility and a good sense of rhythm. (gen. av.)
Pastorale	d1-g2	g1-e2	Not too suitable for very heavy, low voices	Light. Demands facile articulation.
Vieille chanson	e♭1-a♭2	a♭1-f2	Most suitable for light, high voices	Delicate. Demands some flexibility.
Agnus Dei	d1-b♭2	a1-f2 (H)	All voices	Very sustained. Has effective climaxes. Latin and English texts. (GS)

ERNEST BLOCH
(1880–1959)

The very remarkable songs of Ernest Bloch, while written in a most individual idiom, never seem obscure or experimental. Few in number, they are for the most part written for voice and orchestra. Bloch's music is in its essence Hebraic. He has achieved a peculiar and striking musical language of his own which could perhaps be termed nationalistic, but only in the widest sense of the word, since this language is hardly based on folk material.

The three Psalms and the four "Poèmes d'Automne" are among his most remarkable works. They are all written for rather heavy voices, and are musically and interpretatively fairly complex. The accompaniments, being ordinarily scored for full orchestra, demand considerable ingenuity and a well-developed sense of dynamics from the pianist.

Edition: G. Schirmer

TITLE	COMP.	TESS.	TYPE	REMARKS
Invocation (Poèmes d'Automne)	c1-f2	g1-e2	Most suitable for medium voices	Slow, subdued, somewhat declamatory. Demands good command of p. Interpretatively not easy.
La vagabonde (Poèmes d'Automne)	e1-e2	same	Most suitable for medium voices	Slow, somber, somewhat declamatory. Interpretatively not easy. Demands an accomplished pianist.
L'abri (Poèmes d'Automne)	c#1-g2	f#1-e2	Not too suitable for very light, high voices	Slow, somewhat declamatory. In parts demands considerable dramatic intensity. Interpretatively not easy. Demands an accomplished pianist.
Le déclin (Poèmes d'Automne)	c1-eb2	db1-db2	Most suitable for medium voices	Slow, somewhat declamatory, subdued. In parts demands considerable dramatic intensity. Interpretatively not easy. Demands an accomplished pianist.
Psaume 22	c#-f1	f-d1	Baritone	Dramatic, somewhat declamatory. Musically and interpretatively not easy. The English version by Waldo Frank is very good.
Psaume 114	a1-a2	a1-f2	High voices	Dramatic, somewhat declamatory. Musically and interpretatively not easy. Demands an excellent pianist. The English version by Waldo Frank is very good.

TITLE	COMP.	TESS.	TYPE	REMARKS
Psaume 137	gb1-a#2	bb1-g2	High voices, except a very light tenor or soprano	Dramatic, some-what declamatory. Musically and in-terpretatively not easy. Demands an excellent pia-nist. The English version by Waldo Frank is very good.

See also: "Historiettes au crépuscule," four songs for medium voice, published by Demets, Paris.

CHARLES BORDES
(1863–1909)

TITLE	COMP.	TESS.	TYPE	REMARKS
Danson la gigue	e1-e2	same	High or medium voices	Rapid. Demands an excellent pia-nist. See Poldow-ski, Carpenter. (Hamelle)
Promenade matinale	d#1-a2	g1-e2	Not too suitable for very low voices	Not slow; sustained. Interpretatively not easy. (Rouart)

NADIA BOULANGER
(b. 1887)

TITLE	COMP.	TESS.	TYPE	REMARKS
Cantique	f1-f2	f1-d2	All voices	Sustained; for the most part subdued. (Hamelle)

ALFRED BRUNEAU
(1857–1934)

TITLE	COMP.	TESS.	TYPE	REMARKS
La pavane (Chansons à danser)	d1-f#2	e1-d2	High or medium voices	Sustained, rather subdued. (Choudens)
La sarabande (Chansons à danser)	db1-f2	f1-d2	Not too suitable for very light voices	Animated. Inter-pretatively not easy. Demands in parts con-siderable dramatic intensity. (Choudens)

TITLE	COMP.	TESS.	TYPE	REMARKS
Le sabot de frêne (Les lieds de France)	d1-e2	a1-d2	Women's voices	Spirited and gay. Demands facile articulation. (40 IMC)
L'heureux vaga-bond (Les lieds de France)	eb1-g2	g1-eb2 (H)	Men's voices	Vigorous. Inter-pretatively not easy. (40 IMC)

HENRI BÜSSER
(b. 1872)

La meilleure pensée	f#1-a2	a1-e2	Not suit-able for very low voices	Animated. The vocal line is very sustained. (Durand)

ANDRÉ CAPLET
(1878-1925)

Forêt (Les Vieux Coffret. 4 songs.)	d1-gb2	f1-eb2	High or medium voices	Slow, somewhat declamatory. In parts demands con-siderable dramatic intensity. Musical-ly not easy. De-mands an accom-plished pianist. (Durand)
La ronde (Cinq Ballades Françaises)	d1-f#2	e1-e2	Most suit-able for high voices	Rapid, light. De-mands facile artic-ulation and an ac-complished pianist. Musically not easy. (Durand)
Le Corbeau et le Renard (Trois Fables de La Fontaine)	a#-g2	c#1-d#2	High or medium voices	Humorous, some-what declamatory, in the manner of a free recitative. Musically and inter-pretatively not easy. Demands an accom-plished pianist. (Durand)

389

TITLE	COMP.	TESS.	TYPE	REMARKS

Les Prières:
1. Oraison
   Dominicale
2. Salutation
   Angélique
3. Symboles des
   Apôtres
	d♯1-g2	d♯1-d♯2	High or
			medium
			voices
				Sustained. A set-
				ting of three pray-
				ers. The last one
				has an imposing
				final climax. De-
				mand an accom-
				plished pianist.
				(Durand)

Prière normande	d1-f♯2	e1-e2	Medium or high voices	Not fast; rather sustained. Mu- sically not easy. (Durand)

See also "Le Pain Quotidien," fifteen vocalises for <u>soprano</u>. Musically quite complex. (Durand)

EMMANUEL CHABRIER
(1841–1894)

The four delightful "animal songs" listed here could be considered as forerunners of Ravel's "Histoires Naturelles." Chabrier's
wit, droll humor and originality in setting these texts to music are
the more astonishing considering the fact that in his treatment of
other texts (like "L'île heureuse" and "Romance de l'étoile") he does
not seem to rise above the conventional pattern of the mid-nineteenth
century French "Romance."

TITLE	COMP.	TESS.	TYPE	REMARKS
Ballade des gros dindons	b-f2	f1-b♭1	All voices	Humorous. De- mands an accom- plished pianist. (40 IMC)
Les cigales	c1-f♯2	f♯1-e2	Not too suitable for very low voices	Rapid and light. Demands facile articulation and an accomplished pianist. (40 IMC)
L'île heureuse	b-f2	d1-d2	Medium or low voices	Animated. The vocal line is sus- tained. Has ef- fective climaxes. (Enoch, Paris)
Pastorale des cochons roses	c1-e2	d1-d2	Most suit- able for medium voices	Humorous. De- mands facile ar- ticulation. A trifle long. (Enoch, Paris)

TITLE	COMP.	TESS.	TYPE	REMARKS
Romance de l'étoile	(b♭)c1-g2	e♭1-b♭1	All voices	Delicate. Requires a good command of high pp. (Enoch, Paris)
Villanelle des petits canards	c♯1-f♯2	e1-d2	All voices	Very light, humorous. Demands facile articulation and a good sense of rhythm. (40 IMC)

CÉCILE CHAMINADE
(1861–1944)

Chant slave	c1-g2 (b♭2)	d1-f2	Alto or mezzo-soprano	Sustained, effective. (GS)
L'anneau d'argent	c1-g2	f1-d2	Women's voices	Delicate and sustained. (GS)
L'été	e1-a2	f1-f2	Most suitable for soprano	Animated, effective. Demands considerable flexibility. (GS)
Trahison	b-a2	e1-e2	Not too suitable for very light, high voices	Animated, dramatic. Has effective climaxes. (GS)

GUSTAVE CHARPENTIER
(1860–1956)

Les chevaux de bois	e1-a2	a1-g2	High voices	Very animated, in parts quite vigorous. Demands an accomplished pianist. See Debussy. (HEUG)

ERNEST CHAUSSON
(1855–1899)

The songs of Chausson, with the exception of a few ("Les papillons," "Le temps des lilas," "Le colibri"), are infrequently performed.

Such masterpieces as "La caravane," "Les heures," "La chanson bien douce," "Chanson perpétuelle," to name but a few, are for some unknown reason neglected by the great majority of singers, who are sufficiently well equipped to perform "Le temps des lilas" or "Les papillons."

Most of Chausson's songs are neither musically nor interpretatively easy. Although his harmonies and rhythms are never over-complex, his use of them is so highly individual as to be almost startling at first acquaintance. "La dernière feuille," "Le charme," "Le colibri" and "Les morts" are perhaps the simplest of his songs and can be recommended to those who wish to acquaint themselves with his style of writing.

Editions: Rouart, Lerolle, original key
Hamelle, original key
20 songs, high and low, edited by S. Kagen. Published by International Music Co.
Numerous reprints of single songs.

TITLE	COMP.	TESS.	TYPE	REMARKS
Amour d'antan	d1-f♯2	b1-e2	All voices	Sustained, somber. Interpretatively not easy.
Apaisement	e♭1-g2	g1-e2	Most suitable for light, high voices	Very sustained. See "La lune blanche" by G. Fauré and "L'heure exquise" by R. Hahn and Poldowski. Demands good command of pp.
Cantique à l'épouse	c1-f2	f1-c2	Men's voices	Slow and sustained.
Chanson d'amour	e1-g2	a1-f2	All voices	A setting of "Take, o take, those lips away." In parts demands considerable dramatic intensity. Sustained.
Chanson de clown	d-e♭1	g♭-c1	Baritone	A setting of "Come away, come away, death." Grave.
Chanson d'Ophélie	c1-e2	e1-c2	Mezzo-soprano or alto	A setting of "He is dead and gone, lady." Slow.

392

TITLE	COMP.	TESS.	TYPE	REMARKS
Chanson perpétuelle	c♯1-g♯2	g♯1-e2	Mezzo-soprano or dramatic soprano	Slow, somewhat declamatory. Interpretatively and musically not easy. In parts very dramatic.
Dans la forêt du charme et de l'enchantement	c1-g2	g1-d2	Not too suitable for very heavy or low voices	Not fast. Interpretatively not easy. Demands lightness of tone, facile articulation, and an accomplished pianist.
Fauves las (Serres Chaudes)	e1-g♭2	f1-d2	All voices	Sustained. Interpretatively not easy.
L'aveu	f1-g♭2	a1-e♭2	Men's voices	A song of contrasting moods and tempi. In parts demands considerable dramatic intensity.
La caravane	c♯1-a2	a1-f2	Not suitable for light voices	Dramatic. Interpretatively not easy. Demands an excellent pianist.
La chanson bien douce	d1-e2	f1-c2	All voices	Not fast. Interpretatively not easy. Demands facile articulation, lightness of tone, and an accomplished pianist.
La dernière feuille	b-d♯2	f♯1-b1	Most suitable for low or medium voices	Somber, sustained.
Lassitude (Serres Chaudes)	c♯1-f♯2	f♯1-c♯2	All voices	Slow and sustained. Interpretatively not easy.
Le charme	b♭-e♭2	e♭1-c2	All voices, except a very light soprano	Sustained.

TITLE	COMP.	TESS.	TYPE	REMARKS
Le colibri	f1-f2	ab1-db2	All voices	Sustained.
Le temps des lilas	d1-g♯2	a1-f2	All voices, except a very light soprano	Excerpt from "Poème de l'amour et de la mer" for high voice and orchestra. Sustained. In parts demands considerable dramatic intensity. Demands an accomplished pianist.
Les heures	d1-d2	f1-c2	Most suitable for low or medium voices	Grave and sustained.
Les morts	c♯1-g2	e1-c♯2	Not too suitable for very light, high voices	Grave and sustained.
Les papillons	c1-f2	g1-e2	Not too suitable for very low voices	Rapid and light. Demands facile articulation and an excellent pianist.
Nanny	b-g2	g1-e2	All voices, except a very light soprano	Slow and sustained.
Nocturne	e1-g♯2	b1-e2	All voices	Very sustained. Demands good command of p and an accomplished pianist.
Nos souvenirs	d♯1-e2	f♯1-c♯2	Most suitable for medium or low voices	Somber. Interpretatively not easy. Demands an accomplished pianist.
Oraison (Serres Chaudes)	eb1-g2	bb1-f2	All voices	Very sustained. Interpretatively not easy.

TITLE	COMP.	TESS.	TYPE	REMARKS
Sérénade	d1-a2	g#1-e2	Most suitable for light, high voices	Very sustained.
Sérénade italienne	c1-e2	g1-d#2	Most suitable for medium or low voices	Sustained. Demands an accomplished pianist. Rhythmically not easy.
Serre chaude (Serres Chaudes)	d1-g2 (a2)	a1-f#2	All voices	Animated. Musically and interpretatively complex. Demands an accomplished pianist.
Serre d'ennui (Serres Chaudes)	b-f2	a1-e2	All voices	Sustained. Interpretatively not easy. Demands good command of p.
Printemps triste	c1-g2	ab1-f2	Not too suitable for very light, high voices	Somber and slow. Interpretatively not easy. Demands an accomplished pianist.

CLAUDE DEBUSSY
(1862–1918)

The importance of Debussy as a composer of songs can hardly be overestimated. Although he wrote only some 60 songs (including his earliest, imitative efforts), his style of writing for the voice has had and is still having a most profound and pronounced influence on much, if not most, of contemporary vocal music. With the exception of a very few, his songs demand much musically and interpretatively from singer and pianist. Vocally they present few problems; one, and perhaps the most important of these, is the demand he makes upon the singer to find an exact and most delicately adjusted balance between the spoken word and the sung tone, so that neither dominates the other. Often, to insure this effect, he deliberately uses the very edges of a voice's limits, writing, for instance, whole passages between c1 and e1 for a light, high voice from which he may expect an a2 a few bars later. The singer who would attempt to produce a cantilena tone in such passages would, of course, demand an impossible and artistically most undesirable effect from himself.

Three considerations must be kept in mind when approaching

his songs: First, in the treatment of his poetic texts Debussy is as much of a musical dramatist as Liszt or Hugo Wolf, though in his own somewhat veiled and oblique manner, and unlike the two latter composers he is hardly an illustrative realist. Second, the fact that Debussy wrote most expertly for the voice and knew to the minutest detail every shade of sonority that the combination of the human voice and the piano could produce. And, third, that he was one of the most fastidious composers in so far as the notation of his songs is concerned. Everything is marked, every accent, every dynamic shading, every rubato, every shade of tempo change. It will also help to remember that a most exacting rhythmic precision is demanded at all times unless otherwise indicated. Generally speaking most of Debussy's songs seem to lend themselves best to rather light voices, commanding a good pianissimo.

Editions: Durand, original key
37 songs, high and low. Edited by S. Kagen. Published by International Music Co.

TITLE	COMP.	TESS.	TYPE	REMARKS
Ballade de Villon à s'amye	c1-f2	d1-c#2	Most suitable for medium voices	Slow. Musically and interpretatively not easy. Demands an accomplished pianist.
Ballade des femmes de Paris	b-e2	e1-c2	All voices, except a very light soprano	Rapid, humorous. Demands facile articulation and an excellent pianist. Musically not easy.
Ballade que Villon feit à la requestre de sa mère	bb-e2	d1-d2	Mezzo-soprano or alto	Slow. Interpretatively not easy. Demands facile articulation and an accomplished pianist.
Beau soir	c1-f#2	f#1-d#2	All voices	Slow, sustained.
C'est l'extase langoureuse	c#1-a2	f#1-d#2	Not suitable for very low voices	Slow and delicate. Has a dramatic climax. Demands an accomplished pianist. See Fauré.
Chevaux de bois	c1-g2	g1-e2	High or medium voices	Spirited. Interpretatively not easy. Demands

396

TITLE	COMP.	TESS.	TYPE	REMARKS
				facile articulation and an excellent pianist. See Charpentier.
Clair de lune	c♯1-f♯2	f♯1-d♯2	Most suitable for high voices	Delicate, very sustained. Demands good command of high pp and an accomplished pianist. See Fauré and Szulc.
Colloque sentimental	a-f♭2	e1-d♭2	All voices	Very slow, declamatory dialogue. Interpretatively quite complex. Demands in parts considerable dramatic intensity. Musically not easy.
Crois mon conseil, chère Climène	c1-f♯2	c♯1-d♯2	Not too suitable for very low voices	Slow, very delicate. Demands good command of pp and an accomplished pianist. Musically and interpretatively not easy.
Dans le jardin	c1-f♯2 (g♯2)	f1-c♯2	Not too suitable for very low voices	Animated, delicate. Demands facile articulation, good command of pp and an accomplished pianist. Interpretatively not easy.
En sourdine	c1-f♯2	g♯1-d♯2	Not too suitable for very low voices	Slow, delicate. See Fauré, Hahn, Poldowski.
Eventail	d1-f♯2	f1-c♯2	Not too suitable for very low voices	Rapid, light. Demands very facile articulation, good command of pp and an accomplished pianist. Musically and interpretatively quite complex.

TITLE	COMP.	TESS.	TYPE	REMARKS
Faites silence! Ecoutez tous! (L'Enfant Prodigue)	B♭-f1	f1-d1	Baritone	Sustained, majestic.
Fleurs de blés	c♯1-g2	a1-f2	Most suitable for high voices	Sustained, delicate.
Fantoches	d1-a2	g1-f2	Most suitable for high voices	Rapid, light. Demands very facile articulation, good command of high pp and an accomplished pianist. Often taken at too fast a tempo.
Green	c1-a♭2	a♭1-f2	Not too suitable for very low voices	Animated, delicate. Demands good command of high pp and an accomplished pianist. See Fauré and "Offrande" by Hahn.
Harmonie du soir	b-f♯2	e1-e2	Most suitable for high voices	Slow. Interpretatively and musically not easy. Demands good command of high pp and an accomplished pianist.
Ici-bas	e♯1-f♯2	f♯1-d♯2	All voices	Sustained, delicate. See Fauré. This song was composed by Paul and Lucien Hillemacher, published as by Debussy. Another song, "Chanson d'un fou," composed by Emile Pessard was also published under Debussy's name. (SCH)
Il pleure dans mon coeur	c♯1-g♯2	g♯1-d♯2	Not too suitable for very low voices	Sustained. Interpretatively not easy. Demands good command of pp and an accomplished pianist.

TITLE	COMP.	TESS.	TYPE	REMARKS
Je tremble en voyant ton visage	a♭-f2	d♭1-d♭2	Not too suitable for very high voices	Slow, sustained. Demands an accomplished pianist.
La chevelure (Chansons de Bilitis)	c♭1-f♯2	e1-c2	Women's voices, except a very light soprano	Slow, interpretatively not easy. Demands an accomplished pianist.
La flûte de Pan (Chansons de Bilitis)	b-b1	e1-b2	Women's voices	Slow, very delicate. Demands facile articulation and an accomplished pianist. Interpretatively not easy.
La grotte	b-d♯2	d♯1-b1	Medium or low voices	Slow and very subdued. Musically and interpretatively not easy.
La mer est plus belle	d1-g2	f♯1-e2	All voices	Animated. Vocal line is sustained. Demands good command of occasional high pp.
La mort des amants	b♭-a2	g♭1-f♯2	Not too suitable for very low voices	Sustained. Musically and interpretatively not easy. Demands a good command of high pp and an accomplished pianist. See Charpentier.
Le balcon	b♯-a2	g1-g2	Most suitable for high voices	Animated. A song of uncommon complexity, interpretatively. Musically and vocally not easy. Demands an excellent pianist.
L'échelonnement des haies	e♯1-f♯2	g♯1-d♯2	Most suitable for high voices	Animated, delicate. Demands facile articulation, good command of high pp, and an accomplished pianist.

TITLE	COMP.	TESS.	TYPE	REMARKS
Le faune	c1-c2	c1-a1	Medium or low voices	Animated. Interpretatively not easy. Demands an accomplished pianist.
Le jet d'eau	c1-g♯2	e1-e2	Not too suitable for very low voices	Sustained. Musically and interpretatively not easy. Demands good command of p and an accomplished pianist.
Le son du cor s'afflige	d♭1-e2	same	Medium or low voices	Slow, subdued, somewhat declamatory.
Le temps a laissié son manteau	b-f♯2	e1-c♯2	All voices	Spirited. Demands facile articulation.
Le tombeau des Naïades (Chansons de Bilitis)	c1-f♯2	d1-a1	Women's voices	Slow and delicate. Musically and interpretatively not easy. Demands an accomplished pianist.
Les Angélus	c♯1-f♯2	f♯1-d♯2	Not too suitable for very low voices	Very sustained and delicate. Demands good command of pp.
Les cloches	d♯1-g♯2	f♯1-d♯2	All voices	Delicate, sustained.
Les ingénus	c1-f2	e1-d♭2	All voices	Delicate. Interpretatively and musically not easy.
l'ombre des arbres	d♯1-a♯2	e♯1-d♯2	Most suitable for high voices	Slow, demands good command of high pp. Interpretatively not easy. See "Brûme" by Poldowski.
Mandoline	c1-g2	g1-e2	All voices	Rapid and light. Demands facile articulation and an accomplished pianist. See Fauré and "Fêtes galantes" by Hahn.

TITLE	COMP.	TESS.	TYPE	REMARKS
Noël des enfants qui n'ont plus de maisons	c1-g2	f1-e2	Not too suitable for very low voices	Animated, dramatic. Interpretatively not easy. The text (dealing with German aggression during World War I) is by Debussy.
Nuit d'étoiles	d1-g2	g1-eb2	All voices	Very sustained. See Widor.
Placet futile	c1-g2	same	High or medium voices	Not fast. Demands very facile articulation. Interpretatively and musically quite complex. Demands an accomplished pianist. See Ravel.
Pour ce que plaisance est morte	c1-e2	e1-c2	All voices	Slow, musically and interpretatively not easy.

Proses Lyriques. Four songs, texts by the composer.

TITLE	COMP.	TESS.	TYPE	REMARKS
(1) De rêve	b-a2	e1-e2	High or medium voices	Musically and interpretatively quite complex. Demands an excellent pianist.
(2) De grève	c#1-a2	f#1-d#2	High or medium voices	Animated. Musically and interpretatively not easy. Demands an excellent pianist.
(3) De fleurs	c1-ab2	e1-e2	High or medium voices	Slow. Demands in parts considerable dramatic intensity. Musically and interpretatively quite complex. Demands an accomplished pianist.
(4) De soir	c#1-g#2	g#1-e2	High or medium voices	Animated. Interpretatively not easy. Demands an accomplished pianist.

TITLE	COMP.	TESS.	TYPE	REMARKS
Recueillement	c1-g♯2	e1-d♯2	Most suitable for high voices	Very slow. Musically and interpretatively not easy. Demands good command of high pp and an accomplished pianist.
Rondeau	e1-a2	a1-f2	Most suitable for high voices	Sustained, delicate.
Romance	d1-f♯2 (g♯2)	f♯1-d2	All voices	Sustained.
Soupir	c1-f2	g1-e♭2	High or medium voices	Slow, very sustained. Demands good command of pp and an accomplished pianist. Musically and interpretatively not easy.
Spleen	d♭1-b♭2	e1-e2	Not too suitable for very light, high voices	Slow, dramatic. Musically and interpretatively not easy.
Voici que le printemps	(c♯1)d1-g2	f♯1-e2	High or medium voices	Very light and delicate. Demands facile articulation. Interpretatively not easy. In parts gently humorous.

Trois Chansons de Charles d'Orléans
Originally written for mixed chorus, transcribed for solo
voice and pianoforte by Lucien Garbau.

Dieu, qu'il la fait bon regarder	d♯1-f♯2	f♯1-e2	High or medium voices	Slow, sustained, delicate. Demands good command of high pp.
Yver, vous n'estes qu'un villain	e1-f♯2	f♯1-d2	All voices	Rapid, rhythmic. Has an effective ending. Demands facile articulation.
Quand j'ai ouy le tabourin	d1-e2	c1-c♯2	Not too suitable for very	Originally an alto solo with choral accompaniment.

TITLE	COMP.	TESS.	TYPE	REMARKS
			light, high voices	Animated, delicate, gently humorous. Demands good command of pp and facile articulation.

MARCEL DELANNOY
(1898–1962)

TITLE	COMP.	TESS.	TYPE	REMARKS
Ballade des vingt mineurs	c1-f2	e1-e2	Heavy medium voices	Vigorous, animated, narrative. Demands facile articulation and an accomplished pianist. (HEUG)
La Joueuse (Cinq Quatrain de Fr. Jammes)	e1-a2	a1-e2	High voices	Delicate, light, not fast. Demands some flexibility. (HEUG)
Le soleil de la rue de Bagnolet (Etat de Veille)	c1-f2	f1-eb2	Medium or low voices	Animated, gay. Demands an accomplished pianist. (Eschig)
Les Portes (Etat de Veille)	b-e2	e1-c2	Medium or low voices	Sustained, grave. (Eschig)
Reprise (Cinq Quatrain de Fr. Jammes)	e1-bb2	f1-g2	High voices	Animated, forceful. In parts demands considerable flexibility. (HEUG)

LÉO DÉLIBES
(1836–1891)

TITLE	COMP.	TESS.	TYPE	REMARKS
Bonjour Suzon	c1-f2	f1-d2 (H)	Men's voices	Light and rapid. Demands facile articulation. Of no particular distinction. (GS)
Chant de l'almée	(b)d1-e3	a1-a2	Coloratura soprano	A very florid, bravura song. (GS)
Jours passés (also called Regrets)	f#1-ab2	a1-e2	Most suitable for high voices	Slow and sustained. (GS)

403

TITLE	COMP.	TESS.	TYPE	REMARKS
Le rossignol	(a#)b-c3	d1-b1	Soprano or mezzo-soprano	Light. Has florid cadenzas. (GS)
Les filles de Cadix	c#1-c#3	f#1-e2	Coloratura or lyric soprano	Light and brilliant. Demands facile articulation and an accomplished pianist. See "Cadix" by Castelnuovo-Tedesco. (gen. av.)
Myrto	c1-a2	f1-d2	High or medium voices	Rather animated, rhythmical. (GS)

<h2 style="text-align:center">PAUL DUKAS
(1865–1935)</h2>

Sonnet	db1-d2	eb1-b1	Most suitable for men's voices	Sustained, subdued. Musically and interpretatively not easy. (Durand)

<h2 style="text-align:center">HENRY DUPARC
(1848–1933)</h2>

Duparc songs occupy a position of such generally acknowledged eminence that it seems unnecessary to discuss their excellence and importance here.

All of his 13 songs are listed below. They are neither vocally nor interpretatively easy and cannot be recommended to inexperienced singers or pianists, with the possible exception of "Lamento" or "Chanson triste." Musically they present hardly any difficulties.

Editions: Rouart, Lerolle (high and medium).
12 Songs (high, medium and low), edited by S. Kagen.
Published by International Music Co.
Numerous reprints of single songs.

Au pays où se fait la guerre	c1-ab2	f1-eb2	Women's voices, except a very light soprano	Slow. Demands considerable dramatic intensity in parts and an accomplished pianist. (Rouart)

TITLE	COMP.	TESS.	TYPE	REMARKS
Chanson triste	c#1-a2	bb1-f2	All voices	Very sustained. Interpretatively not easy. Demands an accomplished pianist.
Elégie	c1-f2	f1-d2	All voices	Slow and sustained. Interpretatively not easy.
Extase	g1-a2	a1-f#2	Most suitable for high voices	Slow and sustained. Demands good command of high pp. Interpretatively not easy. See "Nocturne" by Hahn.
La vague et la cloche	(ab)b-e2	e1-c#2	Not suitable for light, high voices	Dramatic. Interpretatively complex. Demands an excellent pianist.
La vie antérieure	(bb)eb1-ab2	bb1-f2	Not suitable for very light, high voices	Slow and grave. Has a magnificent climax. Interpretatively not easy. Demands an excellent pianist.
Lamento	d1-f2	f1-d2	All voices	Slow and somber. Demands an accomplished pianist. See Berlioz's "Au cimetière."
Le manoir de Rosemonde	d1-ab2	a1-f2	Not suitable for very light, high voices	Rapid, dramatic, somewhat declamatory. Demands an accomplished pianist.
L'invitation au voyage	f1-ab2	g1-f2	All voices	Very sustained. Interpretatively not easy. Demands an accomplished pianist. See Charpentier.
Phidylé	eb1-ab2	ab1-f2	All voices	Slow and sustained. Interpretatively complex. Has a magnificent climax. Demands an excellent pianist.

TITLE	COMP.	TESS.	TYPE	REMARKS
Sérénade florentine Soupir	eb1-f2	g1-eb2	All voices	Sustained, very delicate.
Soupir	e1-ab2	a1-f2	Most suitable for high voices	Slow. Interpretatively not easy.
Testament	c1-gb2	eb1-d2	Not suitable for very light, high voices	Animated. In parts demands considerable dramatic intensity. Interpretatively not easy. Demands an excellent pianist.

GABRIEL DUPONT
(1878–1914)

TITLE	COMP.	TESS.	TYPE	REMARKS
Chanson des noisettes	e1-a2	g1-e2	High voices	Light, animated. Demands facile articulation. (HEUG)
Mandoline	eb1-a2	g1-eb2	Most suitable for high voices	Rapid, light. Demands an accomplished pianist. See Debussy, Fauré, Szulc, Poldowski, and "Fêtes galantes" by Hahn. (40 IMC)
Les caresses	d1-g2	a1-e2	High voices	Sustained. (HEUG)

LOUIS DUREY
(b. 1888)

TITLE	COMP.	TESS.	TYPE	REMARKS
La métampsychose (Trois Poèmes de Pétrone)	c#1-g#2	f#1-d2	High voices	Sustained, delicate. (Durand)
Le bestiaire	c1-ab2	e1-e2	Medium or high voices	Twenty-six very short, amusing songs about animals. Musically and interpretatively not easy. Demand an accomplished pianist. See seven of

these texts set to
music by Poulenc
("Le Bestiaire")
and Auric. (CHES)

GABRIEL FAURÉ
(1845–1924)

The songs of Gabriel Fauré, with the exception of a very few,
are but little known outside of France. The reason for this is hard
to understand, for one could hardly imagine songs more deserving
of greater popularity, on every conceivable ground.

Fauré's idiom cannot be considered experimental, yet it is
never ordinary and always decidedly and unmistakably his own; his
mastery as a musical craftsman is astonishing, his poetic and musical taste impeccable, and his manner of writing for the voice is
perhaps the most graceful and cultivated among the late nineteenth
century composers. In his songs he combines an extremely sensitive poetic perception with a remarkable melodic gift, an uncommonly pliable and individual harmonic construction, and a rare elegance
of form. It seems incomprehensible that so many of his masterly
songs are rarely performed. Vocally and musically his songs cannot
be considered exacting. A competent performance of a song by
Fauré is none the less not so easy as it may sometimes seem, for
Fauré demands simplicity, elegance and clarity in execution as well
as in intention from both the singer and the pianist, which necessitates an ensemble of considerable excellence.

· Fauré's accompaniments are uncommonly transparent in their
texture and demand excellent pedaling. Pianistically they are expertly handled and should be played with considerable attention to
accuracy of detail.

Most of his songs are suitable for all types of voices, if performed by a singer possessing the requisite polish and simplicity.

Editions: Hamelle, 3 volumes (high and medium), reprinted by
          E. Marks.
          30 Songs (high, medium and low), edited by S. Kagen.
          Published by International Music Co.
          25 songs with very good English translations by M.
          Farquhar (high and medium), G. Schirmer.

TITLE	COMP.	TESS.	TYPE	REMARKS
Après un rêve	d1-g2	a1-f2	All voices	Very sustained.
Arpège	e1-f#2	f#1-e2	All voices	Delicate. Inter-pretatively not easy. Demands an accomplished pianist.

TITLE	COMP.	TESS.	TYPE	REMARKS
Au bord de l'eau	c♯1-f♯2	e1-e2	All voices	Delicate, sustained. Demands lightness of tone.
Au cimetière	d1-f2	f1-d2	Not suitable for light voices	Somber, slow. Interpretatively not easy. The middle section is very dramatic.
Aurore	c1-f2	f1-c2	All voices, except a very light soprano	Sustained.
Automne	d1-f♯2	f♯1-d2	Not too suitable for very light voices	Sustained. Interpretatively not easy. Demands considerable dramatic intensity in parts, and an accomplished pianist.
C'est l'extase	c1-f♭2	a♭1-d♭2	All voices	Slow. Interpretatively and musically not easy. Demands an accomplished pianist. See Debussy.
Clair de lune	f1-f2	a1-d♭2	All voices	Delicate. Demands lightness of tone and an accomplished pianist. Interpretatively not easy. See Debussy and Szulc.
Dans les ruines d'une abbaye	e1-f♯2	f♯1-e2	Not too suitable for very low voices	Light, very delicate. Demands very facile articulation and great lightness of tone.
En prière	e♭1-e♭2	g1-e♭2	All voices	Delicate, sustained.
En sourdine	c1-e♭2	f1-d♭2	All voices	Slow. Interpretatively and musically not easy. See Debussy, Hahn, Poldowski.

TITLE	COMP.	TESS.	TYPE	REMARKS
Fleur jetée	db1-a2	f1-f2	Not suitable for very light, high voices	Very rapid, dramatic. In some editions a curious misprint, MM♩.-172 instead of MM ♩.-72 has caused many a singer and pianist to attempt the impossible. Demands an excellent pianist.
Green	d♯1-ab2	ab1-f2	All voices	Animated. Interpretatively and musically not easy. See Debussy, and "Offrande" by Hahn.
Ici-bas	f♯1-g2	g1-eb2	All voices	Slow, delicate. See Debussy.
La fleur qui va sur l'eau	b-e2	f♯1-d2	Not suitable for very light, high voices	Animated. Demands considerable dramatic intensity in parts, and an accomplished pianist.
La lune blanche luit dans les bois (La Bonne Chanson. Nine songs to text by Paul Verlaine)	d1-f♯2	f♯1-e2	Most suitable for high voices	Sustained; for the most part subdued. See Szulc, "Appaisement" by Chausson, "L'heure exquise" by Hahn, and Poldowski.
Larmes	c♯1-g♯2	g♯1-e2	Not too suitable for very light, high voices	Somber, dramatic. Demands an accomplished pianist.
Le parfum impérissable	c♯1-e2	e1-c♯2	All voices	Slow, sustained. Interpretatively not easy.
Le plus doux chemin	eb1-eb2	g1-db2	All voices	Delicate.
Le secret	db1-eb2	ab1-db2	All voices	Very delicate, sustained. Demands lightness of tone.
Les berceaux	(ab)bb-f2	f1-db2	Not suitable for very light, high voices	Slow and very sustained.

TITLE	COMP.	TESS.	TYPE	REMARKS
Les roses d'Ispahan	d1-f♯2	f♯1-d2	All voices	Delicate, sustained.
L'hiver a cessé (La Bonne Chanson. Nine songs to text by Paul Verlaine)	c♯1-g2	g1-e2	High voices, except a very light soprano	Very animated. In parts demands considerable dramatic intensity. Requires an excellent pianist.
Lydia	g1-g2	a1-f♯2	All voices	Delicate, very sustained.
Madrigal	f1-f2	a1-f2	Most suitable for men's voices	Delicate, sustained.
Mandoline	e♯1-e2	g1-d2	Medium or high voices	Animated. Demands considerable flexibility, very facile articulation, and an excellent pianist. See Debussy, and "Fêtes galantes" by Hahn.
Nell	f♯1-a♭2	b♭1-f2	Not too suitable for very low voices	Graceful, very delicate. Demands an accomplished pianist.
Nocturne	a♭-c2	d♭1-a♭1	Low or medium voices	Slow and sustained.
Noël	e♭1-a♭2	g♭1-e♭2 (H)	All voices	Animated. Has a vigorous and effective ending.
Notre amour	d♯1-a2 (b2)	e1-e2	All voices	Light and animated. Demands facile articulation and an accomplished pianist.

Poèmes d'un Jour
(Three Songs)

(1) Rencontre	c♯1-f♯2	f♯1-d♯2	All voices	Very sustained. Interpretatively not easy. Demands an accomplished pianist.

TITLE	COMP.	TESS.	TYPE	REMARKS
(2) Toujours	e1-g2	g1-e2	Not too suitable for very light, high voices	Rapid, dramatic. Demands facile articulation and an accomplished pianist.
(3) Adieu	e1-e2	g#1-d#2	All voices	Very delicate, sustained. Demands lightness of tone. Interpretatively not easy.
Prison	eb1-f#2	g1-eb2	Not too suitable for very light, high voices	Slow. In parts demands considerable dramatic intensity. See "D'une prison" by Hahn.
Puisque l'aube grandit (La Bonne Chanson. Nine songs to text by Paul Verlaine)	c1-f#2	f#1-e2	Medium or low voices	Animated. Interpretatively not easy.
Rêve d'amour	d1-g2	f1-f2	Not too suitable for very low voices	Light and graceful. Demands facile articulation. See "S'il est un charmant gazon" by Liszt.
Seule!	f#1-eb2	g1-d2	Not suitable for light, high voices	Grave, very sustained. See Hahn.
Soir	c1-f#2	f1-db2	All voices, except a very light soprano	Slow and sustained. Musically and interpretatively not easy. Demands an accomplished pianist.
Spleen	d1-e2	same	All voices, except a very light soprano	Delicate, sustained. Interpretatively not easy. See "Il pleure dans mon coeur" by Debussy.
Sylvie	g1-ab2	ab1-f2	Not too suitable for very low voices	Light and delicate. Demands facile articulation and an accomplished pianist.

411

TITLE	COMP.	TESS.	TYPE	REMARKS
Tristesse	d1-f2	a1-f2	Not too suitable for very low voices	Animated. Demands facile articulation. Interpretatively not easy.
Vocalise	b-g♯2	e1-e2	High voices	Slow. Has some rather intricate florid passages. (Leduc)

See also: La Chanson d'Eve — 9 songs for mezzo-soprano or alto.
(HEUG)
Le Jardin Clos — 8 songs for medium voice. (Durand)
L'Horizon Chimérique — 4 songs for medium voice.
(Durand)
Mirages — 4 songs for medium voice. (Durand)

JEAN FAURE
(1830–1914)

TITLE	COMP.	TESS.	TYPE	REMARKS
Alleluia d'amour	e1-g♯2	g♯1-e2	All voices	Animated, effective. Demands some flexibility. (GS)
Les rameaux	e1-g2 (a2)	g1-e2	All voices, except a very light soprano	A sustained, majestic religious song. Has effective climaxes. (GS)

GUSTAVE FERRARI
(1872–1948)

TITLE	COMP.	TESS.	TYPE	REMARKS
Le miroir	c♯1-d2	e1-a2	All voices	Slow, delicate. (Marks)

HENRI FÉVRIER
(b. 1875)

TITLE	COMP.	TESS.	TYPE	REMARKS
L'intruse	b-d♭2	c1-c2	Not too suitable for very light, high voices	Dramatic, declamatory, very subdued. Interpretatively not easy. (HEUG)

TITLE	COMP.	TESS.	TYPE	REMARKS
Prière pour qu'un enfant ne meure pas	db1-g#2	same	Not suitable for very low voices	Not fast. Interpretatively not easy. In parts dramatic. Demands an accomplished pianist. (Leduc)

ANGE FLÉGIER
(1846–1927)

TITLE	COMP.	TESS.	TYPE	REMARKS
Le cor	E#(D)-d1	c#-b	Bass	An effective descriptive song in several contrasting movements interspersed with recitative passages. (40 IMC)

FÉLIX FOURDRAIN
(1880–1923)

Edition: Ricordi

TITLE	COMP.	TESS.	TYPE	REMARKS
Carnaval	c1-f2 (a2)	a1-e2	All voices	Very rapid, effective. Demands facile articulation.
Chanson norvégienne	e1-a2	g1-eb2	Women's voices, except a very light soprano	A dramatic, effective song. Animated.
Le long des saules	c1-a2	g1-d2	High voices	Rapid, light. In parts declamatory. Demands good command of high pp.
Mon jardin	eb1-f2	g1-d2	Medium or high voices, except a very light soprano	Sustained.

See also "Le papillon" and "Impression basque" among a great number of other effective songs.

413

CÉSAR FRANCK
(1822–1890)

César Franck exercised an immense influence on the development of French music in the late nineteenth century and especially on French song of that period. The contemporary French school may easily be considered as having received its impetus from Franck and his pupils, among whom were Duparc, Chausson, and d'Indy. His very few songs, however, with the exception of "La Procession" and "Nocturne," can hardly be considered as representative of his style of writing and his genius.

Edition: Six Songs. Published by Boston Music Co.

TITLE	COMP.	TESS.	TYPE	REMARKS
La procession	e1-g♯2	g♯1-e2	Not suitable for very light, high voices	Majestic, sustained. Demands an accomplished pianist. Interpretatively not easy. One of the most remarkable of Franck songs. (40 IMC)
Le mariage des roses	e1-f♯2	f♯1-d♯2	All voices	Delicate.
Le vase brisé	(c1)d1-g2	g1-e♭2	Not too suitable for very light voices	Sustained. In parts demands considerable dramatic intensity.
Les cloches du soir	f1-a♭2	g1-e♭2	All voices	Sustained; for the most part subdued.
Lied	f♯1-f♯2	a1-e2	All voices	Delicate, sustained.
Ninon	e1-f♯2	a1-e2	All voices	Delicate, graceful.
Nocturne	d♯1-d♯2	e♯1-c♯2	Not too suitable for very light, high voices	Slow and sustained. (40 IMC)
Panis Angelicus (Messe Solennelle)	a1-f♯2	a1-e2	Tenor or soprano	Very sustained. Latin and English texts. (GS)

ALEXANDRE GEORGES
(1850–1938)

TITLE	COMP.	TESS.	TYPE	REMARKS
Hymne au soleil	e1-a2	c♯2-g♯2	Dramatic soprano or mezzo-soprano	Declamatory, very effective. (40 IMC)
La pluie	e1-e2	a1-c♯2	Women's voices	Very delicate and light. Demands good command of pp. (40 IMC)

BENJAMIN GODARD
(1849–1895)

TITLE	COMP.	TESS.	TYPE	REMARKS
Chanson de Florian	d1-f♯2	f♯1-d2	Women's voices	Light, in the style of a bergerette. (gen. av.)

CHARLES GOUNOD
(1818–1893)

Editions: G. Schirmer
O. Ditson

TITLE	COMP.	TESS.	TYPE	REMARKS
Au printemps	d♭1-a♭2	a♭1-e♭2	All voices	Animated, effective. At one time extremely popular.
Au rossignol	e1-g2	g1-d2	All voices	Sustained, delicate.
Envoi de fleurs	g1-g2	g1-e2	All voices, except bass	Graceful. Demands lightness of tone.
Le vallon	e1-g♯2	g♯1-e2	Not suitable for very light voices	Somewhat declamatory. In parts dramatic.
Medjé	g1-g2	g1-d2	Men's voices	Sustained, "Oriental" in character, effective.
Primavera	f1-g2	a1-e2	Not too suitable for very low voices	Animated, graceful.

TITLE	COMP.	TESS.	TYPE	REMARKS
Venise	f1-g2	g1-eb2	All, except very low, heavy voices	An animated, subdued barcarolle. (40 IMC)

See also "Chanson de la glu" and "Mignon."

GABRIEL GROVLEZ
(1879–1944)

TITLE	COMP.	TESS.	TYPE	REMARKS
Créole	f1-g2	g1-e2	High voices	A sustained, habanera-like song. Interpretatively not easy. Demands an accomplished pianist. (Gallet)
Guitares et mandolines	eb1-g#2	g#1-f#2	High voices	Brilliant and effective. Musically and interpretatively not easy. Demands an excellent pianist. See Saint-Saëns. (Durand)

REYNALDO HAHN
(1875–1947)

Hardly any of Hahn's songs present any vocal or musical problems. Expertly and gracefully written, they seem to suit practically any type of voice and are musically anything but complex. None the less, most of his songs are not to be recommended to inexperienced singers. Hahn's songs demand considerable elegance and delicacy in phrasing and rhythm, a most sensitive delivery of the poem, effortless articulation, and a definite aptitude for the style of expression that he represents. Sung clumsily and ploddingly, these slight and charming songs lose too much of their substance to be enjoyed.

Editions: Heugel.
    12 Songs (high and low), International Music Co.
    Numerous reprints of single songs.

TITLE	COMP.	TESS.	TYPE	REMARKS
A Chloris	d#1-f#2	g#1-e2	All voices	Slow and sustained.
Chanson au bord de la fontaine	a1-e2	same	All voices	Delicate.

TITLE	COMP.	TESS.	TYPE	REMARKS
D'une prison	b♭-e♭2	f1-d2	Not too suitable for very light, high voices	Sustained. Demands in parts considerable dramatic intensity. See "Prison" by G. Fauré.
Fêtes galantes	b-g♯2	g1-d2	Most suitable for high voices	Rapid and light. Demands an excellent pianist. See "Mandoline" by Debussy and by G. Fauré.
Fumée	e1-e2	g1-c2	All voices	Very delicate. Demands good command of pp.
Infidélité	c1-e♭2	f1-c2	All voices	Sustained. Interpretatively not easy. Demands good command of p.
L'heure exquise (Chansons grises)	b-d♯2	d♯1-d♯2	All voices	Very delicate and sustained. Demands good command of pp. See "Apaisement" by Chausson, "La lune blanche" by G. Fauré, and "L'heure exquise" by Poldowski.
Le printemps	f♯1-a2	b1-f♯2	Most suitable for high voices	Spirited and effective. Demands an accomplished pianist.
Le rossignol des lilas	e♭1-a♭2	a♭1-f2	Most suitable for high voices	Delicate and sustained.
Le souvenir d'avoir chanté	e1-f♯2	f♯1-d2	All voices	Very sustained. Interpretatively not easy.
Les cygnes	b♭-f2	f1-e♭2	All voices	Very sustained. Interpretatively not easy.

TITLE	COMP.	TESS.	TYPE	REMARKS
Nocturne	e1-f♯2	a1-e2	All voices	Very delicate. Demands good command of pp. See "Extase" by Duparc.
Offrande	c1-c2	e1-a1	All voices	Subdued, some-what declamatory. Interpretatively not easy. Demands good command of pp. See "Green" by Debussy and by G. Fauré.
Paysage	c1-e2	e1-c2	All voices	Sustained.
Quand je fus pris au pavillon	f♯1-f♯2	g♯1-d♯2	All voices	Rapid and light. Demands very fac-ile articulation and an accomplished pianist.
Seule	b-e2	g♯1-d♯2	Most suit-able for medium voices	Animated. Inter-pretatively not easy. See G. Fauré.
Si mes vers avaient des ailes	b-f♯2	f♯1-d2	Not too suitable for very heavy, low voices	Delicate and sus-tained. Demands good command of high pp.
Sur l'eau	c♭1-e2	f♭1-c♭2	All voices	Very delicate. Demands good command of pp.

AUGUSTA HOLMES
(1847–1903)

Noël d'Irlande	b-e2	d1-a1	All voices	Slow, somewhat declamatory. (OD)

ARTHUR HONEGGER
(1892–1955)

The very remarkable songs of Honegger are to be most emphati-cally recommended to any one interested in contemporary music. One must be, however, sufficiently well equipped musically to be able to perform them.

TITLE	COMP.	TESS.	TYPE	REMARKS
Berceuse de la Sirène	c♭1-e♭2	g♭1-d♭2	Mezzo-soprano or alto	Slow and sustained. Musically not easy. (Senart)
Chanson (Ronsard)	a-e2	f1-d2	Low or medium voices	Slow and sustained. A rather simple song recommended as a splendid introduction to songs by Honegger. (Senart)
Chanson de fol	d♯1-f♯2	f♯1-d♯2	High or medium voices	Light and rapid. Musically not easy. (Senart)
Cloche du soir	b-f2	d1-d2	Medium or low voices	Sustained. Musically not easy. (Senart)
Le chasseur perdu en forêt	c1-e♭2	f1-d♭2	Medium or low voices	Animated, vigorous. Musically very complex. Demands an accomplished pianist. (Senart)
Les cloches (Six Poèmes de G. Apollinaire)	c♯1-f♯2	f♯1-d♯2	Women's voices, except a very light soprano	Animated. In parts demands considerable dramatic intensity. (Senart)
Mimaamaquim	f♯-e♭2	c1-b♭1	Heavy, low voices	Sustained, grave. Demands some flexibility. In parts has the style of a free chant on a vowel. Oriental flavor. Hebrew text based on Psalm 130. (Salabert)
Petit cours de morale	c♯1-g2	f1-d2	Not suitable for very low voices	Five very short songs whose titles are names of women. Demand considerable flexibility and an accomplished pianist. (Salabert)

Quatre chansons pour voix grave
Four songs for low voices. (Salabert)

TITLE	COMP.	TESS.	TYPE	REMARKS
(1) La douceur de tes yeux	c#1-e2	e1-d2		Sustained, rhythmically not easy.
(2) Derrière Murcie en fleurs	a-c2	b-g1		Short recitative-like song. Low tessitura. Guitar-like pianoforte part.
(3) Un grand sommeil noir tombe	g-c#2	c1-g#2		Sustained, very subdued. Demands excellent command of pp.
(4) La terre les eaux va buvant	a#-e2	e1-c#2		Short, animated, humorous. Demands some flexibility and facile articulation. Demands an accomplished pianist.
Quatre poèmes	a-f#2	e1-d2	Four songs for medium voices	Generally sustained. Poems by different authors. (CHES)
Trois poèmes de Claudel	bb-ab2	e1-d2	Three songs for high voices	(Salabert)

Trois psaume
Three settings on texts from the Book of Psalms. (Salabert)

TITLE	COMP.	TESS.	TYPE	REMARKS
(1) Psaume XXXIV	c1-c2	same	Medium or low voices	Rather sustained. Short, simple, straightforward in the treatment of the text.
(2) Psaume CXL	bb-ab2	eb1-eb2	High or medium voices	Slow, sustained. Short. Has subdued ending.
(3) Psaume CXXXVIII	e1-g2	f1-f2	High and medium voices	A short song requiring the sustained, straightforward, grand manner type of delivery.

See also "Six poésies de Jean Cocteau," published by M. Senart.

King David

Solo excerpts from the cantata, with English versions by Edward Agate. Vocal score is published by E. C. Schirmer, Boston.

TITLE	COMP.	TESS.	TYPE	REMARKS
In the Lord I put my faith	c-f♯1	e-e1	Tenor	Not fast. In parts declamatory. Short.
O had I wings like a dove	f♯1-a2	a1-e2	Soprano	Short, slow, sustained. In parts demands considerable dramatic intensity. Musically not easy.
O shall I raise mine eyes	d-g1	g-e1	Tenor	Short, slow, majestic; somewhat declamatory.
Pity me, Lord	d-a1	e-f♯1	Tenor	Short, slow, sustained. The second section is vigorous and animated. Demands some flexibility. Musically not easy.
Song of the handmaid (Oh, my love, take my hand)	b♯-e♭2	e1-c2	Alto	Short, sustained, subdued. Musically not easy.
The song of David (God shall be my shepherd)	b-e2	e1-c♯2	Alto	Short, sustained. Musically not easy.

GEORGES HÜE
(1858–1948)

Hüe, a somewhat conservatively inclined composer, has written a considerable number of tasteful and expertly executed songs. The short list here seems quite representative of his manner of writing, with the possible exception of the very popular, yet hardly deserving "J'ai pleuré en rêve."

TITLE	COMP.	TESS.	TYPE	REMARKS
A des oiseaux	e1-g2	g1-d2	Most suitable for light, high voices	Light and delicate. Demands facile articulation and a good command of pp. (40 IMC)

Chansons du Valet de Coeur
Four songs

TITLE	COMP.	TESS.	TYPE	REMARKS
(1) Tête de femmes est légère	e1-g2	g1-d2	All voices	Spirited. Demands facile articulation and a good sense of rhythm. (Durand)
(2) Sur la tour de Montlhéry	db1-f2	gb1-eb2	All voices	Very rapid, dramatic. (Durand)
(3) A la croisée	db1-fb2	g1-eb2	Soprano or mezzo-soprano	Very sustained. Interpretatively not easy. (Durand)
(4) Le passant	d1-g2	g1-e2	Most suitable for men's voices	Light and rapid. Demands facile articulation. (Durand)
Il a neigé des fleurs	eb1-ab2	ab1-eb2	Most suitable for light, high voices	Light and delicate. (Baudoux)
J'ai pleuré en rêve	e1-f#2 (a2)	a1-e2	All voices, except a very light soprano	Dramatic, effective. See "Ich hab' im Traum geweinet" by Schumann, R. Franz, and C. Löwe. (40 IMC)
La fille du roi de Chine	f#1-g#2	b1-e2	Most suitable for tenor	Rapid and brilliant. Demands an accomplished pianist. (HEUG)
L'âne blanc	eb1-g2	g1-eb2	Most suitable for light, high voices	Light and delicate. Demands an accomplished pianist. (HEUG)
Les clochettes des muguets	e1-gb2	b1-e2	Most suitable for light, high voices	Delicate and animated. (40 IMC)
Par la fenêtre grande ouverte	db1-f2	ab1-eb2	All voices	Slow and sustained. Requires good command of p. (Baudoux)
Sonnez les matines	f#1-g2	f#1-e2	All voices	Sustained. Demands in parts considerable intensity. (HEUG)

JACQUES IBERT
(b. 1890)

TITLE	COMP.	TESS.	TYPE	REMARKS
Chanson du rien	c1-e♭2	d1-d2	All voices	Animated, light. Has folk quality. (Leduc)
Complainte de Florinde	d1-d2	g1-d2	All voices	Animated. Strophic, each verse ending with a spoken phrase. (Leduc)

Deux Chansons de Mèlpomène. Two songs for soprano. (HEUG)

TITLE	COMP.	TESS.	TYPE	REMARKS
(1) Mon bien aimé	e♭1-b♭2	g1-f2	Soprano, most suitable for light, high voices	Sustained. In parts demands facile articulation.
(2) Je pensais épouser	d1-g2	f1-e2	Soprano	Has waltz sections. Ending has optional hummed parts by women's voices.

Quatre chants. Four songs for high voices. (HEUG)

TITLE	COMP.	TESS.	REMARKS
(1) Romance	e1-g2	f♯1-e2	Sustained. Demands an accomplished pianist.
(2) Mélancolie	d♭1-f♯2	e♭1-d♯2	Slow, sustained. Generally subdued.
(3) Familière	d1-a♭2	g1-g2	Animated, fast. Demands facile articulation, flexibility, and an accomplished pianist.
(4) Fête nationale	d♯1-g2	a1-f♯2	Animated, fast. Demands an accomplished pianist.

VINCENT d'INDY
(1851–1931)

TITLE	COMP.	TESS.	TYPE	REMARKS
Lied maritime	b-g2	g1-f2 (H)	Not too suitable for very light, high voices	Sustained. Demands in parts considerable dramatic intensity. Interpretatively not easy. (40 IMC)
Madrigal dans le style ancien	e1-e2	same	All voices	Sustained. Has a severely contrapuntal accompaniment. (40 IMC)
Mirage	c#1-e2	g1-d#2	Most suitable for men's voices	Somewhat declamatory. In parts demands considerable dramatic intensity. (Hamelle)

ÉMILE JACQUES-DALCROZE
(1865–1950)

TITLE	COMP.	TESS.	TYPE	REMARKS
La chère maison	f1-g2	a1-f2	Most suitable for high voices	Graceful, delicate. (Marks)
Le coeur de ma mie	f#1-f#2	g1-d2	All voices	Delicate, light. (GS)
L'oiseau bleu	e#1-a2	a1-f#2	Light soprano	Graceful, delicate. Demands facile articulation and some flexibility. (CF)

ANDRÉ JOLIVET
(b. 1905)

TITLE	COMP.	TESS.	TYPE	REMARKS
Nous baignons dans une eau tranquille . . . (Poèmes Intimes)	c1-fb2	eb1-c2	Medium voices	Sustained, calm, subdued. Third in the cycle of five songs. (HEUG)
Pour te parler . . . (Poèmes Intimes)	bb-f2	db1-db2	Medium voices	Sustained. Has one long cadenza. Subdued ending section. Last in the cycle of five songs. (HEUG)

424

Trois chansons de ménestrels
Three songs for high voices. (HEUG)

TITLE	COMP.	TESS.	TYPE	REMARKS
(1) Chanson de coeur dolent	c1-g2	f1-d2		Sustained. Demands good command of high pp. Strophic.
(2) Lamento de Jésus-Christ	d1-d2	e1-d2	Most suitable for men's voices	Sustained. Strophic.
(3) Amour me nuit	c1-f2	e1-eb2		Rather brisk, lively. Strophic.

See also "Les Trois Complaintes du Soldat," a cycle of three songs for baritone, published by Durand.

CHARLES KOECHLIN
(1867–1950)

The songs of Charles Koechlin, a somewhat conservatively inclined composer, could easily be considered among his outstanding works. Tasteful, distinctive and expertly written, they deserve an esteemed place in every singer's French repertoire.

TITLE	COMP.	TESS.	TYPE	REMARKS
L'air	f1-f#2	a1-f2	High voices	Sustained, for the most part subdued, delicate. (Rouart)
La lune	c1-f2	f1-d2	High or medium voices	Very light, animated. Demands facile articulation. (Rouart)
La prière du mort	db1-e2	g-db2	Not suitable for very light, high voices	Slow. In parts very dramatic. (Hachette)
Le thé	e1-g#2	g#1-d#2	Not suitable for very low voices	Animated, light. Demands an accomplished pianist. (40 IMC)
L'hiver	e1-e2 (g2)	same	Not suitable for very low voices	Very delicate. Has a curious accompaniment in which a glissando figure, e2-b3 and b3-e2, is used incessantly. Interpretatively not easy. (BMC)

TITLE	COMP.	TESS.	TYPE	REMARKS
Si tu le veux	f#1-e2	f#1-c#2	Most suitable for high voices	Animated, delicate. The vocal line is sustained. Demands good command of high pp. (40 IMC)
Villanelle (Le temps, l'étendue et le nombre)	a-d#2	c1-a1	Low or medium voices	Rather slow, very subdued. (Hachette)
Vocalise	a-e2	c1-c2	Low or medium voices	Rather sustained. (Leduc)

EDOUARD LALO
(1823–1892)

TITLE	COMP.	TESS.	TYPE	REMARKS
Ballade à la lune	c1-d2 (g2)	f1-c2	All voices	Rapid, humorous. Demands facile articulation. (Hamelle)
Chant breton	e1-e2	same	Women's voices	Sustained, plaintive. (Hamelle)
Guitare	f#1-f#2	f#1-d2	All voices	Animated, light. See "Comment, disaientils" by Liszt. (Hamelle)
La chanson de l'alouette	eb1-b2	b1-g2	Light soprano	Rapid and light. (GS)
L'esclave	e1-f#2 (H)	f1-d2	Women's voices, except a very light soprano	Slow and sustained. (GS)
Marine	d#1-f#2	g#1-d#2	Most suitable for men's voices	Sustained, somewhat declamatory. In parts demands considerable dramatic intensity. (Hamelle)
Oh! quand je dors	e1-g2	a1-f2	All voices	Sustained. See Liszt. (Hamelle)

RAOUL LAPARRA
(1876–1943)

TITLE	COMP.	TESS.	TYPE	REMARKS
Les pas de sabots	d1-f2	e1-e2	Soprano	Rapid, delicate. Demands facile articulation. (Enoch)

TITLE	COMP.	TESS.	TYPE	REMARKS
Lettre à une Espagnole	e♭1-f2	g♭1-e♭2	All voices	Animated, light, rhythmical. (Enoch)

GUILLAUME LEKEU
(1870–1894)

TITLE	COMP.	TESS.	TYPE	REMARKS
Ronde	d1-g♯2	f♯1-e2	High or medium voices	Animated. Interpretatively not easy. Demands an accomplished pianist. (Rouart)
Sur une tombe	d1-e♭2 (g2)	f1-d2 (H)	Not too suitable for very light, high voices	Slow and somber. (GS)

RENÉ LENORMAND
(1846–1932)

TITLE	COMP.	TESS.	TYPE	REMARKS
Berceuse	c1-f2	f1-c2	Medium or high voices	Sustained and delicate. (Hamelle)
Le petit gardeur de chèvres	f1-d♭2	same	All voices	Sustained and delicate. (Hamelle)
Quelle souffrance	(b♭1)d1-g2	e♭1-c2	Most suitable for men's voices	Very sustained, effective. Demands good command of sustained forte. (Hamelle)

XAVIER LEROUX
(1863–1919)

TITLE	COMP.	TESS.	TYPE	REMARKS
Le Nil	e1-a2	g1-e2	All voices	Sustained. (GS)

JULES MASSENET
(1842–1912)

More widely known as one of the outstanding operatic composers of France, Massenet has written a great number of tasteful and charming songs like "Bonne nuit," "Crépuscule," "Les femmes de Magdalia," "Que l'heure est donc brève," to mention but a few which seem to deserve to be as popular as some of the more famous excerpts from his operas.

TITLE	COMP.	TESS.	TYPE	REMARKS
Editions:	Collection, 2 volumes, published by G. Schirmer. Numerous reprints of single songs by various publishers.			
Bonne nuit	f1-g2	bb1-f2	All voices	Delicate, sustained.
Chant provençal	c1-f2 (a2)	f1-d2	All voices	Delicate, sustained.
Crépuscule	d1-e2	e1-c2	All voices	Delicate, sustained. (40 IMC)
Elégie	c1-f2	f1-c2 (H)	All voices	Very slow and sustained. Perhaps the most widely known, though by no means one of the best songs of Massenet.
Les femmes de Magdala	d1-f#2	g1-d2	All voices	Delicate, sustained.
Ouvre tes yeux bleus	e1-g2	f1-d2	All voices	Animated, effective.
Première danse	e1-g2	a1-e2	All voices	Light, rapid, effective. Demands facile articulation.
Que l'heure est donc brève	e1-e2	a1-d2	All voices	Very delicate.
Roses d'octobre	d1-g2	g1-d2	All voices	Sustained, very subdued.
Si tu veux, Mignonne	e1-f#2	g#1-e2	Most suitable for men's voices	Animated, delicate. The vocal line is very sustained.
Sonnet	e1-f#2	f#1-e2	All voices	Sustained. Demands in parts considerable dramatic intensity.

OLIVER MESSIAEN
(b. 1908)

The songs of Oliver Messiaen, one of the most prominent of contemporary French composers, present formidable rhythmic and ensemble problems, even though harmonically they are not overly complex.

TITLE	COMP.	TESS.	TYPE	REMARKS
Chants de terre et de ciel	c1-a#2	e1-e2	A cycle of six songs for sopra-no, except light, high voices	Rhythmically very complex for both singer and pianist. Demands an ex-cellent pianist. Musically diffi-cult. Text by the composer. (Durand)
Harawi	b♭-b2	c1-g2	A cycle of twelve songs for heavy, high voices	Very difficult; vocally and musi-cally demanding. Demands an ac-complished pia-nist. Text by the composer. (Leduc)
La fiancée perdue	d1-a2	f#1-e2	High voices	Fast, animated. The vocal line is sustained. Demands an accomplished pianist. (Durand)
Le sourire	e1-d2	same	High voices	Slow, very sub-dued. Short. (Durand)

Poèmes pour mi

A cycle of nine songs for <u>high voices,</u> published by Durand. Only the fifth, sixth, and ninth are given here.

(5) L'Epouse	e♭1-a♭2	f1-d♭2		Sustained, some-what slow.
(6) Ta voix	e1-g2	g#1-f#2		Sustained, some-what slow. De-mands an accom-plished pianist.
(9) Prière exaucée	d♭1-a2	a1-e2		Sustained. Has cantabile and par-lando sections, and florid passages. Forceful and florid ending. Demands an accomplished pianist.
Pourquoi?	c1-f#2	e1-c#2	High voices	Slightly animated. Demands an accom-plished pianist. (Durand)

DARIUS MILHAUD
(b. 1892)

One of the most remarkable of the contemporary French composers, Milhaud has written a very considerable number of songs, ranging from the rather inconsequential "Soirées de St. Pétersbourg" to the extraordinarily forceful "Poèmes Juifs." As a rule his songs are musically quite complex, although vocally they present few difficulties. Anyone interested in contemporary vocal music would do well to acquaint himself thoroughly with Milhaud's songs.

TITLE	COMP.	TESS.	TYPE	REMARKS
Berceuse (Chants Populaires Hébraïques. 6 songs)	e1-d2	same	All voices	Subdued, delicate. Demands somewhat facile articulation. (HEUG)
Catalogue de fleurs	c1-f2	same	Most suitable for medium voices	Six delightful, very short songs. Musically and interpretatively not easy. Demands an accomplished pianist. (Also orchestrated by the composer.) (Durand)

Chansons de Ronsard
A cycle of four songs for <u>coloratura soprano</u> and orchestra.
Demands an accomplished pianist. (BH)

TITLE	COMP.	TESS.		REMARKS
(1) A une fontaine	e1-c3 (b2)	a1-a2		Sustained. Demands flexibility.
(2) A cupidon	e1-d3 (c3)	a1-a2		Sustained, florid.
(3) Tais-toi, babillarde	a1-e3 (c3)	c2-a2		Animated, light, florid. Demands facile articulation and flexibility. Has a short cadenza at the end.
(4) Dieu vous gard'	eb1-c3	a1-b2		Animated, demands flexibility and facile articulation. Has a few short florid passages.
Chant hassidique (Chants Populaires Hébraïques)	c1-d2	same	Medium or low voices	Animated. Interpretatively not easy. (HEUG)

TITLE	COMP.	TESS.	TYPE	REMARKS
La tourterelle (Quatre poèmes Léo Latil)	b-g2	d♯1-d2	All except very low voices	Animated. Demands facile articulation and an accomplished pianist. Musically not easy. (Durand)
L'aurore (Trois poèmes de Lucile de Chateaubriand)	d♯1-f2	f1-d♯2	All voices	Delicate, subdued. Musically not easy. (Salabert)

Poèmes Juifs
(published by Eschig)

TITLE	COMP.	TESS.	TYPE	REMARKS
Chant d'amour	c1-g♭2	e♭1-d♭2	Not suitable for very low voices	Rapid. Demands an accomplished pianist. Musically somewhat complex.
Chant de forgeron	c1-f♯2	c1-c2	Not suitable for light, high voices	Very vigorous, rhythmic. Demands an accomplished pianist. Musically somewhat complex.
Chant de la pitié	c1-e♭2	e1-c2	Medium or low voices	Sustained. Musically complex.
Chant de nourrice	c1-g2	e1-c♯2	Soprano or mezzo-soprano	Delicate, slow. Musically very complex. Interpretatively not easy.
Chant de résignation	f1-d2	same	Medium or low voices	Very sustained, delicate. Musically somewhat complex.
Chant de Sion	e♭1-e♭2	a♭1-d♭2	All voices	Sustained. Musically somewhat complex.
Chant du laboureur	b-f2	d1-d2	Not suitable for very light, high voices	Animated. Has a vigorous and rapid ending. Musically somewhat complex.
Lamentation	a-e2	e1-c♯2	Medium or low voices	Animated. Musically somewhat complex.

Trois chansons de troubadour
Three songs for high or medium voices. (Salabert)

TITLE	COMP.	TESS.	TYPE	REMARKS
(1) Rassa	d1-g2	g1-e2		Sustained. Demands some flexibility. Short.

TITLE	COMP.	TESS.	TYPE	REMARKS
(2) Belle dame de mon émoi	c1-d♭2	e♭1-d♭2		Sustained, light.
(3) Je suis tombé de mal en peine	g1-a♭2	g1-e♭2		Brisk, spirited, rhythmic.

ERNEST MORET

TITLE	COMP.	TESS.	TYPE	REMARKS
Le Nélumbo	e1-d♭2 (g♭2 or b♭2)	same	Not suitable for very low voices	Slow, very subdued, delicate. Demands good command of pp. (HEUG)

ÉMILE PALADILHE
(1844–1926)

TITLE	COMP.	TESS.	TYPE	REMARKS
Lamento provençal	c♯1-f♯2	f♯1-d2	Not too suitable for very light, high voices	Slow, somewhat declamatory. Demands in parts considerable dramatic intensity. (Homeyer)
Le roitelet	d♯1-g♯2	g♯1-e2	Light soprano	Rapid and light. Demands facile articulation. (GS)
Les trois prières	d♭1-a♭2	g♭1-e♭2 (H)	All voices	Slow and sustained. (GS)
Psyché	b♭-f2 (g♭2)	g♭1-e♭2	All voices	Delicate, sustained. (40 IMC)

ÉMILE PESSARD
(1843–1917)

TITLE	COMP.	TESS.	TYPE	REMARKS
L'adieu du matin	d1-f♯2	a1-e2	All voices	Delicate. Demands rather facile articulation. (GS)
Requiem d'un coeur	d1-f2	same	Most suitable for men's voices	Not fast. In parts demands considerable dramatic intensity. Effective. (Leduc)

432

TITLE	COMP.	TESS.	TYPE	REMARKS

GABRIEL PIERNÉ
(1863–1937)

TITLE	COMP.	TESS.	TYPE	REMARKS
A Lucette	g♯1-g2 (H)	a1-f2	Not too suitable for very low voices	A song in antique style. Delicate and sustained. (Leduc)
Ils étaient trois petits chats blancs	e1-f♯2	e1-e2	High or medium voices	Rapid, light, humorous. Demands facile articulation. (Marks)
La rieuse	c♯1-f♯2	e1-e2	All voices	A delicate narrative song. Interpretatively not easy. (Leduc)
Le moulin	d1-f♯2	g1-e2	All voices	Animated. Demands an accomplished pianist. A little long. Perhaps one of Pierné's best songs. (Leduc)
L'oeillet rouge	c♯1-d2	e1-b♭1 (L)	All voices	Slow and sustained. (Leduc)
Villanelle	d1-e2	g1-d2 (L)	All voices	A light, delicate song in eighteenth century style. See also "Chanson de berger" by Pierné, set in the same style. (Leduc)

POLDOWSKI
(Lady Dean Paul)
(1880–1932)

Editions: Chester, unless otherwise marked.

TITLE	COMP.	TESS.	TYPE	REMARKS
Colombine	d1-g♭2	g♭1-d2	Not too suitable for very light, high voices	Rapid, very effective. Demands an accomplished pianist. Interpretatively not easy.
Cortège	d1-f♯2	e1-c2	Medium or high voices	Rapid. Demands facile articulation and an accomplished pianist. Interpretatively not easy.

TITLE	COMP.	TESS.	TYPE	REMARKS
Cythère	e1-eb2	f#1-c#2	Medium or low voices	Rapid. Demands facile articulation.
Dansons la gigue	d1-g2	g1-d2	Not too suitable for low voices	Rapid, dramatic. Demands facile articulation. See Carpenter. (40 IMC)
En sourdine	d1-a2	f#1-d2	All voices	Sustained. Demands in parts considerable dramatic intensity. See Debussy, Fauré, and Szulc.
Impression fausse	a-e2	d1-a1	Medium or low voices	Rapid, subdued. Demands facile articulation. The entire middle section is sustained and declamatory. Very effective; interpretatively not easy.
L'heure exquise	db1-ab2	gb1-db2	All voices	Slow, sustained. Demands in parts considerable dramatic intensity. See Hahn, "Apaisement" by Chausson, "La lune blanche" by Fauré, and Szulc. (40 IMC)
Mandoline	f1-f2	g#1-c#2	All voices	Light and rapid. Demands facile articulation and an accomplished pianist. See Debussy, Fauré, and "Fêtes galantes" by Hahn.

FRANCIS POULENC
(1899–1963)

It could be said that perhaps no outstanding contemporary French composer would seem to have achieved as complete a liberation from the influence of Debussy as Poulenc.

Poulenc's harmonic scheme varies considerably. Some of his songs, like the "Tel jour, tel nuit" series, are dissonant and rather complex experimentations; others, like the well-known "Airs chantés" are deliberately confined to the tonic-subdominant-dominant harmonic scheme, and are almost mocking in their simplicity.

His songs, as a rule, demand a great deal of vocal and stylistic elegance and are interpretatively rather complex.

Poulenc was a prolific composer, and this list is primarily intended for those who are not at all familiar with his manner of writing.

TITLE	COMP.	TESS.	TYPE	REMARKS
A sa guitare	d1-f♯2	f♯1-eb2	Not too suitable for very light, high voices	Very sustained. (Durand)

Airs Chantés. Published by Rouart, Lerolle

TITLE	COMP.	TESS.	TYPE	REMARKS
(1) Air romantique	c1-e2	e1-c2	Not suitable for very light, high voices	Very rapid, spirited, and vigorous. Demands an accomplished pianist.
(2) Air champêtre	c♯1-b2	b1-g2	High, light voices	Very animated, delicate. Demands an accomplished pianist.
(3) Air grave	e1-ab2	ab1-f2	High voices	Sustained.
(4) Air vif	c1-ab2	g1-d2	Not suitable for low voices	Very rapid. Demands some flexibility and an accomplished pianist.
Attributs (Cinq Poèmes de Ronsard, for mezzo-soprano)	c1-gb2	f1-eb2	Not too suitable for very low voices	Animated, amusing. Interpretatively not easy. Demands an accomplished pianist. (HEUG)
Avant le cinema (Quatre poèmes d'Apollinaire)	c♯1-eb2	f1-d2	All voices	A fast, mordant satirical song. Interpretatively not easy. Demands facile articulation. (Rouart)

TITLE	COMP.	TESS.	TYPE	REMARKS

Banalités

A cycle of five songs for medium voices.

Published by Eschig.

TITLE	COMP.	TESS.	TYPE	REMARKS
(1) Chanson d'Orkenise	c1-g♭2	f1-f2		Animated, graceful.
(2) Hotel	c1-e2	e1-c2		Slow, sustained. Subdued.
(3) Fagnes de Wallonie	b-f♯2	d1-d♯2		Animated. Demands facile articulation and flexibility.
(4) Voyage à Paris	f1-g♭2 (g2)	g1-e♭2		Graceful waltz.
(5) Sanglots	b♯-g♭2	f1-e♭2		Sustained. Demands some flexibility.
Bleuet	d♯1-a♭2	g1-e2	High voices	Sustained, in parts dramatic. Interpretatively not easy. (Rouart)
C (J'ai traversé les ponts de Cé)	e♭1-a♭2	a♭1-f2	Most suitable for high voices	Sustained. Requires good command of high pp. Interpretatively not easy. (Rouart)
Chanson	e♭1-a2	g1-f♯2	High voices	Animated. (Rouart)
Chanson à boire	B-e1	c-a♭	Bass or baritone	A slow, mock-solemn song. No. 2 of the "Chansons Gaillardes" for baritone. (HEUG)

Chansons Villageoises

A cycle of six songs for <u>high or medium voices.</u> Piano
transcription of the orchestral score is available.

Published by Eschig.

TITLE	COMP.	TESS.	TYPE	REMARKS
(1) Chanson du clair Tamis	b♭-g2	e♭1-e♭2		Very brisk. Demands facile articulation, flexibility, and an accomplished pianist.

TITLE	COMP.	TESS.	TYPE	REMARKS
(2) Les gars qui vont à la fête	b♭-g♭2	f1-e♭2		Spirited, fast. Demands facile articulation, flexibility, and an accomplished pianist.
(3) C'est le joli printemps	e♭1-f2	f1-e♭2		Slow, sustained, gentle, very calm. Demands good command of high pp.
(4) Le mendiant	c1-g2	e1-e♭2		Sustained, has some slightly animated passages. Demands an accomplished pianist.
(5) Chanson de la fille frivole	d♭1-g2	g1-e♭2		Very brisk, demands facile articulation, flexibility, and an accomplished pianist.
(6) Le retour du sergent	b♭-f2	e1-e2		In parts demands facile articulation.
Fleurs (Fiançailles pour rire)	d♭1-f2	f1-e♭2	All voices	Slow, sustained, subdued. (Rouart)
Hier (Trois Poèmes de Louise Lalanne)	e♭1-f2	g1-e2	Most suitable for high voices	Sustained, subdued. Demands a good command of high pp. (Rouart)
Hymne	G♭-d♯2	c-c♯1	Bass or bass-baritone	Slow, sustained. Religious text by Racine. (Salabert)
Il vole	d1-g2	g1-e♭2	High or medium voices	Fast, spirited, demands facile articulation and considerable flexibility. Demands an excellent pianist. (Rouart)
Je n'ai plus que les os (Cinq Poèmes de Ronsard, for mezzo-soprano)	b-f2	e1-d2	Not too suitable for very light, high voices	Very slow, somber. Musically complex. Demands an accomplished pianist. (HEUG)

TITLE	COMP.	TESS.	TYPE	REMARKS
La belle jeunesse	d-f1	f-eb1	Baritone or a heavy tenor	A very animated, rowdy song. Demands facile articulation. No 7 of the "Chansons Gaillardes" for baritone. (HEUG)
La courte paille	d1-g2	f1-e2		A cycle of seven songs for <u>high or medium</u> voices. (Eschig)
Le bestiaire (6 short songs)	b-e2	same	Most suitable for medium or low voices	These six amusing, very short songs — "Le Dromadaire," "La Chèvre de Thibet," "La Sauterelle," "Le Dauphin," "L'Ecrevisse" and "La Carpe" are originally scored for string quartet, flute, clarinet and bassoon. Interpretatively not easy. See Durey. (Sirène Musicale)
Le présent	c1-ab2	e1-eb2	High or medium voices	Brisk, demands facile articulation and flexibility. The vocal line is mostly sustained. Demands an accomplished pianist. (Rouart)
Le travail du peintre	bb-f#2	f1-db2	A cycle of seven songs for medium voices	The title of each song is the name of a painter: Picasso, Chagall, Braque, Gris, Klee, Miró, and Villon. (Eschig)
Paganini (Métamorphoses)	c#1-g2	gb1-eb2	Most suitable for light, high voices	Animated, light. Demands a good command of high pp, facile articulation, and an accomplished pianist. (Rouart)

TITLE	COMP.	TESS.	TYPE	REMARKS
Priez pour paix	e♭1-e♭2	f1-d2	All voices, except bass	Sustained, subdued, in parts very delicate. (Rouart)
Reine des mouettes	e♭1-f2	g1-e♭2	High or medium voices	Animated, demands facile articulation, good command of high pp and an accomplished pianist. (Rouart)
Violon (Fiançailles pour rire)	c♯1-g♭2	e♭1-e2	Most suitable for medium or high voices	Sustained. Interpretatively not easy. Demands an accomplished pianist. (Rouart)

See also "Le bal masqué," a cycle for baritone or mezzo-soprano and a chamber orchestra. (Rouart)

HENRY RABAUD
(1873–1949)

Instant	c1-e2	same	All voices	Somewhat declamatory, very subdued. (HEUG)

RENÉ RABEY

Tes yeux	e♭1-g2	b♭1-e♭2	All voices	Very sustained, effective. (Durand)

MAURICE RAVEL
(1875–1937)

In his songs Ravel's extraordinary mastery is as apparent as it is in his instrumental and orchestral works. Precise to an astonishing degree is his notation, almost uncanny in his knowledge of the variety of unexpected sonorities that the combination of the human voice and the pianoforte or a group of instruments are able to produce, fastidiously exact in his treatment of French prosody, Ravel in his songs demands a most exacting precision on the part of the performer.

Always fully aware of the possibilities as well as of the limitations of the human voice, his treatment of the vocal line is extraordinarily effective, not perhaps from the traditional point of view of a vocalist who is in search of a suitable vehicle for the purpose of exhibiting his vocal equipment, but from the point of view of the composer. In other words, Ravel writes for the voice in a manner that unfailingly ensures the exact musical effect he desires, provided, of course, both singer and pianist follow his instructions.

Most of his songs are musically and interpretatively difficult, though vocally not exacting, and demand an extraordinarily sensitive ensemble.

Only a few could possibly be recommended to inexperienced singers, among them the delightful and ingenious arrangement of the five Greek songs, and the four "Chansons Populaires."

Chansons Populaires

Editions: Durand
International Music Co.

TITLE	COMP.	TESS.	TYPE	REMARKS
Chanson espagnole	d1-bb1	same	Medium or low voices	An arrangement of a Spanish folk song. Animated, rhythmical.
Chanson française	g1-f2	g1-d2	All voices	Delicate. An arrangement of a French folk song.
Chanson hebraïque	e1-e2	e1-c2	Not too suitable for very light, high voices	Has contrasting tempi and moods. An arrangement of a Hebrew folk song.
Chanson italienne	c1-f2	eb1-eb2	All voices	Slow, very sustained, plaintive. An arrangement of an Italian folk song.

Cinq Mélodies Populaires Grecques

Editions: Durand
International Music Co.

(1) Chanson de la mariée	g1-eb2	same	Not suitable for very low voices	Rapid, delicate. Demands facile articulation, good command of pp, and an excellent pianist. The five

TITLE	COMP.	TESS.	TYPE	REMARKS
				Greek folk tunes arranged by Ravel are vocally quite simple. They are very short songs provided with extremely interesting accompaniments. They can be sung separately.
(2) Là-bas, vers l'église	g#1-e2	same	All voices	Slow, very sustained, plaintive.
(3) Quel galant m'est comparable	d1-f2	a1-d2	All voices	Spirited. If sung by itself, it should preferably be sung by a man.
(4) Chanson des cueilleuses de lentisques	a1-e2	same	All voices	Slow and very sustained.
(5) Tout gai!	eb1-f2	ab1-eb2	All voices	Animated, rhythmical. Demands an accomplished pianist.
D'Anne jouant de l'espinette	(b)c#1-g#2	f#1-d#2	High voices	Delicate. Musically not easy. Demands an accomplished pianist. (IMC)
D'Anne qui me jecta de la neige	c#1-f#2	f#1-d#2	High or medium voices	Very slow, delicate. Musically not easy. (IMC)

Don Quichotte à Dulcinee

Three songs for <u>baritone</u> and orchestra. Also available in a transposed edition for <u>tenor</u>. Published by Durand.

TITLE	COMP.	TESS.	TYPE	REMARKS
(1) Chanson romanesque	Bb-f	f-c1		Not fast. Interpretatively and rhythmically not easy.
(2) Chanson épique	A-f1	c-c1		Very slow and sustained. Interpretatively not easy.

441

TITLE	COMP.	TESS.	TYPE	REMARKS
(3) Chanson à boire	B-f1	e-eb1		Very rapid and spirited. Musically and interpretatively complex. Demands some flexibility and an excellent pianist.

Histoires Naturelles

A series of songs which are most suitable for <u>medium or high</u> voices. Published by Durand.

TITLE	COMP.	TESS.	TYPE	REMARKS
(1) Le paon	c1-f2	same		Rather slow. Musically and interpretatively complex. Demands an accomplished pianist.
(2) Le grillon	db-f2	same		Delicate. One of the simpler songs of this series.
(3) Le cygne	d#1-e#2	same		Slow. Musically very complex. Demands an excellent pianist.
(4) Le martin-pêcheur	c#1-e2	same		Slow. Musically complex.
(5) La pintade	c#1-f2	same		Rapid. Musically and interpretatively very complex. Demands an excellent pianist.

L'Enfant et les Sortilèges

Edition: Durand

It seemed best to list the following three airs from "L'enfant et les Sortilèges" in this section instead of in that devoted to the operatic excerpts, as they are more frequently encountered on the concert programs than on the operatic stage and could hardly be classed as standard operatic material.

TITLE	COMP.	TESS.	TYPE	REMARKS
Air de l'enfant	eb-d2	f1-bb1	Mezzo-soprano or soprano	Sustained, delicate. Vocally not taxing.
Air de l'horloge	Bb-g1	same	Baritone or mezzo-soprano	Rapid, vigorous. Demands very facile articulation.

442

TITLE	COMP.	TESS.	TYPE	REMARKS
				Humorous. Musically and interpretatively not easy. Demands an accomplished pianist.
Air du feu	d1-c3	g1-g2	Coloratura soprano	Fast, rather vigorous. In parts very florid. Musically and interpretatively not easy. Demands an accomplished pianist.
Les grands vents venus d'outremer	c♯1-f♯2	d♯1-d♯2	Most suitable for medium voices	Musically complex. Demands an excellent pianist. (Durand)
Manteau de fleurs	(a♯)c♯1-g♯2	d♯1-d♯2	Most suitable for high or medium voices	Animated, delicate. Demands facile articulation. Musically not easy. Demands an accomplished pianist. (Durand)
Nicolette	b-f♯2	f♯1-d2	All voices	Animated. Demands facile articulation. Interpretatively not easy. (Durand)
Noël des jouets	b♯-f♯2	d1-b1	All voices	Not fast. Musically and interpretatively not easy. Demands an accomplished pianist. Has an effective ending. (IMC)
Rêves	d1-f2	d1-d2	All voices	Very sustained, subdued. Demands good command of pp. Has an uncommonly sparse accompaniment. (Durand)

TITLE	COMP.	TESS.	TYPE	REMARKS
Ronde	c♯1-a2	f♯1-f♯2	High voices	Rapid. Demands facile articulation. (Durand)
Ronsard à son âme	c♯1-e2	f♯1-c♯2	Medium or low voices	Sustained, subdued. Has an uncommonly sparse accompaniment. (Durand)
Sainte	c1-g2	f1-d2	Not suitable for very low voices	Slow, sustained, very delicate. Demands good command of pp and an accomplished pianist. (Durand)

Shéhérazade

Three songs for voice and orchestra. Published by Durand and by International Music Co.

(1) Asie	d♭1-g2	same	Most suitable for medium or high voices	The longest of the three songs, the most complex musically and interpretatively, and the least suitable for a performance with piano.
(2) La flûte enchantée	d♯1-f♯2	g♯1-e2	Most suitable for high voices	Delicate. The most performed of the three songs. When sung separately one should remember that the text calls for a woman singer. Demands an accomplished pianist.
(3) L'indifférent	c♯1-e2	d♯1-b1	Most suitable for medium voices	Slow. Demands good command of pp. Interpretatively complex.
Sur l'herbe	c1-g2	same	Most suitable for medium or high voices	Musically and interpretatively very complex. (Durand)

444

TITLE	COMP.	TESS.	TYPE	REMARKS
Trois beaux oiseaux du paradis	b♭-g2	e♭1-e♭2	High or medium voices	Sustained, delicate. (Durand)
Vocalise	b♭-g2	e♭1-e♭2	High or medium voices	A vocalized habanera. Has some rather intricate florid passages. (Hettich, Répertoire moderne de vocalises, Leduc, Paris) Reprinted by Marks.

See also: "Trois Poèmes de Mallarmé" for medium voices.
"Chansons Madécasses," three songs for high or
medium voices, flute, cello and piano.

RHENÉ-BATON
(1879–1940)

TITLE	COMP.	TESS.	TYPE	REMARKS
Berceuse	b-d2	d1-b1	Most suitable for medium or low voices	Delicate, sustained. (From Chansons Douces, 12 songs for medium or low voices, Durand)
L'âme des iris	d1-e2	a1-e2	All voices	Slow, sustained, subdued. (Durand)
Il pleut des pétales de fleurs	c♯1-e2	e1-b1	Medium or low voices	Slow, somewhat declamatory. Demands in parts considerable dramatic intensity. (Durand)
Tendresse ·	b-f2	e♭1-d♭2	All voices	Delicate, sustained. (Durand)

GUY ROPARTZ
(1864–1955)

TITLE	COMP.	TESS.	TYPE	REMARKS
Berceuse	c1-e2	e1-c2	Women's voices	Very sustained. (OD)

445

MANUEL ROSENTHAL
(b. 1904)

TITLE	COMP.	TESS.	TYPE	REMARKS
Le marabout	c1-eb2	ab1-db2	High or medium voices	An amusing, monotonous character song. Musically and interpretatively not easy. (No. 4 of the "Chansons de Bleu," a set of twelve children's songs, published by Eschig)
Le petit chat est mort	db1-f2	f1-eb2	High or medium voices	Slow, musically and interpretatively not easy. (From "Chansons de Bleu," published by Eschig.)

Ronsardises

A cycle of five songs for high or medium voices. Only the first, third and fifth songs are listed here. (Eschig)

TITLE	COMP.	TESS.	TYPE	REMARKS
(1) Epitaphe de Thomas	c1-bb2	g1-f2		Slow, sustained. Demands an accomplished pianist.
(3) Epitaphe pour luymesmes	e1-a2	a1-g2		Sustained, tranquil but not slow. Effective ending. Demands an accomplished pianist.
(5) L'Arondelle	c#1-a#2	f#1-f#2		Fast, animated, lively. Demands facile articulation, some flexibility, a good command of high pp and an accomplished pianist.

ALBERT ROUSSEL
(1869–1937)

TITLE	COMP.	TESS.	TYPE	REMARKS
A un jeune gentilhomme	c1-g2	f1-d2	Soprano or mezzo-soprano	Rapid and light. Demands facile articulation and an

TITLE	COMP.	TESS.	TYPE	REMARKS
				accomplished pianist. See "Don't come in, sir, please" by J. A. Carpenter, and also by Cyril Scott. (Rouart)
Amoureux séparés	c1-g♭2	g1-e2	High or medium voices	Rather animated. Has a vigorous middle section. (Rouart)
Le bachelier de Salamanque	c1-g2	g1-e♭2	Medium or high voices, except a very light soprano	Animated. Demands facile articulation and an accomplished pianist. Musically not easy. (Durand)
Le jardin mouillé	c1-f♯2	g1-e♭2	All, except very low voices	Delicate. Musically not easy. Demands an accomplished pianist. (Rouart)
Nuit d'automne	d♭1-g2	f1-d2	Not suitable for very light, high voices	Slow, somewhat declamatory. Musically not easy. (Rouart)
Réponse d'une épouse sage	d♯1-a2	f♯1-e2	Soprano	Sustained, somewhat declamatory. Interpretatively not easy. (Durand)

CAMILLE SAINT-SAËNS
(1835–1921)

Almost all of Saint-Saëns' many songs are effective and masterfully written. "Danse macabre," "L'attente," "Tournoiement" and "Le bonheur est chose légère" are particularly recommended, being perhaps among his most characteristic songs.

Editions: Durand
         Collection of 12 songs published by G. Schirmer.

TITLE	COMP.	TESS.	TYPE	REMARKS
Aimons-nous	g♭1-a♭2	c2-f2	All voices	Very sustained, effective. (40 IMC)

447

TITLE	COMP.	TESS.	TYPE	REMARKS
Au cimetière (Mélodies Persanes)	e1-a2	a1-f2	Most suitable for high voices	Sustained. Demands good command of high pp.
Clair de lune	db1-eb2	eb1-bb1	Not too suitable for very light, high voices	Delicate.
Danse macabre	bb-eb2	d1-bb1	Medium or low voices	Very rapid and dramatic. Demands facile articulation and an excellent pianist. (40 IMC)
Domine, ego credidi (Christmas Oratorio)	f-a1	g-f1	Tenor	Solo with chorus. Sustained. (Score, GS)
Expectans dominum (Christmas Oratorio)	b-f#2	e1-c#2	Alto or mezzo-soprano	Sustained. (Score, GS)
Guitares et mandolines	g1-g2	a1-e2	Not too suitable for very heavy, low voices	Light and rapid. Demands flexibility and an accomplished pianist. See G. Grovlez.
La cloche	dbb1-ab2	ab1-f2	All voices	Very sustained. Has an effective climax.
La feuille de peuplier	b-e2	g1-e2	All voices	Delicate and animated. Requires good command of pp.
La libellule	c1-d3 (e3)	f#1-f#2	Coloratura soprano or light soprano	An effective waltz song. Somewhat florid.
La sérénité	c1-f2	f1-d2	All voices	Very sustained.
La solitaire	d1-g#2	f#1-d#2	Women's voices, except a very light soprano	Rapid. Demands facile articulation and some flexibility. Effective.
L'attente	e1-g2	a1-f2	All women's voices, except a light soprano	Rapid and dramatic. Demands facile articulation. (40 IMC)

TITLE	COMP.	TESS.	TYPE	REMARKS
Le bonheur est chose légère	d1-b2	g1-g2	Most suitable for high voices	Animated, light, delicate. (40 IMC)
Le lever de la lune	b-f♯2	f♯1-d♯2	Not too suitable for very light, high voices	The vocal line is very sustained.
Mai	g1-f♯2 (a2)	a1-e2	Medium or high voices	Light and rapid. Demands facile articulation and an excellent pianist.
Tournoiement (Songe d'opium, from "Poésies Persanes")	d1-g2	f1-f2	Not too suitable for very low voices	Very rapid. Demands facile articulation and an excellent pianist. Interpretatively not easy.
Tristesse	c1-g2	e1-c2	Not suitable for very light, high voices	Demands in parts considerable dramatic intensity. Slow.
Vocalise (The nightingale and the rose)	d1-d3	g1-g2	Coloratura soprano	Slow, florid. Demands good command of high pp. (CF)

ERIK SATIE
(1866–1925)

TITLE	COMP.	TESS.	TYPE	REMARKS
Daphénéo	d1-d2	f♯1-b1	All voices	An amusing, delicate song. Interpretatively not easy. (Rouart)
La statue de bronze	b♭-f2	d1-d2	Not suitable for very light, high voices	An amusing song. Interpretatively not easy. (Rouart)
Le chapelier	a-a2	f♯1-e2	All voices	A parody on Gounod to the words from Alice in Wonderland. (Rouart)

TITLE	COMP.	TESS.	TYPE	REMARKS

HENRI SAUGUET
(b. 1901)

TITLE	COMP.	TESS.	TYPE	REMARKS
Chasse	b-a2	f#1-f2	High or medium voices	Sustained, with animated middle section. (Rouart)
Printemps	d1-a2	a1-f#2	Most suitable for light, high voices	A lively pastoral with some florid passages. (Rouart)
Songe	c1-a2	g1-f2	All voices	Sustained. (Rouart)

See also "Cirque," five songs, published by Rouart, Lerolle; "Six Mélodies sur des Poésies Symbolistes," published by Amphion; "La Voyante," three songs, published by Dyer.

FLORENT SCHMITT
(1870–1958)

TITLE	COMP.	TESS.	TYPE	REMARKS
Il pleure dans mon coeur	c#1-f#2	f#1-d2	High or medium voices	Sustained, subdued. See Debussy, Fauré, and Carpenter. (Durand)
Lied	c#1-e2	d#1-c#2	Medium or low voices	Slow, subdued, delicate. (Durand)
Nature morte	c#1-f#2	f1-d2	High or medium voices	Sustained, somewhat declamatory, subdued. (Baudoux)

DÉODAT DE SÉVERAC
(1873–1921)

TITLE	COMP.	TESS.	TYPE	REMARKS
Chanson de Blaisine	c1-g2	e1-c2	High voices	Sustained, delicate. (Demets)
Chanson pour le petit cheval	(b)d1-g2	same	All voices	Animated. Demands facile articulation and an accomplished pianist. In parts dramatic. (Rouart)
L'aube dans la montagne	d1-g2	f1-e2	High voices	Slow, subdued. Has very effective final climax. Demands an accomplished pianist. (Rouart)

TITLE	COMP.	TESS.	TYPE	REMARKS
Le ciel est pardessus le toit	e♭1-g♭2	g♭1-e♭2	High voices	Slow, somewhat declamatory. See "Prison" by Fauré, and "D'une prison" by Hahn. (Rouart)
Ma poupée chérie	d1-f♯2	f♯1-d2	Women's voices	Sustained, delicate, subdued. (Rouart)
Temps de neige	d1-g2	e1-d2 (H)	All voices	Delicate, subdued. (Rouart)
Les hiboux	c1-g2	g1-d2 (H)	Most suitable for men's voices	Slow, somber, sustained. (Rouart)

VICTOR STAUB

TITLE	COMP.	TESS.	TYPE	REMARKS
L'heure silencieuse	e♭1-g2	a♭1-e♭2	Most suitable for light, high voices	Delicate, sustained. Demands good command of pp. (Durand)

JOSEPH SZULC
(1874–1935)

TITLE	COMP.	TESS.	TYPE	REMARKS
Clair de lune	d♭1-g♭2	b♭1-f2	Not too suitable for very low, heavy voices	Slow, sustained. Demands good command of pp. See Debussy and Fauré. (40 IMC)
En sourdine	c1-f2 (a♭2)	e♭1-e♭2	Not too suitable for very low voices	Slow, sustained, subdued. Demands in parts considerable dramatic intensity as well as a good command of high pp. See Debussy, Fauré, and Poldowski. (Durand)
La lune blanche	d♭1-g2	g♭1-e2	All voices	Sustained, very subdued. Demands good command of high pp. See Fauré, "L'heure exquise" by Hahn and also by Poldowski, and "Apaisement" by Chausson. (Durand)

TITLE	COMP.	TESS.	TYPE	REMARKS
Mandoline	d1-a2 (b2)	g#1-e2	Soprano	Rapid, light. Demands some flexibility and an accomplished pianist. See Debussy, Fauré, Poldowski, and "Fêtes galantes" by Hahn. (Rouart)
Menuet	c1-g2	g1-d2	Not too suitable for very low voices	Delicate, rhythmically somewhat complex. (RIC)

AMBROISE THOMAS
(1811–1896)

Le soir	d1-ab2	ab1-f2	All voices	Delicate, sustained. (OD)

PIERRE VELLONES

Cinq épitaphes

Five short, amusing songs for medium or low voices. Demand
in parts very facile articulation and an accomplished pianist. Should
be sung without interruption as one piece. (Rouart)

(1) . . . d'une femme par son mari	c1-e2	g1-d2		Sustained section followed by one in recitative style.
(2) . . . d'une dévote	(b)d#1-e2	e1-c2		Sustained. Strong ending section.
(3) . . . d'un paresseux	d1-d2	eb1-bb1		Sustained, majestic.
(4) . . . du pauvre Scarron, par luimême	c1-e2	e1-c#2		Sustained.
(5) . . . d'un grand médecin	(a)c#1-f2	g1-c2		Animated, fast, has some sustained passages. Demands facile articulation. In grand manner almost throughout.

CHARLES MARIE WIDOR
(1845–1937)

Je ne veux pas autre chose	d1-f2	f1-d2	All voices	Sustained, subdued. (Hamelle)

TITLE	COMP.	TESS.	TYPE	REMARKS
L'aurore	d♯1-f♯2	f♯1-d♯2	All voices	Sustained. The pianoforte part is animated. (Hamelle)
Le plongeur	c♯1-f♯2	f♯1-d2	Most suitable for men's voices	Very animated, rhythmical. Vigorous narrative song. Demands facile articulation and an accomplished pianist. (Hamelle)
Nuit d'étoiles	d♭1-g♭2	a♭1-f2	Not too suitable for very heavy, low voices	Delicate and sustained. Demands a good command of high pp. See Debussy. (GS)

AMERICAN AND BRITISH

The selection of American and British songs for this volume presented a not inconsiderable problem. American and British composers of the nineteenth century, the century in which the song experienced its greatest growth as a form of musical expression, produced few songs that were accorded a more than fleeting and local success. This is a fact which cannot be denied, no matter what interpretation one attaches to it or to what causes one attributes it. Yet, since the beginning of the twentieth century American and British composers seem to have produced a veritable avalanche of songs. These songs, like songs in all countries and at all times, seem to fall into three categories: (1) Purely imitative songs, well made, flattering to the voice and effective, but as a rule of little musical value. (2) Purely experimental songs: as a rule somewhat awkwardly written and often overly insistent on being "modern" at any cost. (3) Songs of undeniable individuality and musical merit, even though not necessarily on the same level of inspiration as, for instance, Schubert or Debussy.

The songs belonging to the first category naturally outweigh all others in numbers, in so far as the published material is concerned. Their success is often considerable at the moment, but after a few years they seem to appear less and less frequently on concert programs and soon seem to disappear into the limbo of forgotten music, to be supplanted by more recent productions of the same kind. They fulfill a certain definite need, especially as teaching material, and, though often excellent in their own way, cannot be classed as anything of a more permanent nature. It seemed only fair to include many such songs in this list, though no doubt in a few years a considerable number of them will be justly forgotten. Only a few songs of purely experimental nature have been included. Musical experimentation, necessary and welcome as it is, can hardly command general attention, unless the emotional and technical persuasiveness of the composer makes the fact that such experimentation has been attempted seem of small import in comparison with the impact it carries as an emotionally satisfying or stimulating work.

Thus, the majority of the songs listed below are chosen from the first and third categories. This selection like any other, can and will no doubt be criticized on many grounds, and even if accepted will seem incomplete, for admittedly many a song of merit has not been listed. This, however, is only natural in view of the fact that it is an inhumanly arduous task to examine, even superficially, all the American and British songs published in the past fifty years, for their number is startlingly large.

It seems only fair to add that in the opinion of this writer American popular music abounds in songs written in a much more indigenous idiom and often immeasurably superior in content as well as in workmanship to some of the examples of the so-called concert and teaching songs listed below. It seems a pity that songs from the musical comedies by composers like George Gershwin, Cole Porter and Jerome Kern are, for some unknown reason, not as yet considered serious music, while many an imitative, empty, bombastic and poorly executed ballad is still charitably referred to as an "art song."

NOTE: (Br.) indicates a British composer.

For songs with original English texts see the lists of the following composers: Castelnuovo-Tedesco and Hindemith.

TITLE	COMP.	TESS.	TYPE	REMARKS

ERNST BACON

TITLE	COMP.	TESS.	TYPE	REMARKS
A clear midnight	G♯-c♯1	B-g♯	Alto or bass	Slow, very sustained, subdued. Poem by W. Whitman. (New Music) See Vaughan Williams' "Nocturne."
Ancient Christmas carol	b♯-e2	same	Medium or low voices	Slow, sustained, subdued. (New Music)
Five poems by Emily Dickinson	c1-g2 (a2)	e1-e2	High voices	Five short, delicate songs. Interpretatively not easy. (GS)
Gentle greeting (Quiet Airs)	c♯1-g2	d1-f2	Most suitable for high voices	Slow, sustained, subdued. Demands good command of high p. Poem by E. Brontë. (Mercury)

TITLE	COMP.	TESS.	TYPE	REMARKS
Is there such a thing as day?	d#1-f#2	g#1-d#2	Most suitable for light, high voices	Sustained, very delicate. Poem by E. Dickinson. (AMP)
Omaha	c1-f2 (ab2)	e1-c2	Not suitable for light voices	Vigorous. Musically not easy. Demands an accomplished pianist. Poem by C. Sandburg. (New Music)
The grass so little has to do	c1-f#2 (a2)	d1-d2	Most suitable for light soprano	Very delicate, graceful. Poem by E. Dickinson. (AMP)
The little stone (Quiet Airs)	c#1-g2	e1-e2	Most suitable for high voices	Sustained. Poem by E. Dickinson. (Mercury)
To musique, to becalme his fever (Quiet Airs)	c#1-g2	f#1-e2	Most suitable for high voices	Slow, sustained, generally subdued. In parts demands some facile articulation. Poem by R. Herrick. (Mercury)
Velvet people	c1-e2	c#1-c2	All voices	Fast, animated. The vocal line is sustained. (CF)

See also "Along Unpaved Roads," arrangements of American folk songs published by Leeds.

GRANVILLE BANTOCK (Br.)

A feast of lanterns	f#1-a2	a1-f#2	All voices	Rapid. Demands facile articulation and an accomplished pianist. (Elkin)
Silent strings	f1-g2	g1-eb2 (H)	All voices, except a very light soprano	Sustained, somewhat declamatory. Has an effective final climax. (BH)
The celestial weaver	b#-f#2	e1-e2	Medium or low voices	Slow, declamatory. (CHES)
Yung-Yang	e1-g2	f1-e2	All voices	Animated, graceful. (Elkin)

456

SAMUEL BARBER

Samuel Barber, one of the outstanding American composers, has written a considerable number of excellent songs which ought to be welcomed by every serious singer as valuable additions to his repertoire.

A complete list of his songs may be obtained from his publishers, G. Schirmer.

TITLE	COMP.	TESS.	TYPE	REMARKS
A nun takes a veil	g1-g2 (H)	bb1-f2	Women's voices	Slow, somewhat declamatory. Poem by G. Hopkins.

Hermit Songs

A cycle of ten settings of anonymous Irish texts of the eighth to the thirteenth centuries written by monks and scholars. Best performed as a cycle. Originally written for soprano.

TITLE	COMP.	TESS.	TYPE	REMARKS
(1) At Saint Patrick's purgatory	c#1-f#2	e1-d#2	All voices, except bass	Animated. Rhythmically complex.
(2) Church bell at night	d#1-c#2	same	All voices	Very slow and sustained. Subdued. Short.
(3) St. Ita's vision	c1-ab2	eb1-g2	All voices, except bass	A recitative and a sustained song. Demands excellent command of high pp and an accomplished pianist.
(4) The heavenly banquet	d1-g2	f1-f2	Not too suitable for very light, high voices	Lively, rather robust, rhythmically complex. Demands facile articulation and an excellent pianist.
(5) The crucifixion	d1-f2	e1-d2	All voices, except bass	Slow, sustained, plaintive, for the most part subdued.
(6) Sea-snatch	c1-bb2	g1-g2	Not suitable for very light voices	Fast, robust, dramatic. Musically not easy. Demands an accomplished pianist.
(7) Promiscuity	g1-c2	same	All voices	A very short parlando piece.

TITLE	COMP.	TESS.	TYPE	REMARKS
(8) The monk and his cat	d1-e2	f1-d2	All voices	Delicate, gently humorous, rhythmically complex.
(9) The praises of God	e1-g2	g1-e2	All voices	Animated. Has florid passages.
(10) The desire for hermitage	d1-g2	f1-f2	All voices	Sustained. Not musically easy. Has dramatic climaxes and demands in parts good command of high pp. Demands an accomplished pianist.
I hear an army	db1-ab2	g1-eb2	Not too suitable for very light, high voices	Animated, vigorous, dramatic. Demands an accomplished pianist. Poem by J. Joyce.
Lord Jesus Christ!	e1-a2	f♯1-f2	Soprano	Slow and very sustained. Demands good command of high pp. Short but powerfully evocative. Text is from the famous "Prayers of Kierkegaard."
Monks and raisins	db1-f2 (L)	d1-e2	All voices	Animated, light. Rhythmically difficult. Demands flexibility and facile articulation.
Nocturne	d♯1-g♯2	same	All voices	Sustained. Has a dramatic climax. Demands an excellent pianist. Musically not easy.
Nuvoletta	b♯-b♯2	e1-f♯2	Soprano	A rather extended setting of an excerpt from "Finnegans Wake" by J. Joyce. For the most part a sort of a waltz. Has a florid cadenza. Demands excellent

458

TITLE	COMP.	TESS.	TYPE	REMARKS
				command of high pp. Interpretatively not easy. Demands an accomplished pianist.
Rain has fallen	d1-e2	d1-c2	All voices, except a very light soprano	Sustained, delicate. In parts demands considerable dramatic intensity. Musically not easy. Demands an accomplished pianist. Poem by J. Joyce.
Sleep now	c1-f2	e1-d2	Not too suitable for very low voices	Delicate. Demands some flexibility. Musically and interpretatively not easy. Poem by J. Joyce. See Kagen.
Sure on this shining night	b-e2	e1-d2	All voices	Sustained.
The daisies	c1-f2 (L)	f1-d2	All voices	Graceful and light. Delicate. Has a folk-song character.
With rue my heart is laden	e1-f2	f#1-e2 (H)	All voices	Sustained, subdued. Poem by A. E. Housman.

See also "Mélodies passagères," a cycle of five songs to the French poems by R. M. Rilke; "Knoxville, Tenn. 1915" for soprano and orchestra; "Dover Beach" for medium voice and string quartet.

ARNOLD BAX (Br.)

The songs of Arnold Bax belong undoubtedly among the most significant and interesting songs of contemporary composers written to English texts.

The sixteen songs listed below are sufficiently characteristic of his manner of writing to suit the purposes of this volume. "I heard a piper piping," "Cradle song," and "The pigeons" are most highly recommended to those who wish to acquaint themselves with his songs.

Editions: Chester
Murdoch & Murdoch

TITLE	COMP.	TESS.	TYPE	REMARKS
A Christmas carol	d1-a2	f1-d2	Not too suitable for very light, high voices	Very sustained, majestic.
A lullaby	b-f♯2	e1-e2	Soprano or mezzo-soprano	Delicate. Demands some flexibility and an accomplished pianist.
A milking sian	d1-g2	e1-e2	Soprano	Slow and delicate. Demands an accomplished pianist.
Across the door	c1-f2	eb1-cb2	Women's voices	Musically and interpretatively not easy. Demands an excellent pianist.
As I came over the grey, grey hills	bb-gb2	eb1-eb2	Most suitable for medium or low voices	A solemn, march-like song. Demands an accomplished pianist.
Beg Innish	c1-g2	e1-e2	Most suitable for men's voices	Spirited and rhythmical. Demands facile articulation and an accomplished pianist.
Cradle song	db1-gb2	eb1-eb2	Soprano or mezzo-soprano	Subdued, delicate. Demands good command of high pp and an accomplished pianist.
I heard a piper piping	b-e2	e1-d2	All voices	Slow. Demands good command of pp and an accomplished pianist. See Norman Peterkin.
In the morning	e1-f2	same	High or medium voices	Sustained, subdued. (OX)
Rann of exile	d1-g2	e1-d2	Not too suitable for very light, high voices	Sustained, somber. Demands in parts considerable dramatic intensity.

TITLE	COMP.	TESS.	TYPE	REMARKS
Rann of wandering	bb-f2	eb1-eb2	Not suitable for light, high voices	Vigorous.
Shieling song	c#1-a2	d1-d2	Soprano	Animated, light. Demands some flexibility.
The enchanted fiddle	c1-a2	d1-d2	Most suitable for men's voices	Very rapid and gay. Demands facile articulation and an accomplished pianist.
The pigeons	b-d2	f1-db2	Women's voices	Slow and subdued. Musically and interpretatively not easy.
The white peace	eb1-gb2	g1-eb2	All voices	Very slow and sustained.
To Eire	c1-f2	f1-eb2	All voices, except a very light soprano	Sustained, grave. Demands an accomplished pianist.

See also a Celtic song cycle — five songs. (Chester)

MRS. H. H. A. BEACH

TITLE	COMP.	TESS.	TYPE	REMARKS
Ah, love but a day	eb1-a2	ab1-f2 (H)	All voices	Sustained. Has effective climaxes. Poem by R. Browning. (Schmidt)
The year's at the spring	ab1-ab2	ab1-f2 (H)	All voices	Rapid, has an effective final climax. Poem by R. Browning. (Schmidt)

ARTHUR BENJAMIN (Br.)

TITLE	COMP.	TESS.	TYPE	REMARKS
Before dawn	e1-f2	f1-d2	High voices	Animated, subdued. Demands facile articulation. Christmas song. (CUR)
Calm sea and mist	c1-f2	c1-c2	High or medium voices	Sustained and subdued. (CUR)

TITLE	COMP.	TESS.	TYPE	REMARKS
Hedgerow	d♯1-f2	f1-c2	High or medium voices	Very animated, subdued. (CUR)
The piper	e1-a2	f♯1-e2	Most suitable for high voices	Rapid. Demands facile articulation and an accomplished pianist. See M. Head. (BH)
The wasp	c1-f2	e1-e2	High or medium voices	Animated, delicate. Demands an accomplished pianist. (CUR)

WILLIAM BERGSMA

Six Songs to Poems by e. e. cummings
Published by Carl Fischer

(1) When God lets my body be	e1-a2	f1-f♯2	High voices	Slow, sustained. Somewhat declamatory. Demands an excellent pianist.
(2) Doll's boy's asleep	e1-b♭2	f♯1-f♯2	High voices	Slow, sustained. Somewhat declamatory in parts.
(3) Hist whist little ghost-things	d♯1-f2	f♯1-e2	High voices	Declamatory style throughout. Demands facile articulation and some characterization. Demands an accomplished pianist. See Duke.
(4) Thy fingers make early flowers	e1-a2	f♯1-f♯2	High voices	Sustained, very subdued. Demands good command of high pp and an accomplished pianist.
(5) It may not always be so	e1-a♭2	g♯1-g2	Tenor	Some parts are sustained, others somewhat declamatory. Demands good command of high pp.
(6) Jimmie's got a goil	g1-a2	same	High voices	Rapid. Demands facile articulation. Has an effective ending. Demands an accomplished pianist.

462

TITLE	COMP.	TESS.	TYPE	REMARKS

LORD BERNERS (Br.)

Theodore or the pirate king	c#1-f#2	eb1-eb2	Medium voices	A short, amusing song. (CHES)

LEONARD BERNSTEIN

Afterthought	a-g#2	d1-e2	Most suitable for dramatic soprano or mezzo-soprano	Sustained and grave. Demands considerable dramatic intensity, as well as a good command of high pp. (GS)
La Bonne Cuisine (1) Plum Pudding (2) Ox-tails (3) Tavouk gueunksis (4) Rabbit at top speed	b-b2		Most suitable for soprano or very high mezzo-soprano	Four very amusing "Recipes for Voice and Piano." Original text is French. The excellent English version by the composer seems preferable. Demands in parts very facile articulation and an accomplished pianist. (GS)
Lamentation (Jeremiah Symphony)	c1-a2	f#1-f2	High mezzo-soprano	Sustained; in declamatory style. Demands considerable dramatic intensity. Hebrew text. (Harms)

MAURICE BESLY (Br.)

An epitaph	(ab)cb1-eb2	eb1-c2	Medium or low voices	Sustained. See Ivor Gurney. Poem by W. de la Mare. (CUR)
Listening	e1-a2 (b2)	g1-g2	High voices	Animated. Demands some flexibility and, in parts, some dramatic intensity. (CUR)
Three little fairy songs	db1-f2	eb1-eb2	Most suitable for soprano	Three short, animated, light songs. Demand some flexibility. (CHAP)

TITLE	COMP.	TESS.	TYPE	REMARKS

ARTHUR BLISS (Br.)

TITLE	COMP.	TESS.	TYPE	REMARKS
A child's prayer	f1-f2	a1-d2	Most suitable for soprano	Sustained, delicate. (CUR)
Lovelocks (Three Romantic Songs)	d1-f2	eb1-d2	High voices	Sustained, delicate. Demands good command of high pp. (Goodwin & Tabb)
Rich or poor	e1-f2	e1-d2	Most suitable for tenor or high baritone	Sustained and for the most part subdued. (CUR)
Seven American songs	bb-eb2	d1-eb2	All voices	Short songs and mostly sustained. Poems by E. St. Vincent Millay. (BH)
The buckle	b-f#2	e1-e2	Women's voices	Rapid and light, gently humorous. Demands an accomplished pianist. Poem by W. de la Mare. (CUR)
The hare (Three Romantic Songs)	e1-g#2	g1-e2	Soprano	Delicate. Demands good command of high pp and an accomplished pianist. (Goodwin & Tabb)
Three jolly gentlemen	eb1-gb2	f1-f2	High voices	Rapid, amusing. Demands some flexibility and an accomplished pianist. Poem by W. de la Mare. (Composer's Music Corp., New York)

CARRIE JACOBS BOND

TITLE	COMP.	TESS.	TYPE	REMARKS
A perfect day	g1-f2 (H)	same	All voices	Sustained, effective. (BMC)
I love you truly	f1-eb2 (H)	same	All voices	Sustained, effective. (BMC)

PAUL BOWLES

Blue Mountain Ballads

Poems by T. Williams. Published by G. Schirmer.

TITLE	COMP.	TESS.	TYPE	REMARKS
(1) Heavenly grass	b-e2	e1-d2	All voices	Sustained. Folk-like. Demands good command of high pp.
(2) Lonesome man	db1-eb2	same	Men's voices	Animated, in the manner of a rag-time.
(3) Cabin	c#1-c#2	same	All voices	Sustained, in folk vein.
(4) Sugar in the cane	d1-f#2	e1-e2	Not suitable for very light voices	Animated, in folk vein. Employs jazz rhythms.
Letter to Freddy	eb1-eb2	same	Women's voices	Interpretatively not easy. Text by Gertrude Stein. (New Music)
On a quiet conscience	bb-f2	eb1-c2	Medium voices	Sustained, generally quiet. Has frequent changes of meter. Poem by Charles I. (Music Press)
Once a lady was here	c1-eb2	same	All voices	Sustained, calm. Alternating 4/8 and 5/8 meter. Text by the composer. (GS)

FRANK BRIDGE (Br.)

TITLE	COMP.	TESS.	TYPE	REMARKS
Fair daffodils	c1-d2	e1-c2	All voices	Animated, graceful. (Winthrop Rogers)
Love went a-riding	f1-g2	bb1-f2	Not too suitable for very light voices	Animated, vigorous, effective. Demands an accomplished pianist. (Winthrop Rogers)

TITLE	COMP.	TESS.	TYPE	REMARKS
Mantle of blue	d1-f2	g1-d2	Most suitable for women's voices	Sustained, subdued. See "Cradle song" by Arnold Bax. (Winthrop Rogers)
O that it were so	d1-g2 (b2)	a1-f#2 (H)	All voices	Sustained. Has an effective climax. (CHAP)
When you are old	d1-g2	e1-e2	High or medium voices	Sustained. Demands in parts considerable dramatic intensity as well as a good command of high pp. (CHAP)

BENJAMIN BRITTEN (Br.)

A Charm of Lullabies

A cycle for <u>mezzo-soprano</u>. Demands an accomplished pianist. This cycle, as well as all other Britten songs, is published by Boosey & Hawkes.

(1) A cradle song	bb-e2	eb1-c2		Sustained, quiet. Demands good command of ppp. Text by W. Blake.
(2) The highland balou	b#-e#2	d#1-d#2		Rhythmic. Demands some flexibility. Generally quiet. Marked rhythm in the accompaniment. Text by R. Burns.
(3) Sephestia's lullaby	a-e2	b-c2		Slow, somewhat sustained sections interspersed with light allegretto movements.
(4) A charm	a#-e2	d1-db2		A song of several very contrasting moods and tempi. Demands flexibility and facile articulation.
(5) The nurse's song	a-e1	bb-c2		Sustained. Starts and ends with unaccompanied passages. Demands some flexibility.

TITLE	COMP.	TESS.	TYPE	REMARKS
Canticle I. My beloved is mine and I am his	c♯1-g2	e1-f♯2	Not suitable for very light, high voices	A lengthy song of contrasting moods and tempi. Has recitative and sustained sections and florid passages. Demands good command of high pp, flexibility, and an accomplished pianist.
Canticle III. Still falls the rain	c1-g2	g1-f2	High voices	Originally written for tenor, horn and piano. Except for the last section (Var. VI) which is slow and sustained, the vocal part is mainly in the style of a free recitative. Demands facile articulation and an accomplished pianist. Text is based on the crucifixion.
Fish in the unruffled lakes	c♯1-a♯2	d1-f♯2 (H)	All voices	Animated. Demands considerable flexibility and facile articulation. Demands an accomplished pianist.
Les Illuminations	b-b♭2	f1-f2		A cycle in nine movements for <u>soprano</u> or <u>tenor</u> and string orchestra. Piano score available. Demands a highly accomplished pianist. French text by A. Rimbeau.

On This Island

A cycle of five songs most suitable for <u>high voices</u>, with poems by W. H. Auden. Demands an accomplished pianist.

(1) Let the florid music praise	c♯1-a2	f♯1-g2		Sustained, majestic. Has one long bravura cadenza.

TITLE	COMP.	TESS.	TYPE	REMARKS
(2) Now the leaves are falling fast	ab(c1)-bb2(ab2)	f1-f2		Slow. First section is somewhat agitated and demands flexibility and facile articulation. Last section is subdued and sustained.
(3) Seascape	c1-ab2	f1-f2		Generally sustained vocal line. Animated and forceful middle section. Last section is generally subdued and demands good command of high pp.
(4) Nocturne: Now thro' night's caressing grip	c1-g♯2	c1-e2		Sustained, generally subdued. Accompaniment consists mainly of sustained chords.
(5) As it is, plenty	d1-g2	e1-e2		Rhythmic, marked.
Our Hunting Fathers	g-b2	e1-g2		A symphonic cycle for soprano and orchestra. Piano-vocal score is available. Text by W. H. Auden and others.
Serenade	bb-bb2	f1-g2		A cycle of six songs for tenor, horn and string orchestra (or piano) with poems by Tennyson, Blake, Ben Jonson, Keats, and others.
Seven Sonnets of Michelangelo	c1-b2	g1-f♯2	Tenor	Seven songs on Italian texts. In parts demand some dramatic intensity, flexibility, and a good command of high ppp.
The birds	b-f2	e1-e2	Medium or low voices	Sustained. Folklike. Very soft. Text by H. Belloc.

TITLE	COMP.	TESS.	TYPE	REMARKS

The Holy Sonnets of John Donne

<u>For high voices, except a very light soprano.</u> Demand an excellent pianist.

TITLE	COMP.	TESS.	REMARKS
(1) Oh my blacke soule!	c♯1-g2	e♯1-f♯2	Very slow and sustained. Emotionally intense and heavy.
(2) Batter my heart	c♯1-a2	d1-g2	Rapid, highly agitated. Demands facile articulation and flexibility.
(3) O might those sighes and teares	g1-a2	b1-f♯2	Somewhat slow, sustained. For the most part subdued.
(4) Oh, to vex me	c1-g♯2	d1-f♯2	Rapid. Demands flexibility and facile articulation. Somewhat declamatory in parts. Ends with long cadenza.
(5) What if this present	d1-b♭2	e♭1-f2	Marked; in march tempo. Has a florid passage. Demands in parts dramatic intensity.
(6) Since she whom I loved	e1-a♭2	f1-f2	Very slow and sustained.
(7) At the round earth's imagined corners	d1-a2	g1-g2	Very slow, sustained, somewhat declamatory. Ends in unaccompanied passage.
(8) Thou hast made me	d1-a♭2	e♭1-g2	Rapid, animated. Vigorous for the most part. Demands flexibility.
(9) Death, be not proud	d♯1-g2	d♯1-f♯2	Sustained. Has contrasts in mood; in parts has dramatic intensity. Demands flexibility. Imposing ending.

TITLE	COMP.	TESS.	TYPE	REMARKS

War Requiem

(Oratorio)

TITLE	COMP.	TESS.	TYPE	REMARKS
After the blast of lightning	A-f1	d-e♭1	Baritone	Sustained. Has recitative passages and an animated middle section. (Score)
Bugles sang	A-f♯1	c-e♭1	Baritone	Sustained, generally subdued. (Score)
What passing-bells	f1-a♭2	g♭1-g♭2	Tenor	Brisk, animated. Vocal part is mostly sustained. (Score)
Winter Words	c1-a2	e1-e2		A cycle of eight songs for <u>high voice</u> and piano. Demands an accomplished pianist. Poems by T. Hardy.

GEORGE BUTTERWORTH (Br.)

TITLE	COMP.	TESS.	TYPE	REMARKS
Is my team plowing? (Shropshire Lad)	e♭1-e♭2	same	Men's voices	Sustained, somewhat declamatory. Text by A. E. Housman. (AUG)
Loveliest of trees (Shropshire Lad)	c♯1-e2	e1-e2	High or medium voices	Sustained. See John Duke. Text by A. E. Housman. (AUG)
Requiescat	d1-g2	g1-e2	High or medium voices	Delicate, subdued. Text by A. E. Housman. (AUG)
The lads in their hundreds	c♯1-e2	e1-c♯2	High or medium voices	Graceful, subdued. Text by A. E. Housman. (AUG)
Think no more, lad (Shropshire Lad)	c♯1-f2	e1-d2	Men's voices	Vigorous, spirited. Demands facile articulation. Text by A. E. Housman. (AUG)
When I was one-and-twenty (Shropshire Lad)	d1-e2	same	High or medium voices	Animated. In folk vein. Text by A. E. Housman. (AUG)

TITLE	COMP.	TESS.	TYPE	REMARKS
With rue my heart is laden (Bredon hill and Other Songs)	c#1-e2	e1-c#2	High or medium voices	Sustained, somber. Text by A. E. Housman. (AUG)

CHARLES WAKEFIELD CADMAN

TITLE	COMP.	TESS.	TYPE	REMARKS
At dawning	eb1-g2 (H)	f1-eb2	All voices	Sustained. Effective. (OD)
From the land of the sky blue water (Four American Indian Songs)	f1-f2 (H)	same	All voices	Sustained, effective. (E. H. Morris Co.)

LOUIS CAMPBELL-TIPTON

TITLE	COMP.	TESS.	TYPE	REMARKS
A spirit flower	db1-a2 (H)	f#1-gb2	All voices	Sustained. Has effective climaxes. Demands good command of high p. (GS)
The crying of water	f#1-g#2 (H)	b1-f#2	All voices	Sustained. In parts demands considerable dramatic intensity as well as a good command of pp. (GS)

JOHN ALDEN CARPENTER

The songs of John Alden Carpenter are too well known to need any introduction. With the exception of the "Gitanjali" cycle, however, few of his songs seem to have attained the popularity they deserve. The following list, though not complete, would seem sufficiently representative for the purposes of the volume.

Editions: G. Schirmer
A few songs published by O. Ditson

TITLE	COMP.	TESS.	TYPE	REMARKS
A cradle song	c1-eb2	eb1-c2	Women's voices, except a very light soprano	Slow, very sustained, subdued.

471

TITLE	COMP.	TESS.	TYPE	REMARKS
Berceuse de guerre	c1-g2	c1-bb1	Women's voices, except a very light soprano	Dramatic, interpretatively not easy. French text.
Bid me to live	bb-d2	db1-bb1	Medium or low voices	Slow, sustained.
Chanson d'automne	b-c#2	b-a1	Low voices	Slow, sustained, somewhat declamatory. See Hahn, "Les sanglots longs." French text.
Dansons la gigue	b-e1	f#1-d2	Medium or low voices	Rapid. French text. See Poldowski.
Don't ceare	c1-d2	same	Medium or low voices	An amusing, light Dorsetshire dialect song in folk vein. Demands facile articulation. Can be sung in English.

Gitanjali

A cycle of six songs on texts by Rabindranath Tagore.

	COMP.	TESS.	TYPE	REMARKS
(1) I am like a remnant of a cloud in autumn	bb-f2	eb1-eb2	Not suitable for light, high voices	Dramatic and declamatory.
(2) Light, my light	c1-g2	g1-e2	Not suitable for very light voices	Very animated, effective. The vocal line is very sustained.
(3) On the day when death will knock at my door	c1-f2	eb1-eb2	Not suitable for very light, high voices	Dramatic and declamatory.
(4) On the seashore of endless worlds	c1-f#2	eb1-c2	Not too suitable for very light, high voices	Musically and interpretatively not easy. Demands an accomplished pianist.
(5) The sleep that flits on baby's eyes	b-f#2	f#1-d2	High or medium voices	Slow, very delicate. Demands good command of high pp.

TITLE	COMP.	TESS.	TYPE	REMARKS
(6) When I bring to you colour'd toys	c♯1-f♯2	f♯1-c♯2	High or medium voices	Animated and light. Demands an accomplished pianist.
Go, lovely rose	c♯1-e♭2	f1-d♭2	Most suitable for medium voices	Graceful, delicate. See Roger Quilter.
If	d1-e2	g1-d2	All voices	Light and humorous.
Il pleure dans mon coeur	d1-d2	g1-c2	All voices	Delicate, very subdued. See Debussy, and "Spleen" by Fauré. French text.
Le ciel	c♯1-f♯2	g♯1-d♯2	High or medium voices, except a very light soprano	Slow. In parts demands considerable dramatic intensity. See "Prison" by Fauré and "D'une prison" by Hahn. French text.
Les silhouettes	c1-g2	f1-d2	Most suitable for high voices	Slow, somewhat declamatory. Demands good command of high p. English text.
Looking-glass river	b(a)-d2	d1-b1	Medium or low voices	Slow and sustained.
May the maiden	d1-g2	g1-d2	All voices	Slow, sustained, subdued.
Rest	c1-g2	e1-d2	Not too suitable for very low voices	Slow, sustained, very subdued. Demands good command of high pp.
Serenade	e♭1-a2 (c3)	f1-f2 (H)	Not too suitable for very low voices	Animated. Interpretatively not easy. Demands an accomplished pianist. Published also in a low key, which is quite suitable for high voices (c1-a2).

TITLE	COMP.	TESS.	TYPE	REMARKS
Slumber song	b-g♯2	e1-e2	All voices	Slow, sustained. In parts demands considerable dramatic intensity. Musically and interpretatively not easy.
The cock shall crow	b-e2	e1-d2	Medium or low voices	Animated and light. Demands facile articulation.
The day is no more	g♯-d♯2	d♯1-d♯2	Low voices	Slow, sustained, subdued. Interpretatively not easy. Text by Rabindranath Tagore.
The green river	b-e2	f♯1-b1	Medium or low voices	Slow, sustained, somewhat declamatory. In parts demands considerable dramatic intensity.
The player queen	b♭-e♭2 (g♭2)	e♭1-b♭1	Mezzo-soprano or alto	Sustained.
The pools of peace	d1-f2	f1-d2	Not too suitable for very low voices	Slow, sustained, delicate.
To one unknown	a-d♯2	b-b1	Medium or low voices	Sustained. Has an imposing climax in the middle section.

Watercolors

Four Chinese tone poems

(1) On a screen	b♭-d♭2	d♭1-c2	Medium or low voices	Slow, sustained, very subdued.
(2) The odalisque	e♭1-e♭2	same	All voices	Light, delicate.
(3) Highwaymen	c1-f2	d1-d2	All voices, except a very light soprano	Slow, somewhat declamatory.
(4) To a young gentleman	c1-f2	e♭1-d♭2	All voices	Animated, light, humorous. See also Cyril Scott.

TITLE	COMP.	TESS.	TYPE	REMARKS
			ELLIOT CARTER	
The rose family	e♭1-f2	f1-d2	Most suitable for men's voices	Sustained vocal line. Accompaniment for the most part is detached and with constant graceful movement. (AMP)
Voyage	c♯1-g2	c♯1-f♯2	All voices	Sustained. Demands good command of high pp. Subdued last section. (Valley Music Press)
Warble for lilac-time	b♭(e1)-a2	e♭1-f2	Not suitable for very low voices	Rapid, brilliant. A song with contrasting moods. Demands flexibility, facile articulation, and an accomplished pianist. Vocally not easy. Text by W. Whitman. (Peer International)
			GEORGE W. CHADWICK	
A ballad of trees and the master	G-e♭1	c-c1	Baritone	A narrative song. Religious text. (OD)
Allah	c♯1-g♯2	e1-c♯2 (H)	Not too suitable for very light, high voices	Slow and sustained. (Schmidt)
			THEODORE CHANLER	
Eight epitaphs	b-f2	d1-d2	High or medium voices	Eight short songs to poems by Walter de la Mare. Musically and interpretatively not easy. (Arrow Music Press)

TITLE	COMP.	TESS.	TYPE	REMARKS

Four Rhymes from Peacock Pie

Poems by Walter de la Mare. Published by Associated Music Press.

TITLE	COMP.	TESS.	TYPE	REMARKS
(1) The ship of Rio	b-f#2	c#1-c#2	Most suitable for men's voices	Brisk, demands facile articulation. In the style of a sea chanty. Demands an accomplished pianist.
(2) Old shellover	eb1-fb2	ab1-fb2	Medium voices	Sustained. Demands a good command of high pp.
(3) Cake and sack	eb1-f2	f1-f2	High or medium voices	Light. Demands a good command of high pp and flexibility. Demands an accomplished pianist.
(4) Tillie	d1-f#2	e1-d2	All voices, except bass	Sustained, in waltz rhythm. Text is narrative.
I rise when you enter	c#-g1	e-e1	Tenor or high baritone	Very animated, light. Effective. (GS)
Memory	c#1-f#2	c#1-c#2	Not suitable for very low voices	Animated, somewhat delicate, with a fast and constantly moving line in the accompaniment. Demands facile articulation and an accomplished pianist. (AMP)
The doves	c1-f2	f1-eb2	Most suitable for high voices	Vocal line is sustained and graceful. Accompaniment is percussive throughout except for occasional sustained bass line. (Hargail Music Press)
The lamb	c1-d2	eb1-c2	All voices	Graceful, in the style of a carol. (AMP)

TITLE	COMP.	TESS.	TYPE	REMARKS
The policeman in the park	ab-d2	bb-d2	Most suitable for men's voices	Slow, sustained. In parts slightly declamatory. Narrative. (GS)

See also "The Children," a cycle of nine songs for <u>high and medium</u> voices. (GS)

ERNEST CHARLES

TITLE	COMP.	TESS.	TYPE	REMARKS
My lady walks in loveliness	e1-g2 (a2)	a1-eb2	Most suitable for men's voices	Sustained, has an effective climax. (GS)
When I have sung my songs	d1-g2	f1-d2	All voices	Sustained. Effective encore song. (GS)

REBECCA CLARKE (Br.)

TITLE	COMP.	TESS.	TYPE	REMARKS
Down by the Salley Gardens	d1-e2	same	Most suitable for men's voices	Sustained, delicate. In folk vein. Text by W. Yeats. (WR)
Eight o'clock	db1-f2	f1-bb1	Not too suitable for very light, high voices	Slow, somewhat declamatory. Has a very dramatic final climax. (WR)
June twilight	c1-f#2	f1-c2	High or medium voices	Sustained, for the most part subdued. (WR)
Shy one	c1-a2	g1-d2	Not too suitable for very low voices	Delicate, graceful. Text by W. Yeats. (BH)
The seal man	c1-g2	c1-c2	High or medium voices	Declamatory, in the manner of a free recitative. Interpretatively and musically not easy. Has dramatic climaxes. Demands an accomplished pianist. (WR)

AARON COPLAND

Twelve Poems by Emily Dickinson

A cycle for <u>mezzo-soprano</u>, published by Boosey & Hawkes

	COMP.	TESS.	REMARKS
(1) Nature, the gentlest mother	b-g2	eb1-eb2	Slow and sustained. Soft last section; ends in cascading vocal line. A song with contrasting moods and tempi. Demands an accomplished pianist.
(2) There came a wind like a bugle	b-g2	b-f#2	Animated, vigorous. In parts dramatic, declamatory.
(3) Why do they shut me out of heaven?	bb-ab2	eb1-f2	Dramatic, declamatory. Effective ending. Slow.
(4) The world feels dusty	a#-f#2	bb-e2	Very slow and sustained.
(5) Heart, we will forget him	bb-g2	f1-e2	Slow, sustained. Demands a good command of high pp.
(6) Dear March, come in!	a-f#2	d#1-e2	Rapid and brilliant. Interpretatively not easy. In parts declamatory. Demands facile articulation and an accomplished pianist.
(7) Sleep is supposed to be	bb-bb2	c1-g2	Slow, sustained. Emphatic and dramatic ending, somewhat declamatory.
(8) When they come back	c1-g2	e1-eb2	Slow and sustained at the beginning and ending; animated and vigorous middle section.
(9) I felt a funeral in my brain	c#1-g2	d1-f2	Highly accented and heavy throughout, leading toward a somewhat sustained ending.

TITLE	COMP.	TESS.	TYPE	REMARKS
(10) I've heard an organ talk	bb-f2	db1-db2		Slow, sustained. Narrative.
(11) Going to heaven!	a-f2	d1-d2		Animated. Has sections in recitative and sustained styles.
(12) The chariot	b-f#2	d1-e2		Not fast. Has dotted rhythms throughout. Demands a good command of high pp. See "Because I could not stop for death" by Sergius Kagen.
Vocalise	c1-bb2 (a2)	e1-g2	High voices	An extended vocalise for high voice. Demands flexibility and agility. (BH)

See also "Old American Songs," two volumes — excellent arrangements of folk songs. Published by Boosey & Hawkes.

BAINBRIDGE CRIST

TITLE	COMP.	TESS.	TYPE	REMARKS
Chinese Mother Goose rhymes	c1-g2	e1-e2	Mezzo-soprano or soprano	Seven short, amusing songs. (CF)
O come hither	d1-b2 (d3)	g1-g2	Coloratura soprano	Animated, light, quite florid. In the style of an eighteenth century pastorale. (CF)

PEARL G. CURRAN

TITLE	COMP.	TESS.	TYPE	REMARKS
Nocturne	eb1-g2 (bb2)	g1-eb2 (H)	All voices	Sustained. Effective encore song. (GS)

FREDERICK DELIUS (Br.)
(1862–1934)

The songs of Delius seem to be much more rarely performed in Great Britain and the United States than his symphonic and choral works.

It is possible that the fact that in his choice of texts Delius did not limit himself to poetry in English is somewhat responsible for this. He set to music a considerable number of German translations of Scandinavian poems as well as of original German and French texts; their available English translations, for the most part, leave much to be desired.

Delius' harmonic scheme is not orthodox, though it is by no means experimental. Some of his songs are neither musically nor vocally easy. The short list below is primarily designed for those who are not at all acquainted with his style of writing.

TITLE	COMP.	TESS.	TYPE	REMARKS
I-Brasil	c1-f2	d1-d2	Medium or high voices	Slow, rhythmical. In parts demands a good command of pp. (OX)
Indian love song (I arise from dreams of thee)	eb1-bb2	g1-f2	Most suitable for high, dramatic voices	Sustained, delicate. The middle section is rapid and has an effective climax. Text by P. Shelley. (OX)
Le ciel est pardessus le toit (Three Poems by Paul Verlaine)	db1-gb2	f1-eb2	High voices	Slow. In parts demands considerable dramatic intensity. See Séverac, "D'une prison" by R. Hahn, and "Prison" by G. Fauré. French text. (OX)
Longing	cb1(a)-f#2	e1-d2	Heavy voices	Very animated, vigorous. (AUG)
Lullaby (for a modern baby)	c#1-g2	e1-e2	Soprano	A sustained, subdued vocalise. (UE)
So white, so soft, so sweet is she	b-f#2	g1-e2 (H)	All voices	Sustained, delicate. From "Four Old English Lyrics." See "Have you seen but a white lily grow," Anon. (WR)
The homeward journey (Heimkehr)	eb1-f2	eb1-c2	Not too suitable for very light, high voices	Sustained, somewhat declamatory. The English translation by F. S. Copeland is good. (OX)

480

TITLE	COMP.	TESS.	TYPE	REMARKS
The nightingale	d1-g2	f#1-e2	Not too suitable for very low voices	Sustained. Demands a good command of high pp. (AUG)
To daffodils	c#1-g#2	e1-e2 (H)	All voices	Slow, sustained. Has effective climaxes. (WR)
To the queen of my heart	d#1-a#2	f#1-f#2	Most suitable for heavy tenor	Very animated. Has very imposing climaxes. (OX)
Twilight fancies (Abendstimmung)	d1-f#2	g1-d2	Not too suitable for very light, high voices	Subdued, somewhat declamatory. Demands in parts some dramatic intensity. See Grieg, Kjerulf. The English translation by F. S. Copeland is good. (OX)

TERESA DEL RIEGO (Br.)

TITLE	COMP.	TESS.	TYPE	REMARKS
Homing	d1-ab2	g1-e2 (H)	All voices	Sustained. Effective encore song. (CHAP)

NORMAN DELLO JOIO

TITLE	COMP.	TESS.	TYPE	REMARKS
Eyebright	eb1-f2	f1-e2	All voices	Demands in parts facile articulation. (CF)
Lament	c1-f2	eb1-eb2	Most suitable for medium or low voices	Very slow. In parts declamatory, in others demands considerable dramatic intensity. Demands an accomplished pianist. Very somber 16th century text. (CF)
Mill doors	d1-e2	e1-d2	Medium or low voices	Very slow, sustained, somber. Very subdued ending. Text by C. Sandburg. (CF)

TITLE	COMP.	TESS.	TYPE	REMARKS
New born	c1-d2	e1-c2	Mezzo-soprano or contralto	Slow, sustained, subdued. Has the character of a lullaby. Ends with humming. (CF)
The assassination	bb-d2	same	Low voices	A dramatic conversation between two characters. Slow, declamatory. Interpretatively not easy. (CF)
The dying nightingale	db1-gb2	g1-e2	All voices	Very slow, sustained, mostly subdued. Somber text. (CF)
The listeners	bb-f2	eb1-eb2	Most suitable for baritone	An extended song of contrasting moods and tempi. Narrative. Interpretatively not easy. Text by Walter de la Mare. (CF)
There is a lady sweet and kind	c1-f2	f1-d2	All voices	Vocal line is slightly animated; accompaniment is on sustained chords. A setting to the well-known Elizabethan text. (CF)

DAVID DIAMOND

TITLE	COMP.	TESS.	TYPE	REMARKS
Brigid's song	c1-g2	g1-e2	High voices	Slow, sustained. Demands a good command of high mp. Poem by J. Joyce. (Music Press)
David weeps for Absalom	d1-a2	d1-f2	Not suitable for light, high voices	Slow, sustained. Intensely dramatic. Biblical text. (Music Press)

TITLE	COMP.	TESS.	TYPE	REMARKS
For an old man	d1-f2	d1-d2	Most suitable for men's voices	Rapid, declamatory. Demands facile articulation, flexibility and an accomplished pianist. Vigorous ending. (SMP)
If you can't	d1-g♯2	d1-d♯2	All voices	Animated. Voice part ends on hummed cadenza and spoken phrase. Accompaniment is entirely percussive. Text by e. e. cummings. (Leeds)
Monody	b♭-e♭2	d1-c2	Most suitable for medium or low voices	Sustained. (EV)
The mad maid's song	d1-a2	g1-g2	Soprano	Animated, quasi-modal. Demands facile articulation and some characterization. Score for voice, flute, and harpsichord (or piano). Text by R. Herrick. (SMP)
The midnight meditation	F-f1	B-c1	Bass-baritone	A cycle of four songs on poems by E. Olson. Vocally not easy. Demands an accomplished pianist. (SMP)
The shepherd boy sings in The Valley of Humiliation	c♯1-b2	d1-e2	High voices	Graceful, folk-like, almost in the character of a slow dance. Text by J. Bunyan. See also Vaughan Williams' "The Woodcutter's Song" from "The Pilgrim's Progress." (SMP)

TITLE	COMP.	TESS.	TYPE	REMARKS
This world is not my home	d1-f2	d1-d2	Most suitable for medium or low voices	Sustained. Somber text. (EV)

TOM DOBSON

TITLE	COMP.	TESS.	TYPE	REMARKS
Cargoes	d1-f2	a1-e2	All voices, except a very light soprano	Lively, effective. An amusing poem by J. Masefield. (GS)

CELIUS DOUGHERTY

TITLE	COMP.	TESS.	TYPE	REMARKS
Hush'd be the camps today	b♭-g2	e♭1-c2	Not suitable for light, high voices	Sustained, grave. Demands in parts considerable dramatic intensity. Text by Walt Whitman. (GS)
Listen! The wind	b-g2	g1-e2	High or medium voices	Animated, fast. Demands an accomplished pianist. (BH)
Love in the dictionary	c1-g2	e♭1-f2	High voices	Spirited waltz rhythm; jovial, somewhat humorous. Amusing setting of dictionary definitions of "love." (GS)
Loveliest of trees	e♭1-g♭2	g♭1-e♭2	All voices	Slow, sustained, graceful, delicate. Demands a good pianist. Text by A. E. Housman. (BH)
Madonna of the evening flowers	c1-g2	e1-e2	High or medium voices	Generally sustained. A song of contrasting moods. Large climax. Demands a good pianist. (BH)

TITLE	COMP.	TESS.	TYPE	REMARKS
The bird and the beast	c1-e2	c1-c2	All voices	An amusing setting of a child's awkward "essay" about birds and beasts. (GS)
The k'e	d1-f2	e1-e2	Women's voices, except a light soprano	Slow, sustained. Mostly subdued. A setting of an ancient Chinese poem. (GS)
The song of the jasmine	db1-ab2	eb1-f2	High voices	Sustained. (BH)

JOHN DUKE

TITLE	COMP.	TESS.	TYPE	REMARKS
A piper	c#1-b2	f1-a2	Light soprano	Very lively. Has optional coloratura in the introduction and postlude. See M. Head. (GS)
Central Park at dusk	e1-g2	e1-e2	High voices	Slow, sustained. Delicate, subdued. Demands a good command of high pp. (BH)
For a dead kitten	d1-f2	d1-d2	Medium voices	Slow march tempo, slightly declamatory. Subdued and somewhat somber throughout. (SMP)
hist . . . whist	b(a)-f#2 (g2)	e1-e2	Medium voices	Rapid, very lively. Humorous. Demands facile articulation and an accomplished pianist. Text by e. e. cummings. (SMP) See Bergsma.
I can't be talkin' of love	c#1-g2	e1-e2	Most suitable for soprano	Gently animated, delicate, rhythmical. (GS)
I ride the great black horses	b-f#2	d1-e2	Not suitable for light, high voices	Vigorous, fast. Demands considerable dramatic intensity, and an accomplished pianist. Effective. (GS)

TITLE	COMP.	TESS.	TYPE	REMARKS
Just spring	d1-bb2	e1-g2	High voices	Lively, gently humorous. Effective. Demands a good command of high pp (bb2) and an accomplished pianist. Text by e. e. cummings. (CF)
Loveliest of trees	c1-d2	f1-c2	All voices, except a very light soprano	Graceful, delicate. Text by A. E. Housman. (GS)
Spray	c#1-a2	d1-d2	High voices	Lively, bright. Demands a highly accomplished pianist. Text by S. Teasdale. (BH)
The last word of a bluebird	a-f2	c1-eb2	Medium voices	Somewhat declamatory; narrative. Animated. Demands flexibility. Poem by R. Frost. (GS)
White in the moon the long road lies	c1-eb2	d1-d2	All voices	Vocal line is sustained. Contrapuntal accompaniment is in unison most of the time. Text by A. E. Housman. (Valley Music Press)

THOMAS F. DUNHILL (Br.)

TITLE	COMP.	TESS.	TYPE	REMARKS
To the queen of heaven	c1-g2	f1-d2	Not too suitable for very light, high voices	Very sustained, majestic. (CUR)
The cloths of heaven	eb1-g2	g1-eb2 (H)	All voices	Sustained, very delicate. Demands a good command of high pp. Poem by W. Yeats. See Rebecca Clarke. (S & B)

JOHN EDMUNDS

TITLE	COMP.	TESS.	TYPE	REMARKS
Have these for yours	e1-g♭2	f1-e♭2	High voices	Sustained vocal part, subdued throughout. Demands an accomplished pianist. (SMP)
O death, rock me asleep	d1-e2	same	All voices	Slow, sustained. A setting of a text credited to Anne Boleyn. (SMP)
The Isle of Portland	e1-e2	same	All voices, except a very light soprano	Very slow, sustained. Text by A. E. Housman. (BH)
The lonely	e♭1-f2	f1-e2	All voices	Graceful, light. Vocal line is sustained. (CF)

CLARA EDWARDS

TITLE	COMP.	TESS.	TYPE	REMARKS
By the bend of the river	g♭1-a♭2 (b♭2)	g♭1-e♭2 (H)	All voices	Sustained. In popular vein. (GS)
Into the night	e1-f2 (g2)	g1-e2	All voices	Sustained. Effective. (GS)

SIR EDWARD ELGAR (Br.)

Edition: Novello

TITLE	COMP.	TESS.	TYPE	REMARKS
Pleading	d1-f♯2	e1-e2	All voices	Sustained. Effective.

Sea Pictures

A cycle of five songs for <u>alto</u>

TITLE	COMP.	TESS.	REMARKS
(1) Sea slumber song	b-d2(g)	e1-b1	Sustained.
(2) In haven	c1-c2	e1-c2	Animated, delicate.
(3) Sabbath morning at sea	b-f2(g2)	e1-c2	Sustained, somewhat declamatory, solemn.
(4) Where corals lie	(a♯)d1-d2	d1-d2	Light, delicate. Demands a good command of pp and facile articulation.

TITLE	COMP.	TESS.	TYPE	REMARKS
(5) The swimmer	(g)a-f2 (a2)	e1-e2		Very animated, vigorous, some- what declamatory.
The pipes of Pan	d1-f♯2	f♯1-d♯2	All voices	Spirited. Effec- tive.

Airs from Oratorios

TITLE	COMP.	TESS.	TYPE	REMARKS
King Olaf				
And King Olaf heard the cry	e♭-a1 (b♭1)	f1-f2	Dramatic tenor	A vigorous, ani- mated, dramatic narrative solo.
The Light of Life				
As a spirit didst Thou pass before mine eyes	e♭-a1 (b♭1)	a♭-f1	Tenor	Sustained, rather animated. Has a short, slow middle section; has effec- tive climaxes.
The Light of Life				
Be not extreme, O Lord	c1-a♭2	f1-f2	Dramatic soprano or lyric soprano	Animated, in parts dramatic. The vocal line is sus- tained.
The Light of Life				
I am the good shepherd	c-e♭1	f-d♭1	Baritone	Sustained.
The Light of Life				
Thou only hast the words of life	(a)c1- d2	e1-b1	Alto or mezzo- soprano	Sustained, rather subdued.

NOTE: "The Dream of Gerontius," "The Apostles," and "Caractacus," although abounding in solo passages, do not seem to have soli suit- able for separate performance, since the numerous solo passages are for the most part only sections of larger musical forms.

HERBERT ELWELL

TITLE	COMP.	TESS.	TYPE	REMARKS
In the mountains	d♭1-f2	g♭1-e♭2	High voices	Sustained, rather subdued. (BMI)
The road not taken	b-f♯2	c♯1-c♯2	Medium or high voices	Animated, some- what declamatory. Poem by R. Frost. (GS)

TITLE	COMP.	TESS.	TYPE	REMARKS

CARL ENGEL

TITLE	COMP.	TESS.	TYPE	REMARKS
Sea shell	eb1-eb2	gb1-db2	Most suitable for women's voices	Delicate. Poem by A. Lowell. (GS)

GERALD FINZI (Br.)

TITLE	COMP.	TESS.	TYPE	REMARKS
A Young Man's Exhortation	c1-a2	f1-f2	Tenor	A cycle of ten songs to poems by Thomas Hardy. Demands an accomplished pianist. (OX)
Before and After Summer	(ab)g-f2	b1-e2	Baritone	A cycle of ten songs to poems by Thomas Hardy. Demands an accomplished pianist. (BH)
Earth and Air and Rain	(a)f#-f#2	b-e2	Baritone	A cycle of ten songs to poems by Thomas Hardy. Demands an accomplished pianist. (BH)
I Said to Love	a-f#2	c#1-e2	Low voices	A cycle of six songs to poems by Thomas Hardy. Demands an accomplished pianist. (BH)
Rollicum-rorum	a-e2	a-d2	Baritone	Fast, vigorous, rhythmic. Demands facile articulation. Folklike. (BH)
Till Earth Outwears	c1-a2	d1-f2	High voices	A cycle of seven songs to poems by Thomas Hardy. Demands an accomplished pianist. (BH)

Two Sonnets

A set of two songs to poems by John Milton for <u>tenor (or soprano)</u> and a small orchestra. Piano reduction available. (OX)

TITLE	COMP.	TESS.	TYPE	REMARKS
(1) When I consider	c1-b2 (a2)	d1-g2		Slow, sustained. Dramatic climax.
(2) How soon hath time	db1-a2	f1-f2		Slow, sustained. Stately, imposing ending.

WILLIAM FLANAGAN

TITLE	COMP.	TESS.	TYPE	REMARKS
Go and catch a falling star	e1-bb2	g1-g2	High voices	Sustained. Has contrasts in mood and dynamics. Very subdued last section. Poem by John Donne. (PI)
Heaven haven	f1-f#2	a1-e2	High and medium voices	Slow, sustained. Generally subdued, nostalgic. Text by G. M. Hopkins. (PI) See "A nun takes a veil" by Barber.
The dugout	d#1-g2	eb1-e2	High voices	Slightly declamatory. Frequent and sudden changes of meter. Demands good command of high p and facile articulation. (PI)
Valentine to Sherwood Anderson	b-e2	d1-d2	Low voices	Animated, graceful. Frequent meter changes, closely tied to speech rhythm. Text by Gertrude Stein. (PI)

ARTHUR FOOTE

TITLE	COMP.	TESS.	TYPE	REMARKS
An Irish folksong	d1-g2	g1-e2	All voices	Sustained. In folk vein. Demands some flexibility. (Schmidt)

490

TITLE	COMP.	TESS.	TYPE	REMARKS
Constancy	eb1-ab2	f1-f2 (H)	All voices	Animated. See "I cannot help loving thee" by Clayton Johns. (Schmidt)
I'm wearing away	db1-f2	f1-db2	Most suitable for men's voices	Sustained. In folk vein. (Schmidt)
On the way to Kew	c1-e2	e1-c2	Not suitable for very light, high voices	Sustained. (Schmidt)
The lake isle of Innisfree	eb1-a2	g1-e2	High voices	Sustained. Poem by W. Yeats. (Schmidt)

STEPHEN FOSTER

All songs are generally available

Ah! May the red rose live alway!	c#1-f#2	e1-d2	All voices	Sustained.
Come where my love lies dreaming	e1-a2	f1-f2 (H)	All voices	Sustained.
Jeannie with the light brown hair	c1-f2	f1-d2	Most suitable for tenor	Sustained, graceful.
Katy Bell	c1-f2	e1-e2	All voices	Sustained.
Little Belle Blair	c1-e2	e1-e2	All voices	Sustained.
Nell and I	c1-e2	c1-c2	All voices	Sustained.
Open thy lattice, love	d1-f#2	e1-d2	All voices	Graceful.
Sweetly she sleeps, my Alice fair	d1-f2	f1-d2	All voices	Sustained.
The old folks at home	d1-e2	d1-d2	All voices	Sustained.

RUDOLF GANZ

Memory	e1-g2	g1-d2	All voices	Sustained, very delicate. (GS)

TITLE	COMP.	TESS.	TYPE	REMARKS

EDWARD GERMAN (Br.)

TITLE	COMP.	TESS.	TYPE	REMARKS
Charming Chloe	d1-g2	f1-f2 (H)	All voices	Animated, graceful. Demands facile articulation. (NOV)
My song is of the sturdy North	d1-f2	g1-e2	Men's voices	Spirited, vigorous, effective. (Cramer)
Rolling down to Rio	A-e1	d-d1	Bass or baritone	A spirited, vigorous ballad. Demands some flexibility. (NOV)

VITTORIO GIANNINI

Edition: Ricordi

TITLE	COMP.	TESS.	TYPE	REMARKS
Far above the purple hills	c#1-a2	f#1-e2	High voices, except a very light soprano	Sustained. In parts demands considerable dramatic intensity.
Heart cry	eb1-bb2	eb1-eb2	High voices	Somewhat declamatory. Dramatic, effective.
I shall think of you	d1-g2	g1-e2	Most suitable for men's voices	A free recitative song.
If I had known	e1-a2	g#1-d#2	High voices, except a very light soprano	Sustained. Has effective climaxes.
Tell me, oh blue, blue sky!	f#1(c#1)-g#2	g#1-d#2	High voices	Sustained. In parts dramatic. Demands a good command of high pp. Effective.

See also Giannini's arrangements of Italian and Neapolitan folk songs published by Ricordi, among them the very effective "Zompa llari lira."

G. ARMSTRONG GIBBS (Br.)

TITLE	COMP.	TESS.	TYPE	REMARKS
Five eyes	f1-f2	f1-db2 (H)	All voices	A rapid, amusing song. Demands facile articulation. Text by W. de la Mare. (W)

TITLE	COMP.	TESS.	TYPE	REMARKS
Joan of Arc	c1-b♭2	f1-f2		A cycle of five songs for <u>soprano</u>. (BH)
On Duncton hill	f♯1-f♯2	f♯1-d2	High voices	Sustained, subdued. (CUR)

Songs of the Mad Sea Captain

A cycle of four songs for <u>bass-baritone</u>. (BH)

(1) Hidden treasure	g(b♭)-d2	d1-c2		Animated.
(2) Abel Wright	a♭-d♯2	b-c2		March style. Narrative.
(3) Toll the bell	a-d2	b-d2		Slow, sustained.
(4) The golden ray	b-d2	c1-d2		Animated, rhythmic, carefree.
Take heed, young heart	e1-g2	e1-e2	High voices	Sustained and for the most part subdued. Poem by W. de la Mare. (CUR)
The market	a-e2	e1-c2	Most suitable for baritone	Animated, humorous. (CUR)
To one who passed whistling through the night	f1-g2	g1-e♭2	Most suitable for light, high voices	Somewhat declamatory, subdued. Demands some flexibility. (CUR)

HENRY F. GILBERT

Pirate song	c-g1	e♭-d1	Men's voices, except a light tenor	Vigorous, effective. (NOV)

GUY GRAHAM (Br.)

Callao	c1-f2	f1-d2	Men's voices	Spirited, vigorous. Effective. (BH)

CHARLES T. GRIFFES

Griffes, perhaps one of America's outstanding composers, has written twenty-eight songs to English and German texts. No American singer can afford to neglect Griffes and would profit greatly by a closer acquaintance with songs other than the well-known "By a lonely forest pathway."

Edition: G. Schirmer

TITLE	COMP.	TESS.	TYPE	REMARKS
An old song resung	e♭1-f2	e♭1-e♭2 (H)	Most suitable for men's voices	A vigorous narrative song. Poem by J. Masefield.
Auf dem Teich dem regungslosen (O'er the tarn's unruffled mirror)	b-g♯2	e1-c♯2	High voices, except a very light soprano	Very sustained, subdued. Demands a good command of high pp. The English translation by H. G. Chapman is fairly good.
Auf geheimem Waldespfade (By a lonely forest pathway)	e♭1-a♭2	g1-a♭2 (H)	All voices	Slow and sustained. See Robert Franz. The English translation by H. G. Chapman is good.
Auf ihrem Grab (Upon their grave)	c1-g2	f1-e♭2	Not too suitable for very low voices	Sustained. Demands a good command of high p. Excellent English translation by Louis Untermeyer.
Der träumende See (The dreamy lake)	b♯-g♯2	d♯1-c♯2	High voices, except a very light soprano	Very sustained, subdued. The English translation by Dole is very good.
Elfe (Elves)	f-a♭2	a♭1-f2	High voices	Rapid, light. Demands facile articulation and an accomplished pianist. Excellent English translation by Louis Untermeyer.

TITLE	COMP.	TESS.	TYPE	REMARKS
Evening song	d♯1-g♯2	g♯1-e2	High voices	Sustained. Demands in parts considerable dramatic intensity. Demands an accomplished pianist.
In a myrtle shade	f♯1-a2	g♯1-f♯2	Most suitable for light, high voices	Slow, sustained. Demands a good command of high pp. Poem by W. Blake.
Könnt ich mit dir (If I could go with you)	e1-g♯2	g♯1-e2	Most suitable for high voices	Sustained, delicate. Excellent English translation by Louis Untermeyer.
La fuite de la lune (To outer senses there is peace)	c♯1-f2	e♭1-d♭2	All voices, except a bass or a very light soprano	Slow. Interpretatively not easy. French text.
Phantoms	b♭-f2	e♭1-d2	Not suitable for light, high voices	Dramatic, somewhat declamatory. Musically not easy.
Sorrow of Mydath	b-f♯2	g1-e♭2	Not suitable for light, high voices	Dramatic. Musically and interpretatively not easy. Demands an accomplished pianist. Poem by J. Masefield. See R. Ward.
Symphony in yellow	d♯1-g♭2	f♯1-e♭2	Not too suitable for very low voices	Slow and very subdued. Demands a good command of high pp. Poem by O. Wilde.
The first snowfall	d1-f2	a1-e2	Not too suitable for very low voices	Slow, very delicate. Demands a good command of high pp.
The half-ring moon	d♯1-e2	same	Women's voices, except a light soprano	Rapid. The vocal line is very sustained. Demands considerable dramatic intensity.

TITLE	COMP.	TESS.	TYPE	REMARKS
The lament of Ian the Proud	d♯1-a♯2	f♯1-f♯2	Most suitable for tenor	Slow, somewhat declamatory. Demands in parts considerable dramatic intensity. Musically and interpretatively not easy. Demands an accomplished pianist.
The rose of the night	c♯1-a2	g♯1-e2	Most suitable for high voices	Sustained. In parts demands considerable dramatic intensity. Musically and interpretatively not easy. Demands an excellent pianist.
This book of hours	c♯1-f♯2	e1-c♯2	Not too suitable for very low voices	Slow and very sustained. Demands good command of pp.
Thy dark eyes to mine	e♭1-a♭2	a♭1-f2	High voices	Sustained. Musically not easy. Demands in parts considerable dramatic intensity as well as a good command of high pp. Demands an accomplished pianist. See Arnold Bax.
Wai Kiki	d♯1-g♯2	e1-e2	Most suitable for high voices	Musically and interpretatively not easy. Demands considerable dramatic intensity, in parts, and an accomplished pianist. Poem by R. Brooke.
We'll to the woods and gather May	d♭1-f2	f1-d♭2	Women's voices, except a light soprano	Rapid and vigorous. Of no particular distinction.

TITLE	COMP.	TESS.	TYPE	REMARKS
Wohl lag ich einst in Gram und Schmerz (Time was when I in anguish lay)	e1-g♯2	f♯1-d♯2	Not suitable for light, high voices	Rapid, vigorous. The English translation by Chapman is very good.
Zwei Könige sassen auf Orkadal (Two kings sat together in Orkadal)	b♭-e2	b-b1	Low voices	A dramatic narrative song. The English translation is fair.

See also "Five Poems of the Ancient Far East" for <u>medium voice</u> and piano.

LOUIS GRUENBERG

TITLE	COMP.	TESS.	TYPE	REMARKS
Animals and insects	a-a2	same	Most suitable for soprano	Seven short songs to very amusing words by Vachel Lindsay. Musically quite complex. Demand an excellent pianist. (UNIV)

DAVID W. GUION

TITLE	COMP.	TESS.	TYPE	REMARKS
At the cry of the first bird	d1-g2	f♯1-d2	High or medium voices	Sustained, effective. Religious text. (GS)
Mam'selle Marie	d1-e2	e1-b1	Women's voices	Sustained, subdued dialect song. (GS)

IVOR GURNEY (Br.)

The songs of Ivor Gurney, whom some critics consider one of the most gifted of contemporary song composers, are practically unknown outside of Great Britain. This short list is primarily designed for those who are not familiar with his songs.

TITLE	COMP.	TESS.	TYPE	REMARKS
All night under the moon	d♯1-f♯2	d♯1-d♯2	Most suitable for high voices	Slow, sustained, subdued. (OX)

TITLE	COMP.	TESS.	TYPE	REMARKS
An epitaph	d1-e2	e1-d2	All voices	Slow, very sustained, subdued. (OX)
Bread and cherries	e1-f#2	g1-e2	Not too suitable for very low voices	Animated, light. (OX)
Down by the Salley gardens	db1-f2	eb1-c2	Most suitable for men's voices	Sustained. (OX)
Hawk and buckle	d1-eb2	d1-d2	Men's voices	Spirited, rhythmical. Demands facile articulation. (OX)
Last hours	bb-e2	e1-d2	Medium or low voices	Slow, sustained, subdued, somber. (OX)
The scribe	bb-e2	e1-c2	Not too suitable for very light, high voices	Not slow, sustained. (OX)
Under the greenwood tree	c1-f#2	e1-d2	Medium or high voices	Graceful. (WR)
The folly of being comforted	c#1-f#2 (g#2)	e1-e2	Most suitable for high voices	Rather slow, somewhat declamatory. Interpretatively not easy. Demands in parts considerable dramatic intensity. (OX)

See also: "Ludlow and Teme" — seven poems by A. E. Housman for voice, string quartet and pianoforte (Stainer & Bell).

RICHARD HAGEMAN

At the well	db1-ab2 (cb3)	gb1-gb2	Not too suitable for very low voices	An effective, light song. Demands an excellent pianist. (GS)
Christ went up into the hills	eb1-gb2 (ab2)	gb1-eb2	All voices	Slow, sustained. Has effective climaxes. Religious text. (CF)

TITLE	COMP.	TESS.	TYPE	REMARKS
Do not go, my love	d#1-g2	f#1-d2 (H)	All voices	Slow, sustained. In parts demands considerable dramatic intensity as well as a good command of high pp. (GS)
Miranda	e1-a2	a1-e2 (H)	All voices	A rapid, effective song. Demands an accomplished pianist. See an excellent setting of this Belloc poem "The Inn," by Francis Toye (baritone). (GAL)
Music I heard with you	f1-a2	a1-e2 (H)	All voices	Sustained. Has effective climaxes. (GAL)

ROY HARRIS

TITLE	COMP.	TESS.	TYPE	REMARKS
Fog	d1-f2	f1-d2	Medium voices	Slow, sustained, subdued. Demands an accomplished pianist. Poem by C. Sandburg. (CF)

VICTOR HARRIS

TITLE	COMP.	TESS.	TYPE	REMARKS
A man's song	F#-c1	c-c1	Men's voices	Vigorous, effective. (GS)
The hills o'Skye	d1-g2	a1-f2	All voices	In Scottish folk song vein. Sustained, rhythmical. (OD)

FREDERIC HART

TITLE	COMP.	TESS.	TYPE	REMARKS
Grass	c1-eb2	eb1-c2	All except very light, high voices	Slow, declamatory, dramatic. Stately in some parts. Soft and sustained final passages. Text by C. Sandburg. (Mercury)

HERBERT HAMILTON HARTY (Br.)

TITLE	COMP.	TESS.	TYPE	REMARKS
Across the door	b-f2	d1-d2	Women's voices, except a very light soprano	Animated. Interpretatively not easy. Demands an accomplished pianist. See A. Bax. (NOV)
Homeward	C-e1	c-c1	Bass or baritone	A vigorous, spirited sailor's song. In folk vein. (NOV)
My Lagan love (from "Three Traditional Ulster Airs")	d1-g2	e1-e2	All voices	Sustained. In folk vein. (BH)
Sea wrack	c1-f2	e1-e2	Women's voices, except a light soprano	Sustained. Has dramatic climaxes. (BH)

See also "Three Irish Folksongs" arranged by Hamilton Harty. (OX)

MICHAEL HEAD (Br.)

TITLE	COMP.	TESS.	TYPE	REMARKS
A piper	eb1-g2	f1-eb2	All voices	Animated. Demands facile articulation and an accomplished pianist. (BH)
Money, O!	b-f#2	f#1-e2	Men's voices	An animated, effective ballad. (BH)
Nocturne (from "Over the rim of the moon")	e1-g#2	g1-d2	All voices	Somewhat declamatory. In parts dramatic. Demands a good command of high pp. (BH)
The sea gipsy	e1-g#2	g1-e2 (H)	Men's voices	An effective, vigorous ballad. (BH)
The ships of Arcady	d1-g2	a1-f#2 (H)	All voices	Sustained, for the most part delicate and subdued. (BH)
When I think upon the maidens	d1-g2	g1-eb2 (H)	Men's voices	A very rapid, humorous character song. Demands facile articulation. (BH)

TITLE	COMP.	TESS.	TYPE	REMARKS
You shall not go a-Maying	e♭1-g2	g1-e♭2	All voices	Sustained, effective. (BH)

V. HELY-HUTCHINSON (Br.)

TITLE	COMP.	TESS.	TYPE	REMARKS
Old Mother Hubbard	d1-g2	g1-e♭2 (H)	All voices	A parody on Handel. Demands some flexibility. (CF)
Three nonsense songs: (1) The owl and the pussy cat (2) The table and the chair (3) The duck and the kangaroo	c1-f2	d1-d2	High or medium voices	Three settings of Edward Lear's nonsense poems. Light and humorous. (Pate··son)

JOHN C. HOLLIDAY (Br.)

TITLE	COMP.	TESS.	TYPE	REMARKS
Chumleigh fair	c1-d2	same	Men's voices	Animated, gently humorous. In folk vein. Demands facile articulation. (BH)

GUSTAV HOLST (Br.)

TITLE	COMP.	TESS.	TYPE	REMARKS
A little music	d1-g2	f1-f2	High voices	Animated. Demands facile articulation. (AUG)
In the street of lost time	e1-g2	g1-f2	High voices	Sustained. Short. (AUG)
Journey's end	c1-g♭2	g1-e2	High or medium voices	Sustained, somewhat declamatory. (AUG)
Now in these fairy lands	d1-f2	f1-d2	High or medium voices	Very sustained, rather subdued. (AUG)
Persephone	d1-g♭2	f1-f2	Most suitable for men's voices	Fast, animated. Forceful, effective climax. Demands facile articulation and an accomplished pianist. (AUG)

TITLE	COMP.	TESS.	TYPE	REMARKS
Rhyme	d1-g2	g1-f2	High voices	Rapid, animated, has contrasts in dynamics. Demands facile articulation, a good command of high pp and an accomplished pianist. Meter alternates between 9/8 and 12/8. (AUG)
The floral bandit	c#1-a♭2	g#1-f#2	Most suitable for light, high voices	Rapid, animated, light. Demands an accomplished pianist. (AUG)
The heart's worship	c1-e2	e1-b1	Not suitable for very light, high voices	Slow, sustained, somewhat declamatory. (S & B)
The sergeant's song	A-e1	e-e1	Baritone or bass	A vigorous, spirited ballad. (Ashdown)
The thought	c#1-f#2	e1-e2	High or medium voices	Sustained; declamatory in the manner of a recitative. (AUG)
Things lovelier	d1-g2	f#1-f#2	Most suitable for men's voices	Sustained; somewhat declamatory. Short. (AUG)

See also "Four Songs for Voice and Violin" (medium voice) and "Hymns from the Rig Veda" (high or medium voices). (CHES)

SIDNEY HOMER

The songs of Sidney Homer (over a hundred in number) need no introduction, as they are sufficiently well known to every American singer. The scant selection listed here, though in some ways representative of his style of writing, is admittedly in no way complete. It is hoped that this short list may serve as a point of departure for those who do not happen to be familiar with his songs.

Edition: G. Schirmer

TITLE	COMP.	TESS.	TYPE	REMARKS
A banjo song	e1-f2	g1-e2	Most suitable for men's voices	Sustained. Effective, tuneful song in popular vein.
Dearest	eb1-ab2	eb1-eb2	All voices	Sustained. Demands in parts considerable dramatic intensity.
General William Booth enters into heaven	c1-eb2	eb1-c2	Low or medium voices	A vigorous narrative song. See Ives. Poem by V. Lindsay.
Lullaby, oh lullaby	eb1-eb2	bb1-eb2	Women's voices	Very delicate and sustained. See C. Scott.
Mary's baby	e1-f2	g♯1-e2	All voices	Slow and subdued.
Requiem	eb1-db2	f1-cb2	Men's voices	Slow, sustained, and rather vigorous.
Sheep and lambs	eb1-e2	eb1-bb1	Not too suitable for very high, light voices	Very sustained. In parts demands considerable dramatic intensity.
Sweet and low	c1-c2	db1-ab1	Women's voices	Sustained, delicate.
The fiddler of Dooney	d1-g2	d1-d2	Most suitable for men's voices	Rapid and spirited.
This is the house that Jack built	a-f2	bb-bb1	All voices	An amusing setting of the old nursery rhyme. Very animated. Demands very facile articulation. (JCC)
When death to either shall come	e1-e2	g♯1-e2	All voices	Slow and sustained.

EDWARD HORSMAN

TITLE	COMP.	TESS.	TYPE	REMARKS
The bird of the wilderness	db1-ab2 (bb2)	ab1-eb2	Not too suitable for very light voices	Sustained. Has effective climaxes. (GS)

TITLE	COMP.	TESS.	TYPE	REMARKS

TITLE	COMP.	TESS.	TYPE	REMARKS
Cato's advice	G-c1 (d1)	c-a	Bass	A vigorous, spirited drinking song in eighteenth century style. (GS)
Invictus	bb-db2	f1-c2	Not suitable for light voices	Very vigorous, somewhat declamatory. (GS)

JOHN IRELAND (Br.)
(1879–1962)

Among contemporary British songs those of John Ireland, in the opinion of this writer, occupy a highly honored position. Tastefully and skillfully written, neither experimental nor tritely effective, yet possessing an idiom of their own, they present no particular problems.

TITLE	COMP.	TESS.	TYPE	REMARKS
A report song	eb1-eb2	same	All voices	Animated, graceful. Demands facile articulation. (WR)
Bed in summer	eb1-f2 (H)	same	All voices	Animated, graceful. Poem is from "Child's Garden of Verses" by Stevenson. (CUR)
Epilogue	f1-ab2 (H)	g1-g2	High or medium voices	Sustained. (AUG)
Five XVIth Century Poems	bb-e2	d1-d2		Five songs for medium or low voices. (BH)
Great things	d-f#1	d-d1	Men's voices	Animated, vigorous. (AUG)
Hope the hornblower	e1-e2 (f#2)	e1-e2	Men's voices	Animated, vigorous. (BH)
I have twelve oxen	d1-f#2	e1-d2	Most suitable for men's voices	Animated. In folk vein. See Warlock. (WR)
I was not sorrowful	eb1-gb2 (H)	g1-c2	Most suitable for men's voices	Sustained, for the most part subdued, somber. (BH)

504

TITLE	COMP.	TESS.	TYPE	REMARKS

Marigold

A cycle of three songs for <u>medium or low voices.</u> Demands an accomplished pianist. Published by Winthrop Rogers.

TITLE	COMP.	TESS.	TYPE	REMARKS
(1) Youth's spring-tribute	bb-g2	d1-eb2		Sustained. Has imposing climaxes.
(2) Penumbra	a-f2	d1-d#2		Sustained. Chromatic. Starts with a recitative section.
(3) Spleen	a-db2	eb1-bb1		Sustained. Chromatic vocal line.
My true love hath my heart	f#1-a2	g1-g2	Most suitable for women's voices	Animated. Effective and forceful ending. Accompaniment is highly chromatic. (AUG)
Sea fever	e1-g2	a1-e2 (H)	Men's voices	Somewhat declamatory. Perhaps the best setting of this famous Masefield poem. (AUG)

Songs Sacred and Profane

A collection of songs published by Schott & Co.

TITLE	COMP.	TESS.	TYPE	REMARKS
(1) The advent	d1-g2	g1-e2	All voices	Slow, sustained. Has some declamatory passages.
(2) Hymn for a child	c#1-f2	e1-e2	All voices	Animated, narrative, chromatic.
(3) My fair	e1-g2	g1-e2	All voices	Slow, sustained, chromatic.
(4) The Salley gardens	e1-e2	g1-e2	All voices	Graceful, folk-like.
(5) The soldier's return	d1-e2	g1-eb2	Most suitable for men's voices	Rhythmic, accented, vigorous. March tempo.
(6) The scapegoat	e1-f2	f#1-e2	All voices	Animated. Demands facile articulation and an accomplished pianist.
Spring sorrow	eb1-f2	f1-eb2	All voices	Sustained. (WR)

TITLE	COMP.	TESS.	TYPE	REMARKS
The bells of San Marie	f1-g2	g1-f2	Most suitable for men's voices	Sustained. (AUG)
The heart's desire	f1-a♭2	f1-f2 (H)	All voices	Sustained. Demands in parts considerable dramatic intensity. (WR)
The holy boy	d1-a2 (g2)	e♭1-f2 (H)	All voices, except bass	Slow, quiet, modal, in folk vein. (BH)
The Land of Lost Content	e1-a♭2	f1-g2	High or medium voices	A cycle of six songs to poems of A. E. Housman. AUG)
The rat	b-e2	c♯1-e♭2	Medium voices	Very slow, sustained. Chromatic. Somewhat declamatory. Abounds in triplet figures. (CHES)
Vagabond	f1-f2	g1-d2 (H)	Men's voices	Rather slow, declamatory, subdued. (AUG)
We'll to the woods no more	d1-f2	f1-d2	High or medium voices	Slow, somewhat declamatory. (OX)

See also "Five Poems by Thomas Hardy"—for baritone.

CHARLES IVES

One of America's most individualistic composers, Ives had begun to experiment with unorthodox harmonies and sonorities long before such experimentation was fashionable among American composers. Although he has written over a hundred songs, most of them have been printed privately and only a few are generally available. Of these only eight have been listed below, since most of Ives' mature songs are extraordinarily complex and do not seem as yet to be generally acceptable to the majority of singers or music lovers.

TITLE	COMP.	TESS.	TYPE	REMARKS
Ann street	e1-e2	e1-d2	All voices	Fast, short. Demands a good pianist. (New Music)

TITLE	COMP.	TESS.	TYPE	REMARKS
August	c1-e2	d1-d2	All voices	Graceful, rhythmically intricate. Irregular meter. Demands flexibility, facile articulation and an accomplished pianist. (PI)
Autumn	bb-f2	db1-c2	All voices	Slow and generally sustained. In parts delicate. Has impressive climax. (PI)
Charlie Rutlage	d1-d2	same	Men's voices	A narrative song, much of which is spoken. Demands an accomplished pianist. Some of the piano part is supposed to be played with the fist. Musically complex. (Cos Cob)
Evening	c#1-d2	e1-b1	Medium or low voices	Slow, sustained, subdued. Musically not easy. Poem by J. Milton. (Cos Cob)
From "Lincoln, The Great Commoner"	c1-e2	e1-e2	All except light, high voices	Sustained, stately, declamatory. Except at the end, the music is unmetered. In parts demands considerable dramatic intensity. Demands an accomplished pianist. (PI)
The greatest man	e1-g2	e1-e2	Men's voices, except a very light, high tenor	Narrative, humorous. Demands some flexibility and characterization. Effective encore song. (Cos Cob)
Walking	d1-f#2	d1-e2	All voices	Fast, spirited, marked. The poem is by the composer. (Arrow)

TITLE	COMP.	TESS.	TYPE	REMARKS

SERGIUS KAGEN

TITLE	COMP.	TESS.	TYPE	REMARKS
A June day	f♯1-b♭2	b1-g2	Light, high soprano	Sustained, delicate. Demands a good command of high pp. Poem by S. Teasdale. (Weintraub)
All day I hear	f1-f♯2	f1-d♭2	Not suitable for light, high soprano	Animated, somber. Demands an accomplished pianist. Poem by J. Joyce. (Weintraub)
Because I could not stop for death	c1-f2	d1-d2	All voices, except bass	Mostly subdued. Demands rhythmic precision from both singer and pianist. Poem by E. Dickinson. See Copland's "The chariot." (Leeds)
Drum	b♭-e♭2	b-c2	Medium or low voices	A song which demands very strict observance of rhythmic pulsation. Mostly subdued, fast. Poem by L. Hughes. (Mercury)
I think I could turn	A-d1	B-b1	Bass or bass-baritone	Somber, heavy, in parts demands considerable dramatic intensity. Poem by W. Whitman. (Mercury)
I'm nobody	d1-g2	f♯1-d2	Not suitable for heavy, low voices	Humorous. Demands facile articulation and an accomplished pianist. Poem by E. Dickinson. (Weintraub)
Let it be forgotten	f1-f2	f1-e♭2	All voices, except bass	Slow, sustained. Mostly subdued, with gentle declamation. Accompaniment consists of

TITLE	COMP.	TESS.	TYPE	REMARKS
				sustained, muted chords. Poem by S. Teasdale. (Weintraub)
London	b-f2	eb1-e2	Medium voices; most suitable for baritone	Sustained. Has intense dramatic climaxes. Interpretatively not easy. Poem by W. Blake. (Mercury)
Mag	Bb-e1	e-c♯1	Baritone	Somber, tragic, heavy. In parts intensely dramatic. Poem by C. Sandburg. (Weintraub)
Maybe	d1-g2	g1-e2	Women's voices	Gentle, in folk vein. Poem by C. Sandburg. (Weintraub)
Memory hither come	d1-f♯2	a1-e2	All voices, except bass	Sustained, subdued, gentle. Poem by W. Blake. (Mercury)
Miss T	e1-e2	same	All voices, except bass	Sprightly, humorous. Poem by W. de la Mare. (Weintraub)
Prayer	eb1-bb2	ab1-f2	High voices	Sustained, in parts intensely dramatic. Poem by L. Hughes. (Leeds)
Sleep now	a-e2	e1-c2	Low voices	Sustained, for the most part subdued. Poem by J. Joyce. (Leeds)

Three Satires (Mercury)

TITLE	COMP.	TESS.	TYPE	REMARKS
(1) Persons of intelligence and culture	a-e2	bb-d2	Medium or low voices	Humorous and satirical. Demands facile articulation. Accompaniment is mainly percussive. Text by L. MacNeice.

TITLE	COMP.	TESS.	TYPE	REMARKS
(2) Yonder see the morning blink	d1-e2	d1-eb2	All voices	Slow. Somewhat declamatory. Humorous. Text by A. E. Housman.
(3) How pleasant it is to have money	c1-e2	same	All voices	Demands facile articulation. Has a waltz section. Humorous. Text by A. H. Clough.
Upstream	c#1-f2	f1-eb2	Not suitable for light, high voices	Energetic, broad. Demands considerable dramatic intensity. Poem by C. Sandburg. (Weintraub)

FREDERICK KEEL (Br.)

TITLE	COMP.	TESS.	TYPE	REMARKS
Trade winds	bb-eb2	eb1-bb1	Men's voices	Sustained, gently animated. (BH)

WENDELL KEENEY

TITLE	COMP.	TESS.	TYPE	REMARKS
The Aspen	d1-f#2	e1-d2	Not suitable for very light, high voices	Slow, somber. Demands an accomplished pianist. (GS)

A. WALTER KRAMER

TITLE	COMP.	TESS.	TYPE	REMARKS
Swans	eb1-bb2	ab1-f2	Most suitable for light, high voices	Sustained. Demands a good command of high pp. (RIC)
The faltering dusk	eb1-gb2	eb1-c2	Women's voices	Dramatic, effective. (OD)

FRANK LA FORGE

TITLE	COMP.	TESS.	TYPE	REMARKS
Come unto these yellow sands	f#1-b2 (d3)	b1-a2	Coloratura soprano	Animated, light. Has florid passages. (GS)

TITLE	COMP.	TESS.	TYPE	REMARKS
Hills	e1-g2 (b2)	g1-e2	Not suitable for very light voices	Animated, effective. (RIC)
Song of the open	eb1-ab2 (c3)	f1-f2	Not suitable for very light voices	Very animated, effective. Demands an accomplished pianist. (OD)

BENJAMIN LEES

Cyprian Songs

A cycle of four songs for <u>baritone</u>. Demands an accomplished pianist. Published by Boosey & Hawkes.

(1) From what green island	Bb-d1	d-c1	Sustained.
(2) Wake! for the night of shadows	A-d1	e-c1	Sustained, in parts declamatory.
(3) Still is it as it was	c-d#1	e-b	Very sustained.
(4) Over me like soft clouds	Bb-f#1	eb-d1	Sustained. In parts demands some dramatic intensity.

Songs of the Night

A cycle of six songs most suitable for <u>light, high voices</u>. High tessitura. Published by Boosey & Hawkes.

(1) O shade of evening	gb1-bb2	bb1-f2	Sustained. Demands good command of high p and an accomplished pianist.
(2) A star fell in flames	ab1-a2	b1-g2	Sustained. Has sudden changes in dynamics. Demands good command of high p.
(3) The enemies	f1-g2	g1-e2	Sustained.
(4) A whisper of rain	f1-g#2	a1-f2	Sustained vocal line. Demands a good command of high pp.
(5) Fall to the night wind	f1-bb2	bb1-g2	Sustained.

TITLE	COMP.	TESS.	TYPE	REMARKS
(6) On eastern hills	e♭1-b♭2	b♭1-d2		Very sustained, slow. Imposing climax.

LIZA LEHMANN (Br.)

In a Persian Garden A cycle for four solo voices — <u>soprano, alto, tenor, bass</u>. The solo excerpts from this cycle have been much used for teaching purposes and still enjoy considerable popularity. Expertly written for the respective voices, they are melodious and effective. (GS)

THURLOW LIEURANCE

TITLE	COMP.	TESS.	TYPE	REMARKS
By the waters of Minnetonka	e1-f♯2	e1-e2	All voices	Sustained. Effective imitation of an Indian song. (TP)

CHARLES MARTIN LOEFFLER

TITLE	COMP.	TESS.	TYPE	REMARKS
Les paons	d1-f2	g1-e2	High or medium voices	Slow. Interpretatively not easy. Demands a good command of pp and an accomplished pianist. French text. (GS)
To Helen	d♭1-f2	f♯1-e2	Medium or high voices	Sustained. In parts demands considerable dramatic intensity. Demands an accomplished pianist. Text by E. A. Poe. (GS)
Sonnet	d♭1-f2	f1-e♭2	Medium or high voices	Sustained. Demands in parts considerable dramatic intensity. Demands an excellent pianist. Musically not easy. (GS)

EDWARD MacDOWELL

The songs of Edward MacDowell have not attained the popularity of his pianoforte works. Unpretentiously melodic in character, they possess all the qualities which would seem to ensure a lasting popularity, were it not for the fact that, for the most part, his songs are vocally somewhat awkward. The almost uninterrupted vocal line seldom allows the singer a breathing space, and thus makes rather severe demands upon the singer's technique and endurance.

    Editions: Arthur Schmidt
               G. Schirmer
               Breitkopf & Härtel

TITLE	COMP.	TESS.	TYPE	REMARKS
A maid sings light	e1-g2	ab1-f2	All voices	Light and animated. Demands facile articulation.
As the gloaming shadows creep	e1-g2	g1-d2	All voices	Very sustained. Demands a good command of high pp.
Cradle hymn	e1-d2 (f♯2)	a1-d2	Women's voices	Delicate and sustained. Demands a good command of pp.
Deserted (Ye banks and braes)	f1-f2	a1-e2	All voices	Slow and sustained.
Fair springtide	c♯1-f♯2	d1-d2	All voices	Very slow and sustained.
Long ago	d1-g2	f1-f2	All voices	Very sustained. Demands a good command of pp.
Menie	d1-f2	f1-d2	All voices	Sustained. Demands a good command of pp.
The sea	d1-d2	d1-bb1	Not suitable for very light, high voices	In parts demands considerable dramatic intensity.
The swan bent low to the lily	d1-f2	g1-e2	All voices, except a very light soprano	Very sustained.
Thy beaming eyes	c1-f2	same	All voices; not suitable for very light soprano	Sustained.

TITLE	COMP.	TESS.	TYPE	REMARKS
To a wild rose	db1-gb2	gb1-f2	All voices	Very sustained.

ROBERT MacGIMSEY

TITLE	COMP.	TESS.	TYPE	REMARKS
Shadrack	d-g1 (a1)	g-d1 (H)	Most suitable for men's voices	Vigorous ballad in the manner of a Negro spiritual. A considerable number of effective spiritual songs have been written by MacGimsey, of which this is among the most popular. (CF)

DERMOT MacMURROUGH (Br.)

TITLE	COMP.	TESS.	TYPE	REMARKS
The shepherdess	e1-f2	f1-e2 (H)	All voices	Sustained, delicate. Demands a good command of high pp. (Enoch)

EASTHOPE MARTIN (Br.)

TITLE	COMP.	TESS.	TYPE	REMARKS
Come to the fair	g1-g2 (H)	same	All voices	Gay, spirited ballad. (Enoch)

DANIEL GREGORY MASON

TITLE	COMP.	TESS.	TYPE	REMARKS
A grain of salt	A-d1	c-bb	Bass or baritone	Animated, humorous. (GS)
A sea dirge	d1-eb2	g1-c2	Medium or low voices	Animated, vigorous. (Witmark)
I ain't afeared o' the admiral	A-e1	c-c1	Bass or baritone	Humorous character song. (GS)
Take, o take those lips away	d1-f2	e1-e2	Medium or high voices	Sustained. Demands in parts considerable dramatic intensity. (Witmark)

TITLE	COMP.	TESS.	TYPE	REMARKS
The constant cannibal maiden	c-f♯1	e-c♯1	Baritone	Humorous. Demands in parts considerable dramatic intensity. (GS)

ROBIN MILFORD (Br.)

TITLE	COMP.	TESS.	TYPE	REMARKS
If it's ever spring again (from "Four Hardy Songs")	d1-g2	g1-e2	High voices	Animated, light. (OX)
The colour (from "Four Hardy Songs")	e1-g2	g1-e2	High voices	Sustained. In folk vein. Demands in parts considerable dramatic intensity. (OX)

E. J. MOERAN (Br.)

"Seven Poems" by James Joyce (one is omitted here). (Publisher: Oxford)

TITLE	COMP.	TESS.	TYPE	REMARKS
Bright cap	d1-e2	e1-d2	Medium or high voices	Animated. Demands some flexibility.
Donnycarney	e♭1-f2	f1-e♭2	Men's voices	Sustained, delicate.
Rain has fallen	c♯1-f♯2	e1-d♯2	High or medium voices	Slow, sustained, subdued.
Strings in the earth and air	d1-f2	f1-d2	Medium or high voices	Sustained and delicate.
The merry green wood	e1-e2	same	Most suitable for men's voices	Animated, rather vigorous.
The pleasant valley	c1-f2	f1-d2	Medium or high voices	Sustained.

JAMES L. MALLOY (Br.)

TITLE	COMP.	TESS.	TYPE	REMARKS
Love's old sweet song	d1-f2 (a♭2)	e♭1-e♭2	All voices	Sustained, tuneful encore song. (GS)

TITLE	COMP.	TESS.	TYPE	REMARKS
The Kerry dance	c1-g2	f1-d2	All voices	Animated, rhythmical. Demands facile articulation. In folk vein. Has attained the popularity of a folk song. (gen. av.)

DOUGLAS MOORE

TITLE	COMP.	TESS.	TYPE	REMARKS
Adam was my grandfather	c1-f♯2	e♭1-d♭2	Men's voices	Vigorous, spirited, somewhat humorous. (GAL)
Sigh no more, ladies	d1-e2	e1-c2	Medium voices	Sustained. (BH)
Three Sonnets of John Donne	d1-a2	f1-f2		Three songs for high voice. (GS)

CHARLES NAGINSKI

Among the young American composers, few have shown such remarkable promise, especially in the field of vocal music, as Charles Naginski, who died so tragically at the very outset of his career. The few songs listed below are unfortunately almost all of the vocal music he had completed before his death, except the "Nonsense Alphabet" for soprano and pianoforte (later orchestrated) and another three or four songs as yet unpublished. It is hoped that his songs will find as wide a public as, in the opinion of this writer, they seem to deserve.

Edition: G. Schirmer

TITLE	COMP.	TESS.	TYPE	REMARKS
Look down, fair moon	d1-e2	g1-d2	Not too suitable for very light, high voices	Slow, very sustained, somber. Poem by W. Whitman.
Mia Carlotta	c1-f2	d1-d2	Men's voices	A comic dialect song. Demands very facile articulation.
Night song at Amalfi	d1-e♭2	f♯1-d2	Women's voices	Slow, somewhat declamatory and subdued. Poem by S. Teasdale.

TITLE	COMP.	TESS.	TYPE	REMARKS
Richard Cory	a-e2 (g2)	c1-c2	Not suitable for light, high voices	A somber, satirical narrative song. Demands facile articulation.
The pasture	bb-eb1	eb1-bb2	Most suitable for women's voices	Light, very delicate. Poem by R. Frost.
The ship starting	bb-bb1	same	Medium or low voices	Sustained, somewhat declamatory. Demands an accomplished pianist. Poem by W. Whitman.
Under the harvest moon	d1-e2	e1-b1	Most suitable for medium or high voices	Sustained, rather delicate. Poem by C. Sandburg.

ETHELBERT NEVIN

At twilight	d1-e2	same	All voices	Sustained, subdued, effective. (GS)
The rosary	d1-e2	e1-bb1	All voices	Sustained, effective. At one time very popular. (GS)

JOHN JACOB NILES

Gambling Songs

Five songs most suitable for <u>men's voices</u>. Published by G. Schirmer.

(1) Gambler, don't lose your place	c1-f2	f1-d2		Sustained.
(2) Gambler's song of the Big Sandy River	c#1-f#2	f#1-c#2		Rapid, demands facile articulation.
(3) The gambler's lament	d1-g2	g1-d2		Slow, sustained, somber.
(4) The gambler's wife	db1-gb2	gb1-eb2		Slow, sustained, gentle.
(5) The rovin' gambler	db1-gb2	gb1-eb2		Spirited, bold. Strophic.

517

TITLE	COMP.	TESS.	TYPE	REMARKS
Go 'way from my window	c1-g2	f1-eb2	All voices	Sustained, gentle. In folk vein. Strophic, with refrain. (GS)
I wonder as I wander	bb-d2	d1-bb1 (L)	All voices	Sustained, gentle, graceful. A setting of a well-known Appalachian carol. (GS)
The blue madonna	g1-bb2	g1-eb2	High voices	Sustained vocal line. Dancelike, in imitation to the Spanish pavane. Narrative text by the composer. (GS)

PAUL NORDOFF

TITLE	COMP.	TESS.	TYPE	REMARKS
Dirge for the nameless	bb-gb2	eb1-eb2	Not suitable for light, high voices	Very slow, sustained. A song with contrasting moods. Demands a good command of high pp and an accomplished pianist. (AMP)
Embroidery for a faithless friend	c1-a2	f#1-e2	Most suitable for high voices	Fast. Vocal line is sustained. Accompaniment has animated passages. Effective ending. (AMP)
Fair Anette's song	c1-f2	f1-f2	Soprano	Animated, delicate. (AMP)
Lacrima Christi	c1-f2	same	All voices, except bass	Very slow and sustained. Uses ostinato figures. In parts demands dramatic intensity and a good command of high pp. Religious text by M. Mannes. (Mercury)

TITLE	COMP.	TESS.	TYPE	REMARKS
Serenade	c♯1-f♯2	f♯1-f♯2	Soprano	Delicate, demands a good command of high pp. (AMP)
There shall be more joy	c♯1-f♯2	f♯1-e♭2	High voices	Animated. Demands some flexibility and an accomplished pianist. (SCH)
White nocturne	e1-e2	same	All voices	Sustained, very subdued. (OD)
Willow river	d1-g2	e1-e2	All voices	Sustained, somewhat graceful. (SCH)

HORATIO PARKER

Excerpts from HORA NOVISSIMA, an Oratorio (Latin text)

(Score published by Novello)

TITLE	COMP.	TESS.	TYPE	REMARKS
Gens duce splendida	c1-e2	c1-c2	Alto or mezzo-soprano	Vigorous. In parts demands considerable dramatic intensity.
O bona patria	e♭1-a♭2	a♭1-f2	Dramatic soprano (lyric soprano)	Sustained. In parts demands considerable dramatic intensity as well as a command of high pp.
Spe modo vivitur	A-e1	e-d1	Bass or baritone	Sustained, vigorous. In parts demands considerable dramatic intensity.
Urbis Syon aurea	d-a1	g-e1	Tenor	Very sustained. In parts demands considerable dramatic intensity.

See also "Six Old English Songs" (J. Church Co.), among them the well-known "The lark now leaves his wat'ry nest."

C. HUBERT PARRY (Br.)

TITLE	COMP.	TESS.	TYPE	REMARKS
A Welsh lullaby	f1-f2	a1-f2	Most suitable for soprano	Sustained, delicate. (NOV)

TITLE	COMP.	TESS.	TYPE	REMARKS
Love is a bauble	c1-eb2	eb1-bb2	Medium or low voices	Rapid, vigorous, humorous. Demands some flexibility. (NOV)
Under the greenwood tree	c1-e2	e1-d2	Most suitable for men's voices	Spirited, vigorous. (NOV)
Why so pale and wan	c#1-e2	d1-d2	All voices, except a very light soprano	Animated, humorous. (NOV)

VINCENT PERSICHETTI

TITLE	COMP.	TESS.	TYPE	REMARKS
Brigid's song	c1-d2	d1-bb1	All except light, high voices	Sustained in 5/4 meter. Somber. Poem by J. Joyce. (EV)
Harmonium	c1-c3	e1-g2	Soprano, except very light, high voices	A cycle of twenty songs to poems by W. Stevens. Vocally demanding. Demands an excellent pianist. One hour performance. (EV)
Noise of waters	c#1-e2	e1-d2	All voices	Sustained vocal line. Poem by J. Joyce. (EV) See "All day I hear" by S. Kagen.
The grass	db1-f2	e1-d2	All voices, except bass	Sustained, gentle. Demands some flexibility. Poem by E. Dickinson. (EV)
Unquiet heart	d#1-f#2	f#1-e2	High or medium voices	Slow, sustained. Demands a good command of high pp. Poem by J. Joyce. (EV) See "Sleep now" by S. Barber and S. Kagen.
When the hills do	d1-d2	e1-d2	All voices	Slow, sustained. Poem by E. Dickinson. (EV)

TITLE	COMP.	TESS.	TYPE	REMARKS

NORMAN PETERKIN (Br.)

TITLE	COMP.	TESS.	TYPE	REMARKS
I heard a piper piping	g1-f2	g1-d2	All voices	Somber, subdued. See Arnold Bax. (OX)
So, we'll go no more a-roving	db1-d2	same	Medium or low voices	Sustained, rather subdued. (OX)
The fiddler	f1-f2 (ab2)	f1-eb2	High or medium voices	Animated, rhythmical. (OX)
The galliass	c1-e2	e1-b1	Medium or low voices	Slow, somewhat dramatic. Interpretatively not easy. (OX)
The garden of bamboos	eb1-f2	f1-eb2	Women's voices, except a heavy alto	Delicate, sustained. (OX)

EDWARD PURCELL (Br.)

TITLE	COMP.	TESS.	TYPE	REMARKS
Passing by	f#1-f#2 (H)	a1-e2	Most suitable for men's voices	Sustained, graceful. (OD) This pleasant, tuneful little song is, curiously enough, often attributed to the pen of the great Henry Purcell and is even sometimes programmed as such.

ROGER QUILTER (Br.)

The songs of Roger Quilter have attained a wide popularity in the United States as well as in Great Britain. Effective, well written and possessing excellent texts, they need little introduction.

TITLE	COMP.	TESS.	TYPE	REMARKS
Blow, blow, thou winter wind	e1-g#2	g#1-e2	All voices, except a very light soprano	Vigorous. Poem by W. Shakespeare. (BH)

TITLE	COMP.	TESS.	TYPE	REMARKS
Come away, death	e1-g2	g1-e2	All voices	Sustained. Poem by W. Shakespeare. (BH)
Dream valley (from "Three Songs of William Blake")	eb1-gb2	gb1-eb2	Most suitable for high or medium voices	Sustained, delicate. (WR)
Fair house of joy (from "Seven Elizabethan Lyrics")	f1-ab2	ab1-f2 (H)	All voices, except bass or alto	Sustained. Has effective climaxes. (BH)
Fill a glass with golden wine	e1-g#2	g#1-e2 (H)	Most suitable for men's voices	Very vigorous. (BH)
Go lovely rose	f1-gb2	gb1-eb2 (H)	All voices	Sustained. See J. A. Carpenter. (CHAP)
It was a lover and his lass	f1-ab2	ab1-f2	All voices	Animated, light. Poem by W. Shakespeare. (BH)
I will go with my father a-ploughing	d1-f2 (g2)	g1-d2 (H)	Men's voices	Not slow. In folk vein. (Elkin)
Love's philosophy	d1-a2	a1-f2 (H)	All voices	Very animated, effective. Demands an accomplished pianist. (BH)
Music when soft voices die	f1-g2	bb1-f2 (H)	All voices	Sustained. (WR)
Now sleeps the crimson petal	eb1-gb2	gb1-eb2 (H)	All voices	Slow, very delicate. (BH)
O mistress mine	d1-g2	g1-e2	All voices	Animated, light. (BH)
Song of the blackbird	e1-g2	g1-e2 (H)	Not suitable for very low voices	Very animated, effective. See "The Nightingale has a Lyre of Gold" by Whelpley. (BH)
The fuchsia tree	c#1-g#2	g#1-e2	All voices	Graceful. (WR)
To daisies	eb1-ab2	ab1-f2	Not too suitable for very low voices	Sustained, delicate. (BH)

TITLE	COMP.	TESS.	TYPE	REMARKS

JAMES H. ROGERS

TITLE	COMP.	TESS.	TYPE	REMARKS
At parting	c#1-f#2	g#1-d#2	All voices	A sustained, graceful encore song. (GS)
The star	c1-ab2	ab1-f2 (H)	All voices	Sustained, effective. (GS)

LANDON RONALD (Br.)

TITLE	COMP.	TESS.	TYPE	REMARKS
Down in the forest (A Cycle of Life)	e1-a2	g1-f#2	All voices	Sustained, for the most part subdued, effective. (RIC)
O lovely night	eb1-g2 (bb2)	f1-eb2	All voices	Sustained, effective. (Enoch)

NED ROREM

TITLE	COMP.	TESS.	TYPE	REMARKS
A Christmas carol	c1-f2	e1-d2	High and medium voices	Sustained, generally subdued and plaintive. Poem is dated c. 1500. (EV)
Alleluia	b-g#2	e1-g2	Soprano, except a light, high voice	Animated, vigorous. Has some florid passages. Effective ending. (Hargail)
Cycle of Holy Songs	b-a2	f1-f2		A cycle of four songs for <u>high voices</u> with texts from Psalms 134, 142, 148 and 150. (SMP)
Early in the morning	d1-f2	f1-d2	All voices	Sustained, folklike. (Henmar)
Echo's song	eb1-f2	f1-eb2	All voices	Sustained, somewhat slow. (BH)
Epitaph	d1-f2	same	All voices	Very slow, sustained. Short. Recitative style. Fifteenth century text. (EV)

TITLE	COMP.	TESS.	TYPE	REMARKS
Flight for Heaven	F#-eb1	B-b	Bass	A cycle of ten short songs. Text by R. Herrick. (Mercury)
Rain in spring	a-eb2	d1-d2	All voices	Very sustained, gentle. (BH)
Requiem	c#1-f#2	d1-d2	Medium voices	Slow, sustained, generally subdued. Somewhat plaintive melody. Poem by R. L. Stevenson. (PI)
Spring	c1-a2	e1-f#2	High voices	Animated, light. Poem by G. Hopkins. (BH)
Spring and fall	d#1-f#2	e1-e2	All voices	Sustained. Music follows speech rhythm. Demands facile articulation. (Music Press)
The call	d1-e2	same	All voices	Very slow, sustained. Short. In parts declamatory. Fifteenth century text. (EV)
The lordly Hudson	db1-g2	f1-f2	All voices	Animated. Demands facile articulation and some characterization. Impressive ending. (Mercury)
The nightingale	c#1-f#2	e1-e2	High or medium voices	Fast, delicate, light. Demands flexibility and facile articulation. (BH)
The silver swan	e1-c3	g1-a2	Soprano	Slow, sustained. Has florid passages. Demands a good command of high p. (PI)
What if some little pain	c1-f2	f1-eb2	All voices, except bass	Slow, sustained. (Hargail)

TITLE	COMP.	TESS.	TYPE	REMARKS

ALEC ROWLEY (Br.)

A Cycle of Three Mystical Songs

<u>High voice</u>. Published by Boosey & Hawkes.

TITLE	COMP.	TESS.	TYPE	REMARKS
(1) Three jolly shepherds	d1-g2	f♯1-f♯2		Lively, rhythmic, folk-like. Traditional text.
(2) The prophecy	e1-g2	f♯1-f2		Sustained. Traditional text.
(3) The birthday	e1-a2	e1-g2		Sustained. The last half is a strong, somewhat vigorous Allelujah section.
Pretty Betty	d♭1-e♭2	same	Men's voices	Sustained, rather delicate. (OX)
The toll-gate house	c1-e2	e1-b1	All voices	Very animated, for the most part very subdued. (WR)

EDMUND RUBBRA (Br.)

TITLE	COMP.	TESS.	TYPE	REMARKS
A Duan of Barra	d1-g2	e1-e2	All except heavy, dark voices	Animated and delicate. Demands lightness of tone and facile articulation. Religious text. (Lengnick)
A widow bird sat mourning	e1-g2	g1-e2	Most suitable for high voices	Slow, sustained, subdued. (OX)
Amoretti	c1-a♭2	f1-f2		A cycle of five songs for <u>high voice</u> and string quartet or piano. The poems are sonnets by Edmund Spenser. (Joseph Williams)
In dark weather	b-g2 (b2)	e1-e2	Not suitable for very light, high voices	Slow, somber. Demands in parts considerable dramatic intensity, especially in the final climax. (AUG)

TITLE	COMP.	TESS.	TYPE	REMARKS
The night	b-e2	c#1-d#2	Medium or low voices	Sustained, quiet. (OX)

Three Psalms

Three songs for <u>contralto or bass.</u> (Lengnick)

TITLE	COMP.	TESS.	TYPE	REMARKS
(1) Psalm VI	f#-eb2	c1-d2		Slow, sustained. Rhythmically intricate; the melody follows speech rhythm. In parts demands some dramatic intensity. Demands facile articulation.
(2) Psalm XXIII	a-d2	b-c2		Sustained. Rhythmically intricate; the melody follows speech rhythm. Demands facile articulation and flexibility.
(3) Psalm CL	bb-f2	d1-d2		Fast and vigorous. Has some florid passages. Demands considerable flexibility. Imposing ending.

WALTER M. RUMMEL

TITLE	COMP.	TESS.	TYPE	REMARKS
Ecstacy	gb1-ab2	ab1-f2 (H)	All voices	Very animated, the vocal line is sustained. Effective. (GS)

JOHN SACCO

TITLE	COMP.	TESS.	TYPE	REMARKS
Brother Will, brother John	c1-f2	f1-eb2	All voices	Animated, in parts demands facile articulation. Humorous, rhythmic. (GS)
Mexican serenade	f1-gb2	a1-f2	All voices	Animated, light, humorous. Demands facile articulation. (BMC)

TITLE	COMP.	TESS.	TYPE	REMARKS
Never the nightingale	e♭1-g♭2	f1-f2	High voices	Sustained. Demands in parts considerable dramatic intensity. (GAL)
Rapunzel	f♯1-b♭2	b♭1-f♯2	Women's voices	Animated, effective. The vocal line is sustained. (GS)
Strictly germ-proof	d1-f2	a1-e2	High or medium voices	Animated, light. Humorous. Demands facile articulation and some flexibility. (GS)

MARY TURNER SALTER

TITLE	COMP.	TESS.	TYPE	REMARKS
Cry of Rachel	c1-a♭2	f1-f2	Women's voices, except a very light soprano	Animated, dramatic, effective. (GS)

WILFRED SANDERSON (Br.)

TITLE	COMP.	TESS.	TYPE	REMARKS
Captain Mac'	A-f♯1	d-d1	Men's voices	Spirited, effective, humorous ballad. (BH)

WILLIAM SCHUMAN

TITLE	COMP.	TESS.	TYPE	REMARKS
Holiday song	c1-f2	e1-e2	All voices	Animated, gay. Demands some flexibility. (GS)
Orpheus with his lute	c1-f♯2	f1-e2	High or medium voices	Sustained, subdued. See Vaughan Williams. (GS)

ALICIA ANN SCOTT (PERRENOT)

TITLE	COMP.	TESS.	TYPE	REMARKS
Think on me	f♯1-g2	a1-d2 (H)	All voices	Very sustained encore song. (GAL)

527

CYRIL SCOTT (Br.)

Cyril Scott, a prolific British composer, has written a great number of songs, many of which have attained wide popularity. His harmonic scheme is mildly influenced by Debussy, but his vocal line is always conventionally singable and effective.

TITLE	COMP.	TESS.	TYPE	REMARKS
Blackbird's song	d1-g2	f1-f2	Most suitable for high voices	Animated, effective. Demands some flexibility. (Elkin)
Lullaby	d1-f2 (g#2)	f1-d2 (H)	Women's voices	Very sustained, graceful, very subdued. (GAL)
Night song	c1-f2	eb1-d2	All voices	Delicate, not fast. (Elkin)
Rain	d#1-f#2	f#1-d2 (H)	Not too suitable for very low voices	Very delicate. Demands a good command of high pp. (Elkin)
Songs without words (1) Tranquillity (2) Pastorale	d1-c3	f1-f2	Soprano	Two vocalises for soprano. (RIC)
Time of day	e1-g2	a1-e2 (H)	Men's voices	Rapid, rhythmical. Demands some flexibility and facile articulation. (Elkin)
The sands of Dee	eb1-g2	eb1-eb2 (H)	All voices	A short narrative song. (Elkin)
The unforeseen	d1-a2	f#1-e2 (H)	All voices	Sustained. Has an effective climax. (Elkin)
Water-lilies	eb1-g2	f1-d2 (H)	All voices	Sustained, delicate. Demands a good command of high pp. (Elkin)

MARTIN SHAW (Br.)

TITLE	COMP.	TESS.	TYPE	REMARKS
Cuckoo		f1-f2	same	All voices	Light, delicate. (CUR)
Down by the Salley gardens	b-d1	e1-b1	Most suitable for men's voices	Sustained, subdued and delicate. See Rebecca Clarke, and the

TITLE	COMP.	TESS.	TYPE	REMARKS
				Hughes arrange-ment of an old Irish folk tune with these words added. (CUR)
Heffle cuckoo fair	e♭1-e2 (a2)	same	Not suit-able for very low voices	Animated, light. Demands facile articulation. (CUR)
Lullaby	c1-d2	e1-c2	Women's voices	Sustained, deli-cate. See Cyril Scott. (CUR)
O Falmouth is a fine town	c1-e2	e1-c♯2	Most suit-able for baritone	Animated. De-mands facile ar-ticulation. (CUR)
Over the sea	d1-f2	f1-d2	All voices	Sustained. (CUR)
Song of the palanquin bearers	e1-f2	b1-e2	Most suit-able for high, light voices	Light and ani-mated. Demands good sense of rhythm and facile articulation. (CUR)
The cavalier's escape	B♭-d1 (f1)	d-d1	Baritone	A spirited, vigorous ballad. Demands facile articulation. (CUR)
The land of heart's desire	c1-e2 (g2)	e1-b1	Most suit-able for medium or low voices	Sustained, subdued, somewhat declama-tory. (CUR)

OLEY SPEAKS

TITLE	COMP.	TESS.	TYPE	REMARKS
Morning	c♯1-g2 (a2)	a1-f2 (H)	All voices	A slow introduction and an animated, ef-fective main section. (GS)
On the road to Mandalay	B♭-e♭1 (f1)	e♭-e♭1	Baritone	A vigorous, spir-ited ballad. (GS)
Sylvia	d1-g2	d1-d2 (H)	All voices	Sustained, effective. (GS)

ROBERT STARER

TITLE	COMP.	TESS.	TYPE	REMARKS
Advice to a girl	d1-g2	f1-e♭2	High voices	Animated. Demands some flexibility. Poem by S. Teasdale. (Leeds)

TITLE	COMP.	TESS.	TYPE	REMARKS
Dew	e1-ab2	e1-e2	Soprano	Sustained, generally subdued. Poem by S. Teasdale. (Leeds)
'my sweet old etcetera'	A-eb1	Bb-c1	Baritone	Spirited, brisk. In parts declamatory. Humorous. Text by e. e. cummings. (Leeds)

SIR ARTHUR SULLIVAN (Br.)

TITLE	COMP.	TESS.	TYPE	REMARKS
Orpheus with his lute	d1-g2 (bb2)	f1-f2	All voices	Spirited. Demands occasionally a good command of high pp. (gen. av.)
Sigh no more, ladies	e1-g2 (a2)	f#1-e2	Not too suitable for very low voices	Not fast. Demands some flexibility. (gen. av.)
The lost chord	eb1-ab2	g1-db2	Not too suitable for very light, high voices	Sustained. Has a very effective final climax. (gen. av.)
The willow song	b-e2	b-b1	Most suitable for alto	Slow, subdued. (gen. av.)

HOWARD SWANSON

TITLE	COMP.	TESS.	TYPE	REMARKS
A death song	bb-eb2	c1-bb1	Low voices	Subdued, in the manner of a Negro spiritual. The text by P. L. Dunbar can be sung either in dialect or not. (Leeds)
Cahoots	bb-db2	same	Baritone or bass	A declamatory character song set as blues. Poem by C. Sandburg. (Weintraub)

TITLE	COMP.	TESS.	TYPE	REMARKS
Four Preludes	eb1-ab2	f1-eb2		A cycle of four songs for <u>high voices</u> to poems by T. S. Eliot. (Weintraub)
In the time of silver rain	d1-a2	f1-g2	Light, high voices	Sustained, graceful. Demands a good command of high pp. Poem by L. Hughes. (Weintraub)
Joy	bb-eb2	eb1-eb2	Medium or low voices	Rapid, demands facile articulation. Effective climax. Demands an excellent pianist. Poem by L. Hughes. (Leeds)
Night song	d1-g2	f1-g2	High voices	Sustained, generally delicate. Uses some jazz idiom. Poem by L. Hughes. (Weintraub)
Pierrot	a#-d2	b-c#1	Low voices	Fast, animated. Demands facile articulation. Demands an accomplished pianist. Effective climax. Poem by L. Hughes. (Weintraub)
Songs for Patricia	e1-bb2	g1-f2		A cycle most suitable for <u>light, high voices</u>. Demands an accomplished pianist. Poems by L. Rosten. (Weintraub)
The junk man	e1-g2	f1-eb2	All voices	Mainly declamatory. subdued ending. Demands an accomplished pianist. Narrative text by C. Sandburg. (Weintraub)
The Negro speaks of rivers	g-d2	d1-bb1	Low voices	Grave, heavy, somber, in parts demands

TITLE	COMP.	TESS.	TYPE	REMARKS
				considerable dramatic intensity. Demands an accomplished pianist. Poem by L. Hughes. (Leeds)
The valley	d♭1-f♭2	g♭1-e♭2	All voices	Sustained, subdued, somewhat meditative. Poem by E. Markham. (Leeds)

COLIN TAYLOR (Br.)

TITLE	COMP.	TESS.	TYPE	REMARKS
The windmill	d1-c2	same	All voices	A gently humorous character song. (OX)

DEEMS TAYLOR

TITLE	COMP.	TESS.	TYPE	REMARKS
A song for lovers	d1-f2	g1-e♭2	All voices	Sustained, very subdued. (CF)
Captain Stratton's fancy	B♭-f1	d-d1	Bass or baritone	Vigorous, spirited, humorous. (CF)
The rivals	e1-g2	g1-e2	Not too suitable for very low voices	Animated, light. (CF)

RANDALL THOMPSON

TITLE	COMP.	TESS.	TYPE	REMARKS
My master hath a garden	e♭1-e♭2	f1-c2	All voices	Sustained, graceful. (ECS)
Velvet shoes	c1-e2	f1-c2	All voices	Delicate. Demands a good sense of rhythm and an accomplished pianist. (ECS)

DAVID CLEGHORN THOMSON (Br.)

TITLE	COMP.	TESS.	TYPE	REMARKS
Epitaph	b-d2	d1-d2	Most suit-	Sustained, sub-

TITLE	COMP.	TESS.	TYPE	REMARKS
			able for medium or low voices	dued. See Ivor Gurney. (Cramer)
The birds	c1(a)-e2	e1-c2	Not too suitable for very light, high voices	Sustained. In the manner of a chorale. See Alec Rowley, B. Britten. (Cramer)
The knight of Bethlehem	eb1-g2	eb1-c2	All voices	Sustained. Interpretatively not easy. (NOV)

VIRGIL THOMSON

Dirge	d1-f2	d1-d2	Medium or low voices	Sustained, rhythmically strict. Somber. (GS)

Five Songs from William Blake

A cycle of five songs for <u>baritone.</u> Demands an accomplished pianist. Published by Ricordi.

(1) The divine image	Ab-eb1	c-d1		Sustained. Has effective climaxes.
(2) Tiger! Tiger!	A-g1	e-e1		Pompous, declamatory. Effective ending. Interpretatively not easy.
(3) The land of dreams	c-f#1	e-eb1		Sustained. Demands some characterization and a good command of high pp.
(4) The little black boy	Ab-f1	c-d1		Slow, sustained. Some parts have folk-like simplicity.
(5) And did those feet	A-g1	c#-e1		Stately; in parts has dramatic intensity.
Four Songs to Poems of Thomas Campion	c#1-ab2	eb1-eb2		A group of four songs for <u>men's voices, except bass.</u> (RIC)

TITLE	COMP.	TESS.	TYPE	REMARKS
If thou a reason dost desire to know	c1-f2	d1-e2	Most suitable for men's voices	Slow, recitative-like. (SMP)
John Peel	B-e1	e-e1	Baritone	Stately, marked. Some passages are imitative of the hunting horn. Abounds in triplet figures. (SMP)
Preciosilla	eb1-a2	f1-f♯2	High voices	A long recitative section followed by an "aria." Nonsense rhymes by G. Stein. (GS)
Shakespeare Songs	d1-a2	f1-f2		A cycle of five songs for <u>all voices, except bass</u>. (SMP)
Stabat Mater	d1-bb2	g1-f2		A song for <u>high soprano</u> and string quartet; piano reduction available. Sustained. French and English text. (BH)
The bell doth toll	b-e1	d1-d2	Medium or low voices	Sustained for the most part. Accompaniment consists entirely of slow-moving chords. (SMP)
Tres estampas de niñez	d1-g2	e1-f2	High or medium voices	A little cycle of three songs, "Three Sketches of Childhood," to texts by Reyna Rivas. Has Spanish rhythms. (SMP)

MICHAEL TIPPETT (Br.)

Boyhood's end	c1-a2	f1-g2	Tenor	A solo cantata which is not vocally nor musically easy. Has some long, florid passages. Demands an accomplished pianist. (SCH)

The Heart's Assurance

A cycle for <u>high voice</u> to poems by S. Keyes and A. Lewis. Demands a highly accomplished pianist. (SCH)

TITLE	COMP.	TESS.	TYPE	REMARKS
(1) Song	d1-a2	f♯1-f♯2		Animated. Sustained vocal line. Demands some flexibility.
(2) The heart's assurance	c1-a♭2	f♯1-f♯2		Animated, joyous. Has some florid passages. Demands flexibility.
(3) Compassion	c1-b2 (a2)	f♯1-e2		Slow, very sustained. In parts demands some dramatic intensity and flexibility.
(4) The dancer	d1-a2	e1-f2		Fast, has some florid passages. Demands flexibility. Interpretatively not easy.
(5) Remember your lovers	d♭1-g2	f1-f2		Sustained, demands flexibility and a good command of high p.

FRANCIS TOYE (Br.)

TITLE	COMP.	TESS.	TYPE	REMARKS
The inn	B♭-e1	d-d1	Baritone	Very animated, rhythmical. Interpretatively not easy. Has a somber, sustained final section. Demands an accomplished pianist. (CUR)

CHARLES VALE (Br.)

TITLE	COMP.	TESS.	TYPE	REMARKS
Litany to the Holy Spirit	a♭-f2	c1-e♭2	Medium voices	Sustained. Based on 5/4 ostinato bass. Somewhat declamatory in parts. Text by R. Herrick. Illustrative setting. (OX)

RALPH VAUGHAN WILLIAMS (Br.)
(1872–1958)

In his songs Vaughan Williams, one of the foremost contemporary British composers, attempts to fuse the melodic and rhythmic patterns of the folk songs of the British Isles with contemporary harmonic and poetic material. Since most of his songs do not demand an extensive range, are nearly impeccable in prosody, and are excellently written for the voice, they present hardly any vocal problems. Some of his songs, however, like the admirable "Water Mill" may prove interpretatively somewhat complex, because of the purely descriptive and rather impersonal character of the text.

Vaughan Williams has made admirable arrangements of a great number of English folk songs, most of which are published in the Novello collection of English folk songs. The five English folk songs containing the well-known arrangement of "Rolling in the Dew" are published by Oxford University Press.

TITLE	COMP.	TESS.	TYPE	REMARKS
How can the tree but whither	a-e♭2	c1-e♭2	Medium or low voices	Sustained. (OX)
In the spring	c♯1-e2	e1-d2	All voices	Sustained. (OX)
Let us now praise famous men	e1-g♯2	g♯1-e2	All voices	Sustained, majestic. Imposing ending. Sacred text from Ecclesiasticus XLIV. (CUR)
Linden Lea	e1-f♯2	a1-e2 (H)	All voices	Sustained. In folk vein. (BH)
On Wenlock Edge	d1-a2	f1-f2	Tenor	A cycle of six songs for tenor, piano, and string quartet (ad lib.). Poems by A. E. Housman. (BH)
The House of Life	a-f2	d1-d2		A cycle of six songs for medium or low voices to sonnets by D. G. Rossetti. Demands an accomplished pianist. "Silent Noon," mentioned here, is the best-known of the songs in this work. (Ashdown)

536

TITLE	COMP.	TESS.	TYPE	REMARKS
Silent noon	c1-eb2	g1-d2	All voices	Slow and sustained. See Wilfred Sanderson. (Homeyer)

Seumas O'Sullivan Poems

TITLE	COMP.	TESS.	TYPE	REMARKS
(1) The twilight people	c1-f2	c1-c2	Medium or low voices	Subdued, somewhat declamatory. (OX)
(2) A piper	c1-eb2	d1-d2	Medium or low voices	Rapid and light. Demands facile articulation. See M. Head and A. Benjamin. (OX)

Shakespeare Poems

TITLE	COMP.	TESS.	TYPE	REMARKS
(1) Take, O take those lips away	b-d2	d1-d2	All voices	Slow and sustained. (OX)
(2) When icicles hang by the wall	eb1-f2	f1-eb2	All voices	Animated, light, graceful. Demands a good command of high pp. (OX)
(3) Orpheus with his lute	d1-g2	g1-f#2	All voices	Very sustained, subdued. Perhaps one of the most beautiful contemporary settings of this poem. (OX, Keith Prowse)

Fredegond Shove Poems

TITLE	COMP.	TESS.	TYPE	REMARKS
(1) Motion and stillness	c1-d2	ab1-c2	All voices	Slow, very sustained, subdued. (OX)
(2) Four nights	cb1-gb2	eb1-eb2	All voices	Sustained, with an animated middle section. (OX)
(3) The new ghost	d1-f2	f1-d2	All voices	A sustained narrative. Has some declamatory passages. Demands flexibility and an accomplished pianist. (OX)

TITLE	COMP.	TESS.	TYPE	REMARKS
(4) The water mill	c1-d2	e1-c2	All voices	A descriptive, tranquil narrative song. Demands facile articulation and an accomplished pianist. (OX)

Walt Whitman Poems

TITLE	COMP.	TESS.	TYPE	REMARKS
(1) Nocturne	b-f2	f♯1-d2	Not suitable for light, high voices	Not fast, somewhat declamatory, very subdued. Demands a good command of high pp. Interpretatively not easy. See Ernst Bacon's "This is thy hour, o soul." (OX)
(2) A clear midnight	e1-f2	g1-d2	All voices	Slow, very sustained, subdued. (OX)
(3) Joy, shipmate, joy!	e1-f2	g1-e2	Not suitable for light voices	Animated, vigorous. (OX)

Five Mystical Songs

A cycle of five songs to poems by George Herbert, set to music for baritone, chorus (ad. lib.), and orchestra. Piano reduction is available. Published by Stainer & Bell.

TITLE	COMP.	TESS.	REMARKS
(1) Easter	e♭1-f2	g1-e♭2	Sustained, majestic. Possibly the best solo setting on the Easter subject. Demands an excellent pianist.
(2) I got me flowers	d♭1-e♭2	e♭1-e♭2	Sustained. In parts slightly declamatory. Has frequent changes in meter.
(3) Love bade me welcome	d1-f2	e1-d2	Sustained. Narrative. A song of varied moods and tempi.

TITLE	COMP.	TESS.	TYPE	REMARKS
(4) The call	eb1-f2	f1-db2		Slow and very sustained. Generally subdued.
(5) Antiphon	eb1-f2 (g2)	f♯1-d2		Spirited, vigorous, bold. Ostinato bass. Imposing ending.

Songs of Travel

Selections from the work published in two parts by Boosey & Hawkes. Text by R. L. Stevenson.

TITLE	COMP.	TESS.	TYPE	REMARKS
Bright is the ring of words	db1-gb2	f1-d2 (H)	All voices, except a very light soprano	Very sustained.
The roadside fire	eb1-ab2	ab1-f2 (H)	Most suitable for men's voices	Animated, delicate. The vocal line is sustained.
The vagabond	d♯1-g2	e1-e2 (H)	Men's voices	Vigorous, rhythmical.

The Pilgrim's Progress

Solo excerpts from the opera based on Paul Bunyan's famous work, "The Pilgrim's Progress." Arranged for concert performance and therefore differ considerably from the opera score. Published by Oxford University Press.

TITLE	COMP.	TESS.	TYPE	REMARKS
(1) Watchful's song	c♯1-e2	d1-e2	Medium voices	Slow, sustained, somewhat subdued. Has some unaccompanied sections.
(2) The song of the pilgrims	d1-e2	same	Medium voices	Spirited, vigorous.
(3) The pilgrim's psalm	d1-f2	f1-e2	Medium voices	Spirited, vigorous. Declamatory in parts.
(4) The song of the leaves of life and the water of life	d1-e2	e1-e2	High or medium voices	Sustained, generally subdued. Plaintive.
(5) The song of Vanity Fair	c1-fb2	c1-eb2	Most suitable for high voices	Animated, lively. Demands facile articulation, flexibility. Interpretatively not easy.

TITLE	COMP.	TESS.	TYPE	REMARKS
(6) The wood-cutter's song	d1-e2	d1-d2	High or medium voices	Sustained, somewhat subdued. Plaintive.
(7) The bird's song	db1-f2	eb1-eb2	High or medium voices	Slow and sustained. Generally subdued. Rhythmically varied and complex.

See also: Along the Field, eight songs for <u>high voice</u> and violin.
Poems by A. E. Housman. (OX)
Four Hymns for <u>tenor</u> and viola. Poems by Taylor, Watts, Crashaw and Bridges. (BH)
Ten Blake Songs for <u>high voice</u> and oboe. (OX)

BERNARD WAGENAAR

From a very little sphinx	c1-f2	same	Most suitable for women's voices	Seven short, amusing poems by Edna St. Vincent Millay. Interpretatively not easy. (GS)

Three Songs from the Chinese

Three songs for <u>soprano</u>, flute, harp and piano. (Kalmus)

(1) The three princesses	c1-a2	e1-f2		A song of various moods and tempi. Somewhat narrative.
(2) The mystic flute	e1-b2	g#1-f#2		Slow, sustained. Plaintive.
(3) On the water	d1-a#2	f1-f2		Very slow, sustained. For the most part subdued.

ROBERT WARD

As I watched the ploughman ploughing	c1-a2	e1-f2	Not suitable for light, high voices	Sustained, in parts declamatory and somewhat dramatic. Poem by W. Whitman. (PI)

TITLE	COMP.	TESS.	TYPE	REMARKS
Rain has fallen all the day	c1-a2	e1-e2	High voices	Sustained. Has an impressive climax. Short. Poem by J. Joyce. (PI) See Barber.
Sorrow of Mydath	e1-a2	e1-g2	High voices	Slow and very sustained. Somber. In parts demands considerable dramatic intensity. Demands an accomplished pianist. (PI) See Griffes.
Vanished	d1-g2	e1-c2	High voices	Sustained. In parts subdued. Short. Poem by E. Dickinson. (PI)

PETER WARLOCK (Philip Heseltine) (Br.)

In his songs Peter Warlock seems to attempt a fusion of Elizabethan poetry, English folk melos and a contemporary harmonic idiom. Well written for the voice, impeccable in prosody, his settings of old English poems have become very popular since his death. They present no particular performance problem except that of style, which involves the successful blending of the three elements mentioned above, and which may not always be instantly achieved.

As ever I saw	d♭1-g♭2	f1-d♭2	Most suitable for men's voices	Spirited. The melody of the first verse is inverted (backwards) in the second verse. (WR)
Captain Stratton's fancy	c-f1	c-d1	Men's voices	Vigorous, spirited ballad. See version by Deems Taylor. (AUG)
Consider	c1-g2	f1-d2	Not too suitable for very light, high voices	Very animated, effective. Demands an accomplished pianist. (OX)
Cradle song	d1-f2	f1-d2	Women's voices	Delicate, sustained. (OX)

TITLE	COMP.	TESS.	TYPE	REMARKS
Good ale	c-f1	d-d1	Men's voices	A rapid, rollicking drinking song, very effective. Demands facile articulation and a good sense of rhythm. (AUG)
In an arbour green	d1-g2	e1-e2	Men's voices	Fast and gay. Demands an accomplished pianist. (Paterson)
Jillian of Berry	d1-f2	f1-d2	Most suitable for men's voices	A short jolly song. Rhythmically difficult. Demands an accomplished pianist. (OX)
Passing by	d1-g2	g1-e2	Most suitable for men's voices	Sustained. See the famous setting of this poem by Edward Purcell. (OX)
Pretty ring time	d1-g2	eb1-eb2	All voices	Light and spirited setting of Shakespeare's "It was a Lover and His Lass." (OX)
Rest sweet nymphs	f-f2	g1-eb2	Most suitable for men's voices	Delicate, sustained. (OX)
Sleep	d1-eb2	g1-d2	All voices, except a very light soprano	Slow and very sustained. Musically and interpretatively not easy. (OX)
The fox	d1-f♯2	f1-c2	All voices	Very slow, sustained. Subdued ending section. (OX)
The passionate shepherd	d1-g2	f♯1-e2	High or medium voices	Very animated, light. (Elkin)
The toper's song	B-e1	e-b	Baritone	A vigorous, amusing drinking song. (WR)

TITLE	COMP.	TESS.	TYPE	REMARKS

ELINOR REMICK WARREN

TITLE	COMP.	TESS.	TYPE	REMARKS
White horses of the sea	f1-g2	bb1-f2	Not suitable for very light, high voices	Animated, effective. (GS)

WINTTER WATTS

TITLE	COMP.	TESS.	TYPE	REMARKS
Blue are her eyes	f♯1-f♯2	a1-e2	Not suitable for very low voices	Sustained. (OD)
Little shepherd's song	g1-bb2	g1-e2	Most suitable for soprano	Light, effective. (RIC)
Stresa (Vignettes of Italy)	d1-bb2	ab1-f♯2 (H)	Women's voices	Sustained. Demands in parts considerable dramatic intensity. (OD)
Wings of night	c♯1-g2	f♯1-f♯2	Most suitable for high voices	Sustained, subdued. Demands a good command of high pp. (GS)

POWELL WEAVER

TITLE	COMP.	TESS.	TYPE	REMARKS
Moon-marketing	e1-g2	g1-e2	All voices	Light, sprightly encore song. (GS)

BENJAMIN WHELPLEY

TITLE	COMP.	TESS.	TYPE	REMARKS
The nightingale has a lyre of gold	f♯1-g♯2	g♯1-e2	All voices	Animated, effective. See Delius. (BMC)

JACQUES WOLFE

TITLE	COMP.	TESS.	TYPE	REMARKS
De glory road	A-f1	d-d1	Medium or low men's voices	Effective ballad in Negro dialect. (GS)

TITLE	COMP.	TESS.	TYPE	REMARKS
Gwine to hebb'n	B-e1	e-e1	Medium or low men's voices	Effective ballad in Negro dialect. (GS)
The janitor's boy	eb1-f2	same (H)	Women's voices	A sprightly encore song. (GS)

AMY WORTH

Midsummer	e1-a2	a1-f♯2 (H)	All voices	An effective encore song. (GS)

ITALIAN

The song literature of Italy is comparatively small, most of the
vocal music having been written for the stage. Only a few Italian
composers, mostly contemporary, have written songs more than occasionally. The foremost among them are perhaps Respighi, Pizzetti,
and Castelnuovo-Tedesco.

Very few songs of the nineteenth century are included in this list
as most of them seem to possess only historical interest at the present
time. The few songs of Rossini and Donizetti, still used as display
pieces, are listed below; songs of Verdi are perhaps among his most
unrepresentative compositions; songs of Sgambati, Martucci and Bossi,
historically of no inconsiderable importance, can be highly recommended to those who are interested in tracing the emergence of contemporary song in Italy, but are otherwise of little practical value in
so far as the present-day singer and the public outside of Italy are
concerned. The inclusion of some songs by Tosti, musically no doubt
inferior to the former, seemed warranted, however, in view of the
fact that they are extraordinarily singable and effective, and can be
used to great advantage as teaching material.

Only a few songs of Malipiero and Casella, two of the foremost
contemporary Italian composers, have been included in this list, as
they are for the most part very complex and of obviously experimental
nature.

Those who are particularly interested in the development of the
Italian song literature may be interested in acquainting themselves
with songs by Alaleona, Alfano, Davico, Rocca and Tommasini among
the contemporary composers, and with songs and arrangements of
folk songs of Wolf-Ferrari, Pick-Mangiagalli, Pierraccini and Sini-
gaglia among the Italian composers of the late nineteenth and early
twentieth century.

LUIGI ARDITI
(1822–1903)

TITLE	COMP.	TESS.	TYPE	REMARKS
Il bacio	c#1-b2 (d3)	f#1-f#2	Light soprano	A somewhat florid waltz song. (GS)
Parla	c#1-b2 (d3)	g1-g2	Coloratura soprano	A florid waltz song. (GS)

ALBERTO BIMBONI
(b. 1882)

Sospiri miei	e1-e♭2	f1-d2	All voices	Sustained. (RIC)

GAETANO BRAGA
(1829–1907)

O quali mi risvegliano (Angel's serenade)	d1-g2	g1-e2	All voices	Sustained, effective. (gen. av.)

RENATO BROGI
(1873–1924)

Gotine gialle	d1-g2	g1-e2	Most suitable for women's voices, except a very heavy contralto	Sustained, very delicate. Demands a good command of high pp. (Homeyer)

ALFREDO CASELLA
(1883–1947)

Il bove	d♭1-f2	d1-d2	Medium or low voices	A robust, vigorous, sustained hymn in praise of an ox. Musically not easy. (RIC)

TITLE	COMP.	TESS.	TYPE	REMARKS
Sonnet	b-g2	e1-e2	All voices	Slow, for the most part subdued, sustained. French text. (Mathot, Paris)

Tre Canzone Trecentesche
(Ricordi)

TITLE	COMP.	TESS.	TYPE	REMARKS
(1) Giovane bella, luce del mio core	c1-g♯2	e1-e2	High voices	Delicate, sustained. Demands some flexibility.
(2) Fuor de la bella gaiba	c♯1-a2	a1-f♯2	Light soprano	Slow, delicate, subdued. Demands considerable flexibility and a good command of high pp. Musically not easy. Demands an accomplished pianist.
(3) Amante sono, vaghiccia di voi	d♯1-g2	f♯1-e2	High voices, except a very light soprano	Animated, declamatory, vigorous. Musically and interpretatively not easy. Demands an accomplished pianist.

MARIO CASTELNUOVO-TEDESCO
(b. 1895)

Castelnuovo-Tedesco, one of the most noteworthy of contemporary Italian composers, has written a considerable number of very excellent songs to English, French, Spanish, as well as, of course, to Italian texts. His harmonic idiom is somewhat more complex than that of Respighi and Pizzetti, yet hardly as frankly experimental as that of Casella or Malipiero.

"Ninna Nanna," "L'infinito," "Tamburino," and the delightfully humorous "La ermita de San Simon" are particularly recommended to those who wish to acquaint themselves with his style of writing.

Editions: Ricordi
         Forlivesi

TITLE	COMP.	TESS.	TYPE	REMARKS
Ballatella	d1-g2	e1-e2	Most suitable for high voices	Light, animated. Demands very facile articulation and an accomplished pianist. Interpretatively not easy.

TITLE	COMP.	TESS.	TYPE	REMARKS
Cadix	c1-g2	g1-eb2	Soprano or mezzo-soprano	Spirited. Demands some flexibility. Musically not easy. See "Les filles de Cadix" by Délibes. French text.

Coplas

Out of the eleven "coplas," traditional Spanish folk poems, that Castelnuovo-Tedesco has set to music, only three are listed, selected almost at random. Any singer interested in contemporary music and able to cope with some of its difficulties will find these songs very worthy of his attention.

See also "Stelle cadenti" (twelve traditional Tuscan Folk poems) set to music in somewhat similar manner.

TITLE	COMP.	TESS.	TYPE	REMARKS
En medio de lo mar	f1-g2	g#1-f2	High voices	Slow. Musically not easy. Demands considerable dramatic intensity in parts and an accomplished pianist.
Gitano, porque vas preso	e#1-g2	g#1-d#2	High voices, except a very light soprano	Declamatory, dramatic. Musically and interpretatively not easy. Demands an accomplished pianist.
Hermosa blanca	c#1-f2	g1-e2	All voices	Slow. Has a characteristic rhythm of a Spanish folk song. Musically not easy. Demands an accomplished pianist.
Il passo delle Nazarene (from "Briciole")	c1-e2	e1-c2	All voices	Slow, subdued, somewhat declamatory. Demands facile articulation.
Leggenda	d1-f2	f1-d2	Soprano or mezzo-soprano	Interpretatively and musically not easy.

TITLE	COMP.	TESS.	TYPE	REMARKS
La ermita de San Simon	eb1-g2	f1-f2	Most suitable for high voices	Light and humorous. Demands some flexibility. Interpretatively not easy. Demands an accomplished pianist.
L'infinito	c1-f2 (g2)	eb1-c2	Not too suitable for very light, high voices	Slow, subdued. Musically and interpretatively not easy.
Ninna Nanna	d1-f2	g1-e2	Soprano or mezzo-soprano	Sustained, delicate.
Recuerdo	d1-g2	a1-f2	Most suitable for high voices	Rather animated. Demands an accomplished pianist. English text.
Tamburino	d1-f2	d1-d2	Not suitable for very light, high voices	Very rapid, rhythmic. Demands very facile articulation and an accomplished pianist. Musically not easy.

Twelve Shakespeare Songs

(Chester)

TITLE	COMP.	TESS.	TYPE	REMARKS
Old song (Come away, come away, Death)	e1-f2	f#2-d2	Most suitable for medium voices	Slow and sustained.
O mistress mine	e1-g2	g1-e2	Most suitable for tenor	Animated. Demands an excellent pianist.
Orpheus	c#1-a2	g1-e2	Most suitable for light soprano	Slow and sustained. See "Orpheus with his Lute" by Vaughan Williams among many other settings of this poem.

PIETRO CIMARA
(b. 1887)

Pietro Cimara, chiefly known in this country for his charming "Fiocca la neve" has written a great number of very effective songs. Among those listed below, the "Non più" and the "Scherzo" are perhaps musically most rewarding.

Editions: Forlivesi
Ricordi
Some reprints by G. Schirmer

TITLE	COMP.	TESS.	TYPE	REMARKS
A una rosa	eb1-g2	f1-d2	All voices	Sustained.
Canto di primavera	d1-g2 (a2)	a1-f2	Not too suitable for very light voices	A spirited, very effective song. Demands an accomplished pianist.
Fiocca la neve	g1-g2	a1-e2	All voices	Sustained, delicate.
Melodia autumnale	eb1-g2	g1-e2	All voices	Sustained.
Non più	e1-f#2	f#1-d#2	All voices	Sustained, subdued. Interpretatively not easy.
Ondina	d#1-a2	b1-g2	Not too suitable for low voices	Light and delicate.
Paesaggio	db1-f2	gb1-eb2	All voices	Sustained. Demands a good command of high pp and an accomplished pianist.
Scherzo	d1-g2	g1-d2	Women's voices	Light and animated. See Respighi.
Stornellata marinara	d1-g2	bb1-f2	All voices	An effective barcarole.
Vecchia chitarra	c#1-f#2	f#1-d2	Most suitable for medium voices	Sustained. Demands an accomplished pianist.

LUIGI DALLAPICCOLA
(b. 1904)

Luigi Dallapiccola, an outstanding Italian twelve-tone composer, has not written many songs for voice and pianoforte. All of his songs are musically very complex and difficult but extremely well-written for the voice.

TITLE	COMP.	TESS.	TYPE	REMARKS
An Mathilde	g–b2	c1–g2	Soprano	A cantata in three movements. Vocally demanding and difficult. German text. (Zerboni)
Quattro liriche di Antonio Machado	b♭–c♭3	d1–g2	High voices	Four short songs, vocally demanding and difficult. Demand good command of high ppp and an accomplished pianist. (Zerboni)

See also "Goethe-Lieder," seven short songs for mezzo-soprano and three clarinets. Vocally demanding and musically difficult. German text. (Zerboni)

VINCENZO DAVICO
(b. 1889)

TITLE	COMP.	TESS.	TYPE	REMARKS
Come un cipresso notturno (No. 3 of "Tre Liriche")	d♭1–c2	same	Most suitable for low or medium voices	Slow, very subdued. (RIC)

STEPHANO DONAUDY
(1879–1925)

The charming imitations of the eighteenth century Italian airs and canzoni by Donaudy have long been popular among teachers and singers. Unpretentious, well written for the voice and expertly made they fully deserve their popularity.

The question why one should not prefer the genuine examples of this style, of which so many are now available, to even the most successful imitation of it, is one that only the individual singer can seem to answer.

Editions: Ricordi
G. Schirmer

TITLE	COMP.	TESS.	TYPE	REMARKS
Ah mai non cessate	eb1-ab2	g1-eb2	High voices	Rapid. Demands considerable flexibility and facile articulation.
Amorosi miei giorni	c1-g2	f1-d2	All voices	Slow and sustained. Demands some flexibility.
Cuor mio, cuor mio non vedi	c1-g2	f1-d2	All voices	Light and animated.
Freschi luoghi	db1-ab2	ab1-f2	Most suitable for high voices	Delicate, graceful. Demands some flexibility.
O bei nidi d'amore	db1-ab2	ab1-f2	All voices	Slow, very sustained.
O del mio amato ben	eb1-f2	ab1-eb2	All voices	Slow and sustained.
Perduto ho la speranza	d1-bb2	g1-eb2	All voices	Very sustained.
Quando ti rivedrò	d1-f#2	f#1-d2	Not too suitable for very light, high voices	Very slow and sustained.
Se tra l'erba	d#1-f#2	e1-c#2	All voices	Light and animated.
Spirate pur, spirate	eb1-g2	g1-eb2	All voices	Animated. Demands considerable flexibility.
Vaghissima sembianza	e1-a2	a1-f#2	All voices	Slow and sustained.

GAETANO DONIZETTI
(1797–1848)

TITLE	COMP.	TESS.	TYPE	REMARKS
La Zingara	d#1-a2	a1-f2	Light soprano	Rapid, florid, brilliant. (GS)

RUGGIERO LEONCAVALLO
(1858–1919)

TITLE	COMP.	TESS.	TYPE	REMARKS
Mattinata	c1-ab2	g1-f2 (H)	All voices	Animated, very effective. (gen. av.)

GIAN FRANCESCO MALIPIERO
(b. 1882)

TITLE	COMP.	TESS.	TYPE	REMARKS
Ballata	d1-g2	f#-e2	High or medium voices	Declamatory, not fast. Demands facile articulation. (CHES)
Inno a Maria nostra donna	eb1-f2	f#1-eb2	All voices	Slow, declamatory, grave. (CHES)
La madre folle (from "Sette Canzoni")	d1-ab2	g1-g2	Soprano	Dramatic, declamatory. Vocally, musically, and interpretatively quite complex. (CHES)
L'eco	e1-g2	a1-f#2	Most suitable for high, light voices	Delicate, animated. Demands a good command of high pp and an accomplished pianist. (CHES)

Quattro Sonetti del Burchiello

(Pizzi & Co., Bologna)

TITLE	COMP.	TESS.	TYPE	REMARKS
(1) Cacio stillato	d1-e2	f#-d#2	Soprano; not suitable for very light, high soprano	Interpretatively and musically not easy. Demands facile articulation.
(2) Va in mercato, Giorgin	e1-g2	a1-e2	Soprano; not suitable for very light, high soprano	Rapid, rhythmical. Demands facile articulation. Musically not easy. Demands an accomplished pianist.
(3) Andando a uccellare	c#1-g2	f#1-d#2	Soprano; not suitable for very light, high soprano	Interpretatively and musically not easy.
(4) Rose spinose	d1-e2	f#1-d#2	Soprano; not suitable for very light, high soprano	Very rhythmical, vigorous. Musically not easy. Demands facile articulation.

TITLE	COMP.	TESS.	TYPE	REMARKS
Se tu m'ami (No. 2 of "I Tre Canti di Filomela)	d1-g2	g1-e2	Light soprano	Delicate, light. Demands some flexibility and an accomplished pianist. See "Se tu m'ami" by Pergolesi. (UE)

ILDEBRANDO PIZZETTI
(b. 1880)

TITLE	COMP.	TESS.	TYPE	REMARKS
Il Clefta prigione	c1-g2	eb1-c2	Not suitable for light voices	Vigorous, dramatic, somewhat declamatory. Musically and interpretatively not easy. Demands an accomplished pianist. (Forlivesi)
I pastori	d1-g2	e1-e2	Most suitable for high voices	Slow, subdued. Interpretatively not easy. Demands a good command of high pp and an accomplished pianist. (Forlivesi)
La madre al figlio lontano	d1-g2	e1-bb1	Women's voices, except a light soprano	Sustained, somewhat declamatory. Demands in parts considerable dramatic intensity. Musically and interpretatively not easy. (Forlivesi)
La vita fugge e non s'arresta un'ora	b-e2	e1-c#2	Most suitable for medium or low voices	Slow, somber, somewhat declamatory. Interpretatively not easy. (RIC)
Levommi il mio pensier	c1-g2	g1-f2	Most suitable for high voices	Slow, somewhat declamatory. Interpretatively not easy. (RIC)
Passeggiata	d1-a2	g1-e2	High voices,	Somewhat declamatory. Demands in

TITLE	COMP.	TESS.	TYPE	REMARKS
			except a very light soprano	parts considerable dramatic intensity. Musically and interpretatively not easy. Demands an accomplished pianist. (RIC)
Quel rosignuol che sì soave piagne	b♯-a2	f♯1-e2	Most suitable for high voices	Slow, sustained and subdued. Musically and interpretatively not easy. Demands an accomplished pianist. (RIC)
San Basilio	d1-g2	a1-e2	Not too suitable for very light, high voices	Vigorous. Demands some flexibility and an accomplished pianist. (RIC)

OTTORINO RESPIGHI
(1879–1936)

Resphighi, perhaps one of the most important contemporary Italian composers, has written a great number of excellent songs. "Nebbie" is, of course, one of the most famous and popular.

Among those listed below, "Abbandono," "Canto funebre," "E se un giorno tornasse," "Io sono la madre," "Mattino de luce," "Notte," "Pioggia" and "In alto mare" deserve, in my opinion, an equal popularity. Hardly any of his songs are musically difficult, though his harmonic and melodic idiom is contemporary. They are beautifully written for the voice and demand for the most part an accomplished pianist. His five "Canti all'antica," although written in old style, are by no means outright imitations of old masters in the Donaudy manner and are excellently suited for teaching purposes.

Edition: Ricordi

TITLE	COMP.	TESS.	TYPE	REMARKS
Abbandono	f1-g2	a♭1-f2	All voices	Slow and sustained.
Au milieu du jardin	d1-f♯2	a1-f♯2	Most suitable for high, light voices	Slow and sustained. Demands a good command of high pp. Respighi has a number of songs to French texts. Another one listed here is "Le repos en Egypte."

TITLE	COMP.	TESS.	TYPE	REMARKS
Ballata	d1-f2	g1-d2	All voices	Slow. (From "Cinque canti all'antica," 5 simple songs in old style).
Bella porta di rubini	e1-g2	g1-e2	All voices	Sustained, graceful. ("Cinque canti all'antica.")
Canto funebre	b♯-g♭2	f♯1-d♯2	Heavy voices	Animated, somber and dramatic. Demands an accomplished pianist.
Canzone di Re Enzo	e1-g2	a1-d2	Men's voices	Sustained, rhythmical.
Contrasto	e♭1-f2	f1-d2	All voices	Very sustained, delicate.
E se un giorno tornasse	c1-f2	f1-d♭2	Women's voices	A free recitative. Interpretatively not easy.
In alto mare	c♯1-g♯2	b1-e2	Not suitable for light voices	Dramatic, animated.
Invito alla danza	e♭1-a♭2	a♭1-f2	Most suitable for men's voices	A light, graceful waltz song.
Io sono la madre	e1-e2	f♯1-d2	Mezzo-soprano or alto	Slow, dramatic (from "Quattro liriche su poemi Armeni").
La najade	c♯1-f♯2	f♯1-d♯2	Most suitable for high voices	Delicate. Musically not easy.
L'udir tal volto	d1-g2	g1-d2	All voices	Sustained ("Cinque canti all'antica").
Le repos en Egypte	c♯1-g2	f♯1-e♭2	All voices	Sustained and subdued. Demands a good command of high pp. Interpretatively not easy. French text.
Ma come potrei	f1-f2	g1-d2	All voices	Slow, sustained ("Cinque canti all'antica").

TITLE	COMP.	TESS.	TYPE	REMARKS
Mattinata	c1-ab2	d#1-d#2	Not too suitable for very light voices	Animated.
Mattino di luce	c1-gb2	f1-d2	Not too suitable for light voices	A solemn, very sustained prayer.
Nebbie	d#1-g#2	g#1-e2 (H)	Not too suitable for light voices	Slow and very sustained, dramatic. (gen. av.)
Nevicata	eb1-g#2	eb1-c2	All voices	Slow and sustained.
Notte	db1-e2	f1-db2	Soprano or mezzo-soprano	Slow and sustained. Demands a good command of pp.
Pioggia	f1-g2	a1-e2 (H)	Women's voices	Rapid. Demands an accomplished pianist.
Razzolan, sopra a l'aja, le galline	d1-g2	bb1-f2	Soprano	Rapid, gently humorous. Demands some flexibility and an accomplished pianist.
Scherzo	eb1-db2	g1-db2	Women's voices	Light. See Cimara.
Stornellatrice	eb1-ab2	ab1-eb2	All voices	A free, recitative-like song.
Venitelo a vedere	e1-g2	bb1-g2	Soprano	Sustained. Demands a good command of high pp.
Viene di là lontan, lontan	c1-g2 (a2)	ab1-f2	Soprano	Very delicate, animated. Demands an accomplished pianist.

See also "Il tramonto," a cycle of songs for mezzo-soprano and string quartet.

GIOACCHINO ROSSINI
(1792–1868)

TITLE	COMP.	TESS.	TYPE	REMARKS
La danza	e1-a2	a1-f2	Most suitable for tenor	A bravura tarantella. Demands very rapid articulation

TITLE	COMP.	TESS.	TYPE	REMARKS
				and a good sense of rhythm. Note Rossini's metronome mark of ♩ . -152; often taken at too fast a tempo. (gen. av.)
La pastorella	e1-c3	g1-g2	Coloratura soprano or lyric soprano	Animated, light. Demands flexibility. (Arr. by La Forge, CF)

La regata Veneziana

A set of three canzonette in Venetian dialect. (RIC)

TITLE	COMP.	TESS.	TYPE	REMARKS
(1) Anzoleta avanti la regata	d1-ab2	eb1-eb2	High voices, except light, high soprano	Sustained. Demands some flexibility. Has an effective ending.
(2) Anzoleta co passa la regata	e1-a2	e1-e2	High voices, except light, high soprano	Animated, in parts demands facile articulation and flexibility.
(3) Anzoleta dopo la regata	c1-g2	f1-e2	High voices, except light, high soprano	Spirited, demands flexibility.

TITLE	COMP.	TESS.	TYPE	REMARKS
Stabat Mater Cujus animam	eb-db2	ab-f1	Tenor	Dramatic, majestic. The db2 is touched only once, so that the compass is really eb-bbb1.
Stabat Mater Fac ut portem	b-g#2	e1-e2	Alto or mezzo-soprano	Sustained. Demands some flexibility.
Stabat Mater Inflammatus et accensus	c1-c3	g1-g2	Dramatic soprano (lyric soprano)	Solo with chorus. Majestic, dramatic. Demands some flexibility.

TITLE	COMP.	TESS.	TYPE	REMARKS

Stabat Mater

| Pro peccatis | A-e1 | e-c#1 | Bass | Majestic. Demands some flexibility.and, in parts, considerable dramatic intensity. |

The "Stabat Mater" score is generally available.

FRANCESCO SANTOLIQUIDO
(b. 1883)

Santoliquido's very effective songs are musically not difficult, although contemporary in feeling and idiom. The three "Poesie Persiane" to the Italian translations of Omar Khayyam seem perhaps most individual and representative of his songs.

Edition: Forlivesi

Alba di luna sul bosco	c#1-e2 (g#2)	f#1-d#2	All voices	Delicate and sustained. Has an effective ending (from "Canti della Sera").
Melancolie	c-eb2	g1-eb2	Women's voices, except a very light soprano	Slow and subdued. Interpretatively not easy. French text.
Nel giardino	c1-f2	a1-e2	All voices, except a very light soprano	Sustained (from "7 poemi del Sole").
Poesia Persiana:				
1.	f1-f#2	f#1-eb2	All voices, except a very light soprano	Grave, declamatory.
2.	c1-g2	g1-eb2	All voices, except a very light soprano	Grave, declamatory, very effective. Demands an accomplished pianist.
3.	e1-g#2	e1-e2	All voices, except a very light soprano	Sustained, declamatory.

TITLE	COMP.	TESS.	TYPE	REMARKS
Riflessi	e1-g♯2	b1-f♯2	High voices	Spirited, effective (from "7 poemi del Sole").
Tristezza crepuscolare	c1-g♭2	d♭1-d♭2	Not too suitable for very light, high voices	Slow and sustained (from "Canti della Sera").

FRANCESCO PAOLO TOSTI
(1846-1916)

TITLE	COMP.	TESS.	TYPE	REMARKS
Aprile	e♭1-e♭2	same	All voices, except a very light soprano	Sustained, effective. (RIC)
Good-bye	e♭1-a♭2	a♭1-e♭2	All voices	Sustained, very effective. At one time extraordinarily popular. English text. (gen. av.)
L'ultima canzone	d1-f2	f1-d2	All voices	Animated. The vocal line is sustained. Effective. (RIC)
Mattinata	d1-f2	e1-d2	All voices	Sustained, effective. (RIC)
Non m'ama più	e1-f♯2	g♯1-d♯2	All voices	An effective, melodious drawing-room song. (RIC)

Note: See also other songs by Tosti, equally effective, among them: "Lamento d'amore," "Verrei morire," "Ninon," etc.

GIUSEPPE VERDI
(1813-1901)

TITLE	COMP.	TESS.	TYPE	REMARKS
Requiem Confutatis maledictis	A-e1	e-c♯1	Bass or baritone	Dramatic, in parts very sustained. (Score, GS)

TITLE	COMP.	TESS.	TYPE	REMARKS
Requiem Ingemisco	f-bb1	bb-f1	Tenor	Sustained. In parts requires a good command of high pp. (Score, GS)
Requiem Liber scriptus	b-ab2	d1-f2	Alto or mezzo-soprano	Dramatic, sustained. (Score, GS)
Requiem Libera me	b-ab2	eb1-eb2	Dramatic soprano (lyric soprano)	Dramatic, somewhat declamatory. (Score, GS)

SPANISH AND PORTUGUESE

The following list of songs by Spanish and Portuguese composers is admittedly a sketchy one. Contemporary composers of these two cultures seem to be so influenced by and so steeped in their native folklore that, as a consequence, a great number of their songs could be easily considered modernized concert transcriptions of folk songs and popular airs. It seems almost impossible, especially for one who is not an authority on Spanish and Portuguese folk music, to draw a line between the original compositions in folk vein, on the one hand, and the conscious transcription of folk songs and old popular airs, on the other. Because of this, as well as because of the decision to exclude folk songs in languages other than English (the reasons for this decision are obvious, and have been discussed in the preface), it seemed best to list the examples of the most prominent composers not in detail, as has been done in other instances, but in a broader manner, which could be termed primarily bibliographical.

The composers represented below include:

Albéniz (who curiously enough does not seem to have written any songs to Spanish texts)
De Falla (whose most famous songs are his transcriptions of Spanish folk songs)
Granados
Nin (who apparently devoted his energies almost entirely to transcribing old Spanish music and folk songs)
Turina
Obradors (whose remarkable "Canciones Clásicas" seem to be based for the most part on Spanish folk songs and old popular airs)

In closing I would like to remark that no South and Central American composers are represented in this book except Camargo Guarnieri (Brazil), Alberto Ginastera (Argentina) and Heitor Villa-Lobos (Brazil). For those who would like to become acquainted with the vocal music of South and Central America the following list of composers may be of some help:

562

See also the catalogues of Associated Music Publishers, Peer International, and Southern Music Publishing Company.

Note: Subirá in parentheses refers to "Spanish Songs of the 18th Century," edited by José Subira, published by International Music Co. Publisher's name in parentheses indicates that the song is available singly in that edition.

ISAAC ALBÉNIZ
(1860–1909)

TITLE	COMP.	TESS.	TYPE	REMARKS
Crépuscule	e♭1-g♭2	e♭1-e♭2	Most suitable for high voices	Sustained, subdued. Demands good command of high pp. French text. (Rouart)
Il en est de l'amour	d1-f2	f1-d♭2	High or medium voices	Sustained, subdued. French text. (Rouart)
Pepita Jiménez Romance de Pepita: Hélas! Soir parfumé	e♭1-a♭2	a♭1-f♭2	Lyric soprano (coloratura soprano)	Sustained. Demands good command of high pp. French text. (Eschig)
The caterpillar	e1-f♯2	g1-d2	Most suitable for high voices	Sustained, delicate. See also "Four Melodies," text by F. M. Coutts. English text. (Rouart)

ANONYMOUS
(18th Century)

Canción de cuna (El Gurrumino)	g♯1-e2	a1-e2	Most suitable for women's voices	Sustained, somewhat slow, gentle. (Subirá)

TITLE	COMP.	TESS.	TYPE	REMARKS

MARIANO BUSTOS
(c. 1790)

TITLE	COMP.	TESS.	TYPE	REMARKS
Canción contra los violetistas (La Necedad)	f#1-g2	g1-e2	High voices	Spirited. Demands facile articulation. (Subirá)

JOSÉ CASTEL
(c. 1776)

Canción de la gitana habilidosa (La Gitanilla en el Coliseo)	e1-f2	f1-e2	Women's voices	Rhythmic, dance-like, graceful. (Subirá)

PABLO ESTEVE
(c. 1730–1794)

Canción satírica de pronósticos (El Juicio del Año)	d1-e2	g1-d2	All voices, except bass	Animated, graceful. Humorous, satirical. (Subirá)

MANUEL DE FALLA
(1876–1946)

El Amor Brujo (Chanson du Feu Follet) Lo mismo que er fuego	b-b1	f#1-b1	Alto	Rapid, light. In folk vein. Demands facile articulation. Demands an accomplished pianist. (CHES)
El Amor Brujo (Canción del amor dolido) Yo no sé qué siento	c1-c2	c1-g1	Alto	Rapid, rhythmical, vigorous. In folk vein. Demands facile articulation and some flexibility. Demands an accomplished pianist. (CHES)

TITLE	COMP.	TESS.	TYPE	REMARKS
La Vida Breve				
Air de Salud: Vivian los que rien!	b-a2	f#1-f2	Soprano (dramatic, possibly lyric)	In folk vein. Slow. Has many florid embellishments. For the most part sustained. Demands an accomplished pianist. (Eschig)
Soneto a Córdoba	d1-a2	f#1-e2	High voices, except a light soprano or tenor	Sustained, majestic. The accompaniment is either pianoforte or harp. (OX)

Three songs. French text. (IMC)

(1) Les colombes	d1-g#2	f#1-e2	High voices	Not fast, somewhat declamatory. For the most part subdued, somber. Musically not easy. Demands an excellent pianist.
(2) Chinoiserie	b-f#2	f#1-e2	Most suitable for high voices	A recitative and a delicate song demanding good command of pp. Demands an accomplished pianist.
(3) Seguidille	c1-g#2	e1-e2	High or medium voices	Animated, rhythmical. In folk vein. Demands an excellent pianist.
Tus ojillos negros	d1-g2	a1-e2	Most suitable for high voices	Animated. Demands very facile articulation. (GS)

See also "Siete Canciones Populares Españolas" (Seven Spanish Folk Songs, high and medium). Not too suitable for very light, high voices. Demand an excellent pianist. (AMP)

1. El paño moruno	3. Asturiana	5. Nana
2. Seguidilla murciana	4. Jota	6. Canción
		7. Polo

FERNANDO FERNANDIERE
(c. 1778)

TITLE	COMP.	TESS.	TYPE	REMARKS
Minueto en alabanza de la música seria (La Consulta)	c1-f2	f1-e2	All voices, except bass	A graceful minuet. Vocal line is florid. (Subirá)

VENTURA GALVAN
(c. 1770)

TITLE	COMP.	TESS.	TYPE	REMARKS
Seguidillas del oficial cortejante (Vagamundos y ciegos fingidos)	c1-eb2	f1-c2	Women's voices	Sustained, somewhat humorous. Spoken ending. Accompaniment is in imitation of the guitar. (Subirá)

ALBERTO E. GINASTERA
(b. 1916)

TITLE	COMP.	TESS.	TYPE	REMARKS
Canción al arbol del olvido	g1-g2	a1-d2	All voices	Slow, sustained. (RIC)

Five Argentine popular songs. High or medium voices. (RIC)

TITLE	COMP.	TESS.	REMARKS
(1) Chacarera	e1-g2	g1-d2	Animated, demands facile articulation.
(2) Triste	d1-g2	g1-eb2	Slow, sustained, somewhat free recitative.
(3) Zamba	f1-f2	a1-d2	Sustained.
(4) Arrorró	g1-g2	g1-d2	Slow, sustained, subdued. A lullaby.
(5) Gato	g1-g2	g1-f2	Lively. Effective ending.

Las Horas de Una Estancia

A cycle of five songs for <u>high voices</u>. Published by Southern Music Publishing Co.

TITLE	COMP.	TESS.	REMARKS
(1) El alba	eb1-g2	g1-d2	Sustained, in recitative style.

TITLE	COMP.	TESS.	TYPE	REMARKS
(2) La mañana	f1-g2	g1-e2		Sustained. High tessitura.
(3) El mediodía	f♯1-g2	g1-e2		In recitative style. Pastoral setting.
(4) La tarde	e♭1-a2	g1-e2		Sustained, somewhat slow. Demands a good pianist.
(5) La noche	e1-a♭2	g1-e2		Slow, very sustained. In parts quite subdued.

ENRIQUE GRANADOS
(1867–1916)

TITLE	COMP.	TESS.	TYPE	REMARKS
Amor y odio (Tonadillas)	d1-a2	f♯1-e2	Women's voices, except low, heavy alto	Animated. Demands flexibility and facile articulation. (IMC)
Callejeo (Tonadillas)	c♯1-f2	e1-e2	Women's voices, except a very light soprano	Animated. Demands some flexibility. (IMC)
Canción del Postillón	d-g1	f-e♭1	Baritone	Spirited, vigorous. (GS)
Cantar	c♯1-a2	f♯1-e2	High voices	Animated. Demands some flexibility and an accomplished pianist. (GS)
Descúbrase el pensamiento	d♯1-b2	f♯1-f♯2	High, light voices .	Sustained. Demands considerable flexibility. The tessitura is quite high. (GS)
El majo discreto (Tonadillas)	(c♯1)e1-a2	e1-e2	Most suitable for high voices	Animated, light. Demands some flexibility. (IMC)
El majo olvidado (Tonadillas)	c-f1	f-c1	Men's voices, except bass	Sustained. (IMC)

TITLE	COMP.	TESS.	TYPE	REMARKS
El tra la la y el punteado (Tonadillas)	e1-g2	g1-e2	High voices	Animated. Demands some flexibility. (IMC)
La maja dolorosa No. 1 (Tonadillas)	g-ab2	same	Mezzo-soprano or dramatic soprano	Dramatic, sustained. (IMC)
La maja dolorosa No. 2 (Tonadillas)	e1-e2	a1-e2	Mezzo-soprano	Sustained. (IMC)
La maja dolorosa No. 3 (Tonadillas)	f#-f#2	f#1-e2	Mezzo-soprano or high alto	Sustained, wide range. Demands flexibility. (IMC)
La maja y el ruiseñor (Porqué entre sombras el ruiseñor —from Goyescas)	b#1-a2	f#1-e2	Soprano or tenor	Very sustained. Demands some flexibility and an accomplished pianist. (GS)
Mañanica era	d1-f#2 (a2)	e1-e2	High voices	Delicate, sustained. (GS)

CAMARGO M. GUARNIERI
(b. 1907)

(Portuguese texts)

TITLE	COMP.	TESS.	TYPE	REMARKS
Declaração	c1-f2	e1-c2	All voices	Sustained, calm. (Music Press)
Quando embalada	d1-f2	f1-eb2	Medium voices	Animated. Interesting melodic bass line in the accompaniment. (AMP)
Quando te vi pela primeira vez	db1-f2	f1-db2	All voices	Sustained. (Music Press)
Tanta coisa a dizer te . . .	d1-d2	f#1-d2	All voices	Sustained, somewhat slow. (Music Press)
Vai, azulão	eb1-eb2	same	Most suitable for men's voices	Sustained, melancholic. Generally subdued, but with precise rhythm. (AMP)
Vou-me embora	b-f2	d1-d2	All voices	Animated, light. Demands facile articulation and some flexibility. (AMP)

ERNESTO HALFFTER
(b. 1905)

TITLE	COMP.	TESS.	TYPE	REMARKS
La corza blanca	f1-f2	b♭1-e♭2	High or medium voices	Sustained. In the manner of a free arioso. (Eschig)
La niña que se va al mar	d1-a2	g♯1-e2	Most suitable for soprano	Animated. Has florid passages. Demands an excellent pianist. (Eschig)

BLAS DE LASERNA
(1751-1816)

TITLE	COMP.	TESS.	TYPE	REMARKS
Seguidillas majas (El Majo y la Italiana fingida)	e♯1-e2	g♯1-d2	Women's voices	Animated. (Subirá)

LUIS MISÓN
(?-1766)

TITLE	COMP.	TESS.	TYPE	REMARKS
Sequidilla dolorosa de una enamorada (Una Mesonera y en Arriero)	d1-e2	f♯1-b1	Women's voices	Sustained, somewhat slow. Somber text. (Subirá)

JOAQUÍN NIN
(1879-1949)

(See the Spanish section, Songs and Airs before the 19th Century)

See also: Nin, "Dix Noëls Espagnols"—medium or high voices.
    Transcriptions of ten old Spanish Christmas carols.
    (Eschig)
    Nin, "Vingt Chants Populaires Espagnol"—not too suitable for very light, high voices. Demand an accomplished pianist. Transcriptions of Spanish folk songs.
    (2 volumes, Eschig)

FERNANDO J. OBRADORS
(1897-1945)

"Canciones Clásicas Españolas," twenty-three songs for high voices. Demand an excellent pianist. (2 volumes, Unión Musical Española; first volume reprinted by International Music Co. under the English title "Classical Spanish Songs.")

TITLE	COMP.	TESS.	TYPE	REMARKS

JOSÉ PALOMINO
(c. 1769)

TITLE	COMP.	TESS.	TYPE	REMARKS
Canción Picaresca (El Canape)	c♯1-e2	f♯1-d2	All voices	Animated, humorous. Demands facile articulation. (Subirá)

MANUEL PLA
(c. 1857)

TITLE	COMP.	TESS.	TYPE	REMARKS
Seguidillas religiosas (La Lepra de Constantino	d1-e2	f♯1-d2	All voices	Sustained. Religious text. (Subirá)

ANTONIO ROSALES
(c. 1775)

TITLE	COMP.	TESS.	TYPE	REMARKS
Canción contra las madamitas gorgoriteadoras (El Recitado)	d1-g2	g1-e2	All voices	Animated, humorous. Has florid passages. (Subirá)

JOAQUIN TURINA
(1882-1949)

Poema en Forma de Canciónes

Four songs and an introductory piece for pianoforte. Only numbers 3 and 5 are given here. (Unión Musical Española)

TITLE	COMP.	TESS.	TYPE	REMARKS
(3) Cantares	d1-a2	a1-f2	High voices	Rapid, brilliant. In folk vein. Has florid passages. Demands an accomplished pianist.
(5) Las locas por amor	e1-a2	g1-e2	High voices	Very animated, brilliant. Demands an accomplished pianist.
Rima (Yo soy ardiente)	e1-a2	a1-e2	Soprano	Animated, has brilliant climaxes and a slower, somewhat

TITLE	COMP.	TESS.	TYPE	REMARKS
				declamatory middle section. Demands an accomplished pianist. (Demets, Paris)

Triptico

Edition: Unión Musical Española

TITLE	COMP.	TESS.	TYPE	REMARKS
(1) Farruca	a-f2	d1-eb2	Alto or mezzo-soprano	Animated, rhythmical; in parts very florid.
(2) Cantilena	c1-eb3	a1-a2	Coloratura soprano	Delicate, graceful. Has florid passages. Demands an accomplished pianist.
(3) Madrigal	d1-bb2	a1-f2	Soprano or high tenor	Animated. The vocal line is sustained for the most part. Has a brilliant final climax.

JACINTO VALLEDOR
(c. 1768)

TITLE	COMP.	TESS.	TYPE	REMARKS
Canción de timida (El Apasionado)	e1-e2	g1-e2	All voices	Sustained, graceful. (Subirá)

HEITOR VILLA-LOBOS
(1887–1959)

(Portuguese texts)

TITLE	COMP.	TESS.	TYPE	REMARKS
A Cascavél	c♯1-f2	f♯1-e2	High or medium voices	Animated, bright. Demands facile articulation and an accomplished pianist. (Sampaio Araujo)

TITLE	COMP.	TESS.	TYPE	REMARKS
Aria (Cantilena, from Bachianas Brasileiras No. 5)	d1-bb2	f1-f2	Soprano	Vocalized, some-what florid opening section, followed by semi-chanting on text; third section is hummed. (AMP)
Big Ben	eb1-gb2	f1-eb2	Most suitable for men's voices	Declamatory. Demands some characterization and facile articulation. Interpretatively not easy. Demands an accomplished pianist. English text by the composer. (SMP)
Canção do carreiro (Serésta No. 8)	e1-f♯2	a1-e2	Soprano	Animated, demands facile articulation. Sustained middle section. (Arthur Napoleão)
Canção do poeta do Século XVIII	d1-f2	g1-e2	All voices	Slow, sustained. (SMP)
Cantiga do viúvo (Serésta No. 7)	f1-gb2	ab1-eb2	High or medium voices	Sustained. Has rhythmic complexities. Demands an accomplished pianist. (Arthur Napoleão)
Desejo (Serésta No. 10)	e1-f2	f1-d2	All voices	Graceful, short. (Arthur Napoleão)
Eis a vida! (Epigrammas ironicos e sentimentaes)	e1-f♯2	g♯1-d♯2	High or medium voices	Animated. Vocal line is mostly sustained. Short. (Sampaio Araujo)
Epigramma IV (Epigrammas ironicos e sentimentaes)	fb1-f2	g1-f2	High or medium voices	Animated, light, subdued. Short. Demands an accomplished pianist. (Sampaio Araujo)
Filhas de Maria	eb1-f2	f1-db2	All voices, except bass	Sustained. Atmospheric, plaintive. (SMP)

TITLE	COMP.	TESS.	TYPE	REMARKS
Fleur fanée	a♯-f2	e♭1-e♭2	All voices	A song of contrasting moods and tempi. In parts demands flexibility and facile articulation. Demands an accomplished pianist. French text. (Sampaio Araujo)
Les mères	c1-e♯2	f♯1-d♯2	All voices	Sustained, calm. Short, slightly animated middle section. Demands an accomplished pianist. French text by Victor Hugo. (Arthur Napoleão)
L'Oiseau	c1-e2	f1-d♭2	All voices	Sustained. Demands an accomplished pianist. French text. (Arthur Napoleão)
Louco	a-f2	e1-d♯2	All voices	Somewhat declamatory. In parts demands facile articulation. Demands an accomplished pianist. (Sampaio Araujo)
Mal secreto	b-f♯2	e1-d2	All voices	Sustained. In parts demands facile articulation. Demands an accomplished pianist. (Sampaio Araujo)
O anjo da guarda (Serésta No. 2)	e1-e2	same	All voices	Sustained. (Arthur Napoleão)
Pai-do-mato	c1-f2	c1-c2	All voices	Voice part is sustained. A song of contrasting moods and tempi. Narrative. Demands an excellent pianist. (SMP)
Realejo (Serésta No. 12)	e1-d2	e1-b2	All voices, except a light, high soprano	Animated. (Arthur Napoleão)

TITLE	COMP.	TESS.	TYPE	REMARKS
Sertão no estio	e1-a2	a1-e2	High voices	Sustained. In parts demands facile articulation. (Arthur Napoleão)
Sonho de uma noite de verão (Epigrammas ironicos e sentimentaes)	e1-g2	g1-d2	High or medium voices	Sustained. Demands an accomplished pianist. (Sampaio Araujo)
Vióla (Miniaturas No. 2)	e1-f♯2	g1-d2	All voices	Sustained. Demands an accomplished pianist. (Arthur Napoleão)

See also "Chansons Typiques Brésiliennes" (10 Indian Chants), published by Arthur Napoleão.

RUSSIAN
(in English)

The listing of songs by the Russian composers available in English translations presented a number of not inconsiderable problems. To begin with, only an infinitesimally small part of the extraordinarily varied and rich song literature of Russia is available in English translations. Thus, a great number of representative and significant Russian songs of great importance had to be omitted. Then the available English translations had to be considered. The rhythmical differences between the two languages make the problem of translating a Russian poem into English a difficult one. A virtuoso versifier can sometimes retain the original metric pattern, but even a most well-intentioned and erudite translator will find a number of seemingly insoluble problems when this metric structure is accentuated by the rhythmic pattern of the melodic line of a song. The use of extraordinarily colorful folk idioms and folk metaphors encountered in Russian poetry complicates the matter still further. If translated literally, such metaphors become almost meaningless in English, or at least very obscure, especially during the performance of a song, where the listener does not have time to consult footnotes or to accustom himself to the strange and peculiar imagery of the text; such a translation may have a disturbing effect upon the listener, or even appear senseless and ridiculous. The subject matter of the poems themselves may often seem strangely unfitting as song texts for an English-speaking audience, accustomed as it is to an entirely different poetic climate. In view of all these, and in view of the fact that, at least in so far as I know, no British or American poet of distinction has ever tried to collaborate with a musician in translating the texts of the Russian songs, it seemed very gratifying to have been able to list even the few songs given here, the English versions of which are usable and can be sung without embarrassment. It seemed utterly ridiculous to try to l'st these songs in French or German translations, which are for the most part as clumsy and inaccurate as their English counterparts, especially as this volume is primarily designed for the use of English-speaking singers. A performance of a Russian song by a British or an American singer in a clumsy and inaccurate French or German translation for the benefit of an English-speaking audience seems to border on a farce, to which even a vocalized or instrumental version of the song would seem preferable.

Whenever a song happens to be originally written to a French or German poem (as is often the case with songs of Rubinstein, and sometimes of Tchaikovsky and Borodin) the title of the poem in the original language and not in English has been given.

The very extensive and musically most valuable field of solo excerpts from the Russian operas (Glinka, Serov, Dargomijsky, Tchaikovsky, Mussorgsky, Rimsky-Korsakov) has had to be most regretfully omitted from this volume almost in its entirety, since the available English versions are for the most part too inadequate to be recommended, and since with the exception of the two examples by Tchaikovsky the listing of such excerpts in translations other than English seemed inadvisable for the reasons discussed above. The few excerpts listed are to be found appended to the song lists of the respective composers.

The name found in parentheses after the remarks indicates one of the following collections:

Century: A Century of Russian Song. Edited by K. Schindler, published by G. Schirmer.
Masters: Masters of Russian Song. Edited by K. Schindler, published by G. Schirmer.
Newman 1; 2: Modern Russian Songs, 2 volumes, high and low. Edited by E. Newman. Published by O. Ditson.
Slonimsky: 50 Russian Art Songs. Edited by N. Slonimsky, published by Leeds.

ANTON STEPANOVICH ARENSKY
(1861–1906)

Out of a great number of charming and effective songs of Arensky, only five seem to be available in fairly good English translations.

TITLE	COMP.	TESS.	TYPE	REMARKS
Deep hidden in my heart	d1-e2	e1-b1	All voices	Sustained, rather delicate. The English version by Constance Purdy is fairly good. (Newman 1)
Oh, do not light that lamp	c1-a2	e1-d2	All voices	Animated. Has an imposing climax.

TITLE	COMP.	TESS.	TYPE	REMARKS
Revery	d♯1-f♯2	f♯1-d♯2	All voices	The English version by Nicolas Slonimsky is good. (Slonimsky) Slow, sustained, subdued. The English version by Constance Purdy is good. (Newman 1)
The eagle	a♭-f♯2	d♭1-d♭2	Not suitable for light, high voices	Slow, in parts very sustained, dramatic, effective. The English version by H. G. Chapman is fairly good. (GS) The English version by F. H. Martens is fairly good. (Newman 1)
The little fish's song	d1-a2	a1-f♯2	Most suitable for light soprano	Sustained, graceful, light. The English version by R. H. Hamilton is good. (Newman 1)

MILI BALAKIREV
(1837–1910)

Most of Balakirev's great number of remarkable songs are not available in English versions. This is a great pity, since practically all of them deserve to be much more widely known than many an inferior, effective song by some otherwise undistinguished Russian composer, which through sheer accident of having been adequately translated and properly distributed represents "Russian vocal music" outside of Russia.

TITLE	COMP.	TESS.	TYPE	REMARKS
A rose in autumn	e♭1-f2	f1-d♭2	All voices	Sustained. The English version by Rosa Newmarch is good. (Six Russian Songs, NOV)
Burning out is the sunset's red flame	a♯-d♯2	d♯1-c♯2	Not suitable for light, high voices	Sustained. The English version by Constance Purdy is fairly good. (Newman 1)

TITLE	COMP.	TESS.	TYPE	REMARKS
Invocation (To Russia)	(b)e1-a2	f♯1-d2	All voices, except a very light soprano	A rather free recitative-like sustained song in folk vein. The English version by George Harris, Jr., is good. (Masters)
The pine tree	c♯1-f♯2	c♯1-c♯2	Not too suitable for very light, high voices	Slow, somewhat declamatory. The English version by Constance Purdy is good. (Newman 1)

ALEXANDER PORPHYRIEVITCH BORODIN
(1833–1887)

The most important works of Borodin are his orchestral compositions and his one opera, Prince Igor.

He has written only a few songs, out of which only a handful is available in English translations.

A dissonance	e♭1-f2	f1-d♭2	All voices	Sustained. In parts demands considerable dramatic intensity. The English version by K. Schindler is fair. (Century) The English version by F. H. Martens is fair. (Newman 1)
Fleurs d'amour	e1-f♯2	f♯1-d2	All voices	Graceful, sustained. French text. The poem is a French version of Heine's "Aus meinen Tränen spriessen." See Schumann's "Dichterliebe." The English version by H. G. Chapman is good. (Century)

TITLE	COMP.	TESS.	TYPE	REMARKS
La reine de la mer	e1-a2	a1-e2	Women's voices	Animated. The vocal line is sustained. French text. The English version by H. G. Chapman is fairly good. (Century)
My songs are envenomed and bitter	b♭-f♯2	e♭1-e♭2	Not too suitable for very light, high voices	Sustained, dramatic, somewhat declamatory. The English version by Charles F. Manney is good. (Newman 1)
Song of the dark forest	b-f2	e1-c♯2	Heavy voices	Vigorous, somber, in parts dramatic. In folk vein. Has very interesting 7/4, 5/4, 3/4 rhythm. The English version by H. G. Chapmen is good. (Century)
The sea	d♯1-g♯2	f♯1-e♭2	Not suitable for light voices	A very animated, vigorous, dramatic narrative song. Demands an accomplished pianist. The English version by Grace Hall is fairly good. (Newman 1)
The sleeping princess	d♭1-f2	e♭1-d♭2	Most suitable for women's voices, except a very light soprano	A delicate narrative song. The English version by H. G. Chapman is good. (Century)
Your native land	d1-a2	f♯1-e2	Not suitable for very light voices	Sustained. One of Borodin's most striking songs. The English version by Nicolas Slonimsky is good. (Slonimsky)

CÉSAR CUI
(1835–1918)

TITLE	COMP.	TESS.	TYPE	REMARKS
Dusk fallen	b♯-e2	d♯1-c♯2	Most suitable for men's voices	Sustained, subdued. The English version by Constance Purdy is good. (Newman 1)
The statue at Tsarskoe Selo	d♭1-e♭2	f1-c2	All voices	Delicate, sustained. The English version by Slonimsky is good. (Slonimsky)

ALEXANDER DARGOMIJSKY
(1813–1869)

Most of Dargomijsky's nearly one hundred remarkable songs are as yet unavailable in English versions. A composer of extraordinary power and individuality, Dargomijsky has influenced the vocal music of Russia to a degree hardly appreciated in Western Europe or America. Those who are familiar with Mussorgsky's vocal music and admire it ought to acquaint themselves with the vocal music of Dargomijsky, who has perhaps influenced this great master to a greater degree than is often assumed.

TITLE	COMP.	TESS.	TYPE	REMARKS
An Eastern song	c♯1-d2	f♯1-b1	Most suitable for men's voices	Slow, somewhat declamatory, sustained. The English version by Rosa Newmarch is good. (Six Russian Songs, NOV)
Heavenly clouds	a♯-f♯2	d1-d2	All voices	Sustained; in parts, however, quite florid. Has a spirited, somewhat florid final section. The English version by H. G. Chapman is fairly good. (Century)
I will tell no one	d1-g2	f♯1-e2	All voices	Sustained. The English version by Nicolas Slonimsky is good. (Slonimsky)

TITLE	COMP.	TESS.	TYPE	REMARKS
Look, darling girl	d1-g2	g1-e2	Women's voices	Graceful. In folk vein. The English version by Nicolas Slonimsky is good. (Slonimsky)
O thou rose maiden	e1-g2	a1-e2	Most suitable for tenor	Sustained, delicate. Demands some flexibility. The English version by Constance Purdy is fair. (Newman 1)
Silent sorrow	c♯1-f♯2	e1-c♯2	All voices, except a very light soprano	Sustained, not slow. The English version by Rosa Newmarch is good. (Six Russian Songs, NOV)
Ye dear, fleeting hours	c1-f2	e♭1-c2	All voices, except a very light soprano	Slow, very sustained. Has effective climaxes. The English version by H. G. Chapman is good. (Century)

Operatic Excerpt

Rusalka

Alas! All you young girls are stupid (The miller's song)	A-d♯1	d-d1	Bass or bass-baritone	Animated, demands facile articulation. Somewhat humorous. An "advice to young girls." The English version by L. Finley is good. (K. Adler, Operatic Anthology, GS)

ALEXANDER GLAZUNOV
(1865–1936)

Oriental romance	b-e♭2	e♭1-d2	All voices	Slow, sustained. Somewhat florid. In parts demands some flexibility. The English version by Nicolas Slonimsky is good. (Slonimsky)

TITLE	COMP.	TESS.	TYPE	REMARKS
The Nereid	f#1-a2	a1-e2	High voices	Sustained, effective. The English version by H. G. Chapman is good. (Century)

REINHOLD GLIÈRE
(1875-1956)

TITLE	COMP.	TESS.	TYPE	REMARKS
Ah, twine no blossoms	d1-ab2	f1-db2	Not too suitable for light, high voices	Sustained, effective, in parts dramatic. The English version by Deems Taylor is fairly good. (Newman 1; also sheet, OD)
Sweetly sang a gentle nightingale	c1-g2	f1-eb2	High or medium voices	Sustained. Demands good command of high pp. The English version by Nicolas Slonimsky is good. (Slonimsky)

MICHAEL GLINKA
(1805-1857)

Since only two adequate English versions of Glinka's songs and operatic excerpts seem to be available it seemed best not to try to list any other examples of the great Russian master.

TITLE	COMP.	TESS.	TYPE	REMARKS
Doubt	d1-g2	g1-eb2	All voices	Sustained. The English version by Nicolas Slonimsky is good. (Slonimsky)
So clearly I remember seeing	e1-f2	f1-e2	All voices	Sustained. The English version by Nicolas Slonimsky is good. (Slonimsky)

ALEXANDER TICHONOVICH GRETCHANINOV
(1864–1956)

The songs of Gretchaninov enjoy a well-deserved popularity everywhere. The five songs listed below are among his most representative ones. They also happen to be available in good English versions. All of them are beautifully written for the voice and are neither musically nor interpretatively complex.

TITLE	COMP.	TESS.	TYPE	REMARKS
My native land	e1-g2	g1-e2	Not suitable for light, high voices	A free, recitative-like, short song in folk vein. Most effective. The English version by Deems Taylor and Kurt Schindler is good. (Masters)
Over the steppe	c1-g2	d1-b1	Not too suitable for light, high voices	Slow, declamatory. In parts demands considerable dramatic intensity. The English version by Deems Taylor and Kurt Schindler is good. (Masters)
The captive	b#-f#2	e1-c#2	Heavy voices	Slow, sustained, in parts dramatic. Has an effective final climax. The English version by Grace Hall is fairly good. (Newman 1)
The snowdrop	b♭-f2	e♭1-b♭	All voices, except bass	Very animated, graceful. The English version by A. M. von Blomberg is good. (OD)
The wounded birch	d#1-g2	a1-e2	All voices	Sustained, somewhat declamatory. The English version by Deems Taylor and Kurt Schindler is good. (Masters)

583

THEODOR KOENEMAN

TITLE	COMP.	TESS.	TYPE	REMARKS
When the king went forth to war	A-e1	c#-c#1	Bass or bass-baritone	A vigorous, spirited ballad. The English version by Rosa Newmarch is good. (Marks)

LEONID MALASHKIN
(1842-1902)

TITLE	COMP.	TESS.	TYPE	REMARKS
O could I but express in song	d1-g2 (b2)	e1-e2 (H)	All voices	Sustained. Has effective climaxes. The English version by Rosa Newmarch is good. (CHES)

NICOLAI MEDTNER
(1880-1951)

The songs of Medtner, one of the least nationalistically inclined Russian composers, are well represented in a comprehensive collection of his songs with English translations by Henry Drinker, published by G. Schirmer. In addition, his very unusual "Sonate Vocalise" is listed below.

TITLE	COMP.	TESS.	TYPE	REMARKS
Elegy	b-g2	f#1-e2	All, except light, high voices	Sustained. A song of contrasting moods and tempi. Has passages demanding dramatic intensity. Demands an accomplished pianist.
Sleepless	a-ab2	eb1-eb2	All, except very light, high voices	A song of contrasting moods and tempi. Demands flexibility and an accomplished pianist.
Sonate vocalise	c1-ab2	same	Most suitable for lyric soprano	The setting of a poem by Goethe "Geweihter Platz" serves as an intro-

TITLE	COMP.	TESS.	TYPE	REMARKS
				ductory "Motto" (d1-a2) to the "Sonata" which is sung on vowels only. A difficult piece of vocal chamber music. Demands an excellent pianist. (Edition Russe de Musique)
The angel	d#1-g2	g1-e2	High or medium voices	Sustained. Demands good command of high p, messa di voce, and an accomplished pianist.
The butterfly	db1-gb2	f1-eb2	Most suitable for women's voices, except a heavy alto	
The coach of life	d1-ab2	g1-eb2	All, except light, high voices	Animated, for the most part vigorous. Last section is sustained and calm. Demands an accomplished pianist.
The muse	c1-g2	f1-e2	All voices	Sustained. Demands some flexibility and an accomplished pianist.
The rose	a-eb2	d1-c2	All voices	Slow, sustained.
The singer	d1-f#2	f#1-e2	All voices	Sustained.
Waltz	f1-bb2	f1-f2	High voices	Demands good command of high pp, and an accomplished pianist.

NIKOLAI MIASKOVSKY
(1881–1950)

TITLE	COMP.	TESS.	TYPE	REMARKS
At times it seems to me	g1-ab2	a1-e2	All voices	Sustained, short. The English version by Nicolas Slonimsky is good. (Slonimsky)

TITLE	COMP.	TESS.	TYPE	REMARKS
Her picture	d1-f2	f1-eb2	All voices	Animated, graceful. The English version by Nicolas Slonimsky is good. (Slonimsky)

MODEST PETROVICH MUSSORGSKY
(1839-1881)

Mussorgsky's genius as a composer of vocal music is of a stature that has perhaps no equal among his contemporaries, Russian or otherwise. His manner of setting a text to music is unique, and even now almost shocking in its utter lack of conventionality and the disdain for any facile formula. He is perhaps the only composer who has ever succeeded in welding the native folk melos with a seemingly utterly uninhibited and musically unbridled manner of dramatic recitation. In his choice of texts, many of which stem from his own pen, he is perhaps as remarkable as he is in his musical treatment of them. None of Mussorgsky's contemporaries seems to have dared to choose such unconventional texts for their songs. No composer of his time seems to have aimed at and attained the variety of Mussorgsky's expression ranging from starkly objective realism and mordant social satire to naïve, childlike humor, an almost mystically introspective lyricism, and fantasy.

Mussorgsky's extraordinary songs are as yet not fully appreciated or widely known in the English-speaking countries. One of the primary reasons for this neglect is undoubtedly the lack of adequate English translations of his texts. It is a great pity that perhaps the most adequate English versions of his songs, those by Edward Agate, are but little known to the English-speaking singers, being available only in the Bessel-Breitkopf & Härtel edition. The texts that Mussorgsky uses are so direct and simple that it would seem not at all impossible to translate them into idiomatically correct English. In the original Russian, the texts are for the most part almost crude in their lack of traditional poetic flights of fancy. Their verbal material is simple and everyday. In the available English translations, however, including even those by Mr. Agate, this quality is unfortunately too often lacking, so that the mood of the music seems not to be quite in accord with the elaborate, almost bookish English of the texts. It seems obvious that in songs of a composer like Mussorgsky, who is a musical dramatist above everything else, such a discrepancy between the text and the music is bound to produce a most incongruous effect. It is sincerely to be hoped that some enterprising American or British publisher will soon find it possible to make all of Mussorgsky's songs available to the English-speaking public, translated into idiomatically normal English.

586

Vocally, Mussorgsky's songs present no problems, being written for the most part within a limited range most suitable for medium voices. Interpretatively, of course, they demand a great deal from both the vocalist and the pianist. An acquaintance with Russian literature would undoubtedly benefit any singer attempting to perform these songs.

Edition: Bessel - Breitkopf & Härtel; complete, English texts.

TITLE	COMP.	TESS.	TYPE	REMARKS
A child's song	c♯1-f♯2	g♯1-d♯2	Most suitable for light voices	Delicate, graceful. The English version by Edward Agate is fairly good. (Bessel, B & H)
A vision	g-d♭2	e♭1-c♭2	Low or medium voices	Somewhat declamatory; subdued, not fast. The English version by Edward Agate is good. (Bessel, B & H)
After the battle	b♭-e♭2	e♭1-b♭1	Medium or low voices	Grave, dramatic. The English version by George Harris, Jr., and Kurt Schindler is good. (Masters)
By the river Don	c-f1	f-c1	Men's voices	Graceful. In folk vein. The English version by Edward Agate is fairly good. (Bessel, B & H)
Cradle song of the poor	b-d♯2	e1-b1	Women's voices, except a light soprano	Slow. Interpretatively not easy. The English version by Rosa Newmarch is fairly good. (Bessel, B & H)
Hopak	c♯1-f♯2	f♯1-c♯2	Women's voices, except a light soprano	Vigorous, grim, spirited dance song. Interpretatively not easy. Demands an accomplished pianist. The English

TITLE	COMP.	TESS.	TYPE	REMARKS
				version by Constance Purdy is fair. (Newman 1)
I fain would pour forth all my sorrow	(a)d1-e2	f♯1-d2	All voices, except a very light soprano	Sustained, delicate. The English version by Edward Agate is good. (Bessel, B & H) The original German words by Heine, "Ich wollt' meine Schmerzen ergössen," can be substituted.
Joyless	c1-f2	e♭1-c2	Not suitable for light, high voices	Somber, somewhat declamatory; not fast. The English version by Edward Agate is fairly good. (Bessel, B & H)
King Saul	e1-g2	a1-e2	Most suitable for men's voices	Vigorous, martial. The English version by Edward Agate is good. (Bessel, B & H)
Little star, where art thou?	d1-f♯2	f♯1-d2	All voices	Sustained. In folk vein. Demands some flexibility; slow. The English version by Constance Purdy is good. (Newman 2; sheet, OD)
Master Haughty	c1-d2	f1-c2	Not suitable for light, high voices	Not fast, somewhat declamatory. Interpretatively not easy. The English version by Edward Agate is good. (Bessel, B & H)
Misfortune	d1-f2	a1-d2	Not suitable for light, high voices	Somber, rather slow, somewhat declamatory. The English version by Edward Agate is good. (Bessel, B & H)

TITLE	COMP.	TESS.	TYPE	REMARKS
Night	c#1-g2	f#1-d#2	High or medium voices	Slow. A free recitative song. Demands good command of high pp. The English version by Edward Agate is good. (Bessel, B & H)
On the river Dnyéper	c1-gb2	f1-db2	Most suitable for men's voices, except a very light tenor	Sustained, vigorous. In folk vein. The English version by George Harris, Jr., is good. (Masters)
Oriental chant: Hear ye Amorea's daughters (from the cantata, Josua Navine)	bb-e2	f#1-d2	Alto or baritone	Slow, sustained. In parts quite florid. The English version by H. G. Chapman is good. (Century)
Peasant cradle song	bb-f1	f1-db2	Not suitable for light, high voices	Slow, somber. The English version by H. G. Chapman is fairly good. (Century) The English version by Edward Agate is fairly good. (Bessel, B & H)
Silently floated a spirit	db1-eb2	eb1-cb2	Medium or low voices	Sustained, somewhat declamatory, subdued. The English version by George Harris, Jr., is fairly good. (Masters)
Song of the flea	A#-g1	f#-d1	Men's voices, except a very light tenor	A sardonic narrative song. Interpretatively not easy. The English version by M. C. N. Collet is good. (CHES) See Beethoven's "Aus Goethe's Faust."

TITLE	COMP.	TESS.	TYPE	REMARKS
Song of the harp-player	e♭-e♭1	same	Baritone	Slow, sustained. The English version by Edward Agate is good. (Bessel, B & H) See "An die Türen will ich schleichen" of Schubert, Schumann, and Wolf.

Songs and Dances of Death

A cycle of four songs. The English version by Marion Farquhar is excellent. Published by International Music Co.

(1) Lullaby	a-f♯2	c♯1-c♯2	Low or medium voices, preferably alto or mezzo-soprano	Slow, dramatic, somewhat declamatory. Interpretatively not easy.
(2) Serenade	c♭1-f2	f1-e♭2	All voices, except a very light soprano	Sustained. Interpretatively not easy. Demands an accomplished pianist.
(3) Trepak (Russian dance)	d1-f2	e1-d2	Not suitable for light voices	Dramatic. Interpretatively not easy. Demands an excellent pianist.
(4) Commander-in-chief	d1-f♯2	f♯1-e2	Heavy voices	Very dramatic. Interpretatively not easy. Demands an excellent pianist.
Sphinx	b-e2	e1-c♯2	Medium or low voices	Slow, declamatory. Interpretatively not easy. The English version by Edward Agate is fairly good. (Bessel, B & H)
The classic	b-d2	g1-d♭2	Medium or low voices	A satirical character song. The English version by

TITLE	COMP.	TESS.	TYPE	REMARKS
The goat	b♯-e2	c♯1-c♯2	Most suitable for men's voices	Edward Agate is fairly good. (Bessel, B & H) Satirical. Interpretatively not easy. The English version by George Harris, Jr., is good. (CF)
The grave	c-c1	f-b♭	Baritone or bass	Slow, sustained, somber. Demands an accomplished pianist. The English version by Edward Agate is good. (Bessel, B & H)
The magpie	c1-f♯2	f1-d2	Medium or high voices	Light and animated. Demands facile articulation. The English version by Edward Agate is good. (Bessel, B & H)

The Nursery

A cycle of seven songs. The English version by Edward Agate is good. Published by International Music Co.

	COMP.	TESS.	TYPE	REMARKS
(1) With nursery	c♯1-f2	e♭1-d♭2	Most suitable for soprano or high mezzo-soprano	Animated. Musically and interpretatively not easy. Demands an accomplished pianist.
(2) In the corner	c1-f2	f1-d2	Most suitable for soprano or high mezzo-soprano	Rapid. Interpretatively not easy. Demands an excellent pianist.
(3) The beetle	d♭1-f2	a1-e2	Most suitable for soprano or high mezzo-soprano	Animated. Demands facile articulation and an accomplished pianist. Interpretatively not easy.

TITLE	COMP.	TESS.	TYPE	REMARKS
(4) With the doll	e♭1-e♭2	g1-d♭2	Most suitable for soprano or high mezzo-soprano	Sustained, subdued.
(5) Evening prayer	c1-e2	e♭1-c2	All voices, except bass	Not fast. Demands facile articulation Interpretatively not easy.
(6) The hobby horse	c#1-g2	a♭1-e♭2	Most suitable for soprano or high mezzo-soprano	Rapid. Interpretatively not easy. Demands facile articulation and an excellent pianist.
(7) The naughty puss	c#1-g#2	a1-f#2	Most suitable for soprano	Rapid, light. Demands facile articulation and an accomplished pianist. Interpretatively not easy.
The orphan	c1-f2	g1-e♭2	Women's voices, except a very light soprano	Somewhat declamatory. In parts demands considerable dramatic intensity. The English version by Edward Agate is fairly good. (Bessel, B & H)
The tempest	A-e1	d#-c#1	Baritone	Dramatic, animated, vigorous. Demands an accomplished pianist. The English version by Edward Agate is fairly good. (Bessel, B & H)
The wanderer	f#1-f#2	a1-e2	All voices	Slow, sustained. The English version by Edward Agate is good. (Bessel, B & H)

Without Sun

A cycle of six songs for medium or low voices. The English version by Humphrey Procter-Gregg is good. Published by International Music Co.

TITLE	COMP.	TESS.	TYPE	REMARKS
(1) Within four walls	c♯1-d2	d1-b♭1		Sustained, subdued, somewhat declamatory.
(2) In the crowd	a-e♭2	c♯1-b♭1		Somewhat declamatory, not fast.
(3) An end at last to senseless day	b-e2	c1-c2		Sustained, somewhat declamatory. In parts demands considerable dramatic intensity. Interpretatively not easy.
(4) Ennui	b-d♯2	e1-c2		Rather slow, somewhat declamatory, somber.
(5) Elegy	c♯1-f2	f♯1-c♯2		Dramatic. Interpretatively not easy. Demands an accomplished pianist.
(6) On the river	c♯1-d2	e1-c♯2		Slow, sustained, subdued, somber. Interpretatively not easy.

See also the following important songs, the available English versions of which seem inadequate:
Calistratus, Darling Savishna (Love song of an idiot), Gathering mushrooms, Minstrel's song, The country feast, The musical peep show, and The Ragamuffin.

Operatic Excerpts

Boris Godunov

	COMP.	TESS.	TYPE	REMARKS
A peaceful monk (Pimen's narrative, Act III)	c-e1	d-d1	Bass or bass-baritone	Sustained, somewhat declamatory. The unidentified English version is good. (K. Adler, Operatic Anthology, GS)

Boris Godunov

	COMP.	TESS.	TYPE	REMARKS
Ah, poor Marina! (Marina's aria, Act II)	a-g♯2	e1-e2	Mezzo-soprano or alto	Animated. Interpretatively not easy. The unidentified English version is good. (K. Adler, Operatic Anthology, GS)

TITLE	COMP.	TESS.	TYPE	REMARKS
Boris Godunov				
Farewell, my son, I am dying (Act III)	e♭-e1	e♭-c1	Bass-baritone	A dramatic, declamatory scena. The unidentified English version is good. (Bessel, B & H)
Boris Godunov				
I have attained to power (Boris' monologue, Act II)	B♭-g♭1	d♯-e♭1	Bass-baritone	A dramatic, somewhat declamatory scena. In parts very sustained. The English version by Anna Heifetz is good. (K. Adler, Operatic Anthology, GS)
Boris Godunov				
Long ago at Kazan (Act I)	f-e1	f-d1	Bass or bass-baritone	Vigorous, spirited, dramatic narrative song. The unidentified English version is fairly good. (K. Adler, Operatic Anthology, GS)
The Fair of Sorochinsk				
No, good honest people (Khivria's song and hopak)	b-f♯2	c1-f♯2	Mezzo-soprano or alto	A song of contrasting moods and tempi. Interpretatively not easy. Energetic ending. (K. Adler, Operatic Anthology, GS)

SERGEI PROKOFIEFF
(1891–1953)

The songs of Prokofieff, one of Russia's foremost composers, are unfortunately almost totally unavailable in English translations. Prokofieff wrote a considerable number of remarkable songs and it is hoped that at least some of them will soon be published in America or Great Britain and provided with adequate English versions.

TITLE	COMP.	TESS.	TYPE	REMARKS
Five vocalises (Op. 35)			All for soprano	Vocally and musically not easy. Demand an accomplished pianist.
(1) Andante	eb1-a2	g1-g2		
(2) Lento, ma non troppo	b♯-a2	e1-e2		
(3) Animato, ma non allegro	c1-bb2	gb1-gb2		
(4) Andantino, un poco scherzando	b♯-a2	f♯1-f♯2		
(5) Andante non troppo	b-b2	f♯1-g♯2		
I will wander down the blood-stained path (Song after the battle, from the cantata Alexander Nevsky)	c1-e2	eb1-c2	Mezzo-soprano or alto	Sustained. Interpretatively not easy. In parts has dramatic intensity. The English version by Elaine de Sinçay is good. (Russian-American Music Publishers)
Into your chamber	d1-g2	eb1-eb2	All voices	Sustained, gentle, subdued. The English version by Nicolas Slonimsky is good. (Slonimsky)
The ugly duckling	b-a2	e1-e2	High voices	A setting of Andersen's fairy tale for voice and pianoforte (29 pages long). Interpretatively not easy. Demands an accomplished pianist. The English version by Robert Burness is good. (Gutheil, B & H)

SERGEI VASSILIEVITCH RACHMANINOFF
(1873–1943)

Rachmaninoff's songs and pianoforte pieces are perhaps among his best known as well as representative and appealing compositions.

His songs are beautifully written for both voice and pianoforte; they seem to be nearer to Tchaikovsky's manner of writing than to that of Mussorgsky. For the most part, they are written for rather heavy voices and demand an accomplished pianist.

The nineteen songs listed below seem to be sufficiently representative of his style of writing. Most of them are available in good English versions.

Editions: Gutheil - Breitkopf & Härtel, 2 volumes (71 songs), Russian and English texts.
G. Schirmer
O. Ditson
Carl Fischer
Boston Music Co. (6 songs)

TITLE	COMP.	TESS.	TYPE	REMARKS
As fair is she as noonday light	A-f1	d-d1	Baritone	Slow, sustained. In parts demands considerable dramatic intensity. The English version by George Harris, Jr., and Deems Taylor is fairly good. (Masters)
Before my window	e1-a2 (b2)	a1-e2	Most suitable for high voices	Slow, subdued. Demands good command of high pp. The English version by Constance Purdy is good. (Newman 2) The English version by H. G. Chapman is also good. (Century)
By a new made grave	c1-e2	e1-c2	All voices	Slow, in parts dramatic, somewhat declamatory. The English version by Constance Purdy is good. (Newman 2)
Christ is risen	d1-f2	a1-eb2	Not suitable for light voices	Sustained, dramatic. The English version by Rosa Newmarch is good. (GAL

TITLE	COMP.	TESS.	TYPE	REMARKS
Daisies	f1-ab2	a1-f2	Most suitable for high voices	Slow, rather delicate. Demands an accomplished pianist. The English version by Kurt Schindler is good. (Gutheil, B & H)
Floods of spring	(ab)db1-g♯2	db1-db2	Not suitable for light voices	Very animated. Has imposing climaxes. Demands an excellent pianist. The English version by Constance Purdy is good. (Newman 2)
God took from me mine all	f♯1-e2	same	Not suitable for light, high voices	Animated, dramatic, very effective. The English version by Deems Taylor and Kurt Schindler is good. (Masters)
Here beauty dwells	d1-b2	g1-e2	All voices	Sustained. Demands occasionally good command of high pp. Vocally not easy. The English version by Geraldine Farrar is good. (CF)
In the silence of the night	e1-a2	a1-f2	Not too suitable for very light, high voices	Sustained. Has very effective climaxes. Demands good command of high p and an accomplished pianist. The English version by Carl Engel is good. (Masters)
Lilacs	eb1-g2	g1-eb2	Most suitable for women's voices	Animated, very delicate. The English version by H. G. Chapman is good. (Century)
O, do not grieve!	bb-ab2	db1-c2	Not suitable for light, high voices	Sustained. Has dramatic climaxes. The English version by Rosa Newmarch is good. (Gutheil, B & H)

TITLE	COMP.	TESS.	TYPE	REMARKS
Oh, no, I pray, do not depart!	a#-e2	c#1-b1	Not suitable for very light, high voices	Animated, dramatic. The English version by Constance Purdy is fairly good. (Newman 2)
Sorrow in spring	d1-bb2	g1-eb2	Most suitable for high voices	Animated, dramatic. Demands an accomplished pianist. The English version by Arthur Westbrook is good. (Newman 2)
The harvest of sorrow	g1-bb2	a1-f2	High or medium voices	Slow, sustained. In folk vein. In parts demands considerable dramatic intensity. The English version by Rosa Newmarch is good. (Gutheil, B & H) Also available in G. Schirmer edition ("O thou billowy Harvest Field") in a fair translation.
The raising of Lazarus	c1-f2	eb1-c2	Low voices	Grave, somewhat declamatory. The English version by Edward Agate is good. (Gutheil, B & H)
The soldier's bride	f#1-g2	g1-d2	Women's voices, except a very light soprano	Very slow, sustained. In folk vein. Demands considerable dramatic intensity. The English version by Deems Taylor and George Harris, Jr., is good. (Masters)
The songs of Grusia	e1-a2	a1-f2	High voices	Sustained. In parts demands considerable dramatic in-

TITLE	COMP.	TESS.	TYPE	REMARKS
				tensity and some flexibility. Demands an accomplished pianist. The English version by Deems Taylor and Kurt Schindler is good. (Masters)
To the children	e1-f2	f1-c2	All voices	Slow, somewhat declamatory. Demands in parts considerable dramatic intensity. The English version by Rosa Newmarch is good. (Newman 2; sheet, OD)
Vocalise	c#1-a2 (c#3)	g#1-e2	Not suitable for very low voices	Slow, very sustained. (GS) Also published in a transposed edition (a-f2).

NICOLAI RIMSKY-KORSAKOV
(1844–1908)

The songs of Rimsky-Korsakov are for the most part much less representative of his manner of writing than his operas. He has written a considerable number of songs of which only a few seem to equal his operatic excerpts in content as well as in workmanship.

TITLE	COMP.	TESS.	TYPE	REMARKS
A flight of passing clouds	e1-a2	f#1-e2	High or medium voices	Slow, sustained. Demands an accomplished pianist. The English version by Nicolas Slonimsky is good. (Slonimsky)
Hebrew love song	c#1-e2	f#1-c#2	Women's voices	Slow, sustained, subdued. Demands some flexibility. The English version by H. G. Chapman is good. (Century)

599

TITLE	COMP.	TESS.	TYPE	REMARKS
I have come to you this morning	e1-a2	g1-f2	High or medium voices	Animated, gay. Effective ending. The English version by Nicolas Slonimsky is good. (Slonimsky)
In silent woods	f1-f2	ab1-eb2	All voices	Sustained, very subdued. The English version by George Harris, Jr., and Kurt Schindler is very good. (Masters)
Like mountains the waves	d1-g2	g1-e2	Not suitable for very light, high voices	Animated. In parts demands considerable dramatic intensity. Demands an accomplished pianist. The English version by Constance Purdy is fairly good. (Newman 2)
On the Georgian hills	d#1-f#2	f#1-c#2	All voices, except a very light soprano	Sustained. Demands in parts considerable dramatic intensity. The English version by Nicolas Slonimsky is fairly good. (Slonimsky)
The cloud and the mountain	b-g1	same	All voices	Sustained, subdued. The English version by Deems Taylor is fairly good. (Masters)
The maid and the sun	c#1-a2	a1-e2	Women's voices	Sustained. Demands some flexibility. The English version by Charles F. Manney is fairly good. (Newman 2)
The nightingale and the rose	f#1-f#2	a1-d2	All voices	Very sustained. The English version by Deems Taylor is good. (Newman 2)

TITLE	COMP.	TESS.	TYPE	REMARKS
The octave	e1-a2	f1-e2	All voices	Sustained. The English version by Constance Purdy is good. (Newman 2)

Operatic Excerpts

Golden Cockerel

TITLE	COMP.	TESS.	TYPE	REMARKS
Hymn to the sun (To me give answer)	f#1-b2	a1-f#2	Coloratura soprano (lyric soprano)	Sustained. Has rather intricate florid passages. The English version by George Harris, Jr., and Deems Taylor is fairly good. (Masters)

Sadko

TITLE	COMP.	TESS.	TYPE	REMARKS
Song of Glorification (Blue is the ocean)	e-a1	g#-f#1	Tenor	Sustained. The English version by George Harris, Jr., and Deems Taylor is fairly good. (Masters)

Sadko

TITLE	COMP.	TESS.	TYPE	REMARKS
Song of India (Unnumbered diamonds)	d-g1	g-d1	Tenor	Sustained. Demands some flexibility and a good command of pp. The English version by Constance Purdy is fairly good. (Newman 2)

Snow Maiden

TITLE	COMP.	TESS.	TYPE	REMARKS
Song of the Shepherd Lehl (Snegourotchka)	eb1-f2	f1-eb2	Mezzo-soprano or alto	Light, animated. In folk vein. The English version by H. G. Chapman is fairly good. (Century)

ANTON RUBINSTEIN
(1829–1894)

Rubinstein's songs, with the exception of a very few like "Der Asra" and "Es blinkt der Tau," have been for the most part forgotten outside of Russia.

601

All his songs are effective and are well written for the voice. As his style is rather uniform and as a great number of his songs have been written to the original German texts, it seemed best to list below only his German songs, especially in view of the fact that the available English versions of his Russian songs seem, as a rule, rather poor.

Editions: G. Schirmer, 2 volumes
Novello
Many single songs issued by most publishers

TITLE	COMP.	TESS.	TYPE	REMARKS
Clärchens Lied	c1-f2	ab1-eb2	Women's voices	Sustained. See "Freudvoll und Leidvoll" by Beethoven and Liszt, and "Die Liebe" by Schubert.
Der Asra	d1-ab2	g1-d2	Most suitable for men's voices	Sustained. In parts demands considerable dramatic intensity.
Die Lerche	eb1-g2	f1-eb2	All voices	Animated. The vocal line is very sustained.
Die Rose (Persian songs, Op. 34)	c1-f2	g1-c2	All voices	Sustained, delicate. Demands some flexibility. See "Es hat die Rose sich beklagt" by Robert Franz.
Du bist wie eine Blume	e1-g2	g1-d2	All voices	Sustained, subdued. See Schumann and Liszt.
Es blinkt der Tau	eb1-gb2	a1-f2	All voices	Sustained, effective.
Frühlingslied (Die blauen Frühlings-Augen)	d#1-g#2	f#1-d#2	All voices	Delicate. See Robert Franz.
Gelb rollt mir zu Füssen (Persian songs, Op. 34)	d1-g2	f1-eb2	All voices	Very sustained. Demands some flexibility.
Lied (Es war ein alter König)	d1-g2	g1-d2	All voices	Sustained, somewhat declamatory.

TITLE	COMP.	TESS.	TYPE	REMARKS
Nicht mit Engeln (Persian songs, Op. 34)	eb1-f2	ab1-db2	Most suitable for men's voices	Very sustained. Demands some flexibility.
Nun die Schatten dunkeln	db1-f2	f1-eb2	All voices	Sustained. See A. Jensen, and "Für Musik" by Robert Franz.

DMITRI DMITRIEVITCH SHOSTAKOVITCH
(b. 1906)

TITLE	COMP.	TESS.	TYPE	REMARKS
Bitterly sobbing	e1-f2	g1-eb2	All voices	Animated. Demands a good command of pp. Has gentle humor. The English version by Nicolas Slonimsky is good. (Slonimsky)
Renaissance	c1-f2	g1-e2	All voices	Sustained, somewhat subdued. Demands a good command of high pp. The English version by Nicolas Slonimsky is good. (Slonimsky)

IGOR STRAVINSKY
(b. 1882)

Stravinsky, one of the foremost composers of our time, has written very few songs. With the exception of his earliest efforts ("Song of the dew," "Pastorale," "The Cloister") most of his songs are of great complexity and are not recommended to inexperienced singers.

TITLE	COMP.	TESS.	TYPE	REMARKS
Con queste paroline	G-e1	d-d1	Bass or bass-baritone	A very animated arietta after Pergolesi. Demands some flexibility. Italian text. (CHES)

Le Faune et la Bergère

A cycle of three songs in French for high or medium voices.
(M. P. Belaieff, BH)

TITLE	COMP.	TESS.	TYPE	REMARKS
(1) La bergère	b-f2	f1-eb2		For the most part sustained and subdued. Demands an accomplished pianist.
(2) Le faune	d1-g2	f♯1-eb2		Sustained. In parts vocally complex. Demands an accomplished pianist.
(3) Le torrent	d1-a2	e1-f♯2		A song of contrasting moods and tempi. In parts has dramatic intensity. Musically complex. Demands an accomplished pianist.

Oedipus Rex

Excerpts from the opera-oratorio. Text in Latin. Score is published by Boosey & Hawkes.

Nonn' erubeskite reges (Jocaste's aria)	a-a2	eb1-eb2	Mezzo-soprano	Has both cantabile and recitative passages. In parts demands some flexibility and great dramatic intensity.
Nonne monstrum reskituri (Oedipus' aria)	e1-g2	g1-f2	Tenor	Sustained, dramatically intense. Has florid passages.
Respondit deus (Creon's narrative)	Ab-eb1	B-c1	Bass or bass-baritone	Heavy, dramatic, ponderous. Demands command of double forte, some flexibility, and facile articulation.
Song of the dew	c♯1-f♯2	g1-e2	Mezzo-soprano or soprano	Dramatic. Interpretatively quite complex. Demands

TITLE	COMP.	TESS.	TYPE	REMARKS
				an accomplished pianist. The English version by Nicolas Slonimsky is good. (Slonimsky)
The cloister	d♯1-g2	a1-f♯2 (H)	Women's voices	Animated. In parts demands some flexibility and considerable dramatic intensity. Interpretatively not easy. Demands an accomplished pianist. The English version by M. D. Calvocoressi is fairly good. (Newman 2)
Three Japanese lyrics	g♯1-b♭♭2	g♯1-g2	Light soprano	Three short songs of considerable musical complexity. Originally scored for voice and chamber orchestra. The piano arrangement is by the composer. Demand an excellent pianist. The English version by Robert Burness is good. (Edition Russe de Musique)

PETER ILIYTCH TCHAIKOVSKY
(1840–1893)

One could hardly consider most of Tchaikovsky's many songs as being among his most representative and important compositions. As a rule, they tend to follow a rather facile formula; at present many of them seem to have lost much of the appeal that made them so popular at one time. Yet no matter how insignificant some of his songs may seem when compared with his symphonic music, one cannot help but admit that they could not have been written by anyone but a great master. Any composer of a smaller stature would have undoubtedly earned world-wide renown with songs like "Nur wer die Sehnsucht kennt," "The pilgrim's song," "A ball room meeting," "Don Juan's serenade," "The legend," and "Was I not a blade of grass" to name but a few.

The available English versions of Tchaikovsky's songs are for the most part rather poor. This seems strange in view of the fact that neither his texts nor his treatment of them seems to demand any extraordinary rhythmic virtuosity on the part of the translator.

Tchaikovsky's songs present hardly any problems vocally, musically, or interpretatively, being extraordinarily well written for the voice and for the most part purely melodic in character.

Editions: O. Ditson (Forty Songs, Musician's Library)
Novello (Twenty-five Songs)
G. Schirmer (Twelve Songs)
Many single songs published by Carl Fischer, Augener, and other publishers

TITLE	COMP.	TESS.	TYPE	REMARKS
A ball room meeting	b-e2	f♯1-d2	All voices	A delicate, subdued waltz song. One of the most appealing of Tchaikovsky's songs. The English version by Rosa Newmarch is good. (NOV)
A legend	d1-e2	e1-b1	All voices	Sustained. The English version by H. G. Chapman is fairly good. (Century)
By the window	e1-g2	a1-e2	Most suitable for high voices	Animated, very effective. The English version by Deems Taylor and Kurt Schindler is good. (Masters)
Cradle song	d1-g2	g1-d2	Women's voices	Sustained. Demands good command of high pp. The English version by Charles F. Manney is fair. (OD)
Death	d1-g2	f1-d2	Not suitable for very light, high voices	Sustained, grave. The English version by Isidora Martinez is fairly good. (OD)

606

TITLE	COMP.	TESS.	TYPE	REMARKS
Don Juan's serenade	b-e2 (f♯2)	f♯1-d2	Men's voices	Animated. The vocal line is sustained. Has very effective climaxes. Demands an accomplished pianist. The German version by F. Gumbert and the English version by Isabella Parker are good. (OD)
Evening	c1-f2	d1-c2	All voices	Sustained, somewhat declamatory, rather delicate. The English version by Kurt Schindler is good. (Century)
Farewell	c1-a2	d1-c2	Not suitable for light, high voices	Sustained, somewhat declamatory, in parts dramatic. The English version by F. H. Martens is fairly good. (OD)
Linger yet!	d♯1-f♯2	f♯1-e♭2	All voices	Sustained, subdued. The English version by A. Westbrook is good. (OD)
No tidings came from thee	c-f1	g-d1	Baritone	Sustained. In parts demands considerable dramatic intensity. The English version by Lady Macfarren is fairly good. (NOV)
Nur wer die Sehnsucht kennt	c1-f2	e♭1-c2	All voices	Sustained. In parts demands considerable dramatic intensity. German text. See Beethoven, Schubert, Schumann, and Wolf. (GS)
O my child, in the silence of night	d1-a2	e1-e2	Most suitable for men's voices	Animated, rather delicate serenade. The English version by F. H. Martens is good. (OD)

607

TITLE	COMP.	TESS.	TYPE	REMARKS
Oh, could you but for one short hour	c#-eb1	f#-c#1	Baritone	Very animated. Demands considerable dramatic intensity in parts, and an accomplished pianist. The English version by Lady Macfarren is good. (NOV)
Pilgrim's song	B-e1	g#-c#1	Bass or baritone	Sustained. Has a very imposing final climax. The English version by Paul England is good. (GS)
Regret	e1-g#2	e1-e2	All voices	Sustained. Demands in parts considerable dramatic intensity. The English version by Rosa Newmarch is good. (NOV)
Sérénade	b-f#2	e1-c#2	Not too suitable for very light, high voices	Animated, delicate. French text. (OD)
So soon forgotten	e1-ab2	f1-f2	All voices	Sustained. Demands good command of pp and ppp. Demands some flexibility. The English version by Nicolas Slonimsky is good (Slonimsky)
Song of the gipsy girl	d1-f2	e1-c2	Women's voices	Sustained. The English version by F. H. Martens is good. (OD)
Tears	d1-e2	d1-c2	Medium or low voices	Sustained. In parts demands considerable dramatic intensity. The English version by Charles F. Manney is good. (OD)

TITLE	COMP.	TESS.	TYPE	REMARKS
To sleep	b♭-f2	f1-d♭2	Not suitable for very light, high voices	Sustained. In parts demands considerable dramatic intensity. The English version by Isidora Martinez is fair. (OD)
'Twas you alone	c1-a2	g1-e♭2	All voices	Sustained, somewhat declamatory. Demands in parts considerable dramatic intensity. The English version by F. H. Martens is fairly good. (OD)
Was I not a blade of grass	b-b2	f♯1-e2	Women's voices, except a very light soprano	Sustained, in parts dramatic. Perhaps one of Tchaikovsky's most characteristic songs. The English version by Charles F. Manney is rather poor. (OD)
When spring was in the air	e♭1-g2	f1-e2	All voices, except bass	Animated, gay. In parts has some dramatic intensity. The English version by Nicolas Slonimsky is good. (Slonimsky)
Wherefore?	d1-g2 (a2)	g1-d2	Most suitable for men's voices	Sustained. In parts demands considerable dramatic intensity. The English version by Charles F. Manney is fairly good. (OD)
Whether day dawns	d♯1-a2	g♯1-d♯2	Not suitable for light voices	Very animated, effective. Demands an excellent pianist. The English version by Charles F. Manney is fairly good. (OD)

TITLE	COMP.	TESS.	TYPE	REMARKS
Why?	d1-a2	a1-d2	All voices, except a very light soprano	Sustained. Demands considerable dramatic intensity. The English version by A. Westbrook is fair. (OD)

Operatic Excerpts

TITLE	COMP.	TESS.	TYPE	REMARKS
Eugene Onégin All men should once with love grow tender (Gremin's aria)	G♭-e♭1	d♭-d♭1	Bass or bass-baritone	Sustained. Has some declamatory passages. The English version by Henry Chapman is good. (K. Adler, Operatic Anthology, GS)
Eugene Onégin How far ye seem behind me (Lenski's aria)	e1-a♭2	f♯1-g2	Tenor	Sustained. In parts has some dramatic intensity. The English version by Henry Chapman is good. (K. Adler, Operatic Anthology, GS)
Eugene Onégin If in this world a kindly fortune (Onégin's aria)	d-f1	f-e♭1	Baritone	Sustained. The English version by Henry Chapman is good. (K. Adler, Operatic Anthology, GS)
Eugene Onégin Though I should die for it (Tatiana's letter scene)	d♭1-b♭2	f1-f2	Soprano	A dramatic scena. Has recitative-like passages. The English version by Henry Chapman is fairly good. (K. Adler, Operatic Anthology, GS)

Two operatic airs in French translations (for soprano and alto or mezzo-soprano) are listed in the "Operatic Excerpts" section.

ALEXANDER TCHEREPNIN
(b. 1899)

TITLE	COMP.	TESS.	TYPE	REMARKS
Cradle song	f1-g2	bb1-eb2	Most suitable for soprano	Slow, sustained, subdued. The English version by Constance Purdy is fairly good. (Newman 2) See Gretchaninov.
I would kiss you	d1-a2	g1-f2	All voices	Animated. The English version by Nicolas Slonimsky is good. (Slonimsky)
Quiet night	eb1-ab2	ab1-f2	Not too suitable for very low voices	Sustained, subdued, delicate. The English version by Constance Purdy is good. (Newman 2)

SERGEI VASSILENKO
(1872–1956)

TITLE	COMP.	TESS.	TYPE	REMARKS
In the cathedral a girl sang prayers	d#1-g2	e1-e2	Most suitable for high voices	Sustained, delicate. The English version by Nicolas Slonimsky is good. (Slonimsky)
Longing	e1-a2	a1-f#2	Most suitable for soprano	Slow, sustained. Demands some flexibility and good command of high pp. The English version by Deems Taylor is good. (Newman 2)

SCANDINAVIAN
(in English)

The following list of songs by Scandinavian compososers is pitifully small, since apparently only a few of their songs have been published with adequate English translations.

It is possible that after a most exhaustive research more material could have been listed. However, it seemed best to limit this
list to songs available in the United States, although this decision
was made with great reluctance and much regret, for the song literature of Norway, Sweden, Denmark, and Finland is rich and musically
very significant.

The name in parentheses indicates one of the following collections:

Stub: Songs from the North, edited by Stub, published by O.
Ditson.

Werrenrath: Modern Scandinavian Songs, edited by Werrenrath,
published by O. Ditson.

Publisher's name in parentheses indicates that the song is available singly.

AGATHE BACKER-GRÖNDAHL
(1847–1907)

TITLE	COMP.	TESS.	TYPE	REMARKS
At sea (Tilsjös)	b♭-e♭2	f1-c2	Medium or low voices	Vigorous and spirited. English version by C. Purdy is good. (Werrenrath)
In dance you met me	c1-g♭2	f1-d♭2	High or medium voices	A delicate, graceful waltz song. Demands an accomplished pianist.

612

TITLE	COMP.	TESS.	TYPE	REMARKS

| When the linden's in flower (Lind) | d♯1-f♯2 | f♯1-d♯2 | Not too suitable for very low voices | English version by G. Sundelius is fairly good. (Homeyer) Delicate, sustained. English version by A. Forestier is fairly good. (Stub) |

I. A. BERG

| The herdsman's song (Herdegossen) | c♯1-a2 | f♯1-c♯2 | All voices | Slow and very sustained. English version by A. Forestier is good. (Stub) |

EDVARD GRIEG
(1843–1907)

Grieg's mode of musical expression, predominantly melodic in character, seems perhaps best suited to the smaller forms in which he excelled. His songs could be easily considered among his most characteristic and remarkable compositions.

Grieg's idiom, greatly influenced by the Norwegian folk melos, is always peculiarly and unmistakably his own. All of his songs are beautifully written for the voice and can hardly be considered either musically or vocally taxing. An acquaintance with Scandinavian folk-lore and literature, however, would be helpful to any singer seeking to establish a stylistically satisfactory mode of their interpretation. It is a great pity that most of Grieg's songs have been known in English-speaking countries practically exclusively in German versions, and that the available English versions are for the most part rather poor. The following list, therefore, can by no means be considered representative, omitting as it does many of Grieg's most remarkable songs because of the lack of available English versions, among them the celebrated cycle "Haugtussa."

Editions: C. F. Peters (German texts only)
        O. Ditson (Musicians' Library — German and English texts)
        G. Schirmer (German and English texts)
        Many reprints of single songs by various publishers.

TITLE	COMP.	TESS.	TYPE	REMARKS
A swan (En Svane)	d1-f2	f1-d2	All voices	Slow, sustained. In parts demands considerable dramatic intensity. I have found no satisfactory English translation of this celebrated song. (gen. av.)
Cradle song	b-d♯1	b-g♯1	Most suitable for medium or low voices	Animated, somber. English version by N. H. Dole is fair. (OD)
Die verschwiegene Nachtigall	d1-e2	g1-e2	Women's voices	Light and delicate, sustained. German text. (OD)
Ein Traum	c1-ab2	ab1-f2	Not too suitable for very light soprano	Sustained. Ends in an effective climax. German text. (gen. av.)
Eros	c1-f2	e1-c2	Not too suitable for very light voices	Declamatory and effective. English version by N. H. Dole is fairly good. (OD)
Good morning (God morgen)	d1-f♯2	a1-e2	All voices	Rapid and rhythmical. English versions by A. Forestier and N. H. Dole are fair. (OD)
I love thee (Jeg elsker dig)	e1-f2	g1-e2	All voices	Very sustained. Demands in parts considerable dramatic intensity. English version by R. Werrenrath is good. (Werrenrath)
In the boat	d1-e♯2	g1-d2	All voices	Light and delicate. English version by N. H. Dole is fair. (OD)

TITLE	COMP.	TESS.	TYPE	REMARKS
Lauf der Welt	d1-f♯2	f♯1-e2	Most suitable for men's voices	Light and animated. Demands facile articulation. German text. (OD)
Love's first meeting (Det förste Möde)	c1-ab2	f1-f2	All voices	Slow, sustained. English version by A. Forestier is fairly good. (Stub)
Margaret's cradle song	c1-f2	e1-c2	Women's voices	Slow and subdued. English version by A. Westbrook is good. (OD)
My dear old mother (Gamif mor)	d1-f♯2	f♯1-d2	Not too suitable for very light, high voices	Sustained. English version by A. Forestier is fairly good. (Stub)
Solveig's song (Solvejgs sang)	e1-a2	a1-e2	Women's voices	Sustained. Demands in parts considerable flexibility and good command of high pp. English version by A. Westbrook is good. (OD)
Springtide	d♯1-f♯2	f♯1-d♯2	All voices	Slow and sustained. English version by N. H. Dole is fair. (OD)
Thanks for thy counsel (Tak for dit råd)	c1-a2	a1-f♯2	Most suitable for men's voices	Rapid and vigorous, very effective. English version by R. Werrenrath is good. (Werrenrath)
The mother sings (Moderen synger)	db1-eb2	f1-db2	Women's voices	Slow and somber. English version by N. H. Dole is good. See Sinding. (OD)
The princess	d1-g2	f♯1-eb2	All voices	Somewhat declamatory. Demands in parts considerable dramatic intensity. English version by N. H. Dole is rather poor. The Forestier

615

TITLE	COMP.	TESS.	TYPE	REMARKS
				translation used in the Kjerulf setting could be successfully substituted. See "Twilight Fancies" by Delius and "Twilight Musing" by Kjerulf. (OD)
To Norway (Til Norge)	e1-f2	f1-d2	All voices	Slow and sustained. English version by A. Forestier is good. (Stub)
'Twas on a lovely eve in June	c♯1-f♯2	f♯1-d2	All voices	Delicate. English version by C. F. Manney is fair. (OD)
With a water lily	d♯1-f2	e1-c♯2	All voices	Delicate, animated. Demands an accomplished pianist. I have found no satisfactory English translation of this, perhaps one of the best songs of Grieg. (gen. av.)

See also "Seven Children's Songs," op. 61. (Boston Music Co.)

SVERRE JORDAN
(b. 1889)

TITLE	COMP.	TESS.	TYPE	REMARKS
Finland	d1-g2	f1-d2	All voices	Sustained. English version by C. Purdy is good. (Werrenrath)

YRJÖ KILPINEN
(1892–1959)

The songs of Kilpinen, a Finnish composer, comparatively unknown outside of Scandinavia, England and Germany, should, in the opinion of this writer, occupy one of the foremost places in any singer's contemporary repertoire. Extraordinarily individual in their musical structure, yet hardly ever musically or vocally complex, terse, precise, and almost overpoweringly direct in their dramatic impact, Kilpinen's songs seem to be never subject to any intellectually conceived formula and thus avoid the pitfalls of experimentalism as well as of triteness.

Kilpinen's choice of poetic material as well as his treatment of it seems to be well-nigh impeccable. None of his songs makes any extraordinary demands upon the singer, except of course the demand for extreme sensitiveness for the poetic text. For the most part, Kilpinen seems to write for medium voices, within a short compass seldom exceeding c1-g2.

His accompaniments are perhaps among the most transparent and sparse of the contemporary composers, although harmonically bold and by no means elementary. Never afraid of dissonance, Kilpinen is sparing in its use, relying primarily on the melodic line and not on the harmonic effect for his expression.

For the list below only songs written originally in German (texts by Morgenstern, Sergel and V. Zwehl) have been considered. Kilpinen has written a great number of magnificent songs to Finnish and Swedish texts.

Editions: Bote & Bock, Berlin
Associated Music Publishers, New York

Lieder der Liebe I
Opus 60
(Christian Morgenstern)

TITLE	COMP.	TESS.	TYPE	REMARKS
(1) Mein Herz ist leer	c1-e2	f#1-c#2	Medium or low voices	Slow, somewhat declamatory. Musically and interpretatively not easy.
(2) Es ist Nacht	g1-f2	bb1-f2	High or medium voices	Animated, somber. The final section slow and sustained. Interpretatively not easy. Demands an accomplished pianist.
(3) Unsere Liebe	f1-fb2	ab1-eb2	Medium or low voices	Sustained. Musically and interpretatively not easy.
(4) Wir sitzen im Dunkeln	c1-f2	g1-eb2	Medium or low voices	Sustained, subdued, very short.

TITLE	COMP.	TESS.	TYPE	REMARKS
(5) Schicksal der Liebe	d1-f♯2	g1-d♯2	High or medium voices	Animated, for the most part subdued. The final section slow and sustained. Interpretatively not easy. Demands an accomplished pianist.

Lieder der Liebe II
(Opus 60)
(Christian Morgenstern)

TITLE	COMP.	TESS.	TYPE	REMARKS
(1) Heimat	f♯1-d♯2	same	All voices	Slow, sustained, subdued.
(2) Kleines Lied	d1-e2	same	All voices	Sustained, delicate, very simple.
(3) Deine Rosen an der Brust	e♭1-f2	f1-d♭2	Soprano or mezzo-soprano	Delicate, animated.
(4) Über die tausend Berge	f♯1-f♯2	f♯1-d♯2	High or medium voices	Animated. Has a brilliant final climax.
(5) Anmutiger Vertrag	d♯1-f♯2	f♯1-e♯2	Not too suitable for very heavy, low voices	Rapid, light, gently humorous. Demands facile articulation and an accomplished pianist.

Lieder nach Gedichten von Albert Sergel
Opus 75

TITLE	COMP.	TESS.	TYPE	REMARKS
(1) Im Walde liegt ein stiller See	e♭1-e♭2	same	High or medium voices	Very sustained, subdued, delicate.
(2) Tausend stille weisse Blumen	e♭1-g♭2	g1-d2	High or medium voices	Animated, delicate. The vocal line is sustained.
(3) Heiligendamm	f♯1-f♯2	g♯1-d2	Women's voices, except a heavy alto	Sustained, for the most part subdued. Demands good command of high pp.
(4) Mein Herz der wilde Rosenstrauch	c♯1-f♯2	f♯1-c♯2	High or medium voices	Animated, delicate.

TITLE	COMP.	TESS.	TYPE	REMARKS
(5) Sommersegen	c1-g2	g1-eb2	High or medium voices	Very sustained, for the most part subdued.
(6) Unter Blüten	c#1-f#2	f#1-d#2	High or medium voices	Very sustained.

Lieder um den Tod
Opus 62
(Christian Morgenstern)

TITLE	COMP.	TESS.	TYPE	REMARKS
(1) Vöglein Schwermut	d1-f2	f#1-d2	Medium or high voices	Sustained, subdued, somber. Interpretatively not easy.
(2) Auf einem verfallenen Kirchhof	c#1-fb2	eb1-db2	Medium or low voices	Very sustained, somber. Demands in parts some flexibility. Musically and interpretatively not easy.
(3) Der Tod und der einsame Trinker	c1-f2	f1-e2	Medium or low voices	A dramatic dialogue. Interpretatively quite complex.
(4) Winternacht	eb1-f2	f1-d2	Medium or high voices	Sustained, subdued, somber.
(5) Der Säemann	f1-f2	f1-c2	Medium or low voices	Very animated, dramatic, rather vigorous. Demands an accomplished pianist.
(6) Unverlierbare Gewähr	c#1-e2	f1-c#2	Low or medium voices	Slow, sustained, for the most part subdued. Musically and interpretatively not easy.
Nachts am Posten (op. 79, no. 6)	c1-f2	eb1-eb2	Most suitable for men's voices, except a very light tenor	Sustained, grave. Has a more animated, lyrical middle section.

TITLE	COMP.	TESS.	TYPE	REMARKS
Siehe, auch ich-lebe (op. 59, no. 5)	f♯1-f♯2	a1-d2	Medium or high voices	Very animated. Has vigorous climaxes.
Thalatta! (op. 59, no. 6)	d♯1-f♯2	f♯1-d♯2	Heavy voices	Very vigorous, animated.
Von zwei Rosen (op. 59, no. 3)	e♭1-g2	a♭1-e♭2	Most suit-able for high voices	Animated, for the most part delicate. The vocal line sus-tained.
Vorfrühling (op. 79, no. 3)	d1-f♯2	f♯1-e2	Most suit-able for high voices	Animated, deli-cate, graceful.

See also "Spielmannslieder," op. 77 — eight songs most suitable for men's voices (c♯1-f♯2)

HALFDAN KJERULF
(1815–1868)

TITLE	COMP.	TESS.	TYPE	REMARKS
In days of yore (Det var då)	d1-f♯2	a1-e2	Not too suitable for very light, high voices	Grave, somewhat declamatory. En-glish version by A. Forestier is fairly good. (Stub)
Ingrid's song (Ingrids Vise)	c1-f2	f1-d2	Women's voices	Light, rhythmical folk dance tune. English version by C. Purdy is fairly good. (Werrenrath)
Longing (Last night the nightingale woke me) (Laengsel)	e♭-g2	e♭1-e♭2	All voices	Sustained, deli-cate, English ver-sion by A. Forestier is good. (Stub)
My heart and lute (Mit Hjerte og min Lyre)	e1-f♯2 (a2)	g♯1-e2	All voices	Slow and sus-tained. English version by A. Forestier is good. (Stub)
Sing! sing, nightingale, sing! (Syng, Syng)	e1-f♯2	g1-e2	All voices	Sustained. English version by A. Forestier is good. (Stub)

TITLE	COMP.	TESS.	TYPE	REMARKS
Synnöve's song	c1-f2	f1-c2	Women's voices	Slow and sustained. English version by A. Forestier is fairly good. (Stub)
Twilight musing	d1-f2	a1-d2	All voices	Sustained. English version by A. Forestier is good. (Stub) See "Twilight Fancies" by Delius and Grieg.

PETER E. LANGE-MÜLLER
(1850–1926)

Autumn (Efteraar)	d1-b1	same	All voices	A free recitative-like song. English version by C. Purdy is fairly good. (Werrenrath)
Shine bright and clear (Skin ud, du klare solskin)	a-e2	e1-c2	All voices	Animated, rhythmical. English version by C. Purdy is good. (Werrenrath)

SIGURD LIE
(1871–1904)

Snow (Sne)	db1-eb2	eb1-c2	All voices	Sustained and very subdued. Demands good command of pp. English version by Westbrook is good. (Werrenrath)

LILLJEBJORN

When I was seventeen (Arranged by A. W. Kramer)	c#1-b2	f#1-g#2	Light soprano	Sustained, graceful. Has some florid passages. (RIC)

621

SELIM PALMGREN
(1878-1951)

In the willows (Ivassen)	c1-eb2	e1-c2	All voices	Delicate. The C. Purdy translation is good. (Werrenrath)

See also a collection of six songs published by Boston Music Co. with English texts by Carl Engel.

JEAN SIBELIUS
(1865-1957)

Although Sibelius has written a great number of songs to Swedish and Finnish texts and although many of them have been published by Breitkopf & Härtel and provided with English translations, most of such copies are now unavailable and his songs are but rarely heard in America or Great Britain, notwithstanding the fact that his symphonic music has found a large public in both countries.

It seemed therefore best to list the few of his songs which are at present available in English translations reprinted by American publishers, and to list the few very famous songs published abroad, although such an exceedingly scant list can in no way be considered representative of the foremost Finnish composer of our time.

A maiden yonder sings (Tuol laulaa Neitonen)	d#1-d#2	same	All voices	Slow, very sustained and subdued. English version by C. Purdy is good. (Werrenrath)
Black roses (Svarta Rosor)	c1-g#2	e1-e2	Not suitable for light, high voices	Sustained. Has a very dramatic final climax. Unidentified English version in the Breitkopf & Härtel edition is poor.
Die Stille Stadt (German text)	db1-d2	f1-e2	All voices	Sustained and very subdued. (Werrenrath)
From the North	d#1-g2	a1-f2	High voices	Sustained. Demands some flexibility. English version by Dr. Th. Baker is fair. (GS)

TITLE	COMP.	TESS.	TYPE	REMARKS
Longings vain are my heritage (Längtan heter min arfvedel)	d1-g2	g1-e2	High voices	Sustained. English version by Elizabeth E. Lockwood is fairly good. (AMP)
The first kiss	b♭-g♯2	e1-e2	High or medium voices	Not fast, rather sustained. Unidentified English version is fair. (B & H)
The tryst (Flickan kom)	c♯1-g♯2	f1-d♭2	Women's voices, except a light soprano	A dramatic narrative song. English version by W. Wallace is fairly good. (B & H)
Was it a dream?	b-g♯2	f♯1-e2	High or medium voices	Sustained. Has effective climaxes. Demands an accomplished pianist. Unidentified English version is fair. (B & H)

CHRISTIAN SINDING
(1856-1941)

TITLE	COMP.	TESS.	TYPE	REMARKS
Alb	e♭1-f2	a♭1-d♭2	Not too suitable for very light, high voices	Slow, somber, sustained. German text. (GS)
Amber (Rav)	c1-f2	f1-e2	All voices	Animated, somber. English version by A. Forestier is good. (Stub)
A May night (Majnat)	d1-f2	f1-d2	All voices	Sustained. English version by A. Forestier is good. (Stub)
Ein Weib	b-g♯2	c♯1-d2	Not suitable for very high, light voices	Dramatic. Demands in parts some flexibility, and an accomplished pianist. German text. (Hansen)

TITLE	COMP.	TESS.	TYPE	REMARKS
Schmied Schmerz	d1(a)-f2	d1-d2	Not suitable for light, high voices	Vigorous, somber. German text. (GS)
Sylvelin	e1-e2	a1-e2	All voices	Sustained, rather subdued. English version by F. H. Martens is fairly good. (GS)
The mother sings (Moderen Synger)	d1-f2	g1-d2	Women's voices	Sustained, somber. English version by A. Forestier is fairly good. (Stub) See Grieg.
There cried a bird (Der Skreg en Fugl)	bb-f2	c1-c2	Not suitable for very light, high voices	Sustained. Unidentified English translation is good. (GS)

WILHELM T. SÖDERBERG
(1845–1939)

TITLE	COMP.	TESS.	TYPE	REMARKS
Cradle song (Vaggvisa)	d1-e2	g1-d2	Women's voices	Slow and sustained. English version by A. Forestier is good. (Stub)
The bird's song (Fågelns Visa)	d1-f#2	e1-c#2	Most suitable for women's voices	Delicate, sustained. English version by A. Forestier is fair. (Stub)

VALDEMAR THRANE
(1790–1828)

TITLE	COMP.	TESS.	TYPE	REMARKS
The Norwegian echo song	d1-b2	a1-f#2	Soprano	Animated. Has florid passages. One of Jenny Lind's famous songs. Best for coloratura soprano. English version by A. Forestier is fair. (GS)

MISCELLANEOUS
(in English)

BÉLA BARTÓK
(1881–1945)

Edition: Universal Edition

Béla Bartók, one of the great composers of the twentieth century, is unfortunately represented here by a few songs, since these seemed to be the only ones available in acceptable English translations.

TITLE	COMP.	TESS.	TYPE	REMARKS
In the valley	db1-eb2	e1-c2	All voices	Sustained, generally quiet. Demands an accomplished pianist. The English version by Eric Smith is good.
In vivid dreams	d1-f2	f#1-d2	All voices	Sustained. Demands an accomplished pianist. The English version by Eric Smith is good.
My love	b-g2	e1-e2	High or medium voices	Sustained. Starts with a parlando section. Imposing climax. Demands an accomplished pianist. The English version by Eric Smith is fairly good.

TITLE	COMP.	TESS.	TYPE	REMARKS
Night of desire	c1-f2	e1-d2	All voices	Sustained, rhythmically complex. Musically difficult. Last section is very sustained; demands a good command of pp. Demands an excellent pianist. The English version by Eric Smith is fairly good.
Summer	d1-e2	f1-d2	All voices	Sustained. Demands an accomplished pianist. The English version by Eric Smith is good.
Village Scenes	c1-f♯2	f1-e2	Women's voices	A cycle of five songs in the folk vein. Musically not easy. Demands an accomplished pianist. The English version by Martin Lindsay is fairly good.

FRÉDÉRIC CHOPIN
(1810–1849)

Chopin's seventeen songs to Polish texts, although generally available, are provided with English versions which seem too poor to be recommended. The German versions seem almost equally clumsy. French versions are for the most part fair.

Editions: G. Schirmer (German and English texts)
Durand (French texts)

ANTONIN DVOŘÁK
(1841–1904)

Dvořák is perhaps the only Czech composer whose songs are widely known in English-speaking countries. Among his many songs the two sets, "Gipsy Songs" (Op. 55) and "Biblical Songs" (Op. 99), are perhaps the most remarkable. It is fortunate that the texts of at least these two sets of songs are available in adequate English versions.

In texture his songs remind one of Brahms, although Dvořák has of course an idiom unmistakably his own, and the point of similarity is primarily confined to the marked influence which folk melos and folk rhythms exercised upon the formation of the vocal line in the songs of both composers. All of Dvořák's songs are beautifully written for the voice. For the most part they seem best suited to rather heavy voices, and they are predominantly melodic in their conception.

Biblical Songs, Op. 99

Edition: International Music Co. The English version by H. Procter-Gregg is good.

TITLE	COMP.	TESS.	TYPE	REMARKS
(1) Clouds and darkness	d♯1-f♯2	f♯1-d♯2 (H)	Not too suitable for very light, high voices	Sustained, somewhat declamatory. Demands in parts considerable dramatic intensity.
(2) Lord, thou art my refuge	e1-f2	g♯1-e2 (H)	All voices	Sustained.
(3) Give ear, O God, unto my prayer	e♭1-a2	g1-e♭2 (H)	All voices, except a very light soprano	Sustained. Demands in parts considerable dramatic intensity.
(4) God the Lord my shepherd is	e1-f♯2	f♯1-d♯2 (H)	All voices	Very sustained for the most part; subdued.
(5) Lord, a new song I would fashion	g1-g2	g1-e2 (H)	All voices, except a very light soprano	Animated, majestic, vigorous.
(6) Lord, O harken unto my crying	e1-g2	g1-e2 (H)	All voices	Sustained. Demands good command of high pp.
(7) By the still waters of Babylon	d1-g2	g1-e2 (H)	All voices	Sustained. In parts demands considerable dramatic intensity.
(8) Turn unto me and have mercy	f1-f2	g1-e2 (H)	All voices	Sustained, grave.
(9) I lift up mine eyes	f♯1-g2	a1-e2 (H)	All voices	Not fast, subdued, somewhat declamatory.

627

TITLE	COMP.	TESS.	TYPE	REMARKS
(10) Sing a new song	f1-g2	g1-d2 (H)	All voices	Animated, gay.

Gipsy Songs

A cycle of seven songs, Op. 55

Edition: International Music Co. The English version by H. Procter-Gregg is good.

TITLE	COMP.	TESS.	TYPE	REMARKS
(1) My song of love	d1-g2	b♭1-f2	Not too suitable for very light voices	Sustained, vigorous. Demands an accomplished pianist and an occasionally good command of high pp.
(2) Ei! Triangle be chiming	g1-a2	b♭1-f2	All voices	Rapid, rhythmical. Demands an accomplished pianist.
(3) Here in the wood	d1-g2	f♯1-e♭2	Not too suitable for very light voices	Very sustained and subdued.
(4) Songs as mother sang them	f♯1-g2	b1-g2	All voices	Very sustained. The accompaniment is rhythmically complex.
(5) Set the fiddles scraping	a1-a2	a1-f2	All voices	Animated, rhythmical. Demands an accomplished pianist.
(6) Flowing sleeve and trouser	e1-g2	a1-e2	All voices	Light and animated. Rhythmical. Demands an accomplished pianist.
(7) The cliffs	f1-g2 (b♭2)	f1-f2	Not too suitable for light voices	Animated, vigorous. Demands an accomplished pianist.
Goin' home	c1-g2	g1-e♭2 (H)	All voices	Slow and very sustained. Adapted from the Largo of the "New World Symphony" and sup-

TITLE	COMP.	TESS.	TYPE	REMARKS
				plied with text by W. A. Fisher. (OD)
Stabat Mater Inflammatus et accensus	a-e♭2	c1-c2	Alto	Sustained, in parts dramatic. Demands in parts some flexibility. (NOV)

LEOS JANAČEK
(1854–1928)

No songs of Leos Janaček, one of Czechoslovakia's greatest composers, seem to be available in English translations.

See "The Diary of One Who Vanished," a large cycle for tenor, alto, three female voices, and piano. The tenor soloist sings 18 of the 21 songs (there is one piano solo besides) most of which are short. Published by Artia, Prague.

ZOLTÁN KODÁLY
(1882–1967)

Edition: Boosey & Hawkes. The English version by Elizabeth Lockwood is good.

The many songs of Zoltán Kodály, probably the most important Hungarian composer next to Bartók, are beautifully written for the voice and are musically not very complex. The few songs listed below seem to be the only ones provided with acceptable English translations.

TITLE	COMP.	TESS.	TYPE	REMARKS
Farewell carnival!	F♯-e1	c♯-b	Bass or bass-baritone	Animated, rhythmic.
From a lover's letter	b♭-d♯2	c1-c2	Medium voices	Sustained. Has recitative-like passages. Demands an accomplished pianist.
Life's noontide	a-e2	d♯1-d2	Medium or low voices	Slow, sustained. Has a slightly animated middle section.
Sadly rustle the leaves	b-e2	c♯1-d♯2	Most suitable for men's voices	Sustained, somber. Demands an accomplished pianist.

TITLE	COMP.	TESS.	TYPE	REMARKS
Solitude	f-d1	c♯1-c♯2	Medium or low voices	Slow, sustained, grave.
Spring	c1-g2	f♯1-e2	High or medium voices	Animated, exuberant, brilliant. Demands facile articulation, good command of high p and an accomplished pianist.
Weeping	b♭-f♯2	f1-e2	Medium voices	Sustained. In parts demands dramatic intensity.

See also "Three Songs," Op. 14, with English versions by A. H. F. Strangways and Steuart Wilson. Published by Boosey & Hawkes.

JAROSLAV KŘICKA
(b. 1882)

This outstanding Czech composer, who has written a considerable number of remarkable songs, is unfortunately represented here by one song, since "The albatross" seems to be the only one available in English version.

| The albatross | b-f♯2 | e1-c♯2 | All voices, except a very light soprano or tenor | Sustained. Demands in parts considerable dramatic intensity. Interpretatively not easy. The English version by Fr. McAllister is good. (Homeyer) |

BEDŘICH SMETANA
(1824-1884)

No English versions of Smetana's songs seem to be available. The piano score of "The Bartered Bride," provided with an excellent English translation by Marion Farquhar, is published by G. Schirmer.

KAROL SZYMANOWSKI
(1883–1937)

Since no adequate English versions of the very remarkable songs of Szymanowski seem to be available, it was best not to try to list any of the examples of this outstanding Polish composer. Most of his songs with Polish and German texts are published by Universal Edition.

MISCELLANEOUS FLORID DISPLAY PIECES
and arrangements for <u>coloratura soprano</u> not otherwise listed.

For other similar material see the Song Lists of Adam, Dell'-Acqua, Arditi, Bishop, Delibes, Saint-Saëns among many others, as well as Operatic Excerpts for Soprano.

Alabieff

The nightingale	c1-ab2 (c3)	g1-g2	(gen. av.)

Benedict

Carnival of Venice	d1-eb3	g1-g2	Arranged by E. Liebling. (GS)

Benedict

The Gipsy and the bird	d1-d3 (e3)	g1-g2	Arranged by E. Liebling. (GS)

Délibes

Passepied	d♯1-c♯3	g♯1-g♯2	Arranged by A. Aslanoff. (GS)

Eckert

Swiss Echo song	(a)d1-bb2(d3)	a1-a2	Arranged by E. Liebling. (GS)

Glazunov

La primavera d'or	d1-bb2	g1-g2	Arranged by F. La Forge. (GS)

Haydn

Già la notte	c1-a2	f1-f2	Arranged by Viardot-Garcia. An arrangement of a serenade from one of Haydn's string quartets. Suitable for <u>lyric soprano</u>. (gen. av.)

Liadov

The musical snuffbox	c♯1-d3	f♯1-g2	Arranged by A. Aslanoff. (GS)

TITLE	COMP.	TESS.	TYPE	REMARKS
Proch				
Theme and variations (Deh torna mio bene)	b♭-e♭3	f1-g♭2		(gen. av.)
Rode				
Theme and variations (Al dolce canto)	b♭-c3	g1-g2		(Marchesi, "Coloratur Arien." CFP)
Strauss				
Voci di primavera	e1-c3	g1-f2		A florid waltz. (GS)

For cadenzas of the principal operatic airs for coloratura soprano see:
Estelle Liebling, "Coloratura Digest" (GS)
Mathilda Marchesi, "Variantes et Points d'Orgue" (Heugel; reprinted
 by E. Marks, New York.)

FOLK SONGS

FOLK SONGS

Folk songs, in the form in which they are available to the performer of today, fall in four categories:

1. The true folk song, the words and the melody of which have been faithfully recorded and provided with a harmonization.

2. The concert arrangement, in which the harmonization reflects the individual style of the composer-arranger and the accompaniment is pianistically conceived. (Arrangements of folk songs by Benjamin Britten or Aaron Copland could be cited as excellent examples of such.)

3. The folk tune, in which the melody of a folk song has been retained but to which melody a different set of words has been added. As an example of this type of arrangement see any number of Irish songs arranged by Hughes, Irish Melodies by Moore and Balfe, and Songs of the Hebrides arranged by Kennedy-Fraser.

4. A song in folk style or the traditional air, which, because of its similarity to the true folk song, is popularly considered such. ("Killarney" by Balfe or "Down by the Swanee River" by Stephen Foster, for instance.)

It has been my endeavor to concentrate mainly on the first three categories while preparing this list.

A complete or comprehensive list of American, English, Scottish and Irish folk songs would no doubt comprise several thousand entries. The list below does in no way claim to be complete or even very representative. It is primarily based on admittedly personal and no doubt somewhat arbitrary decision to list only such material as this writer considers of practical value to the singer or the vocal student.

Thus this list will not be of much value to those who are primarily interested in the study of folklore and secondarily in concert and teaching material which happens to be of folk origin. Judged by musicological and historical standards, this list is pitifully inadequate and no doubt amateurish. Yet, having been prepared for the use of performers, the selection has to be primarily based on the practical artistic value of the text and music and not on the historical, anthropological and linguistic factors which so often make an artistically insignificant folk song a culturally most valuable, elucidating and interesting example.

The American list is perhaps more adequately treated than any of the others. British singers have long been appreciative of their folk-song heritage, while American singers have as yet paid comparatively slight attention to their native folk music. It seemed therefore advisable to list the American examples more adequately.

As most of the songs listed rarely exceed a compass of a tenth it seemed advisable to dispense with the naming of the tessituras.

No Welsh folk songs have been listed, since in the opinion of this writer it seems preferable to sing them in their original language.

Since many of the American folk songs stem from England, a great number of duplications and slightly different versions of the same tune and the same text exist. In case of such duplication this writer has favored the American version. Thus many a famous ballad and song not found in the English list (such as "Lord Randal" or "Barbara Allen") will be found in the American list.

The performance of folk songs in a present-day concert hall presents a number of problems. In the opinion of this writer it seems most advisable to treat the folk songs primarily as music and not as some "quaint examples" of folklore. In other words, unless the singer can wholeheartedly accept the text and the music of a folk song as such, and unless this text and its musical expression can produce within him an emotional reaction sufficiently strong to warrant a performance, it would be better not to try to perform such songs. Utmost simplicity, understatement rather than a so-called "dramatic projection," clear, unaffected diction not marred by any attempt to imitate a dialect, and a clear delivery of the melodic line seem imperative to a dignified and satisfactory performance of a folk song in a concert hall. Any conscious attempt to inject the so-called "native flavor" into a folk song or to imitate the mannerisms of an untrained singer is almost invariably bound to result in an exaggerated, carricature-like performance, embarrassing alike in its crudeness and insincerity, which are bound to be accentuated by the stage, footlights, grand piano, and the dress of the performers. Folk songs are best accompanied on a guitar or other such instrument, since in its nature the instrumental accompaniment of a folk song is confined to a simple harmonic background accentuating the rhythmic structure of the melody. The accompanist using the modern piano should make his part as inconspicuous as possible.

The name found in parentheses indicates one of the following collections:

(Collections marked with an asterisk contain concert arrangements. Single copies or arrangements are identified by the arranger's name and the publisher's. Example: Burleigh, RIC)

American:
  Downes: A Treasury of American Song. Collected and arranged
    by Downes & Siegmeister, published by Howell, Soskin & Co.
  Bacon: *Along Unpaved Roads. Arranged by Bacon, published by
    Leeds.
  American Series: American Folk Song Series, 25 sets. Edited by
    Niles, Matteson, Sharp, Ring and others, published by G. Schirmer.
  Powell: *Five Virginian Songs. Arranged by Powell, published by
    C. Fischer.
  McGill: Folk Songs of the Kentucky Mountains. Edited by McGill,
    published by Boosey & Hawkes.
  Brockway: *Lonesome Tunes. Arranged by Brockway & Wyman,
    published by H. W. Gray.
  Copland: *Old American Songs, 2 sets. Arranged by Copland,
    published by Boosey & Hawkes.
  Niles 7: Seven Kentucky Mountain Songs. Edited by Niles, published
    by G. Schirmer.
  Sturgis: *Songs from the Hills of Vermont. Edited by Sturgis &
    Hughes, published by G. Schirmer.
  Niles: Songs of the Hill Folk. Edited and arranged by Niles, pub-
    lished by G. Schirmer.
  Sandburg: The American Songbag. Edited by Sandburg, published
    by Harcourt, Brace & Co.
  Brockway 20: *Twenty Kentucky Mountain Songs. Edited and ar-
    ranged by Brockway and Wyman, published by O. Ditson.

American Negro:
  R. Johnson 1: The Book of American Negro Spirituals. Edited by
    J. Johnson & R. Johnson, published by Viking Press.
  R. Johnson 2: The Second Book of Negro Spirituals. Edited by J.
    Johnson & R. Johnson, published by Viking Press.

English:
  Farnsworth: Folk-Songs, Chanteys and Singing Games. Edited by
    Farnsworth & Sharp, published by H. W. Gray.
  Moffat: Minstrelsy of England. Edited by Moffat, published by
    Bayley & Ferguson.
  Sharp 100: One Hundred English Folksongs. Edited by Sharp, pub-
    lished by O. Ditson.
  Bantock: One Hundred Songs of England. Edited by Bantock, pub-
    lished by O. Ditson.
  Vaughan Williams: *Six English Folk Songs. Edited and arranged
    by Vaughan Williams, published by Oxford Univ. Press.
  Sharp Methuen: Songs of the West. Edited by Sharp, published by
    Methuen & Co.

Scottish:
  Hopekirk: Seventy Scottish Songs. Edited by Hopekirk, published
    by O. Ditson.
  Pittman: Songs of Scotland. Edited by Pittman, published by
    Boosey & Hawkes.

Reid: <u>Songs of Scotland</u>. Edited by Reid, published by Boosey & Hawkes.

Kennedy-Fraser: <u>Songs of the Hebrides</u>, 3 vols. with English and Gaelic words. Edited by Kennedy-Fraser & Macleod, published by Boosey & Hawkes.

Irish:

Hughes Country: *<u>Irish Country Songs</u>, 2 vols. Edited by Hughes, published by Boosey & Hawkes.

Page: <u>Irish Songs</u>. Edited by Page, published by O. Ditson.

Hughes: *<u>Old Irish Melodies</u>. Edited by Hughes, published by Boosey & Hawkes.

Fischer 60: <u>Sixty Irish Songs</u>. Edited by Fischer, published by O. Ditson.

Hatton & Molloy: <u>The Songs of Ireland</u>. Edited by Hatton & Molloy, published by Boosey & Hawkes.

Harty: *<u>Three Irish Folk Songs</u>. Edited by Harty, published by Oxford Univ. Press.

Mixed:

Britten: *<u>Folk Song Arrangements</u>, 6 vols. Edited and arranged by Britten, published by Boosey & Hawkes.

Edmunds: *<u>Folk Song Settings</u>. Edited and arranged by Edmunds, published by Row.

Somervell: <u>Songs of the Four Nations</u>. Edited by Somervell, published by Cramer.

AMERICAN

TITLE	COMP.	TYPE	REMARKS
As I walked out (Kentucky)	d1-f2	All voices	Sustained, graceful. (McGill)
At the river (Hymn tune)	eb1-eb2	All voices	Sustained. Religious text. (Copland.
Barbara Allen (Kentucky)	b-d2	All voices	Sustained narrative song. (Brockway)
Barbary Ellen (Kentucky)	b-e2	All voices	Sustained narrative song. (American Series, Set 18)
Billie boy (Kentucky)	eb1-eb2	All voices	Gently humorous, graceful. (Brockway)
Billy boy (American sailor's chanty)	c1-f2	All voices	Animated, demands facile articulation. (Edmunds)

TITLE	COMP.	TYPE	REMARKS
Bird's courting song (Vermont)	c1-eb2	All voices	Animated, gently humorous, rhythmical. (Sturgis)
Black is the color of my true love's hair (Kentucky)	b-e2	Most suitable for men's voices	Sustained, plaintive. (Niles 7)
Bury me not on the lone prairie	b-d2	Most suitable for men's voices	Sustained, somber. (Downes)
Careless love	e1-f#2	All voices	Sustained, plaintive. (Bacon)
Come all you young and handsome girls (Kentucky)	d1-d2	Women's voices	Sustained, plaintive. (Brockway 20)
Come o my love (North Carolina)	c1-c2	All voices	Sustained, plaintive. (American Series, Set 15)
Common Bill	b-f2	Women's voices	Gently humorous, graceful. (Bacon)
Daily growing (Vermont)	d1-d2	Women's voices	Sustained, plaintive. (Sturgis)
Down in that valley (Kentucky)	e1-e2	All voices	Sustained. (American Series, Set 18)
Ef I had a ribbon bow (Kentucky)	g1-f2	Women's voices	Sustained. (Niles 7)
Every night when the sun goes in	c1-f2	All voices	Slow, sustained. (Edmunds)
Fare you well	f1-ab2	All voices	Slow, very sustained, gentle. (Edmunds)
Father Grumble (Ohio)	c1-d2	All voices	Animated, humorous narrative song. (American Series, Set 18)
Foggy, foggy dew	eb1-db2	Men's voices	Sustained. (Sandburg)
Frog went a-courting	d1-d2	All voices	Rapid, humorous. Demands facile articulation and an accomplished pianist. (Brockway) See "Toad's Courtship."
He's gone away	c1-e2	All voices	Sustained, plaintive. (Downes)

TITLE	COMP.	TYPE	REMARKS
I'm sad and I'm lonely	d1-e2	Women's voices	Sustained, plaintive. (Downes)
I wash my face in a golden vase (Kentucky)	d1-d2	Women's voices	A sustained, delicate Christmas carol. (American Series, Set 18)
I wish I was single (Nebraska)	db1-c2	Men's voices	Humorous. Demands facile articulation. (Sandburg)
I wonder as I wander (North Carolina)	c1-e2	All voices	Sustained, plaintive, subdued. Religious theme. (American Series, Set 14)
Jesus, Jesus, rest your head	d1-g2	All voices	Slow, sustained, quiet. A Christmas carol. (Edmunds)
John Riley (Kentucky)	c1-c2	All voices	Sustained, graceful narrative. (Brockway)
Lady Ishbel and the elfin knight (North Carolina)	c1-d2	All voices	Sustained narrative song. (American Series, Set 20)
Little brown jug	e1-e2	Men's voices	Animated, humorous. (Downes)
Little sparrow (Kentucky)	e1-e2	Women's voices	Sustained. (Brockway)
Lonesome road (Indiana, Texas)	d1-c2	All voices	Sustained. (Sandburg)
Long time ago	f1-f2	All voices	Somewhat slow, sustained. (Copland)
Lord Randal (Kentucky)	eb1-f2	All voices, except a light soprano	Dramatic narrative. (McGill)
Lord Thomas (Kentucky)	c1-eb1	All voices, except a very light soprano	Dramatic narrative song. (McGill)
Madam, I have come a-courting (Maine)	c1-c2	All voices	Animated, humorous. (Ring, Folk Songs, Ballads, etc., Set IV, ECS)
My horses ain't hungry (Kentucky)	b-e2	All voices	Gently humorous, graceful. (American Series, Set 14)
Night-herding song	c1-c2	All voices	Sustained, graceful, subdued. (Downes)

TITLE	COMP.	TYPE	REMARKS
O death (Southern Mountains)	b-d2	Not too suitable for light, high voices	Sustained, somber. (Downes)
Oh, who's goin' to shoe your pretty little foot (North Carolina)	b-c2	Men's voices	Graceful. (American Series, Set 18)
On top of old Smokey	e1-f2	All voices	Slow, sustained. (Edmunds)
Poor way faring stranger (Southern Mountains)	c1-e2	Men's voices	Sustained, plaintive. (Downes)
See—Jesus the saviour (Kentucky)	e1-c2	Most suitable for light voices	A sustained, delicate Christmas carol. (American Series, Set 16)
Simple gifts (Shaker song)	eb1-eb2	All voices	Sustained, gentle. (Copland)
Sinful shoe	c1-eb2	Not too suitable for very light, high voices	Sustained. Demands in parts considerable dramatic intensity. (Bacon)
Sourwood mountain (Kentucky)	b-c#2	All voices	Vigorous, animated. (Brockway)
The barnyard song (Kentucky)	eb1-eb2	All voices	Animated, humorous nursery rhyme. (Brockway)
The bee (New England)	d1-d2	All voices	Graceful, humorous. (Downes)
The bed-time song (Kentucky)	c#1-d2	All voices	Graceful, delicate. (Brockway)
The blue-eyed boy (North Carolina)	c1-c2	Women's voices	Sustained. (American Series, Set 15)
The boatmen's dance (Minstrel song — 1843)	e1-f#2	Men's voices	Animated; slow, sustained refrain. (Copland)
The cherry tree (Kentucky)	a1-e2	All voices	A sustained, graceful Christmas carol. (Niles 7)
The daemon lover (Kentucky)	c1-eb2	All voices	Sustained narrative song. (Brockway 20)
The deaf woman's courtship (Virginia)	b-f#2	All voices	Animated, humorous. (Powell)
The dear companion (North Carolina)	e1-c2	Women's voices	Sustained, plaintive. (American Series, Set 21)

641

TITLE	COMP.	TYPE	REMARKS
The dodger (Campaign song)	g1-d2	Men's voices	Animated, humorous. (Copland)
The false young man (Tennessee)	b-d2	Women's voices	Sustained, plaintive. (American Series, Set 21)
The farmer's curst wife (Kentucky)	e1-e2	All voices	A rapid, comic narrative. Demands facile articulation. (American Series, Set 20)
The lass from the low countree (North Carolina)	b-d2	All voices	Sustained, somber. (American Series, Set 20)
The little horses (Lullaby)	b-e2	All voices	Somewhat slow; sustained. Has an animated refrain. (Copland)
The little Mohee (Kentucky)	c#1-d2	Most suitable for men's voices	Sustained narrative song. (Brockway)
The nightingale (Kentucky)	db1-f2	Not too suitable for very low voices	Graceful, sustained. (Brockway)
The old maid (Kentucky)	eb1-eb2	Women's voices	Animated, humorous. (Brockway 20)
The old maid's song (Kentucky)	eb1-f2	Women's voices	Rhythmical, humorous. (Brockway)
The rich old lady (Virginia)	d1-e2	All voices	Animated, comic narrative song. (Powell)
The rich old miser courted me (Maine)	c1-d2	Women's voices	Animated, humorous. (Ring, Folk Songs, Ballads, etc., Set IV, ECS)
The riddle song (Kentucky)	e1-e2	All voices	Sustained, delicate. (American Series, Set 21)
The single girl	d1-e2	Women's voices	Sustained, graceful, humorous. (Downes)
The swapping song (Kentucky)	f1-d2	Most suitable for men's voices	Animated, comic. (Brockway 20)

TITLE	COMP.	TYPE	REMARKS
The toad's courtship (Kentucky)	d1-e2	All voices	Animated, humorous narrative song. (Brockway 20) See "Frog Went A-Courting."
The twa corbies (Kentucky)	b-f2	Women's voices	Sustained, somber. (American Series, Set 18)
The warranty deed (Vermont)	e♭1-e♭2	All voices	Animated comic song. (Sturgis)
The water-cresses (Kentucky)	c1-f2	All voices	Graceful, delicate, rhythmical. (American Series, Set 20)
Tom Bolynn (New England)	d1-d2	All voices	An animated, humorous narrative. (Downes)
Wanderin' (New York)	d1-d2	Most suitable for men's voices	Sustained, subdued. (Sandburg)

AMERICAN NEGRO

TITLE	COMP.	TYPE	REMARKS
Ain't goin to study war no mo'	f1-e♭2	All voices	Rhythmical, graceful. (Burleigh, RIC)
Blind man	c1-c2	All voices	Sustained, somber. (Downes)
By and by	e1-f♯2	All voices	Sustained. (R. Johnson 1)
City called heaven	c1-f2	All voices	Slow, sustained. (Hall Johnson, Robbins)
Crucifixion	b1-b2	Low voices	Slow, very sustained, tragic. (John Payne, GS)
Deep river	a♭-f2	Most suitable for medium or low voices	Very sustained. Demands in parts considerable dramatic intensity. (Burleigh, RIC)
De gospel train	f1-d2	All voices	Spirited, rhythmical. (Burleigh, RIC)
De ol' ark's a-moverin' an I'm goin home	d1-g2	All voices	Animated, rhythmical. (R. Johnson 2)

TITLE	COMP.	TYPE	REMARKS
Dere's no hidin' place down dere	f1-d2	All voices	Rhythmical, animated. (R. Johnson 1)
Don't you weep when I'm gone	db1-eb2	All voices	Sustained. (Burleigh, RIC)
Go down, death	bb-eb2	All voices	Majestic, sustained. (Kennedy, Mellows, A. & C. Boni)
Go down, Moses	f#1-f#2	Not suitable for very light voices	Vigorous, dramatic. (Burleigh, RIC)
Go tell it on the mountain	d1-e2	All voices	Sustained. (Margaret Bonds, Mercury)
Grumbellin' people	d1-e2	All voices	Animated, rhythmical, gently humorous. (Kennedy, Mellows, A. & C. Boni)
Heav'n, heav'n	f1-d2	All voices, except a very light soprano	Spirited, rhythmical, vigorous. (Burleigh, RIC)
He's got the whole world in his hands	c#1-a2	All voices	Sustained. (Margaret Bonds, Mercury)
Hold on	e1-e2	Not suitable for very light voices	Rhythmical and dramatic. (Hall Johnson, Robbins). See also "Sinful shoe," arr. by Ernst Bacon.
Honor! honor!	eb1-g2	All voices	Very spirited. (Hall Johnson, CF)
I cannot stay here by myself (A slave's lament)	c1-e2	Most suitable for low voices	Very somber. (Hall Johnson, CF)
I got a home in a dat rock	d1-f2	All voices	Rhythmical. (Burleigh, RIC)
I'm troubled in mind	c1-c2	Not too suitable for very light, high voices	Slow, sustained. (R. Johnson 1)
I'm goin' to thank God	d1-g2	Most suitable for high voices	Sustained. (R. Nathaniel Dett, J. Fischer)
I stood on the river of Jordan	c1-c2	All voices	Sustained. (Burleigh, RIC)

TITLE	COMP.	TYPE	REMARKS
John Henry (Negro work song)	c1-eb2	Men's voices	Rhythmical. (Hall Johnson, CF)
Joshua fit de battle ob Jericho	d♯1-e2	Not suitable for very light voices	Vigorous. (Burleigh, RIC)
Lis'en to de lam's	e1-g2	All voices	Sustained, delicate. (R. Johnson 1)
Lit'le David, play on yo' harp	d1-g2	All voices, except a very light soprano	Spirited, rhythmical, vigorous. (R. Johnson 1)
My baby in a guinea-blue gown	b-e2	Most suitable for men's voices	Animated, rhythmical, humorous. (Kennedy, Mellows, A. & C. Boni)
My soul's been anchored in the Lord	e1-f2 (a2)	Not suitable for very light voices	Sustained. Demands considerable dramatic intensity. (Florence Price, Gamble Hinged Music Co.)
Nobody knows de trouble I've seen	eb1-eb2	Not too suitable for very light, high voices	Very sustained, somber. (Burleigh, RIC)
Oh Peter go ring-a dem bells	eb1-ab2	All voices	Spirited, rhythmical. (Burleigh, RIC)
On ma journey	c1-c2	All voices	Spirited, rhythmical. (Edward Boatner, RIC)
Sit down, servant, sit down	c1-db2	All voices	Rhythmical. (R. Nathaniel Dett, GS)
Sometimes I feel like a motherless chile	e1-e2	All voices	Very sustained, subdued. (Burleigh, RIC)
Sometimes I feel like I wanna go home	f1-c2	Most suitable for low voices	Sustained, subdued. (J. Fischer & Bros., 70 Negro Spirituals, OD)
Steal away	ab1-f2	All voices	Very sustained, subdued. (Burleigh, RIC)
Swing low, sweet chariot	eb1-f2	All voices	Very sustained, slow. (Burleigh, RIC)
The whale got Jonah down	f1-f2	All voices	A spirited, comic character song. (Dan Lewis, Plantation Songs, White, Smith & Co.)

TITLE	COMP.	TYPE	REMARKS
This is a sin-tryin' world	e1-b1	All voices	Animated, rhythmical. (Downes)
'Tis me, o Lord	ab1-eb2	All voices	Rhythmical, plaintive. (Burleigh, RIC)
Trampin'	f1-d2	Most suitable for medium or low voices	Slow, rhythmical. (Edward H. Boatner, GAL)
Troubles was hard	e1-e2	All voices, except a very light soprano	Animated, gently humorous narrative song about Biblical characters. (Kennedy, Mellows, A. & C. Boni)
Water boy (a Negro convict song)	d1-d2	Men's voices	Sustained. (Avery Robinson, BMC)
Were you there	c1-f2	All voices	Very sustained, subdued. (Burleigh, RIC)
You may bury me in de Eas'	f1-f2	All voices	Sustained, somber. (Burleigh, RIC)

ENGLISH

TITLE	COMP.	TYPE	REMARKS
As down in the meadows	c1-f2	Most suitable for high voices	Graceful. (Moffat)
As I walked out through the meadows	c1-d2	Men's voices	Sustained, graceful. (Sharp 100)
Botany bay	e1-e2	Men's voices	Sustained narrative song. (Sharp 100)
Cross purposes	c1-f2	All voices	Graceful, humorous. (Moffat)
Early one morning	c1-f2	All voices	Sustained, graceful. (Moffat; Britten)
Gently, Johnny my jingalo	d1-d2	Men's voices	Graceful, gently humorous. (Sharp 100)
Henry Martin	d1-e2	Most suitable for men's voices	Sustained narrative song. (Sharp 100)

TITLE	COMP.	TYPE	REMARKS
I'm seventeen come Sunday	d1-e2	All voices	Graceful, animated. (Farnsworth)
In Bibberley town	d1-d2	All voices	Animated, humorous narrative song. (Sharp Methuen)
In search of a wife	d1-e2	Men's voices	Sustained, humorous. (Moffat)
I saw three ships	d1-d2	Not too suitable for light, high voices	A vigorous, spirited Christmas carol. (Arr., Eric Thiman, AUG)
May day carol	d1-g2	Most suitable for men's voices	Sustained. The accompaniment is somewhat elaborate harmonically. (Arr., Deems Taylor, CF)
Mowing the barley	c1-e2	All voices	Graceful, humorous. (Farnsworth)
My mother did so before me	d1-f2	Women's voices	Spirited, humorous. (Sharp Methuen)
O no, John!	d1-d2	All voices	Animated. (Farnsworth)
O Sally, my dear	c1-e2	Men's voices	Graceful, gently humorous. (Sharp 100)
O waly waly	d1-d2	All voices	Sustained, plaintive. (Farnsworth)
Oliver Cromwell	eb1-eb2	All voices	Fast, humorous. Narrative. (Britten)
Praise we the Lord	f1-f2	All voices	Animated. (Edmunds)
Rolling in the dew	d1-e2	All voices	Animated, light, humorous, rhythmical. (Vaughan Williams)
Some rival has stolen my true love away	d1-e2	Most suitable for men's voices	Animated, vigorous. (Lucy E. Broadwood, BH)
Sweet nightingale	d1-d2	Not too suitable for very low voices	Sustained, delicate. (Sharp Methuen)
The ash grove	db1-f2	All voices	Graceful, light. Demands some flexibility. (Britten)
The brisk young bachelor	c1-d2	Men's voices	Very animated, humorous. Demands facile articulation. (Sharp 100)

TITLE	COMP.	TYPE	REMARKS
The brisk young widow	d1-f♯2	All voices	Animated, humorous. Narrative. (Britten)
The blue flame	c1-e2	Women's voices	Sustained, somber, subdued. (Sharp Methuen)
The foggy, foggy dew	e♭1-e♭2	Men's voices	Sustained, narrative. (Britten)
The golden vanity	a-d2	Not too suitable for very light, high voices	A dramatic narrative song. (Broadwood, English County Songs, Schuberth & Co.)
The loyal lover	d1-e2	All voices	Sustained, graceful. (Maitland, English County Songs, Schuberth & Co.)
The mole catcher	d1-d2	Most suitable for men's voices	A comic, parlato song. (Sharp Methuen)
The plough boy	c1-f2	Most suitable for men's voices	Animated, light. (Britten)
The three ravens	d1-f2	All voices	Sustained, subdued, graceful narrative. (Moffat)
The tythe pig	c1-d2	All voices	Animated, comic narrative song. (Sharp Methuen)
Tobacco is an Indian weed	d1-d2	All voices	A mock-serious song. (Sharp Methuen)
Whistle, daughter, whistle	a-d2	Women's voices	Sustained, gently humorous. (Sharp 100)
Yarmouth fair	d1-g2	Men's voices	Rapid, humorous. Demands facile articulation. (P. Warlock, OX)

SCOTTISH

An Eriskay love lilt	d1-e2	All voices	Delicate. (Kennedy-Fraser)

TITLE	COMP.	TYPE	REMARKS
Annie Laurie	c1-e2	All voices	Very sustained. (Hopekirk)
Benbecula bridal procession	f♯1-f♯2	All voices	Delicate, sustained. (Kennedy-Fraser)
Come, all ye jolly shepherds	c1-e2	Most suitable for men's voices	Animated, rhythmical. (Hopekirk)
Coming through the rye	c1-f♯1	Most suitable for women's voices	Sustained, graceful. A Robert Burns poem. (Hopekirk)
Flora Macdonald's love song	c1-f2	Women's voices, except a very light soprano	Sustained. In parts demands considerable dramatic intensity. (Kennedy-Fraser)
Flow gently, sweet Afton	d1-g2	All voices	Sustained. (Hopekirk)
Get up and bar the door	d1-f2	All voices	Animated, humorous. (Pittman)
Heart o'fire-love	g1-a2	All voices	Vigorous. (Kennedy-Fraser)
Here's to thy health	c1-f2	Most suitable for men's voices	Animated. The poem is by Robert Burns. (Somervell)
Isle of my heart	c1-a♭2	All voices	Graceful, delicate. (Kennedy-Fraser)
Land of heart's desire	d1-g2	Not too suitable for low voices	Very sustained. Demands good command of high pp. (Kennedy-Fraser)
Loch Lomond	d1-e2	All voices	Sustained. (Hopekirk)
My boy Tammy	a-d2	All voices	Sustained, graceful. (Reid)
My love, she's but a lassie yet	c1-g2	Men's voices	Spirited, delicate, gently humorous. Demands facile articulation. (Hopekirk)
My nannie's awa	c1-e♭2	Most suitable for men's voices	Sustained, graceful. (Reid)

649

TITLE	COMP.	TYPE	REMARKS
O can ye sew cushions?	g1-g2	Soprano	Very sustained. Demands good command of high pp. (Colin Taylor, OX)
Robin Adair	f1-f2	Women's voices	Sustained. (Pittman)
Speed, bonny boat	d1-d2	All voices	Sustained. (Malcolm Lawson, OD)
The bens of Jura	e1-g2	All voices, except a very light soprano	Very sustained. In parts demands considerable dramatic intensity. (Kennedy-Fraser)
The death farewell	c1-f2	All voices, except a very light soprano	Very sustained, somber. (Kennedy-Fraser)
The hundred pipers	c1-f2	Men's voices	An animated marching song. (MacPherson & Stuart, OD)
The laird o' Cockpen	c1-f2	All voices	Animated, humorous narrative song. (Hopekirk)
The mermaid's croon	e1-e2	Women's voices	Sustained. (Kennedy-Fraser)
The seagull of the land-under-waves	d1-d2	All voices, except a very light soprano	Sustained. (Kennedy-Fraser)
The troutling of the sacred well	g1-g2	Women's voices, except a very heavy alto	Graceful, very delicate. Demands lightness of tone. (Kennedy-Fraser)
The wild swan	e1-g2	All voices	Very sustained. (Kennedy-Fraser)
To people who have gardens	f1-c2	All voices	Animated, delicate. Demands facile articulation. (Kennedy-Fraser)
Turn ye to me	a-d2	Not too suitable for very light, high voices	Sustained. (Reid)
Weaving lilt	d1-e2	Women's voices	Graceful, gently humorous, delicate. (Kennedy-Fraser)

TITLE	COMP.	TYPE	REMARKS
Whar' hae' ye been a' the day	c1-f2	Men's voices	Sustained, rhythmical. (Hopekirk)
Young Jamie lo'ed me weel	d1-g2	Women's voices	A sustained, personal narrative song. (Hopekirk)
Young Lochinvar	a-d2	Not too suitable for light, high voices	Vigorous. Poem is by Sir Walter Scott. (Reid)

IRISH

TITLE	COMP.	TYPE	REMARKS
A Ballynure ballad	b-d2	Most suitable for men's voices	Animated, rhythmical, gently humorous. (Hughes Country)
Barney O'Hea	d1-eb2	Women's voices	Animated, humorous. (Page)
Believe me if all those endearing young charms (otherwise known as: My lodging is on the cold, cold ground)	eb1-eb2	All voices	Sustained. (gen. av.)
Bendemeer's stream	g1-g2	All voices	Sustained. (Arr., Gatty, BH)
Down by the Sally gardens	db1-eb2	All voices	Sustained, delicate. (Hughes Country; Britten)
I have a bonnet trimmed with blue	f1-d2	Women's voices	Graceful, delicate. (Hughes Country)
I know my love	c1-f2	Women's voices	A rapid comic song. Demands facile articulation. (Hughes Country; Edmunds)
I know where I'm goin'	ab1-eb2	Women's voices	Graceful, delicate. (Hughes Country)
I'm not myself at all	d#1-f#2	All voices	Animated, humorous. Demands facile articulation. (Hughes Country)
In Dublin's fair city	d1-e2	Men's voices	Sustained, graceful. (Page)
I will walk with my love	eb1-f2	Women's voices	Sustained, subdued. (Hughes Country)

TITLE	COMP.	TYPE	REMARKS
Johnny, I hardly knew ye	e1-e2	Women's voices	Animated. Demands facile articulation. (Hughes Country)
Katey's letter	b-g2	Women's voices	Humorous, graceful. (Page)
Kathleen Mavourneen	b-f2	Men's voices	Sustained. (Hatton & Molloy)
Kathleen O'More	f1-e2	Men's voices	Sustained, graceful. (Hughes Country)
Kitty my love will you marry me	c1-f2	Men's voices	Rapid, gently humorous. Demands very facile articulation. (Hughes Country)
Lady, be tranquil	d1-d2	Men's voices	Humorous. Demands facile articulation. (Hughes)
Little boats	eb1-eb2	Most suitable for women's voices	Sustained, graceful lullaby. (Hughes)
Loving dark maid	bb-f2	Men's voices	Sustained, subdued. (Hughes)
Londonderry air (Would God I were a tender apple blossom; Danny boy)	b1-g2	All voices	Very sustained. (gen. av.)
Love is cruel, love is sweet	d1-g2	All voices	Graceful. (Fischer 60)
Must I go bound?	c1-d2	Most suitable for men's voices	Sustained. (Hughes Country)
Reynardine	c#1-f#2	Not too suitable for very low voices	Graceful, delicate. (Hughes Country)
She moved thro' the fair	db1-eb2	Men's voices	Sustained. (Hughes Country)
Shule agra	c1-e2	Women's voices, except a very light soprano	Sustained. Demands in parts considerable dramatic intensity. (Somervell)
The banks of the daisies	eb1-eb2	Men's voices	Sustained, graceful. (Page)

TITLE	COMP.	TYPE	REMARKS
The blatherskite	d1-f2	Men's voices	Animated, humorous. (Fischer 60)
The cork leg	b-d2	Not too suitable for very light voices	Animated, vigorous, humorous. (Hughes Country)
The Fanaid grove	b-d2	Not too suitable for very light, high voices	Sustained, narrative, plaintive. (Hughes Country)
The fairy king's courtship	eb1-f2	All voices	Sustained narrative song. Demands an accomplished pianist. (Harty)
The foggy dew	c1-f2	All voices	Sustained. (Page)
The game played in Erin-Go-Bragh	c1-eb2	Men's voices, except a very light tenor	A rapid character song. Demands facile articulation. (Harty)
The Gartan mother's lullaby	d1-e2	Women's voices	Sustained, subdued. (Hughes Country)
The gentle maiden	bb-eb2	Most suitable for men's voices	Sustained. (Somervell)
The harp that once through Tara's halls	db1-eb2	All voices	Very sustained. (Page)
'Tis the last rose of summer	f1-f2	All voices	Sustained. (Fischer 60)
The leprechaun	d1-g2	All voices	Graceful. (Hughes Country)
The light of the moon	c1-f2	All voices	Animated, gently humorous. (Hughes Country)
The lover's curse	bb-eb2	Women's voices, except a very light soprano	Vigorous, in parts dramatic. (Hughes Country)
The minstrel boy	c1-f2	Men's voices	Sustained. (Hatton & Molloy)
The next market day	a-c2	All voices	Rapid, gently humorous. Demands facile articulation. (Hughes Country)

TITLE	COMP.	TYPE	REMARKS
The lowlands of Holland	d1-e2	Women's voices, except a very light soprano	Very animated, dramatic. Demands an accomplished pianist. (Harty)
The meeting of the waters	d1-d2	All voices	Sustained. (Page)

See also Irish Melodies, words by Thomas Moore, airs arranged by M. W. Balfe, 87 Songs, Novello. Among them are such famous songs as "Believe me if all those endearing young charms," "The harp that once thro' Tara's halls," "The meeting of the waters," "'Tis the last rose of summer," etc.

4

OPERATIC EXCERPTS

OPERATIC EXCERPTS

As already mentioned in the preface, the section devoted to nineteenth and twentieth century operatic airs and excerpts is very limited in scope.

One of the considerations which prompted the exclusion from these lists of all but the most celebrated operatic airs was the relative difficulty of obtaining in separate form at the present time any but the most widely used so-called "standard material." It seemed unfair and unnecessary to recommend much rather inconsequential music which could be obtained only in the complete piano score form, and then only with much difficulty and at a great expense. Even some of the airs listed below, celebrated as they are, are at present rather difficult to obtain. Most of them are, however, listed in the catalogues of various American publishers and since, if some of them are at present out of print, it is hoped that they are only temporarily unavailable, the major percentage of the airs listed below are easily obtainable.

There is a great number of collections of operatic airs in their original languages. Some of the most comprehensive anthologies are listed below.

The name found in parentheses after the remarks indicates one of the following collections:

Adler: Operatic Anthology, 5 volumes. Edited by Adler, published
 by G. Schirmer.
Pelletier: Opera Repertoire for Coloratura Soprano, 1 volume. Edited
 by Pelletier, published by Theodore Presser.
Prima Donna: Prima Donna Album for Soprano, 1 volume. Published
 by G. Schirmer.

In addition, see:
 Arien Album, all voices, published by C. F. Peters.
 Arien Album, all voices, published by Breitkopf und Härtel (many in
 German translations only).
 Arien Album, published by Universal Edition.
 Opera Arias, 4 volumes, published by Ricordi.
 Verdi Arias, 5 volumes, published by C. F. Peters.

For opera airs of Gluck, Handel, Mozart, Haydn, see the separate
sections.
For concert airs see the song lists of the respective composers.
Publisher's name in parentheses indicates that the aria is available
singly in that edition.

On Accompanying Operatic Excerpts

The playing of a nineteenth century orchestral accompaniment
on the pianoforte presents a number of problems not encountered in
the ordinary pursuit of pianistic studies. The problems are mainly
those of sonority and omission of unimportant details, which details,
if performed adequately in a pianistically correct manner, may often
obscure and nullify the much more important features of an orchestral-
ly conceived piece of music. Any pianist interested in doing justice to
music of this nature will profit greatly by comparing the available pianoforte reduction with the orchestral score, so that he may establish
the necessary distinction between the relatively unimportant figuration and the main trend of the musical thought (not always clearly dis-
cernible in an average pianoforte arrangement). Listening to orchestral accompaniments in their original form (now made possible by the
multitude of available records) will sometimes be even more profit-
able for the pianist, since the successful comparison of an orchestral
score with its pianoforte counterpart does in its very nature demand
an ability to imagine orchestral sonorities.

Purely mechanical pianistic problems of some complexity are
almost invariably present in any letter-perfect but realistically ill-
considered pianoforte reduction. The pianist should by no means
feel bound always to retain the sometimes awkward doublings, the
often still more clumsy spacing and rapid figuration of some of the
available pianoforte reductions.

A clear delineation of the bass line, a full sonority of the harmonic background, a proportionately prominent treatment of the melodic line, when such line is contained in the accompaniment, and a
very firm rhythm should be his primary aims. In such an attempt
to approximate the outstanding musical features of the orchestral
part, the pianist may sometimes be forced to omit many passages
which may seem pianistically important to him at the moment. Such
deletions and simplifications, totally inadmissable in a song accompaniment where the pianoforte part is conceived as such, is, in the
opinion of this writer, not in the least reprehensible in playing or-
chestrally conceived accompaniments, as long as the general pattern
of the music is not thereby adversely affected.

Some of the pianoforte reductions of accompaniments of songs
for voice and orchestra, however, when made by the composer himself are often admirably executed and are best played as written.

VINCENZO BELLINI
(1801–1835)

OPERA & TITLE	COMP.	TESS.	TYPE	REMARKS
Beatrice di Tenda				
Ah! non pensar che pieno	f1-g2 (bb2)	f1-f2	Soprano	Slow, sustained. Demands some flexibility. (RIC)
Beatrice di Tenda Recitative:				
Oh! Miei fedeli Air: Ma la sola, chimé!	eb1-c3	g1-g2	Lyric soprano (coloratura soprano)	Recitative, andante, allegro. Quite florid. (Prima Donna)
I Capuleti ed i Montecchi				
Ascolta, se Romeo t'uccise un figlio	g-b2	d1-g2	Dramatic soprano or mezzo-soprano	An andante, allegro air. Demands some flexibility. (RIC)
I Capuletti ed i Montecchi Recitative:				
Eccomi in lieta vesta Air: Oh! Quante volte	d1-c3	g1-f2	Soprano	Scena and a sustained air. Has florid passages. (RIC)
I Puritani				
Qui la voce	eb1-db2	g1-f2	Coloratura soprano (lyric soprano)	Andante, allegro. Florid. (Pelletier)
I Puritani				
Son vergin vezzosa	b-b2	a1-f#2	Coloratura soprano	An animated, florid polonaise. (gen. av.)
La sonnambula Recitative:				
Ah! Non credea mirarti Air: Ah, non giunge	d1-eb3	f1-g2	Coloratura soprano (lyric soprano)	Andante, allegro. Quite florid. (Pelletier)

OPERA & TITLE	COMP.	TESS.	TYPE	REMARKS
La sonnambula				
Come per me sereno oggi renaque il di	d1-d♭3	a♭1-g2	Coloratura soprano	An andante, allegro air. Very florid. (RIC)
La sonnambula				
De' lieti auguri a voi son grata	f1-c3	b♭1-g2	Coloratura soprano	Animated, quite florid. (RIC)
La sonnambula				
Tutto è gioia, tutto è festo	e♭1-c3	a♭1-f2	Coloratura soprano (light soprano)	Animated, quite florid. (RIC)
Norma				
Casta Diva	e1-c3	a1-a2	Dramatic soprano (lyric soprano)	A very sustained andante and a brilliant allegro. Demands considerable flexibility. (gen. av.

ARRIGO BOITO
(1842-1918)

OPERA & TITLE	COMP.	TESS.	TYPE	REMARKS
Mefistofelé				
L'altra notte il fondo al mare	d1-b2	e1-e2	Dramatic soprano (lyric soprano)	Slow, dramatic, somber. In parts demands considerable flexibility. (RIC)
Nerone				
A notte cupa	c♯1-b♭2	f1-f2	Dramatic soprano	Somewhat declamatory. Has dramatic climaxes. (RIC)
Nerone				
Invan mi danni	b-c3	a1-f2	Dramatic soprano	Very sustained, very dramatic. (RIC)

ALFREDO CATALANI
(1854−1893)

OPERA & TITLE	COMP.	TESS.	TYPE	REMARKS
La Wally				
Edden? Ne andrò lontano	e1-b2	b1-e2	Dramatic soprano (lyric soprano)	Sustained. Has dramatic climaxes. (IMC)

OPERA & TITLE	COMP.	TESS.	TYPE	REMARKS
Loreley Amor celesto ebbrezza	d1-c3	g1-g2	Lyric soprano	Sustained, grace- ful. Demands a good command of high pp. (RIC)
Loreley Da che tutta mi son data	d1-ab2	g1-eb2	Lyric soprano (dramatic soprano)	Animated, grace- ful. Demands some flexibility. (RIC)

Loreley
Recitative:
  Dove son? D'onde
  vengo?
Air:
  Ma . . . forse è
  un orrido sogno
	d1-c3	f#1-f#2	Dramatic
			soprano
				A dramatic scena
				and a compound,
				dramatic air. Has
				many sustained
				sections. (RIC)

Loreley O forze recondite	d1-c3	f1-g2	Dramatic soprano	Animated, vigor- ous. Demands flexibility. (RIC)

FRANCESCO CILÈA
(1866-1950)

OPERA & TITLE	COMP.	TESS.	TYPE	REMARKS
Adriana Lecouvreur Io sono l'umile ancella	c1-ab2	f1-f2	Dramatic soprano (lyric soprano)	Sustained. Has dramatic climaxes. (IMC)
Adriana Lecouvreur Poveri fiori	d1-a2	g1-g2	Dramatic soprano (lyric soprano)	Sustained. De- mands consider- able dramatic in- tensity. (IMC)
L'Arlesiana Esser madre	c1-a2	g1-eb2	Dramatic soprano (mezzo- soprano)	A slow, sustained, intensely dramatic aria. (Sonzogno; IMC)

GAETANO DONIZETTI
(1797–1848)

OPERA & TITLE	COMP.	TESS.	TYPE	REMARKS
Anna Bolena Al dolce guidami	d1-g2	eb1-eb2	Soprano or mezzo- soprano	Sustained; in parts quite florid. (RIC)

OPERA & TITLE	COMP.	TESS.	TYPE	REMARKS

Don Pasquale
Recitative:
  Quel guardo il
    cavaliere
Air:
  So anch'io la
    virtù magica
	d1–db3	f1–f2	Lyric
			soprano
			(coloratura
			soprano)
				Andante, allegro,
				quite florid. (Pel-
				letier)

Il castello di
  Kenilworth
Par che mi dica
  ancora
	c#1–a2
	(b2)
		a1–f#2	Soprano	Andante, allegro;
				quite florid. (Pri-
				ma Donna)

La Favorita
Recitative:
  Fia dunque vero
Air:
  O mio Fernando
	b–a2	e1–e2	Dramatic
			soprano
			(mezzo-
			soprano)
				Recitative, andante,
				allegro. Has dra-
				matic climaxes.
				(Adler)

La Figlia del **Reggimento** Ciascun lo dice	c1–a2	g1–f2	Lyric soprano (coloratura soprano)	Light, graceful. Demands some flexibility. (gen. av.) In French (Pelletier).
La Figlia del **Reggimento** Convien partir!	e1–a2	ab1–f2	Lyric soprano (coloratura soprano)	Sustained. De- mands some flexi- bility. (gen. av.) In French (Pel- letier).

La regina di
  Golconda
Che val ricchezza
  e trono
	c1–c3	g1–e2	Soprano
			or mezzo-
			soprano
				An andante, allegro
				air. Demands some
				flexibility. (RIC)

L'elisir d'amore Prendi, per me sei libero	c1–c3	a1–f2	Lyric soprano (coloratura soprano)	Andante, allegro; quite florid. (Score, RIC)

Linda di Chamounix
Recitative:
  Ah, tardai troppo
Air:
  O luce di quest'
  anima
	c1–c3	a1–g2	Coloratura
			soprano
			(lyric
			soprano)
				Recitative and a
				light, rather florid,
				animated air. (Pel-
				letier)

OPERA & TITLE	COMP.	TESS.	TYPE	REMARKS
Lucia di Lammermoor Il dolce suono mi colpi di sua voce (The mad scene)	e♭1-b♭2 (e♭3)	g1-g2	Coloratura soprano (lyric soprano)	A florid scena. As a rule sung with many added cadenzas. See cadenzas—Marchesi and Liebling. (gen. av.)
Lucia di Lammermoor Que n'avons-nous des ailes (Per che non ho del vento)	c♯1-d3	g1-a2	Coloratura soprano	A very florid andante, allegro air. From the French edition of Lucia di Lammermoor, edited by La Forge. (CF)
Lucia di Lammermoor Regnava nel silenzio	c1-c3	g1-f♯2	Coloratura soprano (lyric soprano)	Andante, allegro. Florid. For cadenzas see Marchesi and Liebling. (gen. av.)
Lucrezia Borgia Come è belle quale incanto	b♭-c3	g1-g2	Soprano	An andante, allegro air. Very florid. (RIC)
Lucrezia Borgia M'odi, ah m'odi	(b♭)d1-c3	e♭1-f2	Soprano	An andante, allegro air. Quite florid. (RIC)
Maria di Rohan Recitative: Havvi un Dio Air: Benigno il cielo arridere	c1-c3	a♭1-g2	Coloratura soprano	A florid, compound air. Larghetto, recitative, moderato, allegro. (RIC)

UMBERTO GIORDANO
(1867–1948)

OPERA & TITLE	COMP.	TESS.	TYPE	REMARKS
Andrea Chenier La Mamma morta	c♯1-b2	g1-e2	Dramatic soprano (lyric soprano)	Scena and a sustained air. Has many dramatic climaxes. (Sonzogno; IMC)

OPERA & TITLE	COMP.	TESS.	TYPE	REMARKS
Fedora				
Dio di giustizia	c1-a2	f1-f2	Dramatic soprano (lyric soprano)	Very sustained, grave air. Demands in parts considerable dramatic intensity. (Sonzogno)
Fedora				
Se amor ti allena	f♯1-b2	b1-g♯2	Light soprano	Animated, graceful. (Sonzogno)

RUGGIERO LEONCAVALLO
(1858–1919)

Pagliacci				
Recitative:				
Qual fiamma avea nel guardo	c♯1-a2 (a♯2, b2)	g♯1-f♯2	Lyric soprano (dramatic soprano)	Scena and a sustained air. Has dramatic climaxes. (Adler)
Air:				
Stridono lassù				

PIETRO MASCAGNI
(1863–1945)

Cavalleria rusticana				
Voi lo sapete o mamma	b-a2	a1-f♯2	Dramatic soprano (high mezzo-soprano)	Sustained. Has dramatic climaxes. (Adler)
Iris				
Un di ero piccina	d1-b2	e1-e2	Dramatic soprano	Sustained. Has dramatic climaxes. (RIC)
L'amico Fritz				
Son pochi fiori	d1-g2	eb1-eb2	Dramatic soprano (lyric soprano)	Sustained. Has dramatic climaxes. (Score, Sonzogno)

AMILCARE PONCHIELLI
(1834–1886)

La Gioconda				
Suicidio!	c♯1-b2	f♯1-f♯2	Dramatic soprano	Sustained. Has dramatic climaxes. (gen. av.)

GIACOMO PUCCINI
(1858–1924)

OPERA & TITLE	COMP.	TESS.	TYPE	REMARKS
Gianni Schicchi O mio babbino caro	e♭1–a♭2	a♭1–f2	Lyric soprano	Sustained, rather delicate. Demands a good command of high p. (RIC)
La Bohème Donde lieta usci	d♭1–b♭2	a♭1–e♭2	Lyric soprano (dramatic soprano)	Sustained, has effective climaxes. (RIC; IMC)
La Bohème Quando me'n vo	e1–b2 (d♭3)	g♯1–e2	Lyric soprano (dramatic soprano)	Sustained. Has effective climaxes. (RIC; IMC)
La Bohème Si, mi chiamano Mimi	d1–a2	a♭1–e♭2	Lyric soprano (dramatic soprano)	Sustained, delicate. Demands in parts considerable dramatic intensity. (RIC; IMC)
La Fanciulla del West Oh, se sapeste	e1–b2	g♯1–e2	Lyric soprano	A brilliant, sustained waltz song. (RIC)
La Rondine Chi il bel sogno di Doretta	c1–c3	f1–g2	Soprano, most suitable for light, high voices	Sustained. Demands a good command of high pp. (Sonzogno)
Le Villi Se come voi piccina io fossi	d1–a2	f♯1–e2	Lyric soprano (dramatic soprano)	Sustained. Has effective climaxes. (RIC)
Madama Butterfly Ancora un passo, or via	c♯1–b2	f♯1–f♯2	Lyric soprano (dramatic soprano)	Animated. Demands some flexibility. Has an effective final climax. (RIC)

OPERA & TITLE	COMP.	TESS. ·	TYPE	REMARKS
Madama Butterfly				
Che tua madre dovrà prenderti in braccio	db1–ab2 (bb2)	gb1–eb2	Dramatic soprano (lyric soprano)	Sustained. Has dramatic climaxes. (RIC)
Madama Butterfly				
Un bel di vedremo	db1–bb2	f1–f2	Dramatic soprano (lyric soprano)	Sustained. Has dramatic climaxes. (RIC; IMC)
Manon Lescaut				
In quelle trine morbide	db1–bb2	f1–f2	Lyric soprano (dramatic soprano)	Very sustained. Has dramatic climaxes. (RIC; IMC)
Manon Lescaut				
L'ora, o Tirsi, è vaga e bella	d1–a2 (c3)	g1–g2	Lyric soprano (coloratura soprano)	Graceful, light. Demands consider-able flexibility. (RIC)
Manon Lescaut				
Sola . . . perduta abbandonata	c1–bb2	ab1–f2	Lyric soprano (dramatic soprano)	Sustained, some-what declamatory. Has dramatic climaxes. (RIC)
Tosca				
Non la sospiri la nostra casetta	f1–bb2	ab1–f2	Dramatic soprano (lyric soprano)	Sustained; rather animated. Has ef-fective climaxes. (RIC)
Tosca				
Vissi d'arte	eb1–bb2	gb1–eb2	Dramatic soprano (lyric soprano)	Has dramatic climaxes. (RIC; IMC)
Turandot				
Del primo pianto	eb1–a2	f#1–g2	Dramatic soprano	A song of varied moods. Declama-tory, dramatic in parts. (RIC)
Turandot				
Figlio del cielo!	d1–c3	g#1–g2	Lyric soprano (dramatic soprano)	Sustained. In parts has dramat-ic intensity. (RIC)

666

OPERA & TITLE	COMP.	TESS.	TYPE	REMARKS
Turandot In questa reggia	c#1-c3	a1-f#2	Dramatic soprano	Sustained, de- clamatory. Has dramatic climaxes. (RIC)
Turandot Signore, ascolta!	db1-bb2	bb1-gb2	Lyric soprano (dramatic soprano)	Slow, sustained, rather subdued. (RIC)
Turandot Tanto amore segreto	f1-bb2	g1-g2	Lyric soprano (dramatic soprano)	Slow, sustained. Subdued. Demands a good command of high pp. (RIC)
Turandot Tu che di gel sei cinta	eb1-bb2	ab1-f2	Lyric soprano (dramatic soprano)	Sustained. Has dramatic climaxes. (RIC)

GIOACCHINO ROSSINI
(1792–1868)

OPERA & TITLE	COMP.	TESS.	TYPE	REMARKS
Bianca e Falliero Recitative: 　Come sereno è 　il di Air: 　Della rosa il bel 　vermiglio	b-b2	e1-c2	Soprano or mezzo- soprano	Scena, andante, allegro. Very flor- id. (Prima Donna)
Guillaume Tell Recitative: 　Ils s'éloignent 　enfin Air: 　Sombre forêt 　(French text)	d1-ab2	ab1-f2	Lyric soprano	Recitative and a sustained, some- what florid romanza. (B & H, Soprano Arias)
La donna del lago Oh mattutini albori!	b-g2	g1-d2	Soprano or mezzo- soprano	Sustained. Demands some flexibility. (Prima Donna)
La gazza ladra Di piacer mi balza 　il cor	b-a2	f#1-f#2	Soprano or mezzo- soprano	An andante, allegro air. Demands con- siderable flexibility. (Prima Donna)

OPERA & TITLE	COMP.	TESS.	TYPE	REMARKS
Il barbiere di **Siviglia** Una voce poco fa	g#-g#2 (b2)	e1-e2	Coloratura soprano	Andante, allegro. Very florid. In the original key (E major) this air was intended for a very flexible mezzo-soprano or alto. It is now traditionally sung in F major and provided with ca- denzas suitable for a light soprano voice. For the tra- ditional versions see the edition by Liebling published by G. Schirmer.
Mose Ah! d'un' afflitta il duolo	b-b2	e1-g#2	Soprano or high mezzo- soprano	An andante, allegro air. Very florid. (RIC)
Otello Assisa a piè d'un salice	c1-g2	g1-d2	Soprano or mezzo- soprano	Sustained. Has florid passages. (Prima Donna)
Otello Deh calma o ciel	c1-f2	eb1-eb2	Soprano or mezzo- soprano	Sustained, short. Vocally not taxing. Demands some flexibility. (Prima Donna)

Semiramide
Recitative:
  Bel raggio
  lusinghier
Air:
  Dolce pensiero
	c#1-a2	e1-e2	Soprano
			or mezzo-
			soprano
				An andante, allegro
				air. Very florid.
				(gen. av.)

Zelmira
Recitative:
  Eccolo, a voi
  l'affido
Air:
  Ciel pietoso,
  ciel clemente
	c1-bb2	f1-f2	Soprano
			or mezzo-
			soprano
				Recitative, andante,
				allegro. Very flor-
				id. (Prima Donna)

GIUSEPPE VERDI
(1813–1901)

(See also: Verdi Arias, published by C. F. Peters)

Aida
Recitative:

	COMP.	TESS.	TYPE	REMARKS
Qui Radamès verrà Air: O cieli azzurri	b1-c3	a1-f2	Dramatic soprano (lyric soprano)	Scena and a very sustained air. Demands a good command of high pp. The tessitura is quite high. (gen. av.)

Aida
Recitative:

Ritorna vincitor Air: L'insana parola	c1-bb2	ab1-f2	Dramatic soprano (lyric soprano)	Scena and a compound air. In parts very dramatic. (gen. av.)

Don Carlo

Nel giardin dell bello saracin ostello	c#1-a2	e1-e2	Soprano or mezzo-soprano	Animated, brilliant, rather florid. (CFP)

Don Carlo

Non pianger, mia compagna	b-bb2	ab1-f2	Dramatic soprano	Sustained. Demands in parts considerable dramatic intensity. (RIC)

Don Carlo

O don fatale	cb1-cb3	eb1-eb2	Dramatic soprano (mezzo-soprano)	Scena, andante, allegro. In parts very dramatic. Often sung transposed a third lower. (Adler; CFP)

Don Carlo

Tu che le vanità conoscesti	a#-a#2	f#1-f#2	Dramatic soprano	Scena and a sustained air. Has dramatic climaxes. (Adler)

Ernani

Ernani involami	bb-c3	f1-f2	Dramatic soprano (lyric soprano)	Recitative, andante, allegro. Demands considerable flexibility. (gen. av.)

OPERA & TITLE	COMP.	TESS.	TYPE	REMARKS
Falstaff Sul fil d'un soffio etesio	d♯1-a2	a1-f♯2	Lyric soprano	Light, very delicate. Demands a good command of high pp. (RIC)
I due Foscari Recitative: No, mi lasciate Air: Tu al cui sguardo onni possente	b-c3	g1-g2	Dramatic soprano (lyric soprano)	Recitative and a brilliant, rather florid, andante, allegro air. (RIC)
I Lombardi O madre dal cielo	d1-d♭3	a♭1-a♭2	Lyric soprano (coloratura soprano)	Sustained. Has a very florid final section. (CFP)
I Lombardi Preghiera: Te Vergin santa, invoco! Salve Maria!	c♯1-b♭2	f♯1-f♯2	Dramatic soprano (lyric soprano)	Sustained. Demands in parts considerable dramatic intensity. For the most part subdued. (CFP)
Il Trovatore Tacea la notte placida	(a♭)e♭1- d♭3	f1-f2	Dramatic soprano (lyric soprano)	Andante and a florid allegro. (Adler)
Il Trovatore Recitative: Timor di me Air: D'amor sull' ali rosee	c1-d♭3	f1-f2	Dramatic soprano (lyric soprano)	The adagio from the "Miserere" scene. Slow, rather sustained. Has florid passages. The allegro "Tu vedrai" can be sung separately. (Adler)
Il Trovatore Tu vedrai che amor in terra	c1-c3	f1-f2	Dramatic soprano (lyric soprano)	The allegro from the "Miserere" scene. Spirited. Has florid passages. In parts quite dramatic. (Score, gen. av.)

OPERA & TITLE	COMP.	TESS.	TYPE	REMARKS
I masnadieri				
Lo squardo avea degli angeli	d1-c3	g1-g2	Lyric soprano (coloratura soprano)	Graceful. Demands considerable flexibility and a good command of high pp. (RIC)
I masnadieri				
Tu del mio Carlo al seno	f1-c3	g1-g2	Dramatic soprano (lyric soprano)	Sustained. Demands some flexibility. (RIC)
I vespri siciliani				
Mercè, dilette amiche	a-c♯3	e1-e2	Dramatic soprano (lyric soprano)	Very animated, florid. (RIC; CFP)
La forza del destino				
Me pellegrina ed orfana	c1-b♭2	f1-f2	Dramatic soprano	Sustained. Has dramatic climaxes. (CFP)
La forza del destino				
Pace, pace mio Dio	e♭1-b♭2	f1-f2	Dramatic soprano (lyric soprano)	Sustained. The final section is very animated. Demands in parts considerable dramatic intensity. (Adler; CFP)
La forza del destino Recitative: Son giunta Air: Madre, pietosa Vergine	b-b2	f♯1-e2	Dramatic soprano	Scena and a compound aria. Demands in parts considerable dramatic intensity. (Adler; CFP)
La Traviata				
Addio del passato	e1-a2	a1-f2	Lyric soprano (coloratura soprano)	Delicate, subdued. Demands some flexibility and a good command of high pp. (gen. av.)

OPERA & TITLE	COMP.	TESS.	TYPE	REMARKS
La Traviata Recitative: È strano Air: Ah, forse lui	d1-db3	f1-f2	Lyric soprano (coloratura soprano)	Scena and an andante, allegro air with interpolated recitative passages. In parts quite florid. (gen. av.)
Luisa Miller Lo vidi, e'l primo palpito	f#1-c3	b-g2	Lyric soprano (coloratura soprano)	Animated, graceful. Demands considerable flexibility. (RIC; CFP)
Luisa Miller Tu puniscimi, o Signore	c#1-b2	f#1-e2	Lyric soprano (dramatic soprano)	Animated, rather dramatic. Has a florid final cadenza. (RIC; CFP)
Macbeth Un macchia è qui tuttora (Mad scene)	cb1-db3	f1-f2	Dramatic soprano (lyric soprano)	Sustained, somewhat declamatory, dramatic air. (RIC; CFP)
Otello Ave Maria	eb1-ab2	eb1-eb2	Dramatic soprano (lyric soprano)	Slow, very sustained, subdued. Demands a good command of high pp. (RIC; Adler)
Otello Piangea cantando nell' ermalanda (Canzone del Salice)	c#1-a#2	f#1-f#2	Dramatic soprano (lyric soprano)	Sustained, delicate. Demands a good command of high pp. The folk-song-like theme is often interrupted by recitative passages. (RIC; Adler)
Rigoletto Recitative: Gualtier Maldè Air: Caro nome	b-c#3	g#1-g#2	Coloratura soprano (lyric soprano)	Sustained. In parts very florid. (gen. av.)

OPERA & TITLE	COMP.	TESS.	TYPE	REMARKS
Simon Boccanegra				
Come in quest' ora bruna	db1-bb2	f1-f2	Lyric soprano (dramatic soprano)	Sustained. (RIC; Adler)
Un ballo in maschera Recitative:				
Ecco l'orrido campo Air: Ma dall' arido stelo divulsa	(a)b-c3	f1-f2	Dramatic soprano (lyric soprano)	Recitative and a sustained, dramatic air. Has animated, somewhat declamatory middle section. Demands some flexibility. (RIC; CFP)
Un ballo in maschera				
Morrò, ma prima in grazia	a-cb3	eb1-eb2	Dramatic soprano (lyric soprano)	Sustained. Demands some flexibility. Has dramatic climaxes. (RIC; CFP)
Un ballo in maschera				
Volta la terra	d1-c3	f1-f2	Lyric soprano (coloratura soprano)	Animated, graceful. Demands considerable flexibility. (gen. av.)
Un ballo in maschera				
Saper vorresti	d1-b2	g1-e2	Lyric soprano (coloratura soprano)	Very animated. Demands facile articulation. (Adler)

FRENCH

ADOLPHE ADAM
(1803–1856)

OPERA & TITLE	COMP.	TESS.	TYPE	REMARKS
Le Postillon de Longjumeau				
Je vais donc le revoir	d1-c3 (c#3)	a1-a2	Coloratura soprano	Sustained recitative and a very florid display air. (Brandus et Dufours)

OPERA & TITLE	COMP.	TESS.	TYPE	REMARKS
Le Postillon de Longjumeau Mon petit mari	d1-bb2	g1-g2	Lyric soprano (coloratura soprano)	Graceful, animated, and delicate. Demands flexibility. (Brandus et Dufours)
Si j'étais roi De vos nobles aï-eux	g-b2	f1-f2	Soprano (high mezzo-soprano)	A very florid display air. Spirited; has sustained passages, and a complete vocalise at the end. (Leduc)

DANIEL F. E. AUBER
(1782–1871)

OPERA & TITLE	COMP.	TESS.	TYPE	REMARKS
Fra Diavolo Recitative: Ne craignez rien, my lord Air: Quel bonheur, je respire	d1-c3	g1-g2	Lyric soprano (coloratura soprano)	Recitative and a spirited, graceful air; somewhat florid. (Brandus et Dufours)
Fra Diavolo Voyez sur cette roche	d1-g2	g1-e2	Lyric soprano (mezzo-soprano)	Graceful, light soubrette air. (Brandus et Dufours)
Le Domino noir Aragonaise: La belle Inès	db1-ab2	eb1-eb2	Soprano (mezzo-soprano)	Animated. Has some florid passages. (Brandus et Dufours)
Le Domino noir Rondeau: Je l'ai sauvée en fin	b-b2	e1-f2	Coloratura soprano	Very animated air, interrupted by recitative passages. The second half is florid. (Brandus et Dufours)
Le Domino noir Recitative: Mais je suis, grâce au ciel				

OPERA & TITLE	COMP.	TESS.	TYPE	REMARKS
Air: Flamme vengeresse	b-b2	d1-f♯2	Lyric soprano (coloratura soprano)	Recitative and an animated, light, florid air. (OD)
Manon Lescaut C'est l'histoire amoureuse (The laughing song)	d1-d3	a1-f♯2	Soprano	Bright, animated soubrette air. Demands facile articulation. G. Schirmer edition is transposed one tone lower. (GS)

HECTOR BERLIOZ
(1803-1869)

La Damnation de Faust Autrefois un roi de Thulé	c1-f2	f1-d2	Soprano (mezzo- soprano)	Not fast; rather sustained. See "Es war ein König in Thule" — Schu- bert and Liszt. See also the Jewel Song "Je voudrais bien savoir" from Gounod's Faust. (Costellat)
La Damnation de Faust D'amour ardente flamme	c1-a2	g1-f2	Dramatic soprano (lyric soprano)	Sustained. Has a dramatic middle section. (B & H)

GEORGES BIZET
(1838-1875)

Carmen
Recitative:
  C'est des contre-
  bandiers le refuge
  ordinaire

OPERA & TITLE	COMP.	TESS.	TYPE	REMARKS

Air:
  Je dis que rien
  ne m'épouvante
	d1–b2	g1–g2	Lyric
			soprano
			(dramatic
			soprano)
				Recitative and a
				very sustained
				air. Has dramat-
				ic climaxes. (gen.
				av.)

Les Pêcheurs de
perles
Recitative:
  Me voilà seule
  dans la nuit
Air:
  Comme autre fois
Les Pêcheurs de
perles
	c1–c3	f1–f2	Lyric
			soprano
			(coloratura
			soprano)
				Recitative and a
				sustained air.
				Has a florid final
				cadenza. (Chou-
				dens)

O Dieu Brahma	(b)f1– b2(d3)	b1–g2	Lyric soprano (coloratura soprano)	A sustained andante and a light, florid allegro. (Choudens)

EMMANUEL CHABRIER
(1841–1894)

Gwendoline
Blonde aux yeaux
  de pervenche
  (Fileuse, from
  the duet, Act I)
	c♯1–a2	f♯1–e2	Lyric
			soprano
			(coloratura
			soprano)
				Graceful, animated.
				Demands a good
				command of high
				pp. (Enoch)

GUSTAVE CHARPENTIER
(1860–1956)

Louise Depuis le jour	d1–b2	b1–f♯2	Lyric soprano (dramatic soprano)	Sustained. De- mands a good com- mand of high pp. (HEUG; IMC)

FÉLICIEN DAVID
(1810–1876)

Lalla Roukh Si vous ne savez plus charmer	e♭1–c3	f1–f2	Coloratura soprano	Spirited, animated, graceful soubrette air. Has florid pas- sages. (Girod)

La Perle du Brésil

OPERA & TITLE	COMP.	TESS.	TYPE	REMARKS
Charmant oiseau	d1-e3	g1-g2	Coloratura soprano	Delicate, graceful. Has florid cadenzas. (gen. av.)

CLAUDE DEBUSSY
(1862-1918)

L'Enfant prodigue

L'année en vain chasse l'année (Air de Lia)	c1-a2	f#1-e2	Lyric soprano (dramatic soprano)	Recitative and a compound air. Demands in parts considerable dramatic intensity. (IMC)

LÉO DÉLIBES
(1836-1891)

Lakmé

Où va la jeune Indoue (Bell song)	e1-e3	b1-g2	Coloratura soprano	A very florid display piece. (gen. av.)

Lakmé
Recitative:

Les fleurs me paraissent plus belles Air: Pourquoi dans les grands bois	e1-ab2	a1-e2	Coloratura soprano (light lyric soprano)	Recitative and a sustained air. (Score, HEUG; IMC)

Lakmé

Sous le ciel tout étoilé (Berceuse)	g1-g2 (c3)	c2-g2	Coloratura soprano (light lyric soprano)	Sustained. Demands a good command of high pp. (Score, HEUG; IMC)

PAUL DUKAS
(1865-1935)

Ariane et Barbe Bleue

O, mes clairs diamants	f#1-a#2	a#1-f#2	Dramatic soprano (lyric soprano)	A dramatic monologue. Sustained. Has many effective climaxes. (Durand)

BENJAMIN GODARD
(1849–1895)

OPERA & TITLE	COMP.	TESS.	TYPE	REMARKS
La Vivandière				
Viens avec nous petit	c1-g2	f1-e2	Soprano (mezzo-soprano)	An animated, martial verse song. Demands facile articulation. (Choudens)
Le Tasse				
Il m'est doux de revoir la place	eb1-bb2	bb1-gb2	Lyric soprano (dramatic soprano)	Sustained. Has dramatic climaxes. (HEUG; IMC)

CHARLES GOUNOD
(1818–1893)

OPERA & TITLE	COMP.	TESS.	TYPE	REMARKS
Faust Recitative: Je voudrais bien savoir Air: Ah! Je ris de me voir si belle (The Jewel Song)	c#1-b2	e1-e2	Lyric soprano (dramatic soprano)	A scena into which are incorporated a sustained ballad and a brilliant, animated waltz air. Demands some flexibility. (gen. av.)
Faust Recitative: Elles se chachaient! Air: Il ne revient pas	d#1-a#2 (b2)	g1-f#2	Dramatic soprano (lyric soprano)	Scena and a sustained air. Has dramatic climaxes. Omitted in most stage performances. (Score, gen. av.)
La Reine de Saba Recitative: Me voilà seule Air: Plus grand dans son obscurité	(a)c1-b2	f#1-f#2	Dramatic soprano	Recitative and a sustained air. Has many dramatic climaxes. (gen. av.)
Mireille Heureux petit berger	g1-a2	g1-e2	Lyric soprano (coloratura soprano)	Sustained, delicate. (Choudens)

OPERA & TITLE	COMP.	TESS.	TYPE	REMARKS
Mireille				
Le jour se lève	d1-g2	g1-e2	Soprano or mezzo-soprano	Delicate, grace-ful. (Choudens)
Mireille Recitative:				
Trahir Vincent Air: Mon coeur ne peut changer	d1-c♯3 (f3)	g1-g2	Lyric soprano (coloratura soprano)	Recitative, an-dante, allegro. Has florid pas-sages. (Choudens)
Mireilles				
O légères hirondelles	f♯1-d3	b-a2	Coloratura soprano	A florid, animated waltz song. (Pel-letier)
Philémon et Baucis				
Ah! Si je rede-venais belle!	e1-a2	a1-f2	Lyric soprano (dramatic soprano)	Very sustained, rather delicate. (Choudens)
Philémon et Baucis Recitative:				
Il a perdu ma trace Air: O riante nature	e1-d3	a1-a2	Coloratura soprano	Andante, allegro air. Very florid. (Choudens)
Philémon et Baucis				
Philémon m'aime-rait encore	d1-b2	a1-g2	Soprano	Animated, grace-ful. Has a recita-tive and a slow, sustained middle section. (Choudens)
Polyeucte				
A Vesta portez vos offrandes	g1-c3	bb1-f2	Lyric soprano (dramatic soprano)	Sustained. Has dramatic climaxes. (Choudens)
Roméo et Juliette Recitative:				
Dieu! Quel frisson court dans mes veines? Air: Amour, ranime mon courage	c1-c3	g1-g2	Lyric soprano (coloratura soprano)	A dramatic scena. Demands consider-able flexibility. (Score, gen. av.)

OPERA & TITLE	COMP.	TESS.	TYPE	REMARKS
Roméo et Juliette				
Je veux vivre dans ce rêve	c1-d3	a1-f2	Lyric soprano (coloratura soprano)	An animated, light, rather florid waltz song. (Pelletier)
Roméo et Juliette Recitative:				
Depuis hier je cherche en vain mon maître Air: Que fais-tu blanche tourterelle	f1-a2 (c3)	f1-eb2	Soprano or mezzo-soprano	Animated, light. Demands considerable flexibility. Usually assigned to a high mezzo-soprano in stage performances. (gen. av.)

JACQUES HALÉVY
(1799-1862)

La Juive				
Il va venir	d1-cb3	bb1-gb2	Dramatic soprano (lyric soprano)	Sustained. Has dramatic climaxes. (gen. av.)

LOUIS J. F. HÉROLD
(1791-1833)

Le Pré aux clercs				
Air de Nicette: A la fleur du bel âge	e1-a2	e1-e2	Lyric soprano (coloratura soprano)	Light, animated, graceful. (Score, Brandus et Cie)
Le Pré aux clercs				
Jours de mon enfance	b-b2	e1-g2	Coloratura soprano	A compound, florid air. Demands in parts considerable dramatic intensity and a good command of low voice. (Score, Brandus et Cie)
Le Pré aux clercs				
Oui Marguerite en qui j'espère	b-b2	e1-f♯2	Soprano	A rather dramatic, florid air. De-

OPERA & TITLE	COMP.	TESS.	TYPE	REMARKS
				mands a good command of low voice. (Score, Brandus et Cie)
Le Pré aux Clercs				
Souvenir de jeune âge	eb1-ab2	ab1-f2	Soprano	A graceful verse song. (Score, Brandus et Cie)

EDOUARD LALO
(1823–1892)

OPERA & TITLE	COMP.	TESS.	TYPE	REMARKS
Le Roi d'Ys				
Recitative:				
De tous côtés j'aperçois dans la plaine	eb1-g2	f1-f2	Dramatic soprano (mezzo-soprano)	Very animated, dramatic. (HEUG)
Air:				
Lorsque je t'ai vu soudain				
Le Roi d'Ys				
Vainement j'ai parlé de l'absence	d1-b2	g1-eb2	Dramatic soprano (lyric soprano)	Very animated, dramatic. (HEUG)

VICTOR MASSÉ
(1822–1884)

OPERA & TITLE	COMP.	TESS.	TYPE	REMARKS
Galathée				
Recitative:				
Que dis-tu? Je t'écoute	c♯1-d3	f♯1-f♯2	Coloratura soprano	Recitative and a graceful, florid andante, allegro air. (Score, Grus)
Air:				
Fleur parfumée				
Galathée				
Sa couleur est blonde	b-b2 (d3)	e1-e2	Soprano (mezzo-soprano)	Spirited. Has florid cadenzas. (Score, Grus)
Les Noces de Jeannette				
Au board du chemin (Air du Rossignol)	eb1-db3	ab1-g2	Coloratura soprano	A very florid, graceful display piece. (OD)

JULES MASSENET
(1842–1912)

OPERA & TITLE	COMP.	TESS.	TYPE	REMARKS
Hérodiade Charmes des jours passés	d1-c3	g1-g2	Dramatic soprano (lyric soprano)	Generally sustained air with an extremely dramatic closing section. (HEUG)
Hérodiade Il est doux, il est bon	e♭1-b♭2	f1-e♭2	Dramatic soprano (lyric soprano)	Sustained, has dramatic climaxes. (Adler)

La Navaraise
Recitative:
  Une dot! Et combien?
Air:
  Ah, mariez donc son coeur
	c♯1-a♯2	f♯1-f♯2	Dramatic soprano	Declamatory, dramatic, effective. (HEUG)

Le Cid
Recitative:
  De cet affreux combat
Air:
  Pleurez! pleurez, mes yeux!
	c♯1-b2	b1-f♯2	Dramatic soprano (lyric soprano)	Recitative and a very sustained air. Has dramatic climaxes. (Adler)

Le Cid Plus de tourments	f1-b♭2	g1-g2	Lyric soprano (dramatic soprano)	Sustained. Demands a good command of high pp. (HEUG)
Manon Adieu notre petite table	d1-f2	g1-d2	Soprano	Sustained, graceful, subdued. (IMC)
Manon Je suis encor tout étourdie	d1-b♭2 (e3)	f1-f2	Lyric soprano (coloratura soprano)	Graceful, sustained, delicate. Has optional florid cadenzas. (Score, GS)
Manon Recitative: Je marche sur tous les chemins				

OPERA & TITLE	COMP.	TESS.	TYPE	REMARKS
Air: Obéissons quand leur voix appelle (Gavotte)	e1-c3 (e3)	g1-g2	Lyric soprano (coloratura soprano)	A brilliant scena and a graceful, light air often sung separately (e1-b2; d3). Has some optional florid cadenzas. (Adler)
Manon Oui dans les bois et dans la plaine (Fabliau)	d1-c♯3 (d3)	g1-g2	Lyric soprano (coloratura soprano)	An alternate air for the gavotte. Animated, light. Demands consider- able flexibility. (Score, GS)
Manon Voyons, Manon, plus de chimères	f♯1-a2	same	Lyric soprano (coloratura soprano)	Graceful. Has ef- fective climaxes. (Score, GS)
Marie Magdeleine Recitative: Aux pieds de l'innocent Air: O bien-aimé	c1-bb2	eb1-eb2	Dramatic soprano (lyric soprano)	Sustained. Has ef- fective dramatic climaxes. Demands some flexibility. (HEUG)
Sapho Recitative: Ces gens que je connais Air: Pendant un an je fus ta femme	f1-bb2	f♯1-e2	Dramatic soprano (lyric soprano)	Sustained. Has ef- fective climaxes. Demands a good com- mand of high pp. (HEUG)
Thaïs Recitative: Ah je suis fatigué Air: Dis-moi que je suis belle	d1-bb2 (d3)	g1-g2	Dramatic soprano (lyric soprano)	A declamatory, ef- fective scena and air. Demands in parts considerable dramatic intensity. (IMC)
Thaïs Recitative: Je ne veux rien garder				

OPERA & TITLE	COMP.	TESS.	TYPE	REMARKS
Air: L'amour est une vertu rare	d♭1-b♭2	f1-f2	Dramatic soprano (lyric soprano)	Sustained. Has effective climaxes. (HEUG)

ANDRÉ MESSAGER
(1853–1929)

Fortunio La maison grise	e1-f2	g1-d2	Soprano	Sustained. Vocally not taxing; suitable for all voices. Often used as a song. (Choudens)
Fortunio Chanson de Fortunio	e1-a2	a1-f♯2	Soprano	Sustained. Has ef- fective climaxes. Originally written for tenor. (Choudens)

GIACOMO MEYERBEER
(1791–1864)

Dinorah Ombra leggiera	d♭1-d♭3 (e♭3)	f1-f2	Coloratura soprano	Animated, very florid, compound air. Italian text. (gen. av.)
L'Africaine D'ici je vois la mer	a♭-b2	f1-f2	Dramatic soprano (lyric soprano)	Demands some flexibility. An extended scena. (Score, B & H)
L'Africaine Recitative: Adieu, mon doux rivage Air: Pour celle qui m'est chère	c♯1-c3	g1-e♭2	Lyric soprano (coloratura soprano)	Animated, grace- ful, somewhat florid. Has a flor- id final cadenza. (Score, B & H)
L'Africaine Sur mes genoux, fils du soleil	b-b2	e1-e2	Dramatic soprano (lyric soprano)	Animated, quite florid. (Score, B & H)

OPERA & TITLE	COMP.	TESS.	TYPE	REMARKS
Le Prophète Mon coeur s'élance et palpite	b♭-c3	f1-f2	Coloratura soprano	Animated, brilliant, in parts very florid. Has a short, sustained middle section. (Score, B & H)
Les Huguenots Nobles seigneurs, salut!	c1-c3	g1-f2	Lyric soprano (coloratura soprano)	Graceful, light, florid. Sometimes sung by high mezzo-soprani. (gen. av.)
Les Huguenots O beau pays de la Touraine	d1-b2	g1-g2	Lyric soprano (dramatic soprano)	Sustained. In parts quite florid. (Score, B & H)
Les Huguenots Recitative: Un autre avait mon coeur Air: Parmi les pleurs	d♭1-c3	f1-f2	Soprano	Graceful. Demands considerable flexibility. (Score, B & H)
L'Etoile du nord La, la, la, air chéri	(a)c♯1-c♯3	a1-g2	Coloratura soprano	A once-famous display piece. Very florid. Two flutes obbligato. (Score, Brandus et Cie)
Roberto il Diavolo Nel lasciar la Normandia	d1-c3	f1-f2	Lyric soprano (coloratura soprano)	Animated, in parts quite florid. Italian text. (Prima Donna)
Roberto il Diavolo Roberto, o tu che adoro	c1-b♭2	f1-f2	Dramatic soprano (lyric soprano)	Sustained. Has dramatic climaxes and florid passages. Italian text. (Prima Donna)

JACQUES OFFENBACH
(1819−1880)

OPERA & TITLE	COMP.	TESS.	TYPE	REMARKS
Les Contes d'Hoffman Elle a fui, la tourterelle	d1-a2	f1-f2	Lyric soprano (dramatic soprano)	Recitative and a sustained "romance." (gen. av.)
Les Contes d'Hoffman Les oiseaux dans la charmille	eb1-eb3	ab1-f2	Coloratura soprano	A very florid display piece. (gen. av.)

MAURICE RAVEL
(1875−1937)

OPERA & TITLE	COMP.	TESS.	TYPE	REMARKS
L'Heure Espagnole Oh! La pitoyable aventure (Scene 17)	c#1-a2	e1-e2	Lyric soprano (dramatic soprano)	Not fast; declamatory. Demands in parts considerable dramatic intensity. Musically not easy. (Durand)

See also the list of songs by Ravel.

PETER I. TCHAIKOVSKY
(1840−1893)

OPERA & TITLE	COMP.	TESS.	TYPE	REMARKS

Jeanne d'Arc
Recitative:
  Oui, Dieu le veut
Air:
  Adieu, forêts
	db1-a2	f#1-eb2	Dramatic soprano (mezzo-soprano)	Recitative and a sustained air. Has dramatic climaxes. Often sung by mezzo-soprani or alti a minor third lower than the original. (Adler)

AMBROISE THOMAS
(1811–1896)

OPERA & TITLE	COMP.	TESS.	TYPE	REMARKS
Hamlet				
Recitative:				
Sa main depuis hier n'a pas touché ma main!	c#1-c#3	f#1-e2	Lyric soprano (coloratura soprano)	Scena and an animated air. Demands some flexibility. (HEUG)
Air:				
Les Serments ont des ailes				
Hamlet				
Recitative:				
A vos jeux, mes amis	e1-e3	f#1-f#2	Coloratura soprano	A florid scena and a very florid display air in several sections. (HEUG)
Air:				
Pâle et blonde				
Mignon				
Recitative:				
A merveille! J'en ris d'avance	d1-c3 (d3)	g1-g2	Coloratura soprano	Animated, light, very florid. An alternate air for Filina. The middle section is more sustained. (Score, gen. av.)
Air:				
J'avais fait un plus doux rêve!				
Mignon				
Je connais un pauvre enfant	c#1-a2 (e3)	a1-f#2	Lyric soprano (coloratura soprano)	An animated "styrienne." Quite florid. (Score, gen. av.)
Mignon				
Recitative:				
Ah! pour ce soir	c1-eb3	g1-g2	Coloratura soprano	Recitative and a brilliant, very florid polonaise. (gen. av.)
Air:				
Je suis Titania				
Psyché				
Ah! si j'avais jusqu'à ce soir	c1-c3	gb1-f2	Lyric soprano (coloratura soprano)	An andante, allegro air. Rather florid. (Lévy Frères)
Psyché				
O toi, qu'on dit plus belle	(b)c#1-g#2	f#1-c#2	Soprano or mezzo-soprano	Sustained. (Lévy Frères)

GERMAN

LUDWIG VAN BEETHOVEN
(1770–1827)

OPERA & TITLE	COMP.	TESS.	TYPE	REMARKS
Fidelio				
Recitative:				
Abscheulicher, wo eilst du hin?	b-b2	e1-e2	Dramatic soprano	Recitative, andante, allegro.
Air:				Demands some
Komm, Hoffnung				flexibility and considerable dramatic intensity. (gen. av.)
Fidelio				
O wär ich schon mit dir vereint	g1-a2	g1-f2	Lyric soprano (coloratura soprano)	Graceful. Demands lightness of tone and some flexibility. (Score, gen. av.)

MAX BRUCH
(1838–1920)

Das Feuerkreuz				
Ave Maria	d1-b♭2	f1-g2	Dramatic soprano (lyric soprano)	Dramatic, for the most part sustained. Has a recitative for a middle section. (Simrock)

FRIEDRICH VON FLOTOW
(1812–1883)

Martha				
Den Theuren zu versöhnen	b♭-d3	g1-g2	Lyric soprano (coloratura soprano)	Delicate, in parts quite florid. (Score, gen. av.)

ERICH WOLFGANG KORNGOLD
(1897–1957)

OPERA & TITLE	COMP.	TESS.	TYPE	REMARKS
Die Tote Stadt Glück das mir verblieb (Marietta's Lied)	f1–bb2	bb1–g2	Dramatic soprano (lyric soprano)	Slow, very sustained. Demands a good command of high pp. (AMP)

KONRADIN KREUTZER
(1780–1849)

OPERA & TITLE	COMP.	TESS.	TYPE	REMARKS
Das Nachtlager in Granada Leise wehet, leise wallet rings der Tau	c#1–a2	e1–e2	Lyric soprano (dramatic soprano)	Graceful. Vocally not too taxing. (B & H, Arias for Soprano)

Das Nachtlager in Granada
Recitative:
  Da mir alles nun entrissen
Air:
  Seine fromme Liebesgabe
	d1–b2	f1–f#2	Lyric soprano (dramatic soprano)	Recitative, andante, allegro. Demands some flexibility. (B & H, Arias for Soprano)

OTTO NICOLAI
(1810–1849)

OPERA & TITLE	COMP.	TESS.	TYPE	REMARKS

Die lustigen Weiber von Windsor
Recitative:
  Nun eilt herbei, Witz, heitre Laune
Air:
  Verführer! Warum stellt ihr so
	c1–bb2	f1–f2	Lyric soprano (dramatic soprano)	Recitative, andante, allegro. Quite florid. (Score, CFP; B & H)

Die lustigen Weiber von Windsor Recitative: Wohl denn! Gefasst ist der Entschluss	d1–b2	f#1–f#2	Dramatic soprano (lyric soprano)	Recitative, andante, allegro. Demands considerable flexibility. (Score: CFP, B & H)

FRANZ SCHUBERT
(1797-1828)

Fierrabras
Die Brust gebeugt   f♯1-g2   a♯1-f♯2   Dramatic   Very animated,
von Sorgen   soprano   vigorous. (B & H,
                                                    Soprano Arias)

ROBERT SCHUMANN
(1810-1856)

Genoveva
Recitative:
  Dort schleichen   e♭1-g2   g1-e♭2   Lyric   An animated, reci-
  über'n Hof sie   soprano   tative-like intro-
  sacht   (dramatic duction and a slow,
Air: soprano)   very sustained aria.
  O du der über   (B & H, Soprano
  Alle wacht   arias)

LOUIS SPOHR
(1784-1859)

Faust
Recitative:
  La notte fugge   b♭-b♭2   f1-f2   Lyric   Scena, larghetto,
  ormai   soprano   and a rather florid
Air: (dramatic allegro. Italian
  Si lo sento   soprano)   text. (CFP, So-
                                                        prano Arias)

Jessonda
Recitative:
  Als in mitter-   e1-b♭2   g1-f2   Lyric   Recitative, vigorous
  nächtger Stunde   soprano   allegro and a sus-
Air: (dramatic tained, somewhat
  Die ihr Fühlende   soprano)   florid larghetto.
  betrübet   (CFP, Soprano
                                                        Arias)

Jessonda
Hohe Götter   e1-b♭2   g1-f2   Lyric   Larghetto and a
                                    soprano   florid allegro.
                                    (coloratura (CFP, Soprano
                                    soprano)   Arias)

Zemire und Azor

Opera & Title	COMP.	TESS.	TYPE	REMARKS
Die Rose (Rose softly blooming)	e1-f#2 (a2)	f#1-d2	Lyric soprano (coloratura soprano)	Slow, delicate. Demands some flexibility. Generally sung in English. (gen. av.)

JOHANN STRAUSS
(1825–1899)

Die Fledermaus

Opera & Title	COMP.	TESS.	TYPE	REMARKS
Klänge der Heimat	c#1-d3	f#1-g2	Coloratura soprano (lyric soprano)	Aria in the form of czárdás. Has some florid passages. Brisk final section demands considerable flexibility. (Adler)

Die Fledermaus

Opera & Title	COMP.	TESS.	TYPE	REMARKS
Mein Herr Marquis (Laughing song)	d1-b2 (d3)	g1-g2	Coloratura soprano (lyric soprano)	Animated, light waltz song. Has florid passages. (gen. av.)

Zigeunerbaron

Opera & Title	COMP.	TESS.	TYPE	REMARKS
Ein Mädchen hat es gar nicht gut	d1-a2	g1-e2	Light soprano	Graceful, light, animated, and humorous. Demands facile articulation. (Score, A. Cranz)

Zigeunerbaron

Opera & Title	COMP.	TESS.	TYPE	REMARKS
So elend und treu	c#1-b2	f1-f2	Soprano	A "gypsy song." Rather vigorous, the final part quite animated. (Score, A. Cranz)

RICHARD STRAUSS
(1864–1949)

Ariadne auf Naxos
Recitative:
  Grossmächtige
  Prinzessin

Air:

	COMP.	TESS.	TYPE	REMARKS
Als ein Gott kam jeder gegangen	db-e3	f1-a2	Coloratura soprano	A strict form recitative, andante, allegro air. In parts very florid. Musically not easy. A bravura display piece. (Score, BH)

Der Rosenkavalier

	COMP.	TESS.	TYPE	REMARKS
Da geht er hin, der aufgeblasne, schlechte Kerl (Monologue of Marschallin, Act I, score mark "269")	c1-f2	same	Dramatic soprano	Declamatory. Interpretatively not easy. (Score, BH)

RICHARD WAGNER
(1813–1883)

Soprano Excerpts from Wagner's Music Dramas

Note: None of these excerpts is suitable for light soprano voices. In the instances where "lyric soprano" is indicated as a second choice, a rather heavy type of lyric voice is meant.

Der Fliegende
Holländer

	COMP.	TESS.	TYPE	REMARKS
Jo-ho-hoe! Traft ihr das Schiff? (Act II, Scene 3)	bb-g2	d1-d2	Dramatic soprano (high mezzo soprano)	A vigorous "balade." The second section of each verse is sustained and rather subdued. (gen. av.)

Die Götterdämmerung

	COMP.	TESS.	TYPE	REMARKS
Starke Scheite schichtet mir dort (Act III, Scene 3)	b-b2	e1-f♯2	Dramatic soprano	An imposing, declamatory, dramatic scene. (Score, gen. av.)

Die Götterdämmerung

	COMP.	TESS.	TYPE	REMARKS
Zu neuen Thaten, theurer Helde (Prologue)	c1-g2	eb1-eb2	Dramatic soprano	Sustained, rhythmic, declamatory. (Score, gen. av.)

OPERA & TITLE	COMP.	TESS.	TYPE	REMARKS
Die Walküre Der Männer Sippe	b-a2	e1-g2	Dramatic soprano	Declamatory, with sustained, majestic, dramat- ic ending section. (Adler)
Die Walküre Du bist der Lenz (Act I, Scene 3)	db1-ab2	ab1-f2	Dramatic soprano	Animated, sus- tained. Has an imposing final climax. (Score, gen. av.)
Die Walküre Hojoto-ho! (Act II, Scene 1)	d#1-c3	g1-b2	Dramatic soprano	Very animated, extremely vigor- ous. Demands very facile articu- lation in the middle section. (Score, gen. av.)
Die Walküre War es so schmäh- lich, was ich ver- brach (Act III, Scene 3)	a-g#2	e1-e2	Dramatic soprano	Slow, sustained, somewhat declama- tory. (Score, gen. av.)
Lohengrin Einsam in trüben Tagen (Act I, Scene 2)	eb1-ab2	eb1-eb2	Dramatic soprano (lyric soprano)	Sustained. De- mands in parts considerable dra- matic intensity. (gen. av.)
Lohengrin Euch Lüften die mein Klagen (Act II, Scene 2)	e1-f2	f1-eb2	Dramatic soprano (lyric soprano)	Slow, very sus- tained. Demands a good command of high pp. (Score, gen. av.)
Parsifal Ich sah das Kind (Kundry's Er- zählung, Act II, Scene 2)	c1-a#2	e1-d2	Dramatic soprano (mezzo- soprano)	Rather slow, somewhat sus- tained. Has dra- matic climaxes. (Score, gen. av.)
Rienzi Ich sah die Stadte (Act II, Scene 1)	bb-a2	e1-e2	Dramatic soprano	Sustained. De- mands in parts

OPERA & TITLE	COMP.	TESS.	TYPE	REMARKS
			(lyric soprano or high mezzo-soprano)	some flexibility. (Score, gen. av.)
Siegfried Ewig war ich, ewig bin ich (Act III, Scene 3)	e1-c3	f♯1-e2	Dramatic soprano	Slow and very sustained. Has very imposing climaxes. (Score, gen. av.)
Tannhäuser Allmächtge Jung-frau (Act III, Scene 1)	d♭1-g♭2	g♭1-e♭2	Dramatic soprano (lyric soprano)	Slow, very sus-tained, majestic. (gen. av.)
Tannhäuser Dich, theure Halle (Act II, Scene 2)	d♯1-a2 (b2)	g1-e2	Dramatic soprano (lyric soprano)	Animated, vigor-ous. (gen. av.)
Tristan und Isolde Mild und leise (Isolde's Liebes-tod, Act III, Scene 3)	d♯1-a♭2	f♯1-f♯2	Dramatic soprano	Very sustained. (gen. av.)

CARL MARIA VON WEBER
(1786–1826)

OPERA & TITLE	COMP.	TESS.	TYPE	REMARKS
Abu Hassan Wird Philomele trauern	d1-a2	g1-f2	Light soprano	A graceful, in parts quite florid andante, allegro air. Rather short. (Score, CFP)
Der Freischütz Kommt ein schlanker Bursch	c1-b2	g1-g2	Lyric soprano (coloratura soprano)	Spirited, humor-ous. Demands some flexibility. (gen. av.)
Der Freischütz Recitative: Einst träumte meiner sel'gen Base				

OPERA & TITLE	COMP.	TESS.	TYPE	REMARKS
Air:				
Trübe Augen	d1-b♭2	g1-g2	Lyric soprano (coloratura soprano)	A comic recitative and a graceful, spirited, somewhat florid air. In concert performance the recitative may be omitted. (Score, CFP)
Der Freischütz				
Wie nahte mir der Schlummer	b-b2	f♯1-f♯2	Dramatic soprano (lyric soprano)	Scena and a very spirited allegro. Demands some flexibility. (gen. av.)
Der Freischütz				
Und ob die Wolke	e♭1-a♭2	a♭1-f2	Lyric soprano (dramatic soprano)	Slow, very sustained. (gen. av.)
Euryanthe				
Bethörte! Die an meine Liebe glaubt	a♯-c3	f♯1-g♯2	Dramatic soprano (high mezzo-soprano)	A dramatic scena and a very animated, vigorous air. Has florid passages. (Score, CFP)
Euryanthe				
Glöcklein im Tale	e1-a2	g1-e2	Soprano	Graceful, sustained. (Score, CFP)
Euryanthe				
Recitative:				
So bin ich nun verlassen Air: Hier dicht am Quell	c1-f♯2	f♯1-d2	Soprano or mezzo-soprano	A scena and a slow, declamatory, subdued air. (Score, CFP)
Euryanthe				
O mein Leid ist unermessen	d♯1-g2	same	Dramatic soprano	Animated, vigorous. Demands some flexibility. (Score, CFP)
Oberon				
Recitative:				
Eil' edler Held Air: Ja, o Herr, mein Heil mein Leben	d1-b2	g1-e2	Dramatic soprano	Animated, vigorous. Demands some flexibility. (Score, CFP)

OPERA & TITLE	COMP.	TESS.	TYPE	REMARKS
Oberon Ozean! Du Ungeheuer	(bb)c1- c3	g1-g2	Dramatic soprano	Scena and a very vigorous, dramat- ic, compound air. (GS)
Oberon Traure, mein Herz	b-f2	g1-db2	Dramatic soprano (mezzo- soprano)	Sustained. De- mands some flexi- bility. (Score, CFP)
Preciosa Einsam bin ich nicht allein	d1-f#2	g1-e2	Soprano	Sustained. De- mands some flexi- bility. Vocally not taxing. (Score, CFP)

ENGLISH

SAMUEL BARBER
(b. 1910)

OPERA & TITLE	COMP.	TESS.	TYPE	REMARKS
Vanessa Under the willow tree	b-a2	e1-e2	Soprano (mezzo- soprano)	Sustained. In waltz time. (GS)
Vanessa Must the winter come so soon	eb1-f2	g1-eb2	Soprano (mezzo- soprano)	Sustained, tranquil, mostly subdued. (GS)

BENJAMIN BRITTEN
(b. 1913)

OPERA & TITLE	COMP.	TESS.	TYPE	REMARKS

Peter Grimes
 Child . . . you're
   not too young
   to know (Church
   scene—Ellen's
   aria)
	a#-a#2	f#1-f#2	Soprano	Sustained. Inter-
				 pretatively not
				 easy. Demands
				 flexibility, wide
				 range. Forceful
				 climax. (BH)

Peter Grimes
 Embroidery in
   childhood was a
   luxury
	b-bb2	d1-f#2	Soprano	Mostly subdued.
				 Delicate and florid
				 in parts. Demands

OPERA & TITLE	COMP.	TESS.	TYPE	REMARKS
(Embroidery aria)				flexibility and a good command of high pp. (BH)
The Beggar's Opera				
I'm like a skiff on the ocean	eb1-ab2	ab1-g2	Soprano	Rhythmic, folk vein. (Score, BH)

AARON COPLAND
(b. 1900)

The Tender Land				
Once I thought I'd never grow tall	c1-g2	d1-e2	Soprano	Sustained, gentle. Demands a good command of high p. (BH)

CARLISLE FLOYD
(b. 1926)

Susannah				
Ain't it a pretty night	bb-bb2	eb1-f#2	Soprano	Slow, sustained. (BH)
Susannah				
The trees on the mountains are cold	db1-bb2	g1-g2	Soprano	Somewhat slow; sustained. Demands a good command of high pp. (BH)

GIAN-CARLO MENOTTI
(b. 1911)

Amelia Goes to the Ball				
While I waste these precious hours	d1-bb2	g1-g2	Soprano	Sustained. Demands a good command of high pp. (RIC)
The Consul				
To this we've come	b-bb2	f1-f2	Dramatic soprano	Magda's monologue. Interpretatively not easy. In parts has dramatic intensity. (GS)

OPERA & TITLE	COMP.	TESS.	TYPE	REMARKS
The Medium				
The sun has fallen (The black swan)	d1-g2	f1-f2	Soprano	Sustained, with slight animation. (GS)
The Old Maid and the Thief				
Steal me, sweet thief	c1-b2	g1-f2	Soprano	Narrative recitative and sustained, somewhat melancholic aria. Interpretatively not easy. (RIC)
The Saint of Bleecker Street				
O, sweet Jesus, spare me this agony	d1-c3	f1-f2	Dramatic soprano	A lengthy scena, narrative of the crucifixion. In parts has dramatic intensity. Interpretatively not easy. Has a forceful, dramatic ending. (Score, GS)
The Telephone				
Hello! Hello! Oh, Margaret, it's you	d1-d3	e1-f2	Soprano (lyric coloratura)	Mostly declamatory. Aria ends with "That was Margaret," p. 16 of vocal score. (Score, GS)

DOUGLAS MOORE
(b. 1893)

OPERA & TITLE	COMP.	TESS.	TYPE	REMARKS
The Ballad of Baby Doe				
Ah, willow, where we met together (Willow song)	f1-d3	g1-g2	Soprano	Sustained, in folk style. Ends in vocalized cadenzas. (CHAP)
The Ballad of Baby Doe				
Always through the changing of sun and shadow (Farewell song)	d♯1-b2	f♯1-f♯2	Soprano; not suitable for light, high voices	Sustained, in folk style. Has passages with dramatic intensity. (CHAP)

OPERA & TITLE	COMP.	TESS.	TYPE	REMARKS
The Ballad of Baby Doe Dearest Mama, I am writing (Letter song)	e1-c♯3	f♯1-f♯2	Soprano	Sustained, in folk style. (CHAP)
The Ballad of Baby Doe Please, gentle-men, please (Silver song)	e1-c♯3	g♯1-g♯2	Soprano	Slow, sustained, in folk style. Impressive ending. (CHAP)
The Devil and Daniel Webster Now may there be a blessing	c1-f2	f1-d2	Soprano (mezzo-soprano)	Sustained, in parts gently declamatory. The text is based on Biblical story of Ruth. (BH)

BEDŘICH SMETANA
(1824–1884)

The Bartered Bride How can I live	c1-a♭2	f1-f2	Soprano	Recitative and sus-tained air which starts very gently. Commendable English version by M. Farquhar. (Adler)

IGOR STRAVINSKY
(b. 1882)

The Rake's Progress
Recitative:
  My father!
Air:
  I go, I go to him
	e♭1-c3	g1-g2	Soprano	Recitative and a sustained air. In parts florid. Imposing, climactic ending on high C. (Score, BH)

The Rake's Progress
Recitative:
  How strange!

	COMP.	TESS.	TYPE	REMARKS
Air: O heart, be stronger!	c#1-g2	g1-f#2	Soprano	Recitative and sustained air. (Score, BH)
The Rake's Progress Recitative: No word from Tom Air: Quietly, night	b-b2	f#1-g2	Soprano; not suit- able for light, high voices	Recitative and a sustained air. Demands some flexibility. (Score, BH)
The Rake's Progress Scorned! Abused!	a-a2	d1-eb2	Soprano or mezzo- soprano	Sustained, in parts somewhat florid. Demands flexibility. (Score, BH)

See also the list of songs by Stravinsky.

RALPH VAUGHAN WILLIAMS
(1872–1958)

Hugh the Drover				
Here on my throne	e1-g2	a1-e2	Soprano (mezzo- soprano)	Sustained. A concert arrange- ment of Mary's song.

Note: For excerpts from Russian operas in English translations
see the Russian section of songs (nineteenth and twentieth centuries).

ITALIAN

VINCENZO BELLINI
(1801-1835)

OPERA & TITLE	COMP.	TESS.	TYPE	REMARKS
I Capuletti ed i Montecchi				
Ascolta, se Romeo t'uccise un figlio	g-b2	d1-g2	Mezzo-soprano or dramatic soprano	An andante, allegro air. Demands some flexibility. (RIC)
Norma Recitative:				
Scombra è la sacra selva Air: Deh! Proteggimi, o Dio	bb-gb2	f1-eb2	Mezzo-soprano or soprano	An extended recitative and a short, very sustained, slow air. Demands some flexibility. (RIC)

ARRIGO BOITO
(1842-1918)

Nerone				
Fanuèl. . . Morirò?	c1-eb2	same	Mezzo-soprano or alto	Slow, declamatory. (RIC)
Nerone				
Padre nostro che sei ne' cieli	c1-c2	same	Mezzo-soprano or alto	Sustained. A setting of the Lord's prayer. (RIC)

FRANCESCO CILÈA
(1866-1950)

L'Arlesiana				
Esser Madre	c1-a2	g1-eb2	Mezzo-soprano (dramatic soprano)	A slow, sustained, intensely dramatic aria. (Sonzogno; IMC)

GAETANO DONIZETTI
(1797–1848)

OPERA & TITLE	COMP.	TESS.	TYPE	REMARKS
Anna Bolena Recitative: È sgombro il loco Air: Ah! Parea che per incanto	ab-g2	eb1-db2	Mezzo-soprano or alto	Scena and an animated, rather florid air. (RIC)
Anna Bolena Al dolce guidami	d1-ab2	eb1-eb2	Mezzo-soprano or soprano	Sustained, in parts quite florid. (RIC)
Anna Bolena Deh! non voler costringere	g-g2	eb1-eb2	Mezzo-soprano or alto	Not fast; rather sustained. Demands some flexibility. (RIC)
Don Sebastiano Recitative: Ove celare, oh Dio Air: Terra adorata de' padri miei	b-f2	d1-d2	Mezzo-soprano or alto	Recitative and a slow air. Demands some flexibility. (RIC)
La Favorita Recitative: Fia dunque vero Air: O mio Fernando	b-a2	e1-e2	Mezzo-soprano or alto	Recitative, andante, allegro. In parts demands considerable dramatic intensity. (gen. av.)
Lucrezia Borgia Il segreto per esser felici	c1-f2	e1-c2	Mezzo-soprano or alto	Animated, light. Demands facile articulation. (gen. av.)
Maria di Rohan Per non istare in ozio	g-g2	e1-c2	Mezzo-soprano or alto	Rather vigorous. Not slow. Demands some flexibility. (RIC)
Roberto Devereux All' afflitto è dolce il pianto	b-a2	d1-e2	Mezzo-soprano or alto	Slow, sustained. Has florid cadenzas. (RIC)

UMBERTO GIORDANO
(1867–1948)

<u>Andrea Chenier</u>

Temer? Perche?	f1-g2	g1-e2	Mezzo-soprano or dramatic soprano	Very animated, dramatic. (Score: Sonzogno, IMC)

RUGGIERO LEONCAVALLO
(1858–1919)

<u>La Bohème</u>

Da quel suon soavemento	a-a2	e1-e2	Mezzo-soprano	An animated, brilliant waltz. Demands in parts facile articulation. (Sonzogno)

PIETRO MASCAGNI
(1863–1945)

<u>L'amico Fritz</u>
Recitative:

Povero amico Air: O pallida, che un giorno mi guardasti	e1-g2	g1-d2	Mezzo-soprano	Sustained. Has dramatic climaxes. (Sonzogno)

AMILCARE PONCHIELLI
(1834–1886)

<u>I promessi sposi</u>

È questo della misera	c1-f2	eb1-eb2	Mezzo-soprano	A dramatic, animated air. Demands considerable flexibility. (RIC)

<u>I promessi sposi</u>
Recitative:
  In questo loco
  solitario e mesto

OPERA & TITLE	COMP.	TESS.	TYPE	REMARKS
Air: Involontaria vittima	c1-g2	e1-e2	Mezzo-soprano	Scena and a sustained air. Demands some flexibility. Has dramatic climaxes. (RIC)
La Gioconda Recitative: E il tuo nocchier or la fuga t'appresta Air: Stella del marinar	a♯-a2	e1-e2	Mezzo-soprano	Animated. Has dramatic climaxes. (Adler)
La Gioconda Voce di donna	a-g2	g1-e♭2	Mezzo-soprano or alto	Slow, sustained. Demands in parts considerable dramatic intensity. (Adler)

GIOACCHINO ROSSINI
(1792–1868)

OPERA & TITLE	COMP.	TESS.	TYPE	REMARKS
Bianca e Falliero Recitative: Come sereno è il di Air: Della rosa il bel vermiglio	b-b2	e1-e2	High mezzo-soprano or soprano	Scena, andante, allegro. Very florid. (Prima Donna)
Il Barbiere di Siviglia Recitative: Che vecchio sospettoso Air: Il vecchiotto cerca moglie	c♯1-a2	f♯1-e2	Mezzo-soprano or alto	Recitative and a spirited, comic air. Demands facile articulation and some flexibility. (Score, gen. av.)
Il barbiere di Siviglia Una voce poco fa	g♯-g♯2 (b2)	e1-e2	Mezzo-soprano or alto	An andante, allegro air. Very florid. (See this entry in the soprano section.)

OPERA & TITLE	COMP.	TESS.	TYPE	REMARKS
La Cenerentola Recitative: Nacqui all' affanno Air: Non più mesta	g#-b2	e1-e2	Mezzo-soprano or alto	A very florid andante, and a light, florid allegro. (Adler)
La donna del lago Oh mattutini albori	b-g2	g1-d2	Mezzo-soprano or soprano	Sustained, demands some flexibility. (Prima Donna)
La donna del lago Recitative: Mura felici Air: Oh quante lagrime	g#-f#2	e1-c#2	Mezzo-soprano or alto	An extended recitative, a florid andantino, and a florid, light allegro. (RIC)
La gazza ladra Recitative: Ora mi par che il core Air: A questo seno	c#1-e2	d1-d2	Mezzo-soprano or alto	Recitative and a florid, andante, allegro air. (RIC)
La gazza ladra Di piacer mi balza il cor	b-a2	f#1-f#2	Mezzo-soprano or soprano	An andante, allegro air. Demands considerable flexibility. (RIC)
L'Italiana in Algeri Recitative: Amici, in ogni evento Air: Pensa alla patria	a-b2	b-e2	Mezzo-soprano or alto	Animated, florid air. (RIC)
Mosè Ah! d'un' afflitta il duolo	b-b2	e1-g#2	High mezzo-soprano or soprano	An andante, allegro air. Very florid. (RIC)
Otello Assisa a piè d'un salice	c1-g2	g1-d2	Mezzo-soprano or soprano	Sustained. Has florid passages. (Prima Donna)

OPERA & TITLE	COMP.	TESS.	TYPE	REMARKS
Otello				
Deh calma o ciel	c1-f2	eb1-eb2	Mezzo-soprano or soprano	Short, sustained. vocally not taxing. Demands some flexibility. (Prima Donna)
Semiramide Recitative:				
Ecco come al fine in Babilonia Air: Ah quel giorno	g-g♯2	e1-e2	Alto or mezzo-soprano	Scena, andante, allegro. Very florid. (RIC)
Semiramide Recitative:				
Bel raggio lusinghier Air: Dolce pensiero	c♯1-a2	e1-e2	Mezzo-soprano or soprano	An andante, al-legro air. Very florid. (Prima Donna)
Semiramide In si barbara	g-g2	eb1-c2	Alto or mezzo-soprano	A very florid an-dante and a bril-liant, florid allegro. (RIC; Adler)
Tancredi Recitative:				
O patria dolce Air: Di tanti palpiti	bb-f2	f1-c2	Alto or mezzo-soprano	An extended reci-tative and a rather florid, animated air. (RIC)
Zelmira Recitative:				
Eccolo, a voi l'affido Air: Ciel pietoso, ciel clemente	c1-bb2	f1-f2	Mezzo-soprano or soprano	Recitative, an-dante, allegro. Very florid. (Prima Donna)

GIUSEPPE VERDI
(1813–1901)

(See also: Verdi Arias, published by C. F. Peters.)

OPERA & TITLE	COMP.	TESS.	TYPE	REMARKS
Don Carlo				
Nel giardin del bello saracin ostello	c♯1-a2	e1-e2	Mezzo-soprano or soprano	Animated, brilliant, rather florid. (CFP)

OPERA & TITLE	COMP.	TESS.	TYPE	REMARKS
Don Carlo O Don fatale	cb1-cb3	eb1-eb2	Mezzo-soprano or dramatic soprano	Scena, andante, allegro. In parts very dramatic. Often sung transposed a third lower. (CFP)
Il Trovatore Condotta ell' era in' ceppi	a-bb2	e1-e2	Alto or mezzo-soprano	A dramatic scena, sustained andante, and a declamatory allegro. (CFP)
Il Trovatore Stride la vampa	b-g2	f♯1-b1	Alto or mezzo-soprano	Animated, vigorous. Demands some flexibility. (gen. av.)
Un ballo in maschera È lui! Ne palpiti come risento adesso	g-ab2	f♯1-eb2	Alto or mezzo-soprano	Not fast, somewhat declamatory. Has dramatic climaxes. (RIC)
Un ballo in maschera Re dell' abisso, affrettati	c1-g2	c1-c2	Alto or mezzo-soprano	Very sustained, somber. Has dramatic climaxes. (Adler)

FRENCH

DANIEL F. E. AUBER
(1782–1871)

OPERA & TITLE	COMP.	TESS.	TYPE	REMARKS
Le Domino noir Aragonaise: La belle Inès	db1-ab2	eb1-eb2	Mezzo-soprano or soprano	Animated, has some florid passages. (Brandus et Dufour)

HERMAN (HENRI) BEMBERG
(1858–1931)

OPERA & TITLE	COMP.	TESS.	TYPE	REMARKS
La mort de Jeanne d'Arc Du Christ avec ardeur	db1-ab2	f1-eb2	Dramatic soprano	Sustained, effective. In parts

707

		or mezzo- soprano or alto	demands consider- able dramatic in- tensity. (GS; OD)

HECTOR BERLIOZ
(1803–1869)

Les Troyens à
  Carthage

Monologue de Didon: Ah, je vais mourir	d1-f2	eb1-e2	Mezzo- soprano or dra- matic soprano	A dramatic scena and a slow, sub- dued, sustained air. (Choudens)

GEORGES BIZET
(1838–1875)

Carmen
Recitative:

Voyons que j'essaie à mon tour Air: En vain pour éviter	b-f2	f1-db2	Alto or mezzo- soprano	Sustained, somber. Has dramatic cli- maxes. (Adler)

Carmen

L'amour est un oiseau rebelle	d1-f#2	d1-d2	Mezzo- soprano or alto	A habanera. De- mands very facile articulation. (gen. av.)

Carmen

Près des remparts de Séville	b-f#2 (b2)	d1-d2	Mezzo- soprano or alto	A very animated seguidilla. De- mands very facile articulation and some flexibility. (gen. av.)

Djamileh

Sans doute l'heure est prochaine (Lamento)	e1-f2	e1-d2	Mezzo- soprano	Slow and sustained. (Choudens)

ALFRED BRUNEAU
(1857–1934)

OPERA & TITLE	COMP.	TESS.	TYPE	REMARKS
L'Attaque du Moulin				
La guerre c'est le châtiment	e1-a2	g1-e2	Alto	Spirited, dramatic air. (Choudens)

CLAUDE DEBUSSY
(1862–1918)

OPERA & TITLE	COMP.	TESS.	TYPE	REMARKS
Pelléas et Mélisande				
Voici ce qu'il écrit à son frère Pelléas	a-d2	d1-a1	Alto or mezzo-soprano	A recitative style solo. Not fast; declamatory. Interpretatively not easy. (Score: Durand; IMC)

BENJAMIN GODARD
(1848–1895)

OPERA & TITLE	COMP.	TESS.	TYPE	REMARKS
La Vivandière				
Viens avec nous petit	c1-g2	f1-e2	Mezzo-soprano or soprano	An animated, martial verse song. Demands facile articulation. (Choudens)

CHARLES GOUNOD
(1818–1893)

OPERA & TITLE	COMP.	TESS.	TYPE	REMARKS
Cinq-Mars				
Recitative: Par quel trouble profond	d1-g2	f#1-e2	Mezzo-soprano or alto	Very sustained. Has effective climaxes. (Choudens)
Air: Nuit resplendissante				
Faust				
Faites-lui mes aveux	d1-g2	g1-e2	Mezzo-soprano or soprano	An animated, graceful air with a recitative for a middle

OPERA & TITLE	COMP.	TESS.	TYPE	REMARKS
				section. Demands facile articulation. (Adler)
Faust Si le bonheur	c♯1-e2	e1-c♯2	Mezzo-soprano or alto	A short, sustained romance. Omitted in most stage per-formances. (Score, gen. av.)
Mireille Le jour se lève	d1-g2	g1-e2	High mezzo-soprano or soprano	Delicate, graceful. (Choudens)
Roméo et Juliette Recitative: Depuis hier je cherche en vain mon maître Air: Que fais-tu blanche tourterelle	f1-a2 (c3)	f1-e♭2	Mezzo-soprano or soprano	Animated, light. Demands consider-able flexibility. (Adler)
Sapho Recitative: Où suis-je? Air: O ma lyre im-mortelle	c♭1-g♭2 (b♭2)	f1-f2	Mezzo-soprano or alto	Very sustained. Has dramatic cli-maxes. (Choudens)

JACQUES HALÉVY
(1799-1862)

OPERA & TITLE	COMP.	TESS.	TYPE	REMARKS
Charles VI Recitative: Sous leur sceptre de fer Air: Humble fille des champs	g♯-g♯2	e1-e2	Mezzo-soprano or alto	A very dramatic scena and an an-dante, allegro aria. Demands considerable dra-matic intensity. (GS)
La Reine de Chypre Le gondolier dans sa pauvre nacelle	a-a♭2	e♭1-e♭2	Mezzo-soprano or alto	A sustained an-dante, recitative, and a vigorous, dra-matic allegro. (GS)

EDOUARD LALO
(1823–1892)

OPERA & TITLE	COMP.	TESS.	TYPE	REMARKS
Le Roi d'Ys Recitative: De tous côtés j'aperçois dans la plaine Air: Lorsque je t'ai vu soudain	e♭1-g2	f1-f2	Mezzo- soprano or dra- matic soprano	Very animated, dramatic. (HEUG)

VICTOR MASSÉ
(1822–1884)

OPERA & TITLE	COMP.	TESS.	TYPE	REMARKS
Galatée Sa couleur est blonde	b-b2 (d3)	e1-e2	Mezzo- soprano or soprano	Spirited. Has flor- id cadenzas. (Grus)
Galatée Tristes amours	g-f2	c1-c2	Alto or mezzo- soprano	A sustained andante and a vigorous al- legro. (Grus)
Paul et Virginie Dans le bois à ma voix tout s'éveille	b-f♯2	e1-e2	Mezzo- soprano	Graceful. In parts rather florid. (Grus)
Paul et Virginie Parmi les lianes	c1-b♭2	d1-e♭2	Soprano or mezzo- soprano	Animated, rather dramatic. Demands considerable flexi- bility. (OD)

JULES MASSENET
(1842–1912)

OPERA & TITLE	COMP.	TESS.	TYPE	REMARKS
Don César de Bazan Dors, ami (Berceuse)	b♭-g♭2	d1-d2	Mezzo- soprano or alto	Sustained, subdued. Demands some flexibility. (HEUG)
Hérodiade Hérode! Hérode! Ne me refuse pas	b♭-a2	f1-f2	Mezzo- soprano or alto	Sustained air with many effective, dra- matic climaxes. (IMC)

OPERA & TITLE	COMP.	TESS.	TYPE	REMARKS

Le Roi de Lahore
Recitative:
  Repose, ô belle amoureuse
Air:
  Ferme les yeux, o belle maîtresse
	b-b♭2	f1-f2	Mezzo-soprano	A sustained andante and a light allegretto. Demands some flexibility. Has some dramatic climaxes. (GS)

Werther Va! Laisse couler mes larmes	c1-f2	f1-d2	Mezzo-soprano or alto	Slow, sustained. Has effective climaxes. (IMC; Adler)
Werther Werther... qui m'aurait dit la place que dans mon coeur	c1-g♭2	e1-e2	Mezzo-soprano or alto	An extended scena. Has dramatic climaxes. (IMC)

GIACOMO MEYERBEER
(1791–1864)

OPERA & TITLE	COMP.	TESS.	TYPE	REMARKS
Le Prophète Ah! Mon fils	b-a♯2	f♯1-d♯2	Mezzo-soprano or alto	Slow, sustained. Demands in parts considerable dramatic intensity and some flexibility. (Adler)
Le Prophète Donnez, donnez	b-g2	e1-e2	Mezzo-soprano or alto	Sustained. In parts dramatic. (Adler)

Le Prophète
Recitative:
  Qui je suis? Moi?
Air:
  Je suis, hélas, la pauvre femme
	a♭-a♭2
	(b♭2)
		e♭1-e♭2	Mezzo-soprano or alto	Animated, dramatic. Has florid cadenzas. (Score, B & H)

Le Prophète
Recitative:
  O prêtres de Baal
Air:
  O toi qui m'abandonne
	a♭-a♭2
	(c3)
		d♭1-e♭2	Mezzo-soprano or alto	Scena and a florid display air. (Score, B & H)

OPERA & TITLE	COMP.	TESS.	TYPE	REMARKS
Les Huguenots				
Non, non, non, vous n'avez jamais, je gage	(f)g-b♭2	e♭1-e♭2	Mezzo-soprano	Animated, graceful, very florid. (Score, B & H)

CAMILLE SAINT-SAËNS
(1835–1921)

Samson et Dalila				
Recitative:				
Samson recherchant ma présence	a♭-g2 (b♭2)	e♭1-d♭2	Mezzo-soprano or alto	Sustained. Has dramatic climaxes. (gen. av.)
Air:				
Amour, viens aider				
Samson et Dalila				
Mon coeur s'ouvre à ta voix	b♭-g♭2	f1-e♭2	Mezzo-soprano or alto	Sustained. (gen. av.)
Samson et Dalila				
Printemps qui commence	b-e2	e1-c♯2	Mezzo-soprano or alto	Sustained. (gen. av.)

PETER I. TCHAIKOVSKY
(1840–1893)

La Dame de Pique				
Romance de Pauline: Oh! Jeunes filles!	a-a♭2	e♭1-c♭2	Alto or mezzo-soprano	Sustained, somber. Has dramatic climaxes. (Noël, Paris) With English translation. (Adler)

AMBROISE THOMAS
(1811–1896)

Hamlet				
Recitative:				
Toi, partir! Non, il t'aime	c1-a♭2	f1-e♭2	Alto or mezzo-soprano	Sustained. Has effective climaxes. (HEUG)
Air:				
Dans son regard plus sombre				

OPERA & TITLE	COMP.	TESS.	TYPE	REMARKS
Mignon Connais-tu le pays	c1-f2	eb1-c2	Mezzo- soprano	Very sustained. (gen. av.)

Mignon
Recitative:
  C'est moi, j'ai
  tout brisé,
  n'importe
Air:
  Me voici dans
  son boudoir
	bb-f2	eb1-db2	Mezzo-
			soprano
			or alto
				A graceful, light
				gavotte. Demands
				facile articulation.
				(gen. av.)

Psyché
Recitative:
  Salut! Divinités
  des champs
Air:
  O nymphes! En
  ces lieux
	a♯-a2
	(b2)
		e1-e2	Mezzo-
			soprano
				Sustained. De-
				mands in parts
				considerable
				flexibility. (Lévy
				Freres)

Psyché
Recitative:
  Non, ne la
  suivons pas
Air:
  Sommeil, ami
  des dieux
	bb-f2	f1-d2	Mezzo-
			soprano
			or alto
				Sustained. Has a
				short cadenza.
				(Lévy Freres)

GERMAN

MAX BRUCH
(1838–1920)

OPERA & TITLE	COMP.	TESS.	TYPE	REMARKS

Odysseus
Recitative:
  Hell strahlender
  Tag
Air:
  O, Atryone
  (Penelope's Trauer)
	c1-f♯2	f1-d2	Mezzo-
			soprano
			or alto
				An extended reci-
				tative and a very
				sustained prayer.
				(Simrock)

Odysseus Penelope ein Ge- wand wirkend (Ich wob dies Gewand)	c1-f2	e1-c2	Mezzo- soprano or alto	Sustained. De- mands in parts considerable dra- matic intensity. (GS)

FRIEDRICH VON FLOTOW
(1812—1883)

Martha				
Esser mesto il mio cor	g♯-b2	f♯1-f♯2	Mezzo- soprano	An andante, allegro air, the latter "Jä- gerin, schlau im Sinn." A rather pretentious display piece. Very effec- tive. Demands con- siderable flexibility. Not suitable for voices limited in range. Italian text. (Score, GS)
Martha Jägerin, schlau im Sinn	c1-a2	e1-c2	Mezzo- soprano or alto	Light, animated. Demands facile ar- ticulation. A very elaborate version of this little air, writ- ten as a display piece for Madame Nautier- Didiée, is usually ap- pended to scores of Martha. (Score, GS)

JOHANN STRAUSS
(1825—1899)

Die Fledermaus				
Chacun à son goût	c1-ab2	eb1-eb2	Mezzo- soprano or alto	Animated, short, rhythmic. (Adler)

RICHARD WAGNER
(1813—1883)

Mezzo-Soprano and Alto Excerpts from Wagner's Music Dramas

Das Rheingold				
Weiche Wotan, weiche (Scene 4)	b♯-e2	c♯1-c♯2	Alto	Sustained, somber, declamatory, vigor- ous. (Score, gen. av.)

OPERA & TITLE	COMP.	TESS.	TYPE	REMARKS
Die Götterdäm- **merung** Höre mit Sinn, was ich dir sage (Act I, Scene 3)	g-g2	eb1-eb2	Alto or mezzo- soprano	Declamatory. Has dramatic climaxes. (Adler)
Die Walküre So ist es denn aus mit den ewigen Göttern (Act II, Scene 1)	d1-g♯2	e1-e2	Mezzo- soprano or dra- matic soprano	Very animated, vigorous, dramat- ic. Demands facile articulation. (Score, gen. av.)
Lohengrin Entweihte Götter! Helft jetzt meiner Rache! (Act II, Scene 2)	f♯1-a♯2	c♯1-f♯2	Mezzo- soprano or dra- matic soprano	An extremely vig- orous, dramatic in- cantation. (Score, gen. av.)
Rienzi Gerechter Gott	c1-a2	g1-g2	Dramatic soprano or mezzo- soprano	An extended, dra- matic recitative, a very sustained andante, and a dra- matic allegro. De- mands some flexi- bility. (Adler)
Tannhäuser Geliebter, komm', sieh' dort die Grotte (Act I, Scene 2)	f1-a2	f1-f2	Mezzo- soprano or dra- matic soprano	Sustained. Has an imposing final climax. (Score, gen. av.)
Tristan und **Isolde** Einsam wachend in der Nacht (Act II, Scene 2)	f♯1-f♯2	g♯1-d♯2	Alto or mezzo- soprano	Very sustained, rather subdued. (Score, gen. av.)

CARL MARIA VON WEBER
(1786-1826)

Euryanthe Recitative: So bin ich nun verlassen Air: Hier dicht am Quell	c1-f♯2	f♯1-d2	Mezzo- soprano or soprano	A scena and a slow, declamatory, subdued air. (Score, CFP)

OPERA & TITLE	COMP.	TESS.	TYPE	REMARKS
Oberon Arabien mein Heimatland	a-f2	d1-d2	Mezzo- soprano or alto	A short, sustained andante and a short, graceful allegro. Demands some flexibility. (Score, CFP)
Oberon Arabiens einsam Kind	d♯1-e2	e1-c♯2	Mezzo- soprano or alto	Sustained. De- mands some flexi- bility. (Score, CFP)
Oberon Traure mein Herz	b-f2	g1-d♭2	Mezzo- soprano or dra- matic soprano	Sustained. Demands some flexibility. (Score, CFP)

ENGLISH

SAMUEL BARBER
(b. 1910)

Vanessa Must the winter come so soon	e♭1-f2	g1-e♭2	Mezzo- soprano or soprano	Sustained, tranquil, mostly subdued. (GS)

BENJAMIN BRITTEN
(b. 1913)

The Rape of
Lucretia
Flowers bring to
  every year
  (Flower song)
	a-e2	f1-d2	Alto	Slow, sustained,
				generally subdued.
				Interpretatively
				not easy. (BH)

The Rape of Lucretia She sleeps as a rose	a-f♯2	e1-e2	Mezzo- soprano	Sustained, very subdued (mostly pp). Gentle. (BH)

GIAN-CARLO MENOTTI
(b. 1911)

Amahl and the
Night Visitors

All that gold!	bb-g2	eb1-f2	Mezzo-soprano	Sustained. Ends with a recitative-like passage. (Score, GS)

The Consul

I shall find for you shells and stars (Lullaby)	(a)f-eb2	c1-db2	Alto	Sustained, gentle. Demands a good command of high pp. (GS)

The Consul

I'm not crying for him (The empty-handed traveler)	a-f#2	d1-d2	Alto	Sustained and intense. (Score, GS)

DOUGLAS MOORE
(b. 1893)

The Devil and
Daniel Webster

Now may there be a blessing	c1-f2	f1-d2	Mezzo-soprano or soprano	Sustained, in parts gently declamatory. Text is based on the Biblical story of Ruth. (BH)

IGOR STRAVINSKY
(b. 1882)

The Rake's Progress

As I was saying	c1-d2	d1-bb1	Mezzo-soprano or alto	Animated, narrative. (Score, BH)

The Rake's Progress

Scorned! Abused!	a-a2	d1-eb2	Mezzo-soprano or soprano	Sustained, in parts somewhat florid. Demands flexibility. (Score, BH)

See also the list of songs by Stravinsky.

718

RALPH VAUGHAN WILLIAMS
(1872–1958)

OPERA & TITLE	COMP.	TESS.	TYPE	REMARKS
<u>Hugh the Drover</u>				
Here on my throne	e1-g2	a1-e2	High mezzo-soprano or soprano	Sustained. A concert arrangement of Mary's song. (CUR)
<u>Hugh the Drover</u>				
Life must be full of care	c1-d2	f1-c2	Mezzo-soprano or alto	Sustained. (CUR)

Note: For excerpts from Russian operas in English translations see the Russian section of songs (nineteenth and twentieth centuries).

FOR TENOR

ITALIAN

VINCENZO BELLINI
(1801–1835)

OPERA & TITLE	COMP.	TESS.	TYPE	REMARKS
Norma Meco all'altar di Venere	d-c2	g-e1	Tenor	A sustained andante and a vigorous allegro. (RIC)

ARRIGO BOITO
(1842–1918)

Mefistofele Dai campi, dai prati	f-bb1	a-f1	Tenor	Sustained. Has effective final climax. (RIC)
Mefistofele Giunto sul passo estremo (Epilogue)	f-ab1	bb-f1	Tenor	Sustained. Has effective climaxes. (RIC)

ALFREDO CATALANI
(1854–1893)

Loreley Recitative: Io resto Air: In franto ogni altro vincolo	e-b1	g#-e1	Tenor	Sustained. Has dramatic climaxes. (RIC)
Loreley Nel verde Maggio, un di	e-a1	a-e1	Tenor	Sustained. (RIC)

FRANCESCO CILÈA
(1866–1950)

Adriana Lecouvreur La dolcissima effigie	f-ab1	g-f1	Tenor	Sustained. Has effective climaxes. (Sonzogno)

720

Adriana Lecouvreur

L'anima ho stanca	e-a1	a♯-f♯1	Tenor	Sustained. Has effective climaxes. (Sonzogno)

L'Arlesiana
Recitative:

È la solita storia	e-a1	a-f1	Tenor	Sustained. Has dramatic climaxes. (Sonzogno; IMC)
Air:				
Anch'io vorrei				

GAETANO DONIZETTI
(1797–1848)

Anna Bolena
Recitative:

Vivi tu, te non scongioro	e-a1	g-g1	Tenor	An andante, allegro air. Demands some flexibility. (GS)
Air:				
Nel veder la tua costanza				

Betly

E fia ver	g-b♭1	b♭-g1	Lyric tenor	A rather florid andante, allegro air. (RIC)

Don Pasquale

Com' è gentil	g♯-a1	a-f♯1	Lyric tenor	A sustained, graceful serenade. (Adler)

Don Pasquale
Recitative:

Povero Ernesto	a♭-b♭1	c-a♭1	Lyric tenor	An andante, allegro air. The tessitura is very high. (RIC)
Air:				
Cercherò, cercherò lontana terra				

Don Sebastiano

Deserto in terra	f-d♭2	b♭-g♭1	Lyric tenor	Sustained. Very high tessitura. (RIC)

La Favorita

Spirto gentil	g-c2	c-f1	Tenor	Sustained. (Adler)

La Favorita
Recitative:
Gran Dio! Che degno io ne divenga or vuol

OPERA & TITLE	COMP.	TESS.	TYPE	REMARKS
Air:				
Si, che un tuo solo accento	e-a1	a-f#1	Tenor	Scena and a vigorous air. (RIC)
La Favorita				
Una vergine, un angel di Dio	e-a1 (c#2)	a-f#1	Tenor	Sustained. Demands some flexibility. (RIC)
La regina di Golconda				
Recitative:				
Adorata regina	f-g1	g-f1	Tenor	Sustained. (RIC)
Air:				
Se valor, rispetto e fede				
L'elisir d'amore	e-g1	g-e1	Lyric tenor	Slow, sustained. (RIC)
Quanto è bella				
L'elisir d'amore	f-ab1	bb-f1	Tenor	Sustained, rather delicate. Demands some flexibility. (gen. av.)
Una furtiva lagrima				
Linda di Chamounix				
Recitative:				
Linda! Si ritirò, povera Linda	f#-ab1	ab-f1	Lyric tenor	Recitative and a sustained air. (RIC)
Air:				
Se tanto in ira				
Lucia di Lammermoor				
Recitative:				
Tombe degl' avi miei	f-a1 (bb1)	a-f#1	Tenor	A dramatic scena and a sustained air. (RIC)
Air:				
Fra poco a me ricovero				
Maria di Rohan				
Recitative:				
Nel fragor della festa	e-a1	a-e1	Tenor	A scena and a sustained air. (GS)
Air:				
Alma soave e cara				
Poliuto				
Recitative:				
Io piego la fronte nella polve	ab-ab1	ab-f1	Tenor	Sustained. (RIC)
Air:				
D'un' alma troppo fervida				

UMBERTO GIORDANO
(1867–1948)

OPERA & TITLE	COMP.	TESS.	TYPE	REMARKS
Andrea Chenier Come un bel dì	e-ab1 (bb1)	a-eb1	Tenor	Sustained, somewhat declamatory. Has dramatic climaxes. (Sonzogno; IMC)
Andrea Chenier Si, fui soldato	f-ab1	g-e1	Tenor	Declamatory, dramatic. (Sonzogno)
Andrea Chenier Un di all' azzuro spazio	f-bb1	a-eb1	Tenor	Sustained, declamatory. Has dramatic climaxes. (Sonzogno; IMC)
Fedora Amor ti vieta	b-a1	c-f1	Tenor	Sustained. Has effective climaxes. (Sonzogno; IMC)
Fedora Mia madre la mia vecchia madre	d-g1	a-e1	Tenor	Animated. The vocal line is sustained. Demands in parts considerable dramatic intensity. (Sonzogno)
Fedora Vedi io piango	g-ab1	a-f1	Tenor	Sustained, subdued. Demands in parts considerable dramatic intensity. (Sonzogno)

RUGGIERO LEONCAVALLO
(1858–1919)

OPERA & TITLE	COMP.	TESS.	TYPE	REMARKS
La Bohème Io non ho che una povera stanzetta	eb-bb1	ab-f1	Tenor	Sustained. Has effective climaxes. (Sonzogno)
La Bohème Testa adorata	f-bb1	gb-f1	Tenor	Sustained. Has dramatic climaxes. (Sonzogno)

OPERA & TITLE	COMP.	TESS.	TYPE	REMARKS
Pagliacci O, Colombina	e-a1	g#-f1	Lyric tenor	Animated, light. Demands in parts very facile articulation. (gen. av.)

Pagliacci
 Recitative:
   Recitar! Mentre
   preso dal delirio
 Air:
   Vesti la giubba
	(d)e-a1	g-g1	Dramatic tenor	Very sustained. Has dramatic climaxes. (gen. av.)

PIETRO MASCAGNI
(1863–1945)

OPERA & TITLE	COMP.	TESS.	TYPE	REMARKS

Cavalleria
 Rusticana
 Mamma, quel vino
   è generoso (Final
   solo in the opera)
	f-bb1	bb-f1	Most suitable for dramatic tenor	A declamatory, dramatic scena. Has very sustained passages. (Score, gen. av.)

Cavalleria **Rusticana** O Lola, bianca come fior	ab-ab1	c1-g1	Tenor	Very sustained. The tessitura is quite high. (Score, gen. av.)
Cavalleria **Rusticana** Viva il vino spumeggiante	g-g1	b-g1	Tenor	A spirited, animated drinking song. Demands facile articulation. (Score, gen. av.)
Iris Apri la tua finestra	e-a1	a-f1	Tenor	An effective serenade. (RIC)
L'amico Fritz Ed anche Beppe amò	gb-bb1	bb-gb1	Tenor	Sustained. In parts demands considerable dramatic intensity. (Sonzogno)
L'amico Fritz O amore, o bella Lace	gb-bb1	ab-f1	Tenor	Very sustained. Has dramatic climaxes. (Sonzogno)

AMILCARE PONCHIELLI
(1834–1886)

OPERA & TITLE	COMP.	TESS.	TYPE	REMARKS
La Gioconda				
Cielo e mar	d-b♭1	g-f1	Tenor	Sustained. Has dramatic climaxes. (gen. av.)

GIACOMO PUCCINI
(1858–1924)

All these excerpts, with the exception of one, "Tra voi belle" from Manon Lescaut, are sustained, somewhat declamatory, and have most effective moments. None of them seems too suitable for a very light lyric voice.

OPERA & TITLE	COMP.	TESS.	TYPE	REMARKS
Il Tabarro				
Hai ben ragione	e♭-b♭1	g-f1		(RIC)
La Bohème				
Che gelida manina	e♭-b♭1 (c2)	a♭-f2		(RIC; IMC)
La fanciulla del West				
Ch' ella mi creda	e♭-b♭1	g♭-e♭1		(RIC)
La fanciulla del West				
Or son sei mesi	e-b♭1	b♭-g1		(RIC)
Le Villi				
Torna ai felici di	f-b♭1	b♭-g♭1		(RIC)
Madama Butterfly				
Addio, fiorito asil	f-b♭1	a♭-e♭1		(RIC)
Madama Butterfly				
Amore o grillo	f-b♭1	g♭-e♭1		(RIC)
Manon Lescaut				
Ah! Manon, mi tradisce	e-b♭1	a-f1		(RIC)
Manon Lescaut				
Donna non vidi mai	e-b♭1	b♭-f1		(RIC; IMC)
Manon Lescaut				
Pazzo son! Guardate, come io piango	e-a1 (b1)	b-g1		(RIC; IMC)
Manon Lescaut				
Tra voi belle, brune e bionde	f-a1	a-f1		Animated, light. Demands facile articulation. (RIC)

725

OPERA & TITLE	COMP.	TESS.	TYPE	REMARKS
Tosca E lucevan le stelle	f#-a1	b-f#1		(RIC; IMC)
Tosca Recondita armonia	f-bb1	c-f1		(RIC; IMC)
Turandot Nessun dorma	d-b1	a-f#1		(RIC)
Turandot Non piangere Liù!	gb-bb1	bb-f1		(RIC)

GIOACCHINO ROSSINI
(1792–1868)

Il barbiere di
  Siviglia
Cessa di più
  resistere
	db-bb1	f-f1	Lyric
			tenor
				A florid maestoso,
				very florid andante,
				and a spirited, very
				florid moderato
				which can be sung
				as a separate piece:
				"Ah il piu lieto."
				(Score, gen. av.)

Il barbiere di Siviglia Ecco ridente	f#-b1	g-g1	Lyric tenor	Graceful andante, allegro air. Very florid. (gen. av.)
Il barbiere di Siviglia Se il mio nome	e-g1	g-f1	Lyric tenor	Sustained, delicate serenade. Has flor- id passages. (gen. av.)

Guilliaume Tell
Recitative:
  Ne m'abandonne
  point
Air:
  Asile héreditaire
	c#-a1	a-e1	Tenor	Scena and an an-
				dante, allegro air.
				Demands some
				flexibility. French
				text. (OD)

GIUSEPPE VERDI
(1813–1901)

(See also: Verdi Arias, published by C. F. Peters)

Opera & Title	COMP.	TESS.	TYPE	REMARKS
Aida Recitative: Se quel guerrier io fossi Air: Celeste Aida	d-b♭1	f-f1	Dramatic tenor	Very sustained. In parts demands considerable dramatic intensity. (gen. av.)
Aroldo Sotto il sol di Siria	d-b♭1	a♭-g♭1	Tenor	Recitative and an andante, allegro air. Has dramatic climaxes and a high tessitura. (CFP)
Attila Recitative: Infida! il di che brami è questo Air: O dolore ed io vivea	a♭-bb♭1	a♭-f1	Tenor	Sustained. Demands in parts considerable dramatic intensity. (RIC; CFP)
Don Carlo Recitative: Fontainebleau! Foresta immensa Air: Io la vidi, e al suo sorriso	f-b1	g-f1	Tenor	Recitative and a sustained air. Demands some flexibility. (Adler)
Ernani Recitative: Mercè, diletti amici Air: Come ruggiada al cespite	g-a♭1	g-f1	Dramatic tenor	Recitative and a sustained air. Demands some flexibility. Has dramatic climaxes. (CFP)
Falstaff Dal labbro il canto estasiato	d♯-b♭1	a♭-f♯1	Tenor	Sustained. Demands a good command of high pp. Has effective climaxes. (RIC)

OPERA & TITLE	COMP.	TESS.	TYPE	REMARKS
I due Foscari				
All' infelice veglio	e♭-b♭1	a♭-f1	Tenor	Sustained. Has dramatic climaxes. (RIC)
I due Foscari				
Recitative:				
Brezza del suol natiò	e♭-b♭1	a♭-f1	Tenor	An andante, allegro air. In parts very vigorous. (RIC)
Air:				
Dal più remoto esilio				
I due Foscari				
Recitative:				
Notte! Perpetua notte	e-b♭1	b-f1	Dramatic tenor	A dramatic scena and an animated, vigorous air. Has a sustained vocal line. (CFP)
Air:				
Non maledirmi, o prode				
I Lombardi				
La mia letizia infondere	f♯-a1	a-f♯1	Tenor	Sustained. Demands a good command of high pp. (CFP)
Il Trovatore				
Ah! che la morte ognora	g-a♭1	c-a♭1	Dramatic tenor	Sustained. Has dramatic climaxes. (RIC)
Il Trovatore				
Ah sì, ben mio coll' essere	f-a♭1	a♭-f1	Dramatic tenor	Sustained. Has dramatic climaxes. (gen. av.)
Il Trovatore				
Deserto sulla terra	b♭-a♭1	c♭1-g♭1	Tenor	A sustained, short serenade. Introduction to the trio finale, Act I. (RIC)
Il Trovatore				
Di quella pira	g-b1 (c2)	c-g1	Dramatic tenor	Animated, vigorous. (gen. av.)
I masnadieri				
Recitative:				
Son gli ebbri inverecondi	a♭-b♭1	a♭-g♭1	Tenor	Sustained. Demands some flexibility. (RIC)
Air:				
O mio castel paterno				

OPERA & TITLE	COMP.	TESS.	TYPE	REMARKS

I Vespri siciliani
Recitative:
  È di Monforte il cenno
Air:
  Giorno di pianto, di fier dolore
	e♭-b1	a-f♯1	Dramatic tenor	Scena, andante, allegro. Has very dramatic climaxes. (CFP)

La forza del destino
Recitative:
  La vita è inferno all' infelice (Della natal sua terra)
Air:
  O tu che in seno agli angeli
	d♭-b♭1	a♭-f1	Tenor	Recitative, allegro moderato, and a very sustained andante. Has dramatic climaxes. (Adler)

La Traviata
Recitative:
  Lunge da lei
Air:
  De' miei bollenti spiriti
	e-a♭1	g-f1	Tenor	Scena and a sustained air. (gen. av.)

Luisa Miller Quando le sere al placido	d-a♭1	a♭-e♭1	Tenor	Sustained. Has dramatic climaxes. (CFP)

Macbeth
Recitative:
  O figli miei
Air:
  Ah la paterna mano
	e♭-b♭♭1	a♭-f1	Tenor	Recitative, andante, allegro. In parts very vigorous. (CFP)

Otello Dio! Mi potevi scagliar tutti i mali	e♭-b♭1	e♭-f1	Dramatic tenor	A dramatic scena. Declamatory. (RIC)

Otello
Recitative:
  Tu? Indietro! Fuggi
Air:
  Ora e per sempre addio
	e-b♭1	g-e♭1	Dramatic tenor	A dramatic scena and a sustained, dramatic air. (Castleton, Opera Repertoire for Tenor, TP)

Rigoletto La donna è mobile	f♯-a♯1	b-f♯1	Tenor	Animated, brilliant verse song. Has a florid cadenza. (Adler)

OPERA & TITLE	COMP.	TESS.	TYPE	REMARKS

Rigoletto
Recitative:
  Ella mi fu
  rapita
Air:
  Parmi veder le
  lagrime
	d-b♭♭1	b-g1	Tenor	A scena and a very sustained air. Demands some flexibility. (Adler)

Rigoletto
Recitative:
  Ma dove or
  trovasi
Air:
  Possente amor
  mi chiama
	f♯-a1	a-f♯1	Tenor	Very animated, brilliant. Demands some flexibility. Very short. (Score, gen. av.)

Rigoletto Questa o quella	e♭-a♭1	a♭-f1	Tenor	Rapid. Demands facile articulation and lightness of tone. (gen. av.)

Simon Boccanegra
Recitative:
  O inferno!
  Amelia qui
Air:
  Sento avvampar
  nell' anima
	e-a1	a-f♯1	Dramatic tenor	Recitative, a dramatic allegro, and a sustained largo. (RIC)

Un ballo in maschera Di' tu se fedele il flutto	c-a♭1	e♭-e♭1	Tenor	Animated. Demands facile articulation. (CFP)

FRENCH

ADOLPHE ADAM
(1803–1856)

Si j'étais Roi Elle est princesse	f-c2	b♭-f1	Tenor	Recitative and a sustained air. In parts demands considerable dramatic intensity. (Leduc)
Si j'étais Roi Romance: J'ignore son nom	f-a♭1	a♭-f1	Tenor	Sustained. (Leduc)

OPERA & TITLE	COMP.	TESS.	TYPE	REMARKS
Le Postillon Mes amis écoutez l'histoire	d-b1	g-e1	Tenor	Sustained. (Brandus et Cie)
Le Postillon Romance du Postillon	B-d2	f-f1	Tenor	A difficult display piece. Demands great flexibility and range. (Brandus et Cie)

DANIEL F. E. AUBER
(1782–1871)

OPERA & TITLE	COMP.	TESS.	TYPE	REMARKS
La Muette de Portici Du pauvre seul ami fidèle	g-b1	a-f#1	Most suitable for lyric tenor	Animated, delicate. Demands a good command of high pp. (Adler)
Fra Diavolo Agnès la jouvencelle (Barcarolle)	c#-a1	f#-e1	Most suitable for lyric tenor	Graceful. Demands some flexibility. (Brandus et Cie)
Fra Diavolo Pour toujours disaitelle je suis à tois	d-a1	g-f1	Most suitable for lyric tenor	Sustained and graceful. (Brandus et Dufours)

HECTOR BERLIOZ
(1803–1869)

OPERA & TITLE	COMP.	TESS.	TYPE	REMARKS
La Damnation de Faust Merci, doux crépuscule	e-ab1	g-f1	Tenor	Sustained. Demands in parts a good command of high pp. (Costellat)
La Damnation de Faust Nature immense	f#-a1	g#-e1	Tenor	Slow, sustained, declamatory. Has imposing climaxes. (IMC)

GEORGES BIZET
(1838–1875)

Opera & Title	Comp.	Tess.	Type	Remarks
Carmen La fleur que tu m'avais jetée	f♭-f♭1	a♭-e♭1	Tenor	Sustained. Demands in parts considerable dramatic intensity. (gen. av.)
La jolie fille de Perth A la voix d'un amant fidèle	e-a1	a-f1	Tenor	Animated, graceful, sustained air. (Choudens)
Les Pêcheurs de perles De savanes et des forêts	e♭-a♭1	a♭-f1	Tenor	Short, animated. The vocal line is sustained. (Choudens)
Les Pêcheurs de perles Je crois entendre encore	e-b1	a-f1	Tenor	Very sustained, subdued. Demands a good command of high pp. (Choudens)

ALFRED BRUNEAU
(1857–1934)

Opera & Title	Comp.	Tess.	Type	Remarks
L'Attaque du Moulin Les adieux à la forêt	e-a1	a-f♯1	Tenor	Sustained. (Choudens)

ALFREDO CATALANI
(1854–1893)

Opera & Title	Comp.	Tess.	Type	Remarks
La Wally M'hai salvato	g1-b2	a1-g2	Tenor	Sustained. In parts has dramatic intensity. (RIC)

GUSTAVE CHARPENTIER
(1860–1956)

OPERA & TITLE	COMP.	TESS.	TYPE	REMARKS
Louise Dans la cité lointaine	f♯-g♯1	g♯-e1	Tenor	A sustained sere- nade. (Score, HEUG)

FÉLICIEN DAVID
(1810–1876)

OPERA & TITLE	COMP.	TESS.	TYPE	REMARKS
Lalla Roukh Ma maîtresse a quitté la tente	e-a1	a-e1	Tenor	Sustained, grace- ful air. (Girod)

CLAUDE DEBUSSY
(1862–1918)

OPERA & TITLE	COMP.	TESS.	TYPE	REMARKS

L'Enfant prodigue
Recitative:
   Ces airs joyeux
Air:
   O temps à jamais
   effacé
	d-a1	f♯-f♯1	Tenor	Sustained, some-
				what declamatory.
				Demands consider-
				able dramatic in-
				tensity. (Durand)

LÉO DÉLIBES
(1836–1891)

OPERA & TITLE	COMP.	TESS.	TYPE	REMARKS

Lakmé
Recitative:
   Prendre le dessin
   d'un bijou
Air:
   Fantaisie aux
   divins mensonges
	f-a1	a♭-a♭1	Tenor	Sustained. (Adler)

Lakmé
Recitative:
   Je me souviens
Air:
   Lakmé, dans la
   forêt profonde
	f♯-b1	a♯-f♯1	Tenor	Sustained. (HEUG)

BENJAMIN GODARD
(1849–1895)

OPERA & TITLE	COMP.	TESS.	TYPE	REMARKS
Jocelyn				
Recitative:				
Cachés dans cet asile	f-a1	a-f1	Lyric tenor	Very sustained. Demands a good command of high pp. (gen. av.)
Air:				
Oh! Ne t'éveille pas (Berceuse)				

CHARLES GOUNOD
(1818–1893)

OPERA & TITLE	COMP.	TESS.	TYPE	REMARKS
Faust				
Recitative:				
Quel trouble inconnu	eb-c2	ab-f1	Tenor	Very sustained. (gen. av.)
Air:				
Salut! Demeure chaste et pure				
La Reine de Saba				
Recitative:				
Faiblesse de la race humaine	f-a1	g-g1	Dramatic tenor	A scena and a sustained, vigorous air. Has dramatic climaxes. (Choudens)
Air:				
Inspirez-moi				
Mireille				
Recitative:				
Mon coeur est plein d'un moir souci	g-ab1	c-g1	Tenor	Very sustained. Has effective climaxes. (Choudens)
Air:				
Anges du paradis				
Polyeucte				
Nymphes attentives	f-bb1	a-f1	Lyric tenor	A sustained barcarolle. (Choudens)
Polyeucte				
Source délicieuse	f-a1 (bb1)	bb-f1	Tenor	Very sustained. The final section is more animated and demands considerable dramatic intensity. (Choudens)

734

OPERA & TITLE	COMP.	TESS.	TYPE	REMARKS
Roméo et Juliette Recitative: L'amour! Oui son ardeur Air: Ah, lève toi, soleil	f-bb1	a-f1	Tenor	Sustained. Has effective climaxes. (gen. av.)
Sapho Recitative: J'arrive le premier Air: O jours heureux	eb-bb1 (db2)	ab-f1	Lyric tenor	Sustained. The optional db1 is contained in the final cadenza. (Choudens)

JACQUES HALÉVY
(1799–1862)

OPERA & TITLE	COMP.	TESS.	TYPE	REMARKS
La Juive Rachel, quand du Seigneur	eb-c2	ab-g1	Tenor	Sustained. In parts very dramatic. Usually sung a tone lower. (gen. av.)
L'Eclair Quand de la nuit	b-g1	e-e1	Tenor	Sustained. (GS)

LOUIS J. F. HÉROLD
(1791–1833)

OPERA & TITLE	COMP.	TESS.	TYPE	REMARKS
Le Pré aux clercs Recitative: Ce soir j'arrive donc Air: O ma tendre amie	f-c2	g-g1	Tenor	Short recitative and a sustained air which has some very florid passages. (Brandus et Cie)

EDOUARD LALO
(1823–1892)

OPERA & TITLE	COMP.	TESS.	TYPE	REMARKS
Le Roi d'Ys Recitative: Puisqu'on ne peut: fléchir Air: Vainement, ma bien—aimée	eb-a1	a-e1	Lyric tenor	Light, graceful. Demands a good command of high pp. (gen. av.)

735

JULES MASSENET
(1842–1912)

OPERA & TITLE	COMP.	TESS.	TYPE	REMARKS

Hérodiade
Recitative:
  Ne pouvant ré-
  primer les élans
Air:
  Adieux donc vains
  objets
	d–b♭1	a–f1	Tenor	Recitative and a compound, dramatic monologue. Has many sustained sections. (HEUG; GS)

Le Cid Ô souverain, ô juge, ô père	e♭–b♭1	a♭–f1	Tenor	Sustained. Has dramatic climaxes. (HEUG)

Le Roi de Lahore
Recitative:
  Aux troupes du
  Sultan
Air:
  Promesse de mon
  avenir
	e♭–a♭1	g♭–e♭1	Tenor	Sustained. Demands in parts considerable dramatic intensity. (HEUG)

Manon
Recitative:
  Je suis seul
Air:
  Ah! fuyez douce
  image
	f–b♭1	g–g1	Tenor	Sustained. Has very dramatic climaxes. (gen. av.)

Manon
Recitative:
  Instant charmant
Air:
  En fermant les
  yeux
	e–a1	a–e1	Most suitable for lyric tenor	Sustained, delicate. Demands a good command of high pp. (gen. av.)

Werther
Recitative:
  Un autre est son
  époux
Air:
  J'aurais sur ma
  poitrine
	g–b♭♭1	b♭–f1	Tenor	Scena and an animated air. The vocal line is sustained. Has effective climaxes. (HEUG)

Werther
Recitative:
  Oui! Ce qu'elle
  m'ordonne				

OPERA & TITLE	COMP.	TESS.	TYPE	REMARKS

Air:
  Lorsque l'enfant
  revient d'un
  voyage
	f#-g#1
	(b1)
		b-f#1	Tenor	Sustained. Has effective climaxes. (HEUG)

Werther
Recitative:
  Je ne sais si
  je veille
Air:
  O nature pleine
  de grâce
	f#-a1	a-f#1	Tenor	Sustained. Has effective climaxes. (HEUG; IMC)

Werther
Recitative:
  Traduire! Ah!
  Bien souvent
  mon rêve
Air:
  Pourquoi me
  réveiller
	f#-a#1	g#-d#1	Tenor	Sustained. Has effective climaxes. (HEUG; IMC)

ANDRÉ MESSAGER
(1853–1929)

OPERA & TITLE	COMP.	TESS.	TYPE	REMARKS
Fortunio Chanson de Fortunio	e-a1	a-f#1	Tenor	Sustained. Has effective climaxes. Sometimes sung by soprani. (Choudens)
Fortunio La maison grise	e-f1	g-d1	Tenor	Sustained. Vocally not taxing. Suitable for all voices; often sung as a song. (Choudens)

GIACOMO MEYERBEER
(1791–1864)

OPERA & TITLE	COMP.	TESS.	TYPE	REMARKS

L'Africaine
Recitative:
  Pays merveilleux
Air:
  O paradis
	f-bb1	bb-gb1	Tenor	An andante, allegro air with interpolated recitative passages. (gen. av.)

737

OPERA & TITLE	COMP.	TESS.	TYPE	REMARKS
Les Huguenots Recitative:				
Aux armes, mes amis	e-a1 (c2)	a-f1	Tenor*	Recitative, andante, allegro. (Score, B & H)
Air: A la lueur de leurs torches funèbres				
Les Huguenots Recitative:				
Ah! Quel spectacle enchanteur	e-b1	a-f#1	Lyric tenor	Sustained. In parts demands considerable flexibility. (GS)
Air: Plus blanche que la blanche hermine				

*Many tenor arias by Meyerbeer do not seem to be suitable for any but exceptionally high voices possessing the d♭2 and the d2 notes.

JACQUES OFFENBACH
(1819–1880)

OPERA & TITLE	COMP.	TESS.	TYPE	REMARKS
Les Contes d'Hoffman Recitative:				
Allons! Courage et confiance	e-g1	b♭-f1	Tenor	Recitative and a sustained air. Has effective climaxes. (Score, gen. av.)
Air: Ah, vivre deux				

AMBROISE THOMAS
(1811–1896)

OPERA & TITLE	COMP.	TESS.	TYPE	REMARKS
Hamlet				
Pour mon pays	f-b♭1	a♭-f1	Tenor	Sustained. Has effective climaxes. (HEUG)
Mignon				
Elle ne croyait pas	g-a1	a-e1	Lyric tenor	Sustained. In parts demands considerable dramatic intensity. (gen. av.)

738

LUDWIG VAN BEETHOVEN
(1770–1827)

OPERA & TITLE	COMP.	TESS.	TYPE	REMARKS

Fidelio
Recitative:
  Gott! Welch
  Dunkel hier
Air:
  In des Lebens
  Frühlingstagen
	eb-bb1	ab-g1	Tenor	An extended reci-
				tative followed by
				an andante, allegro
				air. The tessitura
				in the allegro is
				very high. In parts
				very dramatic.
				(gen. av.)

PETER CORNELIUS
(1824–1874)

Der Barbier von
  Bagdad
Recitative:
  So leb' ich noch
Air:
  Vor deinem
  Fenster die Blumen
	f#-a1	a-f1	Tenor	A scena and a sus-
				tained air. Has ef-
				fective climaxes.
				(B & H)

FRIEDRICH VON FLOTOW
(1812–1883)

Martha Ach, so fromm, ach, so traut (or, as usually sung in the Italian version: M'appari)	f-bb1	a-f1	Tenor	Sustained. The tes- situra is somewhat high. (gen. av.)

OTTO NICOLAI
(1810–1849)

Die Lustigen Weiber
  von Windsor
Horch, die Lerche
  singt im Hain
	g-g#1	b-e1	Lyric
			tenor
				Sustained, rather
				delicate. (Score, CFP)

RICHARD WAGNER
(1813-1883)

Tenor Excerpts from Wagner's Music Dramas

All these excerpts are most suitable for the heavy, dramatic type of voice, with the exception of the excerpts from Die Meistersinger and Lohengrin, which are not too unsuitable for less robust voices.

OPERA & TITLE	COMP.	TESS.	TYPE	REMARKS
Der Fliegende Holländer Willst jenes Tag's (Act III, Scene 4)	f-bb1	a-f1		Sustained. Demands in parts considerable dramatic intensity. (gen. av.)
Die Meistersinger von Nürnberg Am stillen Herd (Act I, Scene 3)	d-a1	g-e1		Sustained. Has vigorous climaxes. (gen. av.)
Die Meistersinger von Nürnberg Fanget an! So rief der Lenz (Act I, Scene 3)	f-a1	g-g1		Animated, vigorous. (Score, gen. av.)
Die Meistersinger von Nürnberg Morgentlich leuchtend (Preislied. Act III, Scene 5)	d#-a1	b-g1		Has vigorous climaxes. (gen. av.)
Die Walküre Ein Schwert verhiess mir der Vater (Act I, Scene 3)	c-g1	f-f1		Majestic, vigorous. Somewhat declamatory. (Score, gen. av.)
Die Walküre Winterstürme wichen dem Wonnemond (Act I, Scene 3)	c-g1	f-f1		Sustained. Demands in parts considerable dramatic intensity. (gen. av.)
Lohengrin Atmest du nicht mit mir die süssen Düfte (Act III, Scene 2)	g-ab1	g-f1		Very sustained. (Score, gen. av.)

OPERA & TITLE	COMP.	TESS.	TYPE	REMARKS
Lohengrin				
In Fernem Land (Act III, Scene 3)	e-a1	a-e1		Slow, somewhat declamatory. (gen. av.)
Lohengrin				
Mein Lieber Schwan (Act III, Scene 3)	f#-a1	b-g1		Sustained. Has dramatic climaxes. (gen. av.)
Rienzi				
Allmächt'ger Vater (Act V, Scene 1)	f-ab1	bb-f1		Very sustained, majestic. Has dramatic climaxes. (GS)
Rienzi				
Ihr nicht beim Feste? (Act IV, Scene 2)	f-ab1	g-f1		Animated, vigorous. (Score, CFP)
Siegfried				
Nothung! Nothung! Neidliches Schwert (Act I, Scene 3)	d-a1	f-f1		Very vigorous. (Score, gen. av.)
Siegfried				
Schmiede mein Hammer, ein hartes Schwert (Act I, Scene 3)	g-a1	a-g1		Very vigorous. (Score, gen. av.)
Tannhäuser				
Dir töne Lob! Die Wunder sein gepriesen (Act I, Scene 2)	e#-g1	a-f#1		Animated, vigorous. In the opera the three verses of this song are respectively in the keys of db, d, and eb. (Score, gen. av.)
Tristan und Isolde				
Wie sie selig hehr und milde wandelt durch des Meer's Gefilde (Act III, Scene 1)	d#-f#1	g#-e1		Sustained. (Score, gen. av.)

CARL MARIA VON WEBER
(1786–1826)

Abu Hassan
Recitative:
   Was nun zu machen?

OPERA & TITLE	COMP.	TESS.	TYPE	REMARKS
Air:				
Ich gebe Gaster-eien	c-g1	e-e1	Tenor	Very spirited, gay compound air. The middle section is sustained and delicate. Demands some flexibility. (Score, CFP)
Der Freischütz				
Recitative:				
Nein, länger trag' ich nicht die Qual	(c)d-a1	g-f1	Tenor	Recitative, andante, allegro. In parts dramatic and vig-
Air:				orous. (gen. av.)
Durch die Wälder				
Euryanthe				
Unter blühenden Mandelbäumen	f-b♭1	a-f1	Tenor	Sustained. Demands some flexibility. (gen. av.)
Euryanthe				
Wehen mir Lüfte	e♭-a♭1	a♭-f1	Tenor	An andante, allegro air. In parts quite vigorous. Demands some flexibility. (Score, CFP)
Oberon				
Ich jub'le in Glück und Hoff-nungen	c-g1	g-f1	Tenor	Very animated, vig-orous. Demands considerable flexi-bility. (Score, CFP)
Oberon				
Recitative:				
Ja selbst die Liebe weicht dem Ruhm	d♯-a1	f-e1	Tenor	Scena, andante, al-legro. In parts very vigorous. Demands some flexibility.
Air:				(Score, CFP)
Klag' du Tochter des Morgenlands				
Oberon				
Schreckensschwur!	c-g1	f-d1	Dramatic tenor	Very vigorous, ani-mated, dramatic. (Score, CFP)
Oberon				
Vater, hör' mich flehn zu dir	e-g1	g-e1	Tenor	Slow, sustained, very short. (Score, CFP)

OPERA & TITLE	COMP.	TESS.	TYPE	REMARKS
Oberon Von Jugend auf in dem Kampf-gefild'	d–b1	b–f♯1	Tenor	Very vigorous, animated. Demands considerable flexibility. (Score, CFP)

ENGLISH

BENJAMIN BRITTEN
(b. 1913)

OPERA & TITLE	COMP.	TESS.	TYPE	REMARKS
Billy Budd I am an old man (Prologue)	e♭1–a2	f♯1–g2	Tenor	Sustained, recitative-like. In parts has some dramatic intensity. (Score, BH)
Peter Grimes In dreams I've built myself	d1–b2	f♯1–f♯2	Tenor	Slow, sustained. Ends with a slightly marked and florid section. Demands flexibility and a good command of high pp. (BH)
Peter Grimes Picture what that day was like	d1–a2	e1–f2	Tenor	Declamatory and sustained sections. Demands facile articulation, flexibility, a good command of high pp. In parts has dramatic intensity. (BH)
The Rape of Lucretia Tarquinius does not wait (The ride)	e♭1–b♭2	f♯1–f2	Tenor; not suitable for light, high voices	Vigorous, animated, in parts heavily marked. Has florid passages. Demands facile articulation and flexibility. (BH)

CARLISLE FLOYD
(b. 1926)

Susannah
It must make	e-a2	f♯1-f♯2	Tenor	Sustained, gentle.
the good Lord				(BH)
sad				

GIAN-CARLO MENOTTI
(b. 1911)

Amelia Goes to
   the Ball
| 'Twas at midnight | e♭1-a2 | f1-f♯2 | Tenor | Sustained. (Score, |
| in a dream | | | | RIC) |

DOUGLAS MOORE
(b. 1893)

The Devil and
   Daniel Webster
I summon the jury	e♭1-a♭2	a1-f2	Tenor	Somewhat ani-
				mated and declama-
				tory. (Score, BH)

BEDŘICH SMETANA
(1824–1884)

The Bartered Bride
You are caught!	e1-a2	g1-g2	Tenor	Recitative and a
				very sustained air.
				Imposing climax.
				Good English ver-
				sion by Marion
				Farquhar. (Adler)

IGOR STRAVINSKY
(b. 1882)

The Rake's Progress
Love, too frequent-	f♯1-g♯2	g♯1-f♯2	Tenor	Sustained, short.
ly betrayed				Demands some flexi-
				bility. (Score, BH)

744

OPERA & TITLE	COMP.	TESS.	TYPE	REMARKS

The Rake's
  Progress
Prepare your-
  selves, heroic
  shades
	g1-a2	b1-f♯2	Tenor	Sustained arioso.
				Short. (Score,
				BH)

The Rake's
  Progress
Recitative:
  Here I stand
Air:
  Since it is not
  by merit
	e1-a2	g1-f2	Tenor	Recitative and a
				sustained air.
				Imposing climax.
				(Score, BH)

See also the list of songs by Stravinsky.

RALPH VAUGHAN WILLIAMS
(1872–1958)

Hugh the Drover Alone and friend- less	d1-a♭2	f1-f2	Tenor	Sustained. A con- cert arrangement of Hugh's song.

Note: For excerpts from Russian operas in English translations see
       the Russian section of songs (nineteenth and twentieth centuries).

ITALIAN

VINCENZO BELLINI
(1801–1835)

OPERA & TITLE	COMP.	TESS.	TYPE	REMARKS
Beatrice di Tenda O divina Agnese	d-f1	f♯-d1	Baritone	An andante, allegro air. Demands some flexibility. (RIC)
Beatrice di Tenda Qui m'accolse	d-f1	f-eb1	Baritone	An andante, allegro air. (RIC)
La sonnambula Vi ravviso o luoghi ameni	G-eb1	eb-c1	Bass	An andante, allegro air. Demands some flexibility. (gen. av.)

ARRIGO BOITO
(1842–1918)

Mefistofele Ave Signor	Bb-eb1 (f1)	f-d1	Baritone or bass-baritone	Animated, satirical song. Demands facile articulation. In parts very vigorous. (Score, RIC)
Mefistofele Sono lo spirito che nega	G-e1	c-c1	Bass or bass-baritone	A dramatic monologue. In parts demands facile articulation. (RIC)

EUGÈNE DIAZ
(1837–1901)

Benvenuto
Recitative:
    Quante volte
    alla notte

OPERA & TITLE	COMP.	TESS.	TYPE	REMARKS
Air: O splendore infinito	A-f1	f-d1	Baritone	Recitative and a sustained effective air. (Grus)

GAETANO DONIZETTI
(1797–1848)

OPERA & TITLE	COMP.	TESS.	TYPE	REMARKS
<u>Don Pasquale</u> Ah! un foco insolito	c-e1	g-c1	Bass	A rapid buffo air. Demands facile articulation. (RIC)
<u>Don Pasquale</u> Bella siccome un angelo	Ab-f1	f-db1	Baritone	Slow, sustained. In parts demands considerable flexi- bility. (gen. av.)

<u>Don Sebastiano</u>
Recitative:
  Sente il cielo
  pietade
Air:
  O Lisbona,
  alfin ti miro
	d-f1	g-d1	Baritone	Recitative and a
				sustained larghetto.
				Demands some flexi-
				bility. (RIC)

<u>La Favorita</u>
Recitative:
  Fernando, ei
  del suo cor la
  brama
Air:
  A tanto amor
	c#-e1	f#-c#1	Bass or
			bass-
			baritone
				Recitative and a
				sustained air. (Adler)

<u>La Favorita</u>
Recitative:
  Alcun gli fea
Air:
  Vien, Leonora
	c-f1	f-d1	Baritone	Scena and a compound
				aria. Has dramatic
				climaxes. (RIC)

<u>L'elisir d'amore</u> Udite, udite, o rustici	A-e1	e-c#1	Bass	An andante, allegro buffo air. Demands facile articulation. (RIC)

<u>Le Rénégat</u>
Recitative:
  J'ai renié ma
  foi
Air:
  Ange adoré
	G-d1	d-b	Bass	Recitative, a short
				larghetto, and a very
				vigorous, spirited
				allegro. French
				text. (CFP)

OPERA & TITLE	COMP.	TESS.	TYPE	REMARKS
Linda di Chamounix				
Ambo nati in questa valle	c#-e1	g-d1	Baritone	Sustained. (RIC)
Lucia di Lammermoor				
Cruda, funesta smania	c#-f#1 (g1)	g-e1	Baritone	A sustained larghetto and a spirited allegro. Demands some flexibility. (gen. av.)
Lucia di Lammermoor				
Dalle stanze, ove Lucia	A#-e1	d#-c#1	Bass or bass-baritone	A dramatic narrative. Forceful ending section. (Adler)
Lucrezia Borgia				
Vieni la mia vendetta	Ab-eb1	eb-db1	Bass	An andante, allegro air. Vigorous. Demands some flexibility. Has dramatic climaxes. (RIC)
Maria di Rohan				
Voce fatal di morte	f-f1 (g1)	a-e1	High baritone	Sustained air for very high baritone. (RIC)
Maria di Rudenz				
Recitative: Egli ancora non giunge	e-g1	g-eb1	Baritone	Sustained. Demands some flexibility. (RIC)
Air: Ah, no avea più lagrime				
Poliuto				
Di tua beltade immagine	c-fb1	eb-db1	Baritone	An andante, allegro air. Demands some flexibility. (RIC)

UMBERTO GIORDANO
(1867–1948)

Andrea Chenier				
Compacente a' colloquii	c#1-f#1	f#-c#1	Baritone	Sustained, declamatory. The final sec-

OPERA & TITLE	COMP.	TESS.	TYPE	REMARKS
				tion is very animated, the vocal line sustained. Has dramatic climaxes. (Score: Sonzogno; IMC)
Andrea Chenier Nemico della patria?	c#-f#1	f#-d1	Baritone	A dramatic scena and a sustained air. Has dramatic climaxes. (Score: Sonzogno; IMC)
Fedora La donna Russa	eb-f1	g-eb1	Baritone	Spirited, brilliant. Has some florid passages. (Sonzogno)

RUGGIERO LEONCAVALLO
(1858–1919)

OPERA & TITLE	COMP.	TESS.	TYPE	REMARKS
Pagliacci Si può? Signore! (Prologue)	B-f1 (ab1)	e-eb1	High baritone	A dramatic scena followed by a very sustained andante. (gen. av.)
Zazà Zazà, piccola zingara	f-gb1	ab-f1	High baritone	Sustained. Has effective climaxes. (Sonzogno; IMC)

PIETRO MASCAGNI
(1863–1945)

OPERA & TITLE	COMP.	TESS.	TYPE	REMARKS
Cavalleria Rusticana Il cavallo scalpita	eb-f#1	g-eb1	Baritone	Vigorous, animated. Demands facile articulation. (gen. av.)
L'amico Fritz Per voi ghiottoni inutili (Song of the Rabbi)	d-f1	g-eb1	Baritone	Sustained, vigorous, dramatic. (Sonzogno)

749

ITALO MONTEMEZZI
(1875–1952)

OPERA & TITLE	COMP.	TESS.	TYPE	REMARKS
L'amore dei tre re Italia, è tutto il mio ricordo	A–f1	f–d1	Bass- baritone or baritone	Dramatic, declama- tory. Has an im- posing final climax. (RIC)

AMILCARE PONCHIELLI
(1834–1886)

OPERA & TITLE	COMP.	TESS.	TYPE	REMARKS
La Gioconda Ah! Pescator	eb–f1	g–eb1	Baritone	Spirited. Demands some flexibility. (Adler)
La Gioconda O monumento!	d–g1	g–d1	Baritone	A dramatic scena, declamatory and grave. (RIC)

La Gioconda
Recitative:
  Si, morir
  ella de'
Air:
  Ombre di mia
  prosapia
	G–eb1
	(f1)
		c–c1	Bass	A dramatic scena
				and a compound
				dramatic air. (Ad-
				ler)

GIACOMO PUCCINI
(1858–1924)

OPERA & TITLE	COMP.	TESS.	TYPE	REMARKS
Il Tabarro Scorri fiume eterno	Bb–g1	eb–eb1	Baritone	Sustained, declama- tory. Has dramatic climaxes. (RIC)
La Boheme Vecchia zimarra	B–eb1	c#–c#1	Bass	Sustained vocal line. In parts slightly declama- tory. (Adler)
La Tosca Se la giurata fede	db–gb1	f–eb1	Baritone	Sustained. Has dramatic climaxes. (RIC)

OPERA & TITLE	COMP.	TESS.	TYPE	REMARKS
Le Villi Recitative: No! Possibil non è Air: Anima santa della figlia mia	B♭-f1 (g1)	f-e♭1	High baritone	A dramatic scena and a sustained air. Has dramat- ic climaxes. (RIC)

GIOACCHINO ROSSINI
(1792–1868)

OPERA & TITLE	COMP.	TESS.	TYPE	REMARKS
Guillaume Tell Sois immobile	c-f1	f-d♭1	Baritone	Very sustained. French text. (RIC)
Il barbiere di **Siviglia** A un dottore	B♭-f1	e♭-e♭1	Bass	A spirited buffo air. Demands very facile articulation and con- siderable flexibility. Rather high tessitura. Usually omitted in stage performances of the opera, when an air by Pietro Romani, "Manca un foglio," is substituted. For Romani's air see the G. Schirmer edition of "Il Barbiere di Siviglia," page 319.
Il barbiere di **Siviglia** La calunnia	c♯-f♯1	d-d1	Bass or bass- baritone	A spirited, comic air. Interpretatively not easy. Demands facile articulation. (gen. av.)
Il barbiere di **Siviglia** Largo al factotum	d-g1(a1)	g-e1	High baritone	Very rapid. De- mands very rapid articulation. (gen. av.)

OPERA & TITLE	COMP.	TESS.	TYPE	REMARKS
La Cenerentola				
Recitative:				
Miei rampolli femminini	c-f1	e-d1	Bass or baritone	A spirited buffo air. Demands facile articulation. (RIC)
Air:				
Mi sognai fra il fosco e il chiaro				
La Gazza Ladra				
Il mio piano è preparato	A-e1	c#-c#1	Bass or bass-baritone	A florid andante, allegro buffo air. Demands facile articulation. (RIC)
Le Siège de Corinthe				
Recitative:				
Qu'â ma voix la victoire s'arrête	Bb-f1	c-c1	Baritone	Recitative, andante, allegro. Demands some flexibility. French text. (GS)
Air:				
La gloire et la fortune				
Robert Bruce				
Recitative:				
Le roi someille	Bb-eb1	eb-c1	Bass or bass-baritone	Animated. Demands some flexibility. French text. (GS)
Air:				
Que ton âme si noble				

GIUSEPPE VERDI
(1813-1901)

(See also: Verdi Arias, published by C. F. Peters)

OPERA & TITLE	COMP.	TESS.	TYPE	REMARKS
Attila				
Recitative:				
Tregua è cogl' uni	c-g1	eb-eb1	Baritone	An extended recitative, a very sustained andante, and a vigorous allegro. (CFP)
Air:				
Dagli immortali vertici				
Don Carlo				
Recitative:				
Ella giammai m'amò!	G-e1	d-bb	Bass	Scena and a sustained air. Has dramatic climaxes. (gen. av.)
Air:				
Dormirò sol nel manto mio regal				

OPERA & TITLE	COMP.	TESS.	TYPE	REMARKS

Don Carlo
Recitative:
  Convien qui
  dirci addio
Air:
  Per me giunto è
  il di supremo
	c-g♭1	f-d1	Baritone	For the most
				part sustained.
				In parts declama-
				tory. Has dramat-
				ic climaxes. (Ad-
				ler)

Don Carlo
Recitative:
  Son io mio
  Carlo
Air:
  Per me giunto
	c-g♭1	g-e1	Baritone	Recitative, a very
				sustained andante,
				a dramatic declama-
				tory middle section,
				and a broad, sus-
				tained final moderato.
				(gen. av.)

Ernani
Recitative:
  Che mai vegg'io
Air:
  Infelice! E tuo
  credevi
	G-e♭1	e♭-c1	Bass or
			bass-
			baritone
				Recitative and a
				sustained air. De-
				mands some flexi-
				bility. Has dramat-
				ic climaxes. (gen.
				av.)

Ernani Infin che un brando vindici	c-f1	e♭-d♭1	Baritone or bass- baritone	Recitative and a spirited, martial- type air. Dramatic. (Adler)
Ernani Lo vedremo, veglio audace	d-f♯1	a-e1	Baritone	Animated. Has dra- matic climaxes. De- mands some flexi- bility. (gen. av.)

Ernani
Recitative:
  Gran Dio
Air:
  Oh de verd'
  anni miei
	c-g♭1	f-e♭1	Baritone	Recitative and a
				sustained air. De-
				mands flexibility.
				Has dramatic cli-
				maxes. (RIC)

Falstaff
È sogno? O
  realtà? (Monologo
  di Ford)
	c-g♭1	e♭-e♭1	Baritone	A dramatic, declam-
				atory scena. (Adler)

OPERA & TITLE	COMP.	TESS.	TYPE	REMARKS
Falstaff				
L'onore! Ladri!	A♭-g1	e-e1	Baritone	A declamatory scena. Interpretatively not easy. (Adler)
I due Foscari				
Recitative:				
Eccomi solo al fino	e♭-f1	f-e♭1	Baritone	Sustained. Demands some flexibility. Has dramatic climaxes. (RIC)
Air:				
O vecchio cor che batti				
Il Trovatore				
Di due figli vivea	B-e1	c♯-c♯1	Bass or bass-baritone	An andante, allegretto narrative song. For the most part subdued. Has dramatic climaxes. Demands some flexibility. (Score, gen. av.)
Il Trovatore				
Recitative:				
Tutto è deserto	A-f1(g1)	f-e♭1	Baritone	An extended recitative, and a very sustained largo. Demands some flexibility. (gen. av.)
Air:				
Il balen del suo sorriso				
I masnadieri				
Recitative:				
Tradimento! Risorgono i defunti	B♭-f1	f-e♭1	Baritone	A very dramatic scena and a vigorous, dramatic, animated air. (CFP)
Air:				
Pareami che sorto da lauto convito				
I vespri siciliani				
In braccio alle dovizie	c♯-f♯1	f♯-d♯1	Baritone	A vigorous, dramatic allegro and a sustained meno mosso. (CFP)
I vespri siciliani				
Recitative:				
O patria, o cara patria				

OPERA & TITLE	COMP.	TESS.	TYPE	REMARKS
Air: O, tu Palermo	A-e♭1	d♭-d♭1	Bass or bass- baritone	Recitative and a sustained air. Has dramatic climaxes. De- mands some flex- ibility. (CFP; RIC)

La Forza del
  Destino
Recitative:
  Morir! Tremen-
  da cosa
Air:
  Urna fatale
	c-g1	f-e♭1	Baritone	Scena and a sus-
				tained air. De-
				mands some flex-
				ibility. Has dra-
				matic climaxes.
				(gen. av.)

La Traviata
Recitative:
  Mio figlio!
Air:
  Di Provenza il
  mar, il suol
	d♭-g♭1	a♭-e♭1	Baritone	Very sustained.
				(gen. av.)

Luisa Miller Il mio sangue, la vita darei	B♭-g♭1	e♭-d♭1	Baritone	A dramatic, vig- orous andante, al- legro air. Has florid final cadenza. (CFP)
Luisa Miller Sacra la scelta è d'un consorte	d-g♭1	f-f1	High baritone	A dramatic an- dante, allegro air. Demands some flexibility. (Adler)

Macbeth
Recitative:
  Studia il passo,
  o mio figlio!
Air:
  Come dal ciel
  precipita
Macbeth:
Recitative:
  Perfidi! All'
  Anglo contro
  me v'unite
	A-e1	b-b1	Bass or
			bass-
			baritone
				Recitative and a
				sustained air. Has
				dramatic climaxes.
				(Adler)

OPERA & TITLE	COMP.	TESS.	TYPE	REMARKS

Air:
  Pietà, rispetto,
  onore
	c-f1	f-d♭1	Baritone	Recitative and a sustained air. Demands in parts considerable dramatic intensity. (Adler)

Nabucodonosor
  (Nabucco)
Chi mi toglie il
  regio scettro?
  (Finale II)
Nabucodonosor
  (Nabucco)
	c-f1	f-e♭1	Baritone	Animated, vigorous, dramatic. (CFP)

Recitative:
  Vieni, o Levita
Air:
  Tu sul labbro
  de' veggenti
Otello
	G-e1	d-c1	Bass	Recitative and a sustained air. (CFP; RIC)

Recitative:
  Vanne, la tua
  meta gia vedo
Air:
  Credo in un
  dio crudel
Rigoletto
	A♯-f♯1	f-e♭1	Baritone	A very dramatic declamatory scena. (gen. av.)

Recitative:
  Si, la mia figlia
Air:
  Cortigiani, vil
  razza
	c-f1	f-d♭1	Baritone	Recitative, a dramatic, declamatory andante agitato, and a final very sustained andante. (gen. av.)

Simon Boccanegra Fratricidi! Plebe! Patrizi!	e♭-f♯1	a♭-e♭1	Baritone	Sustained, short. Has a dramatic opening section. (RIC)

Simon Boccanegra
Recitative:
  A te l'estremo
  addio
Air:
  Il lacerato
  spirito
	F♯-d1	c♯-b	Bass or bass-baritone	Slow, grave, sustained. (Adler)

OPERA & TITLE	COMP.	TESS.	TYPE	REMARKS
Un ballo in maschera				
Recitative: Alzati! Là tuo figlio	c-g1	f-e1	Baritone	Scena and a dramatic, vigorous, sustained air.
Air: Eri tu che macchiavi				(gen. av.)

FRENCH

ADOLPHE ADAM
(1803–1856)

OPERA & TITLE	COMP.	TESS.	TYPE	REMARKS
Le Chalet				
Recitative: Arrêtons-nous ici	B♭-e♭1	e♭-c1	Bassbaritone	A scena and a sustained, dramatic air. Has
Air: Vallons de l'Helvétie				very florid passages. (GS)
Si j'étais Roi				
Dans le sommeil	e♭-a♭1	a♭-e♭1	High baritone	Sustained. (Leduc)

HECTOR BERLIOZ
(1803–1869)

OPERA & TITLE	COMP.	TESS.	TYPE	REMARKS
La Damnation de Faust				
Certain rat, dans une cuisine	A-d1	c-c1	Bass	A spirited, vigorous, satirical song. (IMC)
La Damnation de Faust				
Recitative: Maintenant, chantons à cette belle	B-d♯1	e-c♯1	Baritone or bassbaritone	A satirical, animated serenade in waltz tempo. Demands some
Air: Devant la maison (Sérénade de Méphisto)				flexibility. (Costellat)

OPERA & TITLE	COMP.	TESS.	TYPE	REMARKS
La Damnation de Faust				
Une puce gentille (Chanson de la Puce)	d-f1	f-d1	Baritone	A spirited, satirical verse song. See "Song of the Flea" by Mussorgsky and "Aus Goethe's Faust" by Beethoven. (Costellat; IMC)
La Damnation de Faust				
Voice de roses	c♯-e1	e-c♯1	Baritone	Sustained, subdued. (Costellat)

GEORGES BIZET
(1838–1875)

OPERA & TITLE	COMP.	TESS.	TYPE	REMARKS
Carmen				
Votre toast (Song of the Toreador)	B♭-f1	f-d♭1	Baritone	Vigorous, spirited. (gen. av.)
La jolie fille de Perth				
Quand la flamme de l'amour	B-e1	e-d1	Bass or bass-baritone	Animated, vigorous. (Choudens)
Les Pêcheurs de perles				
Recitative: L'orage s'est calmé	B-f♯1	d-d1	Baritone	Recitative and a sustained air. Has effective climaxes. (Choudens)
Air: O Nadir, tendre ami				

GUSTAVE CHARPENTIER
(1860–1956)

OPERA & TITLE	COMP.	TESS.	TYPE	REMARKS
Louise				
Recitative: Les pauvres gens	A♯-f1	f-d1	Baritone	A dramatic monologue. (Score, HEUG)
Air: Voir naître un enfant				

CLAUDE DEBUSSY
(1862–1918)

OPERA & TITLE	COMP.	TESS.	TYPE	REMARKS
L'Enfant prodigue				
Faites silence! Ecoutez tous!	Bb-f1	f-d1	Baritone	Sustained, majestic. (Durand; IMC)

LÉO DÉLIBES
(1836–1891)

OPERA & TITLE	COMP.	TESS.	TYPE	REMARKS
Lakmé				
Lakmé, ton doux regard se voile	eb-f1	f-db1	Bass or bass-baritone	Sustained. (gen. av.)

CHARLES GOUNOD
(1818–1893)

OPERA & TITLE	COMP.	TESS.	TYPE	REMARKS
Faust				
Avant de quitter ces lieux	c-g1	eb-eb1	Baritone	Sustained. In some editions transposed a whole tone lower. (gen. av.)
Faust				
Ecoute-moi bien, Marguerite (The Death of Valentine)	c-f1	f-d1	Baritone	Dramatic, declamatory. (Score, gen. av.)
Faust				
Le veau d'or	c-eb1	eb-d1	Bass	A spirited, vigorous verse song. (gen. av.)
Faust Recitative:				
Il était temps Air: O nuit étends sur eux ton ombre	G-c1 (db1)	g-c1	Bass	Slow and very sustained. (Score, gen. av.)
Faust				
Souviens-toi du passé	G-d1	c-c1	Bass	Very sustained, somber. Omitted in most stage performances. (Score, gen. av.)

OPERA & TITLE	COMP.	TESS.	TYPE	REMARKS
Faust				
Vous qui faites l'endormie	(A)G-g1	d-d1	Bass or bass-baritone	A spirited, satirical serenade. Demands facile articulation and some flexibility. (Score, gen. av.)
La Reine de Saba				
Recitative:				
Oui, depuis quatre jours	E-d1	B-b	Bass	Sustained. Demands some flexibility. (GS)
Air:				
Sous les pieds d'une femme				
Mireille				
Si les filles d'Arles	c-f1	e-d1	Baritone	An animated, rather vigorous verse song. (Choudens)
Philémon et Baucis				
Au bruit des lourds marteaux	Ab-eb1	d-db1	Bass	Spirited, vigorous. Demands some flexibility. (gen. av.)
Philémon et Baucis				
Que les songes heureux	E-c#1	e-b	Bass	Very subdued, sustained. (GS)
Roméo et Juliette				
Recitative:				
Buvez donc ce breuvage	G-d1	eb-bb	Bass	Sustained, somber. The final section is more animated, the vocal line is sustained. (Score, gen. av.)
Air:				
C'est là qu'après un jour				
Roméo et Juliette				
Mab, la reine des mensonges	d-f#1	f#-c#1	Baritone	Very animated, light. Demands facile articulation. (gen. av.)

JACQUES HALÉVY
(1799–1862)

OPERA & TITLE	COMP.	TESS.	TYPE	REMARKS
La Juive				
Si la rigueur	E-c1	c-bb	Bass	Very sustained. (gen. av.)

OPERA & TITLE	COMP.	TESS.	TYPE	REMARKS
La Juive				
Vous qui du Dieu vivant outragez la puissance	G-eb1	d-d1	Bass	Grave, majestic, somber. (Brandus et Cie)

JULES MASSENET
(1842–1912)

OPERA & TITLE	COMP.	TESS.	TYPE	REMARKS
Hérodiade				
Recitative:				
Dors, ò cité perverse	c-f1	eb-d1	Bass or baritone	A dramatic mono- logue. Has many sustained sections. (HEUG)
Air:				
Astres étincilants				
Hérodiade				
Recitative:				
Elle a fuit le palais	db-f1	g-eb1	Baritone	Recitative and a sustained, in parts very dramatic air. (Adler)
Air:				
Salomé, Salomé				
Hérodiade				
Recitative:				
Ce breuvage pourrait me donner un tel rêve	c-gb1	f-db1	Baritone	An extended recita- tive and a very sus- tained air. Has dra- matic climaxes. (Adler)
Air:				
Vision fugitive				
Le Jongleur de Notre Dame				
Légende de la Sauge (Marie avec l'Enfant Jésus)	c#-f1	f-d1	Baritone	A sustained, narra- tive air. (HEUG)
Le Roi de Lahore				
Recitative:				
Aux troupes du Sultan	db-gb1	f-eb1	Baritone	An extended recita- tive and a sustained air. Has dramatic climaxes. (HEUG)
Air:				
Promesse de mon avenir				
Manon				
Recitative:				
Les grand mots que voilà!	c-f1	e-d1	Bass or baritone	Sustained. Has ef- fective climaxes. (Score, gen. av.)

OPERA & TITLE	COMP.	TESS.	TYPE	REMARKS

Manon
Air:
  Regardez-moi
  bien dans les
  yeux
	c-e1	e-c♯1	Baritone	Rather vigorous;
				rhythmical.
				(Score, gen. av.)

Thaïs Voila donc la terrible cité	B-f1	e-c♯1	Baritone	An animated, dra- matic monologue. The vocal line is quite sustained. (HEUG)

GIACOMO MEYERBEER
(1791–1864)

OPERA & TITLE	COMP.	TESS.	TYPE	REMARKS

L'Africaine
Adamastor, roi
  des vagues
  profondes
	A♯-e1
	(f♯1)
		e-e1	Baritone	Vigorous, spirited.
				Demands facile ar-
				ticulation and some
				flexibility. (GS)

L'Africaine Fille des rois	d-f1(g1)	f♯-e♭1	Baritone	A very sustained andante and a spir- ited, vigorous al- legro. (GS)

Le Pardon de
  Ploërmel
Ah, mon remords
  te venge
	d♭-g♭1	g♭-e♭1	High
			baritone
				Sustained. Has ef-
				fective climaxes.
				The g♭1 is very
				frequently employed.
				(GS)

Le Pardon de
  Ploërmel
Recitative:
  En chasse!
Air:
  Le jour est levé
	B-e1	d-d1	Bass or
			bass-
			baritone
				Spirited. Demands
				facile articulation
				and some flexibility.
				(GS)

Le Prophète Aussi nombreux que les étoiles	G♯-e1	e-c♯1	Bass or bass- baritone	An animated verse song. Demands fac- ile articulation and considerable flexi- bility. (Score, B & H)

OPERA & TITLE	COMP.	TESS.	TYPE	REMARKS
Les Huguenots				
Recitative:				
Piff, paff	F#-e1	c-c1	Bass	An animated verse
Air:				song. Demands
Pour les couvents,				some flexibility
c'est fini! (Chan-				and facile articula-
son Huguenotte)				tion. (Score, B & H)
L'Etoile du nord				
Recitative:				
Pour fuir son	(Eb)Gb-	eb-c1	Bass	Demands some
souvenir	eb1			flexibility. Sus-
Air:				tained. (GS)
O jours heureux				
Robert le Diable				
Recitative:				
Voici donc le	B-d#1	d-b	Bass or	Dramatic, vigor-
débris du monas-			bass-	ous, declamatory.
tère antique			baritone	(GS)
Air:				
Nonnes qui				
reposez				

JACQUES OFFENBACH
(1819–1880)

Les Contes d'Hoffman				
Scintille diamant	Bb-f#1 (g#1)	e-c#1	Baritone	Sustained. Has effective climaxes. (gen. av.)

CAMILLE SAINT-SAËNS
(1835–1921)

Henry VIII				
Qui donc com- mande quand il aime!	d#-f#1	f#-d#1	Baritone	A sustained larghet- to. The middle sec- tion is a vigorous allegro. (GS)

AMBROISE THOMAS
(1811–1896)

Hamlet				
Comme une pâle fleur	Bb-f#1	f#-d#1	Baritone	Sustained. Has dra- matic climaxes. (HEUG)

OPERA & TITLE	COMP.	TESS.	TYPE	REMARKS
Hamlet Recitative:				
J'ai pu frapper le misérable	c#-d#1	e-c#1	Baritone	A dramatic scena (a setting of the famous monologue).
Air:				
Etre ou ne pas être				(HEUG)
Hamlet				
Je t'implore	Eb-eb1 (f1)	c-c1	Bass	Sustained. Has dramatic climaxes. (HEUG)
Hamlet				
O vin, dissipe la tristesse	c-f1(g1)	f-d1	Baritone	A vigorous, spirited drinking song. (gen. av.)
Le Caïd				
Le Tambour-Major tout galonné d'or	A-e1	d-d1	Bass or bass-baritone	Spirited, robust and florid air. Demands facile articulation. (OD)
Mignon				
De son coeur j'ai calmé la fièvre	A-d1	e-b	Bass	Sustained, very subdued. (Adler)

GERMAN

LUDWIG VAN BEETHOVEN
(1770–1827)

Fidelio				
Ha! Welch ein Augenblick	Ab-e1	d-d1	Bass or bass-baritone	Very animated, vigorous. (Adler)
Fidelio				
Hat man nicht auch Gold beineben	Bb-d1	d-bb1	Bass	Animated, in parts quite rapid. Demands in parts facile articulation. (Adler)

PETER CORNELIUS
(1824–1874)

Der Barbier von Bagdad				
Mein Sohn	D#(F#)-e1	A-c#1	Bass	Slow, sustained first section,

				followed by a brisk, somewhat declamatory section. Dramatic and sustained ending. (Adler)

FRIEDRICH VON FLOTOW
(1812–1883)

Martha				
Lasst mich euch fragen	G-f1	c-c1	Bass	A spirited drinking song. (gen. av.)

ALBERT LORTZING
(1801–1851)

Undine				
Es wohnt am Seegestade	A-e1	g-d1	Bass or bass-baritone	A sustained verse song. Demands some flexibility. (CFP, Arias for Bass)
Zar und Zimmermann				
O sancta justitia	G-e1	d-d1	Bass-baritone	An animated buffo air. Demands facile articulation. Has florid passages. Rather long. (CFP, Arias for Bass)
Zar und Zimmermann				
Sonst spielt' ich mit Scepter	d-f1	g-d1	Bass-baritone or baritone	A sustained verse song. (GS)

HEINRICH MARSCHNER
(1795–1861)

Hans Heiling				
An jenem Tag	c#-f#1	g#-e1	Baritone	A sustained allegro, andante, and a vigorous final allegro. (CFP)

FELIX MENDELSSOHN
(1809–1847)

Die Heimkehr
aus der Fremde

OPERA & TITLE	COMP.	TESS.	TYPE	REMARKS
Ich bin ein viel-gereister Mann	G-f♯1	d-d1	High baritone	A rapid comic air. Demands very facile articulation. (OD)

VICTOR NESSLER
(1841–1890)

Der Trompeter
von Säckingen

OPERA & TITLE	COMP.	TESS.	TYPE	REMARKS
Es hat nicht sollen sein	c-e1	g-d1	Baritone or bass-baritone	Very sustained. (GS)

OTTO NICOLAI
(1810–1849)

Die Lustigen Weiber
von Windsor

OPERA & TITLE	COMP.	TESS.	TYPE	REMARKS
Als Büblein klein	E-e1	c♯-c♯1	Bass	A vigorous drinking song. (Adler)

LOUIS SPOHR
(1784–1859)

Faust
Recitative:

OPERA & TITLE	COMP.	TESS.	TYPE	REMARKS
Che l'orco dia giustitia Air: Tu che sei quel dolce fiore	(G)A-d1(f1)	d-d1	Bass or baritone	Recitative and a compound air. Demands considerable flexibility. Italian text. (CFP, Arias for Bass)

Jessonda

OPERA & TITLE	COMP.	TESS.	TYPE	REMARKS
Der Kriegeslust ergeben	c-f1	d-d1	Bass or baritone	Animated, vigorous. Demands considerable flexibility. (CFP, Arias for Bass)

RICHARD WAGNER
(1813–1883)

Baritone and Bass Excerpts from Wagner's Music Dramas

OPERA & TITLE	COMP.	TESS.	TYPE	REMARKS
Das Rheingold				
Abendlich strahlt der Sonne Auge (Scene 4)	B-f1	db-db1	Bass-baritone	Majestic, sustained. (gen. av.)
Der Fliegende Holländer				
Die Frist ist um (Act I, Scene 3)	G-f1	d-d1	Baritone	An extended recitative and a dramatic, vigorous compound air. (gen. av.)
Der Fliegende Holländer				
Mögst du mein Kind (Act II, Scene 6)	A-d1	e-d1	Bass-baritone or bass	Animated, rather vigorous. The vocal line is sustained. (Score, gen. av.)
Die Meistersinger von Nürnberg Recitative: Jerum! Jerum! Air: Als Eva aus dem Paradies (Act II, Scene 5)	c-f1	d-d1	Bass-baritone	Vigorous. In parts sustained, gently humorous. (gen. av.)
Die Meistersinger von Nürnberg				
Nun hört und versteht mich recht! (Pogner's Address. Act I, Scene 3)	A-f1	e-c1	Bass-baritone or bass	Animated, vigorous. (gen. av.)
Die Meistersinger von Nürnberg				
Wahn! Wahn! (Hans Sachs' Monologue. (Act III, Scene 1)	A-e1	d-c1	Bass-baritone	Declamatory. In parts vigorous, sustained. (gen.-av.)
Die Meistersinger von Nürnberg				
Was duftet doch der Flieder (Hans Sachs' Monologue. Act II, Scene 3)	A-e1	e-d1	Bass-baritone	Sustained. Somewhat declamatory. (gen. av.)

OPERA & TITLE	COMP.	TESS.	TYPE	REMARKS
Die Walküre				
Leb' wohl, du kühnes, herrliches Kind (Wotan's Abschied. Act III, Scene 3)	Bb-e1	e-c#1	Bass-baritone	Declamatory, majestic, vigorous, sustained. (gen. av.)
Die Walküre				
Nicht send' ich dich mehr aus Walhall (Act III, Scene 2)	c-f1	f-db1	Bass-baritone	Animated, majestic. The vocal line is sustained. (Score, gen. av.)
Götterdämmerung				
Hier sitz' ich zur Wacht (Act I, Scene 2)	Bb-d#1	c-c1	Bass	Slow, somber, declamatory. (Score, gen. av.)
Lohengrin				
Mein Herr und Gott nun ruf' ich dich (Act I, Scene 2)	F-eb1	eb-c1	Bass	Majestic, very sustained. (Score, gen. av.; Adler)
Parsifal				
Mein Vater! (Gebet des Amfortas. Act III, Scene 2)	A-eb1	eb-c1	Bass-baritone or baritone	Slow, declamatory, grave. (gen. av.)
Siegfried				
Auf wolkigen Höhn (Act I, Scene 2)	c-f1	db-db1	Bass-baritone	Sustained, majestic. (gen. av.)
Tannhäuser				
Als du in kühnem Sange uns bestrittest (Act I, Scene 4)	d-e1	f#-d1	Baritone	Very sustained. (Score, gen. av.)
Tannhäuser				
Blick' ich umher (Act II, Scene 4)	B-eb1	d-d1	Baritone	Very sustained. (Score, gen. av.)
Tannhäuser				
Recitative: O Himmel lass' dich jetzt erflehen Air: Dir, hohe Liebe (Act II, Scene 4)	eb-f1	f#-eb1	Baritone	Very animated. The vocal line is sustained. (Score, gen. av.)
Tannhäuser				
Recitative: Wie Todesahnung				

OPERA & TITLE	COMP.	TESS.	TYPE	REMARKS
Air:				
O du mein holder Abendstern (Act III, Scene 2)	B♭-e♭1	d-d1	Baritone	An extended, sustained recitative and a very sustained, rather subdued air. (gen. av.)
Tristan und Isolde				
Darf ich die Antwort sagen (Act I, Scene 2)	A-f1	d-d1	Baritone	Vigorous, animated. (Score, gen. av.)
Tristan und Isolde				
Tatest du's wirklich? (Act II, Scene 3)	G♯-e1	c-c1	Bass	Sustained, somewhat declamatory. Has a few dramatic passages. (Adler)

CARL MARIA VON WEBER
(1786–1826)

Der Freischütz				
Hier im ird'schen Jammertal	d-f♯1	f♯-d1	Baritone or bass-baritone	A vigorous verse song. Demands some flexibility. (gen. av.)
Der Freischütz				
Schweig, damit dich niemand warnt	F♯-e1	d-d1	Baritone or bass-baritone	A vigorous dramatic air. Has florid passages. (gen. av.)
Euryanthe				
Recitative: Wo berg' ich mich Air: So weih' ich mich	G-f1	d-d1	Baritone or bass-baritone	A very extended recitative, a sustained and vigorous andante, and a dramatic final allegro. Has florid passages. (GS)

BENJAMIN BRITTEN
(b. 1913)

OPERA & TITLE	COMP.	TESS.	TYPE	REMARKS
Billy Budd And farewell to ye, old 'Rights o' Man'!	c-f1	g-d1	Baritone	Animated, lively. High tessitura. Has some dramatic intensity toward the end. (Score, BH)
Billy Budd Look! Through the port comes the moonshine astray!	c-e1	d-c1	Baritone	(Score, BH)
Billy Budd O beauty	G-f♯1	c-d1	Bass or bass-baritone	A dramatic scena. Interpretatively not easy. (Score, BH)

NORMAN DELLO JOIO
(b. 1913)

OPERA & TITLE	COMP.	TESS.	TYPE	REMARKS
The Trial at Rouen I call on Thee, eternal God (The Creed of Pierre Cauchon)	B♭-f1	e♭-d1	Baritone	Recitative-like throughout. In parts has some dramatic intensity. (RIC)

CARLISLE FLOYD
(b. 1926)

OPERA & TITLE	COMP.	TESS.	TYPE	REMARKS
Susannah Hear me, O Lord, I beseech Thee (Blitch's prayer of repentance)	G-e1	c-d1	Bass or bass-baritone	Sustained, intense. In parts demands some dramatic intensity. (BH)

GIAN-CARLO MENOTTI
(b. 1911)

OPERA & TITLE	COMP.	TESS.	TYPE	REMARKS
Amelia Goes to the Ball				
Dearest Amelia (Letter aria)	B♭-f1	c-e♭1	Baritone	Sustained. (Score, RIC)
The Old Maid and the Thief				
When the air sings of summer	A-f1	d-d1	Baritone	Sustained. (Score, RIC)

DOUGLAS MOORE
(b. 1893)

OPERA & TITLE	COMP.	TESS.	TYPE	REMARKS
The Ballad of Baby Doe				
Warm as the autumn light	B-e1	d♯-c♯1	Baritone	Sustained, in folk style. (CHAP)
The Devil and Daniel Webster				
I wanted clothes . . . well, that was a day	F♯-d1	B-b	Bass	Somewhat declamatory. Narrative. (Score, BH)
The Devil and Daniel Webster				
I've got a ram	B♭-g♭1	d-d1	Baritone	Sustained, somewhat majestic, eloquent. Imposing ending. (BH)

BEDŘICH SMETANA
(1824–1884)

OPERA & TITLE	COMP.	TESS.	TYPE	REMARKS
The Bartered Bride				
Lovers everywhere fatuously swear	B-d1	d-d1	Bass or bass-baritone	Lively, humorous air. Vigorous in parts. Demands facile articulation. Commendable English version by M. Farquhar. (Adler)

IGOR STRAVINSKY
(b. 1882)

The Rake's Progress

In youth the panting slave	eb-e1	g-d1	Baritone	Sustained, short. (Score, BH)

See also the list of songs by Stravinsky.

Note: For excerpts from Russian operas in English translations see
the Russian section of songs (nineteenth and twentieth centuries).

INDEX OF COMPOSERS

776

777